CAMBRIDGE STUDIES IN LINGUISTICS

General Editors · W. SIDNEY ALLEN · C. J. FILLMORE
E. J. A. HENDERSON · F. W. HOUSEHOLDER · J. LYONS
R. B. LE PAGE · F. R. PALMER · J. L. M. TRIM

Principles of diachronic syntax

In this series

1 DAVID CRYSTAL: *Prosodic systems and intonation in English**

2 PIETER A. M. SEUREN: *Operators and nucleus*

3 RODNEY D. HUDDLESTON: *The sentence in written English*

4 JOHN M. ANDERSON: *The grammar of case**

5 M. L. SAMUELS: *Linguistic evolution**

6 P. H. MATTHEWS: *Inflectional morphology**

7 GILLIAN BROWN: *Phonological rules and dialect variation**

8 BRIAN NEWTON: *The generative interpretation of dialect*

9 R. M. W. DIXON: *The Dyirbal language of North Queensland**

10 BRUCE L. DERWING: *Transformational grammar as a theory of language acquisition**

11 MELISSA BOWERMAN: *Early syntactic development**

12 W. SIDNEY ALLEN: *Accent and rhythm*

13 PETER TRUDGILL: *The social differentiation of English in Norwich*

14 ROGER LASS and JOHN M. ANDERSON: *Old English phonology*

15 RUTH M. KEMPSON: *Presupposition and the delimitation of semantics**

16 JAMES R. HURFORD: *The linguistic theory of numerals*

17 ROGER LASS: *English phonology and phonological theory*

18 G. M. AWBERY: *The syntax of Welsh*

19 R. M. W. DIXON: *A grammar of Yidiɲ*

20 JAMES FOLEY: *Foundations of theoretical phonology*

21 A. RADFORD: *Italian syntax: transformational and relational grammar*

22 DIETER WUNDERLICH: *Foundations of linguistics*

23 DAVID W. LIGHTFOOT: *Principles of diachronic syntax**

* Issued in hard covers and as a paperback

PRINCIPLES OF DIACHRONIC SYNTAX

DAVID W. LIGHTFOOT

Reader in English Linguistics
Rijksuniversiteit, Utrecht

Cambridge University Press

CAMBRIDGE

LONDON : NEW YORK : MELBOURNE

Published by the Syndics of the Cambridge University Press
The Pitt Building, Trumpington Street, Cambridge CB2 1RP
Bentley House, 200 Euston Road, London NW1 2DB
32 East 57th Street, New York, NY 10022, USA
296 Beaconsfield Parade, Middle Park, Melbourne 3206, Australia

First published 1979

Printed in Great Britain at the
University Press, Cambridge

Library of Congress Cataloguing in Publication Data
Lightfoot, David.
Principles of diachronic syntax.
(Cambridge studies in linguistics; 23)
Bibliography: p.
Includes indexes.
1. Grammar, Comparative and general – Syntax.
2. Historical linguistics. I. Title. II. Series.
P291.L48   415   78–54717
ISBN 0 521 22082 3 hard covers
ISBN 0 521 29350 2 paperback

P
291
L48

Contents

Foreword   vii

I PRELIMINARIES
1.1 Some general observations   I
1.2 Pre-theoretical reflections   4
1.3 Early generative approaches to syntactic change   21
1.4 A theory of grammar   42
1.5 Grammatical theory within the logic of markedness   71

2 A PARADIGM CASE: THE ENGLISH MODALS
2.1 Modals in Modern English   81
2.2 Historical re-analysis   98
2.3 Appendix: periphrastic *do*   115

3 A THEORY OF CHANGE
3.1 The Transparency Principle   121
3.2 A theory of change   141
3.3 Syntactic reconstruction   154

4 MORE CATEGORY CHANGES
4.1 English quantifiers   168
4.2 The English infinitive   186
4.3 Redistribution of existing categories   199
4.4 Serial verbs in Kwa   213

5 CHANGES IN THE LEXICON
5.1 Impersonal verbs in Middle English   229
5.2 Passive constructions   239
5.3 The Greek moods   282

6 ON CYCLIC TRANSFORMATIONS
  6.1 NP Preposing   295
  6.2 *wh* Movement   313

7 THE CAUSES OF RE-ANALYSIS
  7.1 Role of surface structure and analogies   343
  7.2 Independent causation   374
  7.3 Conclusion   405

Bibliography (*and index of references*)   409

Citation index   428

Foreword

The aim of this book is to develop a perspective within which one may profitably study how and why the syntax of a language changes in the course of time. In that sense it concerns the *principles* of diachronic syntax. Research on syntactic change has always played a minor role in the activities of historical linguists, taking a back seat to phonological, lexical and morphological change. There are good reasons for this. I shall argue that the poverty of the field is a function of inadequate theories of *synchronic* syntax on the part of neogrammarians, American structuralists and transformational generative grammarians alike. However, there has been a recent resurgence of interest in diachronic syntax, as indicated by the papers from the first and second International Conferences on Historical Linguistics (Anderson & Jones 1974, Christie 1976) and the publication of several books on the subject (Jacobs 1975, Friedrich 1975, Lehmann 1974, and the anthologies edited by Li 1977 and Steever, Walker & Mufwene 1976).

Three developments suggest grounds for some optimism: (a) a renewed interest in surface structure implicational universals, stemming most directly from the work of Greenberg (1966) on word order relationships; such 'universals' have formed the basis for claims about how languages change and have led to more extensive catalogues of diachronic changes in various languages; (b) the publication of Visser's compendious study of the history of many construction-types in English, which makes certain kinds of crucial data far more readily accessible; (c) the recent re-orientation of work in generative grammar, following the results of Peters & Ritchie (1973); work within the so-called Extended Standard Theory of generative grammar tries to provide a definition of what kind of formal object will count as a possible grammar of a particular natural language and seeks a universal template, prescribing explicit constraints on the form of grammatical rules and on the way in which such rules may function.

A definition of a possible grammar will provide the upper limits to the way in which a given grammar may change historically, insofar as it cannot change into something which is not a possible grammar. Such a definition, i.e. a *restrictive* theory of grammar, provides interesting and non-trivial predictions about the way in which grammars change; these predictions are derived via a simple theory of change which states, for example, that grammars are liable to undergo a radical re-analysis as they come close to the limits prescribed by the theory of grammar, and that the outputs of two grammars holding for the language of two 'adjacent' generations must be sufficiently similar to permit communication. With a theory of grammar and a theory of change along these general lines, one can view linguistic change progressing as a function of chance and necessity, much as Monod (1970) viewed genetic change. Certain changes may take place in a given grammar, which have the effect of making that grammar more 'marked', closer to the limits prescribed by the theory of grammar. As these limits are approached, so a re-analysis becomes necessary. The re-analysis itself must fall within certain bounds, such that the necessary therapy is performed and communication is preserved across generations. Within these limits, imposed by an interaction of the theories of grammar and change, it is a matter of chance which of the possible re-analyses is adopted. Whatever change is adopted in a given dialect may itself contribute to the need for further changes, rendering the grammar more marked in certain areas, despite performing the necessary therapy in other areas. In this way, the restrictions imposed by the theory of grammar play a crucial role in accounting for the causes of change.

Therefore, much of this book will deal with radical re-analyses. As a paradigm case, I take a change whereby the grammar of sixteenth-century English developed a new syntactic category of 'modal verb', which manifested itself in a variety of changes in possible utterances. The simultaneity of those overt changes argues for the singularity of the change in the abstract grammar. In the light of such re-analyses we shall gradually develop a Transparency Principle as a statement in the theory of grammar, requiring that derivations be minimally complex and that deep structures be fairly 'close' to their corresponding surface structures. I shall treat the English modals and the Transparency Principle like the task of peeling an onion, constantly returning to them from different points of view in the light of an examination of more re-analyses and the development of a rather simple theory of change. Finally in chapter 7, our perspective on diachronic change will be laid out in full.

The Transparency Principle will constrain possible particular grammars and contribute to the explanation of why such radical re-analyses occur. Conversely, the point at which radical re-analyses occur in history might be expected to tell us about the limits to possible grammars (particularly about the precise form of the Transparency Principle) and thus to inform work on the theory of grammar, conceived as a set of restrictions on possible descriptions. In this way data from diachronic change can be brought to bear on questions arising within the theory of grammar, and the study of diachronic syntax will be fully integrated within the general enterprise of providing restrictions on possible grammars, a central empirical task of linguistics. This will be an innovation for syntax, although data from phonological change often figure crucially in arguments about possible synchronic descriptions.

I see this view of diachronic syntax as having three merits: (a) it relates various simultaneous but superficially unconnected changes by claiming that they are the manifestations of a single change in the abstract grammar. It thereby contributes to our understanding of the internal history of a given language by explaining (and perhaps discovering, as with the English modals) the simultaneity of the changes; (b) it provides a novel approach to questions about the causes of change; (c) it introduces a new style of argumentation for choosing between competing theories and synchronic descriptions, by requiring that the theory of grammar should be responsive to diachronic data insofar as it should interact with a theory of change to account for the point at which grammars undergo re-analyses or 'catastrophic' changes in the sense of Thom (1972). This is a matter of some considerable methodological importance at a time when many linguists seem to believe that generative theories of grammar have no empirical consequences for domains of enquiry other than morpheme distribution and the pairing of phonetic and semantic representations. Such criticisms are often based on a failure to distinguish a theory of grammar, a particular grammar and 'interpretive' mechanisms deriving predictions about the nature of historical change, language acquisition, pathology, etc. I hope that developing such an interpretive mechanism for diachronic change may be helpful for similar work in the domain of language acquisition, etc., and suggest some caution in dealing with questions of the 'psychological reality' of grammatical descriptions – a term which has led to much confusion.

This view of diachronic change has provided the basis for my research programme over the last five years. The work has been supported by grants from McGill University and the Canada Council and has been reported in earlier papers by myself and some of my assistants. Several students have collaborated on these research projects, and I am particularly grateful for the work of Michael Canale, Anita Carlson, Elan Dresher, Norbert Hornstein, Monica Koch, Amy Weinberg and Lydia White.

This book has been written in the course of sabbatical leave granted by McGill and funded in part by a Canada Council Leave Fellowship. I am thankful for the gracious hospitality of Clare Hall and the Department of Linguistics at the University of Cambridge. I owe a debt of gratitude to Edward Klima, Elizabeth Traugott and other diachronic syntacticians whose pioneering work has been a necessary prelude to what I have done here, even if I criticize it on some methodological points. I am also grateful to several audiences who have helped me to see defects in some of my earlier conceptions and to many scholars who have discussed various aspects of it: Harry Bracken, Ray Dougherty, Joe Emonds, Henry Hiż, Henry Hoenigswald, Jay Keyser, Paul Schachter, Bob Stockwell and John Trim. More immediately, a word of public thanks goes to my wife for her assistance in typing from a semi-legible manuscript; to Sidney Allen, Rudolf Botha, Noam Chomsky, Paul Kiparsky, Roger Lass, and Anthony Warner, each of whom read the whole text and made many useful comments which have made it into a better book; and finally to Sari Hornstein for helping me through the proofs.

Cambridge, July 1977   DAVID LIGHTFOOT

I *Preliminaries*

1.1 Some general observations

Most linguists hold opinions about the ways in which either a language or a grammar may change in the course of time. These opinions are often invoked as the basis for an argument supporting some synchronic analysis. This is sufficiently common for citation to be almost redundant, but consider two recent examples for the sake of illustration. Carden (1976: p77) seeks to choose between two analyses of a given range of data concerning the scope of quantifiers and negatives, although he finds neither analysis very attractive. He considers three dialects and notes that under an analysis using derivational constraints one dialect, which he labels 'AMB', can be characterized as the simplest of the three, whereas under the competing analysis, appealing to interpretive semantic rules, the AMB dialect is the most complicated.[1] He then proceeds: 'if we assume that linguistic change represents a simplification of the grammar, at least at the point at which the initial change takes place', an argument for the derivational-constraint analysis can be constructed on the basis of two facts: (a) the AMB dialect is the most common, and (b) speakers of the other dialects 'have been known to change to AMB over a period of months', while no changes have been

[1] The notion of a 'more simple' grammar is crucial to Carden's account and it is not explicated. It seems to be based on the number of rules in the grammars but then he observes in a note that if one looks at a wider range of data it might be the case that under the derivational-constraint analysis the grammar of the AMB dialect has as many (more general) rules as the other two dialects. In any case, 'until both derivational-constraint and interpretive analyses of scope determination have been worked out in some detail, it will be possible for a partisan of either side to devise a plausible-looking analysis in which the theory he favours gives AMB the simplest grammar of the three dialects' (p77). Carden's argument therefore seems to be devoid of any actual content, but here we are concerned with its internal logic, which will turn out to be based on similarly unwarranted assumptions.

observed in the other direction, from AMB to one of the other two. He then calls attention to the _form_ of the argument, choosing between synchronic analyses but based on 'a theory of linguistic change motivated by historical data'. Indeed, in his Introduction he notes that 'an argument combining dialect-variation evidence with an historically-motivated theory of linguistic change will be crucial to the eventual solution', and he concludes the book with the comment that 'this sort of argument, if it proves to be widely applicable, offers an approach to the old problem of the synchronic relevance of historical data and the possibility of a genuinely unified linguistic theory'. Despite the importance attached to the argument, no further discussion is offered either of the theory of linguistic change assumed, or the relation between it and the choice between competing synchronic analyses, or the way in which a theory of grammar and a theory of linguistic change may combine to yield a unified linguistic theory. It is crucial to this argument that grammars change only by inexorable simplification and that they cannot become more complicated. From this theory of linguistic change, as Carden describes it, it follows that the grammar of Modern English will be simpler and, presumably, more highly valued than the grammar of any earlier stage of English – a most improbable consequence.

Radford (1976) has quite a different approach to diachrony. In discussing certain complement constructions with causative verbs in Romance, he postulates and compares two grammars, which he labels 'relational' and 'transformational'. One argument offered in favour of the relational grammar is that the transformational counterpart 'fails to provide any adequate account of the notion of "ongoing linguistic change"...Over the course of time, there has been a gradual "fusion" of an original two-clause structure into a mono-clause structure' and in a relational grammar of Latin and its daughter languages 'it is possible to discern an ongoing historical process, a unitary "theme" or "direction" of change which makes what has been happening look anything other than arbitrary'. It is by no means clear in what sense the ongoing historical process is discernible in a relational grammar of some synchronic stage of a language, but the notion that the historical _process_ is represented in some more or less transparent way is adduced as support for that general form of grammar. Again, there is no further discussion of the theory of change presupposed, but it is clear that Radford will prefer a particular grammar which represents historical processes in some form; such discussion as there is is conducted in terms of particular grammars rather than of theories of grammar.[1]

Certain aspects of underlying forms postulated by transformational generative grammarians, whether the lexical item which is the input to the phonological rules or the initial phrase marker (or 'deep structure') which is the input to the transformational sub-component, sometimes recapitulate their history and take on a form which was actually attested at an earlier stage of the language. Many people have observed that some of the underlying forms postulated by Chomsky & Halle (1968) actually occurred in Middle English. In syntax it has been proposed that in the grammar of Modern English initial phrase markers may contain complementizers with two members, as in *I wonder [whether that]*$_{\text{COMP}}$ *Linda left*, where *that* must be deleted subsequently by a transformational rule. This underlying form recapitulates the fact that in Middle English such double-barrelled complementizers were attested and a sentence of the form *I wonder whether that Linda left* was well-formed. In such a situation there is a tendency, to which many linguists have succumbed, to point to the 'historical validity' of the underlying forms postulated, as if the fact that they reflect an earlier stage of the language contributes to their plausibility as abstract constituents of a formal, synchronic grammar. It is, of course, not surprising that a grammar should reflect its history to some extent but there is no reason to suppose that ontogeny recapitulates phylogeny as a matter of general

---

[1] Radford makes even stronger requirements of grammars, that they should reflect 'the relevance of universalist considerations to language-particular descriptions'. He claims that there is a rule of Subject Raising to higher object position in Latin, cites Postal's (1974) arguments for 'a precisely parallel rule' in English and Japanese, and asserts that 'there is simply no way of capturing the similarities between these different rules in transformational terms, and thereby attaining a substantively universal characterization of the rule . . . Thus, universalist considerations argue strongly against a transformational characterization of syntactic rules.' A *substantive* universal based on three languages is not a basis for a very persuasive argument and, in any case, I have argued that Postal's arguments for Subject Raising in English have no force (Lightfoot 1976a). Radford assumes that in a relational theory of grammar one can formulate a set of universal rules, i.e. substantive universals. One would like to see one such rule carefully formalized before evaluating the claim (Radford gives the 'universal' Subject Raising only what he calls an informal characterization). But if there is such a set of rules, it is not clear that this in itself reduces the class of grammars available to the language learner, which is the basic task of a generative theory of grammar. Unless it is shown that there is such a reduction, the discussion has no bearing on the comparison and evaluation of transformational and relational theories.

For a demonstration that the factual basis of Radford's claim is also false, see the analysis of Old French by Morin & St Amour (1977).

principle. Therefore, pace Radford, there is no reason for a linguist to view historical recapitulation, when it does occur in an analysis, as lending support or further plausibility.[1]

Arguments of the type invoked by Carden and Radford are not uncommon in the linguistic literature. Evidently, diverse opinions are held about the nature of diachronic change in grammars and about the manner in which a synchronic grammar and a theory of grammar should be responsive to data from diachronic change, even if these opinions are often not supported by evidence or even articulated with much care or clarity. Some might argue that there is a causal relationship between the willingness of some linguists to introduce diachronic wild cards into arguments about the nature and form of a synchronic syntactic description and the fact that very little work has been published on the nature of syntactic change and particularly on methodological principles for research in this area. We shall return to an account of the poverty of this domain of enquiry, but in the meantime it is clearly necessary to pose some rather fundamental questions about the investigation of syntactic change and to attempt some straightening up of a few of the basic concepts involved in the enterprise.

1.2   Pre-theoretical reflections

There are several pre-theoretical difficulties for the study of diachronic syntax, such that one must ask whether it is possible to do useful work on historical change and, if so, in what way. If one is to formulate a theory of syntactic change, what will the goals be for such a theory? How can these goals be attained? How will the theory interact with theories of other domains, such as theories of grammar and perceptual strategies? Before providing some answers to these questions, we shall

---

[1] This has been widely misunderstood. For example, Makkai & Makkai (1976) assume that a transformational grammar of Modern English should provide a model of its history in a very strong sense. They argue that the fact that it fails to do this entails that it should be discarded in favour of a 'stratificational' grammar, which, presumably, provides the desired model. They argue that because a transformational grammar is organized in such a way that the phonological rules operate on the output of the syntax, it is in some sense disconfirmed by the alleged fact that certain diachronic syntactic changes in Middle English followed from and were caused by some historically prior phonological changes. If interpreted as a historical model in this way, transformational grammar is apparently consistent with syntactic changes entailing subsequent phonological change, but not with the reverse direction of causation. Needless to say, this is a bizarre interpretation of grammatical models and imposes far too strong a requirement on the predictions which should follow from a synchronic grammar.

look first at some of the pre-theoretical difficulties posing problems which by and large do not arise in the study of diachronic phonology. We shall consider five such problems.

(i) A fundamental prerequisite for work in diachronic syntax is that one should be able to compare the grammars of at least two stages of a language. The phonetic and phonological segments of a language are finite and can be listed. But this is not true of sentences, which are potentially infinite, numerically indefinite, and this presents special difficulties for writing a grammar of an early stage of a language. Classical Greek and Early Modern English, for example, are among the most copiously attested of the ancient languages and have extensive corpuses of many different literary genres; also the transitions into Modern Greek and Modern English are well documented at most stages. But even in these cases, there must be severe limitations on the extent to which one can delve into the problems of an ancient language without the aid of a native speaker's intuition, particularly when one is concerned with the area of the grammar where syntax and semantics interact. Usually one has no knowledge of ungrammatical 'sentences', except in the rare instances where a contemporary grammarian may report that certain forms and constructions are not used; one is thus in the position of a child acquiring its first language, who hears sentences being uttered but does not know whether certain other hypothetical sentences are not uttered because they would be grammatically deviant in some principled way or because they have not occurred in his experience simply as a function of chance. One is therefore bound to the texts, which are usually deficient and often lack the crucial examples which will choose one grammatical hypothesis over another. Also, the available texts must be used with caution and with philological skill, since they may represent different dialects or styles. Particular value might be assigned to texts indicating colloquial language, such as letters and dramatic characters like Shakespeare's Mistress Quickly and Pompey; see Salmon (1965) for a judiciously selected corpus. One must be prepared to allow a grammar to characterize a certain sentence as ill-formed, even though that sentence is actually attested in the surviving documents. The sentence might have been consciously used as an archaism, as an imitation of a foreign construction, or even as deliberately ungrammatical. Thus P. G. Wodehouse puts ill-formed English into the mouth of Monsieur Antoine, the French cook, in *Right ho, Jeeves*, indicating his non-English origins: 'Make some attention a little. Me, I have hit the hay, but I do not sleep so good, and presently I wake and up I look, and there is one who make faces against me through the dashed window.' Similarly, Thorne (n.d.) argues that the language of Leontes in the early part of *The Winter's Tale* is at times extremely awkward and occasionally downright ungrammatical. He claims convincingly that this is a dramatic device to convey the private delusions and incoherence engendered by Leontes' jealousy. Critics from Samuel Johnson to Dover Wilson have commented on Shakespeare's occasional 'syntactical incoherence' and 'ungrammatical style'. In a similar vein, Naro (1976) illustrates the proper use of philological criteria to avoid what might appear to be contrary data.

On the other hand, progress can be made without conjuring up a native speaker of a dead language, if the linguist is prepared to use his own intuitions where obvious generalizations can be made. That is, we reject the traditional restriction that one may use only attested sentences of Classical Greek, Early Modern English, etc., as evidence for one's hypotheses. Enough is known about Classical Greek for one to make a large number of generalizations, enough to allow most college curricula to include courses on prose composition, where the student composes and the teacher corrects original and otherwise unattested Greek sentences, based on their trained intuitions about the language. We make no apology for doing the same here. To do otherwise is to impose an unrealistic limitation on one's analyses. Thus, although one is bound to the texts, they must be used with philological skill and one must be ready to characterize certain unattested sentences as well-formed and some attested sentences as ill-formed.

Even with this treatment of the texts, it is probably impossible to write a full grammar of a dead language, albeit as richly attested as Classical Greek and Early Modern English. There will always be crucial gaps in a finite corpus and questions which must be left unresolved. These problems are less acute in diachronic phonology, where one does not need such copious texts in order to do useful work. This was illustrated nicely in the 1971 discovery of a new page of the Gothic Bible, reported and discussed in Szemerényi (1972). Our knowledge of Gothic is based on no more than 280 printed pages, all but ten of which are New Testament translations. The new page added significantly to our knowledge of inflectional morphology and lexical items, but did not permit us to make new inferences about Gothic syntax. King (1969: p141) observes that 'a corpus of a fixed size will permit statements about phonology at confidence levels significantly higher than the confidence levels associated with syntactic statements based on the same corpus. We would all feel safer drawing phonological conclusions from the Rosetta stone or the Horn of Gallehus rather than syntactic conclusions.' One simply needs more data to write a syntactic description. This points to the importance of working with a reasonably well-understood area of grammar and it unfortunately entails severe limitations on the number of languages wherein one can work on diachronic syntax. There are very few languages, apart from Chinese, Tamil, Kannada and those of the Indo-European and Semitic families, which have a rich attestation over a long enough period of time. In order to write a grammar of an early stage of a language, one needs many texts covering many literary genres, and in order to discuss subsequent changes one needs a grammar of a later stage and usually some attestation of a substantial intervening period. The Bantu and Iroquoian languages, for example, do not fulfil this requirement and therefore will not be an appropriate basis for work on syntactic change (reconstruction of the grammars of pre-historical languages is, of course, a very different matter, and something we shall attend to in chapter 3). This limits the number of language-types which can be examined from the viewpoint of syntactic change.

(ii) There are further pre-theoretical difficulties for diachronic syntax beyond those of writing a grammar of a dead language. Students of syntactic change have virtually no legacy from the neogrammarians, and for good reason. The neogrammarians and their contemporaries handed down formidable lists of phonological correspondences related by rules, and discussions of 'natural' phonological changes (Vendryes 1902), whereas in syntax the notions of a corresponding form or a diachronic rule made no sense. That is, one can reasonably claim that *chapter, captain* are in a way the same word as their historical antecedents, *chapiter, capitain*, and further that these ultimately are derivable (by different routes) from the same (Latin) stem *capit-*; or even that *brother, pal* are (again by different routes – the latter a loan from Romani, derivable from Sanskrit *bhrātā*) in a sense the 'same' as their reconstructed Proto-Indo-European antecedent **bhrater-*, the forms being related by historical rules mapping phonemes or allophones into other phonemes or allophones. Basing a theory of phonological change on such correspondences may turn out to be inadequate (as argued by Jakobson, Halle, Kiparsky, Andersen et al.), but it leaves scope for much useful work and is not obviously senseless. An analogous view of syntax, however, is incoherent: there is no clear basis for saying that a certain sentence of Old English 'corresponds' to some sentence of Middle English, and there is no reason to claim that a surface structure is mapped by a historical rule into another form occurring in a later stage of the language. Nonetheless there is a good deal of misleading discussion in the more recent literature, which is couched in terms of 'diachronic processes'. Traugott (1969) speaks of a 'diachronic grammar'; Givón (1971), Li (1975a) and Warburton & Prabhu (1975) talk of 'diachronic processes', and seem to visualize some formal device which takes a sentence of an early stage of the language as input and yields a sentence of a later stage. The best one can do is to specify what was a possible sentence at a given stage of a language, and this is the main concern of Delbrück's work.

Of course, there is much more to be said about the neogrammarian view of language. I use 'syntax' differently from the neogrammarians, who used it to cover also what one would now call morphology. Under the rubric of syntax they studied changes in inflections and changes in the use of morphological categories such as subjunctives, infinitives, etc. Jankowsky (1972: p167) points out that 'neither Brugmann nor Paul could conceive of a clear-cut differentiation between morphology and syntax...investigating syntax in its own right simply presupposed a completed morphological analysis'.[1] Moreover, the nineteenth-century view of language was pre-eminently historical; the scientific study of language was in essence a study of its history. Jespersen (1922) began his book with the words: 'The distinctive feature of the science of language as conceived nowadays is its historical character.' So any neogrammarian dealing with syntax would naturally look to history for an explanation of what occurred in their various synchronic descriptions. Historical change in turn was to be explained by the speaker's

[1] In fact, it seems that the neogrammarians did not have a generally agreed definition of the boundaries of syntax. Reviewing Delbrück's Vedic syntax, Whitney (1892: p281) was 'a little surprised to find the formation and value of compound words among the matters discussed at some length . . . in this work on syntax; the subject is not ordinarily classed as syntactical'. The boundaries were actively disputed. Ries had considerable influence on Brugmann, who abandoned a separate, comparative Indo-European syntax in the second edition of the Grundriss. Ries' (1894) attempt to define the subject argued that syntax should not properly encompass Delbrück's material, only part of which was included in the second volume: *Lehre von den Wortformen und ihrem Gebrauch*. Lane (1949) claims that it was a result of these disputes 'that, of the actual syntax (by Ries' definition) planned for the Grundriss, only one small volume ever appeared: *Die Syntax des einfachen Satzes* (1925)'.

psychological activity, his ability to see proportional analogies and to create new forms out of old ones by borrowings, blends, etc. At some points one finds such relationsips being explicitly drawn in syntax and Paul (1880) sometimes wrote as if he had in mind a notion of synchronic relationships among sentences. For instance, he wrote of the 'transition' from verbs to action nouns like *transportation, liberation*; 'these may approach the verbal construction; as *my transportation from England to Ireland* ("I was transported from England to Ireland")'. There were precedents for this view, as for example in the Port Royal (synchronic) 'derivation' of *invisible God created the visible universe* from three 'underlying' propositions which were in the mind. But the neogrammarians never made these ideas as precise as they did many other analytical concepts and it is indisputable that they did not leave behind syntactic discoveries in any way comparable to Verner's Law or Saussure's postulation of coloured schwas, or what came to be known as the PIE laryngeals. By and large, despite Paul, they did not use any concept of an abstract formal grammar, with a level of representation distinct from surface structures or with a set of devices to relate one sentence or phrase to another. Also they did not employ recursive rules even for surface structures, and lacked any notion of a 'generative grammar', not just of some particular version distinguishing a more abstract level than surface structure. Therefore they were unable to compare the grammars of different stages and to discuss the possible formal relationships between these grammars. Without a theory of syntax along these lines, they could only set up constructional classes and compare the sentences of the various stages, which Delbrück, Brugmann, Löfstedt, Hirt, Wackernagel and others did with characteristic thoroughness and skill. Clearly they understood that it was senseless to write rules mapping a sentence or construction-type of Old English into a 'corresponding' Middle English form. Any rate, they did not make the attempt, and the lack of a syntactic legacy in any way comparable to what they left to phonologists can be viewed as a consequence of the theory of language they presupposed.

(iii) A further and related difficulty for diachronic syntacticians is that they cannot begin their work with any useful notion of what constitutes a natural kind of historical change. Given all the phonetic correspondences of the neogrammarians, a phonologist has certain expectations of what kinds of changes to look for in examining a new language. The same types of phonetic changes keep recurring in language after language and this provides analysts with notions of natural changes. They know that a vocalic segment like *a* cannot change across the board into a consonantal such as *p*; that is, there will be no direct historical correspondence mapping *aïtar* into *pitar*. Some linguists (e.g. Postal 1968) extrapolate from this and conclude that there can be no synchronic phonological rule changing an *a* to a *p*, on the grounds that synchronic rules are subject to a 'naturalness condition' that they may not effect an operation which has no correlate from historical change. Some may argue that these intuitive notions usually turn out to be ill-founded, but, given the absence of such historical correspondences in syntax, there can be no basis for parallel notions of natural changes or of natural rules, whatever the merits of such notions.

(iv) Furthermore, given the lack of clear ideas on what constitutes a natural change in syntax, there will be obstacles to reconstructing proto-forms or elements of a grammar of an unattested parent language. Work in historical reconstruction has always presupposed at least an intuitive evaluation metric which would prescribe, for example, that a language with an asymmetric vocalic system or irregular nominal declensions is not highly valued. In reconstructing proto-languages, linguists have presupposed definitions of simplicity of paradigms, naturalness of rules and of changes which must be postulated in order to map the proto-language into one of its daughters, naturalness of certain aspects of grammars, implicational universals. Whatever the validity of these definitions, they have served as essential pre-requisites for phonological reconstruction. There would appear to be no useful analogues for syntax. Most of the candidates for implicational universals, e.g. those of Greenberg (1966), have many unexplained exceptions and virtually nothing is known about the naturalness of syntactic changes or of synchronic rules. We shall return to the viability of syntactic reconstruction in chapter 3, after making some claims about the nature of syntactic change and about a methodology for the study of diachronic syntax. However, on a merely pre-theoretical level, it is clear that the specific techniques used in the reconstruction of the phonological and morphological structure of proto-languages do not hold for similar reconstruction work in syntax.

(v) Many of the difficulties we have discussed stem from the lack of an adequate theory of possible (synchronic) syntactic descriptions. What work has been done by historical syntacticians, although usually thorough and sometimes insightful, has rarely gone beyond observational adequacy, listing sentence-types, word order in various clauses, etc. Noting this, King (1969: p141) claimed that the application of transformational grammar to syntactic change promised to be extremely fruitful, because 'the substantial core of agreement about the form and substance of transformational grammar is certainly enough to support its application to historical problems'. As an aid to work on the grammars of dead languages he offers 'the universal or near-universal status of many features of syntax'. He provides four theory-bound but 'trivial' examples: (a) no known language lacks transformations, (b) most languages have some means of deriving questions from underlying declarative sentences, (c) most languages have a rule to create one co-ordinating sentence from two or more simple ones, and (d) most languages transformationally derive complex complement constructions from two or more sentences:

> John saw the boy
> ⇒ John saw the boy who is playing
> the boy is playing

If this was supposed to represent the core of substantial agreement in 1969, it is salutary to note that eight years later few linguists would assent to any of these claims. I shall argue in chapter 6 that transformations play only a minimal role in a generative grammar of English, and it is quite conceivable that languages with a rich morphological system, like Eskimo or Japanese, have no syntactic transformations in the usual sense. Furthermore, no proponent of the Extended Standard Theory would permit any of the derivations mentioned in (b)–(d), or conceive of transformations as mappings between sentences as opposed to mappings between abstract structures. Nor, in fact, would (b)–(d) have been accepted in the earliest work on generative grammar, e.g. Chomsky (1955, 1957), where it was explicit that transformations do not operate on sentences.

Thus the prospect for work in diachronic syntax is not encouraging and one may question whether it is worthwhile to embark on the enterprise. In phonology some phenomena cry out for explanation: certain changes keep recurring in a given language, such as the nasalization of vowels before a nasal consonant; the same rules re-appear in many different languages. In the present state of our knowledge, we cannot point to analogous phenomena in syntax which require explanation. Nonetheless, although prescribing goals for a theory of syntactic change will not be a trivial matter, there are reasons for attempting to formulate a principled approach to syntactic change.

Firstly, from the viewpoint of the internal history of particular languages, there are historical facts which require description and, if they are not accidental, also demand explanation. For example, one finds clusters of simultaneous changes, changes which appear prima facie not to be related. The question then arises of whether their simultaneity is merely accidental or a function of abstract principles. Also there is some evidence for implicational sequences of changes, whereby it is said that if a language undergoes a certain change then it will subsequently develop some other property. A good deal of work has been conducted along these lines recently, building on the cautious pioneering work of Greenberg (1966). For example, it is said that if a language develops a verb-object surface word order, it will also have auxiliary-verb order, and that if languages develop certain word order patterns they will also acquire an Extraposition transformation. We shall examine some of this 'typological' work in §7.2.

Secondly, historical data can provide a way to choose between competing synchronic hypotheses. This is by no means obviously so and we shall need to build some theoretical machinery before demonstrating the proposition in chapter 3. I take it that there are two fundamental problems in linguistic research: to argue for the correctness of grammatical descriptions and to constrain the excessive 'power' of grammars, restricting the class of grammars available for the description of any given language. These two concerns are inextricably related and really two faces of the same basic problem. Generative grammar, as usually defined, seeks a formal model which will generate all the grammatical sentences of a language and no ungrammatical forms, assigning the correct structural descriptions and relating the forms so generated to some kind of (partial) semantic representation. Such a model will correctly characterize the *substance* of a native speaker's linguistic competence. However, there can be no conclusive evidence for claiming to have captured the correct *form* of that competence. After all, there are many possible characterizations; whenever one produces an adequate model, one will be able to invoke the wonders of mathematics and re-axiomatize the system. Choosing the correct grammar can be influenced by 'external', non-grammatical criteria, since grammatical criteria alone underdetermine the form of the grammar. That is, invoking external criteria can reduce, although not eliminate, the indeterminacy. This is one of the basic problems addressed by psycholinguists: if a linguist uses an abbreviatory device such as curly brackets to collapse two or more phonological rules, how can one know that this notation in any way represents the form of the native speaker's knowledge? Kiparsky (1968a) noted that psycholinguists were confronted with the problem of syphoning off facts of performance in addressing such questions of competence. He claimed that historical change yields a window on the form of competence, which is not obscured by performance factors because language change is a manifestation of grammar change, change in a model of competence. If there are constraints on possible changes, then through historical change a linguist can discover constraints on the form of people's grammars. This hypothesis, to which we shall return in a moment, has long influenced work in phonology, where synchronic and diachronic analysis have usually proceeded hand-in-hand, and, partly through Kiparsky's own work, evidence from diachronic change has been used to constrain synchronic descriptions, reducing indeterminacy. So far this has not been so in generative syntax for at least two reasons: firstly, as indicated, there is no traditional legacy of data on change or intuitive notions of what constitutes a natural syntactic rule. Secondly, questions of power have been easier to address in phonological analyses, since derivations could be constrained in certain 'obvious' ways (e.g. Kiparsky's Alternation Condition, 1968b) and the problem of non-unique solutions was much less rife than in syntax. However, three recent developments open up a more realistic possibility for serious work in syntactic change from this point of view: (i) the publication of Visser's massive collection of English sentence-types indicating the history of the construction, the dates of its first attestation and of the final appearance of an obsolete form, (ii) the revival of interest in diachronic syntax in terms of simply cataloguing changes which have taken place, and (iii), following the results of Peters & Ritchie (1973), the re-orientation of work in syntactic theory to the aim of imposing severe restrictions on the class of possible grammars, which we shall outline in §1.4. However, even with these encouraging developments, one should re-emphasize the importance of concentrating one's attention on changes affecting well worked out and well understood areas of grammar.

If, despite the difficulties inherent in any work on diachronic syntax, there are prima facie good reasons to attempt research in this area, how can one go about it? We have noted three recent developments which might encourage us. However, despite much activity, the recent attention paid by generativists to diachronic syntax has led to no significant implications for a general theory of grammar and, from a purely historical viewpoint, has failed to focus on any well-defined concepts of historical change. The papers in this field stand largely in isolation from each other and show few common threads of interest or argumentation; there is little agreement on even the most fundamental concepts. Modern diachronic syntacticians, it is true, have no legacy equivalent to that handed down to phonologists, and they must do their own pioneering work. This will preclude rapid progress, but it does not explain the current disarray of the field. The fault for that lies in ourselves and is a consequence of a theoretical approach to syntax precisely as barren as that of the neogrammarians. I have suggested above that the lack of work by the neogrammarians on principles of syntactic change (as distinct from cataloguing permissible sentences at various historical stages of a given language) was a function of their theory of language.

Things *appear* to be different today: diachronic syntacticians have an idea of the status of a grammar and can view syntactic change as change(s) in an abstract system. Hence, if G_1 is a grammar of a language at time t, and G_2 is a grammar of the same language at a later stage of development $t + 1$, one may compare G_1 and G_2, note differences of internal structure and attempt to correlate these internal differences with the fact that a given sentence will be generated by G_1 but not by G_2. Hence there is a descriptive framework within which one can talk about syntactic change. However, most of the work done on syntactic change in a generative perspective has assumed a theory of such power that virtually anything could be expressed as a rule of grammar, and thus almost any imaginable change could be described. If the constraints on grammars are so loose that G_1 or G_2 can take on an unlimited number of forms, then G_1 may differ from G_2 in an unlimited number of ways and we have no method of distinguishing possible from impossible changes, which I take to be a central task of any theory of historical change. If some charlatan announced that a historical change had taken place in his idiolect, such that all constructions involving a Passive transformation underwent a new rule which affixed -*at* to every even-numbered major constituent in the clause containing the passive verb and prefixed *ta-* to every odd-numbered word except the fifth, a grammer could be written for the later stage and thus the change could be described; we would have no way qua linguists of proving that our informant was a charlatan. That is not to say that restrictive theories were unavailable; the theory of Chomsky (1955) would probably suffice to preclude such a non-structure-dependent rule. We shall discuss the expressive power of current transformational generative grammars later on, but for the moment it is noteworthy that most of the work in diachronic syntax has assumed the most powerful versions of transformational grammar and sometimes even a universal base hypothesis (Lakoff 1968). This, I shall argue, is the reason for the present disarray and for the fact that there is no coherent body of theory dealing with syntactic change. Generative work on diachronic syntax has chosen for the most part to describe changes as changes in the transformational component (Klima, Traugott, Lakoff). Robin Lakoff argued for the lexical governance system of transformational rules as being the major locus of syntactic change and reduced the enterprise to a taxonomy. Where claims have been made about changes in the phrase structure rules (e.g. Traugott [Closs] 1965), the changes argued for have been quite arbitrary and presuppose no theory of a possible phrase structure rule. Thus given the looseness of the theories being used, current work reveals no more about possible syntactic changes than did the work of the neogrammarians and their contemporaries. Work in this area will make significant progress when conducted within the context of a restrictive theory of grammar. A restrictive theory will make predictions about possible historical changes; investigation of actual changes will have consequences for the restrictions imposed by the theory. Within this perspective, work on diachronic change will be an integral part of work on syntactic theory in general; there will be a constant interaction.

Before proceeding to discussion of a restrictive theory, I shall spell out how work on diachronic change can be made an integral part of work on general syntactic theory, since it is not obvious that this can be done. Grammatical theories can be responsive to diachronic change in at least two ways: (a) A theory should be interpretable as providing a distinction between possible and impossible changes. If a theory provides a framework within which particular grammars may be constructed, then the extent to which those grammars are permitted to differ from each other will provide the upper limits on the ways in which a given grammar is liable to change historically. Of course, the grammars of two *adjacent* stages of some language will differ only in more restricted ways, and these lower limits will be predicted by a theory of change (as distinct from a theory of grammar); so the structure of a particular theory of change will be in part derivative from a particular theory of grammar. (b) On a more specific level, theories can be made responsive to change in that grammars subsumed by them should be capable of relating simultaneous changes. That is, if some changes occur simultaneously, one will prefer a grammar which can relate these changes, showing that in fact they are simply the surface manifestations of a single change in the grammar and therefore that their simultaneity is not accidental. Of course, one cannot rule out the possibility that a grammar may undergo more than one change at a time, but the idealization that the grammars of two adjacent stages of a language may differ only minimally provides severe restrictions on the form of the grammar for each of those stages. We assume then that things treated alike in a diachronic development are treated alike, where possible, in the synchronic grammar. Making such an assumption turns out to yield fruitful insights into the possible form of grammars; the productivity of the assumption is its 'justification'. In this perspective the examination of simultaneous but superficially unrelated changes will severely restrict the choice of grammars for the earlier and later stages, and therefore provide a window on constraints on grammars. If G_1 is a grammar yielding an output O_1, and G_2 is a grammar producing O_2 (where $O_1 \neq O_2$), then both G_1 and G_2 may each be of many different forms and still be consistent with a given theory, say the Extended Standard Theory in its present stage of development. However, if we impose the requirement that, if possible, G_1 and G_2 may differ only minimally, while still producing O_1 and O_2 respectively, then the form of the grammars is immediately restricted. As an analogy, consider two chess positions, P_1 and P_2. If one asks a spectator to construct the games leading to P_1 and P_2, there will be many different possibilities, all within the limits imposed by the rules of chess. However, if one adds that the games leading to P_1 and P_2 may differ only minimally, i.e. by one move, then the total number of possible games is reduced significantly.

I take it that the immediate goal of a theory of language is to provide a set of constraints on possible grammars, although this approach is not necessarily correct or required a priori, as we shall discuss in §1.4. The ideal theory will be so restrictive that for any given language there will be only one grammar capable of producing the relevant output in a way consistent with the theory. If we hypothesize that a child is equipped with this theory and brings it to the task of acquiring his first language, then in this view the child will be driven to a unique grammar by an interaction of the theory and the data for which he is constructing a grammar. This may turn out to be too strong a position and it may prove necessary to admit a degree of indeterminacy (Lightfoot 1974a); in fact the view of syntactic change to be developed here requires some indeterminacy insofar as more than one hypothesis (or grammar) may be formulated to account for a given area of data. However, the linguist pursuing a research programme on this basis will seek to discover the tightest possible restrictions on available grammars. Like any scientist, he will assume that a theory should account for the maximum amount of data with minimal machinery. If making the theory responsive to data from diachronic change provides insights into restrictions on the theory, then that will contribute to the general research programme. For any area of data, it will be an empirical question whether making the theory responsive to that data will yield a way of restricting it. For example, holding the theory responsive to the class of errors made in the acquisition process and for the class of possible diachronic changes does provide interesting information on apparent restrictions, whereas holding the theory responsive to 'processing time' involved in the comprehension of sentences has no implications at our present stage of understanding.[1] Discussion of such 'external' data bases is often couched misleadingly in terms of 'psychological reality' (Kiparsky 1968a). It is assumed that we may write a variety of formal grammars which 'work', successfully correlating semantic and phonetic representations for a given sentence, and then we may ask which of these grammars is psychologically real. This presupposes that there is psychological evidence which is distinct from linguistic evidence. There seems to be little virtue in deciding that data from language acquisition and diachronic change is inherently psychological and not linguistic, or vice versa. Rather we should seek simply 'the correct grammar' for a certain language, presupposing a restrictive theory.[2] The correct grammar or theory will be the one

---

[1] Another example is 'pragmatics' as distinct from formal semantics. I have argued (Lightfoot 1976c) that one can require a grammar to be responsive to pragmatic considerations but that, if the proper distinctions are made, this simply entails adding to the grammar an extra component designed specifically to deal with pragmatics. This fails to interact in any interesting way with the formal grammar, and therefore does not constrain the choice of grammars or shed any light on their internal structure or properties.

[2] I use 'correct' in a metaphorical and Popperian sense, as a short-hand for a falsifiable but hitherto unfalsified theory which is most truth-like in yielding the greatest

which accounts for the maximum data with minimal machinery; the data will include the distinction between grammatical and ungrammatical sentences, the nature of acquisition by first language learners, diachronic developments. No one area of facts will have privileged status. Data from acquisition, say, will simply constitute one more argument for or against the theory, one more area where the theory makes predictions, and will help to reduce the indeterminacy of the linguistic description; not even all the imaginable data from acquisition could ever totally eliminate indeterminacy. Therefore the question posed earlier 'how can one know that [a given] notation in any way represents the form of the native speaker's knowledge?' does not differ in kind from the question 'how can one know that there are electrons?'.

Interpretive mechanisms will mediate between the theory of grammar and data from acquisition and historical change; these interpretive mechanisms will be theories of acquisition and change and will constitute the evidence for or against theories of grammar, favouring the theory of grammar which permits the simplest interpretive mechanism. When we achieve the correct grammar, it will be as unnecessary to ask the further question of whether the theory is psychologically real as it would be to ask, having constructed a theory accounting for the manner in which radio waves are emitted from a star, whether the theory corresponds to what is physically happening inside the star. Chomsky (personal communication) points out that one can formulate a theory of vision without having to ask whether, in the simplest case of viewing a white square on a black background, the neurological activity involved in defining the righthand vertical side is isomorphic with some component of the theory. It is an unrealistically strong requirement to impose on a theory of language that its various individual components should demonstrably correspond in some strict way to the neurological processes involved in uttering or comprehending some sentence. This kind of view represents the usual procedure in other sciences. Consider this passage from Koyré (1957: pp176–7):

Fortunately, as Newton knew full well, we need not have a clear conception of the way in which certain effects are produced in order to be able to study the phenomena and to treat them mathematically. Galileo was not obliged

number of correct predictions. We shall return to this more carefully in a discussion of refutability in §1.5, arguing that one should stress depth of explanation rather than refutability or coverage of data.

to develop a theory of gravity – he even claimed his right to ignore completely its nature – in order to establish a mathematical dynamics and to determine the laws of fall. Thus nothing prevented Newton from studying the *laws* of 'attraction' or 'gravitation' without being obliged to give an account of the real forces that produced the centripetal motion of the bodies. It was perfectly sufficient to assume only that these forces – whether physical or metaphysical – were acting according to strict mathematical laws (an assumption fully confirmed by the observation of astronomical phenomena and also by well-interpreted experiments) and to treat these 'forces' as *mathematical* forces, and not as real ones. Although only a part of the task, it is a very necessary part; only when this preliminary stage is accomplished can we proceed to the investigation of the real causes of the phenomena.

This is precisely what Newton does in the book so significantly called not *Principia Philosophiae*, . . . but *Philosophiae naturalis principia mathematica*, that is, Mathematical Principles of Natural Philosophy.

We shall simply seek the 'correct' grammar of a language, i.e. the grammar to which the child is driven by the theory of language with which he is endowed, in order to produce the correct output for his native language. This does not deny an interest in mental facts; it denies that there is an independent 'psychological' area of validation for grammars or theories of grammar. Evidence about ambiguity or grammaticalness, etc., is no less evidence about psychological reality than is evidence about language acquisition, pathology, change, etc. It is just different evidence. One must claim that 'the correct grammar' is psychologically real, if one is to make the usual claims for explanatory adequacy (Botha 1973). That is, the theory of grammar must be interpretable as making some predictions about a variety of domains (such as diachronic change, language acquisition or even neurological processes, when we know enough about neurology to pose interesting questions), if it is to achieve explanatory adequacy in the usual sense, a point to which we return in §1.5. For now, at least, the overwhelming mass of crucial evidence bearing on the correctness of grammar (i.e. its psychological reality, its truth in the domain of psychology) comes from what is misleadingly called 'linguistic evidence', data about ambiguity, grammaticalness, etc. But it also turns out that data from diachronic change provides invaluable assistance in the task of providing restrictions on grammars, if one assumes that phenomena undergoing simultaneous changes should ideally be related in the synchronic grammar. Such an approach is the basis for my research programme in syntactic change.

I have argued that diachronic syntax will be studied most profitably in the context of a restrictive theory of grammar. The restrictive theory will provide an upper bound on possible changes; the study of syntactic change will contribute to the formulation of further restrictions. Some version of the Extended Standard Theory (henceforth EST) seems to me to be a good candidate for a suitably restricted theory within which we may profitably study syntactic change. Several changes can be described insightfully in a way consonant with the EST and, to make a stronger claim, arguments can be constructed in favour of such a theory by using data from syntactic change. Working within this framework will immediately change the focus of attention. Following the results of Peters & Ritchie (1973), the thrust of the work since the late 1960s has been to constrain severely the definitions of a possible syntactic rule (both phrase structure and transformational rules) and particularly to limit the activity of the transformational sub-component.[1] By

---

[1] As noted below, conditions on the functioning of rules antedate the Peters & Ritchie results; work on the A-over-A condition, recoverability of deletion, and $\overline{\text{X}}$ conventions for phrase structure rules, dates from the early and mid-1960s. Therefore one may query whether Peters & Ritchie was relevant to the new 'thrust' (Chomsky personal communication). They showed that without further conditions on the deletion of designated elements, a transformational grammar could generate any recursive enumerable set. The same is true, trivially, of context-sensitive phrase structure grammars (and perhaps of context-free phrase structure grammars, although this may be harder to prove). That is, if we take one terminal symbol to be 'blank', then derivations can 'shorten' the terminal string, which generally leads to non-recursive sets. But this is a trivial aspect of the problem of excessive generative capacity and one might argue that their results were almost totally irrelevant to the issue of restricting grammars. In fact, it is not obvious that the theory of grammar should restrict grammars to recursive languages (see Chomsky 1965: ch. 1; 1977). Moreover they proposed some reasonable ways to overcome the generation of non-recursive sets, namely the survivor property on the cycling function. But the fact that the theory they considered allowed an excessive range of structural descriptions, with Boolean conditions, multiple factorizations, etc., did not figure in their proof of non-recursive generation. The importance of their work was: (a) to give a good formalization of the standard assumptions about TG; (b) to show that recoverability of deletion, as formulated, did not suffice to restrict grammars to recursive sets; (c) to suggest an approach to restrict grammars to recursive sets (the survivor property).

The Peters & Ritchie results have been widely misinterpreted and it is no doubt sociologically true that they focussed attention on excessive generative capacity. Chomsky's view of the history is given in the introduction to Chomsky (1955). In the 1950s, a major goal was to devise a notion of 'transformation' rich enough to handle things beyond the capacity of a phrase structure grammar. From the early 1960s, much of his work was devoted to constraints on grammars *in order to improve explanatory adequacy*, and this orientation was independent of the Peters & Ritchie results.

enriching the theory of rule application by developing conditions on the function of rules, one restricts drastically the role played by specific transformational rules. Thus a particular grammar within such a theory would be liable to change in various ways and not just through changes in transformational rules. Furthermore, given a restricted theory of a possible transformational rule, the scope for changes here would be extremely limited. When one notes the most recent proposals of Chomsky (1975: ch. 3; 1976; 1977), that the core of English cyclic syntax consists of two transformational rules, NP Preposing and *wh* Movement, and when one notes the extreme simplicity of the structural descriptions of these rules, it becomes clear that within such a theory transformational rules will play a very minor role as a locus of syntactic change. One will have to look elsewhere. The best work on $\overline{X}$ conventions (e.g. Emonds 1976, Halitsky 1975, Hornstein 1977a) also yields a restricted notion of a possible phrase structure rule in a way that we shall illustrate in §1.4, and the possibilities for change in this area are also correspondingly limited. Even rules of semantic interpretation must meet several fairly restrictive requirements (Chomsky 1976, 1977), and there are grounds for hope that the structure of the lexicon will also be limited (Aronoff 1976, Jackendoff 1975). Given a theory of this form and the desire to restrict further the expressive power of grammars, the possibilities for change are also limited and there begins to emerge a theory of what will constitute a possible historical change in the syntactic or semantic components. Whether or not that theory is correct is, of course, a matter for empirical investigation, but precise, testable hypotheses can easily be derived from it. If these hypotheses yield a productive account of change, showing surprising relationships not hitherto noted, the theory will gain further plausibility. There are grounds to suppose that this is a useful line to pursue; a plausible account of syntactic change seems to be indicated and the general syntactic theory thereby derives further support. In the course of the book we shall ask what kinds of changes would be consistent with such a theory and what would not, assuming an appropriate theory of change.

1.3 Early generative approaches to syntactic change

We have observed in §1.2 that the neogrammarians did little work on syntactic change and we suggested that this was a consequence of the

theory of grammar they presupposed. The American structuralists of
the first half of this century paid even less attention to diachronic
syntax, as witnessed by Lane (1949), who lamented the neglect, argued
that 'most comparatists have been incompetent to attack the problems
involved', and suggested plausible lines of research, identifying a
type of study in Germanic syntax which could be contributed by a
neophyte. In this section we shall look at some of the work on diachronic syntax conducted in a generative perspective, concentrating on
a few pieces which contribute to one's understanding of how to go
about doing diachronic syntax, as opposed to studies which make use of
existing techniques to illuminate aspects of the history of a particular
language.

In many ways the earliest work, by Klima (1964a, b), is the best, at
least from the viewpoint of methodological clarity. He considered the
case markings on pronominal forms, examining four stages of English:
late Middle English (L_1), eighteenth-century (L_2), a colloquial dialect
from the end of the eighteenth century (L_3), and a dialect form of
Modern English (L_4). The facts are illustrated in table 1, which is to

TABLE I

L_1	L_2	L_3	L_4
⎧he and I left			him and me
⎨it was I		it was me	left
⎩who could see him?			
⎰whom could she see?	who could she see?		
⎪whom did he speak	who did he speak		
⎨with?	with?		
⎩who was it?			
⎧he knew who it was			
⎨he knew whom he	he knew who he		
⎩spoke with	spoke with		
⎰the man who saw him			
⎪left			
⎪the man whom I saw	the man who I saw		
⎨left	left		
⎪the man whom he	the man who he		
⎪spoke with left	spoke with left		
⎪the man with whom			(does n〔 〕st)
⎩he spoke left			
Case Marking	*wh* Movement	*wh* Movement	lexical re-
			analysis
wh Movement	Case Marking	Generalized Case	
		Marking	
Subj-Aux Inversion	Subj-Aux Inversion	Subj-Aux Inversion	

be read from left to right in the sense that in the second line *it was I* is grammatical in L_1 and L_2, but not in L_3 or L_4, which permit *it was me* but not *it was I*. In formulating a partial grammar of these four stages, Klima appealed to three rules, which may be written as (1)–(3).[1]

(1)   Case Marking

$$X \quad \begin{Bmatrix} V_t \\ P \end{Bmatrix} \quad \text{Pronoun} \quad Y \Rightarrow 1 \quad 2 \quad 3 + \text{case} \quad 4$$

(2)   *wh* Movement

$$Q \quad X \quad NP \quad Y \Rightarrow 3 \quad 2 \quad 4$$

(3)   Subj-Aux Inversion

$$\begin{Bmatrix} Q \\ NP \end{Bmatrix} \quad NP \quad Aux \quad X \Rightarrow 1 \quad 3 \quad 2 \quad 4$$

These rules apply in the order indicated in table 1. In the grammar of L_1, Case Marking attaches accusative endings to any pronoun immediately following a transitive verb or preposition. This rule applies before *wh* Movement, and so *wh* pronouns are always marked with accusative endings when they originate after a transitive verb or preposition in the initial phrase marker. In the grammar of L_2, *wh* Movement applies before and thereby 'bleeds' Case Marking (in the terminology of Kiparsky 1971), depriving the rule of forms to which it would otherwise have applied. The grammar of L_3 differs from that of L_2 in that Case Marking has been extended to apply not only to pronouns after transitive verbs but also to those following a copula. In the grammar of L_4, Case Marking is lost and a lexical re-analysis has taken place whereby *I* no longer occurs in the grammar and is replaced by *me* in the lexicon. It is assumed that the base rules and the lexicon are otherwise identical for L_1–L_4.

The change from L_1 to L_2 can be interpreted as a development whereby at the time of L_1 case marking was assigned in the initial phrase marker, indicating the *function* of the NP, but later was assigned according to the surface structure *position*. Although Klima describes the change as a re-ordering of Case Marking and *wh* Movement, the same output will be produced if Case Marking applies at surface

---

[1] I do not follow Klima's formulations of the rules closely but amend them so that they are consistent with more recent versions of transformational grammar. For example, I assume that *wh* elements are base-generated and not introduced by transformation. Also I do not distinguish singulary from generalized transformations which embed one S under another.

structure, after Subject-Auxiliary Inversion, etc. This instance of syntactic change looks very much like the descriptions of several phonological changes and takes the form of a re ordering of rules, a simplification of a transformation (whereby in the grammar of L_3, Case Marking has a simpler structural description which will apply to more NPs: X V Pronoun Y), and re-structuring of underlying, lexical forms. In fact, the mode of implementation of the change could also be analogous to what is often assumed to take place with phonological innovations. Halle (1962) suggested that the grammars of adults could change only in superficial ways, perhaps by adding a rule to the end of the phonological component or perhaps at some natural break within the component. Children, however, could carry out a more fundamental re-structuring in the acquisition process, in that a child's grammar could differ quite radically from that of his models. To put it differently, while the grammar of a single adult could change only in minor ways in the course of a life-time, there could be greater differences between the grammar of a child and that of his parents or models. This change in case marking from L_1 to L_2 could be interpreted in similar fashion, although there is no evidence one way or the other. The innovating generation may have introduced a new rule of *whom* Replacement, changing clause-initial *whom* to *who*. If we assume the rule to be cyclic, it can be formulated as (4). Notice that the structural description will not be met if *whom* is preceded by a preposition or is in anything other than clause-initial position. Therefore, adding this rule to the grammar of L_1 will yield L_2. Subsequent generations re-structured the grammar, simplifying it by eliminating *whom* Replacement and re-ordering Case Marking to apply after *wh* Movement.

(4)   *whom* Replacement
       who + case   X ⇒ *who* X

This illustrates some of the earliest work concerning the historical changes which can take place in the transformational sub-component of a generative grammar. Partial grammars are properly formulated for the various stages under examination, but no explanation emerges for why these changes should have taken place and there are no clear implications for the possible form of grammars. Assuming the correctness of the grammatical formulations given for L_{1-4}, the changes in the grammars are akin to what has been postulated for diachronic phonology. From the same period Traugott (1965) and Wang (1965) take a similar orientation in describing the progressive simplification of the phrase structure rule expanding Aux in Old, Middle and Modern English, and a simplification of a rule in Northern Mandarin. Consider now Kiparsky's (1968c) interesting and novel account of the Indo-European injunctive. We shall be concerned here only with his discussion of 'historical presents'. In the modern Indo-European languages a present tense form may refer to past time; it is then labelled a 'historical present'. Such forms carry a sense of immediacy and vividness, and are open to a semantic treatment; one may view their distribution as being semantically conditioned (I gloss over the question of sequence-of-tenses phenomena, which are arguably to be dealt with by syntactic rules). However, in the earliest Indo-European languages, Vedic Sanskrit, Old Irish, early Greek and Latin, etc., the distribution is syntactically governed: a historical present occurs only after a true past tense, as in these examples from Greek, Old Norse and Old Irish.

(5) a. *élabon* dè kaì tò phroúrion kaì toùs phúlakas *ekbállousin* 'they captured the fort and drive out the garrison'. Thucydides VIII 84

b. þeir *hliópo* á hesta sína ok *ríþa* ofan á Fýresvǫllo, þá sǫ́ þeir, at Aþils konungr *reiþ* epter þeim...ok *vill* drepa þá 'they leaped on their horses and ride down to the Fyres-fields; then they saw that King Athils rode after them and wants to kill them' (cited in Heusler 1964: p128)

c. Iar sin *at·racht* [preterite] sūas ocus *no·mbertaigedar* [present] 'after that he arose and exults'. The Tale of MacDatho's Pig IV 1

Similarly a present tense may follow a future and take on the force of a future (6a); a present subjunctive may follow an aorist subjunctive and be interpreted as an aorist (6b). Likewise with optatives (6c) and imperatives.

(6) a. doulṓsete...erēmoûte 'you will enslave...you lay waste'. Thucydides III 58

b. eàn gár tí se *phanô* kakòn pepoiēkốs...eàn méntoi mēdèn *phaínōmai* kakòn pepoiēkốs...'if I shall appear to have done you any wrong...but if I shall not appear to have done you any wrong...'. Xenophon, Cyr. v v 13

c. ei mèn gàr *prosdéksaito*...ei dè mḕ *prosdékhoito*...'if he should accept...but if he should not accept...'. Demosthenes XIX 318

As far as one can tell there there is no semantic distinction between these present tense forms and the corresponding full forms. Thus one might postulate an optional syntactic rule reducing the second mood or tense in a sequence to the 'unmarked' form, a kind of 'conjunction reduction' rule. In Vedic Sanskrit, Celtic and Homeric Greek, the injunctive was the unmarked form; at a later stage of Greek, and in Old Irish, early Latin and Old Icelandic, the unmarked form was the present indicative, what the handbooks have referred to inaccurately as the 'historical present'. Later on in the history of Greek, Latin etc., this conjunction reduction rule was lost and was, in a sense, replaced by a semantic rule interpreting present tenses as 'dramatic' when they violated sequence-of-tenses rules, regardless of whether or not they were preceded by a fully marked form such as a past tense. This semantic rule would have a greater range of applicability compared to the conjunction reduction rule, since it would apply to present tense forms conjoined to a preceding past or future tense, etc., and to present tenses not in a conjoined structure.

This account of the change, loss of a syntactic rule and acquisition of a new rule of semantic interpretation, assumes the autonomy thesis, whereby syntactic rules may not refer to factors of meaning or use. Under this hypothesis, no syntactic rule can be sensitive to a semantic notion such as vividness or dramaticality. However, there are other possible accounts. Even under the autonomy hypothesis, the grammar of, say, Homeric Greek may contain not a syntactic rule of conjunction reduction, optionally changing a fully specified verb into a present indicative if it is preceded by another fully specified verb form, but rather a rule of interpretation assigning past time reference (a semantic notion) to a present indicative conjoined to a preceding past tense form in a closely parallel structure (we leave aside the definition of 'parallel structures'). Under this view, tenses would be assigned randomly by the phrase structure rules and would receive an interpretation, assigning temporal and perhaps aspectual reference; the semantic rules might have a filtering effect, characterizing certain tenses as uninterpretable and thus the structure as ill-formed. If, however, we do not assume the autonomy hypothesis, many more alternatives arise even within a transformational generative grammar consisting of the usual kinds of phrase structure, lexical, transformational and interpretive rules. For example, assuming the grammar of Homeric Greek to have a syntactic transformation of conjunction reduction, as above, the change into later Greek might be characterized in such a way that the transformation loses its syntactic condition (requiring a preceding and conjoined fully specified verb form) and now reduces any verb form to a present indicative, simultaneously assigning to it a feature [+dramatic]. As a further alternative, the semantic feature [+dramatic] might be assigned by the phrase structure rules randomly to any verb form; under this analysis it might prove necessary, depending on the facts, also to invoke some kind of surface filter if verbs cannot be interpreted as [+dramatic] in some contexts.

It can be seen that the way in which a syntactic change may be characterized will vary according to the theory of grammar under which descriptions are written of the two (or more) historical stages being compared. Of the above change we can say that it consists of the loss of some kind of rule dealing with surface examples of the present indicative as the second member of a conjoined structure. This rule may have been a transformational rule changing a fully specified verb form to a present tense indicative, or an interpretive rule assigning to a present tense form the semantic value of a preceding, conjoined verb; no doubt there are further alternatives. This rule was replaced by another rule dealing with surface instances of a present indicative interpreted as denoting dramaticality or vividness. We can conclude that grammars may lose rules and acquire new ones in the course of time, but any further conclusions about the kinds of rules which can be acquired and lost will vary according to one's assumptions about a theory of possible grammars.[1] Therefore, while Kiparsky's article gave a novel and insightful account of the injunctive and of the distribution of so-called 'historic presents' in early Indo-European languages, solving a problem in the internal history of these languages, it was not a significant contribution to a general theory of diachronic syntax (nor was any such claim made for it). This will serve to illustrate the point made in §1.2, that while generative grammarians can talk about syntactic change as change in abstract, formal grammars, they have been no closer than were the neogrammarians to formulating a theory of syntactic change or explaining possible changes. In order to make responsible claims in this area and to avoid widespread indeterminacy, it is imperative to work within the framework of a restrictive theory of

[1] Another example of rule loss would occur with grammars changing from an underlying order Subject-Object-Verb (SOV) to SVO. The innovation characteristically first affects main clauses and later subordinate clauses. For the intermediate stage the grammar presumably contains a transformational rule changing SOV to SVO in main clauses or perhaps SVO to SOV in subordinate clauses. Under either hypothesis the new transformational rule would be lost as SVO order becomes regular and is generated as such in the base component.

grammar. The restrictive theory will allow only one, or, more likely, a small number of possible grammars of one stage of a given language. Thus the formal properties of the change will be a function of the theory of grammar. The theory of grammar will permit (ideally) a unique description of the early stage and a unique description of the later stage; the two descriptions can then be compared with a view to determining the kinds of changes which have taken place. Without a restrictive theory of grammar, the grammars of the stages being compared may take on a wide variety of forms and the means of characterizing the historical changes will increase by a geometric progression depending on the number of stages involved. Therefore I can see no way of doing useful work on the nature of syntactic change without presupposing a highly restrictive theory of grammar.

Traugott's (1965, 1969) careful study of the English auxiliary is instructive from a similar point of view. She argued that in Old, Middle and Modern English there was a progressive simplification of the phrase structure rules expanding a category Aux. These are useful contributions which give a good account of the historical facts, but they contain four methodological errors which vitiate the general conclusions about the nature of syntactic change. I shall comment only on these aspects of her methodology.

First, the papers illustrate the dangers of arguments ex tacito, based on the assumption that if a sentence does not exist in the corpus it must be presumed to be ungrammatical. She discusses the distribution of 'modals', and of *have* and *be* in auxiliary contexts, and cites the Old English data of (7)–(8), amongst others.

(7) a. ic sceal feohtende beon 'I shall be fighting'
     b. ic sceal gefuhten habban 'I shall have fought'
     c. *ic sceal feohtende gebeon habban 'I shall have been fighting'
(8) a. þa Darius geseah þæt he oferwunnen beon wolde 'then Darius saw that he would be conquered'
     b. *...þæt he oferwunnen geworden hæfde 'that he had been overcome'
     c. *...þæt he oferwunnen wesende wæs 'that he was being overcome'

(7) illustrates that perfect or progressive auxiliary verbs, but not both, may occur with a modal. (8) shows that while a modal may co-occur with a passive, perfect and progressive auxiliaries may not. Traugott

then formulates a phrase structure rule of (9), where PP indicates a past participle, PrP a present participle, V_t a transitive verb, V_i an intransitive, and M modal elements like *cunn, mag, sceal*, etc.

(9)
$$\text{Aux} \rightarrow \left(\left\{ \begin{array}{l} \text{PP-}habb, \text{ in env. } V_{t-}, V_{i_{move}} - \\ \text{PP-}wes, \text{ in env. } V_{i-} \\ \text{PrP-BE} \end{array} \right\} \right) \text{(Inf-M)} \quad \text{T}$$

This rule permits the correct auxiliary combinations of (7) and (8), and disallows (7c). However, no predictions are made about (8b) and (8c) because the rule fails to say anything about passive auxiliaries and no transformations such as Passive are formulated or discussed. (9) also does not permit sentences of the form *I have been fighting*, where a perfect and progressive co-occur without a modal; such sentences were well-formed. Furthermore, in the 1969 paper Traugott notes the non-occurrence of sentences like *he wolde gefeohten habban* 'he would have fought' and assumes them to be ungrammatical, although they would be permitted by her 1965 rule (9). Whatever the defects of the rule formulated, its complexity arises from the fact that it is designed to characterize the non-occurring (7c), (8b) and (8c) as ungrammatical. Traugott proceeds to discuss Middle English and notes that while perfects occur with either *have* or *be* followed by the past participle, only *have*, not *be*, precedes the progressive in a perfect tense (10). The progressive always takes the form of *be*-PrP. Her Middle English phrase structure rule (11) is formulated with otherwise unnecessary complexity in order not to generate sentences like (10b). Again, it is assumed that the non-occurrence of (10b) indicates ungrammaticality, although it might be a function of a stylistic avoidance of such sequences of *be*.

(10) a. we haue been waytynge al this fortenyght
      b. *we were been waytynge al this fortenyght[1]

(11) $\text{Aux} \rightarrow \text{T} \quad \text{(M)} \left(\left\{ \begin{array}{l} (have\text{-PP}) \quad \left(\left\{ \begin{array}{l} be\text{-PrP} \\ do \end{array} \right\} \right) \\ be\text{-PP, in env. } -V_{i_{move}} \end{array} \right\} \right)$

In writing the grammar of a dead language, a linguist must appeal to arguments ex tacito, contrasting occurring and non-occurring sentences. However, for each hypothetical, non-occurring sentence, one must ask whether its non-occurrence is accidental or indicative of ungrammati-

---

[1] Traugott actually cites *we been been...*, which I amend to *were been*. It seems irrelevant that the first verb should show no number and person agreement with the subject.

cality. Often this will be a difficult question which will require philological skill and some notions about the naturalness of grammars.
For example, if all known living languages which have feature x also
have feature y, but a dead language with feature x appears not to have
feature y, most linguists would be inclined to assume that the non-
occurrence of y was an accident of the corpus and they would write a
grammar which would characterize sentences with feature y as well-
formed, even though they are not attested. Philological judgment is
required to ascertain whether a non-occurring sentence-type would
in any case be rare in the kinds of texts available. Suppose that a
linguist wrote an optimal grammar based on a corpus of stylized
documents like historical chronicles. If this optimal grammar generated
all the occurring forms and none of the non-occurring ones except
some which were characteristic of a casual style of speech (e.g. tag
questions: *he did it, didn't he?*), it would be unwise to complicate the
grammar just to exclude such forms. One would prefer to ascribe the
absence of such forms to chance or to stylistic incompatibility. In
the case discussed, Traugott may be right to characterize these sentences
as ungrammatical. However, in Modern English the sentences corresponding to those excluded for Old and Middle English (7c, 8b, 8c,
10b) are all grammatical but statistically fairly uncommon, particularly
in literary texts. Furthermore I know of no living language with the
properties that she ascribes to Old and Middle English. That is, no
language I know of has modal, progressive and perfective categories,
and permits modals to co-occur with progressives or perfectives but
not both, while progressives and perfectives may nonetheless co-occur
without a modal. Therefore, I would be inclined to view such gaps as
accidental and not a function of grammatical principles.[1] If this is

---

[1] It is important not to impute 'unnatural' properties to earlier or reconstructed
systems, although this is often done. For example, Palmer (1954) and other Latinists
analyse *impero ut Romam eas* 'I order you to go to Rome' as a complex sentence,
containing a main verb *impero* and a subordinate clause *ut Romam eas*. However,
they claim that a speaker of earliest Latin would have uttered two parallel sentences
for Classical Latin's single complex sentence and would have said *impero; (ut)
Romam eas* 'I give an order; go to Rome'. Thus prehistoric Latin consisted of
independent sentences and only later began to embed complements under main
verbs. This paratactic view of language would seem to be tantamount to saying that
Proto-Indo-European (PIE) consisted of a finite number of sentences, since, of
course, there was only a finite number of words in the language and, in this view,
there were no recursive functions of complementation or relativization (the relative
pronoun is alleged to originate from a resumptive, anaphoric pronoun meaning 'and
he'). If this were so, PIE was a finite language and radically different from all
attested languages, including its descendants.

correct, the apparent complexity of the Old English Aux rule is a result of mis-analysis; therefore the conclusions do not follow that there has been a progressive simplification of the phrase structure rule in the course of the history of English. Of course, nothing has been *demonstrated* here, but there are reasons to regard Traugott's general claim as not persuasive and the discussion illustrates the caution which is necessary in the proper use of texts.

Second, the lack of a sufficiently restrictive theory of grammar entails considerable indeterminacy in the description of each of the stages investigated and, therefore, even greater indeterminacy in the characterization of the formal nature of the change in grammar. The neogrammarians did not write synchronic rules of syntax and limited themselves to fairly weak generalizations. It is no great advance to acknowledge the need for rules, but to make them up and use them arbitrarily. We shall consider two examples of this. Dealing with sentences such as (12), Traugott seems to assume that in earlier English an overt negative marker was introduced by an optional transformation to 'a semantically affirmative subordinate sentence' under inherently negative verbs such as *forbid, prevent, deny*. Under this analysis there would be no negative in the pre-transformational structure of these complement clauses, but one could be inserted transformationally with no ensuing change of meaning. The optionality of the negative is indicated by the existence of (13), which does not have the negative, alongside (12a) which does. The negative in (12b) is equally optional and the author could have omitted it with no apparent difference in meaning; Modern English, of course, does not permit such a negative to have the same sense as the affirmative.

(12) a. forbead þæt mon na ðær eft ne timbrede 'forbade that one never there after not built = forbade anyone ever to build there after'. c. 893 Aelfred, Orosius CCLXII 22
      b. the waves prevented him from not reaching the shore. Swift, Gulliver's Travels

(13) forbead þæt hiene mon god hete 'forbade that him one called God = forbade that anyone called him God'. Aelfred, Orosius CCLIV 8

As an alternative to Traugott's optional *not* Insertion rule, another linguist might argue that *not* was obligatorily present in the complements to such 'negative-meaning' verbs, and that a transformation of *not* Deletion applied optionally in earlier English and obligatorily in

Modern English. Such an analysis has been advocated by Robin Lakoff. One might go on to claim that after the innovating generation made *not* Deletion obligatory, there was a subsequent re-structuring whereby *not* was no longer introduced by the phrase structure rules to the complements of these verbs, although Lakoff did not postulate such a re-analysis. Given the theory of grammar presupposed by Traugott, it is hard to see how any facts would lead one to prefer the deletion analysis over insertion, or vice versa; under the deletion analysis, it would be equally impossible to choose for the later stage between an obligatory deletion of a *not* optionally introduced by the phrase structure rules and a grammar which failed to generate the *not* in the initial phrase marker. Lakoff's analysis was based on the observation that similar 'redundant' negatives were used in the complements to verbs of preventing, denial, etc., in other languages, e.g. Greek *mḗ*, and Latin *nʒ* and *quin* (which is usually analysed as historically descended from an earlier negative marker). She also assumed a version of the universal base hypothesis, claiming that it was at least easier to study diachronic syntax if the phrase structure rules were taken to be not liable to change. Moreover, she was committed to a view that the major locus of historical change in a grammar was not the formulation of rules so much as the governance system of transformations, and this encouraged her to describe the change in the distribution of the negative as a change in the valence of *not* Deletion, formerly optional but obligatory in Modern English. Whatever the merits of this reasoning and whatever the validity of her theories of grammar and of change, this particular description was at least more fully determined than that of Traugott. That is, she assumed (a) that a negative was required in the deep structure complements to inherently negative verbs in Greek and Latin (although that is not obviously correct); (b) that phrase structure rules are unchanging and therefore presumably universal, or at least common to the historically related Greek, Latin and English (a characteristic assumption of 'Generative Semantics', not of generative grammar as developed in §1.4), and (c) that changes usually take place in the governance system of transformational rules rather than in the rules themselves and that changes should be formulated in this way whenever possible. From these assumptions and the facts of English, the description is almost fully determined: there must be a negative in the initial phrase marker, which is deleted optionally in, say, Middle English and obligatorily in Modern.

Another example of an arbitrary use of rules is found in the discussion of split constructions such as (14).

(14)   a.   that was kyng Priamus sone of Troy 'that was King Priam of Troy's son'
       b.   folweth the Prolog of the Clerkes tale of Oxenford 'the clerk of Oxford's tale follows'

Traugott invokes two rules, Genitive Attachment and Grouping, although they are not formulated and it is not clear from the discussion what they are intended to do. She claims only that in Middle English (henceforth ME) Genitive Attachment precedes Grouping, while the reverse order holds for Modern English (NE) to produce constructions such as *the wife of Bath's tale, the mayor of London's mace*. I interpret this to mean that Genitive Attachment adds *'s* to a NP dominated by a Determiner, $[[[\text{Bill}]_{\text{NP}}]_{\text{Det}}[\text{hat}]_{\text{N}}]_{\text{NP}}$, and that Grouping moves the dependent PP leftwards, in under the NP dominated by the Determiner, yielding *the mayor of London's*. In the absence of a clear proposal it is difficult to evaluate the analysis. However, there is obviously an alternative description available, which is compatible with the theory of grammar presupposed insofar as it is made explicit. This alternative would postulate an initial structure (15), and in ME an Extraposition rule (16) would move the PP to the right, in the same way as it can effect the derivation of (17).[1]

(15) $[[[\text{the}]_{\text{Det}}[[\text{clerk}]_{\text{N}}[\text{of Oxford}]_{\text{PP}}]_{\text{N}}]_{\text{Det}}[\text{tale}]_{\text{N}}]_{\text{NP}}$

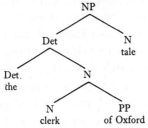

(16) $[[\text{X} \begin{Bmatrix} \text{VP} \\ \text{PP} \end{Bmatrix}]$ Y]   ⇒   1   3   2

(17)   [[John   ]ₛ is likely *to come*]

I am concerned here not so much with the merits of the latter proposal compared to that of Traugott, but I point out that it seems to be a

[1] (16) has a very general formulation but it gives good results on the assumption that it is a cyclic rule and that NP and $\bar{\text{S}}$ are cyclic nodes.

viable alternative, compatible with the theory Traugott operates with. Of course there are further alternatives, particularly if one also admits lexical and interpretive rules. Again, if there are many possible descriptions of the stages compared, the nature of the change can be described in a multitude of ways. Therefore, the fact that this change *may* be described as a re-ordering of transformational rules is of little interest when the theory of grammar presupposed is loose enough to permit several alternative grammars for the two stages compared.

This arbitrary use of rules is compounded by a third methodological error, a tendency to take a rule or some other feature of the grammar of NE and to ask what that rule, etc., looked like in Old English (OE) or ME. Posing questions in this way entails that the formulation of the earlier grammar will be influenced by the claims made for the later one. For example Traugott postulates tense as a deep structure constituent in the grammar of NE. She notes that it seems to behave in the same way in OE and concludes that therefore it should be treated in the same way in the grammar of OE. But this conclusion is fallacious. Before the development of the periphrastic *do* there was no reason to treat tense as a deep structure constituent as opposed to a feature on the first verb of the clause, where 'verb' includes items like *have, be, may, can* and *must* as well as *go, drink* and *roast*. Similarly modals are assumed to constitute a syntactic category for all stages of the language. In chapter 2 I shall argue that while modals are a separate category in NE they were not in OE and ME and that tense, a deep structure constituent in NE, was only a verbal feature until Early Modern English (ENE). Similarly in §4.1 it will be argued that items like *all, some,* and *many,* quantifiers in NE, had an almost identical distribution in OE but at that time were adjectives, there being no separate syntactic category of Quantifier. The point is that given the manner in which Traugott sometimes poses her questions there is no reason to seek out the ways in which 'modals', 'quantifiers', etc., behaved differently in OE and to ask whether they constituted an initial syntactic category. It is important to recognize that while one *theory* of grammar must be presupposed, the particular grammars of OE, ME, NE, etc., must be written independently and then be compared only after the formulation.

The fourth methodological point concerns an apparent confusion between the roles of a particular grammar, a theory of grammar and a theory of change. Traugott (1965: p403) misrepresents Klima (1964b) as claiming that 'a synchronic syntax reflects historical change', and she cites a passage where Klima refers only to the order of his exposition of some dialectal styles, not the order of grammatical rules: 'the order in which the styles are considered does, in fact, recapitulate comparable aspects in the historical development of the pronouns'. On p412f she comments that 'a synchronic grammar cannot account for these changes', although it is not at all clear how a synchronic description of a particular state, whether of a grammar, a biological organ or anything else, can be expected to 'account for' historical changes preceding or following on from that state (see p4n). She continues:

it has been suggested that grammars should provide rules accounting for synchronic relatedness between grammatical systems, such that different systems may be regarded as modifications or extensions of a given basic system. This is essentially what Klima's grammar does for pronouns. In addition, it has been suggested that grammars should provide rules accounting for diachronic relatedness between grammatical systems ... Such grammars would reveal with great clarity the similarities and differences between stages of the language, and would provide in simpler, i.e. more compact, form the same information that separate grammars of different stages of the language provide.

Presumably this is what Traugott has in mind when she speaks in the 1969 paper of a 'diachronic grammar'. However, this confuses a particular grammar and a theory of grammar with in the first instance a theory of variation and in the second instance with a theory of change. I see no reason to devise one formal object, 'a diachronic grammar', which will contain the 'information' of various synchronic grammars and the *formal* relation between those grammars, where the formal relations would include specific instances of rule re-ordering, simplification, loss, addition, etc. It is certainly incorrect to attribute such properties to Klima's description of case marking on pronouns (see above). Klima's description consisted of four separate and independently formulated grammars. An analyst can perceive relationships between those grammars, e.g. that the grammar of L_1 differs from that of L_2 by a different ordering of two transformations; but Klima did not formalize these relationships within a 'diachronic grammar'; nor was there any reason to do so, given the usual goals of linguistic research. We shall return to the essential distinction between a theory of grammar and a theory of change in chapter 3. Clarifying such a distinction has far-reaching consequences for the content of a theory of change and for the appropriate goals for work in diachronic syntax.

The study of diachronic syntax, I have claimed, is best conducted within the framework of a restrictive theory of grammar. In the course of this book it will be argued that underlying representations should be 'close' to their corresponding surface structures and that transformational derivations cannot be complex or effect major changes in the structures operated on. This approach can be contrasted with that of Robin Lakoff (1968: ch. 6), who argued the opposite view: that in order to describe syntactic change one needs a highly abstract notion of deep structure and that it is easier to study the historical evolution of languages if one assumes that deep structures do not change from one stage of a language to another. The major part of her book concerns the Latin complementation system, and to account for various data she postulates 'abstract verbs', which are lexical items which play a role in various syntactic and semantic derivational processes but which have no phonological form and do not appear in surface structures, being deleted obligatorily by a transformational rule. Lakoff assumes a system of rule governance, whereby lexical items, including abstract verbs, will be marked to indicate whether or not they undergo a particular transformation. This permits a characterization of lexical exceptions to rules of grammar, and a set of lexical redundancy rules permits rule features to be assigned to semantic classes of words. If verbs of desire as a class are marked not to undergo a given rule, whose structural description they would otherwise meet, then any specific verb of desire may conform to the normal behaviour of its meaning class or it may be marked as exceptional and be liable, therefore, to undergo the rule in question. Thus the redundancy rules reflect an analyst's expectations about whether or not a given word undergoes a given rule.

Quite apart from the vast extension to the class of available grammars entailed by introducing abstract verbs and arbitrary rule features to the theory, there are many reasons not to adopt abstract verbs as a descriptive device for synchronic grammars, and specifically not Lakoff's abstract verbs in a grammar of Latin. In principle, Lakoff's theory permits special devices and exceptional rule features for abstract verbs, and she and others appeal to such devices in practice. It is true that there are generalizations which can be stated via abstract verbs, but often these abstract verbs lead to false predictions. Lakoff is not disturbed to find that abstract verbs can have exceptions and behave idiosyncratically: when dealing with the abstract verb [*vel*], she says (p179), 'this abstract verb, therefore, does not act like any of the real verbs of its class (though, of course, an abstract verb easily could, as [*imper*] does), but it acts as a verb of its class might act if specially marked'. And of [*oport*]: 'here too the abstract verb does not behave like either of the real verbs in its meaning class' (p184). On p175 she lists a number of special rules needed just for the abstract verb [*imper*] (compare the parenthesized comment in the quotation above). But the whole point of the theory of abstract verbs is that they permit a grammar to capture linguistically significant generalizations in the most economical fashion, by virtue of the fact that they behave exactly like corresponding real verbs and therefore feature only in independently motivated rules. As soon as one postulates special rules to apply only to abstract verbs, the argument for economy begins to wobble, and when abstract verbs show a different syntactic behaviour from the corresponding real verb, it becomes doubtful whether there is any generalization there to be captured in the first place. Given the essentially taxonomic character of a theory of grammar allowing abstract verbs and arbitrary rule features on lexical items, such a theory is interpretable as providing only a taxonomic account of diachronic changes, and not the insightful account which Lakoff attributes to it.

Lakoff considers various changes from Classical Latin to modern Spanish, regrettably with minimal discussion of the intervening stages despite the time-span of about two thousand years. Much of the discussion is vitiated by false claims and analyses of the Spanish data. For example, in a discussion of a putative rule of Raising she analyses sentences like *hacerlo él sería imposible* as having *él* as the subject of the predicate *sería imposible*, *hacerlo* being a complement clause. *El* is alleged to have been transformationally raised from the lower clause, something which was possible with such verbs in Greek but not in Latin; the change having taken place in Spanish was imputed to Greek influence on Latin through bilingual tutors in imperial Rome. However, the correct analysis would treat *hacerlo él* as a constituent acting as the subject of the predicate *sería imposible*. Some evidence for treating *él* as a member of the lower clause is that if *él* were replaced by a plural pronoun, *sería* would remain in the singular: *hacerlo ellos* $\begin{Bmatrix} *serían \\ sería \end{Bmatrix}$ *imposible.*

Lakoff analyses purpose clauses, e.g. *John came in order to see Nero*, as derived from a structure like (18) involving two abstract verbs, [*want*] and [*cause*].

(18)

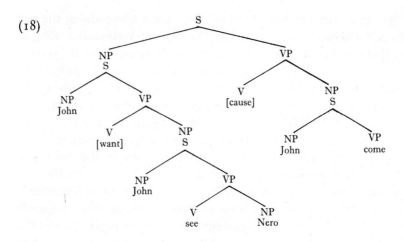

Latin purpose clauses are derived from the same structural configuration but have the abstract verb [*vol*] for English [*want*]. [*vol*] permits a complement clause with *ut* + subjunctive, but not with the accusative + infinitive, although the corresponding real verb *volo* permits both constructions. Therefore the rule features on the abstract [*vol*] differ from those of the real verb *volo*, permitting only the subjunctive construction and thereby describing the fact that its complement clause, which becomes the surface purpose clause, may occur only with a subjunctive.

(19)   a.   Marcus venit ut Neronem videret
       b.   *Marcus venit Neronem videre

Lakoff then notes that a Spanish purpose clause will have its verb in the infinitive if the subject is phonologically null and interpreted as the same as that of the main clause. Otherwise the verb will be in the subjunctive (20). This is precisely how verbs of wishing work, such as *quiero* (21). Since Spanish purpose clauses work in the same fashion as complements to verbs of wishing, the change from Latin can be interpreted in such a way that the abstract verb [*quer*] now permits the same complement-type as the corresponding real verb.[1] Therefore, given the existence of abstract verbs in synchronic grammars, one can view this change as a simplification of the grammar. In this instance

---

[1] Actually Lakoff says 'the only way to account for the behaviour of these sentences in Spanish is to assume an abstract verb [*vol*]' (p232). I change this to [*quer*] because I cannot see how one can justify a Latin abstract verb for Spanish, when the Latin root does not survive into Spanish.

the abstract [*vol*] was specially marked not to undergo a complementation rule normal for its meaning class, whereas the 'corresponding' Spanish abstract verb was not so marked.

(20) a. fuí a Madrid para que Juan me viera 'I went to Madrid in order for Juan to see me'
b. fuí a Madrid para ver a Juan 'I went to Madrid in order to see Juan'
(21) a. quiero que Juan me viera 'I want Juan to see me'
b. quiero ver a Juan 'I want to see Juan'

However, when one turns to imperative constructions, one finds a different situation. Lakoff derives imperatives from complement clauses to a verb of ordering, [*imper*], and is happy to note that Latin imperatives may be in the subjunctive or the infinitive (22), just as the corresponding real verb may take subjunctive or infinitival complements (23).

(22) a. ne abeas [subjunctive] 'do not go away'
b. ne abire [infinitive]
(23) a. impero ne abeas 'I order you not to go away'
b. impero ne abire

However, in Spanish there is an asymmetry between the abstract and the corresponding real verb. Presumably [*mand*] is the abstract verb from the complements of which imperative sentences are to be derived, although Lakoff (p231) seems to assume that the Latin [*imper*] survives into Spanish, despite the fact that the root is otherwise lost. The real verb *mandar* takes complements in *que* + subjunctive or in the infinitive, but the corresponding abstract verb takes only a subjunctive, as indicated by the fact that imperatives are normally expressed with a subjunctive but not an infinitive (24).

(24) a. le mandé a Juan que se fuese: ¡que vaya a Madrid!
b. le mandé a Juan irse: *¡ir a Madrid!

Therefore this historical change is the reverse of the change involving purpose clauses. In this example the Latin abstract verb behaved like the corresponding real verb and had no special rule feature; in Spanish the parallel abstract verb, unlike the real verb, has an idiosyncratic feature precluding infinitival complements. If the change in the purpose clauses represented grammar simplification, this represents grammar complication. Lakoff also argues that some abstract verbs in Spanish retain the irregularity of their Latin counterparts. If abstract verbs can have arbitrary rule features and if these features can be retained, lost or acquired in the course of time, one has only another taxonomy of possible historical changes, not an insightful account. For an insightful account based on this conception of grammar one would need some means of predicting when, say, loss of a rule feature, i.e. grammar simplification, will take place. No attempt is made to formulate such predictive principles, nor is there any discussion of the matter. Even if it is too strong to demand predictions, there should be some way to distinguish natural from impossible changes if the theory has the virtues claimed for it. It is hard to know what kind of principle in even the broadest sense could interact with this conception of grammar to yield an insightful or even partially predictive account of possible diachronic changes. Of course, a *fully* predictive theory of change is beyond anybody's present capacity, and probably will always be so, but Lakoff's theory, as presented, lacks *any* predictive force and therefore does not get beyond the level of a taxonomy.

The work discussed here is typical of generative approaches to diachronic syntax, and it seems appropriate to observe that it has not advanced the field significantly. Klima provided a way of talking about syntactic change as grammar change, but in the framework adopted changes could be of a wide variety of forms, so that there was little that emerged to permit a definition of a possible syntactic change. If rules could be added, lost, re-ordered, simplified and complicated, it was difficult to imagine what would constitute an impossible change, beyond what would contravene restrictions imposed by a theory of grammar. At the same time no implications were drawn for the form of the theory of grammar, partly as a result of the quite loose theories which were generally presupposed by generative linguists working on syntactic change during the 1960s (again, despite the fact that more restrictive theories were available in the literature, e.g. Chomsky 1965). Nor was there any attempt to explain why changes took place. Therefore, although Klima had provided a rigorous way of talking about syntactic change, the results were anticlimactic and no significant consequences emerged for a theory of possible changes or for a theory of possible grammars. After it had been shown that syntactic change *could* be formulated in this fashion, there seemed to be no good reason to pursue the enterprise. Many of the subsequent works introduced serious methodological errors, partly as a result of a failure to distinguish objects such as a particular grammar, a theory of grammar and a theory of change, and of a failure to presuppose a restrictive theory of grammar which would minimize the number of descriptions available for any one stage of a language. Traugott wrote rules and made various clear proposals, but there was a considerable degree of arbitrariness in the proposals put forward. Lakoff wrote very few rules, assuming that not enough was known to permit their useful formulation. There have, of course, been other studies on syntactic change conducted in the framework of a generative grammar. Here I have examined only the most commonly cited studies and those which are methodologically the most illuminating. I have suggested reasons for the current disarray and lack of progress in diachronic syntax and for the fact that no more has been achieved in this area by generativists than by neo-grammarians. With each school it comes down to a failure to work with an appropriate theory of grammar. One of the aims of this book is to demonstrate a methodology for the study of diachronic syntax and to show precisely how that study can have significant consequences for a more general approach to language.

In this section we have emphasized the relationship between a theory of grammar and approaches to diachronic syntax, and the necessity of drawing a clear distinction between theories of grammar and theories of change. There are other areas of diachronic research which are less obviously related to the particular properties of a theory of grammar but interact more directly with accounts of other cognitive domains. For example, there has been interesting work, notably stemming from Bever & Langendoen (1972), involving appeal to perception strategies. On another front, creolization of pidgin languages is a special kind of language change, and the developments which can take place as part of the creolization process will be in part a function of the properties of the pidgin which forms the base. Pidgins clearly have properties not found in other languages and a characterization of those properties will presumably play a role in determining the kinds of changes which take place during creolization. Taking yet another angle, several diachronic studies invoke language contact and foreign influence as causal factors in certain changes. To the extent that such invocations can be justified, one may assume that they will interact with sociological accounts of the societies in question. Furthermore, much work has been done by language typologists on diachronic change, following up the seminal work of Greenberg's (1966) set of implicational universals. Translating these universals into claims about diachrony, analysts have sought to develop hierarchies of change, specifying that if a certain change takes place, something else will follow, which in turn will cause a further change, and so on. This turns out to be related to Sapir's notion of 'drift', as will be shown in §7.2. All of these studies, involving perception strategies, creolization, language contact, typologies and drift, are subsumed under the general rubric of diachronic syntax and, appearances notwithstanding, crucially involve particular theories of grammar. We shall discuss these various kinds of studies at later points, but before we can say much about them we need to spell out the fundamentals of a theory of grammar and of a theory of change, in order to develop a suitable research paradigm. We proceed now to consider the form of a theory of grammar.

1.4   A theory of grammar

There have already been several references to various devices used in transformational generative grammar, and readers who have persevered this far probably have at least a basic acquaintance with phrase structure and transformational rules and the way in which they interact. In this section I shall outline the general theory of grammar which will be presupposed at some points in the book and argued for at other points. This will be a version of the so-called Extended Standard Theory, but it will differ in several ways from the usual descriptions of trans- formational grammar given in the introductory books. Under the view of grammar to be outlined, it will be shown that not only can useful research be conducted on historical change in syntax but also that such research can make an essential contribution to determining some properties of the theory of grammar and to rendering the theory of grammar empirically testable in another domain.

Practising linguists have often engaged in arguments about the correct form of a grammar of some language or even of a theory of grammar, without first agreeing on the *goals* of linguistic research in general or on the theory of grammar in particular. These goals can be formulated in quite different ways. It misses the point for a linguist interested in metaphor to charge that transformational grammar, in the broadest sense, is inadequate because it fails to give any account of metaphor. Equally irrelevant to the usually stated goals of transformational grammar is to charge it with failing to account for the relationship between language and culture or to express the 'intuition' that native speakers normally use language to communicate thoughts. Over recent years there has been much loose talk along these lines and a common predeliction for elevating by fiat pre-theoretical observations into statements about a theory.

For example, several linguists have noted an interaction between syntax and semantics, sometimes incorporating 'presuppositions' and speakers' beliefs, which is an almost self-evident pre-theoretical observation demanding little perspicacity. From this observation some have concluded promptly that therefore syntactic rules must have access to semantics, perhaps to presuppositions, and that no distinction can be sustained between syntax and (presuppositional) semantics; this is a claim about the form of a theory and a very different matter. The autonomy of syntax is a hypothesis about a theory of grammar and therefore cannot be refuted by offering an observation or some unanalysed sentence or phenomenon (see below). This kind of category error is extremely common in the literature. Corum (1975) illustrates the conflation of theoretical and pre-theoretical claims quite graphically: 'to develop such a theory [of syntax and semantics – DWL] independent of pragmatic factors is to claim that such facts of use do not interact with syntactic or semantic facts', adding that 'put against the wall, few linguists would wish to take on the onus probandi of such a noxious claim'. This conclusion is explicitly contradicted in Chomsky (1955, 1957) and elsewhere, but Corum offers no counterargument. To take one more illustration, Searle (*Times Literary Supplement*, September 10, 1976), noting certain facts about the distribution of *please* and imperative verbs and conceding that the facts can be described quite economically in an autonomous syntax, pleads exasperatedly 'but why on earth shouldn't the syntactical rules mention the fact that *please* is used for requests and that the imperative mood only takes verbs that denote voluntary actions?' After all, he notes later, this is 'the intuitively obvious observation' and should therefore appear in the description, although he offers no other argument. Such claims are worthless unless made in the context of a discussion of the appropriate goals for a theory or backed up by an argument to the effect that a description referring to considerations of use is in some way superior to some other description; Searle offers no such argument or discussion of goals. Indeed, if the distribution of *please* can be accounted for by a pragmatic rule, that would support the autonomy thesis, since one would not want the syntax to explain the distribution redundantly. In general, the autonomy thesis (or 'modularity') is supported when one has an independent (e.g. pragmatic) account of some phenomenon, permitting the syntax to avoid any consideration of it. So, if the *intersection* of 'modules' gives the right results, that offers evidence for the correctness of the theory of individual modules (which do not, in isolation, give the right results).

Perhaps one reason for this prevalent looseness has been the tendency to think in terms of a 'theory of *language*' and to assert that a theory of language must deal with metaphor, the interrelationship of language and culture, the ways in which a language can change historically, etc. This seems to me to be not a useful concept. Physicists do not usually formulate their research goals in terms of something as broad as a theory of matter, nor biologists theirs in terms of a theory of living beings. Rather goals are formulated in terms of a theory of electro-magnetism, a theory of genetically determined hereditability or of yet more limited concepts. One formulates one's research goals broadly enough to have interesting intellectual consequences for other domains of enquiry and narrowly enough to permit useful work, not rendered unattainable by excessively ambitious aims. For example, Chomsky (1957) argued that the goals of 'American structuralist' linguistics were too ambitious and therefore unattainable, that it was unrealistic to seek a set of general *analytical* procedures which would permit a linguist to arrive at a grammar of some language; if correct, an argument of this form suggests the need for revised goals. The formulation of goals is partly a matter of choice and of taste, but the success of a research programme and its consequences for other areas of enquiry will depend largely on the skill with which the goals are adumbrated.

Transformational generative grammarians have customarily set up the most general aim of their linguistic work as the characterization of how it is that children can learn their native language in the way that they do, in what appears to be a relatively short time and when provided only with 'degenerate' and limited data, a finite number of utterances with many false starts, speech errors, much extraneous noise ranging from intermittent coughs to phonological redundancy, etc. Such a goal requires a description of the linguistic knowledge which is eventually attained, conventionally called a grammar. In their descriptions of native speakers' linguistic knowledge, or 'competence', transformational generativists have usually sought general organizing principles of grammar which determine what form a grammar may take and how its rules may function; some have attributed these principles to the innate equipment which the child brings to the task of acquiring his native tongue, thus helping to account for the alleged speed of the learning process. Viewed in this way, linguistic research, right or wrong, will have consequences for other domains of enquiry, notably cognitive and developmental psychology and certain branches of philosophy. This is one way of formulating general goals. This is not an area for dogmatism and goals can be set up in many different ways. The appropriateness of one's goals will be determined by the success of one's research programme. Here I shall leave open the fascinating question of how such success is or should be measured. That kind of measurement is not the primary concern of this book but it is the stuff of which scientific revolutions are made. There has, of course, been much discussion in recent years of the proper reasons for a scientist to abandon one research paradigm and to take up another (Kuhn 1962, Popper 1963, and the debate in Lakatos & Musgrave 1970).

If one takes the characterization of how a child comes to learn his native language as the basic goal for linguistic work, one must distinguish now a theory of grammar, as distinct from a theory of language or a theory of metaphor, historical change, etc. A theory of grammar, sometimes referred to as Universal Grammar, delimits the form and functioning of a possible description of a natural language. I assume that the theory of grammar should be as restrictive as possible, but this is by no means a necessary approach and there are alternatives. For example, a theory might have sufficient latitude to allow a wider range of possible grammars than actually occur, but specifying a rich evaluation metric to narrow the range and make the relevant choices. Within this programme the burden of work will lie in the development of an evaluation metric. One cannot show that this is impossible in principle, but as a matter of historical fact very little work has been done in this area by proponents of grammatical theories permitting a wide range of grammars; there seem to be scant grounds for optimism. Since the mid-1950s, fairly straightforward theories have had a considerable effect in ranging grammars in complexity. Therefore it seemed to some that the next development should be to restrict the available devices, holding the evaluation metrics more or less constant. Such evaluation metrics are usually based on notions of 'simplicity', and simplicity criteria may be able to distinguish the 'simplest' of three or four grammars, but it is difficult to imagine them choosing between billions. Again as a matter of historical fact, such simplicity criteria have played a significant role only in resolving more general questions, e.g. the choice between a phrase structure and transformational grammar (Chomsky 1955); on finer questions, competing theories usually turn out to be empirically non-equivalent in such a way that it is unnecessary to appeal to an explicit and carefully defined simplicity metric, even if a general notion of simplicity is tacitly assumed. Another approach might seek to develop a set of perceptual mechanisms to restrict possible grammars. Again one would permit a loose theory of grammar, permitting more kinds of grammars than are attested, but here one would claim that the class of actually available grammars is further restricted by general perceptual strategies affecting cognitive domains other than language.[1] No doubt there are further alternatives to seeking an enrichment of the theory of grammar in order to restrict the class of available grammars.

This study will be conducted within the broad framework of a transformational generative theory of grammar, but it will become clear in this section that we shall permit only a very minimal role for transformations. It is worth observing that 'generative' and 'transformational' are terms of different status. To say that a grammar is transformational means that it contains a particular formal device, namely a rule changing one syntactic phrase marker into another in certain prescribed ways. But to say that a grammar is generative represents a different kind of claim and is a methodological assertion, independent of any particular formal devices in the grammar. A generative grammar will contain explicit and formal rules which will assign to the sentences of a language their correct structural descriptions and associate their phonological form with a representation of their meaning. The ideal generative grammar will so generate all the well-

---

[1] For example, grammatical rules determining the presence or absence of the complementizer *that* seem to be quite complex. Bever & Langendoen (1972) suggest that the distribution of *that* be captured by a perceptual strategy. They propose a left-to-right procedure analysing any NP-VP sequence as a full sentence (not a NP) unless it is preceded by *that* or the NP is morphologically marked to indicate that it is not a subject (e.g. by an oblique case desinence). This is a natural candidate for a perceptual strategy, operating perforce at the level of surface structure. Under this view the grammar would 'overgenerate' and specify as well-formed various structures which would be filtered out by a set of perceptual strategies. Similarly, a grammar might generate structures with multiple centre-embedding, only to find them discarded or characterized as ill-formed by some perceptual strategies.

formed sentences of a given language and none of the deviant ones, although on this score we shall introduce some caveats later in the chapter. Within this framework a distinction is drawn between weak and strong generation, such that a grammar strongly generates a set of structural descriptions and weakly generates a language, assigning one or more structural descriptions to each sentence and, in principle, to all potential sentences.

Such a generative view of grammar can be contrasted with informal grammars or with pedagogical grammars of, say, English written with Dutch and Indonesian speakers in mind (e.g. Poutsma 1914), or with grammars written on historical principles listing construction-types and informally describing their history (e.g. Jespersen MEG), or with grammars classifying elements of language according to co-occurrence and paraphrase (Harris 1957, 1965). Such taxonomic, non-generative grammars essentially classify data according to some selected parameters. Dougherty (1975) has observed that in a sense the problems (e.g. to teach English to Dutch speakers, to demonstrate the historical antecedents of modern sentences, to characterize paraphrase, etc.) define the grammatical model in taxonomic studies, whereas in generative studies not designed for a particular user or practical purpose, the theoretical model defines the problems to be posed. Given the aim of formulating a theory of grammar, some regard generativeness as more or less uncontroversial; Anttila (1975: p72) simply equates generative grammar with 'good grammar'. But others argue that most published analyses are too informal to be classed as contributions to a truly generative grammar, even if most practising linguists would permit themselves to be labelled 'generativist' in the broadest sense.

Summarizing, a person learning a language constructs a system which will correlate meaning with sound over an infinite domain of sentences. An analyst's grammar is an account of the native speaker's fully developed linguistic competence, under the usual idealizations. The theory of grammar imposes restrictions on the possible form a grammar may take and explicit conditions on the way in which grammatical rules may function. So in phonology there are many different physical dimensions which could in principle be exploited by the sound system of a language, but in fact only a small range of the logically possible systems are actually used. Research will be designed to discover the most restrictive principles on the form and function of possible grammars. These restrictive principles, when formulated, can be hypothesized to be part of the innate equipment brought by the child to the task of acquiring his native language, and making language acquisition possible in a short time and with only impoverished primary data. To refute a theory of grammar one will need a grammar or fragment of a grammar which can be shown to be the optimal description of some language but which does not accord with the theory of grammar under challenge; theories, whether of grammar or electro-magnetism or the structure of DNA molecules, cannot be refuted by primary facts or unanalysed data. Therefore refutation is not a trivial business. One must also bear in mind that of the world's languages, past and present, only a tiny fraction have been used as a basis for a serious attempt to write a generative grammar. However, principles of Universal Grammar or a theory of grammar will not be determined by a superficial view of all the world's languages. Linguists may derive courage from the history of genetics, which discovered general principles not by surveying all living species, but by performing extremely detailed experiments on the fruit-fly, which led to results which could be generalized. We can view the theory of grammar as

a common human attribute, genetically determined, one component of the human mind. Through interaction with the environment, this faculty of mind becomes articulated and refined, emerging in the mature person as a system of knowledge of language. To discover the character of this mental faculty, we will try to isolate those properties of attained linguistic competence that hold by necessity rather than as a result of accidental experience, where by 'necessity' I of course mean biological rather than logical necessity. We will therefore be particularly interested in properties of attained linguistic competence that are vastly underdetermined by available experience in general, but that nevertheless hold of the linguistic competence attained by any normal speaker of a given language, and in fact by all speakers of all languages (perhaps vacuously in some cases) on the natural assumption of uniformity across the species. The commitment to formulate a restrictive theory of U[niversal] G[rammar] is nothing other than a commitment to discover the biological endowment that makes language acquisition possible and to determine its particular manifestations. Returning to the matter of 'explanatory adequacy', we can explain some property of attained linguistic competence by showing that this property necessarily results from the interplay of the genetically-determined language faculty, specified by UG, and the person's (accidental) experience. (Chomsky 1976)

We turn now to the specific form of grammar which will provide a basis for the major part of the book. The general model is sketched in (25); this grammar will formally relate phonetic form to logical form for any given sentence. The base sub-component consists of phrase structure rules and a lexicon, which define the initial phrase marker for some structure.[1] The initial phrase marker is the input to the transformational sub-component, where it may be amended in several ways by the successive application of various transformational rules. These two sub-components make up the syntactic component, whose output is a surface structure. The surface structure constitutes the input to the phonological component, which produces a phonetic

(25)

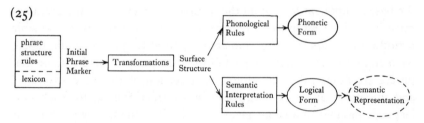

representation; I shall have little to say here about this aspect of the grammar, but I presuppose the general framework of Chomsky & Halle (1968). The surface structure is also the input, and the sole input to the semantic interpretation rules (cf. earlier formulations which permitted interpretive rules to take as input aspects of surface structure, initial structure and even intermediate structure). The interpretive rules will produce a 'logical form', a description of the scope of quantifiers, anaphora relations, thematic functions of NPs, subject-predicate relations, various entailments, etc. I distinguish tentatively between logical form and a fuller semantic representation, assuming that logical form can be fully specified by rules of sentence-grammar but leaving

---

[1] Following Chomsky (1975), I refer to the output of the base component as an 'initial phrase marker' and not as a 'deep structure'. Chomsky drops the latter term because of misleading connotations about 'deep' properties of language being describable particularly at this level as opposed to the levels of surface structure, phonetic representation, etc. But there are other reasons to drop the term. 'Deep structure' was introduced in the 1960s to refer to a level of representation which met certain conditions: this was a unique representation which was (a) the output of the phrase structure rules, (b) the input to the transformations, (c) the input to the semantic rules and the point at which (d) all lexical insertion took place, (e) categories could be assigned, (f) co-occurrence restrictions were stated. In the model (25) there is no single level of representation which meets all six requirements.

open the possibility that there is more to semantic representation, perhaps involving beliefs, expectations, legitimate inferences, conditions of appropriate use and matters beyond what can be usefully formalized. After all, many philosophers have disputed the feasibility of a coherent formal notion of semantic representation. Even admitting the possibility of semantic representation broadly conceived, it may not constitute part of grammar; I leave this as an open question and I shall say nothing more about it here.

To consider aspects of this model in more detail, the initial phrase marker is a configuration specifying an abstract constituent structure, category labels and a lexical entry under each pre-terminal category node. I take the class of initial phrase markers to be infinite, assuming the base component to contain the recursive property that any grammar must have. Bearing in mind that we want the most restrictive possible definition for the class of grammars of natural languages, as discussed, we turn first to the categorial part of the base component. I assume that phrase structure rules are subject to a version of the '$\overline{X}$ convention' and therefore cannot be postulated in arbitrary fashion for each new language or stage of a language examined. Thus the theory of grammar prescribes that phrase structure rules must be written according to the general schema of (26), where X represents any major category such as N, V, P, Adj, etc. The bar notation indicates the hierarchy of dominance relations, and $\overline{\overline{N}}$, $\overline{\overline{V}}$ and $\overline{\overline{P}}$ are equivalent to NP, VP and PP. This schema defines the available phrase structure rules and will permit a particular grammar to contain the rules of (27), for example, which in turn will yield a tree such as (28) (I omit certain lower nodes and assume that for English [Spec(-ifier) $\overline{N}$] dominates determiners, [Spec $\overline{V}$] auxiliaries, etc; Comp(-lement) is an abbreviatory device which subsumes a variety of categories).

(26)   a. $\overline{\overline{X}} \rightarrow \{[\text{Spec } \overline{X}] \ \overline{X}\}$
       b. $\overline{X} \rightarrow \{X \text{ Comp}\}$

(27) $S \rightarrow \overline{\overline{N}} \ \overline{\overline{V}}$
       $\overline{\overline{N}} \rightarrow [\text{Spec } \overline{\overline{N}}] \ \overline{N}$
       $\overline{\overline{V}} \rightarrow [\text{Spec } \overline{\overline{V}}] \ \overline{V}$
       $\overline{\overline{P}} \rightarrow [\text{Spec } \overline{\overline{P}}] \ \overline{P}$

       $\overline{N} \rightarrow N \ \left(\begin{Bmatrix} \overline{\overline{P}} \\ S \end{Bmatrix} \right)$

$$\overline{V} \to V \left(\left\{ \begin{matrix} \overline{\overline{P}} \\ \overline{\overline{N}} \\ S \end{matrix} \right\} \right)$$

$$\overline{P} \to P \ \overline{\overline{N}}$$

(28)

S
- $\overline{\overline{N}}$
  - [Spec $\overline{N}$] — the
  - $\overline{N}$
    - N — dog
- $\overline{\overline{V}}$
  - [Spec $\overline{V}$] — has
  - $\overline{V}$
    - V — gone
    - $\overline{\overline{P}}$
      - [Spec $\overline{P}$] — right
      - $\overline{P}$
        - P — to
        - $\overline{\overline{N}}$
          - [Spec $\overline{N}$] — the
          - $\overline{N}$
            - N — bowl
            - $\overline{\overline{P}}$
              - [Spec $\overline{P}$]
              - $\overline{P}$
                - P — of
                - $\overline{\overline{N}}$
                  - [Spec $\overline{N}$]
                  - $\overline{N}$
                    - N — water

I shall not enter into any debates here about the specific form of the conventions, whether they should be as in (26), which are emendations of the original proposals of Chomsky (1970), or whether they should involve triple bar structures, etc. A good proposal for the categorial base rules of English, formulated in terms of $\overline{X}$ conventions, is to be found in Hornstein (1977a), who outlines clearly the logic behind these conventions; for a general discussion, see Jackendoff (1977). The point is that these conventions provide a template for possible phrase structure rules, thereby restricting their possible form in grammars of particular languages. The rules of (27) accord with the general convention (26) and therefore are possible phrase structure rules. One can imagine many sets of rules which would not accord with the template of (26) and therefore under this theory such sets would not be possible in grammars of natural languages: for example, no grammar could contain both the rules $\overline{N} \to$ [Spec $\overline{N}$] $\overline{N}$ and $\overline{\overline{V}} \to \overline{V}$ [Spec $\overline{V}$]. We thus have a restrictive definition of available phrase structure rules;

in fact this definition (26) would exclude many published rules. Whether or not this definition is correct depends on whether it is compatible with the optimal grammar for each language. Initial results are encouraging but there remain problems, which I shall not discuss here.

These conventions have been widely misunderstood and some clarification is in order. It is essential to note that the conventions themselves are metagrammatical, part of the theory of grammar and not part of particular grammars, and they require that the major categories, NP, VP, PP, AdjP, etc. (here written respectively as $\overline{\overline{N}}$, $\overline{\overline{V}}$, $\overline{\overline{P}}$, $\overline{\overline{A}}$) be expanded in symmetrical fashion. In the convention of (26) the curly brackets are to be read as indicating that the categories are unordered, order being assigned by the particular grammar. This permits a grammar to have specifiers of all categories either preceding or following the head; thus *all* specifiers will be on the same side. On one interpretation of this notation, it follows that in any given grammar, if the specifier precedes the head, the complement will follow it, and vice versa. Thus (26b) permits Comp immediately to precede or immediately to follow the category head, but if the specifier is already determined to precede the head, the Comp will be left with Hobson's choice – on the assumption that [Spec $\overline{X}$] and Comp must each be adjacent to the head. So in English all specifiers precede the head (29) and all complements follow (30). This entails that all phrase nodes (except S) are endocentric, as proposed by Harris (1951).

(29) [*the* dog]$_{\overline{\overline{N}}}$ (30) [the picture *of Mary*]$_{\overline{\overline{N}}}$
      [*has* gone]$_{\overline{\overline{V}}}$ [lies *on the table*]$_{\overline{\overline{V}}}$
      [*right* to the kennel]$_{\overline{\overline{P}}}$ [on *the table*]$_{\overline{\overline{P}}}$

All metagrammatical principles will be either absolute or relative. Thus the theory of grammar might specify that any particular grammar must without exception contain phrase structure rules and that its other rules will be structure-dependent, using structures assigned by these phrase structure rules. On the other hand, some other principles of grammar may be only desirable, the theory of grammar specifying that a grammar conforming to principle P_i will be more highly valued than one which does not. Such an evaluation metric may be quite complex, stipulating that while P_i may be only desirable for some grammars, it may be essential if a grammar conforms to some other principle P_j (we shall return to this in §1.5 and in chapter 7). Given such a distinction, are $\overline{X}$ conventions absolute or relative restrictions on possible grammars? The answer is that some elements of the conventions are probably absolute and others probably relative; there can, after all, be no principled grounds to determine in advance what is absolute and what relative.

For example, the claim (above) emerging from one reading of (26), that specifiers and complements must always be on opposite sides of the category head, may well be an absolute universal. Such a claim corresponds to assertions by Lehmann (1973) and Vennemann (1974) about possible word orders. Vennemann claims that 'operators' precede 'operands' in OV languages, and vice versa in VO languages (see §7.2); while Lehmann put forward a structural principle that 'modifiers are placed on the opposite side of a basic syntactic element from its primary concomitant'. However, the claim that all specifiers must be on the same side of the head may prove to be too strong. There seem to exist languages (e.g. some of the Dravidian group) whose verbal specifiers, auxiliaries of some kind, follow the verb, while nominal specifiers (such as determiners) precede the head noun. Greenberg (1966) noted that OV languages tend to have post-verbal auxiliaries and to be postpositional with respect to case markers on nouns, determiners, etc., whereas a VO language will be prepositional and have auxiliaries preceding verbs. Typologists basing their work on such universals of Greenberg's describe languages violating these claims as unusual and transitional, assuming them to be changing diachronically from one type to another. Similarly under the version of $\overline{\overline{X}}$ conventions given here, they would be regarded as marked and less highly valued than grammars conforming more closely to the conventions. We shall return later to the matter of markedness, the distinction between more or less highly valued grammars, and the way in which such claims can lead to empirically testable predictions about the possible form of grammars.

Notice some dangers inherent in these conventions: it is easy to reduce them to empirically vacuous statements, and some of the proposals in the literature do just that. In particular, any proposal comes close to empirical vacuity which (a) permits different categories in any one grammar to involve different levels of analysis such that for nouns there is a node $\overline{\overline{N}}$ while for verbs there is no analysis higher than a double bar node, $\overline{\overline{V}}$, or (b) allows both [Spec $\overline{X}$] and Comp to be treated as abbreviatory symbols only, not actually appearing in the phrase structure rules of a given grammar as category labels. Under such interpretations it is not clear that the $\overline{X}$ conventions offer any means of restricting possible phrase structure rules from which a particular grammar may draw. For example, if one surveyed all the phrase structure rules which have been proposed in the literature for various languages, it is not clear that any would be eliminated by such a liberal interpretation of the conventions. I leave aside here questions involving specific proposals for universal conventions or for specific rules of, say, English, and I am concerned just to illustrate the logic of the matter.

The phrase structure rules, then, constrained in their formal properties by such metagrammatical conventions, will define the initial phrase marker of a given sentence, which will have the general form illustrated in (28). Lexical items will be inserted at the base of such labelled trees, more or less as proposed in Chomsky (1965). The lexical entry for each item will contain an abstract phonological specification, an indication of its meaning and the syntactic frame in which it can be inserted in a phrase marker. For more details the reader is referred to Aronoff (1976). However, the lexicon may also contain redundancy rules as discussed in Jackendoff (1975) and elsewhere. These rules will express the relationship between morphological items like *decide–decision*, which I shall not discuss, and the relationship between various syntactic constructions that a given lexical item may occur in; this is an alternative to codifying the information in a 'lexically governed transformation'. An example of a proposed lexical entry for *break*, omitting phonological specification, is given in (31), and a lexical redundancy rule in (32). The upper line of the entry specifies the syntactic frame in which it may occur, and the lower line gives a semantic representation. Thus the lexicon expresses the relationship between (33a) and (33b), specifically the fact that in the transitive and intransitive examples the semantic relation between *pot* and *break* is identical. The same redundancy rule will relate the non-homophonous *kill* and *die*, which have the lexical entries of (34).

(31)   a. $[+V, \quad NP_i\text{\_\_\_}]$
          $\quad NP_i \quad \text{BREAK}$
        b. $[+V, \quad NP_j\text{\_\_\_}NP_i]$
          $\quad NP_j \quad \text{CAUSE} \quad (NP_i \quad \text{BREAK})$

(32) $\begin{bmatrix} +V, & NP_i\text{\_\_\_} \\ NP_i & W \end{bmatrix} \longleftrightarrow \begin{bmatrix} +V, & NP_j\text{\_\_\_} \ NP_i \\ NP_j & \text{CAUSE} \ (NP_i \ W) \end{bmatrix}$

(33) a. the pot broke; Bill died
      b. Horace broke the pot; Fred killed Bill

(34) a. *die*

      $[+V, \quad NP_i\text{——}]$

       $NP_i \quad$ DIE

    b. *kill*

      $[+V \quad NP_j\text{——}NP_i]$

      $NP_j \quad$ CAUSE $\quad (NP_i \quad$ DIE$)$

Under this view (33a) and (33b) will have quite different syntactic structures at all levels of analysis and will not be related by a transformational rule deriving one from the structure underlying the other, as in 'generative semantic' analyses (Lakoff 1970a). The transformational approach has been criticized on many grounds, which we shall not go into here (Chomsky 1970, 1972a, Fodor 1970, etc). Also there is much which could be said about the appropriate form for expressing this kind of information in the lexicon; there are various proposals discussed in the literature. I shall say nothing further about this, nor about the motivation for the framework adopted, but some more detail on the general properties of these rules is in order.

It might appear that this is an unwarranted introduction of a new kind of rule to perform operations which could be carried out by syntactic transformations, albeit under a highly permissive definition of transformation. In fact it is a good illustration of a frequent phenomenon, whereby enriching the theory of grammar, in this case by distinguishing two classes of rules, lexical and transformational, restricts the class of available grammars – always a desirable consequence. In general, lexical rules, whatever their precise form of representation, have properties distinguishing them from transformations and transformations can consequently be defined in more restrictive fashion than would otherwise be possible. First, lexical rules may relate items of different grammatical categories, whereas transformations can be defined so that they cannot change category membership. Second, lexical rules do not change structure, whereas transformations characteristically do. Root transformations (see below) can effect fairly radical structural changes and structure-preserving transformations may move lexical entries from one identical node to another, e.g. moving material from one base-generated NP position to another. Third, lexical rules apply only to lexically defined sets of morphemes,

3

while transformations cannot be lexically governed or have genuine lexical exceptions. Fourth, lexical rules apply before any transformations, while transformations may apply to the output of other transformations. Fifth, lexical rules are 'local' and may involve only morphemes which occur in the sub-categorization frame of the lexical items undergoing the rule, while transformations are non-local and insensitive to grammatical relations as such, applying blindly to phrase markers meeting their structural description. This division of properties turns out to make some surprising distinctions. We shall discuss this in more detail in §5.2, as a prelude to arguing for a diachronic change whereby a lexical rule acquires a transformational counterpart. That is, it will be argued that the postulation of such a distinction permits one to relate a set of simultaneous historical changes which would otherwise have nothing in common but their simultaneity, which would presumably have to be regarded as fortuitous.

Thus the categorial rules, rules permitting lexical insertion, and the lexical rules themselves, combine to generate an initial phrase marker, which is the input to a set of transformations. A transformation has a *structural description* specifying the class of phrase markers to which it applies and a *structural change* stating the effect of the transformation on an arbitrary member of this class. So it changes an abstract phrase marker into another phrase marker, not, it is worth noting, sentences into other sentences. A transformation may apply to a phrase marker if its terminal string can be factored in such a way as to meet the structural description of the rule. For example, if the structural description calls for X-A-B-C-Y, where X and Y are (end-) variables covering arbitrary material, the rule may apply to any sequence A-B-C contained in the phrase marker. In fact, the structural descriptions appearing in the literature are often much richer than this and presuppose a theory of transformations allowing reference to be made to disjunctions, dominance relations (applying, for example, to a NP only if it is dominated by S), grammatical relations such as 'subject of', semantic features, derivational history no longer encoded in the phrase marker undergoing the rule (so called 'derivational constraints', Lakoff 1970b), even to aspects of other derivations ('transderivational constraints') and to non-syntactic factors such as beliefs. Also one finds proposals for sub-categorizing transformations into clause-mate/non-clause-mate rules, bounded/non-bounded, etc. All of these extensions to the class of permitted transformations have been discussed in the literature and will not be discussed further here. Following the general orientation of work in the EST, we shall take a much more restrictive definition of possible transformations, assuming that they cannot refer to any of the items listed above.[1] If transformations cannot refer to semantic features, disjunctions or dominance relations, they will be much more limited than most proposals in the literature.

There may be no transformations in a sentence-grammar which delete material under an identity condition, although they may delete designated elements (there may be such rules in discourse grammar, e.g. VP Deletion, Ellipsis). Non-deletion transformations fall into three classes, being root, local or structure-preserving (Emonds 1976). *Root transformations* can effect radical changes but they apply only in 'root' sentences, i.e. to a matrix S or to a S immediately dominated by a matrix S, broadly speaking main clauses. There can only be one root transformation applying in a given derivation and it must move, copy or insert a node such that it is dominated immediately by the root S. A *local transformation* affects only a sequence C'–C or C–C', where C is a non-phrase node and C' is an immediately adjacent constituent, and the rule is insensitive to any condition exterior to the sequence defined. A *structure-preserving transformation* introduces a constituent C into a position in a phrase marker dominated by a node C. Thus a NP may move into a NP position, a PP into a PP, but not a PP into a NP or vice versa. I also assume that rules apply cyclically first to the most deeply embedded domain and then successively to each more inclusive domain, where 'cyclic domain' corresponds to the nodes NP and $\bar{\text{S}}$ (see (35) below).[2]

Not only are transformations maximally simple in form, but they

---

[1] Occasionally our actions will appear to belie our words, as in the formulation of rule (16), which contains a disjunction $\left\{ \begin{matrix} \text{VP} \\ \text{PP} \end{matrix} \right\}$. However, this formulation is adopted simply for ease of exposition. On the assumption that rules should be written in terms of $\bar{\text{X}}$ conventions, this rule would have a structural description operating on $\underset{[\alpha\,\text{F}]}{\bar{\bar{\text{X}}}}$ where F represents the features distinguishing VP and PP from other phrasal categories. Again, this should be viewed in the framework of a markedness theory: as in phonology, features will permit the characterization of natural classes. Therefore if a putative rule affects, say, only determiners and VPs, i.e. elements at different levels in the bar analysis and sharing few or no distinctive features, such a rule will be costly and will necessitate a very complex feature specification.

[2] Some have proposed that VP and AdjP are also cyclic domains. For a suggestion that S and not $\bar{\text{S}}$ is a cyclic node, see Chomsky (1977). Presumably different languages can vary in their inventories of cyclic nodes. The possible cyclicity of VP and AdjP has no effect on the analyses to be discussed in this book and I take no position on that issue.

are also few in number. In fact, following Chomsky (1977), just two rules, NP Preposing and *wh* Movement, will do a great deal of work, the work done by many different transformations under earlier grammars. Given the phrase structure rules of (35) and the formulations of (36), these rules will play a role in the derivations of (37) and (38). That is to say, these transformations are abstract in the sense that they are not associated with any particular construction-type. Contrast this with earlier versions of transformational grammars, wherein there was almost a one-to-one relation between transformations and construction-types. There was a Passive rule and a passive construction, a Pseudo-cleft rule and a pseudo-cleft construction, an Imperative Formation transformation and imperative constructions. Dougherty (1975) has argued that this practice reflected a perpetuation of Harrisian taxonomic transformations into research on generative grammars. There is much more to be said about the rules of (35) and (36), and about the derivations of (37) and (38) (where a 'trace' *t* marks the position from which the italicized NP has been moved by NP Preposing in (37) and *wh* Movement in (38)). For convenience of exposition, the phrase structure rules are simplified and written in a familiar, non-bar notation. Further illustration will be provided later and more details will be filled in as the need arises. For the moment, this will serve to illustrate the form of transformations and the way in which one particular rule may be involved in the derivation of many construction-types.

(35) $\bar{\bar{S}} \rightarrow$ TOPIC $\bar{S}$

$\bar{S} \rightarrow$ COMP   S

S $\rightarrow$ NP   Aux   VP

VP $\rightarrow$ (*have-en*) (*be-ing*)   V $\left(\left\{ \begin{matrix} \text{NP} \\ \text{PP} \\ \bar{\bar{S}} \end{matrix} \right\} \right)$

PP $\rightarrow$ P   NP

NP $\rightarrow$ (Det)   N

Aux $\rightarrow$ T   (M)

(36) NP Preposing

np   X   NP $\Rightarrow$ 3   2   t

wh Movement

COMP   X   wh $\Rightarrow$ 3   2   t

(37)   a. *John* was arrested t

  b. *John*'s arrest t

  c. *John* seems t to be happy

  d. *John* is believed t to be happy

(38)   a. *who* did you see t
       b. the woman *who* you saw t
       c. John is taller than (*what*) Fred is t
       d. John, (*wh*) I like t
       e. John is easy (*wh*) to please t

The output of the transformational sub-component will be a surface structure, which constitutes the input, and the sole input to another class of rules, which will assign a logical form. The feasibility of semantic interpretation off surface structure alone arises under the 'trace theory of movement rules', coupled with some other proposals about the nature of rightward movement rules (chapter 6). Movement rules leave behind a trace, as indicated in (36), and if that trace survives into surface structure it will codify at surface structure the initial position of the moved NP, permitting thematic functions (determined on the basis of initial or 'deep' structure position) to be captured at the level of surface structure (for discussion, see Chomsky 1975: ch. 3). These interpretive rules will specify the scope of quantifiers, anaphoric relations, etc. Although there are limits to what interpretive rules may do and, as we shall see, limits on the way in which they can function, there are as yet no good proposals to restrict the possible form of these rules in the way that phrase structure and transformational rules are formally defined.[1] Here, for illustration, we shall consider two such rules: Bound Anaphora Interpretation and Disjoint Reference. Bound Anaphora Interpretation associates reflexives, reciprocal expressions, 'bound anaphoric' terms like traces (see below), *his* in (39d) and abstract elements like *PRO* in (39e) with a full NP higher and to the left, marking them [+anaphoric].[2] Thus in the surface structures sketched in (39) (with many details omitted), the rule will associate the two italicized items. Notice that (40) are also possible surface structures, since *himself*, *each other*, *PRO*, etc., being lexical NPs, may be generated under any NP position in the initial phrase marker. However, they will not be interpreted by Bound Anaphora Interpretation because they fail to meet its structural description, having no

---

[1] Jackendoff (1972) presents some early proposals for formal restrictions on interpretive rules. In the light of more recent work, one may be able to claim that such rules may only co-index two elements and therefore are highly restricted in their possible form.

[2] 'Bound anaphora' can be viewed as obligatory co-reference. In *Bill said that he left*, *he* may refer to *Bill* or to some other person specified in the discourse setting; but in *Bill lost his way*, a bound anaphoric expression, *his* must refer to *Bill*.

full NP higher and to the left. Therefore the italicized items in (40) will not be associated and *himself*, *each other*, etc. will remain uninterpreted, entailing that the derivation will be classed as defective. In this way the interpretive rules have a filtering function, eliminating certain surface structures which emerge from the syntactic component but cannot be assigned an interpretation.

(39)   a. *John* washed *himself*
      b. *the men* washed *each other*
      c. *John* was washed *t*
      d. *John* lost *his* way
      e. *John* tried *PRO* to become popular

(40)   a. *himself* washed *John*
      b. *each other* washed *the men*
      c. *his* way was lost t by *John*
      d. *PRO* tried *John* to become popular

The rule of Disjoint Reference specifies that no two NPs may be interpreted as intersecting in reference and if they co-refer by their very nature (e.g. if they are both either first or second person pronouns), the sentence is classed as ungrammatical. The rule (41) will specify correctly that *they* and *them* in (42a) do not intersect in reference and that (42b) is ungrammatical. In (43a) the two *they*s may co-refer and (43b) is grammatical, which suggests that these may be counterexamples to the analysis; we shall show in due course that they are not counterexamples when one invokes certain necessary conditions on the application of rules.

(41)   Disjoint Reference
      In a configuration NP_1 X NP_2, enter in the table of co-reference
      NP_1 [−anaphoric] NP_2.

(42)   a. they shot them
      b. *I washed me

(43)   a. they voted that they should get a raise
      b. I said that she disliked me

Some writers assert that interpretive rules of this type are notational variants of transformations, or transformations 'working backwards'. They point to the apparent equivalence of (a) a Pronominalization transformation changing a fully specified NP into a pronoun just in case a 'co-referential' NP precedes and commands the NP to be changed, and (b) an interpretive rule interpreting a base-generated pronoun as anaphoric to a fully specified NP which precedes and commands it. Although these two proposals may look like equivalent mirror-images it has often been shown that they have different empirical consequences. To take just one example, assume that there is a cyclic transformational rule of Dative Movement, relating *the man gave the dog to John* to *the man gave John the dog*. The rule should not apply if the direct object is a pronoun: *the man gave it to John* but **the man gave John it*. However, in a structure like [*the dog bit the man* [*who gave NP to John*]$_{S^1}$]$_{S^2}$, Dative Movement will be free to apply on the lower S^1 cycle. Under the interpretive theory the NP may contain a pronoun *it* and then Dative Movement will not apply, yielding only *the dog bit the man who gave it to John* with *it* interpreted optionally as anaphoric to *the dog* on the higher cycle, or at surface structure. However, under the transformational theory, the NP will contain a full lexical item *the dog*. Therefore Dative Movement will be free to apply on the internal cycle where its structural description is met and there is no pronominal NP; the structural description for Pronominalization will not be met until the higher cycle, when the rule can 'see' the two identical NPs. This will yield **the dog bit the man who gave John it*. No doubt this problem can be handled in a variety of ways, but it suffices to show that even if two rules look like equivalent mirror-images, they may have quite different consequences when embedded in a grammar and interacting with other rules. Wasow (1975) and Lasnik (1976) give several reasons to adopt an interpretive account of pronouns, basing their arguments on empirical consequences of this type.

As noted, this theory of grammar presupposes a version of the autonomy hypothesis, stipulating that syntactic rules operate independently of considerations of meaning and use, and do not have access to any form of semantic information. This has been a recurrent theme throughout the history of transformational generative grammar and constitutes a restriction on the set of available grammars in that it limits the class of syntactic rules. This, coupled with other severe limitations imposed on the transformational sub-component, entails that the syntax will 'overgenerate' and produce many ungrammatical structures. Some of these will be filtered out by the interpretive rules, as we have seen. Such a conception of grammar accords with the fact that there are no valid intuitions, in many cases, about whether a given structure should be characterized as ill-formed by the syntactic or semantic component; this will be a matter of convenience to the grammar (not arbitrary convenience, of course; the formulation of the grammar will have empirical consequences and will make a truth-claim). Any such 'intuitions' that one might have concerning the appropriateness, say, of ruling *himself left* as ill-formed in the semantic component, are a function of one's experience as an analyst and depend in part on where one went to graduate school; they are not part of the primary data to which a theory must be responsible.

However, having restricted the form of rules, one can also restrict the manner in which they function and this will further reduce the problem of over-generation. In addition to the principles of the cycle and structure-preservation already noted, we shall invoke four other conditions on the application of rules. These conditions grow out of work developing some proposals of Ross (1967), who in turn sought to make precise the A-over-A constraint of Chomsky (1962). Ever since 1962 the A-over-A constraint has been another recurrent theme in transformational grammar and Bresnan (1976a) has recently sought to give it a precise account, modifying it significantly to a 'relativized' version. The constraint will play only a minimal role in the rest of the book so we need not appeal to Bresnan's ingenious version. The constraint aims to restrict the access of rules to categories contained within a larger category of the same type. This can be illustrated by the fact that while *John kept the car in the garage* is structurally ambiguous, indicating either where John kept the car (44a) or just what he kept (44b), the corresponding question *what did John keep in the garage?* is unambiguous and correlates only with the locational reading. This suggested that a *wh* NP could not be extracted from within a larger NP; in other words, that (45a) is an interpretable surface structure, but not (45b).

(44) a. John [kept [the car]$_{NP}$ [in the garage]$_{PP}$]$_{VP}$
      b. John kept [the car in the garage]$_{NP}$
(45) a. what did John [keep t [in the garage]$_{PP}$]$_{VP}$
      b. what did John keep [t in the garage]$_{NP}$

The four constraints which will play a significant role here are the Propositional Island Constraint, the Specified Subject Constraint, the Subjacency Constraint and the COMP-to-COMP Condition, which I formulate in (46)–(49) following Chomsky (1977).

In a configuration ...X...[$_\alpha$...Y...]...X..., where α is a cyclic node (S̄ or NP).

(46) Propositional Island Constraint (PIC)
No rule may involve X and Y where α is a finite clause

(47) Specified Subject Constraint (SSC)
No rule can involve X and Y where α contains a specified subject, i.e. a subject not containing Y and not controlled by X, where X is a possible controller

(48) Subjacency Constraint
No rule can move a phrase from position Y to position X, where Y is properly included in a cyclic node other than α

(49) COMP-to-COMP Condition
No rule can involve X and Y where Y is in COMP and X is not in COMP

A transformational rule 'involves' X and Y when it moves a phrase from position X to position Y and an interpretive rule 'involves' X and Y when it assigns to Y the feature [anaphoric to X]. Note that while the PIC and SSC affect all rules, Subjacency applies only to movement rules.

We shall now take a series of examples to illustrate how these four constraints interact with the two transformations and two interpretive rules proposed, in order to avoid the overgeneration mentioned earlier. We begin with PIC. It can now be seen that the apparent counter-examples to the Disjoint Reference rule (43) in fact fall out under PIC. Disjoint Reference involves two NPs, in this case *they...they* and *I...me*; but the lower NP is contained in a finite clause and so PIC prevents the rule from applying. Therefore it is not specified that the two *they*s may not intersect in reference, nor is (43b) classed as un-grammatical; PIC blocks the rule from assigning a star to (43b) or specifying the two NPs of (43a) as non-intersecting. Consider also the rule of Bound Anaphora Interpretation in (50) and (51). The rule cannot associate *each other* with *the men* in (50a), because *the men* is X in the formulation of PIC and *each other* is Y and is contained in a finite clause; therefore PIC blocks application of the rule, ensuring that *each other* remains uninterpreted and therefore that the sentence is ungrammatical because it contains an uninterpretable element. Compare (50b), where *each other* is contained in a parallel non-finite clause and nothing blocks interpretation. Similarly with (51), where in

(51a) by virtue of PIC *t* cannot be associated with a higher NP and therefore remains uninterpreted; compare (51b), where *t* is in a non-finite clause and PIC does not block interpretation. (51) could also serve to illustrate the blocking effect of PIC on NP Preposing, which can apply successfully in (51b) because the lower item involved in the rule, i.e. moved, is not contained in a finite clause, unlike in (51a) where the movements indicated would violate PIC.

(50)   a.   *the men believed [that each other left]
       b.   the men believed [each other to have left]
(51)   a.   *the men were believed [t left]
       b.   the men were believed [t to have left]

Moving on now to the slightly more complex case of SSC, consider first how it interacts with Disjoint Reference. The rule is blocked by SSC from assigning ungrammaticality to (52b) and non-intersecting reference to *they* and *them* in (52a), because intervening between the two elements undergoing the rule is an item *Susan* which is not controlled by *they* or *I* (i.e. *X* in the formulation of SSC (47)) and therefore counts as a specified subject. Compare (53) where the rule is not blocked by the SSC and therefore does apply, assigning a non-intersecting reading in (53a) and ungrammaticality to (53b). In (53) nothing intervenes between the two items involved and in (54) something intervenes which is controlled by the higher of the two items involved in the rule, i.e. *X*, and therefore does not count as a specified subject and does not activate SSC.

(52)   a.   *they* believed [Susan to be corrupting *them*]
       b.   *I* believed [Susan to be corrupting *me*]
(53)   a.   *they* believed [*them* to be corrupting Susan]
       b.   *I* believed [*me* to be corrupting Susan]
(54)   a.   *they* tried [PRO to corrupt *them*]
       b.   *I* tried [PRO to corrupt *me*]

Bound Anaphora Interpretation is also sensitive to SSC. In (55) *t* and *each other* cannot be associated with *Susan* and *the men* because *Mary* intervenes and is a specified subject. Therefore *t* and *each other* remain uninterpreted and the structure is marked ungrammatical. Compare (56), where the italicized items can be associated because in (56a) no subject of any kind intervenes and in (56b) an abstract element is present which is anaphoric to and therefore controlled by *the men* which is involved in the rule, hence not qualifying as a specified subject.

55) a. **Susan* was believed [Mary to like *t*]
     b. **the men* believed [Mary to like *each other*]
(56) a. *Susan* was believed [*t* to like Mary]
     b. *the men* were believed [t to like *each other*]

Compare also (57a) and (57b). SSC blocks Bound Anaphora Interpretation from associating *the men* and *each other* in (57a) because there is an intervening subject *t*, which is controlled by *Susan* (not by the item involved in the rule), and therefore counts as a specified subject and activates the SSC. In (57b) the association is not blocked by the SSC because the intervening *t* subject is controlled by one of the elements involved in the rule and therefore does not count as a specified subject. Notice that this is another instance where the trace theory of movement rules plays a crucial role; for discussion of some interesting questions concerning the nature of traces and the way in which they may affect syntactic and semantic rules, see Chomsky (1977) and Lightfoot (1977a).

(57) a. *Susan seemed to *the men* [t to like *each other*]
     b. *the men* seemed to Susan [t to like *each other*]

Promise and *persuade* have different control properties and in (58a) PRO must be interpreted as referring to *John* and to *Fred* in (58b). That is, the subject of the lower verb is interpreted as anaphoric to the object of *persuade* and the subject of *promise*. Therefore, in (59a) SSC blocks Bound Anaphora Interpretation from associating *the men* and *each other* because there intervenes an abstract element controlled not by the item involved in the rule but by *Susan*. In (59b) PRO is controlled by *the men*, according to the usual control patterns associated with *persuade*, and therefore does not count as a specified subject.

(58) a. John promised Fred [PRO to leave]
     b. John persuaded Fred [PRO to leave]
(59) a. *Susan promised *the men* [PRO to see *each other*]
     b. Susan persuaded *the men* [PRO to see *each other*]

In (60), both *John* and *Fred* meet the structural description of NP Preposing (36) and could therefore be moved into the empty NP position, indicated by lower case np. However, *Fred* would be moved over an intervening specified subject; hence that movement is disallowed by SSC.

(60)   np was expected [John to meet Fred]

The Subjacency Constraint applies only to movement rules and blocks the derivations illustrated in (61) because an element would be moved over two intervening cyclic nodes. Compare the permitted movements of (62), where only one cyclic node intervenes.

(61)   a.   * who did you believe [the claim [that Bill saw t]₅]ₙₚ

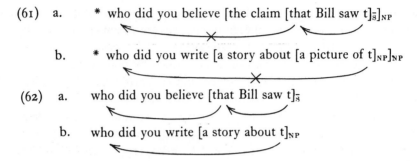

   b.   * who did you write [a story about [a picture of t]ₙₚ]ₙₚ

(62)   a.   who did you believe [that Bill saw t]₅

   b.   who did you write [a story about t]ₙₚ

Notice that in a structure such as (63), Subjacency blocks the *wh* element being moved directly to the highest COMP position, although the structural description of *wh* Movement (36) would permit it. This forces *wh* Movement to apply in 'successive cyclic' fashion, as illustrated.

(63)   who did you think [t Bill wanted[t you to see t]₅]₅

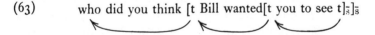

The COMP-to-COMP Condition guarantees that an element in COMP, effectively a *wh* word, can move only to another (higher) COMP. This disbars movements of the type illustrated in (64a). Compare (64b), where the COMP-to-COMP Condition is not violated.

(64)   a.   [   ]꜀ₒₘₚwho was believed [[   ]꜀ₒₘₚ Mary to have seen t]₅

   b.   [who]꜀ₒₘₚt was believed [[   ]꜀ₒₘₚt to have seen Mary]₅

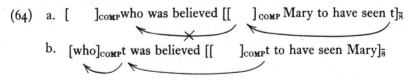

In this survey of the grammatical theory to be presupposed in the following chapters, we have glossed over a myriad of important issues and we have offered virtually no motivation or supportive arguments. Such arguments can be found in the references cited. The book as a whole will offer support of a novel kind for such a theory of grammar: having first developed a basic methodology for work in diachronic syntax and shown how such work can be integrated with research on a theory of grammar, we shall offer several arguments suggesting that a restrictive grammatical theory of this type yields good predictions about the nature of historical change. In some cases we shall argue for revisions to this theory on the basis of an analysis of syntactic change, notably in chapter 6. This survey has aimed at conveying the internal logic of a restrictive theory of grammar. A small number of very simple rules, *formally* prohibited from reference to Boolean conditions, multiple factorizations, etc., can handle a great deal of material when their *functions* are restricted by the four conditions illustrated. The conditions on form and the four conditions on function are to be construed as contributions to Universal Grammar or the theory of grammar, and are to be viewed as defining properties of possible grammars. If the child learning its native language is genetically endowed with this 'knowledge', he then has to postulate only a small number of simple and maximally general rules.

Now, it is certain that the child is not endowed with this knowledge in the specific form given in (46)–(49). The SSC has a certain perceptual naturalness to it since, at the risk of oversimplification, it essentially forces a rule to regard only the closest two elements meeting its structural description or to take the 'most prominent' NP in the embedded structure; if such an account could be made precise, it might emerge that the SSC is just a special case of a more general perceptual strategy affecting cognitive domains other than language. Perhaps a similar suggestion could hold of Subjacency which might be interpreted as a limitation on the extent of the domain over which mental computation can take place (see Koster 1976). The version of the PIC given above is clearly too specific to be regarded as a general defining property. One hopes that work on other languages will suggest a more abstract form of the constraint, a kind of archi-PIC, which particular grammars may draw on and adapt to their own purposes within fixed limits. Chomsky reports that Kim (1976) notes that rules of anaphora in Korean are subject to a condition similar to PIC but with a different condition on α. Korean has no formal distinction between tensed and non-tensed clauses but the complements to certain 'assertive' verbs are islands in the same way as English tensed Ss. Therefore a variant of PIC can be formulated for Korean, which suggests the need for a more abstract formulation of PIC of which the English and Korean versions are special cases. Likewise the SSC depends on the definition of 'subject' in any given language and in some grammars 'one might want to characterize "subject" in terms of primitives such as ergative, absolutive, or non-oblique. Hale (1976) proposes certain conditions on what can be taken as subject in the syntactically "unmarked" situation; in accordance with his approach, a language might characterize the notion "subject" differently, but at a cost in the grammar, in accordance with the logic of markedness' (Chomsky 1977). Therefore, the conditions cited in (46)–(49) should be regarded as instances of archi-conditions or condition-schemata. Recall that the rationale for such research is that of the detailed work by geneticists on the fruit-fly (Dobzhansky 1970) and subsequent generalization to other species.

In the following chapters there will be frequent references to the rules of NP Preposing and *wh* Movement and to the four conditions. A further proposal within this line of research, already alluded to, requires some more description. As indicated earlier, NP Preposing plays a role in the derivation of various construction-types. Recent proposals by Chomsky (1977) eliminate a large number of putative rules and derive a wide range of constructions by application of *wh* Movement. Chomsky noted that sentences which are usually agreed to be derived via *wh* Movement manifest the five properties listed in (65).[1]

(65) a. a gap is left
      b. apparent violation of SSC
      c. apparent violation of PIC
      d. apparent violation of Subjacency
      e. obedience to the Complex NP and other island constraints of Ross (1967)

He proceeds to investigate the strong hypothesis that *all* constructions manifesting these five properties are derived by *wh* Movement: direct and indirect questions, relatives, topicalizations, clefts, comparatives, and various infinitival complements (including '*tough* Movement' sentences). In other words, the properties of (65) were regarded as a diagnostic for *wh* Movement. If the putative rules, hitherto regarded as participating in the derivation of the above constructions are all

---

[1] Firstly, by an 'apparent violation' of SSC and Subjacency I refer to (unanalysed) sentences like *what did Mingus want Miles to ask Rahsaan to play — in New York?*, where *what* is associated with the gap indicated despite two intervening cyclic nodes and two specified subjects. These are not real violations, however, if *wh* Movement applies successive cyclically. Secondly, in (65e) I mean that sentences are consistent with Ross' Complex NP Constraint etc., although the Complex NP Constraint will be subsumed under Subjacency and therefore not be represented in grammatical theory in the form specified by Ross.

properly viewed as instantiations of *wh* Movement, they should have the same properties, obey the same general filters, and be subject to the same anaphora principles.

To examine just one example, consider cases of topicalization, *this book, I like*, which will be derived as illustrated in (66a). The base-generated *wh* element is moved into COMP by *wh* Movement and is subsequently deleted. Compare this with 'left dislocation' sentences, *(as regards) this book, I like it*, which do not involve movement (there is no 'gap' at the surface and transformations cannot 'create' structure like *as regards*) and have an initial and surface phrase marker as in (66b).

(66) a. Topicalization   b. Left dislocation

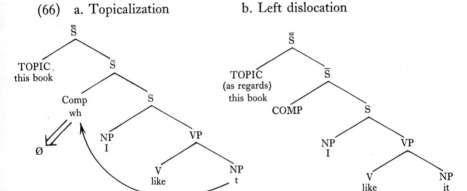

This analysis derives (67) a and b, and not c, d or e. I cite the sentence and the initial phrase marker (omitting morphological details).

(67) a. this book, I asked Bill to read
       this book, [COMP I asked Bill [COMP PRO to read wh]]
   b. this book, I told Bill that he should read
       this book, [COMP I told Bill [COMP he should read wh]]
   c. *this book, I accept the arguments that Bill should read
       this book, COMP I accept [the arguments [COMP Bill should read wh]]
   d. *this book, I met someone who read
       this book, COMP [I met [someone[COMP who read wh]]]
   e. *this book, I wonder who read
       this book, [COMP I wonder [COMP who read wh]]

In (67a) and (67b) *wh* is moved first into the lowest COMP and on the next cycle into the higher COMP, subsequently being deleted; no conditions are violated and the derivation is well-formed. Notice that the second application of *wh* Movement does not violate the SSC because (a) $\bar{S}$, not S, is the binding node for the SSC (and therefore the matrix subject is irelevant) and (b) the embedded subjects, PRO and *he*, are not controlled by the higher item involved in the rule, they do not c-command COMP and are therefore irrelevant to the SSC. In (67c) on the lowest cycle *wh* moves into COMP but now it cannot escape to the higher COMP because that would entail crossing two cyclic nodes, $\bar{S}$ and NP, which would contravene the Subjacency Condition. Likewise in (67d). (67e) is slightly more complex. On the lowest cycle two *wh* elements would satisfy the structural description of *wh* Movement and in such cases an independent convention (the Superiority Condition of Chomsky 1973) requires the rule to apply to the higher item, i.e. the one closer to the dominating S, in this instance the subject NP, which thereby moves into the lower COMP.[1] COMP is now filled and cannot accommodate another *wh* element resulting from a subsequent application of *wh* Movement on the object *wh* element. On the next cycle *wh* Movement might move the object *wh* directly to the higher COMP, but this would violate PIC and is blocked. Notice that if one substitutes a real pronoun *it* for the gap indicated in the sentences of (67), one has 'left dislocation' sentences and all five sentences become grammatical. No movement is involved in the derivation of such sentences and therefore Subjacency is inapplicable, since it applies only to movement operations. Notice also the contrasting anaphora patterns, whereby in a topicalization sentence such as (68a) *John* cannot be in an anaphoric relation with *he*, whereas it can in a left dislocation sentence like (68b). In (68a) *he* may not refer to *John*; in (68b) it may. This follows on the assumption, motivated in Wasow (1972), that for the purposes of anaphoric relations traces behave like names. Just as *he* cannot be epiphoric to *Bill* in (68c), because it precedes and commands, so *he* cannot be epiphoric to *t* in (68a) for the same reason. However, *t* is anaphoric to, or co-indexed with, the deleted *wh* element, which in turn is co-indexed with *John*; therefore if *t* cannot be anaphoric to *he*, then *he* cannot be anaphoric to *John*, even though *John* precedes and commands.

(68)   a. John, he likes t
     b. John, he likes him
     c. he said that Bill left

For detailed discussion of the possibility of treating many disparate

---

[1] Chomsky (1973) motivates the Superiority Condition with the analysis of contrasting sentences like *I don't remember who saw what* vs. **I don't remember what who saw.*

rules as instantiations of *wh* Movement, including motivation and some problems arising, see Chomsky (1977).

The logic of this form of abstract grammar should now be clear. A small number of very simple and general rules will handle a wide range of facts if the functioning of these rules is constrained by the four principles spelled out in (46)–(49). Further restrictions on available grammars will be suggested in chapter 6. Undoubtedly more rules will be needed, but one may regard this as part of the 'core grammar' of English. In this view extrinsic ordering will play a minimal role and it may be possible to eliminate such conventions altogether, thereby imposing a further significant limitation on available grammars (for such a proposal, see Jenkins 1977). Two features of this theory which will prove to be crucial for our work on diachronic changes, are its restrictiveness on the class of available grammars, particularly as regards the syntactic domain, and the enriched conception of surface structure which, under these proposals, contains abstract, phonologically null elements and is rich enough to provide a sufficient input for the semantic rules. Given this richness, there are various generalizations statable at the level of surface structure (some formulated in terms of 'surface filters', in addition to those captured by the semantic rules). Surface structure therefore plays an enhanced role in grammar, serving more functions than in earlier conceptions, and this will have significant consequences for the articulation of analogical principles invoked in work on diachrony (§7.1).

1.5 Grammatical theory within the logic of markedness

Having defined a theory of grammar in this way, I assume that a theory of mind is a wider-ranging object encompassing a theory of grammar as one component. Other components will include a theory of per-

(69)

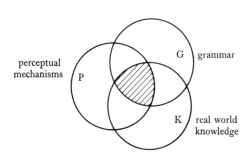

ceptual strategies and an account of knowledge of the real world. One may think of this as three (perhaps more) intersecting domains (69). The circles specify well-formed objects in each domain: the circle P indicates objects which are in accord with natural perceptual strategies, circle G specifies objects which are well-formed grammatically, and circle K sensible beliefs about the world. The shaded area, where all three circles intersect, encompasses objects which are well-formed from all three viewpoints. These will be sentences, i.e. grammatical objects, which accord with perceptual mechanisms and reflect a sensible view of the world. However, some objects are well-formed only from two viewpoints. For example, let us assume that a perceptual mechanism specifies multiple centre-embedding as difficult to interpret and that centre-embedding is usually avoided in various domains such as natural language, music, arithmetic. Thus some objects may be well-formed with respect to grammatical rules and may reflect a coherent world view, but violate restrictions on centre-embedding, thereby being perceptually ill-formed (70).

(70) [[that[that[that the moon is bright]is obvious]disturbs me] surprised Harry]

Other objects may be grammatically and perceptually well-formed but may convey only nonsense, such as Russell's famous *colourless green ideas sleep furiously*. One could also have multiply centre-embedded nonsense which was grammatically well-formed, although perceptually and cognitively deviant. Similarly there are perceptual mechanisms dealing with, say, properties of vision and colour differentiation which do not interact at all with the domain of grammar and may or may not have anything to do with one's knowledge of the world. Circle K specifies people's beliefs about the world (no doubt a rather large circle), factors of language use and perhaps those things which, in discussing the EST model of grammar (25), I tentatively suggested were to be dealt with by some shadowy rules relating logical form to 'semantic representation'. Be that as it may. Under this approach a broad theory of mind encompasses a more limited theory of grammar, which in turn intersects with theories of other cognitive domains. A grammar will generate structures which may be characterized as unacceptable by a set of perceptual strategies or some account of real world knowledge, although one may still say that a grammar generates only *grammatical* sentences if 'grammatical' is taken to mean 'generated by a grammar'.

Perhaps a theory of *language* should be construed as treating not only cognitive domains as in (69) but it should also include theories of dialect variation, historical change, and pathological loss of the language faculty. In which case, one must ask whether it is useful to speak of a 'theory' of language at all, as distinct from 'linguistics', the name given to a group of related areas of study. Certainly, if the theory is conceived as broadly as this, it will not sustain a coherent research programme in the foreseeable future, since it will be virtually impossible to formulate falsifiable hypotheses until more is known about the individual components, theories of grammar, historical change, dialect variation, etc. Even within any one of those components falsification of theories is a difficult matter; discussion is necessarily somewhat abstract and theory-bound. This is a relatively recent development for linguistics, although of course well-established in more mature disciplines such as physics and biology. No physicist would simply offer an unanalysed observed phenomenon as an alleged refutation of Quantum Mechanics or Gauge Theory. As theories of grammar become richer one hopes that the tendency will become less prevalent for linguists to elevate by fiat pre-theoretical observations to the status of claims about the form of a theory, as illustrated in the passage quoted earlier from Corum (1975), and simply to cite unanalysed phenomena as alleged counterexamples to a theoretical claim (Pullum 1975). One will refute a theory of grammar by presenting an analysis and, as noted by Chomsky (1977), the refutation will be as convincing as the fragment of grammar offered. Thus falsification is no longer a trivial matter. However, discussions of potential falsification must now become more abstract and increasingly theory-bound; one must ensure that the theory remains falsifiable in principle and is not rendered immune to empirical disconfirmation. We now turn to that question: is the EST, as outlined, a falsifiable theory of available grammars?

The A-over-A condition and the four principles illustrated here, PIC, SSC, Subjacency and COMP-to-COMP, are all restrictions on the functioning of rules. It is in principle possible to formulate a rule such that it will be immune to one or more of these conditions (see below), but this will render the grammar less highly valued and the complications in the rule necessitated by its exceptional character constitute a 'cost' to the grammar. The logic of this approach is that of markedness. If the existence of a rule designed to violate, say, the SSC simply renders the grammar more marked or less highly valued, but not impossible, how could one ever falsify such a theory? Chomsky (1977) distinguishes a 'core-grammar' of English, whose rules are heavily constrained and have little expressive power, as distinct from peripheral rules deleting *wh* elements, adjusting complementizers, etc., whose properties are less clearly defined. Again, such a distinction must be located in the logic of markedness. This raises questions about the falsifiability of the theory.

I incline towards a *broadly* Popperian viewpoint (Popper 1959, 1963), that scientific theories can be falsified by experience, i.e. must be falsifiable in principle, while no theory can ever be verified in any significant sense.[1] One can never demonstrate the truth of a theory, only its falsity (except in domains like logic and finite arithmetic). Thus progress in scientific endeavours can be viewed as the successive elimination of theories shown through empirical investigation to be false. Theories then can be evaluated for 'verisimilitude'; for example, Ptolemaic models of the universe were verisimilar or truth-like to the extent that they made correct predictions, but Copernican models turned out to be more truth-like. Popper (1973) argues that the alleged truth or correctness of a scientific theory is best viewed as an interim report on attempts to disconfirm it.

Linguists from the neogrammarians to Bloomfield (1926, 1960) and Chomsky (passim) have claimed that their discipline should be

---

[1] This does not entail 'atomic falsificationism', that all statements in a given theory should be falsifiable individually. Quite apart from some general difficulties (see below), many writers have pointed out technical problems with the Popperian approach, notably the impossibility of falsifying any existential statement. C. S. Peirce, in many ways anticipating Popper and Lakatos, offers interesting reflections on refutability:

> It is a great mistake to suppose that the mind of the active scientist is filled with propositions which, if not proved beyond all reasonable cavil, are at least extremely probable. On the contrary, he entertains hypotheses which are almost wildly incredible, and treats them with respect for the time being. Why does he do this? Simply because any scientific proposition whatever is always liable to be refuted and dropped at short notice. A hypothesis is something which looks as if it might be true, and which is capable of verification and refutation by comparison with facts. The best hypothesis, in the sense of the one most recommending itself to the inquirer, is the one which can be most readily refuted if it is false. This far outweighs the trifling merit of being likely. For after all, what is a *likely* hypothesis? It is one which falls in with our preconceived ideas. But these may be wrong. Their errors are just what the scientific man is out gunning for more particularly. But if a hypothesis can quickly and easily be cleared away so as to go toward leaving the field free for the main struggle, this is an immense advantage. (1966: vol. 1 p120)

viewed as an empirical science in some sense of the term.[1] However, if, following Popper, one takes the empirical content of a theory to be a function of its falsifiability, it is clear that many linguistic proposals cannot be regarded as contributions to an empirical science. Botha (1970, 1971, 1973) has argued that much current work fails to meet Popper's 'demarcation criteria' for scientific theory in that the proposals are either too vague to have clear empirical consequences or contain 'blocking devices' which immunize the theory against refutational evidence. I believe that Botha's general claim is correct, but that Popper's (and Botha's) standards are excessive and that, in any case, the situation can be remedied.

It is clear that physics does not meet Popperian standards. At all stages of its history, physics has disregarded contrary data that refuted available theories, hoping that they would somehow be taken care of elsewhere. In general, the Popperian view understates the role of idealization in physics and the dismissal of conflicting evidence. Chomsky (1975) discusses a trivial case of somebody claiming to refute the law of falling bodies by catching a ball before it hits the ground. The physicist would dismiss this 'refutation', on the grounds that he is predicting only for 'mechanical systems' and that 'human intervention' is not part of such a system. But why not? He has no real answer, except that he cannot account for human will. Applying Popper's or Botha's criteria, one would then say that physics is empty, since it works only where it works and has no principled way to exclude counterexamples. Chomsky (personal communication) points out that in fact much less trivial examples have arisen throughout the history of physics. For example, at the time of Galileo it was thought that the universe was finite and that bodies should fall towards 'its centre'. But clearly a body dropped on earth does not drop towards the sun, refuting Copernicus. Similarly the luminescence of the planets did not vary as it should on Copernicus' theory. Lakatos (1970) and Holton (1973) discuss many such examples. Copernican and Newtonian theories were at variance with much of the available observational 'data' and it is by no means clear that they could be seen to give more correct predictions than existing theories. The real point is that they gave deeper explanations within the narrower range in which they were not falsified by clear and impressive data. Application of Popper's

---

[1] For some provocative discussion of the empirical content of most approaches to linguistics see Itkonen (1974) and the Epilogue to Lass (1976).

demarcation criteria would at once destroy any living science, which is why they are never invoked in practice. But if Popper's criteria are too rigorous for physics, it seems unreasonable to apply them to less mature research programmes like linguistics and the psychological sciences. The crucial factor in science is depth of explanation, not data-coverage. Any non-trivial scientific theory is apparently falsified for much of the time, but one persists with it if it is providing explanations within some domain and offers a useful and productive research programme. Therefore, as a working scientist, I favour the less demanding approach of Lakatos (1970), who defines falsifiability in terms of research *programmes*, and distinguishes fundamental from auxiliary hypotheses, where auxiliary hypotheses may be revised or rejected without implicating the basic enterprise or the 'hard core' of the programme. This approach has developed from Popper's work, although it is inconsistent with it in many important respects.

If one adopts such a view of science, stressing depth of explanation rather than coverage of data, the formulation of generative grammars can be shown to have clear empirical consequences. Consider the claim that the PIC, say, is a component of the theory of grammar, conceived within the logic of markedness. Chomsky notes that it is possible to formulate a rule in such a way that it will violate the constraint, but at a cost: the rule would have to specify the relevant structures so that it can apply without falling under the condition. For example, one might claim that transformations and interpretive rules characteristically apply to two constants with only a variable intervening in the structural description and that the two constants are 'involved' in the rule only if the structural description does not require an intervening constant; otherwise they are not 'involved' (notice that 'involve', in the formulation of PIC (46) and SSC (47), is now a technical term). Therefore specification of an intervening constant term will render the conditions inapplicable. Such a specification complicates the rule in order to immunize it against PIC. Therefore a cost is entailed, in accordance with the logic of markedness. In this way the conditions become an integral part of the evaluation metric, rather than absolute restrictions. A similar interpretation should be assigned to $\overline{X}$ conventions, as observed on p57 n1. Therefore, the theory permits a blocking device and appears to immunize itself against refutation. However, if these proposals are couched in terms of markedness they will be empirically refutable to the extent that testable claims are made about the properties of 'marked' or 'less highly valued' grammars. For specific proposals concerning marked values to entail testable claims, these claims will have to hold of an 'external' domain, a domain other than that of the distribution of morphemes or grammatical well-formedness. Claims to explanatory adequacy will have to be grounded in such domains. Natural candidates for such a domain wherein markedness proposals make empirically testable claims are language change and acquisition.

Markedness theory is essentially a function distinguishing more or less highly valued grammars. The markedness conventions of Chomsky & Halle (1968) explain why certain configurations are more 'natural' than others. For example, Convention (xi) (p405) classes [i] and [u] as more natural than [y] and [ɯ], etc.

(xi)
$$[u \text{ round}] \rightarrow \begin{cases} [\alpha \text{ round}]/ \begin{bmatrix} \underline{\quad\quad} \\ \alpha \text{ back} \\ -\text{low} \end{bmatrix} \\ [-\text{round}]/ \begin{bmatrix} \underline{\quad\quad} \\ +\text{low} \end{bmatrix} \end{cases}$$

Such naturalness claims are based at least in part on the frequency of occurrence in natural languages and implicational relations, such as that no language will have [y] if it does not have [i]. That is, no language will have the marked value if it does not also have the unmarked. Following Postal (1968: p170), Lass & Anderson (1975: p285) state that 'the convention...should predict (a) that front round vowels should not arise as innovations (since this represents an increase in markedness, i.e. a "complication" of the grammar), and (b) that if they should arise they will be unstable, and tend to disappear over time especially by merger with similar "unmarked" vowels'. Lass & Anderson then proceed to show that if one assumes this interpretation of markedness this convention yields incorrect predictions in that, under their analysis of the history of English front round vowels (which, it must be said, is by no means uncontroversial; see Dresher 1978), changes in the inventory of these vowels represent sometimes an increase in markedness, sometimes a decrease. They conclude that the convention is of no explanatory value in an account of the history of the English vowel system. They argue that this is a defect not just of this particular convention, but of the whole concept of markedness as used, or alleged to be used, by Chomsky & Halle. However, whatever the merits of their analysis of the English vowels – and their refutation can be no more persuasive than their analysis – they interpret markedness

too narrowly in terms of the way in which it should make predictions
about historical changes.

If a theory of markedness is to make empirically testable claims, those
claims will presumably involve the nature of language acquisition and
diachronic change. Markedness will therefore interact with theories of
acquisition and change to yield relevant predictions. We shall take no
stand here on the nature of the predictions made for acquisition, but
it is not inconceivable that Lass & Anderson's strong interpretation is
appropriate in this domain. It might be the case that marked segments
or marked rules are acquired in different fashion, perhaps later than
unmarked segments and rules. However, markedness must be treated
differently in the historical domain. One cannot simply look at one
segment or rule, note that it is 'marked' and not highly valued and
conclude that therefore it is liable to drop out of the language. One
must make two assumptions; that grammars may contain marked rules
and secondly that grammars did not originate in the Garden of Eden
in a highly marked condition, being simplified inexorably ever since
and gradually becoming less marked and more highly valued. On
these assumptions one can assert that grammars may acquire marked
segments and rules in the course of historical change. Therefore, if
the facts of the English vowel system are as Lass & Anderson describe
them, one should not be surprised to find marked segments being
added to a grammar. It makes sense to regard markedness of the whole
grammar or sections of the grammar, but not of individual segments
or rules.

In the following chapters we shall illustrate examples of piecemeal
changes resulting in steady complication of a grammar, rendering it
as a whole more marked, less highly valued. In the examples discussed,
these piecemeal changes are followed by a catastrophe in roughly
the sense of Thom (1972, 1973), a major re-analysis of the grammar
eliminating the markedness and complexity which had been gradually
accumulating. The symptoms of such a cataclysmic re-structuring will
be a set of simultaneous but apparently unrelated changes. Often we
shall postulate a single change in the abstract grammar which will
(a) eliminate much of the accumulated complexity and marked values
and (b) account for the simultaneity of the surface changes. The
simultaneity of the changes will be the evidence for the uniqueness or
singularity of the change. It will be shown that the re-analysis is
necessitated by an interaction of the earlier changes leading up to the

re-structuring and of an appropriately restrictive theory of grammar, along the lines of the version of the EST outlined in this chapter but incorporating also one further principle, the Transparency Principle, to be discussed in due course.[1] In short, we shall show how a theory of grammar, viewed in the context of the logic of markedness, can predict the point at which these re-analyses occur. It will not predict, however, the precise nature of the re-analysis. In this way, the theory of grammar, properly conceived, will be shown to make empirically testable predictions about the nature of diachronic change. If these promises can be substantiated satisfactorily, the results will be of considerable methodological importance and the study of syntactic change will be firmly integrated with work on the theory of grammar and, indeed, shown to be an essential component of that work, not simply an optional luxury.

I have argued in this chapter that while there are prima facie difficulties confronting any attempt to study syntactic change systematically, the task can be undertaken if one draws a careful distinction between a theory of grammar and a theory of change and if one views a theory of grammar as a set of the tightest possible restrictions on the class of grammars available for particular languages. We outlined such a theory and found that this theory will have further empirical consequences if one extends the data-base so that it can be interpreted as making predictions about diachronic change or language acquisition by native speakers. In other words, not only is it possible to undertake work on syntactic change (given suitable distinctions and methodological principles) but it is also desirable if the theory of grammar is to maximize its empirical content and provide testable claims about markedness. Finally we have claimed that there is a way to make the theory of grammar responsive to data from diachronic change, data concerning the point at which radical re-analyses take place, in such a way that the theory becomes predictive and therefore testable. This

---

[1] In other words some changes, occurring in piecemeal fashion, increase the overall markedness of a grammar, while others simplify, often by introducing a single change in the grammar which has many ramifications at the surface. I assume that the point at which the simplifying re-analyses occur should be predictable by a theory of grammar. This raises the question of how we can tell whether any given change is a 'radical re-analysis' of the type that a theory of grammar should predict, or merely a piecemeal amendment with no further consequences. There may be a problem in drawing such a distinction clearly on a general basis, although this seems not to be a practical problem. This is another question we shall take up after analysing some real examples of change.

is at least in part a promissory note. The logic will become clearer after we have considered one example of various piecemeal changes leading up to a catastrophic re-analysis; this will provide the empirical ground for our conception of a theory of grammar. We now proceed in chapter 2 to such a case, the story of the development of the English modals. Following an account of that change, in chapter 3 we shall reflect on its implications, and formulate the basis of a theory of change, i.e. an interpretive device deriving testable predictions from the theory of grammar about the nature of diachronic change. In the course of those reflections we shall return to the issues raised in this section.

2 A paradigm case: the English modals

In this chapter I shall seek to establish that grammars can undergo radical re-structurings in the course of time, and I shall introduce the Transparency Principle, which will account for when such re-structurings should occur. The argument will be that the grammar of NE, unlike that of OE, has an initial structure syntactic category of 'modal', and that the development of that category sheds much light on the nature of syntactic change.

2.1 Modals in Modern English

As a prelude to the diachronic argument, I shall discuss the status of modals in NE and claim that they should be analysed as originating in the same S as that in which they end up in surface structure. This might be taken as a controversial position since there has been a widespread belief that auxiliaries, and more particularly modals, are to be derived transformationally from higher predicates. This view originated with Ross (1969a), who presented ten arguments that auxiliaries and verbs 'are really both members of the same lexical category, *verb*', and two arguments purporting to show that they must be main verbs. Since this analysis has achieved a certain popularity, it is worth examining with some care. §2.1.1 will show that all of these arguments are badly flawed as they stand, and §2.1.2 will show that there are good reasons to derive modals from within the same S as the verb they 'govern'.

2.1.1 To illustrate Ross' position, *windows may be broken by rioters* is to be derived from one of two initial structures, (1) or (2), which happen to correspond to the two possible semantic readings, i.e. the permission (root) or possibility (epistemic) readings. In each case the modal *may* originates in a higher predicate to the rest of the sentence. *Max was chortling* would come from an initial structure like (3).

(1)

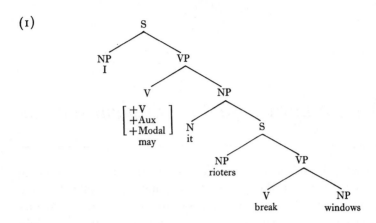

(2)

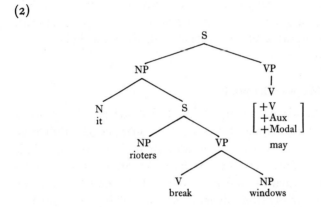

(3)

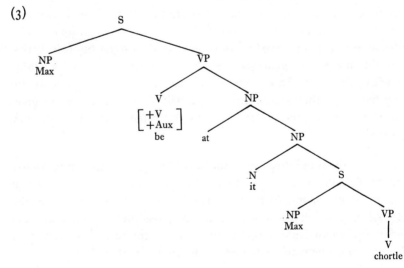

As the first argument for such initial structures Ross points out that

the term T ($\left\{\begin{array}{c} M \\ \textit{have} \\ \textit{be} \end{array}\right\}$) is mentioned in at least three rules of English:

Subject-Auxiliary Inversion, Negative Placement, and VP Deletion. He notes that this is a very odd term, not even being a constituent, and that the standard theory makes the claim that the items mentioned in this term have no similarity which would predispose them to function together. With no more argumentation he concludes: 'I suggest that this term should be replaced in all rules which mention it by the entirely natural constituent... $\begin{bmatrix} + \text{Aux} \\ + \text{V} \end{bmatrix}$.' This is not an argument for anything, but a suggestion for a new labelling convention; furthermore, Ross' feature analysis is essentially the same as the one in Chomsky (1957), except for notation. The 'problem' is that the standard theory has no single label to cover tense and the first auxiliary verb. Ross tries to invent one, but it is not clear how this simplifies the grammar or enables it to capture more generalizations. One price to be paid is that the affixes *-en* and *-ing* will now need to come from quite a different source, presumably introduced by special rules of complementation. It is curious to note, parenthetically, that the fact that T ($\left\{\begin{array}{c} M \\ \textit{have} \\ \textit{be} \end{array}\right\}$) is mentioned in several rules was taken as a positive argument in Chomsky (1955). Under that theory it was assumed that a transformational grammar consists of (i) a list of structural descriptions, (ii) a list of structural changes, and (iii) rules associating them. Thus if a single structural description appeared in many rules, this was a generalization.

There is, in fact, another solution which does not resort to new labels, higher predicates or special complement types. The proposal involves the phrase structure rules of (4). Some justification for this unusual division is that *have* + *en* and *be* + *ing* can occur in infinitives and gerunds but T and modals cannot (5).

(4)   S → NP   Aux   VP
      Aux → T   (M)
      VP → (*have-ɛn*)   (*be-ing*)   V...
(5)   a.   Sam believes Bill to have arrived at noon
      b.   Sam believes Bill to be arriving at noon

    c. *Sam believes Bill to arrived at noon
    d. *Sam believes Bill to can arrive at noon

The proposal includes a rule of *have-be* Raising, which moves *have* or *be* from the VP into Aux position.

    have-be Raising

$$X \quad T \quad \begin{Bmatrix} have \\ be \end{Bmatrix} \quad Y \quad \overset{oblig}{\Rightarrow} \quad 1 \quad 2+3 \quad 4$$

Notice that the rule will not apply if there is a modal intervening between T and $\begin{Bmatrix} have \\ be \end{Bmatrix}$. This means that, after the application of *have-be* Raising, Aux will be able to consist only of T, T M, T *have* or T *be*. Therefore, Subject-Auxiliary Inversion and Negative Placement need mention only the node Aux, and VP Deletion will mention only VP; there will be no need for the T ($\begin{Bmatrix} M \\ have \\ be \end{Bmatrix}$) configuration. Jackendoff (1972: pp79ff) makes extensive use of this framework to capture a series of generalizations about the syntax and semantics of adverbs.[1]

    Ross' second argument is to the effect that the copula *be* should be analysed as a true verb and be assigned the feature [+Aux]. It behaves like a real verb in that it occurs in the same position in the sentence and it undergoes Gapping. On the other hand it behaves like an auxiliary in that certain quantifiers hop over it (6).

(6)   a. they $\begin{Bmatrix} all \\ both \\ each \end{Bmatrix}$ are handsome

     b. they are $\begin{Bmatrix} all \\ both \\ each \end{Bmatrix}$ handsome

---

[1] Jackendoff gives as further evidence the sentences

    (i) for John $\begin{Bmatrix} \text{not to have} \\ \text{*to have not} \end{Bmatrix}$ left disturbs me

    (ii) for John $\begin{Bmatrix} \text{not to be} \\ \text{*to not be} \end{Bmatrix}$ the man I'm looking for disturbs me

Assuming with Chomsky (1973) that infinitival complements are tenseless, the structural description for *have-be* Raising would not be met and so the negative would be placed before the *have* or *be* since it is still in the VP. I am less than happy with this argument because (a) the grammaticality judgments are not clear, and (b) by most formulations *to* replaced Aux, therefore the predicted order would be the less acceptable ... *to not have left*, instead of ... *not to have left*.

It is true that the main verb *be* and the auxiliary *be* share certain properties (e.g. both undergo Subject-Auxiliary Inversion), but it is curious to call the main verb *be* an 'auxiliary' in order to capture these similarities. Moreover, it is scarcely an argument to label the copula $\begin{bmatrix} +V \\ +Aux \end{bmatrix}$ if one shows that it shares properties (word order and Gapping) with 'true verbs', which are $\begin{bmatrix} +V \\ -Aux \end{bmatrix}$, i.e. properties not shared by 'verbs' which are $\begin{bmatrix} +V \\ +Aux \end{bmatrix}$.

The third argument is based on a putative constraint that 'no agent in a *for-to* or poss-*ing* complement can be identical to the subject of a higher sentence, as long as only *for-to* or poss-*ing* sentences intervene'. This is to account for the ungrammaticality (for Ross) of (7b).

(7)   a. he forced me to be examined by Dr Hito
      b. *he$_i$ forced me to be examined by him$_i$

Unfortunately many people do not find (8) to be any better than Ross' (9), to which he assigns ??. (8) has a *that* complementizer intervening between the subject *I* and the agent *me*.

(8)   I want Mary to tell Tom that Peter got Bill to try to force Jack to be examined by me

(9)   I want Mary to convince Tom to get Peter to try to force Jack to be examined by me

So the constraint does not seem to be well-founded. However, Ross assumes its correctness and uses it as evidence that the *may* of permission is a true verb which has a first person subject (when used as a performative) and undergoes a rule of 'Flip'. Such a constraint would then explain the difference between (10a) and (10b), since they would have essentially the same source as (11a) and (11b).

(10) a. you may gladly be examined by Dr. Hito
      b. *you may gladly be examined by me
(11) a. I gladly allow you to be examined by Dr. Hito
      b. *I gladly allow you to be examined by me

Ross concludes that 'the rule of Flip applies only to verbs – hence the fact that it must apply to *may* argues that this modal is also a verb'. The illogic of that needs no comment. Moreover the ungrammaticality of (10b) and (11b) has more to do with the adverb *gladly* than the interaction of the putative constraint and Flip. If *gladly* is deleted the sentences become perfectly well-formed. It is somewhat unusual to use *allow* as a performative but $\begin{Bmatrix} I'll\ allow \\ I\ allowed \end{Bmatrix}$ *you to be examined by me* is quite acceptable. Therefore, the constraint must be abandoned and this argument for treating *may* as a higher verb is no longer valid.

As the fourth argument, Ross points out that *be-ing* and *have-en* can occur under verbs such as *seem*, which normally require the next lowest verb to be [+stative], and not under verbs such as *force*, which require the next lowest verb to be [−stative]. These facts can be captured by treating *be* and *have* as 'true verbs, with the features [+Aux] and [+stative]'.

(12)
I forced him to $\begin{Bmatrix} \text{learn the answer} \\ \text{*know the answer} \\ \text{*be sleeping} \\ \text{*have slept} \end{Bmatrix}$

(13)
he seems to $\begin{Bmatrix} \text{*learn the answer} \\ \text{know the answer} \\ \text{be sleeping} \\ \text{have slept} \end{Bmatrix}$

However, the data are more complicated. One can, in fact, have [−stative] verbs immediately under *secm* and [+stative] verbs under *force* in certain circumstances, for example, if *seem* is in the past tense or if the complement S contains a plural NP or an indefinite adverbial clause.

(14)   a. Bill seemed to learn the answer
　　　 b. Bill seems to learn the answers
　　　 c. Bill seems to kick Floyd whenever he has a chance
　　　 d. Max forced Harry to be washing up when his mother came

Chomsky (1972b) points out that there is no need for any special initial structure constraints on the complements of *seem* and *force*; it is always possible to assign some interpretation. Thus any well-formed sentence can be embedded under *seem*, but no ill-formed sentence: **John reads a book* is unacceptable except as a stage direction, etc., and likewise **John seems to read a book*. Compare *John is reading a book*, which is acceptable, and likewise *John seems to be reading a book*.

The next three arguments are all based on pronominalization, in particular on the assumption that the antecedent of a pronoun must be a constituent. Ross assumes that *so* is a pro-S (as in *I hope that we will win in Vietnam, but no sane man hopes so*) and then shows that *so* may replace *singing, been singing,* or *have been singing*.

(15)   they said Tom may have been singing, and

$$\text{so he} \begin{cases} \text{might have} \\ \text{might have been} \\ \text{might} \end{cases}$$

Ross proposes that the derived structure of the embedded sentence be (16), so that in all cases there is an appropriate antecedent for *so*, namely a S.

(16)

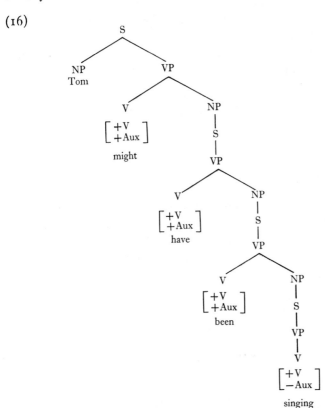

In the other pronominalization arguments Ross is concerned to provide a NP antecedent for *which* and *that* in sentences like (17) and to derive (18) by the rule of S Deletion, where *it* replaces a S which is identical to some earlier S.

(17)   a.   they said that Tom likes ice cream, $\begin{Bmatrix} \text{which he does} \\ \text{and that he does} \end{Bmatrix}$

   b.   they said Tom might have been sleeping,

       $\begin{Bmatrix} \text{which he might (have (been))} \\ \text{and that he might (have (been))} \end{Bmatrix}$

(18)   Max was chortling when I got up yesterday morning and he was still at it when I went to bed that night

At the time that Ross' article was written, many arguments for increasingly abstract underlying syntactic structures were being based on the assumption that an antecedent for Pronominalization should be a constituent at the time that Pronominalization applies. This assumption, of course, was quite a priori. It has since been shown that there are many cases where pro-forms refer back to something which is not a constituent at any point in the derivation.[1] Examples to counter Ross' arguments here would be (19)–(21).

(19)   Tom refused the hot dog, $\begin{Bmatrix} \text{which} \\ \text{and that} \end{Bmatrix}$ wouldn't have happened with filet mignon

(20)   Tom refused the hot dog, and it wouldn't have been so with filet mignon

(21)   Tom refused the hot dog, and it happened again with filet mignon

Two arguments concern S Deletion and word order in German. It is difficult to see what bearing these arguments have on the analysis of auxiliaries in NE. It is entirely likely that in certain languages English modals will be translated by truly verbal forms, but one cannot argue that on universal grounds the English modals are therefore verbs.

There is an interesting argument that *windows may be broken by rioters* should be derived from either a higher transitive verb *may* as in (1) (which gives the permission or 'root' reading) or an intransitive as in (2) (which gives the possibility or 'epistemic' reading). Ross shows that the sentence can be disambiguated by the adverbs *gladly* and *possibly* and then points out that only the *possibly* sentence can undergo *there* Insertion. (Chomsky (personal communication) points

---

[1] This is based on the usual assumption that in *John refused the hot dog* the subject and verb do not form a constituent. Chomsky (1972b) cites *John turned down the hot dog flat, but it (that) wouldn't have happened with filet mignon,* and *half the class flunked physics, which would never have happened in Eng. Lit.*

out that, in fact, the distribution of *gladly* and *possibly* is not a function of the root/epistemic distinction, since the same incompatibility arises with *were* instead of *may be*.)

(22)   *there may gladly be windows broken by rioters
(23)   there may possibly be windows broken by rioters

(23) would be derived by applying Passive and *there* Insertion on the lower S and then raising *there* on the next cycle by Subject Raising. This kind of derivation would be needed independently for sentences like *there seems to be an octopus lying on the quay*, since there is good evidence that *seem* is an intransitive verb. However, Ross' argument does not go through because, as he shows, (22) is also derivable by his theory, an unhappy result. (22) would be derived from an initial structure like (1) by applying Passive and *there* Insertion on the lower cycle, raising *there* on the next cycle and then moving *there* into subject position by Flip. The transitive *may* must be able to undergo Flip in order to derive *Max may gladly be examined by Dr. Hito* (in the permission reading); recall the discussion of Ross' third argument (p85).

A further argument is based on the fact that (24) and (25) 'are felt to be variants of one another' but that in the *Aspects* analysis they must come from quite different initial structures, namely (24a) and (25a) (Ross' trees).

(24)   Ella doesn't need to go

(24)   a.

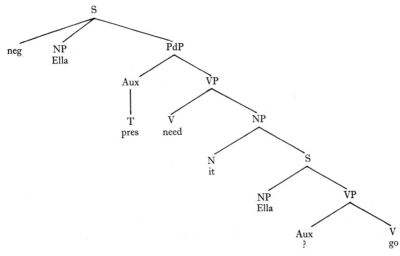

(25)   Ella need not go

(25)   a.

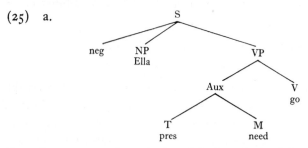

Ross, however, analyses (24) and (25) as derived from the same initial structure, thereby capturing their similarities.

(26)

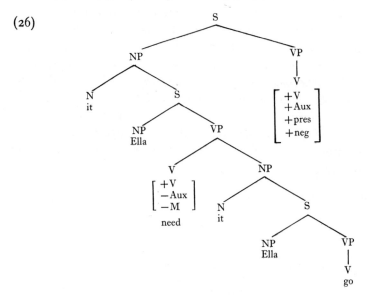

An extra transformational rule is then needed to change the features under certain circumstances. Ross formulates it roughly as (27).

(27)   *dare*   opt $\begin{bmatrix} +\text{Aux} \\ +\text{Modal} \end{bmatrix}$ / negative contexts
       need   ⇒

If this rule fails to apply, *need* is treated as a real verb, and will undergo Number Agreement, *do* Support, normal complementation rules, etc. But if (27) does apply, then *need* will be treated as a modal, i.e. will not trigger *do* Support, will undergo Inversion in questions, allow a negative to be placed on its right, etc. The new [+Aux] *need* will be marked to undergo Equi-NP-Deletion obligatorily. This will necessitate a new kind of marking convention, since this feature complex is introduced transformationally and therefore we cannot take the familiar course of using rule features in the lexicon. Furthermore, the [+Aux] *need* will also have to be marked to undergo a special rule of *to* Deletion to avoid **need he to be so cruel?* Thus Ross will need extra mechanisms to account for the different syntactic behaviour of the two *needs*. It is scarcely clear that this constitutes an improvement in the grammar, but given that there are two *needs* (in Ross' framework one being [+Aux] and the other [−Aux]) and that they have different syntactic properties, it is not unreasonable for the standard theory to posit the two initial structures. The standard theory was concerned with syntactic behaviour as a criterion for initial structures. If one wants to argue that (24) and (25) are synonymous and therefore should come from the same source, one has changed the criteria for positing underlying structures. That was not Ross' position in this paper.

Ross' final argument is based on Greenberg's (1966) observation that in languages whose predominant order is SOV, any auxiliary will follow the verb, whereas in SVO languages an auxiliary will precede the verb. Ross claims that if one treats auxiliaries as main verbs, in *Bill was writing a letter* 'the fact that *was* precedes its object, *writing a letter*, is the same as the fact that *writing* precedes its object, *a letter*, and these facts need only be stated once'.

(28)

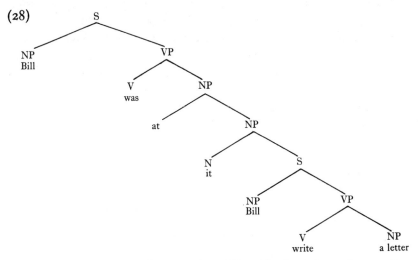

Presumably Ross is re-interpreting Greenberg's universal as a fact about initial structures or 'basic' word order. In which case, it will be a problem for him that several of his 'auxiliaries' are intransitive verbs in initial structure, e.g. *may* in (2), and only after the operation of Subject Raising and Extraposition do they end up to the left of their 'object'. If on the other hand he interprets the universal as a fact about surface structure, then it is a claim about 'predominant' word order and has only the status of a statistical tendency, and it is hard to interpret his claim that treating auxiliaries as main verbs 'explains' the universal.

2.1.2   Having been very negative and shown the faults in the internal logic of Ross' arguments for deriving modals from higher predicates, we turn now to an interesting set of generalizations which can be captured by deriving modals from the same S as they end up in in surface structure. I shall first outline some of Jackendoff's proposals concerning 'speaker-oriented adverbs'. Jackendoff (1972: ch.3) distinguished four classes of -*ly* adverbs: speaker-oriented, subject-oriented, manner, and finally adverbs like *merely*, which do not concern us here. Speaker- and subject-oriented adverbs occur only in S-initial and Aux position or S-final with pause. Speaker-oriented adverbs often have a paraphrase *S is Adj to me, I am Adj that S* or *I consider S Adj* (e.g. *happily, John sang the aria*; cf. the subject-oriented *carefully John drove his car through the crowded intersection*. Each of these is distinct from the manner interpretation in *John sung the aria happily* and *John drove his car through the crowded intersection carefully*). Jackendoff proposed that a rule of semantic interpretation, $P_{speaker}$, assign a semantic structure ADJ (SPEAKER, $f(NP^1, ... NP^n)$). If S is a sentence containing a non-strictly sub-categorized adverb, $f(NP^1, ... NP^n)$ will represent 'its functional structure, that is, the relation between the verb and the strictly subcategorized arguments $NP^1, ... NP^n$'. ADJ is the semantic content of the adjectival counterpart of the adverb undergoing the rule. The rules for subject-oriented and manner adverbs are stated by Jackendoff as follows:

$P_{subject}$:   If Adv_1 is a daughter of S, embed the reading of S . . . as one argument to Adv_1, and embed the derived subject of S as the second argument to Adv_1.

P_{manner}:   If $\begin{Bmatrix} Adv \\ PP \end{Bmatrix}$ is dominated by VP, attach its semantic markers to the reading of the verb without changing the functional structure.

These rules give minimal semantic structures as (29) and (30) respectively.

(29)   ADJ (NP^i, f(NP^1, ... NP^n))   (where $1 \leqslant i \leqslant n$)

(30) $\begin{bmatrix} f \\ ADV \end{bmatrix}$ (NP^1, ... NP^n)

'...adverbs will be marked in the lexicon as to which of the possible semantic structures they can enter into. For example, *certainly* will be a predicate over an S; the reading of *happily* in *happily, Frank is avoiding us* will be a predicate over an S and the argument SPEAKER'. Then, if *evidently*, a speaker-oriented adverb, is in final position without pause (i.e. dominated by VP), as in *John walked in evidently*, only P_{manner} will be applicable, giving $\begin{bmatrix} WALK \\ EVIDENT(S) \end{bmatrix}$ (JOHN, IN), which is ill-formed because of the unfilled variable S. With *evidently* in initial position, $P_{speaker}$ applies giving the correct interpretation: EVIDENT to SPEAKER (WALK (JOHN, IN)). $P_{speaker}$ operates on adverbs dominated by S. The predicted positions in surface structure for adverbs dominated by S are all the possible major constituent breaks. Assuming the base rules of (4), particularly that analysis of Aux, these positions are: initial, before Aux, after the first auxiliary and final with pause.

(31)   a. evidently John could have left before noon
     b. John evidently could have left before noon
     c. John could evidently have left before noon
     d. *John could have evidently left before noon
     e. *John could have left evidently before noon
     f. John could have left before noon, evidently

There are two phenomena which will take on importance for the analysis of modals. Firstly, Jackendoff points out the apparent incompatibility of S adverbs and Subject-Auxiliary Inversion.

(32)   a. *did Frank probably beat all his opponents?
     b. *what has Charley evidently discovered?

VP adverbs are fine in these contexts and so are the higher predicate paraphrases of these S adverbs and tag questions.

(33)   a. did Frank easily beat his opponents?
     b. what has Charley suddenly discovered?
(34)   a. is it probable that Frank beat all of his opponents?
     b. what is it evident that Charley has discovered?
(35)   a. Frank probably beat all of his opponents, didn't he?
     b. Charley evidently discovered a new way, didn't he?

This incompatibility holds not only with Inversion marking interrogatives but also with Inversion conditioned by optionally preposed elements.

(36)   a. Bill (apparently) has never seen anything to compare with that
       b. Tom (probably) ran so fast that he got to Texas in ten minutes
(37)   a. never has Bill (*apparently) seen anything to compare with that
       b. so fast did Tom (*probably) run that he got to Texas in ten minutes

One way to handle this would be to put identical restrictions on *wh* Movement, Negative Adverb Preposing and *so* Adverb Preposing, prohibiting them just if there is a S adverb present. This is very uneconomical and misses the point that the generalization seems to involve Inversion. We cannot require the absence of any S adverb in the structural description of Subject-Auxiliary Inversion, because suppressing the inversion makes things even worse.

(38)   a. *never Bill apparently has seen anything to compare with that
       b. *so fast Tom probably ran that he got to Texas in ten minutes

Jackendoff argued that Inversion introduces a semantic factor not present in the non-inverted forms, which is incompatible with the reading of S adverbs. (The problem may be more general than this, since *who evidently discovered uranium* seems to fall into the same class, although not involving Inversion.)

Secondly, there cannot be more than one subject-oriented adverb, and that one must be the last S adverb in the sentence (excluding final position with pause).[1]

---

[1] Jackendoff treats adverbs of frequency, e.g. *often, never*, as S adverbs (see (39)). But Lydia White has pointed out that such adverbs are not incompatible with Inversion (e.g. (37a), and *never (before) has he been late*). This may stem from a failure to isolate this set of adverbs from other S adverbs, or it may indicate that S adverbs are not, in fact, incompatible with Inversion. Notice that (38a), which is alleged to indicate that suppressing the inversion with S adverbs makes the sentences even worse, involves one S adverb which is an adverb of frequency (*never*) and one which is not (*apparently*); if *apparently* is omitted, the sentence is still ungrammatical, and therefore is irrelevant to the claim that S adverbs and Inversion are incompatible.

(39) a.
$\begin{Bmatrix} \text{probably} \\ \text{happily} \\ \text{often} \\ \text{evidently} \end{Bmatrix}$, Max $\begin{Bmatrix} \text{carefully} \\ \text{cleverly} \\ \text{quickly} \\ \text{stealthily} \end{Bmatrix}$ was climbing the walls

b. * $\begin{Bmatrix} \text{carefully} \\ \text{cleverly} \\ \text{quickly} \\ \text{stealthily} \end{Bmatrix}$, Max $\begin{Bmatrix} \text{probably} \\ \text{happily} \\ \text{often} \\ \text{evidently} \end{Bmatrix}$ was climbing the walls

c. * $\begin{Bmatrix} \text{carefully} \\ \text{cleverly} \\ \text{quickly} \\ \text{stealthily} \end{Bmatrix}$, Max $\begin{Bmatrix} \text{carefully} \\ \text{cleverly} \\ \text{quickly} \\ \text{stealthily} \end{Bmatrix}$ was climbing the walls

Now, a minimal requirement for any treatment of English modals is that it be able to capture the difference between the 'root' and 'epistemic' senses of each modal. Ross' treatment allowed such a distinction on the basis that root modals came from higher transitive predicates and epistemics from higher intransitives (see (1) and (2)); thus he drew the root/epistemic distinction at the level of initial syntactic structure. This involves various problems, as I have shown, and ignores the almost identical syntax of the two types of modal.[1] The

---

[1] The root/epistemic distinction is probably cross-linguistic and independent of variations in syntax. I know of two arguments that the two classes of modal have a different syntax, neither very strong. Ross (class lectures, 1968) claimed that the negative could contract only with root modals.

John mustn't do the shopping tomorrow

*John mustn't have been a student

Not many people agree with Ross on these judgments and, in any case, *this rule can't/couldn't be simplified any further* is well-formed despite the epistemic modals.

Another argument is that the deleted *must* in *John must do the shopping and be a student* can only be read in the same way as the first *must*; the sentence cannot be read as 'John is required to do the shopping and he is certainly a student'. Thus the syntactic deletion rule must 'know' whether both modals are epistemic or root; if one is epistemic and the other root the rule will not apply. This argument is unsound because in the undeleted *John must do the shopping and must be a student* again the modals must be read in the same way. Kuno (1972) has convincingly shown that this kind of thing is not dictated by the grammar but is due to a general perceptual strategy which assigns parallel interpretations to adjacent ambiguous objects. Each of the objects A and B is ambiguous in terms of which is the nearest surface, but when juxtaposed they will generally be interpreted in the same way.

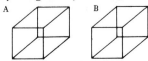

claim made here is that if one derives modals from the same S as they end up in, specifically from an Aux node immediately dominated by S and dominating only T (M), the epistemic readings can be derived by an independently motivated rule, namely Jackendoff's rule for speaker-oriented adverbs. Auxiliaries and S adverbs are in the same syntactic configurations, dominated directly by S and the semantic structures of epistemic modals are identical to those for speaker-oriented adverbs, as advocated by Jackendoff. The scope of epistemics, unlike roots, is the whole of the S in which they occur[1] and epistemics all indicate some degree of possibility. Therefore a minimal semantic structure for epistemic modals, as in *John* $\begin{Bmatrix} must \\ may \\ should \end{Bmatrix}$ *be here*, will have to include something like POSS(JOHN BE HERE). Features indicating the degree of possibility will then be added depending on the particular modal. This semantic structure is identical to that postulated by Jackendoff for speaker-oriented adverbs, and, since the syntax is the same, Jackendoff's $P_{speaker}$ can easily be generalized to epistemic modals. The really convincing evidence for this position comes from the fact that exactly the same conditions obtain for the rule interpreting epistemics as for the one interpreting speaker-oriented adverbs. This suggests that there is probably just one rule involved.

Firstly, if a modal has undergone Subject-Auxiliary Inversion, it cannot be interpreted epistemically. That is, epistemic modals and Subject-Auxiliary Inversion are incompatible, although there is some dialect variation. For many speakers (40a) and (40b) are ambiguous in that the modal may have root or epistemic sense, but in (41) the modals can have only the root reading.

(40)   a. Max $\begin{Bmatrix} may \\ must \end{Bmatrix}$ work at the McGill library

   b. Max $\begin{Bmatrix} may \\ must \end{Bmatrix}$ drive at 90mph

(41)   a. $\begin{Bmatrix} may \\ must \end{Bmatrix}$ Max work at the McGill library?

   b. $\begin{Bmatrix} may \\ must \end{Bmatrix}$ Max drive at 90mph?

---

[1] Interestingly, with the exception of speaker-oriented adverbs, which are outside the scope of the modal. *Evidently John must be a student* means 'it is evident that it must be the case that John is a student' and not 'it must be the case that it is evident that John is a student'.

Presence of *have* + *en* usually forces an epistemic reading, so if our explanation is right, it should not be possible to invert a modal if there is a *have* + *en* in the same S.

(42)   a. $\begin{Bmatrix} \text{Max must} \\ \text{*must Max} \end{Bmatrix}$ have studied at McGill

     b. $\begin{Bmatrix} \text{Max must} \\ \text{*must Max} \end{Bmatrix}$ have driven at 90mph?

(43)   a. Max may never have seen such a show
     b. *never may Max have seen such a show

This incompatibility is of the same status as the incompatibility of Inversion and speaker-oriented adverbs. Parallel to the adverbs, tag questions allow epistemic readings and Inversion can be done on the non-modal paraphrases.

(44)   a. Max must drive at 90mph, mustn't he?
     b. is it possible that Max studies at McGill?

Secondly, like speaker-oriented adverbs epistemic modals can precede but not follow subject-oriented adverbs (46), although there are no such ordering restrictions with speaker-oriented adverbs (45).

(45)   a. $\begin{Bmatrix} \text{John will evidently} \\ \text{evidently John will} \end{Bmatrix}$ have opened the secret door by now

     b. $\begin{Bmatrix} \text{Bill should probably} \\ \text{probably Bill should} \end{Bmatrix}$ have left by now

(46)   a. $\begin{Bmatrix} \text{John will slowly} \\ \text{?? slowly John will} \\ \text{?? John slowly will} \end{Bmatrix}$ have opened the secret door by now

     b. $\begin{Bmatrix} \text{Bill may quietly} \\ \text{?? quietly Bill may} \\ \text{?? Bill quietly may} \end{Bmatrix}$ have left by now

What I hope to have shown in this section is that in a transformational grammar of NE, there is good reason to derive modals from the same S as the one they end up in and not to treat them as underlying verbs. The arguments in the literature for deriving them from higher predicates are faulty and there are significant generalizations to be captured by generating them within their own surface S. Also, the wide range of transformations needed to derive the appropriate surface structures require an extremely permissive, hence undesirable theory of grammar. Given the view of grammar adopted here, my conclusion should not be very surprising, because modals simply do not have the syntactic properties of verbs: they do not undergo Number Agreement or *do* Support but do undergo Subject-Auxiliary Inversion and Negative Placement. They cannot appear in infinitives and gerunds, cannot occur adjacent to each other and cannot take normal complementation forms. No doubt there is much more that could be said about the proper analysis of modals in NE, and there have been more recent arguments supporting a Ross-type analysis (Huddleston 1974, McCawley 1975, Newmeyer 1975, Palacas 1971).[1] Having shown the plausibility of an analysis such as (4), I turn now to the diachronic data and show that this analysis permits an explanation for some historical changes, particularly for their timing. When we have developed a theory of change, this will constitute a further reason to adopt this analysis.

2.2   Historical re-analysis

2.2.1   When we look at Old and Middle English, we find a very different state of affairs. Here verbs such as *sculan, willan, magan, cunnan, motan,* which we usually translate into NE with modals, have all of the characteristic properties of verbs. They have full person–number paradigms (undergoing Number Agreement) and behave like verbs with respect to Negative Placement and Inversion. (Examples will be provided when the historical changes are discussed in §2.2.2 and §2.2.3.) They can occur adjacent to each other in series, and in infinitives and gerunds. They occur in sentence-final position, as one would expect if they were verbs, since at this stage English had an underlying SOV order (see Canale 1976). They can occur with normal complementation types and many can take surface direct objects, although they cannot then be translated in NE with a modal.

(47)   a.   hwæt þær foregange, oððe hwæt þær eftfylge, we ne cunnun
   'what came before, or what comes after, we do not know'.
   Bede

---

[1] Most of these arguments are based in some way on assumptions that there is a one-to-one relation between meaning and deep structure, and are beside the point for the view of grammar adopted here, which permits rules of semantic interpretation and does not require a one-to-one relation between initial phrase markers and semantic representations. Such a theory does not *disregard* semantic facts, but it simply denies a certain theory about them.

b. she koude muche of wandrynge by the weye 'she knew much of wandering by the way'. Chaucer

c. seþe sculde him undred denera 'he who owed him a hundred denarii'. c.975 Rushworth Gospels, Matt. xviii 28

d. ac him sealde ða mihte se ðe mæg ealle ðing 'but he who can do all things gave him the power'. c.1000 Aelfric, Feria vi in Prima Ebdomada Quadragesimae 157

e. ich wille, þat þou suere On auter ... 'I want you to swear ...'. 1300 Havelok 388

f. heora non swaðeah nolde befrinian hwæt heo ðær wolde 'none of them, however, would ask what she wanted there'. c.1000 Aelfric, Feria vi in Tertia Ebdomada Quadragesimae 62

What all this means is that for OE there would be no justification for setting up a syntactic category 'modal'. What we translate with modals in NE, all behave exactly like ordinary, complement-taking verbs in OE. Therefore, it is entirely reasonable and apparently uncontroversial[1] to argue that the initial structure of *ne con ic noht singan* 'I cannot sing' Bede, Cædmon, would be (48), at least insofar as *can* is treated as a main verb. (I omit details such as the constituency membership of Tense, returning to that in §2.4.)

(48)

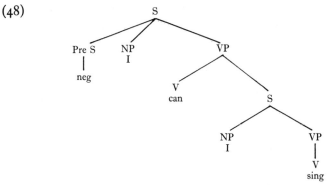

[1] Among generativists, Wagner (1969) and Allen (1975), for example, take this position. Although Traugott (1972a) analyses modals as auxiliaries, she says (p69) 'the predictive use of *will-* and *scul-* is rare in OE, however. Both verbs were originally main verbs, and it is as main verbs that they are most commonly found', and (p109) 'the modal and perfect auxiliaries were originally main verbs that introduced subordinate clauses'. Visser (1963–73: §1565) says of OE *willan*, for example, that it was a 'verb that gradually became toned down to the status of an auxiliary'; of *shall, may, can, will* and *ought* he says (§548) 'originally ... they were not function words, but full or independent notional verbs that syntactically did not differ in any way from the other full verbs'.

If our analyses of OE and NE are correct, a radical re-structuring took place in the development of NE, and when we look at how that came about there are some conclusions to be drawn about the nature of syntactic change and about the abstractness of synchronic syntactic analyses.

We have here a case of a radical change in initial structure. Diachronic syntacticians have often tried to argue that there can be no such thing as a radical re-structuring. Robin Lakoff (1968: ch.6), for example, sought to show that much syntactic change was a function of changes in lexical redundancy rules and not even of changes in transformations. Hence syntactic change took place only or mostly through changes in governed rules. Her claim was that diachronic syntax is at least easier to do if one assumes that the phrase structure rules do not change.

Secondly, Traugott (1972b) has argued that 'there is no such thing as "pure syntactic change" ...', where reference is made exclusively to syntactic rules, and not at all to either semantic or phonological factors'. Stockwell (1976) takes the same position. It seems to me that the initial structure of English modals presents us with a case of pure syntactic change, a change affecting only the syntactic component. One of the striking aspects of changes involving words such as *may*, *must*, *can*, *should*, is that they underwent very many changes in their syntax and in their meaning but that these changes seem to have proceeded quite independently of each other. This would be surprising to proponents of Generative Semantics, or to those who believe that there is a tight correlation between syntactic and semantic properties. For example, *cunnan* (> NE *can*) used to mean 'to have the mental or intellectual capability to, to know how to', and was sometimes contrasted in the same sentence with *magan* (> NE *may*), which meant 'to have the physical capability to'. This semantic distinction was lost and *may* developed a permission reading from ME onwards. At one point in its history *may* denoted ability or capacity not depending on outward circumstances and used to serve in contexts where we now use *can*, e.g. *he can speak Klamath*. Such semantic changes are typical of these words and seem to have taken place without affecting their syntax. On the other hand, a flood of syntactic changes came in the sixteenth century and had no noticeable affect on the meanings of the modals. We shall return to the question of 'pure syntactic change' in §3.2 and §5.1.

2.2.2 There are two stages to the story of the change: a number of apparently isolated changes took place early in the history of English. The net effect of these changes was to lead to a second stage, a re-analysis of *cunnan, magan*, etc., as a new category, 'modal'. Postulating that this re-analysis took place in the sixteenth century accounts for a large number of surface syntactic changes which took place at the time.

The early changes which set the scene for the re-structuring were the following, (i)–(v).

(i) The antecedents of the modern modals (henceforth 'pre-modals') lost the ability to take direct objects. This seems to have been complete in ME, with the exception of *can* which was a good deal more resistant. *Mun* + direct object, meaning 'to think of, remember', was lost early. The last cases attested by the OED for the other object-taking pre-modals are those of (49).

(49) *shall*: the leeste ferthyng þat y men shal. c.1425 Hoccleve, Min. Poems xxiii 695[1]

  can: yet can I Musick too; but such as is beyond all Voice or Touch. 1649 Lovelace, Poems (1659) 120[2]

  may: for all the power thai mocht. 1470 Henry, Wallace iii 396[3]

(ii) Most pre-modals (*sculan, magan, mōtan, agan* and *durran*[4]) belonged to an inflectional class generally known as 'preterite-presents'. These were strong verbs where the preterite forms had taken on present meaning in pre-Germanic and for which new weak preterites had been made. This is analogous to Greek οἶδα 'I know' and Latin *odi* 'I hate', which also are past (more precisely, perfective) in form but present in meaning. Other members of this class were *witan* 'to know', *dugan* 'to be of value', *unnan* 'to grant', *þurfan* 'to need', *munan* 'to think, remember', *benugan* 'to suffice'. The notable thing about this class is that the third person singular (being historically a strong preterite)

---

[1] The OED gives one later reference, which it treats as an archaism of doubtful standing: *by the feith I shall to god*, 1530 Court of Love 131.

[2] This is the last attested direct object but the OED has later references for *can*+ PP and the idiom *can skill of*: *that cunning Kaiser was a scholar wise, and coulde of grammarye*, 1875 Kingsley, Poems, 'Little Baltung' 82; *no skill of Musick can I, simple swain*, 1710 Philips, Pastorals iv 23. Roger Lass points out that these may be conscious archaisms.

[3] This is arguably not a genuine direct object but a 'cognate accusative'. But *may* here clearly acts as an independent verb, so I classify it with the true direct objects.

[4] I classify *durran* (> NE *dare*) as a pre-modal. *Dare* behaves sometimes as a modal (*dare he do it? he dare not do it*) and sometimes as a normal verb (*did he dare to do it? he didn't dare to do it*).

was *sceal, man, ann, dearr*, etc., i.e. it did not have the usual *-eþ* ending, the antecedent of the modern *-s*. Thus the modals are conservative in failing to undergo modern Number Agreement; there never was a *-s* ending for these verbs (although they did have second person singular and plural endings: *þū cannst, wē cunnon, we cūðon*). However, the truly remarkable thing is that all the non-pre-modals of this class were lost. *Benugan* dropped out of the language very early and the last cases of *unnan* and *þurfan* attested by the OED are as in (50).

(50)   *unnan*: Meriadok was a man þat tristrem trowed ay; Miche gode
           he him an. c.1320 Sir Tristrem 1928.
       þurfan: of þis cors ne thar not a-baffle. c.1485 Digby Mysteries
           III 1437.[1]

Witan survived into the nineteenth century, but not as a member of the same inflectional class as the pre-modals. The OED says 'the original conjugation [of *witan*] ... presented many apparent anomalies, and various attempts at normalization were made by means of analogical formations and irregular extension of the use of certain forms, with the result that new infinitive and present-stem forms came into existence ...'. *Witan* was removed from the preterite-present class, or at least abandoned its fricativeless present tense third person singular. The date of this change is not clear but it seems to have happened in ME. The OED says that *wat, what, waht* ... served as the first and third person singular forms but I have found no examples in the OED or elsewhere of such unlevelled third person forms after ME.

   Munan also survives into recent times, particularly in Scots. However, it survives only as a modal: *an' if I mun doy I mun doy*, 1864 Tennyson, The Northern Farmer (Old style, Lincolnshire dialect) xvii. It lost its sense of 'think, remember' very early.

   The history of *dugan* is somewhat more complicated. Stratmann gives its last occurrence as c.1360, but the OED and Visser show it surviving as late as the nineteenth century, although by that time it is very rare and confined to northern dialects. The OED points out that the original inflection *deag* as the singular present was supplanted in the fourteenth century by *dow* for the plural, the third singular becoming *dows* in most cases. Similarly a levelled past tense form *dowed*

---

[1] The OED has one later reference from 1825. This is a dialect citation in Jamieson's Scottish Dictionary, '*ye thursten*', *ye needed not*.

comes in in the fourteenth century. This would indicate that, like *witan*, *dugan* left the preterite-present class and conformed to the most common inflectional pattern. Therefore our hypothesis predicts that it would survive only as a main verb. Unfortunately this is an oversimplification. The history of *dugan* is just like that of *dare* and *need* in that it survived schizophrenically as an independent verb (e.g. *I never dowed to bide a hard turn o' work in my life*, 1816 Scott, Antiquary xxiii; *March grows Never dows*, 1855 Robinson, Whitby Gloss), but also, albeit much less commonly, as a modal (e.g. *ye may not, ye cannot, ye dow not want Christ*, 1637 Rutherford, Letters (1862) vol. I. p203; *she doughtna let her lover mourn*, 1724 Allan Ramsay, Tea-Table Miscellany (1733) vol. I p2).

One can only assume that it was an accident that in this inflectional class only the pre-modals survived. It does indeed seem remarkable that almost all the pre-modals had past forms with present meanings and that modern 'past tense' modals (*should, would, could* and, historically, *must*) generally have present sense. Also in other languages it is often the case that what we have analysed as auxiliaries have some kind of past tense form even in present sense. I have no idea why this should be, but it does not seem possible to define a class of modals (and therefore of preterite-presents) on semantic grounds, and furthermore we have seen that preterite-presents in OE and other languages encompass a very wide semantic range: 'hate', 'know', 'grant', 'be able', 'think', 'need', etc. We need not concern ourselves here with the reason; the crucial effect of the loss of the non-pre-modal preterite-presents was that the pre-modals (including the now uncommon *mun*) became an identifiable class of verbs, with the unique characteristic that they did not have a fricative suffix for the third person singular. This property was shared by OE *willan* which is usually classed as an anomalous verb and not as a preterite-present. It was conjugated *wille, wilt, wil(l)e, willaþ, willaþ, willaþ* and, like the pre-modals descended from preterite-presents, had no third person singular fricative.[1]

(iii) A third change concerns the preterites of the pre-modals. The preterite-presents shared with the weak (and therefore productive) verbs the feature that there was no phonological distinction between

---

[1] OE had the three verbs, *willan, willian* and *wilnian*, which were distinct in most inflectional parts. *Willan* is anomalous and the other two Class II weak verbs. *Wilnian* always had the *n* before the ending, and *willian* had, for example, *þu willast, we williaþ* and a preterite *ic willode* (cf. *ic wolde* for *willan*). Some of these forms coalesced in ME with the decay of inflectional endings.

the preterite indicative and subjunctive except in the second person singular. Hence modern *should* corresponds phonologically to an old preterite indicative or subjunctive. However, the preterites seem to have become unstable from early times, perhaps as a result of competition from the subjunctive. NE *must* and *ought*, historically past tenses, never carry past sense, and the relations of *shall/should*, *will/would* and *can/could* are rarely based on a distinction of tense; for the most part *should*, *would* and *could* carry present-future sense and exist independently of *shall*, *will* and *can*. However, in OE the pre-modals used to have appropriate time reference corresponding to their tense (whereas in NE past time reference is expressed by *he must have gone*, which seems not to have occurred in OE). The breakdown in the productivity of the present-preterite relationship appears to have started quite early and the preterite and present tense forms developed uses independently of each other and the tense relationship between them was steadily eroded, possibly as a result of the demise of the subjunctive mood. This can be illustrated by some uses of *might* and *should*. For example, constructions like *they may intend to do mischief*, where *may* is epistemic and means 'it is possible', are common from early times, but *might* did not occur as a past tense variant of this until the sixteenth century and now it has dropped out again.[1] An example with *might* is *these two respectable writers might not intend the mischief they were doing*, 1762 Bp. Richard Hurd, Letters on Chivalry and Romance 85; nowadays this would have to be *might not have intended*. Constructions such as *you may be right* are common from ME onwards (*be as be may, I make of it no cure*, 1385 Chaucer, LGW 1145) but *you might be right* is not distinct from it in terms of time reference. The past tense of the *may* of permission has become obsolete and *he might do it* cannot mean 'he was permitted to do it'. The opacity of the *may/might* tense relationship was increased by new uses of *might* being introduced into the language with no corresponding use of *may*. An example would be the use in *you might (have) shut the door properly*, which is a suggestion amounting to a request or reproach. The first

---

[1] This statement follows the standard handbooks. However, Peter Collins has pointed out to me the following examples, which seem to be earlier epistemic uses of *might*: *and hiða ealle sæton, swa swa mihte beon fif ðusend wera* 'and they all sat then; it is possible that there were 5000 men', Aelfric, Homilies of the A-S Church, Thorpe (1844–6); *sume beladunge mihte se rice habban his uncyste, gif se reoflica wædla ne læge ætforan his gesihðe* ... 'it was possible that the rich man had some excuse for his stinginess, if the leper did not lie before his sight', ibid.

convincing example of this is *as for these gentlemen . . . I think they might show a little more respect for their benefactors,* 1748 Smollett, Rod. Random (Tauchn.) xlv p287.

Turning now to *should: shall* used to mean 'to be under an obligation, be bound to' and this meaning survives into modern times, although nowadays it sounds a little archaic: *he shall hide himself in a bean-hole, if he remains on Scottish ground without my finding him* (= 'will have to'), 1818 Scott, Heart Midlothian xviii. However, the past tense of this with *should*, became obsolete in the fifteenth century: *Arthour, as he scholde done, Sende lucyes body to Rome* (= 'he had to do'), c.1400 Arthur (EETS) 481. An example of a new use of *should* with no corresponding use of *shall* is that in *I should like to have someone for a help,* where *I should like, suppose, hope,* are just diffident ways of saying *I want, suppose, hope.* This usage seems to have come in in the seventeenth century; the first example I find is *I should be glad to see you at my house,* 1675 Wycherley, Country Wife (Mermaid) I i. Another example is the use of *should* under adjectives expressing some degree of possibility: *is it possible that this shou'd be the true Lord Foppington?* 1695 Vanbrugh, Relapse (Mermaid) IV vi. This seems to have been introduced in the fifteenth century; Visser's first example is *it is impossible . . . þat a soule þat is bleendid in custom of synne schuld see þe foule spot in his concyence,* c.1400 Cloud of Unknowing (EETS) lxxii 10. Even in oratio obliqua *should* does not always appear where required by normal sequence-of-tenses rules: *we shall do it* cannot be reported as *we said we should do it.*

What all this means is that the *shall/should, may/might,* etc., distinctions are not based simply on tense or mood. For NE there is good evidence that *should* and the epistemic *could* are separate modals, distinct from *shall* and *can* and not related to them on the basis of tense. Even in ME there was a certain amount of evidence beginning to accumulate for this analysis, since the *shall/should* distinction was not as transparent as, say, that between *open* and *opened.*

(iv) The standard handbooks usually identify two normal word order patterns for OE: SMVO in main clauses and SOVM in subordinates, where M indicates the pre-modals *cunnan, sculan,* etc. However, if the pre-modals were indistinct from verbs and assuming the underlying order to be SOV, one would expect further possibilities. OE had a rule which moved the verb to between the subject and object; this rule was obligatory in main clauses and optional elsewhere, accounting for the usual SVO order in main clauses, and SOV or SVO in sub-ordinates. In that case one would expect the following orders:

(51)   main clauses: a. NP_s M   V NP_0: John can drink the ale
             b. NP_s M NP_0 V: John can the ale drink
    subordinates: c. NP_s NP_0 V   M
             d. NP_s M NP_0 V
             e. NP_s M   V NP_0

We may assume two possible initial structure configurations, (52a) for root modals and (52b) for epistemics. In (52a) the embedded subject will never be realized in surface structure and in (52b) the embedded subject would normally be raised to become the surface subject of the highest verb, the pre-modal (not affecting the order of elements).

(52)   a. NP_s [(NP_s) NP_0 V]$_0$ M
    b. [NP_s NP_0 V]$_s$ M

Therefore SOVM will emerge if V-Fronting does not apply on either cycle (and hence will occur only in subordinate clauses); SMOV will result from the application of V-Fronting on only the higher cycle in (52a) or by Subject Raising and Extraposition (a special instance of the OE scrambling rules) on (52b); V-Fronting on both cycles will give SMVO from (52a). Each of these orders occurs frequently in OE. I cite one example of each order from Aelfric (c.1000) (examples drawn from Allen 1975).

(53)   a. SMVO: ælc man mæg ðær geseon oðres manes geðoht 'each man might there see other men's thoughts'. Sermo ad Poplum in Octavius Pentecosten Dicendus 558

    b. SMOV: ic ne mæg ðam almihtigan ahwar ætberstan 'I cannot break away anywhere from the Almighty'. The Maccabees 29

    c. SOVM: se ðe hit rædan wyle 'he who will read it'. Domenica Pentecosten 107

So correct predictions are made for OE by adopting an underlying SOV order, a transformational rule of V-Fronting (obligatory in main clauses, optional elsewhere), and, crucially, treating the pre-modals as underlying verbs.[1] However, in early ME there was a base re-

---

[1] There is, in fact, one further possibility which I have not found attested: SVOM in subordinate clauses. This would result from applying V-Fronting on the lower

analysis whereby English became underlyingly SVO (see §7.2 and Canale 1976) and the V-Fronting rule became redundant. So the relevant base structures for root and epistemics would now be those of (54), assuming that the pre-modals were still verbs.

(54) a. NP_s M [(NP_s) V NP_o]
      b. [NP_s V NP_o] M

Thus one would now expect to find only the orders SMVO for root pre-modals and SVOM for epistemics. Following the SOV-to-SVO base change, root and epistemics now occurred in different configurations, which was not the case before the change of underlying order. However, SVOM is attested only rarely and SMVO became the standard order even for epistemics. It is as if the grammar was reluctant to follow through on one of the implications of the earlier SOV-to-SVO change and did not want to distinguish syntactically the root and epistemic pre-modals, perhaps because to do so would endanger mutual communicability between the conservative and innovating generations. Any rate, if we assume, as we must, that the pre-modals were still underlying verbs, then to account for the scarcity of SVOM surface structures we must postulate a further change: a rule is needed which would have the effect of mapping SVOM structures into SMVO. A rule of Extraposition would have the desired effect. However, Extraposition at this time probably did not exist, as we shall show in §4.3, because infinitival subject complements were base-generated in rightmost position (and likewise finite *that* complements although the data is less clear on this count). Therefore there are two possible analyses: (a) to invoke a probably not otherwise needed rule of Extraposition operating only on epistemic modals and in any case operating obligatorily, or (b) to claim that as the SOV-to-SVO word order change took place, there was another simultaneous change affecting epistemic modals such that they became underlying two-place predicates, subcategorized to co-occur with an empty subject: np *may* [NP_s V NP_o]$_s$. In the latter case, in order for the empty np to be filled, NP Preposing

cycle but not on the higher one, a possibility only in embedded clauses. Structures with two levels of embedding, as would be required, are not common and the absence of SVOM, if absence it is, may be accidental. However, one unexpected pattern is attested, SVMO. Fortunately this is not common and seems to occur under restricted conditions, namely when there is also a prepositional or adverbial phrase in the embedded S. I am at a loss to explain this: *ðæt we habban moton ða heofonlican wununge mid him sylfum æfre* 'that we might always have the heavenly dwelling place with himself', Aelfric, Domenica v 6.

would have to apply moving the lower subject up into the subject position of the epistemic verb; the np could not be filled by a dummy *it*, as with similar verbs such as *seem, be likely*. The point is that under either analysis, following the SOV-to-SVO base change some special mechanism would be needed to distinguish the epistemic pre-modals from other one-place predicates, avoiding the expected SVOM or *it* M [NP . . .]$_s$ structures: either a rule of Extraposition or NP Preposing applying obligatorily if the main verb is an epistemic pre-modal. (This discussion is predicated on the common assumption that root and epistemic pre-modals occurred in different initial structure configurations. It is not clear that this is necessarily correct. There might always have been just one (two-place) structure, with the pre-modal allowing either interpretation. If this is correct, one would not expect to find the almost non-existent SVOM structure and there would be no need to invoke a new device which came to affect the epistemic pre-modals. This would avoid the complications noted above.)

(v) Another change which helped to isolate the pre-modals was the introduction of the *to* infinitive. The handbooks usually depict a titanic struggle between the *to* and *to*-less infinitives raging during the late OE and early ME period, with *to* eventually winning out in most places. The exact way in which the *to* infinitive came to prevail is a matter of some argument, but Visser reflects a common view in asserting that in the beginning the introduction of *to* was semantically based, that is, that it first appeared as a true preposition with a sense of 'direction towards' (which changed, for example, *singan* to *singenne*). Gradually the prepositional force of *to* became weakened and the use of the *to* infinitive increased rapidly during the early ME period. However, some ME glossaries and dictionaries alternate between the *to* and bare infinitives and Kellner (1892) points out that 'even in the sixteenth century the simple infinitive tries still to retain part of its old dominion'. The relevance for us is that the *to* form never occurs immediately after a pre-modal (although it often occurs when separated by other material: *to do youre biding ay we wille*, Townley Mysteries 266, or *she tells me she'll wed the stranger knight, Or never more to view nor day nor night*, Shakespeare, Pericles II v 17). As long as *to* was interpreted as a preposition, one could predict that it would never occur after the pre-modals, because they conveyed no notion of 'direction towards'. However, it is not clear to me why the pre-modals consistently resisted the encroachment of *to* after it had lost its prepositional force and was taking over elsewhere. It seems that the pre-modals were already beginning to be identified as a unique class. The conditions for the invasion of *to* are complicated and mysterious. The *to* infinitive is rare in subject position before NE (*to go is necessary*), whereas the plain infinitive is very common in this position. On the other hand, the *to* infinitive in 'extraposed' positions (*it is good to go*) was introduced in OE and became common in ME (see §4.3). Any rate, Visser (1963– 73: §901) concludes that 'it took a long time for the particle *to* to be reduced from a preposition expressing motion, direction . . . to a semantically empty sandhi form, functioning as a mere sign of the infinitive . . . after about 1500 the construction with plain infinitive is on its way towards obsolescence'. So we must conclude that the pre-modals were seen as a unique class by the sixteenth century, if not earlier.

This, then, was the first stage of the story. Five independent changes took place which had the effect of isolating the pre-modals as a distinct class: (i) loss of all the direct object constructions with pre-modals, (ii) loss of all the preterite-presents except the pre-modals, thereby isolating the latter as a unique inflectional class, (iii) increased opacity of the past tense pre-modals *might, could, should, would* and *must*, (iv) special marking of epistemic pre-modals to avoid otherwise expected SVOM or *it* M[NP . . .]$_s$ structures, (v) the development of *to* infinitives with almost all verbs except the pre-modals.[1] In early OE the pre-modals had no characteristics peculiar to themselves, but by the end of the ME period they had become identifiable as a unique class by virtue of these five changes in various parts of the grammar. The changes did not occur simultaneously and were presumably independent of each other; at least, I can see no causal relationship between them. The pre-modals from earliest times shared another unusual but not unique property that the subject NP of the S they dominated was never phonologically realized in surface structure, i.e. was obligatorily PRO. Some other verbs, such as *try*, have this property.

(55) a. Bill could __ do that
      b. it may __ be that Bill left
      c. Bill tried __ to do that

2.2.3 These changes seem to have taken effect by the end of the fifteenth century: all direct objects had been dropped by then, except

[1] Verbs of perception also preserve the plain infinitive: *I heard him play 'Bitches Brew'*.

with *can*; the last surviving non-pre-modal preterite-present is *þurfan* in c.1485; several new non-temporal senses of the preterites of the pre-modals came in before 1500; the Extraposition marking for epistemics developed with the SOV-to-SVO base change, in ME; Visser dates the final obsolescence of the plain infinitive from 1500. The pre-modals were now firmly established as a unique class inflectionally, syntactically and semantically. It was no longer so clear that they were true verbs; if they were, they had several exceptional features. Evidence suggests that at this time they were re-analysed as a new category, which we can call 'modal', being derived as part of an S containing the verb they govern; the grammar did not continue treating them as verbs and piling up more and more 'exception features'. The evidence is a whole series of changes taking place simultaneously in the sixteenth century, all of which follow automatically from a re-analysis along the lines that I have suggested. It is remarkable that all of these changes took place together, within the same short period.

(i) The old pre-modals could no longer appear in infinitival constructions. The last instance attested by Visser is *that appered at the fyrste to mow stande the realm in great stede* . . . 1533 More, Works 885 C1; and Thomas Cooper records the form *to may* in his *Thesaurus Linguae Romanae et Britannicae* of 1565.

(ii) The old pre-modals could no longer occur with *-ing* affixes. The last recorded cases I have found are *the potential mode signyfyeth a thyng as mayyng or owing to be doone*, c.1512 Linacre, Progymnasmata, and *maeyinge suffer no more the loue and deathe of Aurelio*, 1556 Aurelio and Isab. M ix.

(iii) As from the mid-sixteenth century there could be no more than one modal for any verb in the standard dialects. Visser's last attested case of two modals is *I fear that the emperor will depart thence, before my letters shall may come unto your grace's hands*, 1532 Cranmer, Letters. (In fact, some dialects of NE allow such sequences: Scots has *will you can come?* and southern US dialects allow *she might could do it*. I do not know if these are innovative or conservative forms.)

(iv) The old pre-modals could no longer occur with *have* and an *-en* affix. The last case seems to be *if wce had mought conuenient come to-gyther, ye woulde rather haue chosin to haue harde my minde of mine owne mouthe*, 1528 More, Works 107 H6.

These four changes follow automatically from deriving the pre-modals from M, introduced by a rule Aux → T (M). This entails that there can be no more than one M in any S, that it cannot occur ad-jectively in a participle form, that it will never be found in a *for-to* complement type (since in that construction Aux is manifested only as *to*) and that in any one S *have* and *be* will never appear on the left of a modal. It is important to note the simultaneity of the changes. Three further changes took place at about the same time, which, while they are not automatic consequences of the re-analysis of the pre-modals, do nonetheless follow in a natural way which I shall explicate in §7.3.

(v) The Negative Placement rules had previously placed the negative particle immediately after the first verb, whether or not it was a pre-modal. This gave patterns like *John could not take the bread* and *John took not the bread*. With the development of two categories, if the existing rule were preserved, it would yield a new surface structure *John could take not the bread* alongside *John took not the bread*. Under this hypothesis, the grammar had to decide, as it were, whether the negative should be attached to the right of the modal or of the real verb, or whether to change the rule, generalizing to apply to both M and V, thereby maintaining the existing surface structures. It took the former course and retained forms like *John could not take the bread*. For clauses containing just one verb, two patterns developed in the early sixteenth century: *he did not speak* and, without *do* Support, *he not spoke*. In both cases the evidence was that Negative Placement had been re-formulated to place the negative between Aux and V. Constructions like *he not spoke* began to decline sharply in the late seventeenth century and the *do* type became standard. The conservative *I spoke not* survives into modern times in isolated phrases such as *I think not, I hope not* (although these structures represent *I think [not S]*, rather than *I don't think [S]*), but it became much less common from the late seventeenth century and was increasingly confined to poetry and archaisms (see §2.3).

(vi) Parallel changes had to be made in the Subject-Verb Inversion transformation, which had given patterns like *could John take the bread?* and *took John the bread?* Now that *could* and *took* were analysed as members of different categories, the inversion rule either had to be generalized to operate on M and V, in order to maintain the old patterns, or to prepose only auxiliaries.[1] It took the latter course. Jespersen and

---

[1] Logically it is possible that the grammar could have elected to invert only on the V, but this would give new surface structures with very strange cross-over phenomena:

Visser show that *did John take the bread?*, where the verb is not inverted, becomes common in the sixteenth century and the verb-inverted *took John the bread?* is definitely on the decline in the latter half of the seventeenth century.

It is impossible to put precise dates on these last two changes since they are both inextricably intertwined with the development of the *do* Support rule, which was a lengthy and complicated process and not clearly understood by grammarians. Competing forms existed side by side for long periods. *Do* began to develop in ME, but Jespersen (MEG v 25.6) points out that 'the exuberant use of *do*, chiefly unstressed, and having no real grammatical value, was reached in the 16th c. . . . but from the 17th c. a reaction set in and gradually restricted the use of *do* to those three cases' (i.e. with negatives, inversions and to indicate emphasis). Hence these changes occurred at roughly the same time as the postulated re-analysis, but we shall return to the development of *do* Support in §2.3.

(vii) So the old pre-modals were no longer verbs and were no longer to be derived from higher predicates. But now came what is perhaps the most remarkable change of all. As this re-analysis took place, a new set of verbs came into the language. These are often called 'quasi-modals', namely the verbs *be going to, have to, be able to*. Despite some subtle nuances, these verbs are for most purposes semantically identical to the modals *shall/will, must, can* and differ only syntactically in that they have all the usual properties of other verbs. They are true verbs. It is as if the re-analysis of *can, may, must*, etc., as modals created a vacuum, which the grammar immediately filled by creating a new set of semantically equivalent verbs. Again the dates are striking. The first OED references for *have to* are *he told him he had not to beleeve, that the couetousness of Virginio . . . had moved Ferdinand*, 1579 Geoffrey Fenton, Guicciard (1618) 6, and *we have . . . to strive with a number of heavy prejudices*, 1594 Richard Hooker, Of the Laws of Ecclesiastical Polity 1 i I. The first OED reference for *be going to* is *thys unhappy soulè . . . was goyng to be broughte into helle for the synne and onleful lustys of the body*, 1482 Monk of Evesham (Arb.) 43. The situation with *be able to* is more complicated. The OED's earliest reference is to *a felde uþer lyeþ leye . . . or is able to pasture . . .*, 1398 Trevisa's

---

take John could the bread? As the rule was re-formulated, there were also some minor changes in the conditions for application: in NE, but not in ME, Inversion must apply after a negative conjunction, *she did not like Fran, nor did John like Max.*

Englishing of Bartholomaeus de Proprietatibus Rerum xiv p49, where *able* means 'suitable'. The earliest convincing example where *to be able* is equivalent to *can*, is *to be abill to wed hure*, 1440 The Gesta Romanorum, ed. S. J. H. Herrtage (1879), p269. As Strang (1970: p150) puts it, with the development of these forms 'English developed a repertoire of full verbal paradigms to supplement the defective and functionally restricted modals'.

2.2.4 One can summarize the re-structuring in the following (greatly simplified) fragments of grammars, where *must*, *may*, etc., are subsumed under V in OE, under M in ENE.

Fragment of OE grammar	Fragment of ENE grammar
S → NP VP	S → NP Aux VP
VP → V (NP)	Aux → T (M)
NP → $\begin{Bmatrix} N \\ S \end{Bmatrix}$	VP → (*have* + *en*) (*be* + *ing*) V (NP)
	NP → $\begin{Bmatrix} N \\ S \end{Bmatrix}$

Negative Placement

NP   V   X ⇒ NP   V   neg   X   NP   Aux   X ⇒ NP   Aux   neg   X

Inversion

NP   V   X ⇒ V   NP   X   NP   Aux   X ⇒ Aux   NP   X

I have not 'proved' anything here and no doubt there are alternative ways of treating this data; but a radical re-analysis of pre-modals of the kind suggested here accounts naturally for the simultaneity of the seven changes taking place in the sixteenth century, and, as we shall see, it also permits an *explanatory* account of the historical changes. The relevant dates are remarkably uniform and 'clean' and there is no need to idealize the data, in a way that one would ordinarily expect to have to do, abstracting away from different dialects, literary styles, etc. The re-analysis is a genuine syntactic change affecting the base rules of the grammar of English. It is hard to see how the flush of changes taking place at the same time could be treated as anything other than an incredible accident in a more abstract, Ross-type analysis of the modern modals. One assumes that such an analysis would entail the claim that seven exception features were added simultaneously to various parts of the grammar. The historical corollary of abstract analyses of this type is that the base rules do not change and that radical re-structurings like this just do not happen (Lakoff 1968).

On the contrary, I have assumed that a grammar is a system of rules, not a fundamentally taxonomic system with a small number of rules smothered by large sets of rules features; such a view of grammar permits a description of the simultaneity of the surface changes discussed. These rules interlock in complex ways and changing one part of the system will cause 'pressure' on another part. Changes in the membership of an inflectional class, combined with some independent changes elsewhere in the grammar, were followed by the re-analysis of some verbs as a new category (manifesting itself in the changes (i)–(iv), p110), and that in turn precedes changes in certain transformational rules (e.g. Negative Placement and Subject-Verb Inversion) and the introduction of some new lexical items. The re-analysis was provoked by a number of changes which made it unclear whether the pre-modals were verbs or a unique category. Analysing them as a new category would avoid having to treat them as verbs with a cluster of exception features and would in a sense institutionalize their exceptionality. It seems that it did not take many exception features to bring about the re-analysis. Thus the category membership of pre-modals became opaque and the grammar moved to avoid such opacity. What this strongly suggests is that grammars are not as abstract as many transformationalists have been supposing over the last several years. It seems that some kind of transparency principle is at work in syntax and that initial structures are constructed and categories determined on the basis of fairly tangible and superficial alternations. As soon as *may* and, say, *take* started to behave differently with respect to things like inflections, infinitive forms and some other phenomena, there was a wholesale re-analysis of the pre-modals, keeping the initial structures within earshot of the surface structures; the grammar did not just go on acquiring more and more exception features. At least that hypothesis would explain the remarkable chronology of the changes I have discussed.

We shall return to the status of such an explanatory Transparency Principle in §3.1, and in §7.3 we shall specify a causal chain showing how the re-formulation of Negative Placement and Subject-Verb Inversion was a necessary consequence of the introduction of the modal category. The Transparency Principle, therefore, will be a principle of grammar which explains why this re-analysis took place. A theory of grammar, permitting only shallow derivations and incorporating the Transparency Principle, not only accounts for the simultaneity of the various surface changes, as shown in §2.2.3, but also explains why this change should take place, as we shall see after developing a theory of change in chapter 3. Each of these feats is beyond the capacity of a more abstract analysis like that of Ross, or, it can be added, that of McCawley (1975). McCawley, echoed more recently by Pullum & Wilson (1977), argued that *can*, *must*, etc., are really verbs with a defective paradigm, lacking non-finite forms, i.e. participial and infinitival forms. This accounts for their inability to occur with *-ing*, *-en*, or as the (presumably infinitival) complement to another verb. However, it says nothing about why present and past participles and infinitives should be lost at the same time, why it should happen to these verbs and not to, say, *take* and *go*, why as these forms were lost there were at the same time changes in inversion and negative patterns, or why Tag Formation and Number Agreement distinguish these defective verbs from fully endowed verbs (Tag Formation applying to the defective verbs and not to full verbs, and vice versa for Number Agreement). Since this proposal cannot describe simultaneity of the changes, it certainly cannot give an explanation (see §3.1 for some synchronic defects of an almost identical proposal).[1]

2.3 Appendix: periphrastic *do*

The aim of this chapter was to show that changes can take place in the base component of a grammar, in particular that a new category can be introduced, and that changes may affect only the syntactic component. So far I have argued that a modal category was introduced into the grammar of English, and that suffices to validate the general point. However, one may go on to ask whether this was the full extent of the change taking place in the sixteenth century. There is evidence that the change was more extensive and that the categories of Aux and T

---

[1] It is worth noting that such defective paradigms do not necessarily occur in non-finite packages. *Stride*, for example, lacks only the perfect participle: *Susan is striding to victory, wants to stride to victory, *has stridden/strid(d)ed to victory.*

   We have argued for a historical change in the phrase structure rules of English. Under the usual assumptions, that entails a change in the base component. However, if somebody proposed a generative grammar without transformations relating different levels of representation (see §6.2 for a proposal to eliminate structure-preserving rules), one would still hold that there had been a change in the phrase structure rules, which under this view would generate surface structures without the intervention of transformations. Therefore, under certain relatively extravagant assumptions, the claim for an independent, syntactic change is independent of the claim that there was a change specifically in the base component.

were also introduced for the first time. The evidence concerns the periphrastic *do*.

Grammars of English, from *Syntactic structures* onwards, have analysed tense as a deep structure constituent, unlike grammars of, say, French, where tense is best treated as a feature on the first verbal element of a clause. In NE the tense marker has the same distribution as the auxiliary verbs, i.e. modals and aspectual markers: it occurs before the negative, before the subject in inverted questions, in anaphoric VPs, and in tag questions.

(56)   a. John did not leave
        John must not leave
      b. (who) did John leave?
        (who) must John leave?
      c. Mary left and John did too
        Mary will leave and John must too
      d. John left, didn't he?
        John must leave, mustn't he?

It is the availability of the periphrastic *do* which enables the tense marker to have this freedom of movement and independence of its verb. To adopt a transformational analysis, we may say that this was not possible before the development of the rule of *do* Support, which provides a 'support' for tense markers 'stranded' by independently motivated rules (i.e. Negative Placement, Subject-Auxiliary Inversion, VP Deletion and Tag Formation) and no longer situated to the immediate left of a verbal element. *Do* Support applies after Affix Hopping which attaches T to any verbal element to its immediate right; *do* Support operates on all unattached or stranded Ts.

do Support

$$X \quad T \quad Y \quad \overset{\text{oblig}}{\Rightarrow} \quad X \quad do + T \quad Y$$

At a time when there was no periphrastic *do*, the patterns of (56) did not occur and there would be no reason to treat tense as anything other than one of the features on the verb, like number and person. If T was not an initial structure constituent and if *may*, *must*, etc., were verbs, then there would also be no justification for the category Aux (recall that the aspectual markers are analysed as constituents of VP). It seems plausible to claim that *do* Support was introduced at the same time as the modal category, although the evidence is not as clear-cut. If this is correct, the full extent of the rule changes affecting the auxiliary elements in the sixteenth century was a new phrase structure rule Aux → T (M) and a new transformation, *do* Support (in addition to the re-formulations of Negative Placement, Subject-Auxiliary Inversion, and the new lexical items, *have to, be going to, be able to*). The evidence will be sketched only briefly, since I do not intend to take a position on the nature of this change.

Some have claimed that the periphrastic *do* dates from OE or even earlier. There is a similar construction in certain dialects of German, *tun* + infinitive (Erben 1969), but this must be viewed as an independent development. *Do* + infinitive in OE was always a causative and quite unlike the modern usage. Similarly German *tun* occurred frequently in early New High German literary texts of the fourteenth-sixteenth centuries, but was strictly a causative. *Tun* and *do* underwent parallel but presumably independent development and eventually took on similar tense-carrying functions, although *tun* is now vanishingly rare in the standard language. This parallelism does not indicate an ancient ancestry, but rather a common innovation.

In his monumental study Ellegård (1953) argues that the non-causative, periphrastic *do* does not come into existence until the late thirteenth or early fourteenth century. He claims that the change of use took place under the special conditions of the southwestern dialect in the thirteenth century. 'The decisive factor was that causative *do* in this dialect had come to be used almost solely in positions where a periphrastic interpretation was also possible without changing the meaning of the whole context. This 'equivocal' *do* had an exact correspondence in French, which undoubtedly had some influence in the spread of its use' (p208). The equivocal case arises where the infinitive has no subject: *he dude writes sende* 'he caused to send writs', *þai gert seke him in þat sesoune* 'they caused to seek him in that season' (*ger* is the Scandinavian counterpart of English *do*). Out of context such constructions may be causative or periphrastic, such as [*he*] *dude strepe þis Maide naked*, which might mean that he had this maid stripped or that he stripped her himself. Infinitives with subjects can only be causatives: *þai gert hym bere it with envy* 'they made him bear it with envy'. Actual equivocal cases (i.e. cases not disambiguated by the context) were particularly common in texts of western dialects from the thirteenth century. Ellegård showed that the periphrastic *do* was exploited first by poets for rhythmical purposes and rhyming (since its availability often permitted the infinitive to occur at the end of a line), pointing to some eastern writers who used the periphrastic in verse but only the causative in prose. As the periphrastic became more common, so the causative gave way to *make* and *cause*. 'It is not until the end of the fifteenth century that the *do*-form becomes widely used in prose texts. From then on it spreads fast for about two generations' (p209). As noted earlier, *do* was used exuberantly at this time, particularly in learned writings, occurring even with pre-modals: *hit you behouith . . . behold ho* [= *who*] *shall doo gouerne*, c.1475 Partenay (EETS) 2385. This usage survived until St Thomas More: *now if I would then doe . . . tel him that . . .* , 1534 Works (1557) 1192 F4. Sweet (1900: p88) says of this period that the *do*-pattern was used 'according as a caprice, convenience, and clearness of construction, or euphony suggested', although there were constraints, e.g. *do* did not occur before *be* or *have* in 'standard' English (Irish dialects use it even here: *would anyone believe the things they do be saying in the glen?*, Synge, Shadows of the Glen).[1] From the fifteenth century the use of *do* was more strictly confined to its present-day environments, and this state was reached finally in the seventeenth century, although as the periphrastic *do* originated in southwestern dialects, so according to Palmer (1965: p26) those dialects have preserved the 'exuberant' uses more tenaciously. Contemporary grammarians viewed *do* as a mere tense carrier, semantically empty. Ch. Butler in his *English Grammar* of 1633 (p45) says 'The Present tense is formed of the Right case [i.e. the infinitive], either with the sign, [i.e. auxiliary *do*], or without the sign: '*I loove, thou loovest, hee looveth* . . . ; with the sign: *I doo loove, thou doost loove, hee dooeth loove* . . . – The Imperfect is formed either of the oblique Case [i.e. preterite] without the sign, or of the Right case with the sign, thus: *I looved* or *did loove*'. C. Cooper agrees in his *Gramm. Ling. Anglic.* (Pt III Cop4 §5) of 1685: '*I did learn* discebam et *I learned* aequipollent'.

In the light of this, it is plausible to claim that *do* Support became firmly established in the grammar of English by the seventeenth century. As noted in §2.2.3, the rule was established at the same time as Negative Placement and Subject–Auxiliary Inversion were reformulated to accommodate the re-analysis of the pre-modals. Before the re-analysis the canonical surface structure patterns included those

---

[1] The first example of the periphrastic *do* in imperatives is *come, do be a good girl, Sophy*, 1749 Fielding, Tom Jones (Everyman) vol. II p286.

of (57) for negatives and interrogatives, where V encompassed full verbs and pre-modals, and always carried the tense marker.

(57) a. NP   V   not ...
     b. V   NP ...

After the re-analysis the canonical patterns were (58), where Aux included modals and *do*, and carried the tense marker.

(58) a. NP   Aux   not ...
     b. Aux   NP ...

It was possible to assign a fairly precise date to the re-analysis of the pre-modals; this is more difficult for the introduction of *do* Support. There is clear evidence for a *do* Support transformation when the periphrastic *do* becomes limited to interrogatives, negatives, anaphoric VPs and tag questions.[1] There is no evidence for such a rule when *do* occurred only as a causative, when it would be treated as a normal lexical item occurring in the initial phrase marker. What about the intervening period? At this time *do* appears as an optional tense carrier and again, therefore, there is no reason to postulate a *do* Support transformation. However, T does occur as a constituent independent of the main verb of the clause. A grammar could handle this in a variety of ways, including a phrase structure rule Aux → T or treating *do* as a 'higher predicate', a true complement-taking verb. I know of no compelling evidence for a choice between these two options; each adds complications to the grammar. Therefore, while arguing that the present version of *do* Support was introduced just after the re-analysis of the pre-modals, I cannot take a position on the introduction of Aux and T as initial structure constituents: they were

---

[1] If we look at this as the development of a *do* Support transformational rule and T as an initial structure constituent, then it is an unexplained fact that the auxiliary *do* occurs first in anaphoric VPs, as in (i).

(i)   a. reced weardode unrim eorla, swa hie oft ær dydon 'innumerable men guarded the building, as they often did'. Beowulf 1238
      b. he her curseth as other fooles do. c.1503 More, Book of Fortune (Works 1557) 3 D2.

These expressions occur freely in the very earliest texts, and are the only evidence for treating T as a constituent in OE. Perhaps this evidence was sufficient to force the analysis. If so, one might argue that English had a phrase structure rule Aux → T from the earliest times and that *do* was attached first only to a T where there was no verb in the clause, then to any T (except before *be* or *have*), and finally only to a T not immediately preceding its verb. This would account for the relevant chronological stages, whereby *do* occurred (1) only in anaphoric VPs, (2) almost anywhere, and (3) in inverted interrogatives, negatives, anaphoric VPs and tag questions.

certainly introduced by the sixteenth century, but may have been introduced before the re-analysis of the pre-modals, when the periphrastic *do* became widely used as an optional tense carrier in the prose texts at the end of the fifteenth century. In either case one can say (if one rejects the hypothesis in p119n) that Aux was introduced as a category within the period of 1475–1550. This is roughly simultaneous with the introduction of the modal category.

3 A theory of change

By weighing, we know what things are light, and what heavy. By measuring, we know what things are long, and what short. The relations of all things may thus be determined, and it is of the greatest importance to measure the motions of the mind. I beg your Majesty to measure it. (Mencius c. 335 BC)

3.1 The Transparency Principle

At the end of §2.2 I introduced the Transparency Principle, more or less like a rabbit out of a conjuror's hat. I shall attempt to give some fairly precise content to this principle in subsequent chapters, but here we shall consider the status of such a principle and the role it plays in the logic of research outlined for work in diachronic syntax.

The Transparency Principle requires derivations to be minimally complex and initial, underlying structures to be 'close' to their respective surface structures, and it must be conceived as part of the theory of grammar, and not as a component of a theory of (syntactic) change; it helps to define what constitutes a possible grammar of a particular natural language. (As with many principles of grammar (e.g. the Specified Subject and Subjacency Conditions, §1.4), it might eventually turn out to be subsumed under a more general perceptual strategy; while not excluding that possibility, I know of no relevant evidence and treat it here as a grammatical principle. Since perceptual strategies also define possible grammars, the question is of no relevance to the concerns of this book.) In the case of the re-analysis of the English modals, the first part of the story told of five, apparently unrelated changes affecting quite different parts of the grammar. One consequence of these piecemeal changes was a grammar of ENE containing a set of exception markers of one kind or another. One such marker, for example, specified that while all other verbs took a fricative desinence in the third person singular, only the pre-modals did not. Similarly, the assignation of a past *time* interpretation to a verb with a past *tense* suffix was blocked in the case of the pre-modals.[1] Also the infinitive was characteristically formed with a *to* morpheme, except after pre-modals. At this stage, therefore, if the pre-modals were underlyingly verbs, the grammar contained various kinds of exception markers in different components, which could be formulated in various ways. By virtue of the exceptionality which had developed, derivations were now more complex and, adopting the view of markedness outlined in §1.5, one may claim that the grammar of English had become increasingly marked in certain areas. If the Transparency Principle characterizes the limits to the permitted degree of exceptionality or derivational complexity, then it will follow from this principle that as these limits are approached so some kind of therapeutic re-analysis will be necessary to eliminate the offending complexity. Viewed in this way, such a principle of grammar will predict the point at which radical re-analyses will take place. So in the case of the English modals, the first part of the story tells of complexity being developed gradually with an increasing number of exception markers. The second part of the story is a sudden, cataclysmic, wholesale re-structuring of the grammar whereby the exceptionality is, in a sense, institutionalized and the derivational complexity is eliminated at a stroke. That is to say, while the pre-modals continue to be distinguished from true verbs, the exception markers as such are eliminated. The new grammar contains a new category, modal, but the derivations are regular and not complicated by the various exception markers. Such a catastrophic re-analysis which has the effect of eliminating derivational complexity is predicted by a principle of grammar prescribing absolute limits to tolerable degrees of derivational complexity or opacity. If the Transparency Principle can be formulated in such a way as to characterize the last of the five changes leading up to the re-analysis (i.e. the regularization of the *to* form of the infinitive with all verbs except the pre-modals) as breaching the limits to tolerable opacity, this will provide

---

[1] I assume an interpretive rule assigning past time reference, a semantic concept, to a verb with a past tense suffix. This is not a trivial rule and there are several contexts where it does not apply, as in counterfactual conditionals, which refer to present time despite past tense endings: *if Gerry was President today, he would be richer*. See Hornstein (1977b) for discussion of this kind of rule in the context of proposals by Reichenbach (1947). Whatever the details of the rule, in ME it had lexical exceptions, viz. *would, should, could, might* and *must*, which could not be relied on to have past meaning in contexts where other past tense verbs could, such as in simple declarative sentences.

an *explanation* for the re-analysis and for the fact that it took place at this time. Of course, it does not explain the nature and form of the re-analysis, a point to which we shall return. Let us assume that the Transparency Principle can be so formulated. As it stands so far, this 'explanation' is after-the-fact, but in subsequent chapters we shall examine more re-analyses of the type illustrated in chapter 2, arguing that they can be viewed as a consequence of a Transparency Principle so conceived. In this chapter we shall assume that there exists some such principle in the theory of grammar, and examine the function of such a principle.

The Transparency Principle represents an inductive generalization, resulting from an examination of several radical re-structurings of grammars like the one involving the English modals (this is not to claim that induction plays any role in the testing or 'justification' of the principle, which would be contra Popper; the means by which one hypothesizes a principle has no bearing on establishing whether or not it is correct). One examines re-analyses which have the effect of eliminating derivational opacity in certain areas of the grammar, and then seeks to determine the degree of opacity holding as the re-analysis takes place. One explains the re-analyses in terms of a principle of grammar which manifests itself through diachronic change. That is, by looking at the points at which a grammar is driven to a therapeutic re-structuring, one infers something about the limits to possible grammars.

This involves two assumptions, one of which seems to be quite well-founded while the other is somewhat speculative. The first assumption is that grammars practise therapy, not prophylaxis. That is to say, changes may take place which, while perhaps having a therapeutic effect in one area of the grammar, contribute to derivational opacity elsewhere. So, the gradual loss of the non-pre-modal preterite-presents in ME, either by falling into disuse or by being assigned to a new conjugational class, had the effect of isolating the pre-modals inflectionally and, after the levelling of verbal inflections, requiring exception markers to indicate that only the pre-modals lacked a -*s* ending for the third person singular present tense. If grammars practised prophylaxis, such a change might have been blocked because of the fact that it contributed to extra derivational opacity in some area of the grammar. Rather, it seems that grammars may undergo changes which cause derivational opacity up to the limits imposed by the

Transparency Principle. As those limits are approached, therapy is performed by some kind of re-analysis or Thomian 'catastrophe' which eliminates the offending opacity. That seems to be a plausible way of viewing several changes such as those described in chapter 2 and some to be recounted in later chapters. This position has been adopted by some earlier writers: Samuels (1965) observes that it is a commonplace that grammatical ambiguities arising from sound change may be remedied by the selection of new analogical forms, and he cites Sapir (1921: p196), Saussure (1916: p227), Hermann (1931: p128), Jespersen (1941: pp23, 58). The position is illustrated by this passage from Bally (1926: pp40–1):

> une langue est sans cesse rongée et menacée de ruine par l'action des lois phonétiques, qui, livrées à elles-mêmes, opéreraient avec une régularité fatale et désagrégeraient le système grammatical . . . Heureusement l'analogie (c'est ainsi qu'on designe la tendance inconsciente à conserver ou recréer ce que les lois phonétiques menacent ou détruisent) a peu effacé ces differences.

Paul (1880: p251) also denies that languages ever practise prophylaxis and prevent some inconvenience developing: 'es gibt in der Sprache überhaupt keine Präkaution gegen etwa eintretende Übelstände, sondern nur Reaktion gegen schon vorhandene'. Recently Langacker (1977), who in other respects takes quite a different approach from the one adopted here, says that

> a re-analysis occurs in response to a particular set of factors present in a particular class of expressions; it resolves certain structural pressures or exploits the structural potential of those expressions. Speakers do not however redesign their entire language or check the implications of a modification for all other aspects of the linguistic system before adopting the modification. A change which resolves certain structural pressures may therefore create new ones and lead to further changes. (p96)

The second assumption is that these therapeutic re-analyses take place only when necessary and not randomly. That is, they occur only when provoked by some principle of grammar such as Transparency. This is a necessary assumption if one is to claim that such re-analyses provide an insight to the defining properties, the limits to possible grammars. This assumption, while plausible enough, is quite speculative. However, the current state of the art is such that an analyst must take whatever he can get in order to restrict the class of available grammars. Whether or not this assumption is viable will be demonstrated by its consequences for the theory of grammar. Making the theory of grammar responsive to historical change in this way clearly requires a restriction on the class of available grammars of the general type provided by the Transparency Principle. Whether or not that particular restriction is correct remains to be seen. However, this is good methodology because, to take again a broadly Popperian–Lakatosian viewpoint, the proposal is evidently falsifiable in principle. That is, it is in principle possible that an analyst could motivate a grammar for some language which was inconsistent with the Transparency Principle. For example, Ross' analysis of English auxiliaries violates the principle and would constitute a counterexample or a falsification if it were well-motivated; we showed in §2.1.1 that it is not. The principle, whose formulation is based crucially on the assumption that languages undertake radical re-analyses only when forced to do so by some principle of grammar, is falsifiable in essence but hitherto not actually falsified. It is a 'bold' or 'risky' hypothesis, by no means necessarily correct. But it accounts for when several re-analyses take place. Therefore, while the assumption is indeed speculative, it is also productive and one can readily specify what kind of grammar would constitute a falsification. The falsifiability of the assumption on the one hand and its usefulness on the other is sufficient recommendation.

Let us now consider the general role of a theory of grammar in accounting for historical change, elaborating some points made in chapter 1, and then returning to the question of the status of the Transparency Principle from a slightly different point of view. In chapter 1 we stressed the importance of a restrictive theory of grammar for the study of historical syntactic change. The restrictive theory provides an upper bound on possible changes. It was argued that some version of the EST (incorporating $\overline{X}$ conventions, clear distinction between lexical and transformational rules, etc.) was sufficiently restrictive to provide precise, testable hypotheses about the nature of possible and impossible changes. If the expressive power of grammars is limited, the possibilities for change are also limited and there begins to emerge a theory of what will constitute a possible historical change. There are grounds to suppose that this is a useful line to pursue; a plausible account of syntactic change seems to be indicated and the general syntactic theory thereby derives further support. One must ask, then, what kinds of changes would be consistent with such a theory and what would not. If we assume some version of Emonds' structure-preserving hypothesis, then it will follow that non-structure-preserving innovations will enter the language first as root transformations, affecting just root sentences, and only later percolating through the grammar to affect the phrase structure rules and thus the structures in embedded clauses. One can cite numerous examples of changes progressing in this fashion. Consider, for example, the word order changes which occurred independently in most of the Indo-European languages. The SOV-to-SVO change characteristically took place first in main clauses and later in subordinate clauses. Clearly any transformational rule relating SOV and SVO orders would not be structure-preserving and therefore, under Emonds' hypothesis, would affect only root sentences. It seems that Basque is undergoing a similar change in word order, and again the change affects main clauses first. So in main clauses one finds SOV and SVO orders, but only SOV order in relative clauses, etc. (de Rijk 1972). Dillard (1972) argues for a new rule in Black English whereby subject agreement is effected by prefixing *he- she-*, or *they-* to the verb, but this development has taken place only in main clauses: *the man he-came to dinner*. Givón (1976) claims that 'main clauses (and in particular declarative-affirmative ones) are the most progressive, innovative environment in language, where innovations are first introduced and from where they spread later on into other environments'.[1] Such changes are entirely consistent with the theory outlined, unlike, say, a change affecting first relative clauses and then spreading to all other clause-types. It is difficult to see how such a change could be interpreted within this theory, and therefore we may claim that the theory predicts that such a change would be impossible.

Having said this, let me try to forestall possible misunderstanding. The logic of this claim is that a theory of grammar which is restrictive will ipso facto provide limitations on possible diachronic changes. As an illustration, current versions of the EST incorporating Emonds' structure-preserving principle are most naturally interpretable as making predictions (above) which seem to be correct. This *logic* is not

---

[1] A further example is found in Teeter's (1974) discussion of Pronoun-V-Suffix structures in Algonquian. The pronominal prefix occurs only in main clauses and Teeter argues that it represents a common innovation in most of the Algonquian languages. For further discussion of innovations affecting main clauses first, see Givón (1975a).

affected if I leave open the question of the correctness of Emonds'
principle. It may be the case, as I suggest in chapter 6, that there are no
structure-preserving transformations; the domain of root transformations may be semantically based (although I am not persuaded by
Hooper & Thompson (1973) that it has to do with 'assertive' clauses;
see Green 1976); if it is the case, as sometimes suggested, that 'parallel
changes' affect, say, VPs before NPs, it might turn out that under
another theory this will be viewed as a consequence of some more
general principle also predicting the progressiveness of main clauses
(whereas Emonds' principle could not be naturally interpreted as
saying anything about the putative progressiveness of VPs as opposed
to NPs). These are all interesting questions, important areas of research
for diachronic syntacticians, but they are extraneous to the present line
of argument. There is much more to be said about the proper formulation of structure-preservingness, but in this section I am interested
in the general relationship between a restrictive theory of *grammar*
and a theory of *change*. So the present formulation of the structure-
preserving constraint limits the class of available grammars and thereby
limits the class of possible historical changes.

If no grammar can have structure-changing rules operating in non-
root clauses, that restricts the possibilities for change and the restriction
is effected by a principle of grammar, not a principle from a theory of
change. This yields a rather precise claim about the nature of possible
changes. Only structure-changing transformations are restricted to
root clauses, where 'structure-changing' means moving elements
into configurations which could not be generated directly by otherwise
needed phrase structure rules. If a grammar were to acquire such a
structure-changing transformation, its domain of application would
be limited to, broadly speaking, main clauses. On the other hand,
structure-preserving transformations are free to apply in all clause-
types and therefore there is no reason to suppose that if a grammar
acquires such a rule its domain of application will spread from main
clauses to subordinates. Similarly with rules which do not change the
order of underlying elements in the course of a syntactic derivation,
e.g. lexical redundancy rules, phrase structure rules, semantic interpretation rules, morphological and phonological rules. These rules are
not structure-changing transformations and therefore their effects
would not be limited to main clauses by Emonds' constraint; this
entails that there is no reason, at least no reason associated with the

principle of structure-preservation, to suppose that introduction of such rules should be manifested in main clauses before subordinates. Under this view, we can claim that only certain kinds of historical changes, those involving structure-changing transformations, should begin by affecting only main clauses. If a grammar has phrase structure rules generating SOV structures and then acquires a transformational rule permuting SOV into SVO, such a transformational rule will be structure-changing and is therefore limited to root clauses.[1] There may then be a subsequent change whereby the phrase structure rules change, perhaps by some kind of analogical process, and generate underlying SVO structures, and SVO structures will then occur in all clause types. As noted earlier, this is the way in which word order changes characteristically develop. The progression of the new order from main clauses to subordinates can thus be seen as a function of the theory of grammar, not a theory of change. On the other hand, if morphological classes are levelled, the first examples of the new levelled forms do not occur more frequently in main clauses than in subordinates. Similarly new lexical rules and new phrase structure rules (as in the example of the modals discussed in chapter 2) affect all clause-types alike. So it can be seen that a restrictive theory of grammar incorporating some version of the structure-preserving constraint makes predictions about possible changes, and that it sharpens the observations of Givón (1976), who noted a general 'tendency' for innovations to affect main clauses first; under the view of grammar adopted here only certain specifiable changes will progress in this fashion. This illustrates how a restrictive theory of grammar provides the upper bounds to possible changes and makes testable predictions about the way changes may be implemented.

Returning now to the Transparency Principle, we can apply the same logic. In chapter 2 I argued for re-structuring of phrase structure

[1] If Emonds is right in claiming that there can be only one non-structure-preserving transformation applying in any one root clause, then finer predictions are made. For example, it will fall out that innovations will first appear in clauses which do not undergo some radical structure-changing rule. Therefore the predictions following from a theory of grammar incorporating such a definition of transformations will intersect to a large extent with the consequences of a principle of change specifying that 'syntactic change is implemented for sentences that have undergone "superficial" rules before it is implemented for sentences that have undergone "major cyclic" rules' (Chung 1976). Assuming the principle of structure-preservation to be motivated as a constraint on synchronic grammars, if its predictions intersect with those of this principle of change, to that extent the principle of change is rendered superfluous. See §7.2 for further discussion.

rules as a type of syntactic change. I showed that a set of simultaneous but superficially unrelated changes could be viewed as the realization of a single change in the abstract grammar; under the assumptions outlined above, the simultaneity of the changes provides the evidence for the singularity of the change. Such changes follow from the Transparency Principle.[1] Typically, changes in various places in the grammar may occur and happen to have the effect of making existing initial structure analyses more opaque to the language learner. There seems to be a tolerance level for such exceptional behaviour or 'opacity', and when this is reached a radical re-structuring takes place and renders the initial structures more transparent, easier to figure out and 'closer' to their respective surface structures. The re-structuring is entailed by the Transparency Principle and is manifested by a set of simultaneous changes in possible surface structures. That is, only the latter changes result from the Transparency Principle; put differently, if such sets of changes did not take place, one would have no evidence that there had been a re-analysis, instead of just toleration of the complexity. Thus the Transparency Principle will need to quantify the amount of exceptional behaviour needed in order to bring about a re-structuring of the grammar.

Under this view one may set up as a goal for work in syntactic change the formulation of such a Transparency Principle, the determination of the tolerance level for initial structure opacity. How much opacity can a language take before being driven to re-analyse its initial structures to bring them closer to their surface structures and eliminate the exceptionality?[2] How much 'work' can the transformational component perform? To put it differently: how smart are language learners? What is the limit to the abstractions that they postulate? In order to answer these questions and determine the functional load which the transformations may carry, one must examine cases of radical re-analysis which have the effect of eliminating opacity, and seek to establish the conditions for such re-structuring of the grammar.

The Transparency Principle is therefore a component of the theory

[1] More precisely, of the set of seven simultaneous changes, four were the surface manifestations of the introduction of the new modal category and the other three changes followed in a slightly different sense which remains to be discussed.

[2] My notion of 'opacity' would include what Anttila (1975) calls 'SURFACE AMBIGUITY, which is the traditional name for invitation for re-analysis'. The case of the impersonal verbs in ME (§5.1) would involve both 'surface ambiguity' and 'opacity', but the situation leading to the establishment of a category of 'modal' in English involved 'opacity' but not 'surface ambiguity' in the usual sense.

of grammar, just like Emonds' structure-preserving constraint, and it will serve as a basis for choosing between competing analyses. Consider again our tale about the development of the English modals. In §2.1.1 we showed the inadequacy of arguments adduced for an 'abstract' account, deriving the NE modals from underlying main verbs. However, suppose that another linguist could formulate such an abstract analysis in such a way that it avoided the criticisms we levelled against Ross (for an attempt along these lines, see Pullum & Wilson (1977)).[1] In that case we would have two analyses which would 'work' and generate the modals correctly. One analysis might postulate underlying verbs with various 'exception features' in different parts of the grammar which would distinguish 'verbs' like *may, must* from 'regular' verbs in the relevant ways; the other analysis postulates an underlying category modal. Even if these two analyses appeared to be more or less equally well-motivated, one would choose the latter because it accords with the Transparency Principle. This principle, being a restriction on the class of grammars, will thereby resolve certain indeterminacies of description, selecting a description consistent with Transparency over one which is not.

It is important to recognize that while the Transparency Principle is a principle of the theory of grammar, eliminating certain otherwise possible grammatical descriptions, it reveals itself primarily through historical change. That is to say, we have argued for the principle on the basis of certain diachronic changes, claiming that if there were such a restrictive principle in the theory of grammar one would have an explanation for various radical re-analyses. In particular, the re-analysis involving the English modals would be a consequence of this principle. If one requires that a grammar should give an orderly account, where possible, of apparently unrelated but simultaneous changes and that a theory of grammar should provide an explanation for why radical re-analyses eliminating derivational opacity take place at the points

---

[1] The analysis by Pullum & Wilson is a very good example of this. They treat modals as main verbs which are inflectionally irregular and defective, having, for example, no perfective, progressive, infinitival or third person singular -*s* forms. The notion of a defective paradigm seems to be well-motivated and assigning the 'verbs' *can, may, must*, etc., these particular lexical gaps accounts correctly for certain aspects of their distribution. However, the analysis violates the Transparency Principle and yields no understanding of the historical change. Under this account, these various lexical gaps developed inexplicably simultaneously in the sixteenth century. Not only is the simultaneity unaccounted for, but the change appears to be random and follows from no known principle of grammar or change. See also §2.2.4.

where they do, one constructs an argument for a Transparency Principle which has the effect of restricting the class of available grammars and resolving some indeterminacies of description – a desirable consequence. The plausibility of grammars constructed in accordance with Transparency will depend on many factors: the ability to account for the distribution of morphemes and assign semantic descriptions to sentences, the capacity to support an insightful account of the acquisition process by children learning their first language, etc. This accords with the view outlined in chapter 1, that the 'correctness' of a grammar will be determined not only by data from morpheme distribution and the correlation of structural descriptions with semantic representations, but also with data from diachrony, acquisition, language pathology, etc. Since no one area of facts has a privileged status, if data from these different domains seem to support conflicting claims about the 'correct' grammar, one will have a paradox. In that case one behaves like any scientist confronted with a paradox; one worries about it and seeks to resolve the apparent conflict.

To see the same point from a slightly different angle, consider an alternative account of the changes affecting *can*, *may*, *must* etc. In chapter 2 it was shown that the simultaneity of the changes occurring in the sixteenth century can be viewed as the manifestation of the development of a new category. Another possibility would be to treat the various surface changes as a function of the development of a new surface filter. This analysis would continue to treat *may*, *must*, etc., as underlying verbs as in OE, not postulating a new modal category. However, the claim might be made that the grammar develops a new output constraint (1).[1]

(1) the verbs *may*, *might*, *must*, *can*, *could*, *shall*, *should*, *will*, *would* must occur in surface structure immediately preceding a tense marker

It has been argued by Haiman (1974) that the introduction of a new surface filter is a possible form of historical change.[2] On the assumption

[1] Jenkins (1972) suggests such a surface constraint in a somewhat different context, rejecting it after discussion.

[2] We shall return in §6.2 and §7.2 to the role of surface filters as a mechanism of syntactic change, suggesting that they should be invoked only as a last resort, that they cannot be language-specific and therefore that they cannot be acquired or lost by grammars (although they may become vacuous by virtue of new rules of grammar (see §7.2)). Haiman, however, makes an interesting case, based on the notion of 'targets' (the term is due to Hoenigswald (1966), although the idea is much older). Various grammatical devices are viewed as conspiring to some end;

that grammars may have surface filters, one must admit that this is a possible change, as I shall show in §3.2 when I discuss a theory of change. Such a filter would account for the fact that these 'verbs' do not occur in infinitival complements ((2) a, b), if one assumes that such complements are tenseless (I take 'infinitival' in a broad sense, to include the complement to *will* in (2b)). The filter also accounts for the inability of these items to occur in perfective or progressive aspect, since in such a case the only tense marker surviving into surface structure would be attached to the initial *have* or *be*, as indicated in (2) c and d. We showed in §2.2.3 that such constructions were admitted before 1500. I assume in this account that tense is generated as an underlying constituent and is attached transformationally to a verb immediately following it, giving rise to the structures of (2).

(2)   a. *Kirsten want + T [PRO to can do it]$_s$
      b. *Kirsten will + T [PRO can do it]$_s$
      c. *Kirsten have + T [PRO can + en do it]$_s$
      d. *Kirsten be + T [PRO can + ing do it]$_s$

This filter would also account for the ungrammaticality of (3), where the only surviving tense marker is attached to a periphrastic *do* and the relevant 'verb' is left with no tense. Such forms should be contrasted with the acceptable (4).

(3)   a. *do + T you can leave
      b. *you do + T not can leave
(4)   a. can + T you leave
      b. you can + T not leave
      c. you can + T leave

Such a filter does some work in the grammar and from a diachronic viewpoint has the virtue of being a single device added to the grammar accounting for the four surface changes indicated in (2). The singularity of the device serves to describe the simultaneity of the four changes. This filter, however, has many inadequacies. For example, under this analysis one can see no reason why the three further changes should take place at the same time: the new inability of regular verbs to

thus Smyth (1920: §46) notes different processes in Classical Greek which had the net effect of eliminating two-vowel sequences. Haiman seeks to show that in German various devices 'conspire' to a single 'target': that the verb be in second position in main clauses. He shows how such a V-2 constraint might have developed historically.

undergo inversion with the subject (**plays Mingus the flute?*) or to tolerate a negative (**Mingus plays not the flute*), and the introduction of the new lexical items *be going to, have to,* and *be able to.* More seriously it is not clear just how (1) would operate as a surface filter or how it would interact with the rest of the grammar. One assumes that a rule deletes a tense marker in an infinitival complement, leaving the 'modal' unaffected; this gives rise to the surface structures of (2), which are then filtered out by the output constraint (1). This permits 'modals' to be generated in any S and accounts for the fact that they do not surface in an infinitival complement, or after another 'modal', a perfective or progressive marker. The problem lies in the formulation of the inversion and negation rules, yielding (3) and (4). If there is no separate class of modals or auxiliaries, the rules will have to refer to verbs, along the (simplified) lines of (5) and (6).

(5) Inversion
   NP V X $\Rightarrow$ 2 1 3
(6) Negative Placement
   NP V X $\Rightarrow$ 1 2 neg 3

Even if one assumes that the periphrastic *do* is a verb in the initial structure and is not transformationally introduced, while the data of (3) and (4) are handled successfully, some other device will be needed to block Inversion and Negative Placement on a regular verb: **plays Mingus the flute?* Similarly for the other rules which distinguish *may, must, can,* etc., from regular verbs, such as Tag Formation, Number Agreement and VP Deletion (see chapter 2). That is, regular verbs must be marked as exceptional to at least Inversion, Negative Placement, Tag Formation and VP Deletion, and 'modal' verbs are exceptional to Number Agreement. An additional defect of this analysis is that it gives no account of why the 'modal' verbs take special complementation forms and not the usual *to* infinitive, nor why a one-place epistemic 'modal' never occurs with a sentential subject in surface structure (assuming, perhaps controversially, that epistemics are underlyingly intransitive verbs).

This is, nonetheless, an interesting modification of Ross' analysis, which describes the simultaneity of four of the seven sixteenth-century changes. However, even if the other three changes could be shown to be related to the development of the new filter, the analysis of chapter 2 should be preferred. Although the new filter relates some of the simultaneous changes and thereby partly fulfils the basic descriptive requirement, its introduction cannot be shown to follow from any principle of grammar, certainly not from the Transparency Principle. Despite the new filter, derivations are no less complex than before it was added to the grammar and the large number of exception features still stands. The language learner is still confronted with the problem of deciding whether items like *can* and *may* are exceptional verbs or members of a distinct category, and under this analysis they become even more exceptional by virtue of the filter which distinguishes them from other verbs. However, if one looks at the competing analyses, one involving a modal category, the other an output filter and no such category, one finds indeterminacy of description. It could be argued that the modal analysis is to be preferred on grounds of economy, but we shall make no appeal here to Occam's Razor. A theory of grammar incorporating a Transparency Principle obliges one to reject the filter analysis, which involves just as much derivational opacity and exceptionality as Ross' description. The Transparency Principle was arrived at through a study of diachrony but it has consequences for synchronic descriptions and provides a basis for selecting one synchronic grammar over another. A re-analysis involving the introduction of a new modal category eliminates derivational opacity and therefore is explained by a theory incorporating Transparency. However, a re-analysis involving the introduction of a new output filter such as (1) does not eliminate derivational opacity and therefore does not follow from the Transparency Principle. Furthermore, it does not follow from any other principle of grammar known to me, and therefore remains unexplained. Thus the assumption that a theory of grammar should predict the point at which radical re-analyses occur serves to restrict the class of available grammars. From a diachronic point of view a theory incorporating Transparency provides an explanation for a sixteenth-century change whereby a new category is introduced to the grammar, eliminating derivational opacity; it does not explain a change whereby a filter along the lines of (1) is introduced. If the latter change does not follow from any other principle of grammar (e.g. an evaluation measure making a filter simpler than exception features, etc.), it remains unexplained. Such a description of the diachronic facts must be rejected if one assumes that re-analyses of this type should be predicted by the theory of grammar. Secondly from a synchronic point of view the Transparency Principle selects a grammar of NE incorporating a modal category over one which has the surface filter (1) and no categorial distinction between verbs and modals, since the latter entails an intolerable degree of derivational complexity.

The logic of this should now be clear. We assume that clusters of simultaneous changes should be related where possible as being the surface manifestations of a single basic change at some point in the abstract grammar. We also assume that the point at which such re-analyses occur should be predictable by the theory of grammar. Armed with these assumptions, we investigate several historical re-analyses and find as an inductive generalization that in many cases the re-analyses have the effect of institutionalizing the exceptionality and eliminating derivational complexity. We then seek to formulate a Transparency Principle which prescribes the tolerance level for opacity. The Transparency Principle, being a statement in the theory of grammar, selects one synchronic description over another and therefore also selects diachronic descriptions. In particular, it selects a grammar of NE with a modal category over one with a surface filter and no modal/verb distinction. Also the diachronic developments of the early sixteenth century cannot be described as the consequences of the introduction of a new filter, because such a re-analysis appears to be random and not a consequence of any grammatical principle. Therefore a goal for work in diachronic syntax is the sharpening of the Transparency Principle; this principle can be refined and, indeed, falsified, and, therefore, does not constitute part of the 'hard core' of my research programme in the precise sense of Lakatos (1970) (unlike, say, the requirement that grammars be generative, or the assumption that all human beings have the same innate language learning capacity and that there is one linguistic theory specifying the characteristics of all human languages). Assuming that diachronic shifts inform us about the limits to grammars, the study of diachronic change can illuminate how much opacity a grammar can tolerate before being driven to a therapeutic re-analysis, how abstract the initial structures can be. The point at which these re-analyses take place sheds light on the functional load which can be borne by derivational processes; the limits are manifested by the occurrence of the re-analyses. In this way research on syntactic change informs work on a restrictive theory of grammar and is fully integrated with that general enterprise.

In this book we shall be concerned with the role of the Transparency

Principle only with respect to syntactic change. This, however, is not to imply that the principle is effective only in this domain. Anttila (1972: p356), if I understand correctly, claims that there is no principle which affects only syntactic change. This may be correct, and I shall not dispute it here. One can easily imagine an analogue of the Transparency Principle governing phonological derivations. Kiparsky's Opacity and Kaye's Recoverability Principles (Kiparsky 1971, Kaye 1975) are along these lines.[1] In fact this general way of looking at things seems to be quite well-established in diachronic phonology. Posner (1974), for example, invokes a similar notion of opacity, 'where to disinter the underlying form one has to penetrate an incrustation of rules'. She says:

> The task of the historical phonologist is to determine at what points re-structuring has taken place and what circumstances have dictated a radical re-thinking of the systematic phonemic system . . . Reduction of opacity is obviously a major factor, but in the Romance languages this seems to have been effected in two diametrically opposed ways, sometimes both at the same time: items may be re-structured so that the underlying forms are closer to the phonetic representation, or rules may be eliminated to bring the phonetic representation closer to the underlying form.

In syntax there are several more possible ways of eliminating opacity, including changes in phrase structure rules, lexical rules, strict sub-categorization requirements, re-formulation of transformations and semantic interpretation rules, re-ordering of rules, changes in the mode of application of rules, changes in the inventory of lexical items and abstractions like *PRO*, *t*, etc.[2] However, we have required of a theory of grammar that it should predict the point at which a re-analysis is necessary, not its form. We shall consider the possibility of the stronger requirement in the next section.

Throughout this section I have spoken of the Transparency Principle

---

[1] Neither are quite parallel to the Transparency Principle. Kaye (1975) refers to Recoverability as a function of the relationship between surface form and the number of underlying forms from which it could be derived, where one assumes the set of rules and phonotactic constraints and allows no recourse to morphological relation-ships. The fewer the number of potential sources, the greater the recoverability. He goes on to claim that counter-feeding order of rule application often yields greater recoverability, and therefore serves a useful function in grammars.

[2] In phonology too opacity can be eliminated in more ways than Posner indicates. Kiparsky (1971) suggests three fates for opaque rules: loss, re-ordering and morpho-logization. Thomason (1976) adds one further possibility, that in inflectional para-digms there may be an analogical replacement of affixes, whereby a dative ending, say, of a given declension-type may be replaced by that of a different declension.

as an independent principle of grammar, and I shall continue to do so in subsequent chapters. However, this is only for convenience of exposition and it may be possible to regard the principle as a specific consequence of a general evaluation measure. Thus, imagine the admittedly unlikely event that complexity (opacity) gradually mounts in a grammar, but there is no alternative consistent with the theory of grammar and yielding an output sufficiently close to that of the model grammars (i.e. preserving mutual comprehensibility across adjacent generations). Then, presumably, the Transparency Principle will not entail a re-structuring, because none is possible. Rather, the opacity will be tolerated. So the child learning the language will pick the simplest grammar consistent with the data. If the grammar of the models is more complex (opaque) than the data require, then the child will pick a simpler grammar and thereby effect a re-structuring. He may even modify some of the output in the search for a simpler grammar, but not such as to endanger mutual comprehensibility. Under this view, there is really no independent Transparency Principle, beyond the requirement for an evaluation metric and the assumption that it plays a role in language acquisition. If there exists an independent Transparency Principle, re-analyses like that involving the English modals cast light on the limits to tolerable opacity. If one assumes only a more general evaluation metric, such re-analyses help to define 'simplicity', revealing the point at which the re-categorization was preferred to the older verbal analysis, i.e. the point at which it was treated as 'more simple'; thus as opacity mounted to degree x, the re-categorization came to be preferred, whereas it was not preferable when opacity was only at $x - 1$. Under both views, the point at which the re-analyses occur illuminates the limits to possible grammars and thereby contributes to one's hypotheses about the theory of grammar. At this point, I see no reason to prefer one view over the other and I shall continue to speak of an independent Transparency Principle simply for ease of exposition.

Under the assumption that grammars should be responsive to historical change in the manner specified here, one obtains a significant restriction on the set of possible grammars. We have made two requirements: first that simultaneous changes should be related where possible and be shown to be the manifestations of a single change in the grammar, and secondly that that change should be demonstrably provoked by a principle of grammar. That is, one should be able to describe the unity of the simultaneous changes and to explain them. We have shown how the second requirement restricts available descriptions of NE to those which have a modal category as opposed to those having no modal/verb distinction. However, the first requirement also imposes severe restrictions. If two adjacent stages of a language are different, i.e. if there has been a historical change such that the outputs of the grammars differ, then the grammars themselves must be different. Let the grammar G_1 yield the output O_1, and G_2 yield O_2, where $G_1 \neq G_2$ and $O_1 \neq O_2$. G_1 and G_2 could be characterized in many different ways and still generate O_1 and O_2 respectively, but we greatly restrict the choices by requiring that G_1 and G_2 may differ in only one respect. In chapter 1 we compared this to the task of reconstructing games of chess. A slightly more accurate analogy may be drawn from mathematics. Consider the triples of (7) and (8), where all the lines accord with the formula $x^2 + y^2 = z^2$, where x is the first number, y the second and z the third.

(7)				(8)		
3	4	5		3	4	5
5	12	13		15	8	17
7	24	25		35	12	37
9	40	41		63	16	65
11	60	61		99	20	101
?	?	?		?	?	?

There are many different ways of calculating the numbers left blank and of extending each of the two tables indefinitely. For example, if i is the number of the line, the formulae of (9) will serve to generate the numbers of the sixth line of (7), and (10) will do the same for (8).

(9) a. $x_i + z_i + x_{i+1} = z_{i+1}$
     b. $i(x_i) + i = y_i$
(10) $x_i = (2 \times i)^2 - 1$
      $z_i = (2 \times i)^2 + 1$ or $(y_i \times i) + 1$
      $y_i = 4 \times i$

To illustrate (9b), let i be line 4; therefore (x_i) is the first number of line 4, namely 9. The value of the second number of the same line is given by $4 \times 9 + 4$, namely 40. There are many more formulae which will be equally effective, but I shall leave those as an exercise for the reader who enjoys puzzles. However, if one were to impose a further requirement that a single formula should be able to extend both tables, then the possible solutions are restricted. In fact, as far as I know, there is only one reasonably simple solution. The algebraic formula of (11) will extend the tables of (7) and (8), where the value for *m* and *n* are prescribed by (12). The values of (12a) will be used to extend table (7), and (12b) for (8). There are general constraints on the values provided by (12): that *m* and *n* be possible integers, that *m* be greater than *n*, and that *m* and *n* cannot both be odd for any given line. Thus to calculate the sixth line of (7), one takes *n* to be 6 and *m* to be 7, and applies the formulae of (11), deriving the triple 13   84   85. Similarly the sixth line of (8) is generated by taking *n* to be 1 and *m* to be 12; the formula (11) then yields 120   24   145.

(11) $x = m^2 - n^2$
       $y = 2mn$
       $z = m^2 + n^2$

(12)   a.

n	m
1	2
2	3
3	4
4	5
5	6
6	7

b.

n	m
1	2
1	4
1	6
1	8
1	10
1	12

The point of this exercise is that while there are many different methods of extending the tables (7) and (8), there is only one candidate for a straightforward valid solution if one seeks to relate the two tables by deriving them from the same general formula. So with grammars. The grammars G_1 and G_2 may successfully yield their respective outputs, but they can each be of quite different forms. Requiring that G_1 and G_2 may differ in only one respect greatly constrains the indeterminacy. This follows from the methodological requirement that simultaneous surface changes should be shown, where possible, to be the consequence of a single change in the abstract grammar. Notice that this requirement is quite different from the one rejected in chapter 1, whereby indeterminacy might be resolved by demanding that a grammar recapitulate its history wherever possible. An analogy for that kind of requirement would be provided by a scientist confronted by an animal with wide arms, and wondering whether to describe them as arms or wings. It would be faulty methodology to describe them as wings simply on the basis of information that the animal is a direct descendant of a bird in the evolutionary chain.

Summarizing, under the assumption that simultaneous surface changes should be related and that the grammatical re-analyses accounting for them should be seen to follow from the theory of grammar, data from diachronic change can be used to support a Transparency Principle, restricting available (synchronic) grammars in a significant way. In this way diachronic data support plausibility arguments for certain kinds of grammars.[1] Following our earlier discussion, these arguments cannot be said to prove or conclusively validate these grammars and theories of grammar. The strongest claim to be made for a particular hypothesis is that it is so far the least disconfirmed and provides a fruitful and explanatory way of viewing a range of phenomena. To be a candidate for such a designation the hypothesis must fulfil many conditions, providing a good account of morpheme distribution and the association of semantic readings with structural descriptions, and supporting good interpretive devices accounting for diachronic changes, acquisitional phenomena, data from language pathology, etc. Therefore, the proposals made here about the form of a theory of grammar must be viewed as part of that larger enterprise, as suggestions for a theory which will be subject to disconfirmation in many different realms of data. These suggestions will be based on a study of diachronic material and will be informed by current work (within the framework of the EST) on grammars from the viewpoint of morpheme distribution and semantic interpretation. We shall pay almost no attention to language acquisition, pathology, etc., even though our theory of grammar must make predictions for those areas; this limitation is

[1] I do not distinguish here a new kind of argument; one can adduce nothing stronger than a plausibility argument as support for a theory. Again taking a broadly Popperian–Lakatosian view, scientific hypotheses cannot be validated or proved except in mathematics or formal logic (which Popper labels 'demonstrative' and excludes from empirical 'science' proper); hypotheses will be evaluated on the basis of the predictions they make, the extent to which those predictions are both correct and non-trivial. Therefore, to offer an argument for a hypothesis should be regarded charitably as showing that a correct prediction follows from the hypothesis, and a prediction which is surprising and not necessary in some trivial sense. Such a prediction will indicate the plausibility of the hypothesis. For example, the autonomy thesis is a restriction on possible syntactic rules and therefore is falsifiable but not verifiable; it is in principle impossible to construct a proof for the autonomy thesis, except by building a grammar in accordance with it and showing that the grammar fulfils all of the goals set up for it. One might then claim that this theory, in principle falsifiable, is the least falsified theory to date and therefore the most truth-like. Thus 'arguments' for a theory are best regarded as interim reports on its falsifiability, and may suggest the plausibility of the theory under examination. To this extent, all arguments in support of a theory are of equal status, although arguments may, of course, be more or less suggestive of the theory's plausibility.

based entirely on practical considerations, in that there are limits of space and limits to an individual's capacity to construct a theory of grammar and to test it in all relevant domains. Also it must be said that while there are many studies of language acquisition and pathology, there is very little solid work on interpretive machinery deriving predictions from a restrictive theory of grammar about the nature of the acquisitional and pathological processes. Nonetheless one should not lose sight of the wider domain to which a theory of grammar must be responsive.

3.2 A theory of change

If one takes a theory of grammar to specify what counts as a possible grammar of a natural language, this will provide the upper bound to possible diachronic changes: no grammar can change historically into something which is not a possible grammar of natural language. If there are lower bounds, these will presumably be a function of a theory of change. There clearly are lower bounds, since grammars do not change in wholesale fashion, for example changing all lexical entries from one generation to the next. However, I shall now argue that possible changes cannot be *formally* distinguished from impossible ones.

3.2.1 Consider again the re-analysis of the English modals. That change involved new phrase structure rules whereby Aux was introduced as an initial structure node, tense was treated for the first time as a constituent (as opposed to a verbal feature), and a new modal category was introduced. These changes entailed a simultaneous restructuring of the transformations of Subject–Auxiliary Inversion and Negative Placement. Presumably there were also changes in Number Agreement (now applying to all verbs, not only to the non-pre-modals, and assigning a -*s* suffix for the third person singular present tense), Tag Formation (now copying only Aux and not a sub-set of verbs); and VP Deletion (now applying to all verbs). Also entailed by the introduction of the new modal category (in some ill-understood way) were the new lexical items *have to, be going to* and *be able to.* Therefore this example alone serves to illustrate a very wide range of formal changes in grammars; later chapters will establish still more, like changes in strict sub-categorization frames, changes in the meaning of lexical items, introduction of new transformational rules, reformulation of other transformations, categorial changes and changes in lexical redundancy rules. Also we have already alluded to re-ordering of transformations in discussing Klima's work, rule loss (Kiparsky 1968c) and the introduction of new surface filters (Haiman 1974). No doubt there are further possibilities, including various combinations of all these, and the acquisition and loss of lexical items. If these analyses are correct, as I take them to be, one must urge scepticism about the proposition that it is possible to formulate a theory of historical change which describes a possible change in formal terms.

Such a theory might specify that $a \rightarrow b$ is a possible change, whereas $a' \rightarrow b'$ is not. As noted in chapter 1, it is hard to see how this could be a mapping of surface structures or of sentences, such that a sentence of one stage is said to be formally related or mapped into a sentence of the next stage of the language. Rather a and b, a' and b' can only be interpreted as grammars. So now the question is: can there be formal rules whose input will be the grammar of the early stage and whose output will be the grammar of the next stage? If the two entities are formal objects and both are subject to the constraints imposed by a restrictive theory of grammar, then it will certainly be possible to write formal rules deriving one from the other. However, relational rules of this kind will have to map the grammar of the late fifteenth century into that of the sixteenth, which has undergone a re-analysis involving new phrase structure rules, reformulated transformations and new lexical items. In later chapters we shall discuss other re-analyses of comparable formal diversity. Therefore the rules specifying the formal relationship between historically adjacent grammars will have to be loose enough to allow for re-analyses of this type. In the light of the formal diversity of the changes examined in this book, I see no reason to suppose that such rules relating grammars have any interesting formal properties or are in any way constrained by a theory of change in the way that a theory of grammar imposes constraints on possible rules in a particular grammar. If the theory of grammar specifies that G_1, G_j, G_k ... are possible grammars of natural languages, a theory of change might specify lower bounds on possible historical changes, prescribing that G_1 can change directly to G_j in the course of one generation, but that $G_j \rightarrow G_k$ is not a possible change. Under this view, I see no grounds to suppose that such lower bounds are formally characterizable through the articulation of constraints on rules relating adjacent grammars. This, of course, is not to assert that change is entirely random or unpredictable, or to claim that grammars may change in unlimited ways. I claim only that changes are not limited *formally*. The functional requirement that changing grammars must preserve mutual comprehensibility, that speakers of different generations should be able to communicate with each other, blocks a wholesale change replacing all lexical items, or a catastrophic re-analysis changing an underlying SVO order to an underlying VSO when VSO never occurred as a (transformationally derived) surface pattern in the earlier grammar. This is by no means a trivial limitation but it will prevent many kinds of changes of a suddenly radical nature; it will force certain changes to be gradual in the sense that new surface orders, for example, must 'leak' into the grammar, appearing first in restricted environments and then becoming more general – rather than jumping out of thin air into all contexts (see §7.2). However, I doubt that such functional constraints on mutual comprehensibility are statable in formal terms, particularly when one notes the wide range of formal changes which are permitted.

Nonetheless most work on historical change within both a broadly neogrammarian and a generative framework, has sought formal constraints on possible changes. Work couched in the neogrammarian tradition has specified possible changes of surface (usually phonological) forms, invoking various kinds of analogical processes at certain points. Hoenigswald (1960) is a particularly clear and precise example of this work. The generativists frame their discussion in terms of grammar change.[1] Kiparsky (1968a) illustrated various types of grammar change and, discussing phonological change, cited rule addition and loss, rule simplification and complication, re-ordering of rules and re-analysis of the underlying forms which are the input to the rules. He provides convincing examples of each of these types of change, and this kind of work has been widely imitated. However, if these are the permitted changes, it is difficult to imagine what would constitute an impossible change ... defined on formal grounds and beyond the requirements

---

[1] The neogrammarians did not seek a restrictive definition of a possible change: rather the definition would simply follow from the taxonomy. That is, they sought to describe changes with no particular presuppositions about the formal limits, although they surely would have been surprised to find a rule $a \rightarrow p$. Their legacy to early structuralists lay in the fact that they viewed sound change as phonetically conditioned and therefore wrote rules which mapped an early stage of a language into a later stage. What they mapped were 'surface' (phonetic) forms. The generativists, amending earlier ideas of Jakobson (1929, 1931 [1962]) and others, took up this mapping of one stage of a language into another, but viewed it as a mapping of abstract grammars.

imposed by the theory of grammar. Of course, there are limits on possible changes and Kiparsky claims that rules will tend to be re-ordered in certain directions in accordance with his Opacity Principle. The claim has been revised by Kaye (1973) and others, but in any case the Opacity Principle (and Kaye's Recoverability Principle) is a function of the theory of grammar, not a theory of change; like our Transparency Principle, this is another principle of grammar which 'could hardly be discovered from strictly descriptive considerations, but requires evidence from historical linguistics, developmental psycholinguistics, or other external sources' (Kiparsky 1974).

Despite such all-embracing definitions of possible changes, the literature is full of references to 'diachronic processes', conceived as mappings between grammars. The 'diachronic processes' referred to invariably remain unformulated and usually confound claims about theories of grammar and change, not to mention perceptual strategies. For example, while Givón (1976) writes of a diachronic process whereby changes tend to affect main clauses before subordinates, we have shown that when a clear distinction is drawn between a theory of change and a restrictive theory of grammar, the fact that certain changes seem to progress in this fashion is not a function of formal constraints on possible changes imposed by a theory of change, but rather a con-sequence of a principle of a theory of grammar incorporating a structure-preserving constraint on cyclic movement rules. Many of the claims about diachronic processes in the literature are based on a failure to draw proper distinctions between theories of grammar, change and perceptual strategies, as indicated in chapter 1, and elevate pre-theo-retical observations to the stature of theoretical proposals by fiat.

To illustrate this, we shall consider some recent work by Kuno (1974) associating various word order facts with perceptual strategies, parti-cularly the ban on multiple centre-embedding, and a diachronic ob-servation based on this work: that as a grammar changes from an underlying VSO order to SOV, it will also tend to develop a rule of Extraposition. Some linguists require that a theory of change should account for this correlation, whereas in fact it is only a pre-theoretical observation. Kuno argues that

a. certain syntactic patterns (centre-embedding and conjunction juxta-position, in particular) cause perceptual difficulties
b. whether these patterns arise or not is determined primarily by the inter-action of major constituent word orders

c. languages will employ devices to minimize those patterns which cause perceptual difficulties

Following up work of Chomsky (1961) and Yngve (1960), he assumes:

a. centre-embedding is bad in general
b. successive centre-embedding of clauses or phrases of the same grammatical function or of the same shape is worse
c. centre-embedding of clauses or phrases of the same shape or grammatical function with conjunctions next to each other is worst

Taking a variety of constructions (a. subject embedded in subject, b. subject embedded in object, c. object embedded in subject, d. object embedded in object), Kuno now shows that SOV languages with clause-initial conjunctions yield a disastrous situation from this point of view. (C indicates centre-embedding, J conjunction juxtaposition.)

(13)   a. [that [that the world is-round] is-obvious] is-dubious (C & J)
       b. John [that [that the world is-round] is-obvious] says (C & J)
       c. [that everyone [that the world is-round] knows] is-obvious (C)
       d. John [that everyone [that the world is-round] knows] says (C)

VSO languages, on the other hand, with clause-initial conjunctions yield no centre-embeddings and no conjunction juxtapositions.

(14)   a. is-dubious that is-obvious [that is-round the world]
       b. says John that is-obvious [that is-round the world]
       c. is-obvious that knows everyone [that is-round the world]
       d. says John that knows everyone [that is-round the world]

SVO languages 'are like SOV languages in that the subject appears to the left of the verb, but they are like VSO languages in that the object appears to the right of the verb. Therefore, if they use clause-initial conjunctions, they win on the object position, but lose on the subject position'.

(15)   a. [that [that the world is-round] is-obvious] is-dubious (C & J)
       b. John says [that [that the world is-round] is-obvious] (C & J)
       c. [that everyone knows [that the world is-round]] is-obvious (C)
       d. John says [that everyone knows [that the world is-round]]

Now, Extraposition provides a way to avoid these perceptual difficulties. Applying Extraposition to the sentential subject of the embedded clause of (15a) yields (16a), which involves only one centre-embedding and no conjunction juxtaposition. Applying Extraposition twice yields (16b), which has neither centre-embedding nor juxtaposition of conjunctions.

(16)   a. [that it is obvious [that the world is round]] is dubious
      b. it is dubious [that it is obvious [that the world is round]]

So then we may conclude that SOV languages with clause-initial conjunctions would be virtually unspeakable without a rule of Extraposition or some other device to break up the multiple centre-embedding. The situation in SVO languages is somewhat less critical and thus the demand for the therapeutic work of Extraposition is less compelling. German provides a nice test case since it is SOV in subordinate clauses and SVO in main clauses. It turns out to use Extraposition consistently in subordinate clauses.

(17)   a. *ich denke dass dass die Erde rund ist, deutlich ist
      b. ich denke dass es deutlich ist, dass die Erde rund ist
      c. *ich denke dass Maria dass die Erde rund ist, glaubt
      d. ich denke dass Maria glaubt dass die Erde rund ist

Hence Kuno provides us with a perceptual explanation for the compulsory use of Extraposition in SOV languages. Since English in the earliest period was still predominantly SOV, we expect to find logical subject complements invariably in extraposed position, and that is in fact what happens. Then following Kuno's analysis, as the language becomes SVO, the perceptual need for having sentential complements only in extraposed position is less acute and in English we begin to find alternations occurring whereby sentential complements may occur in their 'logical' subject position (see §4.3). Thus one has an explanation for the putative fact that as a language changes from underlying VSO order to SOV it develops a rule of Extraposition, and as a language changes from SOV to SVO alternative positions arise for sentential subjects, which come to be found in subject position as well as in the rightmost slot. Hence the development of an Extraposition rule is a consequence of an earlier VSO-to-SOV word order change. Both of these changes affect only the syntactic component but the causal relationship rests on the perceptual constraint which makes multiple centre-embedding difficult to process. Introducing a new SOV order, while no doubt 'desirable' from certain points of view, introduces multiple centre-embedding. The new Extraposition rule can be viewed as a response to those problems and eliminates the centre-embedding. This is perfectly consistent with the view of grammar and of change outlined here, and with the autonomy hypothesis. The implicational statement that SOV languages usually have an Extraposition rule, while VSO languages do not, is *explained* by the perceptual strategy, which provides the causal relationship. Under this view, there is no reason to require that a theory of change should say anything about the observed diachronic implication wherein a VSO-to-SOV word order change is promptly followed by the development of a rule of Extraposition. These diachronic facts fall out from the interaction of a grammatical description and a perceptual constraint indicating that multiply centre-embedded structures are highly marked. Therefore, it would be quite unwarranted to elevate the pre-theoretical observation of this diachronic implication into a statement in the theory of change distinguishing possible from impossible changes.

Following the lead of the neogrammarians who wrote rules mapping an early stage of a language into a later stage, linguists have traditionally sought to characterize the concept of a possible diachronic development. If we put aside pre-theoretical characterizations, as discussed, the careful work in this area (e.g. Kiparsky 1968a) allows an extremely wide range of formal changes. In the light of the formal diversity of possible changes, I hypothesize that there are no formal constraints on possible changes beyond those imposed by the theory of grammar. As noted several times, a restrictive theory of grammar can be seen to impose severe limits on possible changes, even though this approach to diachrony has by no means been fully explored. However, when one considers the way in which a language is learned, there is no reason to expect lower formal limits to changes beyond those which follow from a grammatical theory. Each generation has to construct a grammar anew, starting from scratch. Speakers of a given grammar construct a grammar on the basis of the primary data available, i.e. the sentences in their experience. A subsequent generation constructs a grammar in the same way, but if the primary data is now slightly different the grammar hypothesized will also be different, and there is no reason why it should have to bear any closer formal relation to that of the parent generation beyond the defining requirements of a theory of grammar; after all, small differences in output may result from large differences in the grammar, and vice versa (see, for example, Fasold 1976 and

Hale 1974). This can be illustrated nicely with Henning Andersen's (1973) diagram.

(18)

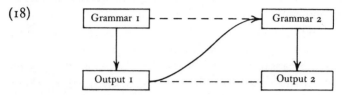

Grammar 1 generates Output 1 and Grammar 2 generates Output 2. Grammar 2 is inferred from the output of the grammar of the earlier generation, subject to the defining properties of grammar. If the two outputs differ, then the grammars will also differ. However, it is also possible that the two grammars may differ even when the outputs are identical, where 'outputs' refers to the sentences generated and their interpretations, not to structural descriptions. Andersen calls this 'abductive change'; we shall return to this in a moment. The outputs, so defined, must be mutually comprehensible, but there are no arrows relating the two grammars or the two outputs, indicated in (18) by dotted lines. There is nothing for such arrows to correspond to and Andersen correctly refers to them as 'pseudo-connections'.[1] For each generation, grammar construction reflects the free activity of the language faculty, and if the output on the basis of which G_1 was inferred differs even minimally from the output on which G_2 is inferred, there is no reason why G_1 and G_2 should be more similar than required by the theory of grammar. Grammars are not objects floating smoothly through time and space, undergoing a continuous, steady metamorphosis. As Andersen (1973: p790) puts it, 'what seems to have been insufficiently appreciated is that the internalized grammars of individual speakers are discontinuous. Since there can be no direct causal relation between discontinuous entities, the mere study of correspondences between consecutive states of a language cannot yield any explanations of change'. Andersen goes on to call for a radical reformulation of the goals for work in diachronic phonology, requiring that analysts do not

[1] Andersen proposes the notion of an 'adaptive rule', permitting speakers to deal with items not featuring in their own core grammar, i.e. items from other dialects, unusual speech styles, non-native features of foreign loanwords, etc. These are accretions to the core grammar, and not mappings taking one grammar as input and yielding another grammar as an output. Even then, no formal constraints are proposed in order to define what is a possible adaptive rule and it is difficult to see how adaptive rules constitute a testable component of grammars.

seek to specify the 'pseudo-connections' but rather to explain why re-analyses should take place in the way that they do: 'early structuralism viewed phonological systems as being more or less at the mercy of phonetic alterations, and consequently could insist only that every phonetic innovation be interpreted in terms of the system that UNDER-GOES it ...; but the theory sketched here shows how it is possible to interpret every phonological innovation ... in terms of the system that GIVES RISE to it'. In a later paper (1974) he underlines the futility of simply comparing the form of successive grammars and noting the possible differences:

It is true that an abductive innovation can be established and defined only on the basis of a comparison of consecutive grammars (ideally a learner's and his models'). But to classify the possible differences between consecutive grammars would be futile; that would yield a classification of results of innovations divorced from their causes, which are surely to be found in the speech data from which learners infer their grammars. It is remarkable how often the investigation of linguistic change has been side-tracked into such sterile classifications of results of innovations. Jakobson's typology of phonemic changes (1931) is such a classification of diachronic correspondences. So is the somewhat fuller classification presented by Hoenigswald (1960).

More recently, Langacker (1977) has repeated the exercise in the domain of morphology, listing the possible differences between grammars of successive generations and classifying them under resegmentation, reformulation, etc., etc. But when one bears in mind that grammars are created anew by each successive generation and that changes may be radical and are to be interpreted in terms of the system which gives rise to them, then one would not expect to find a 'diachronic universal' independent of a theory of grammar (see §7.2).

3.2.2 Having shown in §3.1 that a restrictive theory of grammar imposes severe constraints on possible historical changes, and in this section that there is no reason to expect plausible formal restrictions to be imposed on possible changes by a theory of change, we should consider now the content of a theory of change. Assuming a proper distinction between theories of grammar, change and perceptual strategies, I propose an impoverished theory of change, which contains only four substantive statements (19).

(19) a. communicability must be preserved between generations
      b. grammars practise therapy rather than prophylaxis

    c. less highly valued grammars are liable to re-analysis
    d. certain therapeutic changes are more likely than others
The requirement (19a) that changes may not entail a breakdown of communication constitutes a limitation on possible changes, but a limitation of an informal nature (cf. Halle 1962). I know of no principled or general basis for specifying which of various grammars yield languages which are mutually comprehensible. Although this is the only basis for imposing lower limits on possible changes, I see no grounds to suppose that a formal characterization of 'mutually comprehensible' may be forthcoming and I shall have nothing more to say about this matter, except for the purposes of illustration in chapter 7, where we shall show how this statement restricts significantly the class of possible changes and causes specific changes.

    We have already commented on proposition (19b). From this, in conjunction with the 'interpretive' statement (19c), it will follow that a theory of grammar will predict when a change is likely and what that change must achieve. For example, a principle of grammar (such as Transparency) or the perceptual ban on multiple centre-embedding might lead to a certain grammar being identified as very low rated. (19c) indicates that such a grammar is liable to change and (19b) predicts that the change will be therapeutic and eliminate the intolerable markedness. The particular therapy may cause markedness elsewhere in the grammar, but this will not inhibit the change, because it seems to be the case, as noted earlier, that grammars do not practise prophylaxis. (19b) and (19c) are simple statements which need no elaboration; the real work is done by the theory of grammar and by the set of general perceptual mechanisms, which together define 'less highly valued' grammars in accordance with the logic of markedness, as illustrated in §1.5. These statements will permit predictions to be made about when radical re-analyses may take place. However, even (19b) and (19c) may be redundant if one assumes the hypothesis discussed on p137, that there is no independent Transparency Principle, rather just a refined simplicity metric. Under that view, since the appropriate results would be guaranteed independently by a statement (perhaps in a theory of acquisition) that the child will construct the simplest possible grammar which yields an output close enough to that of his models, the theory of change would then not need to specify (19b) and (19c).

    One might also require of a theory of change that it specify which of

the possible changes is most likely (19d), i.e. of the changes which perform
the desired therapy, solve the existing 'problem' and yield a more
highly valued grammar. This is a legitimate goal to set up, but it
imposes a very strong requirement on a theory of change and I see no
prospect of success. Consider again the modals story. One can imagine
many different ways in which the derivational opacity might have been
eliminated without introducing a new category. For example, the
earlier changes which caused the opacity could have been undone:
the pre-modals might have undergone a morphological levelling with
other verbs, developing a -*s* ending for the present tense third person
singular, have tolerated the *to* infinitive like other verbs and shed the
semantically opaque and idiosyncratic interpretations of their past
tenses. After all, French, German and many other languages do not
have a modal category distinct from verbs. I see no principled basis
for specifying why none of the many alternative solutions was adopted.
Nonetheless there are claims in the literature that certain kinds of
changes are more likely than others. In the framework adopted here,
predictions of this type sometimes fall out from the theory of grammar.
For example, given a highly marked or opaque derivation, where the
degree of opacity is at the limits prescribed by the Transparency
Principle, it falls out from the theory of grammar that a further change
causing further opacity is impossible, and from the theory of change
that one is likely to find a re-analysis eliminating the offensive opacity.
The question is: are there predictions to be made about likely/unlikely
changes which must be independent of a theory of grammar? That is,
are there independent principles of change? To put it differently,
many syntactic changes, as we shall see, result from a new structural
analysis being assigned to an existing string, such that this string has
an ambiguous structural analysis; Andersen (1973) calls this 'abductive
change', Parker (1976) 'mis-assignment of constituent structure'.
A theory of grammar incorporating a Transparency Principle predicts
that, given certain earlier changes, certain surface re-analyses are likely.

   It is often alleged that there are in addition independent principles of
change. For example, clitic pronouns are frequently supposed to be
conservative in their word order position. Therefore, while it is possible
to have a grammar G_p generating SVO order in all sentence-types,
regardless of the nature of the object NP, and another grammar G_q
generating SVO order where the object is a full NP and SOV order
where the object is a clitic pronoun, nonetheless, even though G_p and

G_q are both possible grammars, permitted by the theory of grammar, $G_q \rightarrow G_p$ is a possible change but not $G_p \rightarrow G_q$. The alleged reason for this is that it is a principle of *change* that clitic pronouns are conservative and undergo re-ordering changes *after* full NPs.

(20) G_p: S V O;   S   V O_p ↑↓
       G_q: S V O;   S O_p V ↕

Although it is true that in Romance the SOV-to-SVO word order change affected full NPs before object clitics, this is not a general phenomenon. Steele (1977) argues against the conservative nature of clitic pronouns, although on the basis of reconstructed changes in Uto-Aztecan. But Modern Greek is like G_q, allowing post-verbal full objects and pre-verbal clitic objects. Clitic object pronouns arose long after Greek had undergone its SOV-to-SVO change and therefore, whatever the reason for the positional discrepancy, it is not a function of historical conservatism. One must look elsewhere for the answer. We shall say much more about the implications of changes for other changes, but I see no reason to suppose that there are independent principles of change. Therefore I shall say nothing further here about (19d); we return to this in §7.2. This, of course, is not to say that any grammar can change into any other grammar (even within the limits imposed by the requirement of preservation of communicability). For example, consider the changes taking place between OE and NE. It is not possible, I would claim, for NE to undergo all those changes 'backwards' and arrive back at OE. Many of the OE-to-NE changes were a function of the Transparency Principle. Therefore to undergo these changes backwards would clearly entail massive *increases* in opacity.

If this approach turns out to be fruitful, then the theory of change, as defined in (19), will have much less content than might have been expected, and will hold very little intrinsic interest. Many predictions are made about the nature of possible changes, but these predictions are a function of a severely restrictive theory of grammar and a few simple interpretive statements in an impoverished theory of change. Therefore for historical linguists seeking to delimit possible changes, the focus of attention must shift from a theory of change to a theory of grammar. Compare this to the view of [Closs] Traugott (1965), who began her article by saying 'The objectives of diachronic linguistics have always been to reconstruct the particular steps by which a language changes, and also to hypothesize about processes of language change in general.' The neogrammarian legacy of a search for independent principles of change must be abandoned if this approach proves to be worth adopting. This is not to abandon the general aim of characterizing and predicting changes, but the distinction outlined here between theories of grammar and change requires a change of focus, such that these predictions are derived mostly from a theory of grammar via some simple interpretive statements. Viewed differently, re-analyses will provide tests for a theory of grammar.

It is worth emphasizing that this compartmentalized approach to diachrony is quite consistent with invoking functional causes for changes. For example, one aspect of the grammatical theory adopted in this book is the autonomy thesis, the claim that syntactic rules operate independently of considerations of meaning and use. This restricts the definition of a possible rule of grammar and therefore helps to delimit possible historical changes. The changes discussed in chapter 2 are all instances of 'pure syntactic change', i.e. change affecting only the syntactic component and not reflexes in any direct way of semantic or phonetic factors. It is often claimed that this kind of thing cannot happen. The clearest statement of this is by Stockwell (1976), who asserts that 'the notion of "pure syntactic change" . . . implies that there exists a class of formal changes which are not motivated by semantic change or phonetic change. I do not believe that this is possible. I claim that all syntactic changes are motivated by semantic and/or phonetic considerations.' Contrary to this, I have argued for a notion of pure syntactic change within the framework of an autonomy thesis, but claiming that such changes are consequences of opacity created by earlier changes and of a principle of grammar requiring transparent derivations. Thus changes can be provoked by principles of grammar or by perceptual strategies, what some might refer to as 'functional' factors. To deny the possibility of changes affecting only the syntactic component is to confuse the characterization of the change with its so-called cause.[1]

It should also be clear that such an impoverishment of a theory of change in no sense downgrades the study of historical change. On the

[1] In arguing that there are cases of syntactic change which are unprovoked by semantic or phonetic factors, I do not, of course, claim that there cannot be cases where an earlier change in the phonology creates opacity which may be eliminated in turn by a syntactic change. This view of syntactic change is consistent with and in fact argues for a version of the autonomy thesis.

contrary, the fact that the theory of grammar bears the major burden in the task of making predictions about the point at which radical re-analyses will occur, entails that the degree of its success will provide another means of evaluating the theory. That is to say, diachronic syntax can be studied in order to derive implications for the 'correct' theory of grammar. We have provided a methodology for making grammatical theories responsible to historical change. The point at which re-analyses occur enables one to see the limits to grammars at work, causing re-structurings as the limits are breached, and permits one to formulate a Transparency Principle which characterizes the load which may be borne by the derivational processes. Under this somewhat different approach, research on diachronic change is fully integrated with work on grammatical theory in general.

There is, however, one further consequence of this change of focus away from a theory of change: that any attempt at the reconstruction of pre-historical syntactic systems should be treated with great caution. Reconstruction is arguably the major focus of current work in diachronic syntax, as indicated by the papers in Li (1977). But if there are no formal constraints on 'diachronic processes', on the rules relating grammars, there can be very little basis for reconstruction. I turn to this matter in the next section.

3.3   Syntactic reconstruction

The goal of reconstruction is essentially comparative: to express the relationship between languages by a formal model consisting of proto-forms and relational rules mapping the proto-forms into the attested forms of the languages to be compared. As Anttila (1972: p207) puts it, 'comparative linguistics bases itself on the regularity of sound change either to classify languages or to reconstruct earlier stages. Because sounds develop regularly, it is possible to use well-defined methods to bring them back together regularly.' As a matter of historical fact, the earliest work on the reconstruction of proto-languages by the neo-grammarians and their followers was done in the area of phonology and was based crucially on fairly clear ideas of what constituted a possible or 'natural' change and what did not. Not only is this what happened, but a distinction between possible and impossible changes is in principle a necessary prerequisite for reconstruction (cf. Kiparsky 1974). I shall put aside the question of whether traditional definitions of possible and natural phonological changes were well-founded, but I have argued that in syntax there are no formal constraints on possible changes independent of those which follow from a definition of a possible grammar. Furthermore, while a theory of grammar may be interpreted as predicting when re-analyses are likely to happen, there seems to be no basis for predicting the precise nature of that re-analysis, beyond that it must be therapeutic and eliminate the derivational opacity which offends the Transparency Principle, or remove the multiple centre-embedding which offends a perceptual mechanism, etc. If this is so, a certain caution is in order in undertaking any work in syntactic reconstruction by simply applying to syntax the traditional methods of phonological reconstruction.

In recent years there has been a great deal of work on syntactic reconstruction; witness Friedrich (1975), Jacobs (1975), Lehmann (1974) and several of the papers in Li (1975b and 1977) and references cited there. It is remarkable that there is virtually no serious discussion of an appropriate methodology for syntactic reconstruction despite the self-evident lack of parallelism with phonological work, and despite the fact that Friedrich, Jacobs and Lehmann have offered book-length studies on particular reconstructed systems.[1] Jeffers (1976a) correctly observes that 'the new enthusiasm for historical research in the area of syntax has permitted a widespread failure on the part of historical linguists to confront some of the basic problems that we will have to face as we attempt to reconstruct prehistoric syntactic systems. Little regard has been shown for the establishment of methodological principles, or for the very explication of procedures which might direct work in syntactic reconstruction.' In many cases it is even unclear what the authors claim to be reconstructing, whether sentences or (fragments of) grammars of the proto-language. For example, the claim that Proto-Indo-European was SOV might be a claim about the underlying order of initial structures or a claim about statistical probabilities of surface structures or of sentences. There seems to be a tacit assumption that syntactic reconstruction can be done in more or less the same fashion as reconstruction of phonological systems, and that if there are methodological differences their validity is not worth discussing explicitly. All this ignores the questions raised repeatedly about the viability of

[1] Friedrich (1975: p6) makes a remarkable reference to 'the problems, some of them insuperable, of reconstructing proto-syntax at all'. Apart from this comment, the problems are ignored in the remainder of the book – which deals with a reconstructed syntax!

syntactic reconstruction: Allen (1953), Anttila (1972: pp355ff), Collinge (1960), Dressler (1971), Hoenigswald (1960: p137), King (1969: p140), etc. However, despite the lack of explicit discussion, one can infer something of the methodology followed.

As noted, a conception of possible/impossible changes keeps reconstruction within the bounds of plausibility. Many of the authors in the works cited base such a conception on Greenberg's work on implicational universals, and typological data turn out to play an essential role. It is assumed that the proto-language is a 'consistent' type (for example that Proto-Indo-European is consistently SVO (Friedrich), SOV (Lehmann), VSO (Miller)) and that it is progressing along definable lines to another consistent type.[1] Thus a distinction is drawn between 'consistent' and 'transitional' languages, as if all languages are not in transition from one stage to another. This methodology, used most notably by Lehmann, and referred to by him several times as an *explanatory* historical syntax, has been criticized correctly by Friedrich as a 'misuse of typology'; and Watkins (1976) notes in a powerful critique that Lehmann's theory 'elevates some of Greenberg's extremely interesting quasi-universals to the dubious status of an intellectual straightjacket, into which the facts of various Indo-European languages must be fitted, willy-nilly, rightly or wrongly'. Under this Procrustean approach, where the facts do not fit some ideal 'consistent' type, it is because the language is in transition. This reconstruction procedure seems to begin by establishing the proto-language type, often on the basis of a small set of correspondences. For example, Lehmann assumes Proto-Indo-European to be SOV although this pattern occurs consistently only in Hittite, early Latin and Sanskrit. This type is then taken as a given and any construction in any daughter language which is consistent with the presupposed parent type constitutes an archaism and evidence for the reconstructed type. Jeffers (1976a) points out that:

the method itself demands that the proto-language be considered typologically consistent ... Lehmann, the most notable proponent of this method for

[1] This illustrates what Watkins (1976) refers to as 'Teeter's Law', that the language the analyst knows best always turns out to be the most archaic of the family. Friedrich notes the selectivity of scholars working in syntax: Lehmann bases his reconstructions on Vedic, Hittite and Germanic, with only rare references to Homeric Greek and almost none to Old Irish. Watkins (1963, 1964) bases his work on Vedic, Hittite, Latin, Greek and Old Irish, and while Meillet (1937) is comprehensive in his phonology, his morphologies were based on the languages of India, Iran and Greece, mostly the first 231 lines of the *Iliad*.

reconstruction, admits that languages are commonly not consistent . . .but . . . he proceeds as if this were not so for Proto-Indo-European. That Proto-Indo-European is an OV language is, for Lehmann, an apparent given. And, indeed, what choice does he have? If he allows for any lack of consistency in the parent, the method falters.

Therefore any construction in an attested daughter language which is consistent with OV typology is ipso facto to be regarded as an archaism, even if evidence suggests that it is an innovation. Lehmann's book pays little attention to distinguishing archaic from innovative patterns, beyond what is dictated by the alleged OV typology of the proto-language. Jeffers gives a telling illustration of this neglect of comparative data:

Lehmann (1974: p214ff) denigrates the importance of the striking corres-pondence between forms like Hitt. *nu*, OIr. *no*, Ved. *nu*, Latin *nu-*, etc. and of the significant evidence that these forms reflect one of several sentence connectives in Proto-Indo-European. Lehmann prefers to ignore the impor-tance of the comparative data concerning how these particles pattern in the several IE languages, because sentence connectives are characteristic of VSO languages, not SOV languages. He considers forms like Hittite *nu*, etc. to reflect IE adverbs. That they might develop as sentence connectives in Old Irish, for example, is not surprising, since that language has become VSO. However, their use as sentence connectives in a straightforward OV language like Hittite can only be attributed to contact with Semitic. Here we have a classic case of mixed priorities. Hypotheses based on typological considerations should be made to fit the facts. In some cases, at least, Lehmann and others have seen fit to view the facts only in light of the prejudices which specific typological considerations demand.

Friedrich (1975: p3) makes the same point:

Almost all Indo-Europeanists agree not only on the presence but the precise shape of the PIE relative pronoun (**yo*) and of an appositional comparative morpheme (**-tero-*). Yet it has been argued that (1) since PIE has been shown to be OV(?), and (2) since OV systems often lack a relative and a comparative, that therefore (3) the search for a relative pronoun is 'pointless and unfounded', and that, for similar reasons, one should not even posit a comparative ending. In other words, what remains a hypothesis about the OV variable is used deductively to preclude another variable, although the universal status of these implications has not been established even à la Greenberg.

For further criticism of the methodology of this general approach, the reader is referred to Watkins (1976) and to Jeffers' (1976b) review of Lehmann's book.

However, before we leave this kind of work, consider what it means to assert that Proto-Indo-European was, say, an SOV language. SOV patterns occur to a greater or lesser extent in all the early IE languages. But Dressler (1969) has shown that V-initial order tends to be found in certain contexts: in emphatic declaratives, and in imperative, interrogative and various subordinate clauses. Assuming this to be general, one might conclude that the proto-language had SOV and V-initial sentences. That is, two (and no doubt more) orders are commonly attested in the oldest daughter languages. Lehmann (1974: p21) refers to V-initial structures as marked. This is correct, because these orders carry more semantic information than SOV orders (in, say, Sanskrit and Hittite) and therefore are 'marked' in the same sense as the English past progressive is a marked counterpart of the simple past, in that it identifies a semantic feature which the unmarked form leaves unspecified. However, Watkins observes that Lehmann seems to equate 'marked' with 'non-normal' and clearly implies that when carrying out linguistic analysis one should exclude texts showing marked orders. A grammar constructed on such a basis does violence to the facts and, as Watkins notes, is not observationally adequate, let alone explanatorily adequate. If all the daughter languages showed an unmarked SOV order and a marked V-initial, one could reasonably conclude that the proto-language allowed similar orders. But what can one conclude about the internal structure of the *grammar* of the proto-language? So far, nothing except that it must somehow generate both orders. The mere fact, if fact it be, that SOV is the unmarked, the semantically least loaded order, is not in itself enough to justify a claim that it is the underlying order which may be permuted by transformational rules. For that matter, even if SOV were also the most common or normal order, nothing would follow from that fact alone about the form of the grammar.[1] Grammar construction for a proto-language is a higher order activity which depends on the prior establishment of

---

[1] In fact if Emonds' structure-preserving hypothesis is correct, if there is a conflict between the usual word order of root and subordinate clauses, the latter will in general reflect the underlying order – a non-structure-preserving transformation permuting the elements in the root clause. Doubtless main clauses would outnumber subordinates in most texts and therefore the most commonly attested order would not be the underlying order.

the sentences of that proto-language. Grammars are not transmitted historically but must be created afresh by each new language learner. Therefore it is also fallacious to claim (e.g. Anttila 1972: p358) that when three or even all the daughter languages show a particular rule, that rule can be assigned to the proto-language. Equally fallacious is the claim of Watkins (1963) that 'the underlying syntactic structure of a sentence, for example the rules of arrangement of its constituent elements, can be assumed . . . to form a linguistic system or set of systems functioning in time, and *historically transmittable* [my emphasis – DWL]. As such, it is susceptible to analysis by the comparative method . . . ' King (1969: p142) commits the same error, in saying that if the grammars of several daughter languages 'all have, say, the same or nearly the same embedding transformation, then we need not hesitate to posit such a transformation for [the proto-grammar]'. Since there appear to be no formal constraints on the ways in which a grammar may differ from the grammar of the preceding generation, beyond, again, constraints imposed by the theory of grammar, one can deduce very little about the form of the proto-grammar merely through an examination of the formal properties of the daughter grammars. The grammar of a proto-language, like that of any language, can be constructed only on the basis of an interaction between a theory of grammar and the structure and meaning of sentences of the language. That is a minimal requirement, although in certain areas indeterminacy of description may be resolved by appeal to facts of acquisition and change. As a matter of fact, the work cited does not follow this procedure and therefore can be viewed (charitably) as making responsible claims about proto-sentences, but not about proto-grammars – even if there are pretensions to the contrary. As a matter of principle, claims about a proto-grammar can be made only if a sufficient body of proto-sentences is first established. I shall show that successful reconstruction of proto-sentences must be very limited, given the nature of syntactic change, and that it is most unlikely that there could ever be a sufficient database to make interesting claims about the proto-grammar.

The traditional tools for reconstruction are the comparative method, by far the more important, and internal reconstruction, and these may be supplemented by various philological techniques and principles of dialect geography to establish which forms and constructions are innovations and which are conservative relics. Internal reconstruction can do a certain amount of work and assist inferences about an earlier stage of a given language, if one admits certain assumptions. The following two assumptions, which are sometimes adopted in the literature, would permit such work: (a) morphological patterns will partially recapitulate the syntax of an earlier stage of the language in a consistent way, (b) there are universal principles of change along the lines that word order changes affect certain elements before others. No doubt there are further assumptions which provide a basis for internal reconstruction in syntax, but the ones I could suggest are extremely controversial. I shall briefly examine these two assumptions, which are often invoked, show some problems with them and then point to some deficiencies of the method in general.

Givón (1971) translates the first assumption into the slogan 'yesterday's syntax is today's morphology'. The problem with the assumption as a probe into pre-history is that the morphology is notoriously slow to adapt to changing syntax and may reflect syntactic patterns of such antiquity that the assumption becomes vacuous and untestable. For example, it is claimed that the fact that NE nominal compounds are characteristically OV reflects the earlier OV syntactic word order: *windowcleaner, traindriver, coathanger, meathook, windbreak,* even recent forms such as *car-wash, snowplough*. There is no detectable tendency to replace such forms with VO compounds, even though English has not had a preponderant or even an underlying OV syntax for at least 800 years. While recent OV forms like *car-wash* indicate that this is still a productive pattern, older VO forms such as (first OED citations in parentheses) *breakback* (1556), *breakfast* (1413), *breakstone* (1688), *breakwater* (1721), *pickpocket* (1591) (compare *pickpurse, picktooth, pickquarrel, pickthank,* all dating from Elizabethan times and now obsolete), *turncoat* (1557), *turncock* (1702), *turnkey* (1654), *turnsole* (1375), *turnspit* (1576), *turntail* (as a noun, 1621), *turnwrest* (1653), which date back at least to Elizabethan times, might be taken as evidence for an earlier SVO syntax; but we know that there is no evidence for such a claim and much evidence that there never was an earlier SVO stage (whether for underlying or statistically preponderant order). Consider also French verb morphology, which forms most tenses with post-stem suffixes: *nous aimons, aimions* and the future *aimerons*. However, the perfect tense has a pre-verbal auxiliary: *nous avons aimé*. This can be accounted for as preserving the late Latin pattern *habemus amatum*. But we know that Classical Latin had suffixes for all tenses: *amamus, amabamus, amabimus, amavimus*. The problem is that the late Latin future was also formed with a pre-verbal auxiliary, *habemus amare*, but this is not preserved in modern French verb morphology, while the late Latin perfect is (Pope 1934). Not only is morphology very slow to adapt to syntactic changes, but also it mirrors earlier syntax only in a selective way. Therefore it is a most unreliable way of reconstructing earlier syntax because, while each of the individual forms reconstructed may be accurate, there is no reason to suppose that they each reflect the same earlier stage, whether they reflect the syntax of 500, 1000 or 2000 years ago.

The second assumption is no less doubtful and will be discussed in more detail when we discuss typological studies in §7.2. To give an example, it is commonly supposed that in word order change clitic pronouns are more conservative and reflect the older order more faithfully than full NPs, as noted earlier. If this assumption were correct, one could deduce that when there is a conflict between the order of full NPs and clitic pronouns the latter reflect the older order. Thus French direct object clitic pronouns characteristically precede the verb, while full NPs follow, correctly indicating an earlier SOV order: *je l'aime* vs. *j'aime Pierre*. However, we showed above that this is not a general phenomenon and that in Modern Greek there is a similar conflict but the clitic pronouns are not conservative.

Although the principles actually used as a basis for internal reconstruction are highly doubtful, there is no reason to rule it out a priori.[1] However, if there are no independent formal principles of change it is unlikely that there will ever be much scope for productive assumptions supporting this method. Furthermore, one must always bear in mind that, as often noted, internal reconstruction is not a genuinely historical method. As Anttila (1972: p273) puts it, 'whatever can be captured on the basis of one language is synchronically present in that language. All we get is a higher level of abstraction . . .'. The history of Lachman's Law illustrates that whenever there is a conflict between the comparative method and internal reconstruction, the comparative method wins out.[2]

---

[1] Jeffers (1976c) makes an interesting attempt to find a principled means of distinguishing innovative and archaic patterns with a view to developing the usefulness of typological data as a basis for reconstruction. The logic is that if harmonically SOV constructions in attested daughter languages could be shown to be innovations of secondary origin, and if there was no such evidence for similar SVO constructions, the SVO hypothesis for the proto-language would gain plausibility. This kind of fine analysis would permit rational discussion about the type of the proto-language, replacing the current Cyclopean techniques described below.

[2] That is, by internal reconstruction one might infer that Latin underlying *ag + tus*

Therefore, as a matter of practice, scholars usually apply internal reconstruction simply as a prelude to the comparative method, eliminating the effects of recent changes before the real work begins. For the limitations of internal reconstruction as a historical probe, see Anttila (1972: chs. 12 & 13).

Turning now to the comparative method, we can begin by emphasizing an obvious but often forgotten point: that the items compared should be similar kinds of animals. Watkins (1976) compares relative sentences dealing with athletic contests in Hittite, Vedic Sanskrit and early Greek, and concludes that 'the syntactic agreements are so striking and so precise, that we have little choice but to assume the way you said that sort of thing in Indo-European could not have been very different'. Watkins shows that when one is careful to compare like constructions in like contexts dealing with like subject-matter in texts of a like stylistic genre, one finds extensive similarities between the earliest IE daughter languages, permitting plausible inferences that these similarities reflect sentence-patterns of the parent language. He contrasts this with the 'gross generalizations, the crude Cyclopean techniques of "typological" syntax'. Friedrich, for example, studied a 300 line sample of Homeric Greek and found that SVO and SOV are about equally frequent (although in clauses with a verb and *one* NP, S/O-V predominates by about two-to-one over V-S/O). On the other hand, Fischer (1924) studed a 400 line sample from further on in the same book (*Iliad* v) and found a preponderant SOV pattern. Watkins observes further that 'if we look at other more rigid patterns than in the breathtaking narrative of book 5 of the Iliad (for example proverbs), verb-final, SOV or OSV patterns are far more strongly dominant'. Perhaps these discrepancies may be avoided by taking ever larger samples, but then one bulldozes away finer analyses which might find different orders in different contexts and distinguish, say, proverbs or gnomic expressions, which might be expected to preserve a frozen syntax and by virtue of their non-normal status be particularly valuable evidence for internal reconstruction. By such techniques one may distinguish conservative sentence-types, find parallels between daughter languages when comparing similar sentences from like

underwent vowel lengthening before the voiced consonant and then assimilation of voicing to give the surface *āktus*. However, we know by the comparative method that voicing assimilation was an old rule presumably of Proto-Indo-European (since it affects all the daughters), whereas vowel lengthening was a later rule specific to Latin.

domains, apply the comparative method and impute these patterns to the proto-language. Therefore by factoring out the effects of more recent changes by distinguishing archaic from innovative structures and by applying, where possible, the method of internal reconstruction, one may arrive at identical structures in the daughter languages and then apply the comparative method with some confidence. Jeffers (1976a) shows that the few genuinely successful examples of 'comparative' reconstruction have actually followed this methodology. He shows, for instance, that Watkins (1964) exploits *internal* reconstruction to 'undo' the effects of sound changes, pattern re-analyses, etc., in various Old Irish constructions to arrive at earlier forms which are essentially identical to attested forms in Hittite and Vedic. Therefore, the comparisons with Hittite and Vedic help to explicate the *internal* history of Old Irish. Having factored out various changes, one is left with identical constructions in several languages which one then imputes to the proto-language. Hall (1950) follows the same procedure, and where he is left with non-identical constructions in two languages he posits two proto-forms, reasoning that there is no need to assume a uniform proto-language.

However, problems arise when the most archaic patterns are not alike in the daughter languages. The success of the comparative method in phonology is a function of the putative regularity of sound change. In genetically related languages, a finite set of phonological segments have a regular correspondence, occurring in parallel positions in a finite set of cognate words which are transmitted historically. The alleged regularity of the correspondences permits application of the comparative method. There is no analogous basis in syntax for the comparative method; there is no finite set of sentences occurring in parallel positions across languages in a finite set of cognate (presumably discourse) contexts. As noted in chapter 1, the sentences of a language are not listable in the way that the inventory of sounds is, and they are not transmitted historically in the same way. Many writers have observed that where regular correspondences do not exist, the comparative method is inapplicable, and that would seem to embrace all of syntax except where there is agreement between the attested daughter languages. For example, consider the following statements from two recent works:

whenever an innovation that does not involve regular phonetic change enters the language, the comparative method staggers, or can even be derailed. The principal stumbling blocks are either all kinds of analogy . . . or irregular sound change. (Anttila 1972: p255)

In phonological reconstruction, when sounds do not reflect the continuous tradition which results from the operation of sound changes, e.g. where forms, hence segments, have been replaced because grammatical patterns have been readjusted, [the comparative method] collapses . . . [In morphological reconstruction] we first use the methods of internal reconstruction to discover all those language-specific developments which have produced alterations in the paradigms of the various cognate languages in order to determine the appearance of those paradigms before the said events occurred. The result is, in general, a series of paradigm types which are exact parallels from language to language, but for the reflexes of sound change. Where some anomaly exists in the general identity of pattern types, as in the case of the IE dat.-instr. plural endings in -*mo* for certain languages versus -*bho* for others, we either flip a coin, or throw our hands up in despair. Differing patterns simply don't compare . . . In the comparison of morphological and syntactic systems . . . there exists no correspondence which is not a correspondence of identity. Reconstruction is not possible until the cognate languages can be shown to have or to have had patterns of morphologic and syntactic structure which are essentially identical. (Jeffers 1976a)

The problem is that in syntax there are no principles (independent of a theory of grammar) which define possible changes formally, and syntactic change is in large measure analogical, based on a re-analysis or 'regrammatization' of old surface structure patterns, levelling former distinctions or creating new ones. That is, existing strings are given a new structural analysis, which eventually supplants the former analysis, presumably by some kind of analogical function. We shall see several examples of this in subsequent chapters, discussing its significance in §7.1. Such analogical processes will cause as much interference for the usual methods of reconstruction as they do in phonology and other areas of grammar; but in syntax such changes are the normal type and therefore the methods will be particularly limited. The typical kinds of syntactic change represent exactly the areas where the comparative method breaks down. Sentences can become grammatized (Latin *quam vis* 'as you wish' > 'although'); paratactic clauses can allegedly be re-analysed as a main clause and a subordinate (*impero; ut eas* 'I order; go' > *impero ut eas* 'I order you to go'); etc. One might argue (with King 1969: p142) that working with a restrictive theory of grammar reduces the scale of the problem, because the set of available grammars for the proto-language is thereby limited. But Jeffers (1976a) points to some desperate problems for reconstruction which hold even under such a view of grammar: what does one do when related languages show parallel syntactic patterns but with different meanings, or patterns defying correspondence, or corresponding syntactic patterns without cognate lexical material? For example, what could a comparativist deduce from a demonstration that Hittite had underlying SOV order, Germanic SVO and Celtic VSO? In phonology, Hitt. *p*, Gmc. *f* and Celtic ∅ allow him to deduce a proto-phoneme, but SOV, SVO, and VSO allow no deductions. Also the IE passive has almost as many formal expressions as there are languages. But even if one cannot deduce a morphological realization for the PIE passive, Jeffers asks whether one can fail to reconstruct a grammatical category which occurs in almost all the daughter languages.[1]

Given the lack of an independent and constrained definition of a possible syntactic change and the consequently limited applicability of internal reconstruction and the comparative method, it will be possible to reconstruct very few proto-sentences. Reconstruction will be possible via the comparative method only where the daughter languages show identical constructions either in attested forms or in internally reconstructed abstractions. Consequently it is most unlikely that there will ever be a sufficient data-base of proto-sentences to make responsible claims about the proto-grammar. However, there is no particular reason to seek a proto-grammar. A reconstruction is an artifact to express the precise relationship between genetically related languages. It is a fallacy reminiscent of Schleicher's attempt to compose proto-texts to assume that the proto-language ever existed in the reconstructed form. The methods used require that one reconstructs a uniform, homogeneous, idealized system which is typologically 'consistent' and 'non-transitional', whereas there are no grounds for assuming that these conditions were fulfilled by the 'original' language of the Indo-European peoples or, for that matter, by any natural language. However, this is of no consequence if it is understood that what is reconstructed is an abstract means of expressing relationships with precision. Meillet (1937) makes this point emphatically:

le seule réalité à laquelle elle ait affaire, ce sont les correspondances entre les langues attestées. Les correspondances supposent une réalité commune, mais cette réalité reste inconnue, et l'on ne peut s'en faire une idée que par des

---

[1] The answer is that some linguists, notably Lehmann, do deny a passive in Proto-Indo-European. I do not find this convincing and will deal with the matter in §5.2.

hypothèses, et par des hypothèses invérifiables: la correspondance seule est donc objet de science. On ne peut restituer par la comparaison une langue disparue: la comparaison des langues romanes ne donnerait du Latin vulgaire ni une idée exacte, ni une idee complète . . . ce que fournit la méthode de la grammaire comparée n'est jamais une restitution de l'indo-européen, tel qu'il a été parlé: *ce n'est rien autre chose qu'un système defini de correspondances entre les langues historiquement attestées.* (Meillet's italics)

If there are no formal constraints on possible re-analyses imposed by a theory of change, one cannot use such things as a basis for claiming historical reality for one's reconstructions, nor is the mapping of one grammar into another of any interest in itself as a method of illuminating possible changes. Reconstruction is not, pace Jeffers (1976a), 'an important *tool* in the investigation of language change' (my emphasis – DWL); it is the exploitation of acquired knowledge to express genetic relations. The knowledge is acquired from a study of actual changes where both the earlier and later grammars can be deduced in the usual way from a stock of sentences attested for both stages. One can exploit one's knowledge of diachronic syntax or phonology, by applying it to the comparative work of relating languages, but one can never discover anything new about the nature of change by examining the relationship between attested languages and one's reconstructed abstraction, which one arrives at by internal reconstruction and the comparative method, with all their limitations which are well-known in phonology and extensive in syntax. Therefore, the mapping between a reconstructed language and its attested daughters is not an appropriate basis for illustrating types of changes, much less for acquiring insight into the nature of change.[1]

---

[1] This view may be contrasted with several papers in Li (1977), which assume the contrary although usually with no discussion of methodology. It is likewise opposed to the view of Jacobs (1975), who entitles his book *Syntactic change* when it deals only with reconstructed material.

In this section I have said little about reconstruction of phonological systems. I think there are similar, if less obvious reasons to doubt the viability of reconstruction in this domain also, but I am not concerned with that here.

4 More category changes

Chapter 2 argued that a new category could be introduced into grammars, and there will be similar arguments in this chapter. In §4.1 I shall argue that a certain class of OE adjectives were later analysed as a new category of 'quantifier', and in §4.2 I shall claim that *to* infinitives were once nouns and only later became verbal forms, losing their nominal status.

Traditional grammarians had distributional and morphological criteria for categories. For example, an English noun can occur after a preposition and is marked for number but not tense. Consequently some elements were classified as blends, having some of the properties of one category and some of another. This traditional approach has continued into modern times and I shall appeal to such criteria in what follows. However, it is of vital importance to realize that here a claim is being made about a generative grammar, and 'discovery procedures' can be nothing more than heuristics. Therefore, implicit in all of the discussion which follows is the notion that one can only compare various grammars. In a generative context, to claim that *all* was an adjective in the grammar of OE is a shorthand way of saying that a properly formulated grammar of OE where *all* is an Adj is superior to all grammars treating it as some other category. It is clearly impossible to substantiate such a claim fully. The proponent of such a view will lay out what he regards as critical data and consider in fact only the most plausible alternatives. His success as a generative grammarian will be in part a function of his ability to select and evaluate the most plausible alternatives.

In the ensuing discussion of category changes, I shall follow usual practice and beg an important question. To say that the lexical items x and y are members of the same category implies that they have identical properties to a significant extent, and differ in significant ways from members of other categories. Thus in chapter 2 we claimed that a properly formulated grammar of NE treating *can* and *must* as modals is superior to a similarly well-formulated grammar treating them as verbs. Unlike verbs, they both undergo Inversion, can stand before a negative, etc. However, the fact that *can* has a past tense and *must* does not is usually not regarded as sufficiently significant to assign them to different sub-categories. Again, this is an idealization and, at worst, misleading shorthand. If one adopts the proposals of Chomsky (1970) for a feature analysis of categories, more subtle distinctions can be drawn and one avoids at least some of the problems arising from a lack of criteria for determining which facts are sufficient to motivate a category distinction. Reference to categorial distinctive features also permits one to capture properties shared by different categories and to distinguish the behaviour of items which might otherwise be assigned the same atomic category label like 'verb', 'noun', 'adjective'. The logic is much the same as that involved in the choice between dealing in indivisible phonemes or clusters of phonological distinctive features. While acknowledging the need for finer analyses of this type, I shall deal here with traditional categories, arguing that *to go* was once a noun and became a verb, rather than that it shifted from something like $[+N, -V]$ to $[-N, +V]$.

4.1   English quantifiers

This section will illustrate the importance of viewing historical change as change in a formal system of grammar, something which is generally acknowledged as a matter of principle but often forgotten in practice. It will be shown that items such as *all, any, both, each, either, every, few, more, none, some* have virtually the same distribution in OE as in NE, but that they have undergone a category change and now function differently with respect to the rest of the grammar than they did in OE. With some minor modifications I shall follow the analysis of Anita Carlson's recent MA thesis (Carlson 1976), showing that the elements were once adjectives and were re-analysed as a new category of quantifier in the late sixteenth century. This re-analysis is a consequence of the Transparency Principle and several changes affecting other parts of the grammar, while *all* etc. underwent no significant changes in distribution. The fact that the grammatical re-analysis is indicated by the failure of quantifiers to undergo any change in distribution is thus reminiscent of the Sherlock Holmes story where the vital clue was provided by the fact that the dog did *not* bark.

4.1.1 Quantifiers are distinguished as a category in NE by the unique range of positions they can assume. The corresponding elements in OE, henceforth 'pre-quantifiers', could freely occupy the same slots, as shown in (1).

(1)   a. Preceding the modified noun (and any adjective)
OE: wið *ealle wundela*, genim þas wyrte. c.1000 Sax. Leechd. 1 296
NE: Jerry hated *all books*
      b. Predeterminer
OE: ofer *al his rice*. 855 OE Chronicles
NE: Jerry burned *all his books*
      c. Postnominal
OE: and *þa scipo alle* geræhton. 885 OE Chronicles
NE: *the books all* burned
      d. With a modified noun in the genitive case
OE: ðæt he spræc to *his liornæra sumum*. c. 875 in OE Texts p 178
NE: *some of his books* burned with a blue flame
      e. Floating
OE: *hit* is Adame nu *eall* forgolden. a.1000 Gen. (Grein) 756
NE: *the books* were *all* lost
      f. Nominal
OE: *ælc* hine selfa begrindeþ gastes dugeðum. a.100c Gen. (Grein) 1521
NE: *each* was insured

However in OE, unlike NE, normal adjectives could occur in the same positions and had the same internal morphology; the pre-quantifiers could also occur in the usual adjectival positions and there is no reason to treat the pre-quantifiers as anything but adjectives. This is probably not surprising to a traditional grammarian since the standard handbooks often refer to these elements as adjectives. Sievers-Cook (1903: p215) refer to *eall, monig, genog*, etc. as adjectives and the OED describes, for example, *all* as 'properly adj. but passing on one side into a sb., on the other into an adv.' The remainder of §4.1.1 will be devoted to substantiating these claims.

(*a*) *Prenominal*   This is an extremely common position for adjectives in OE and NE, and citation is redundant. Quantifiers and adjectives have various co-occurrence restrictions, to which we shall return, but it is perhaps worth noting that in this position the OE pre-quantifiers were subject to fewer restrictions than in NE and therefore looked a little more like adjectives (which seem to be less restricted than quantifiers). For instance, *many* and *each* in OE were both free to occur before a singular or plural noun.

(2)   a.   þæt Estland is swyðe mycel, & þær bið swyð *manig burh*. c.893
             Aelfred Orosius 1 i 23
       b.   *Ælc* wunde hyt gehæleþ. c.1000 Sax. Leechd. 1 310

(*b*) *Predeterminer*   Most adjectives were free to occur before a determiner and some normally did so. Quirk & Wrenn (1955: p88) point out, for example, that adjectives in *-weard* usually precede a demonstrative: *of inneweardre his heortan* 'from within his heart'. The pattern declines through the OE period but is attested in early ME: Lawman, in the late twelfth century, has *at æðelen are chirechen, mid deore mine sweorde, mid sele þan kinge*. Possessive adjectives commonly occur predeterminally, *hæleð min se leofa freond*, and numerals normally appear there when there is an adjective in the superlative: *þær wæron þreo þa betstan ele*, *þas forewarde gesworan xii þa betste of þes cynges healfe*. There is discussion in the handbooks about the correct interpretation of these types (see Mustanoja (1958) for a good survey, Carlson (1976) for some analysis), we need only be concerned here with their mere existence. Since the numerals are taken as adjectives (Kellner, OED, Kispert, Sievers-Cook, etc.; see Carlson for discussion), the existence of these patterns serves to reinforce the adjective:pre-quantifier analogy. The ability of quantifiers to occur predeterminally in NE is unique and helps to define them as a class, but in OE this ability was shared by adjectives under various conditions.

(*c*) *Postnominal*   Again, this is a common position for OE adjectives. Quirk & Wrenn (1955: pp88–9) note several sub-classes of these patterns, even with numerals, possessives and emphatic demonstratives: *freoðoburh fægere* 'fair stronghold', *wadu weallendu* 'surging waters', *niceras nigene* 'nine water-demons', *eþel þysne* 'this country', *wine min Unferð* 'my friend U.', *gingran sīnre* 'to her handmaiden'.

(*d*) *With a genitive*   Although it was not usual for a normal adjective to occur as the head of a partitive phrase, nonetheless this construction does not serve to differentiate pre-quantifiers from other adjectives on a categorial basis. A partitive genitive could be governed by various categories: Kellner (1892: p108) lists nouns, comparative and superlative adjectives, numerals, interrogative and indefinite pronouns. Furthermore it could occur with normal adjectives when they are used substantively: *the tall of the Romans*. In short, a partitive could occur under any expression interpretable as denoting a set, a semantic property, and therefore co-occurrence with a partitive cuts across syntactic categorial distinctions. Not all quantifiers tolerated partitive expressions: *every* does not now do so and *all* and *both* did not occur with the *of* form until the late sixteenth century, according to the OED and Jespersen (MEG VII 9.9₂).

(e) Floating Given the relatively free word order of OE, adjectives often 'float' off their NP; the elaborate inflectional system facilitated the association of the adjective with its head noun. So this is another property shared by adjectives and pre-quantifiers. There is, however, another possible analysis which is worth raising: that the 'floating' adjectives are actually adverbs. Adverbs were usually related morphologically to adjectives and most commonly carried a -*e* ending (an old dative-instrumental). An adverb, thus derived, would be identical in form to the strong adjective in the feminine singular accusative or in the nominative or accusative plural of any gender.[1] Thus a floating pre-quantifier (which is usually plural, and almost always nominative and strong) would look like an adverb. Also an adjective, including pre-quantifiers, with any oblique case ending can be used adverbially. Therefore there would be very few contexts where the floating element could not be analysed as an adverb. Furthermore these elements also occur in normal adverbial positions, which at this time included immediately post-verbal: *John won easily the prize*. Not only is this usually a possible syntactic analysis, but very often it is also a possible semantic interpretation. The OED, for example, comments on the structural ambiguity of *Zion our mother is all woful*, where 'all, orginally an attribute or complement of *Zion*, comes to be viewed as qualifying *woful* = altogether woful'. Whether one adopts the floating or the adverbial analysis, no special rules will be needed; the elements will either be derived in place by the phrase structure rules (under the adverbial analysis) or moved there by the general scrambling rules of OE.

---

[1] The relationship is not bi-directional and some adjectives within the categories listed do not show an -*e* suffix: (a) strong adjectives with a neuter *a*-stem have a zero ending in the nominative and accusative, (b) many ō-stem feminines have plurals in *e* or *a*, and (c) adjectives in -*h* (*heāh, fāh, nīh*, etc.) simply lose the -*h* and do not show -*e* in the feminine accusative singular.

(*f*) *Nominal*   In OE, as long as the inflectional system functioned, any adjective could occur substantively.

(3)   a. cwæð þæt *se ælmihtiga* eorðan worhte. 'he said that the almighty created the earth'. Beowulf 92

b. ne geald he *yfel yfele* 'he did not give evil for evil'. c.900 Cynewulf, Elene 493

c. Crist sylfa his *geongrum* sægde 'Christ himself said to his disciples'. 971 Blick. Homilies cix 7

d. twegen landes men and *an ælþeodig* 'two natives and one stranger'. c.1000 Aelfric Homilies ii 26, 20

e. seþe underfehð *rihtwisne* on *rihtwises* naman, he onfehð *rihtwises* mede 'he that receiveth a righteous (man) in the name of a righteous(man) shall receive a righteous (man's) reward'. Matt.x 41 (Gospels in West Saxon, MS cxl Corpus Christi College, Cambridge)

(*g*) *Morphology*   Having established that OE adjectives could occur in the pre-quantifier positions, we shall now show that they were not to be distinguished from the viewpoint of internal morphology. Adjectives were inflected for number, gender and case, and had two sets of endings, 'weak' or 'strong'. Weak endings were used when the adjective followed a demonstrative or possessive, modified a noun in direct address, or occurred in the comparative (regularly) or superlative (usually, but not always); the strong forms are used elsewhere. The same holds for the pre-quantifiers. The weak forms are rare with the pre-quantifiers because they have no comparative or superlative forms and it seems that they seldom occur after demonstratives or possessives (presumably as a result of their indefinite semantics); direct address is not common in the texts. The weak forms are rare enough for some writers (Bright 1935: plv; Sievers-Cook 1903: p215; Quirk & Wrenn 1955: p31) to claim that they are non-existent and that therefore pre-quantifiers are unlike true adjectives inflectionally, but Campbell (1959: p261) cites examples of weak endings, e.g. *þa monigan cyningas*. There is also some confusion in the literature on the conditions for the use of strong and weak forms. For example, Sievers-Cook (p215) say that when the adjective is used substantively it has weak endings whereas pre-quantifiers have strong endings in this context.

(4)   a. on *allum* þam þe him læstan woldon. 874 OE Chronicles

b. *ælc* hine selfa begrindeþ gastes dugeðum. a.1000 Gen.(Grein) 1521

   c. þonne ic winde sceal sincfag swelgan of *sumes* bosme. a.1000
    Riddles (Grein) xv 15

However, the right explanation is that the weak form occurs with a
demonstrative or possessive, and the fact is that adjectives used substantively are almost always preceded by a demonstrative . . . often
enough for Quirk & Wrenn (p88) to state categorically that 'adjectives
used substantively are preceded by a demonstrative: *seo æðele* 'the
noble (woman)'.' However Kispert (1971: p43) gives a crucial example
of an adjective used substantively and in the strong form, where it is
not accompanied by a possessive or demonstrative: *ac se wonna hrefn
fus ofer fægum [sceal] fela reordian* 'but the dark raven, eager over the
doomed ones, shall speak many things'. Carlson (1976: p20) has
unearthed the perfect minimal pair: *se blinda, gyf he blindne læt* 'the
blind, if he lead a blind (man)', Matt. xv 14 (Gospels in West Saxon,
MS cxl Corpus Christi College, Cambridge), where the adjective
blind occurs twice as a substantive, once in the weak form and once
in the strong form without demonstrative or possessive modifiers.
Therefore, one may conclude that the OE pre-quantifiers behaved
morphologically just like tıue adjectives (and unlike nouns and demonstratives, which have different inflections).

   So far we have shown that adjectives could occur in all positions
occupied by the pre-quantifiers; the reverse also holds. The most
common position for an adjective is between determiner and noun, and
the pre-quantifiers could also occur here until the seventeenth century,
although it was not common.[1]

(5) a. in þe al worlde. 1297 R. Glouc. 367
     b. our bather slogh. 14c. Cursor M. 1254
     c. a moche felde. 1338 Robert Mannyng
     d. the bothe endes. 1430 Bk. Hawkyng in Rel. Ant. I 297
     e. leeve you not this eich one. a.1500 Miracle Plays (1838) 17
     f. your some sweete smiles. 1589 Pottenham, Eng. Poesie (Arb.)
       235
     g. your either person. 1615 Chapman, Odyss. IV 79
     h. two rocks . . . whose each strength. 1615 Chapman, Odyss. XIII
       149

---

[1] Three of these expressions survive into NE: *whose every deed, the many men,* and
this much bread, although in the last example *this* is probably not a determiner but
some kind of degree adverb.

Pre-quantifiers sometimes occur in this position alongside another adjective. Pecock's 'The Repressor of over much blaming of the clergy' (Rolls series 1860) (c.1449) has the following permutations: *it upon which the al hool substance of the wal . . . stondith* (I ii 11); *it is open ynoug to alle hem whiche wolen biholde al the hool proces . . . But according to the hool al processe* (II vii 177). Secondly, adjectives can occur adjacent to each other, although this has always been subject to many apparently idiosyncratic restrictions (e.g. *the big black ball* vs. *the black big ball*, see Bever 1970). The modern quantifiers can never occur in sequence but their antecedents were much less restricted and, like regular adjectives, could sometimes occur adjacent to each other. I know of no examples after 1600.

(6)   a.   mid childe hii weren *boþe two.* c.1275 Layamon, Brut 2399

    b.   þey weron as bleynd *all bothe*, y wys, as ever was ony stok or stoune. c.1420 Chron. Vilod. 892

    c.   the scorpyon . . . byteth & styngeth *bothe two* at ones. 1413 Lydg. Pylgr. v xi (1483) 102.

    d.   they all endeuor . . . to kepe still *eyther bothe* kingdome safe. 1561 T. Norton, Calvin's Inst. vol. I Pref.

    e.   yet would he retain with hym still Silan & Sasilas, *all both* Lacedemonians. 1571 T. Fortescue, Forest Hist. p129.

    f.   to endeavour & strain themselves, *both all & some.* 1600 Holland, Livy XXVII xiii 637e.

4.1.2   In the last section, the pre-quantifiers were shown to be non-distinct as a categorial class from normal adjectives in OE. Of course, there are meaning differences amongst *all, some, many,* etc., but they do not warrant a categorial distinction any more than meaning differences between *a* and *the* suggest that they should not be both classed as determiners. It should also be added that I know of no evidence for a semantic interpretation rule which distinguishes adjectives from either NE quantifiers or the pre-quantifiers in earlier English. For example, scope assignment rules apply to determiners, quantifiers, negatives, some adjectives and even to *wh* elements under the proposals of Chomsky (1976, 1977), and therefore they cut across this categorial distinction. During ME and ENE changes affected the distribution and morphology of adjectives in such a way that it became possible to view the pre-quantifiers as a distinct sub-set.

(*a*) *Prenominal* All adjectives, including the pre-quantifiers, have continued to occur freely in this position throughout the history of the language. Therefore there are no relevant changes in this domain.

(*b*) *Predeterminer* This position becomes increasingly rare for adjectives other than the pre-quantifiers. In §4.1.1 three special contexts were identified where adjectives frequently occurred predeterminally. Two of these do not survive the OE period: adjectives in -*weard* almost never occur before a determiner in ME, and likewise predeterminer possessives. The third, numeral–determiner–superlative adjective, survives into ME and is very frequent in the fourteenth and fifteenth centuries (Visser 1963–73: §249). However, the construction becomes obsolete in the Elizabethan period (Mustanoja 1960: pp297–300; Kellner 1892: pp110–11) and Visser (§249) cites (7) as the last attestations.

(7) a. for they be two the prowest knights on ground. 1590–6 Spenser, FQ II iii 15
    b. his stature did exceed The hight of three the tallest sonnes of mortal seed. ibid. I vii 8
    c. he is one The truest manner'd. 1611 Shakespeare, Cymb. I vi 165

For ordinary attributive adjectives, Mossé (1945: §166) cites the Shakespearian vocatives in (8) as the last survivals; they were supplanted by *my dear lord*, etc.

(8) a. Dear my lord. 1601
    b. Gentle my lord. 1605

Jespersen (MEG III 15. 16) and Abbott (1870: p25) claim that in these constructions *my lord* is treated as a compound like French *monsieur* (cf. *milord*). Under this analysis these would not be predeterminer adjectives but adjective-compound nouns. However, there are other examples from the same period where a compound analysis is much less plausible.

(9) a. sweet my childe. 1588
    b. good my glasse. 1588

Therefore, in the sixteenth century the only adjectives which could occur before a determiner were the pre-quantifiers, numerals and attributive adjectives in vocative contexts. The latter two ceased to occur here, leaving only the pre-quantifiers by the end of the century. So by this time the pre-quantifiers were distinct from other adjectives in at least the ability to occur predeterminally.

(*c*) *Postnominal*   Postnominal adjectives continue to occur in ME and became increasingly common. This is often attributed to French influence, but that cannot be right since French adjectives at this time were overwhelmingly prenominal (see §4.3). However, by the sixteenth century adjectives other than pre-quantifiers ceased to occur postnominally, and the pre-quantifiers thereby acquire another distinguishing trait.

(*d*) *With a genitive*   Numerals with a partitive genitive on an indefinite NP continue to occur in ME but as the inflections decayed a competing appositive construction (10) developed rapidly and soon became dominant (Kellner 1892: p162; Mustanoja 1960: p291). In the thirteenth and fourteenth centuries a similar appositive emerged with measure nouns (11) but this gives way rather suddenly to the *of* form at the end of ME (Kellner 1892: pp109–10, Mustanoja 1960: p84); it does not appear in Caxton.

(10)   a.   these hundird shepe that were ther. 14c. Cursor M. 10399
       b.   mani þusend hali saules. c.1200 Vices and Virtues 115
(11)   a.   he . . . lette ænne drope blod. c.1275/c.1205 Lawman A 7650
       b.   a dozeine chickenes. 1362–93 Piers Pl. B iv 37
       c.   no morsel breed. c.1386 Chaucer, Monks Tale 3624

Throughout ME numerals may occur with the *of* form on both definite and indefinite NPs (12), and likewise the pre-quantifiers (13) and superlative adjectives.

(12)   a.   fif & sixti hundred of heþene monnen. a.1225 Lawman A 18256
       b.   of ladies foure & twenty. c.1386 Chaucer, Wife of Bath 992
(13)   a.   ga . . . þer eni of þine cunne lið in. c.1175 Lamb. Hom. 35
       b.   ne choes himm nohht te Laferrd Crist Till nan off hise posstless. c.1200 Orm. 13931
       c.   he . . . maked ech of hem to been his thral c.1386 Chaucer, Monk's Tale 163
       d.   thei token eueryche of hem a peny. 1388 Wyclif, Matt. xx 9

(*e*) *Floating*   In ME word order patterns were rigidified and adjectives were less likely to float away from their head noun; the decay of the inflections would have made it harder to make the correct associations between adjective and noun. However, in §4.1.1 an analysis was suggested whereby adjectives (including pre-quantifiers) never did float but that what are sometimes regarded as floating adjectives were really adverbs. This analysis is quite plausible throughout ME. As the adjectival desinences were restricted to *-e* and *-∅* (see below), adjectives were often indistinguishable from adverbs with the *-e* marker, and confusion arises (14). Adjectives are often used adverbially and adverbs serve for attributive adjectives; this is rare in early ME, but frequent towards the end of the period (Mustanoja 1960: pp648–50). This confusion is increased by contexts where adjectives and adverbs are interchangeable (15).

(14) a. for his wel dede. c.1205/1275
b. the condicioun of mannes goodes . . . ne last nat perpetuel.
c.1386 Chaucer, Boethius ii p4 86

(15) he nas nat right fat, I undertake, But looked *holwe*, and therto *sobrely*. c.1386 Chaucer, CT A. Prol. 289

In this situation 'floating pre-quantifiers' would not look distinct in surface structure; they resembled in form those adverbs which, having lost the *-e*, are identical to their corresponding adjectives. Not only did they look like adverbs morphologically, but they also continued to appear in normal adverbial positions.

The adverbial *-e* suffix became inactive around 1170 and was replaced by the increasingly common *-lice* (> NE *-ly*).[1] This reached a peak in the sixteenth century, when it was added even to adjectives in *-ly* (*earlily, godlily, kindlily, livelily, lovelily, statelily*) and to French loans for the first time (e.g. *princely, scholarly*, which the OED dates from 1548 and 1598 respectively). As adverbs become formally distinct from adjectives, so floating quantifiers (which never had the *-ly* suffix) can no longer be analysed adverbially and must be treated idiosyncratically. Also they become distributionally distinct in that post-verbal position ceases to be viable for lightly stressed adverbs. In ME light

---

[1] *-lice* was not originally an adverbial suffix. *-lic* served for de-nominal adjectives and the *-e* is the old dative-instrumental. However *-lice* became interpreted as an adverbial marker and was added to words where *-lic* alone was not appropriate.

Strang (1970: p273) notes that there has been a steady increase in the *-ly* type, replacing the forms which were morphologically identical to the adjectives. This is another example of the principle mentioned in §3.2 and elsewhere, that languages practise therapy rather than prophylaxis. As a result of the decay of the inflectional system, adverbs became morphologically indistinct and some repair-work became necessary.

adverbs (including the negative) regularly occurred here, but from ENE it ceased to be a possible position: *he wrote well the poem*; *he touched lightly her shoulder*. Therefore a Quantifier Floating rule (24) becomes necessary as the adverbial analysis became impossible. This innovation must be dated from the sixteenth century, which is when adverbs finally became formally identifiable by the -*ly* suffix.

(*f*) *Nominal* ME adjectives continued to occur as head nouns (see Mossé 1945: §113 for details), but by the late sixteenth century the modern restrictions hold. Kellner (1892: pp147–54) shows that sub-stantival adjectives with a singular referent die out in late ME, and reference to an abstract idea in this way becomes rare in the late fifteenth and early sixteenth centuries, revives somewhat in the Elizabethan age but dies out at the end of this period. Mossé, Strang, Jespersen and Kellner all date the development of the prop-word *one* from the four-teenth century, and Jespersen (MEG II Appendix x) proposes (16) as a developmental chronology. The sentences of (17) seem to represent the earliest uses of the indefinite *one* (as opposed to the numerals which could occur with pre-quantifiers in the earliest records: *æt æghwylcum anum þara hongaþ leohtfæt*, 971 Blick. Hom. 127).

(16)   1300 a good one
       1400 the good one
       1550 never a one, such a one, (the) good ones
       1600 one good one
       18c. that one, a silver one
       19c. the one (we) preferred, those ones, a one to keep company,
            the ones that . . . , my one

(17)   a. a moche felde; *so grete a one* never he behelde. 1338 Robert
            Mannyng
       b. wan he was armed on horsebak, a fair knygt a was to see,
            A iolif on wyþ oute lak, boþe strong & fers was hee. a.1380
            Sir Ferumbras 251

The development of the prop-word permitted singular/plural dis-tinctions to be made (Jespersen (MEG II 10.82) points out that the plural *ones* is more common in the early uses), and fills what would otherwise have been a 'gap' in a sentence so that a noun is now an obligatory component of a NP.[1] The prop-word becomes obligatory

[1] It is interesting to note that the 'dummy element' *one* develops in NPs at about the same time as the dummy subject markers *it* and *there*, i.e. in the fifteenth century

with singular adjectives by the end of the sixteenth century (Jespersen MEG II 10.32) and adjectives (other than the pre-quantifiers) lose the ability to occur as a head noun.

(*g*) *Morphology* In late OE the inflectional system, already dys-functional, was simplified enormously by the coalescence of final -*m* and -*n* and the weakening of final unstressed vowels to ə. The northern dialects lead this development, but by the twelfth–thirteenth century adjectives in other dialects as well have only -*e* and -∅ desinences. Monosyllabic, consonant-final adjectives have the -*e* suffix in the strong plural, and weak singular and plural; other adjectives are invariant. The pre-quantifiers also undergo this inflectional levelling (except for the survival, sometimes, of a genitive plural), although the weak forms are as rare as in OE. The weak/strong distinction generally became quite confused in ME and even in the earliest texts (e.g. the Peterborough Chronicle) adjectives tend to be used invariantly. The inflections undergo their eventual demise with the loss of final, unstressed -*e* in the late fifteenth century. Therefore, it can be seen that the pre-quantifiers were not distinct from other adjectives with respect to internal morphology at any point in their history.

4.1.3 From the previous section it emerges that by the end of the fifteenth century the pre-quantifiers are exceptional with respect to certain adjectival properties. By this time the following changes had taken effect: adjectives other than the pre-quantifiers can no longer occur *freely* in (a) predeterminer position, (b) with a partitive, or (c) as a substantive. Adjectives can still occur in these positions, but only subject to severe constraints. Adjectives may occur predeterminally only if they are numerals or if the expression is a vocative; only com-paratives and superlatives appear with a partitive, numeral adjectives having lost this property in the fifteenth century (i.e. with indefinite NPs: **five of pastries*); only plural adjectives occur as substantives. The pre-quantifiers, however, continue to occur freely in all these positions.

As further evidence that they were now treated as a class, *all* and *both* occur with a partitive in *of* for the first time at the end of the sixteenth century. The OED cites (18) as the first examples. As a result of this extension, all pre-quantifiers (including at this time *every*) but no other adjective can occur with a partitive.

(Strang 1970: pp96, 211; Jespersen MEG II 10.12). These elements serve to main-tain the 'integrity' of the larger constituent, in that, for example, sentences usually have subjects in surface structure even if semantically vacuous.

(18) a. yea, *all of them* at Bristow lost their heads. 1593 Shakespeare, Richard II, iii ii 142

b. I am sure you *both of you* remember me. 1590 Shakespeare, Err. v i 291

Some curious and irregular things happen to the pre-quantifiers at this time, as one might expect of a class of elements whose category membership has become opaque. For example, in the late sixteenth and early seventeenth centuries the pre-quantifiers occur with the -*s* genitive, as if they are being treated as nouns.

(19) a. *sommes* consciences. 1565 Cooper, Thesaurus s.v. Capio

b. as great delight in thy company as ever I did in *anyes*. 1580 John Lyly, Euphues and His England in Works vol. ii p76

c. as *eithers* way them led. 1591 Spenser, Mother Hubbard 551

d. of *manies* ouerthrow. 1598 Grenewey, Tacitus, Ann. iv xiii (1622) 110

e. they are both in *eithers* powers. c.1600 Shakespeare, Tempest i ii 450

f. *boths* talke. 1616 B. Parsons, Mag. Charter 26

g. for *somes* unquietness. 1653 Bp. Webbe, Pract. Quiet. 253

Also at this time the pre-quantifiers begin to occur alone after a preposition (20), another position characteristic of a noun. It seems that as pre-quantifiers had what now had become an unusual ability to occur in a noun's position, they began (at least in some dialects) to acquire some further nominal properties. They might have developed as nouns, but there is good evidence that they were re-analysed as a unique category.

(20) a. we be borne for *neither of bothe*. 1544 Ascham, Toxoph. (Arb.) 27

b. *neither of either*, I remit both twain. 1588 Shakespeare, LLL v ii 459

Most of the changes discussed in §4.1.2 occurred at the end of the sixteenth century. They are the following:

(21)   (i) *all* and *both* first appear with *of* partitives

(ii) last occurrences of determiner-pre-quantifier-noun

(iii) last occurrences of multiple pre-quantifiers in sequence

(iv) last occurrences of adjective-determiner-noun

(v) last occurrences of postnominal adjectives

(vi) last occurrences of adjectives used substantively

(vii) *-ly* becomes a productive marker for adverbs (which entails the need for a rule of Quantifier Floating)

This indicates that the phrase structure rules now generated adjectives in pre-nominal position and that a new category of quantifier was introduced. I assume the relevant phrase structure rules to be as in (22), where [Spec $\bar{\bar{\text{N}}}$] subsumes quantifiers and [Spec $\bar{\text{N}}$] determiners.[1]

(22) $\bar{\bar{\bar{\text{N}}}} \rightarrow$ [Spec $\bar{\bar{\text{N}}}$] $\bar{\bar{\text{N}}}$
$\bar{\bar{\text{N}}} \rightarrow$ [Spec $\bar{\text{N}}$] $\bar{\text{N}}$
$\bar{\text{N}} \rightarrow$ (Adj) N ...

Given such a system, (i)–(v) fall out automatically, since quantifiers will now occur in two configurations (23).

(23) a.   b.

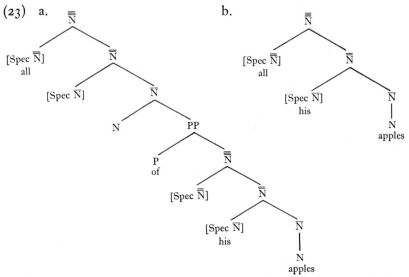

---

[1] Of course, there are many different analyses of quantifiers for NE, but I shall not offer any purely synchronic arguments here for the analysis of (22). My aim in this chapter is to show categorial changes. To the extent that my arguments for a categorial innovation are correct, they militate against any analysis of NE which fails to distinguish quantifiers in underlying structure (e.g. Lakoff 1970c, Carden 1976). The analysis of (22) permits an account of the simultaneity of the changes (i)–(vii). There may be other analyses equally successful in this respect but those analyses will all posit a distinct underlying category of quantifier, and therefore there will have been a category change from OE. If quantifiers are not distinguished from, say, adjectives or verbs, the changes will be characterized as the development of various exception features, for example, prohibiting *all*, *every*, etc., from occurring in

Under these rules, a quantifier could not be generated between a determiner and noun, immediately adjacent to another quantifier; and adjectives could not occur predeterminally or postnominally. (vi) is not explained by the development of a quantifier category; but it is a partial *cause* of the category change in that it contributed to the distinctness of the pre-quantifiers.

As the quantifiers are identified as a distinct category, sentences with floating elements, like *the boys were all unhappy*, will no longer be generable, since *all* can no longer be generated as an adverb and, in any case, under the stricter word order requirements adjectives were confined to the NP domain. These sentences in fact continue to occur, which means that, under this analysis, a further innovation was needed. We shall assume that this took the form of a rule of Quantifier Floating (24).[1]

(24)   Quantifier Floating

$$X \quad [+\text{univ}] \quad \overline{\overline{N}} \qquad (\text{Aux}) \quad Y \quad \langle \text{oblig} \rangle \qquad 1 \quad 3 \quad 4 \quad 2 \quad 5$$
$$\begin{bmatrix} \langle +\text{pro} \rangle \\ +\text{pl} \end{bmatrix} \qquad\qquad\qquad \Rightarrow$$

This rule will move quantifiers to both post-nominal and post-auxiliary position, and applies only to universal quantifiers with a plural noun, accounting for (25).

(25)   a. all the men   the men all
       b. both the men   the men both
       c. every man   *(the) man every
       d. each man   *(the) man each

predicative position; under such an analysis the simultaneity of the changes would be a remarkable accident. For the $\overline{X}$ structures adopted here, see Hornstein (1977a) for details.

   Richard Hogg points out that just as adjectives have never occurred freely with negatives, so the OE pre-quantifiers did not do so. Therefore the introduction of *not many*, *not all* expressions would constitute another reason for the later grammar to distinguish pre-quantifiers from other adjectives.

[1] Again, other analyses are possible, for instance an interpretive rule operating at surface structure and associating the quantifier with a NP under appropriate conditions (Jackendoff 1972). It is difficult to choose between two such analyses as is indicated by the extensive literature on the subject (Fiengo & Lasnik 1973, Dougherty 1974, etc). Carlson (1976) gives a diachronically based argument in favour of the interpretive analysis, and I am inclined to prefer this. Notice that (24) will apply incorrectly to (23a), relating *all of his apples were in the bag* to **of his apples were all in the bag*. This example of 'over-generation' could be ruled out in a variety of ways, e.g. by the resulting lack of a subject NP and therefore the inapplicability of the rules assigning number to the verb.

e. ?   the men each

f. many men   *men many

g. much love   *love much

Note that the rule is obligatory if the noun is a pronoun. In earlier periods, the pre-quantifier occurred frequently before a pronoun (26): *all we*, compared to the modern *we all* or *all of us*. Stratmann (1891) cites many examples.

(26) a. *ealle hi* sind on Godes gesihðe. c.1000 Aelfric, Saints' Lives i 140

   b. þurh heore vuele ræde, *beien heo* beoð dædde. a.1225 Layamon, Brut 10433

   c. *summe hi* weren wyse, and duden al bi his rede. c.1275 Passion of Our Lord 43 in OE Misc. 38

   d. *alle wee* as shep erreden. 1382 Wyclif, Is. liii 6

   e. *both they* Match not the high perfection of my loss. 1594

   f. *alle we* like sheepe haue gone astray. 1611[1]

The handbooks say that these forms died out in ENE and Carlson found no examples later than Shakespeare. Even in Shakespeare, Abbot (1870: p316) claims that they were highly marked and used only for emphasis. So from the end of the sixteenth century postposing of the quantifier is obligatory over a pronoun. The interesting thing from our point of view is that the change occurred at the same time as our postulated re-analysis. While *all, both* and *each* were adjectives, one would expect them to occur pre- and postnominally, giving *we all* and *all we*, since at that time normal adjectives could occur in both positions. After the re-analysis the above restriction became possible (but by no means necessary; the language could have continued quite happily, as far as I can see, with both orders, i.e. without the complication in (24) of the angled brackets).[2]

I have noted that after the re-analysis indicated in (22) quantifiers had to precede determiners. As a special case, I observe instances where the quantifier may be construed as modifying the determiner, as in (27).

---

[1] Although cited as 1611, this is from the authorized version of the Bible, which is usually agreed to be in the language of Tyndale. 1525 would be a more appropriate date.

[2] This apparently unnecessary change may be related to the demise of appositive constructions such as *a bushel venym* and the development of genitival expressions *all of us, both of us*. Both these changes were roughly simultaneous with the loss of *all we*.

(27) a. both our remedies. 1592 Shakespeare, Rom. & Jul. II iii 51
      b. to all our lamentation. 1607 Shakespeare, Coriolanus IV vi 34
      c. both their haire. 1627 Hakewill, Apol. (1630) 167
      d. one brimmer to all your healths. 1738 Swift, Polite Conversation 163
      e. a sister died in both our infancies. 1830 Lamb, Essays of Elia I 127
      f. I think she's been pulling both our legs successfully. 1915 Maugham, Plays vol. II p114
      g. both our mothers. 1601 Shakespeare, All's Well I iii 169

Prior to the re-analysis, one also found the reverse order (again, predictably), but this dies out at the right time.

(28) a. *here elces* riht hand. c.1126 Peterborough Chronicle, anno 1125
      b. *heore beira* gast. c.1175 Lamb. Hom. 99
      c. *their both* assente. c.1430 Lydgate, Bochas I ix (1544) 19b
      d. *our alleris* offence. 1513 Douglas, Aeneis XII i 40
      e. *your bothe* Sovereigne. 1536 St. Papers Hen. VIII vol. I p509

The genesis of the English quantifiers is similar to that of the modals. By virtue of some early changes, adjectives other than the pre-quantifiers ceased to occur freely in predeterminer position, with a partitive or as a substantive. Some adjectives continued to occur in these positions, but only under severe restrictions; pre-quantifiers continued to occur here quite freely and therefore became distinguishable from mainstream adjectives. After these changes the pre-quantifiers came to behave as a class: *all* and *both* were regularized to take partitive *of* expressions so that all pre-quantifiers occurred with a partitive, but no other adjective. They also behaved as a class by being treated as nouns in that they occurred with a novel genitive case form and after prepositions; this proved to be a short-lived and not a widespread development. Then during the sixteenth century a flush of changes took place (21) which distinguished them clearly from adjectives. Five of these seven changes follow from claiming that English introduced the phrase structure rules of (22). The sixth change is not a manifestation of the categorial change and the seventh points to the introduction of a new rule (24), but these two changes contributed to the distinctness of the pre-quantifiers and therefore are partial causes of the re-analysis. Therefore the seven surface changes of (21) are a function of a radical re-analysis consisting of new NP-expansion rules, a limitation on adjectives occurring with an empty N and a new rule (24). Again, the simultaneity of the changes (i)–(v) indicates the singularity of the change in the abstract grammar, the new phrase structure rule.

The data are not quite as clean as that of the modals in two respects: the dates of the changes are somewhat less uniform and the categorial idealization is not as satisfactory, in that there are distributional differences amongst the NE quantifiers: for example, while *all* may occur predeterminally (*all the books*), *some* may not (**some the books*); unlike other quantifiers, *every* does not occur with a partitive (**every of the books*). However, while a finer analysis, dealing in features rather than just gross, shorthand category labels, might draw distinctions amongst quantifiers, nonetheless they clearly share enough distinctive properties to warrant treating them as a class (sharing several categorial distinctive features in the framework of Chomsky (1970)). Again we see changes leaking gradually into the language and being followed by a wholesale re-analysis. The grammar developed various exception markers forcing distinctions between pre-quantifiers and other adjectives, and then these exception markers were eliminated by a re-categorization. Evidence for the re-categorization is, again, the simultaneity of the changes (i)–(v) in (21). If one assumes that the re-analysis must have been provoked by the theory of grammar, the point at which it applied sheds light on the Transparency Principle and on the degree of tolerable opacity. Under this view, the re-categorization would have taken place as the exceptionality breached the limits of permitted derivational complexity. Under the hypothesis outlined on p137, whereby the Transparency Principle is subsumed under a more general evaluation metric, the issue would be not 'tolerable' opacity but just 'complexity'. The grammar eventually became sufficiently complex for the language learners to be able to find a simpler analysis within the bounds of mutual comprehensibility with their models. Again I shall not choose between these two formulations. The point at which the re-analysis occurred helps to define either 'tolerable opacity' or 'simpler analysis'.

One might speculate whether the quantifier categorization is related to that of the modals. Under the analyses presented here, the changes took place at about the same time. Furthermore, if one assumes an $\overline{\overline{X}}$ convention whereby auxiliaries are subsumed under [Spec $\overline{\overline{V}}$] (see §1.4), the two changes are formally parallel in that they involve a new [Spec $\overline{\overline{X}}$]

node, and thereby require a triple bar level. This question must be left open until it can be determined whether there were simultaneous changes affecting PPs and AdjPs which also required the innovation of a triple bar level. If this is correct the introduction of the new quantifier category does not complicate the grammar in any way but simply fills a 'gap' made available by the general $\overline{\overline{X}}$ conventions for phrase structure rules. In any case, the re-analysis illustrates the necessity of viewing change in the context of the grammar as a whole. It is not enough to look at quantifiers in NE and OE, see that they have the same distribution and conclude that there are no relevant changes; one must view 'quantifiers', etc., within the framework of a system of oppositions. Similarly, in the context of generative proposals one cannot look at one rule in the grammar of NE, note that the phenomena handled by that rule are much the same in OE and therefore posit the rule for the grammar of OE – least of all, posit the rule for a reconstructed system. Unfortunately this is fairly common practice (§1.3), but a broader view is necessary. Following Carlson, one might compare this change to a Charlie Chaplin film, where the sergeant-major asks for a volunteer to step forward; everybody else steps back and Chaplin becomes the 'volunteer'.

4.2   The English infinitive

4.2.1   I shall now argue that the *to* infinitive in ME was originally a NP and later lost its NP status as a result of a category change predictable by the Transparency Principle.[1] Consider first some data on the interaction of the *to* infinitive with *for*, which first appeared as a clause-initial morpheme in early ME. Originally it occurred followed directly by the *to* infinitive form and *for to* V is usually regarded as just an alternative form of the infinitive. Only later did it appear in front of a clear case of a NP. I list in (29) constructions, mostly drawn from Visser (vol. 2), without a clear NP following the *for*. All these constructions are now obsolete (except for two, (29c) and (29e), which survive in Ozark English and some rural dialects of England), but the dates cited record the first (A) and last (B) attested examples of the type. (30) is a list of corresponding constructions where there is a

---

[1] Some of the material in this section appeared in Lightfoot (1976b), but the analysis adopted here differs significantly from that of the earlier version. Most of the data on the infinitive in OE is drawn from Callaway (1913). Kenyon (1909) and Poutsma (1923) were helpful for later periods.

clear case of a NP following the *for* and acting as the subject of the infinitival verb. The striking fact is that, although several *for* clause-types are represented (subject complements, extraposed subjects, object complements, adjectivals, *fear* constructions, comparatives, purpose clauses, etc.), the *for NP to V* construction appears consistently about 200 years later than the corresponding *for to V* forms. The constructions in (30) survive to the present day and I cite the date of the first recorded example of the type. To facilitate comparison, under column C in (29) I give the first date of the corresponding *for NP to V*, i.e. the date for the corresponding form in (30). Thus the *for to V* construction in a subject complement (29a) occurs first in 1205, last in 1590, while the *for NP to V* construction in a subject complement (30a) occurs first in 1567, which I enter also in column C in (29).

			A	B	C
(29)	a.	for to go is necessary		1205–1590	1567
		I for to go is necessary		14c. –1607	
	b.	it is good for to go		1300–1590	1534
	c.	it is necessary a man for to go		1300–80	1385
		it is no shame a man for to go		1338–1450	
		it grieves me for to go		1400–dial.	
	d.	that stood in aunter for to die		1205–1623	1391
	e.	the king did it for to have sibbe		1100–dial.	1422
	f.	this is a fouler theft than for to breke a chirche		1205–1601	1534
	g.	he taketh of nought else kepe, but for to fille his bagges		1385–1405	1568
	h.	for to say the sothe, ye have done marvellously		1300–1583	1637
		as for to speken in comune, thei folwen all the favour of Fortune		14c. –14c.	
	i.	hir olde usage as for t' honour hir goddes	1374–1590		1380
	j.	the principle of their vocation is for to defende the faith		14c. –1487	
	k.	there was nothing able for to shake me		1225–1623	
	l.	the king . . . sende for to hine finde		13c.–15c.	
(30)	a.	for us to go is necessary		1567	
	b.	this would make it imprudent for him to . . .		1534	

c. it is necessary $\begin{Bmatrix} \text{to} \\ \text{for} \end{Bmatrix}$ a man (for) to go   1385

d. I'm afraid for them to see it   1391

e. he brought it with him for us to see   1422

f. what would be better than for you to go   1534
   the weight is too heavy for you to lift   1508

g. there is nothing to do but for him to   1568
   marry Amanda

h. for this low son of a shoemaker to talk   1673
   of families

i. this left room for the controversy to   1380
   go on

If one focusses on the *for*, one might entertain a hypothesis along these lines: clause-initial *for* is introduced first in the thirteenth century as a COMP(lementizer) and is never analysable as a preposition followed by a NP – hence phrase structure rules $\bar{S} \rightarrow$ COMP S, $S \rightarrow$ NP VP; *for* later occurs in the fifteenth century where it is analysable also as a preposition with a dependent NP; and finally *for* occurs *only* where analysable as a preposition. This would account for the above data and would have the merit of being a single initial structure (category) change which has consequences for several different surface structures. It might also follow from the Transparency Principle: in the early stage *for* occurs sometimes as a preposition (*I bought it for Mary*, etc.), sometimes as a COMP; thus the *for* in the new constructions of (30) was of unclear category membership and could be analysed as a preposition or as a COMP, causing potential confusion for the language learner. This indeterminacy was removed by the final change, whereby all *for*s were levelled and analysed as prepositions. However, the hypothesis is inadequate because if *for* was a COMP originally, then there is no reason why the forms of (30) should not have occurred from the earliest times alongside those of (29), since the NP subject could have been realized optionally.

In (30) the infinitive is never in a position which could be occupied by a clear case of a NP, without changing constituent structure: **I'm afraid for them scepticism*. If (30a) is construed as [*for us*]$_{\text{PP}}$ [*to go is necessary*]$_{\text{S}}$, then a substitution is possible: *for us scepticism is necessary*; no NP substitution is possible if it is construed as [*for us to go*] [*is necessary*]. However, in all the examples of (29) a NP could be substituted for the infinitive without sacrificing well-formedness or changing constituent structure except the rare pattern in the second case of (29a):

(31) a. *scepticism* is necessary
      b. it is good, *scepticism*
      c. it grieves me, *scepticism*
      d. that stood in aunter for *death*
      e. the king did it for *bad reasons*
      f. this is a fouler theft than *that of the crown jewels*
      g. he takes nothing else to keep, except for *warmth in the night*
      h. for *peace of mind*, you have done marvellously
      i. her old usage as for *honouring her gods*
      j. the principle of their vocation is *the protection of wildlife*
      k. there was nothing (suit)able for *analysis*
      l. the king sent for *him*

Patterns of this type were grammatical in ME. Notice that my substitutions exploit an ambiguity: sometimes the NP has replaced *for to V* (31 a, b, c, f, j), sometimes only *to V* (31 d, e, g, h, i, k, l). This is based on the assumption, mentioned above, that the infinitive in ME was either *to V* or the 're-inforced' *for to V* and therefore that the constituent structures of (29a) and (29l) were (32a) and (32l) respectively.

(32) a. [for to go]$_{NP}$ [is necessary]$_{VP}$
      l. the king sende [[for]$_P$ [to hine find]$_{NP}$]$_{PP}$

This systematic equivocation will not help somebody trying to make NP substitutions in (30). Therefore, deferring discussion of the equivocal treatment of *for*, one can account for the differences between (29) and (30) by saying that the (*for*) *to V* infinitive had the distribution of a NP in earliest times and was later re-analysed as something else, presumably a VP.

  This analysis of the early *to* infinitive as a NP derives some credibility from the fact that the bare infinitive in OE, which the *to* form replaces, had clear nominal properties. It is generally assumed that the infinitive in prehistoric times was a fully inflected verbal substantive. In OE the ending was *-an* (variants *-on*, *-n* for contract verbs, and Northumbrian *-a*) and the only inflected form was the dative *-enne* (later *-anne*, presumably under the influence of *-an*), which occurred after the preposition *to*. The case endings marking the infinitive had gradually decayed and grammarians (Bock, Jespersen) speculate that it required another sort of marker to preserve its substantive character, and the preposition *to* was introduced (and later, also the preposition *for*). The prepositional force of the *to* weakened, entailing the rise of the 'extra' preposition *for*, and the *to* infinitive gradually replaced the bare infinitive during the late OE and early ME period. *To* sometimes occurred with inflectional endings, *to singenne*, but when these finally dropped off the *to* infinitive simply did not look like a NP any more; it did not have the internal structure of a NP. I shall show that it ceased also to have a NP's distribution.

   The gerund in *-ing* or *-ung* has been used as a verbal substantive throughout its history and it has the regular distributional properties of a NP. I list examples of these properties in (33), citing cases from OE. Emonds (1972) carries this claim over into current versions of transformational grammar by arguing that poss-*ing* complements (but not *for-to* or *that* complements) are instances of NPs. Visser (1963–73: §1001) notes that these forms 'were pure nouns and syntactically, did not differ in anything from such nouns as *grund, flot, sceamu* and *ðanc*' and asserts that their NP status 'can be proved in the following ways' (a–j; see Visser §1001 for the sources. I add two further criteria k and l where I have constructed examples, drawing on my own intuitions about ME):

(33)   a. they function as subjects in syntactical units: *þæt is sorgung* and *sargung* and a singal heof
       b. they function as complements to a copula: *nis ðis nan wiglung,* ac is gecyndelic ðincg
       c. they function (in the genitive) as attributive adjuncts to a noun: on andgyte *ihran understandincge*
       d. they function as antecedents to relative clauses: be ðære *acsunge ðe ic ðe ascode*
       e. they function as objects in syntactical units: hit bið unnyt ðæt mon *unweorðunga* forlæte
       f. they take the case endings of a noun: buton ðu forlæte ða *leasinga, wechweorðinga,* and wuldres God ongyte gleawlice
       g. they take adnominal modifiers in the form of adjectives: *gelome spœtunga* oððe *hrœcunga*
       h. they take adnominal modifiers in the form of articles and demonstratives: drihten gehyrð ða *wilnunga* his þearfena

    i. they take adnominal modifiers in the form of possessives: mid earum onfoh *mine halsunge*; for lare and for *tiehtinge his aganes firenlustes*

    j. they can be preceded by prepositions: *in utiomingc* blodes

    k. they occur in passive constructions: hēo wæs on mōde onhryned fram (Sæms) *drincunge*

    l. they occur in cleft constructions: hit wæs (Sæms) *drincung* þe mislīcode me

In fact, properties a–e are not diagnostics for NP status, since they hold also for sentences, including subjectless sentences, i.e. VPs. For details of this the reader is referred to Emonds (1972) and his discussion of the root transformation of Intraposition. Properties f–l, however, are crucial diagnostics. For ease of exposition I shall simply assume here, uncontroversially and with the traditional grammarians, that the old inflected infinitive was a NP. As the *to* form was introduced, it retained most of the NP properties, occurring, for example, quite freely after prepositions (34j), etc. In NE, of course, the *to* infinitive does not behave like a NP, but Visser notes that originally there was 'not much semaseologically' to choose between the infinitive and the gerund. The first three citations in (34b), for example, illustrate the free interchangeability of infinitive and gerund. In (34) I illustrate the distribution of the *to* infinitive with respect to the properties noted for gerunds.

(34) a. subjects: *to rowe* in a barge with a skulle Avayleth not but the flud be at full; *for to foyne* is better than to smyte; for us *to go* on pretending would be a farce

      b. complements to a copula: þe synnes of þe mouthe er thir: *to swere* oftsyth, forswerying, . . . *to heven* his name withouten reverence, agaynsaiyng, . . . grotchyng agayns God . . . , *to say* Goddes servys undevowtly, . . . flytyng, manasyng, sawyng of discorde, . . . to turne gude dedes to ill . . . ; talking is not always *to converse*; *to declaim* on the temporal advantages they enjoy, is only repeating what none either believe or practice; his charge is *to sesoun* the bred and bake it; coueitise is *for to coueite* swiche thynges as thow hast nat; the firste point is . . . A man *to have* pes with himself; the overall strategy was for them *to break* through to Alexandria

      c. attributive adjuncts to a noun: a fygure of thynges *to come*; he hath roume and space *to welde* an axe; I have litil tyme *to doon* it; he broughte a yerde *to scourge* the chile; I have herde of an erbe *to lyss* that peyne; he næfde gyrde hine mid *to sleanne*

d. antecedents to relative clauses: I don't want John to come, which is pretty unlikely anyway

e. objects: I loue the people, But doe not like *to stage* me to their eyes

f. case endings: the bare infinitive had all the usual inflectional endings prehistorically. These endings gradually dwindled until at the time of the re-analysis they had all been dropped

g. adjectival modifiers: do not occur

h. articles, demonstratives: do not occur

i. possessive modifiers: do not occur

j. prepositions: (i) *after*: *after for to speke* of Ierusalem . . . 3ee schull vnderstonde þat it stont full faire betwene hilles. c.1400

(ii) *at*: ne i herd neuer . . . in land Men sua hard *at to understand.* 14c.

(iii) *for* (without *to*): þo þe [h]er doð eni god *for habben* godes are, c.1250; hi gunne *for arise*, c.1300; *for castyn* on the see: Drynke þe iuce . . . or þat þou comyst to þe see, c.1450. For cases with *to*, see (29) above.

(iv) *from*: his fyte him beris *fra* down *to fall*, 14c.; the parteys shalle abstayne hem from alle goodys of werre *to make* a yenste the othyr partys, c.1475; not to affirm is a very different thing from *to deny*, 1879

(v) *in*; *into*: þet byeth zuo . . . sotyl *in* kwednesse to *uind* ine oþren, c.1200; thou shalt not take the sister of thi Wijf *into liggyn* bi hir, 1382; it came into my head, that she might . . . be drawn *into lie* with some of that coarse cursed kind and be with child, 1724

(vi) *instead of*; (*in stead*; *in lieu*): *in stede to healþe* hym to dye well, [he] putteth hym in vayne hope of long lyfe, 1557; people . . . called upon to conform to my taste, *instead of to read* something which is comfortable to theirs, 1834

(vii) *of*: forrþi mann lætepþ litell *off To wunndrenn* ohht tæronne, c.1200; bliss of herte þat comþ *of* god *to louie*, 1340; they impeach him *of* traiterously *to have assumed* the regall power to himself, 1678

(viii) *on*; *upon*: pine ðe seluen for his luue ðe ðolede pine for ðe

anon to ðe deaðe *on fasten* and *on wacchen,* an *on* ðine awene
Wille *to laten,* c.1200; it is a great wonder that men caste Her
herte *upon* such wrong *to winne,* c.1390

(ix) *þurh*: sume sade *ðurh fasten,* sum *herborʒin* wrecche men,
and *feden* and *screden.* Sum sade ðurh seke menn *to lokin,*
c.1200

(x) *till to*; ʒiff þeʒʒ haffdenn lefe *till* All affterr þeʒʒre wille
To takenn off þe laʒherleod, c.1200; rædiʒ *till To wissenn* himm
and lærenn, c.1200

(xi) *to*: bot by hem . . . may a soule neuer come *to for to
knowe* þe vertewe and þe condicions of bodely creatures, c.1360

(xii) *with*: and himm birrþ ʒeornenn aʒʒ þat an Hiss Drihhtin
wel to cwemenn Wiþþ daʒʒsang and wiþþ uhhtennsang . . .
and *wiþþ to letenn* swingenn hemm þe bodiʒ, c.1200

(xiii) *without*: wiþoute eni enihte *forlede* to þan fihte, c.1250;
Dei þai sal wit-ven lite, *Wit-vten* raunscun *for to quitte,* 14c.;
wiþout þe first now seid knowing afore *to be* had parfitly . . . ,
he schal ramble and wandre, 1443; Vyenne salewed parys
wythoute to make ony semblaunce of Love, c.1485

k. passives: hēo wæs on mōde onhryned fram drincan
l. clefts:[1] hit wæs drincan þe ic þorfte

Recall that properties a–e are not crucial diagnostics for NP status,
despite the practice of the traditional grammarians to take them as such.
Therefore we can ignore this data (pace Visser) and it does not trouble
us that these properties hold for *to* infinitives even in NE (see Emonds
1972 for analysis). Properties f–l, however, are crucial. Some of these
nominal properties (g, h, i) seem never to have obtained even for the
bare infinitive. This we can describe neatly in the EST by stating that
the infinitive was a regular NP except insofar as it did not occur with
[Spec $\bar{\text{N}}$], which normally subsumes determiners, adjectives and possessive modifiers: this of course, does not constitute an explanation.
However, the occurrence of the *to* infinitive after prepositions, in passive
and cleft sentences, and with case endings (the dative *-enne*) are clear-cut

---

[1] The examples in (34k) and (34l) are of my own invention; in general, clefts and full
passives are extremely rare in the extant texts of OE. My guess is that these sentences
would be grammatical in OE, although not attested.

A further construction which preserves nominal properties into NE is the infinitive in (indirect) *wh* questions: *how to get there was the question; what I'm thinking
about is how to leave; he was bothered by whether or not to leave.* I regard this as
unrelated to the problem in hand.

indicators of NP status. The transition from NP to VP status would
be marked by the surface changes of (35).

(35)   a. rise of [for NP to V . . .]   see (30)
      b. obsolescence of [for to V . . .]   see (29)
      c. obsolescence of [P to V . . .]$_{PP}$ see (34j)
      d. obsolescence of infinitives in passives   see (34k)
      e. obsolescence of infinitives in clefts   see (34l)
      f. obsolescence of inflectional endings   see (34f)
         (*-enne*) on infinitives

We are now ready to pull the threads together. [for NP to V . . .]
constructions, in a wide variety of sentence-types (35a), were firmly
established by the mid-sixteenth century; see (30). [for to V . . .]
patterns (35b), again regardless of the sentence-type, seem to be
obsolete by the late sixteenth century, despite a very small number of
isolated citations as late as 1623; see (29). Prepositions cease to occur
freely with *to* infinitives (35c) also by the mid-sixteenth century, again
despite a few tenacious idioms.[1] Infinitives in passive and cleft constructions are dead by the sixteenth century, and the last *-enne* inflection
finally disappeared at the same time, after withering slowly since ME.
These dates seem to be relatively clean, when one bears in mind that
we are dealing with data from many different dialects and literary
styles. The uniformity of the dates is striking: all the crucial nominal
properties of the *to* infinitive are lost simultaneously. The conclusion
should be obvious by now: we have here another case of an abstract
re-analysis. Postulating a single initial structure change enables us to
account for the striking simultaneity of the changes listed in (35).

Having established that there was such an initial structure change, we
can ask why it happened. The change can be viewed as following from
the Transparency Principle. The original, inflected infinitive had all the
properties of a NP, or more accurately a NP without [Spec $\overline{\text{N}}$], i.e. a
noun. As inflections were lost generally, so we find the inflected infinitive replaced by two competing forms, the bare infinitive and the
to form, there being a transitional period with forms such as *to singan*
and *to singenne*. The use of the *to* preposition to form the new infinitive

[1] This is harder to date precisely, but as a productive process it seems to me to be
finished by the date given. See Visser (1963–73: §976) for the relevant facts for
individual prepositions; Mustanoja (1960: p540) provides several more examples of
prepositions governing an infinitive.

is alone good evidence for its NP-hood. The NP properties were carried over, and in its early history the *to* infinitive had precisely the same distribution as the earlier inflected form. However, after the development of the *to* form, *to* lost its early prepositional force and came to be seen as a mere 'sandhi form'. Now *to sing* did not look like other NPs and from the late fourteenth century it began to be treated as something different. From this date we begin to find occasional forms which are incompatible with treating *to V* as a NP, e.g. [for NP to V . . .], and forms which require a NP analysis begin to be less common, e.g. [for to V ...], [P to V ...], etc. The NP-hood of the *to* infinitive is now much less clear (it is now a NP with exception features), and in the sixteenth century a series of changes takes place, all of which follow from saying that there was a category re-analysis whereby *to* infinitives lost their NP status. Viewed in this way, the change can be seen as another consequence of the Transparency Principle.

4.2.2 It remains only to consider the status of *for*, and I shall argue that it has been a preposition throughout its history as a clause-introducer. This is not to deny that it also constituted an optional part of the infinitival morphology during ME, re-inforcing the newly established *to* form. In fact, its ability to occur as an infinitival marker seems to be a function of its prepositional status. In a great number of languages the infinitive marker has developed from or is homophonous with a locative preposition or case marking: Greek *-ein* reflecting an old locative, English *to*, German *zu*, Swahili *ku-/kw-*, Hungarian *ni*, Thai *thi*, Tok Pisin *long*, Hebrew *le*. Washabaugh (1975) draws on considerable comparative evidence and argues that in creolization the infinitival complementizer evolves always from a locative preposition, which then serves many syntactic functions as the language is elaborated. Nichols' (1976) work on Gullah lends support to this claim. Bresnan (1972), noting differences between *for* and *that* complements, gives a semantic account, claiming that the key to the meaning of the complementizer *for* lies in the meaning of the preposition *for*. In ME the *for* in, say, (29a) cannot be analysed as a complementizer, because, as pointed out above, such an analysis would permit corresponding sentences like (30a) which did not occur at this time. Nor can it be analysed as a preposition, because PPs cannot in general occur as the subject of a sentence. Therefore it seems best to adopt the traditional analysis and say that it is simply part of the infinitival morphology. This is a plausible analysis on typological grounds, in that this kind of preposition often occurs as an infinitive marker, and it accounts for the second sentence of (29a): the sentential subject of *is necessary* consists itself of a subject (necessarily in the nominative case here) and an infinitival verb.

Consider now *for-NP-to-VP* constructions, as in (30). Sometimes the *for* NP is a PP in a higher clause, as in a surface structure like (36a), where PRO is a phonologically null NP (compare (36b)).

(36)   a. it was disturbing [for John]$_{PP}$ [PRO to leave]$_S$
       b. it was disturbing [for John]$_{PP}$ [for Bill to leave]$_S$

In OE *for John* would have been in the dative case. It is often argued (e.g. Stockwell 1976) that the earliest cases of *for-NP-to-VP* were along the lines of (36a), but that a change took place later allowing a *for-S* analysis, where *for* becomes a complementizer, losing its prepositional nature, and structures like (37) become permissible.

(37)   it was disturbing [for John to leave]

Supporting evidence might lie in the fact that (30c) and (30d) antedate those constructions which require an analysis like (37), i.e. (30f, g, h, i). But there is no evidence for a subsequent change whereby *for*, formerly a preposition, became a complementizer, and even in NE *for* must be treated as a preposition.

The latter point needs amplification. There are good grounds to adopt Emonds' principle of structure-preservation and the analysis of COMP in Chomsky (1973), in particular that, since *wh* Movement applies successive cyclically, COMP may be expanded as PP, to permit phrases such as *the woman to whom you gave the book*. If one also adopts the now well-established practice of assigning lexical material to categories on an optional basis, one can generate initial structures such as (38).

(38)

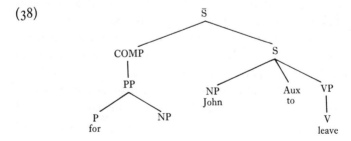

Adapting slightly a proposal of Emonds (1976), one may postulate a local transformational rule of *for* Phrase Formation (39) which will map (38) into (40).

(39)   *for* Phrase Formation
          [for np]$_{\text{COMP}}$ NP   X $\Rightarrow$ 1   3   t   4
(40)   [for John]$_{\text{PP}}$,   t   Aux   VP

Failure to apply the rule will leave a 'dangling preposition' in COMP, which must be disbarred on independent grounds: **who did you say to — Lou gave the shoe*. If both NPs were filled in (38), the structure would fail to meet the surface structure requirement that a NP in COMP must be interpretable as 'associated' with a trace, or a 'gap' (see §6.2). This requirement is needed independently to rule out **who did Kirsten see Heidi?* (see Lightfoot (1977a) for a discussion of *wh* Movement in this approach to grammar). This analysis permits existentials (*it is vital for there to be a conference soon*), weather verbs (*it is irritating for it to rain every day*), and subject complements (*for Zeus to wed Leda would disturb Hera*), which are adduced as evidence for the claim that *for* is a complementizer like *that*. Emonds (1976: p196) supports this kind of analysis by pointing out that while certain adverbial PPs can be interposed between COMP and the subject NP (41), this is not possible after *for* (42). This follows from the above analysis if the preposing rule moves elements to the position immediately after COMP, and because generally it is not permitted to interpose material between a preposition and its NP.

(41)   Mary asked me if, in St Louis, John could rent a house
          he doesn't intend that, in these circumstances, we be rehired
          you should do that so that, when you're old, you'll be protected
(42)   *Mary arranged for, in St Louis, John to rent a house
          *he doesn't intend for, in these circumstances, us to be rehired
          *you should do that in order for, when you're old, us to be able to live well

This analysis also accounts for the necessity of a *to* infinitive in a clause introduced by *for*. Kiparsky & Kiparsky (1970) pointed out that *to* appears in subject-less clauses. If 'subject' is defined as the NP dominated immediately by S, *for* Phrase Formation renders the clause subject-less and hence necessitates the *to*. The analysis also accounts for the accusative case form of pronouns immediately following *for*, if one assumes that a NP takes an accusative marking when immediately following a verb or preposition. We may express this by a rule (43). This yields (44a) and (44b); it is blocked by the Propositional Island Constraint of §1.4 from applying to a structure corresponding to (44c), which explains the nominative *she*. If *for* was not a preposition, one would expect [*for we to go*]. Such patterns never occur at any point in the history of the *for* construction. Those who argue for a historical re-analysis of COMP-to-P would need to find *for we to go* being replaced by *for us to go*, and vice versa for those advocating a P-to-COMP re-analysis.

(43)   X $\begin{Bmatrix} P \\ V \end{Bmatrix}$ NP   Y $\Rightarrow$ 1   2   3   4
$$[+acc]$$

(44)   a. Mary arranged for me to rent the house
        b. Mary considered [her to be conservative]$_{\overline{S}}$
        c. Mary considered [she was conservative]$_{\overline{S}}$

Analysing *for* as a preposition in this way also facilitates the statement of a fairly general correspondence between verbs which take a *for-to* complement-type and nouns requiring a preposition *for*: *she preferred (for Linda) to do it/her preference for gin*; *he hoped (for John) to leave Chicago / his hopes for glory* (see Faraci 1974 for a long list of correspondences). It is, of course, possible that *for* was re-analysed as a COMP some time after the period discussed in this paper, but then there should be some evidence for such an initial structure change along the lines of the evidence here for the re-analysis of infinitives. I know of no convincing evidence for this, but the *that* complementizer was undergoing some important changes at the same time as our postulated re-analysis (see Klima 1964a: §XII; Bresnan 1972), and an argument might be constructed on the basis of parallelism of innovations. This seems unlikely, but I must leave it as an open question for the present time.

4.2.3   A consequence of the change described in this section is that we can see that the wheels of syntactic change grind very slowly. The grammar was ripe for this re-analysis as soon as the *to* of the new infinitive lost its prepositional force and began serving as a mere grammaticized form. The nominal properties did begin to wane, but it was 200–300 years before they waned sufficiently for the final re-analysis to take place. This concept becomes important in studies of word order change and language typologies. Greenberg (1966) has a notion of 'consistent languages': for example, a consistent SVO-type language will show SVO order, N-modifier, preposition-N, Aux-V, VO noun compounds, etc. A language changing from SOV to SVO type may take a long time, often many centuries, to develop all the properties of a 'consistent' SVO language. That is, there may be a considerable lag between the initial changes in the direction of SVO and the eventual completion of the process. Indeed it may even be the case that the process goes faster in VPs than in NPs and that before it is complete in NPs the VP may be starting out towards another typological order. This view of things runs the risk of unfalsifiability as the notion of a consistent language becomes arbitrary. For example, how does one decide whether a consistent SVO language has N-modifier or modifier-N order, when there are SVO languages with both orders? The concept of lag now becomes crucial. It may well be that on further analysis such lags can be shown to be functions of other constraints, that a language cannot follow through on fulfilling all the requirements of the new typological class until it has solved some impeding problems. For example, Li & Thompson (1975: p186) argue that a SVO-to-SOV change in Mandarin Chinese is impeded by the use of word order to mark the definiteness or indefiniteness of nouns. Likewise Givón (1975b: p71) claims that the SOV-to-SVO change in some Niger–Congo languages is retarded by a development of viable case-markings through a process of serialization. We shall return to this matter in §7.2.

4.3 Redistribution of existing categories

The changes investigated so far involve the introduction of a new category, modal and quantifier, or the re-assignment of an inflectional class (infinitives) to a different category. This section will examine another possibility: a simple change in phrase structure rules without introducing a new category or re-assigning lexical material. Without taking a definite stand, I shall examine the plausibility of the introduction of a rule NP → $\bar{\text{S}}$ in ENE. The grammar of English had always included NP and $\bar{\text{S}}$ as categories, and the rules NP → Det NOM, NOM → N $\bar{\text{S}}$. These rules provide the structure characteristic of relative clauses (see Stockwell, Schachter & Partee (1973) for this

analysis of relative clauses and a comparison with its competitors).[1]
But there is some evidence that in ENE the grammar of English for
the first time permitted S̄s to be dominated exhaustively by NP.
Although the discussion will be inconclusive, we shall elaborate some
interesting consequences to the analysis of §4.2 and demonstrate the
logic of using diachronic data as a basis to choose between competing
synchronic analyses.

In the last section various kinds of infinitival expressions were
examined. It was seen that sentences such as *for John to leave is necessary*,
with a *for-to* sentential subject, are rare almost to the point of non-
existence in ME. But subject-less *to* infinitives in the same context
were almost equally rare until towards the end of the ME period.
Visser (1963–73: §901) comments: 'the absence of instances in Old
English and the comparatively small number of examples in Middle
English are in striking contrast to the frequent occurrence of the plain
infinitive in this position in both these periods'. Visser's examples
support this generalization and thereby refute Mustanoja (1960: p523)
who claims counterfactually that the *to* infinitive is more common than
the plain in subject position.

(45) a. miỡ stefne *gespreca* ỡæm dumbe geswald wæs. c.950 Lindisf.
          Gosp. Luke i (Introd.)
      b. feower kynna beon sutol is. a.1030 Interlin. Rule St Benet
          (ed. Logeman) ix 15
      c. *richtcn* hire & *smeỡen* hire is of euch religiun ... þe god &
          alỡe strengỡe. c.1225 Ancr. R. (EETS 1952) ii 18

The bare infinitive could always occur in subject position, including in
embedded clauses, as expected since it was a noun (see §4.2). However,
the first clear case of a *to* infinitive in subject position is in the thirteenth
century and there are only a couple of cases before the end of the
fourteenth. The construction becomes entrenched in the fifteenth
century, where there are very many cases attested:

(46) a. *to late* þi sinne ... nis noht inough. c.1300 Spec. Guy 147
      b. *to be* wedded is no synne. c.1386 Chaucer CT D. 51
      c. *to drede* noght shame makys foly takynge c.1425. Secr. Secr.
          liv 23

---

[1] Other common analyses have derived the relative clause from the determiner (e.g.
Smith 1964) or by a rule NP → NP S (e.g. Ross 1967). A notable advantage of the
analysis cited here is the facility with which the scope of quantifying expressions can
be assigned.

The *for-to* variant also begins to occur in subject position at the same time, which is consistent with the claim in §4.2 that *for to* . . . was simply an alternative form of the *to* infinitive. An early example is (47a). The first case of a (pro)noun + *to* infinitive in subject position (47b) is somewhat later and the construction is never very common. As shown in §4.2, the [*for* (pro)noun *to* infinitive] in subject position developed later and became established only in the sixteenth century, the first attested case being 1567 (47c).

(47)   a. *forto to beon* so angresful nis nout God icweme. c.1225 Ancr. R. 370
       b. *a man to soweyn* kokyl betoknith euelis and stryf (MMED). c.1400 Dreambk. (Förster, Mitteleng. Volkskunde) 80
       c. nowe *for him to become* an Arrian is voluntarily to teache to beleue or to allow the Arrian heresie. 1567 T. Stapleton, A Counterblast to M. Hornes Vayne Blaste (Louvain 1567) 112r

On the other hand, the (*for*) *to* infinitive (without a subject NP) is common in extraposed position from the tenth century. Note that *eallum mannum* (48c), *ænigum* (48d), *þe fader* (48e), and *hym* (48g) are to be construed as datives and members of the higher clause.

(48)   a. hit is god godne *to herianne* 7 yfelne *to leanne*. c.950 Aelfred, Bede, Pref. (1890) p2
       b. hit is sceame *to tellanne* ac hit ne þuhte him nan sceame *to donne*. OE Chronicles anno 1085
       c. hit is earmlic and sorhlic *eallum mannum to gehyrenne* . . . þæt . . . a.1023 Wulfstan, Polity (Just) p245 70
       d. hit is swiðe earfoðe *ænigum to ðeowinne* twam hlafordum. c.1000 Hexameron St Basil (ed. Norman) 36
       e. it is vncuth and vnwon *þe fader to be-cum* þe sun. 14c. Cursor M. 10139
       f. it is no shame *forto swinken*. c.1300 Hauelok 799
       g. it nys nouȝth myd hym *for to stryue* (MMED). c.1300. King Alex. 3021

A clear picture emerges from all of this: from the tenth to the fourteenth century *to* infinitive constructions which act as 'logical' subjects, although they are nouns at this time, occur only in extraposed position. In the fourteenth century they begin to occur also in subject position but only in the fifteenth century does this become a productive variant position. This is a strong argument for claiming that the initial structure of sentences of the form *it is necessary for John to leave*, for the period of the tenth to the fourteenth centuries, is that of (49), where *to leave*, a noun at this time as shown in §4.2, is generated directly in the right-most part of the VP and is not moved there transformationally.[1] If in surface structure the *to* infinitive never occurs in subject position, it is difficult to imagine what could persuade a child or a syntactician (or anybody else who is in the business of postulating underlying syntactic representations) to set up an initial structure such as (50) or (51) with the infinitive in subject position.[2] A rule of Extraposition would then have to be postulated and be obligatory for all circumstances (including for *that* complements; see below); it would be equivalent to a rule of absolute neutralization in phonology and therefore very difficult or perhaps even impossible to learn in the normal way. I claim then that (49) is the correct initial structure for *it is necessary for John to leave* in English of the tenth to fourteenth centuries, but that for this period there was no optional leftward movement rule of 'Intra-position' taking the infinitive into subject position.[3] Notice that (50) is an impossible source if one assumes the conclusions of §4.2. If *to leave* was a noun until the sixteenth century, it could not appear as indicated in (50), where the lower $\bar{\text{S}}$ would have no VP. However (51) is not eliminated as a possible structure merely by the claim that *to* infinitives were nouns at this time; a further restriction will be needed, to which we shall return. That is, it follows from §4.2 that $[John]_{\text{NP}}$ $[to\ leave]_{\text{NP}}$ $[is\ necessary]_{\text{VP}}$ will not be generable in ME, since no independently needed rules would permit $[to\ leave]_{\text{NP}}$ to occur in this position; it also follows that $[to\ leave]_{\text{NP}}$ $[is\ necessary]_{\text{VP}}$ would be generated. This is an incorrect consequence and we shall assume that

[1] Emonds (1972) advocated a similar analysis for NE. Higgins (1974) and Postal (1974) argued against this proposal, and Emonds (1976) adopts the conventional analysis, whereby the clause is generated in subject position.

[2] Such a view is based on the working principle that underlying structure is like surface structure unless there is (syntactic) evidence to the contrary. This principle would not be adopted by most diachronic syntacticians, such as Lakoff and Traugott, who would say (with Postal 1974: p32) that it totally ignores the alleged semantic character of underlying structure. In fact the principle is based on a restriction of the semantic character of the underlying structure to the domain of thematic relations. Recall the view of grammar provided in §1.4.

[3] Furthermore adopting this proposal for ME does not run into the problems of NE which led Emonds to postulate the curious concept of a doubly filled node. As far as I can tell, the relevant structures (*that Jerry has blood on his shirt proves that he killed Dick*) did not appear until well into the modern period.

there is a special surface filter precluding *to* infinitives from occurring in subject position.

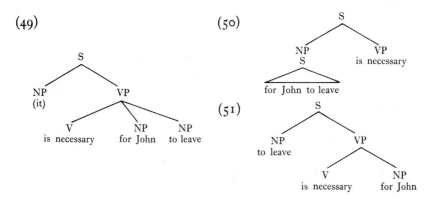

Such an analysis of the earlier stage permits a natural account of later changes, whereby *to leave is necessary* became possible in the thirteenth and fourteenth centuries. We could say that the grammar developed a leftward and optional Intraposition rule which applied very rarely before the fifteenth century. (In §6.1 we shall show that this was a special case of a more general rule, NP Preposing.) Notice that the rule is structure-preserving in that it moves a NP into another NP position. Therefore, it follows from a theory of grammar incorporating some version of Emonds' principle of structure-preservation, that the rule once available would apply in main and embedded clauses. This predicts that sentences such as *Max said that to leave was necessary* and *I saw a man whom to drive fast frightens*, where a *to* infinitive is subject of an embedded clause, should have been generable as soon as Intraposition was introduced to the ME grammar, and this seems to be correct. It is often claimed that changes usually affect main clauses first and spread from there. Under the theory of grammar adopted in chapter 1, it follows that only if a new transformational rule is non-structure-preserving will it operate first in main clauses, later permeating the grammar sufficiently to effect a re-analysis of the phrase structure rules. A new structure-preserving transformation would be expected to operate in all clauses, as in the case of the ME Intraposition (and unlike the similar rule discussed by Emonds (1972), which preposes Ss only in root clauses). See §3.2 for further discussion.

A rule of Intraposition is not required for *to leave is necessary*, because *to* infinitives, being NPs, would be free to occur in subject position after the surface filter (above) banning them from such positions became defunct. But the development of an Intraposition rule in ME and the re-analysis of *to* infinitives as verbal forms in the sixteenth century are sufficient to account for the further change when sentences like *for John to leave is necessary* first occurred in ENE. English already had a rule expanding VP as at least V (NP) (S̄), the source for ordinary complement structures: *John [said [that Mary left]*ₛ*]*ᵥₚ. Therefore, given the sixteenth-century re-analysis of *to* infinitives as verbal forms, initial structures like (52) became possible. The already existing Intraposition was free to apply and this yielded a derived structure such as (50). The fact that such sentences begin to occur in the sixteenth century, i.e. at the same time as the changes in (35) of §4.2, is another correct pre-diction made by the analysis of infinitives in that section.

(52)

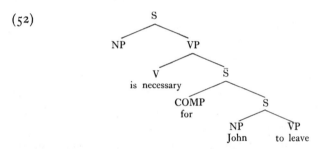

Once initial structures such as (52) became available, one would expect to find structures involving subject-to-subject raising, *John is likely to leave*. Assuming that Intraposition preposes a NP or S̄ (or an adjective; see below), it would be free to apply to the lower subject NP in a structure like (52), and this would derive the relevant structures. This is another correct prediction, since it will be argued in §6.1 that, although there is lexical variation (*likely* acts as a 'bridge' for subject-to-subject raising, but *necessary* does not), these structures appear for the first time in late ME.

Consider now some more evidence for the introduction of Intra-position in ME. During this period one often finds 'split' constructions with NPs modified by a complex genitive construction or by an adjective phrase. Similar split constructions occur with coordinates.

(54)   a.   the King's son of England = NE [[the King of England's] son]
       b.   a constant woman to her husband = NE [a woman [constant to her husband]]
       c.   Xrist slep and his halechen. 1137 Chron. p265 10
             his good men and true

Other examples of the same thing:

(55) a. manye evylle wylled peple to Sir Thomas Tuddenham. 1422–
    1509 Paston Letters vol. II p189 21
  b. his decayed eyes with iniquitie. Nashe, Strange News vol. I
    p262 25
  c. their ouerfraught studies with trifling compendiaries. Nashe,
    Pref. to Green's Menaphon vol. III p318 2

The facts are neutral between two possible analyses: the modifiers
might be generated in prenominal position with an Extraposition rule
moving *of England* and *to her husband* out to the right, or they may be
generated directly in leftmost position with an Intraposition rule moving
the head of the modifier leftwards into prenominal position. This
dilemma can be resolved. OE adjectival modifiers appeared characteristically in prenominal position, particularly for unco-ordinated adjectives and participles. However, in ME postnominal adjectives become
increasingly common. In this period most adjectives can occur as pre-
and postnominals and the latter appear to represent a productive position, because newly borrowed adjectives are often introduced as postnominals. From this productivity I conclude that modifiers may be
generated post-nominally in initial structure at this time. If Greenberg's
(1966) implicational universals are correct, then this is a plausible
change. Greenberg noted that SOV languages usually have prenominal
modifiers, while SVO order correlates most commonly with postnominals. As English changed from underlyingly SOV to become SVO
in the twelfth century, it seems that it also followed through on one of
the implications of this move and developed postnominal modifiers,
later reverting to only the older order. A similar phenomenon took place
with noun compounding, which followed through on the new VO
typology and then reverted to the old OV patterns. We shall return to
this in detail in chapter 7.

(56) a. the los of oure othere goodes temporels. Chaucer, Mel. B.2188
  b. Sumorsæte ealle; his suna twegen; wæter genog
  c. in alle haste resonable. 1425 Paston Letters vol. II p23 3
  d. speak from thy lungs military. Shakespeare, Merry Wives IV v 17

Another interpretation would ascribe the rise of postnominal modifiers
to the influence of French, the source of most of the borrowings. One
might seek support for this by pointing to occasional instances of

number agreement as in (56a). I resist such foreign-influence interpretations on ideological grounds; such 'explanations', which are extremely numerous in the literature, are usually unilluminating (see §7.2). Furthermore, in this case the explanation will not work because in contemporary French adjectives normally occurred prenominally. Wydler (1956) shows that in the *Chanson de Roland* 70 per cent of the adjectives occur prenominally. Wagner's examination of thirteenth- and fourteenth-century prose (reported in Reiner 1968) finds 2393 prenominal and 11 postnominal instances of 'cardinal' adjectives (*beau, grand, gros, haut, long*). He divides non-cardinal adjectives into two categories: 'populaires' and 'savants'. Seventy-five per cent of 'adjectifs populaires' occur always or almost always prenominally, and 70 per cent of 'adjectifs savants' always or almost always postnominally. Also popular adjectives (including cardinals) are 16 times as common as learned ones: he finds 6450 cases of such adjectives (95.4 per cent in prenominal position, 4.6 per cent in postnominal) as against 407 cases of learned adjectives (68.5 per cent postnominals and 31.5 per cent prenominals). The conclusion is inescapable: postnominal adjectives in English cannot be attributed to French influence.

As further evidence that French influence is not an important factor in the rise of postnominal modifiers, I submit the following word count of adjective order in Chaucer, based on Tatlock's Concordance. I have distinguished adjectives which are of French provenience and fairly recent borrowing, from those which are not. I give the total number of occurrences and the percentage of occurrence in prenominal and postnominal position. While the predominant position is prenominal for both English and French adjectives, postnominal occurrence is quite common. French adjectives are no more or less likely to occur postnominally than English. For clarity I have divided the adjectives according to their most common position. The figures in table 1 emphasize the parallelism of English and French when it is noted that where an English passage is modelled closely on a French source adjectives are rendered in the order of the original model. Nonetheless French adjectives are no more likely to occur postnominally than English ones. Consider, for example, the correspondences in Chaucer's *Tale of Melibee* (57).[1]

---

[1] Where possible one would prefer such data based on prose material. But in this case I know of no reason why prose translations should reflect the syntax of the source material more loosely than a poetic translation.

TABLE I

	French				Non-French		
	Total No.	Pre-nominal (%)	Post-nominal (%)		Total No.	Pre-nominal (%)	Post-nominal (%)
certain	103	68		black	40		55
clear	49	53		cold	50	50	50
common	51	98		green	50		52
divine	67	90		red	55		69
false		95		smart	31		100
gay	13	100		soft	29		52
humble	39	97		wet	9		78
jealous	13	100		dear	229		62
large	58	66		yellow	8	50	50
long	104	89		small	85	60	
natural	34	96		strong	47	53	
necessary	6	67		thick	10	60	
perfect	47	96		white	80	59	
piteous	45	89		wide	24	54	
present	25	80		empty	7	71	
pure	25	92		fair		98	
rich	63	90		fat	8	75	
royal	39	60		few	39	77	
strange	33	97		good		99	
temporal	30	83		great		99	
tender	27	96		hard	32	97	
virtuous	18	73		heavy	27	92	
celestial	17		53	high		95	
digne	11		55	idle	25	92	
grey	9		78	last	27	92	
round	12		58	lewd	21	100	
spiritual	16		51	little		100	
				new	109	73	
				next	28	89	
				nice	21	95	
				old	100	90	
				proud	24	92	
				sad	14	100	
				sharp	30	80	
				short	25	100	
				sundry		100	
				sweet	136	71	
				true	91	82	
				wicked		100	
				worldly	44	100	
				worthy		100	
				wretched	31	100	
				young	76	99	

(57)

Tale of Melibee		Le livre de Melibee et Prudence	
(page)		(line)	
201	a young man called M., myghty and riche	B2156	Uns jouvenceaulx appellez M., puissans et riches
202	of oure othere goodes temporels	B2187	de noz autres biens temporelz
	thy trewe freendes alle	B2192	tous tes loyaulx amis
	a fewe woordes moore	B2206	
203	so greet an entryng and so large	B2228	une chose si large et [qui] a si grant entree
205	many a womman ful good and trewe	B2267	en . . . pluseurs bonnes et loyaulx
209	youre trewe frendes olde and wise	B2433	tes loyaulx amis sages et anciens
	enemys reconsiled	B2435	ennemis reconciliez
	every conseil honest and profitable	B2437	
210	youre trewe freendes olde and wise	B2446	tes loyaulz amis sages et anciens
	youre doghter deere	B2463	ta fille
212	cosyns germayns	B2557	cousins germains
217	withouten temporeel goodes	B2744	sanz biens temporele

Returning to the initial structural analysis of adjectives in ME, since postnominal position is quite productive and cannot be attributed to an extraneous factor such as borrowing, I postulate that modifiers may be generated prenominally or postnominally at this time.[1] If this is correct we have an account for the rise of the split constructions of (54) and (55). The modifier phrases would be generated in post-nominal position and the independently needed Intraposition rule would prepose the head of the modifier phrase and give the correct results. One would not expect these sentences to occur before the development of Intraposition in the fourteenth century, nor would one expect them when modifier phrases are generated again only in prenominal position. These predictions seem to be correct. Prenominal position begins to regain its dominance in the fifteenth century and this becomes standard

---

[1] Thus the phrase structure rule might include something like NP → Det (Mod) N (Mod), since both modifier positions may be filled. This is similar to the situation in French, wherein lexical objects are generated post-verbally but pronominal objects occur as pre-verbal clitics. This has led some analysts to permit the phrase structure rules to generate S → (O) V (O) structures (in this case, unlike with the ME modifiers, a proviso must ensure that both O positions are not filled in some single structure).

by the sixteenth, even to the exaggerated point where past participles of intransitives occur prenominally:

(58)   a.   sour turned wine. 1548

      b.   new comen up matter. 1562

      c.   a gone man. 1598

Such an account is unavailable if modifiers are generated only pre-nominally. In that case a not otherwise needed rule of Extraposition[1] would be posited to derive the split constructions and therefore it would presumably be viewed as accidental that the split constructions arise at the same time as sentences like *to leave is necessary* and became obsolete at the same time as the disappearance of postnominal adjectives (disregarding stylistically postposed 'heavy' adjective phrases: *a woman faithful to her husband*).

Having partially motivated the introduction of an Intraposition rule in ME, which in ENE will derive (50) from (52) (additional motivation will be provided in §6.1), we may now address a further question, the one advertised at the beginning of this section: did English at some point acquire a phrase structure rule NP → S̄? To put the same question differently, was there a further re-analysis whereby a structure like

[1] The claim that Extraposition is not needed is partly a function of the theory of grammar presupposed throughout this work and outlined in §1.4. It assumes 'interpretive' rules which can associate elements such as *it* and *John is happy* in *it seems that John is happy*. There appears to be no syntactic motivation for Extraposition.

    As discussed in §3.2.1, Kuno (1974) argues that it is no accident that SOV languages have 'a rule of Extraposition'. The need for such a rule follows, he claims, from the perceptual strategies which find multiple centre-embedding and juxtaposition of conjunctions hard to process. An SOV language (with clause-initial complementizers) faces multiple centre-embedding and juxtaposition of conjunctions if it permits clauses to occur in subject position. A rule of Extraposition therefore has a therapeutic function in SOV languages. This kind of explanation is attractive from certain points of view, and the emergence of clauses in subject position may be a consequence of the earlier base change of SOV-to-SVO underlying order. Unfortunately Kuno's arguments are crucially flawed: he compared VSO languages (again with clause-initial complementizers), which reputedly do not usually have rules of Extraposition. Complementizer-juxtaposition will not arise in base structures, as he noted, but there will be rampant centre-embedding, as illustrated in (i). Kuno did not consider this kind of structure.

(i)

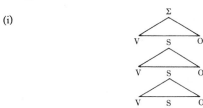

(50) became base-generated without an intervening application of Intraposition? This is a difficult question in principle and I do not have enough critical data to take a clear position.

Surface subject complements can be generated either in place by the putative NP → S̄ rule or by application of Intraposition, and therefore do not choose between the competing analyses. We have established that infinitival clauses did not occur as subjects until the introduction of Intraposition; the same seems to hold of clauses introduced by *that*. If sentences such as *that John left disturbed Jim* occurred before the introduction of Intraposition, they would provide evidence for a rule NP → S̄ in early ME. As far as I know, such sentences do not occur. However, they are so marked stylistically in NE that their absence in early ME may not be indicative of ungrammaticality. *-ing* forms such as *Jim saw the moon rising* are sometimes derived from an S dominated by NP, but Akmajian (1977) has the best analysis, and derives them from [NP VP]$_{NP}$, with no intervening S̄ node. Occurrence of a S̄ in a characteristic NP position, such as after a preposition, or in passive, cleft or pseudo-cleft constructions might be adduced as relevant evidence, but this turns out to be very weak.[1] One can either allow an intervening NP node or change the phrase structure rule or transformational structural description to include a disjunction such as PP → P $\begin{Bmatrix} NP \\ S̄ \end{Bmatrix}$. This clearly would not be an appropriate move if S̄ and NP had identical distribution (subject to selectional restrictions), because it would entail introducing a disjunction wherever NP was mentioned in the grammar, a significant complication and loss of generality. However, since S̄ and NP have only partly parallel distribution, one has to weigh the number of necessary disjunctions against the special statements required in adopting the 'over-general' solution of a phrase structure rule NP → S̄. Emonds (1972), for example, argues that clauses introduced by *for* and *that* are not NPs at any level of analysis. An important argument is that a phrase structure rule NP → S̄ predicts that *for* and *that* clauses should occur as the subjects of embedded sentences. Since by and large they do not occur here, a special

---

[1] Rosenbaum (1967) distinguishes the sentential complements of *tend* and *prefer*, arguing that those of *prefer* are dominated by NP. This is designed to account for the fact that the object complement of *prefer*, but not of *tend*, can be preposed by a rule of Passive and moved by Pseudo-cleft, rules which characteristically operate only on NPs. However, he disavows this basis for the relevant distinction in his preface.

blocking device will be needed, perhaps making Extraposition obligatory in embedded clauses (Ross 1967). The use of empty nodes also renders the decision more difficult, as can be seen from passive sentences. (59a) and (59b) can be derived from (61) by successive application of Agent Postposing and NP Preposing; subsequent application of Intraposition yields (59a) and non-application gives (59b). Similarly (62) is a possible source for (60a) and (60b).

(59)   a. that Fred left was noted by everyone
       b. it was noted by everyone that Fred left
(60)   a. everyone was disturbed that Fred left
       b. it disturbed everyone that Fred left

(61)

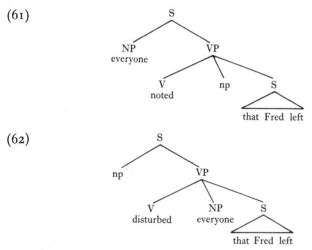

(62)

If NP and $\bar{\text{S}}$ were shown to be cyclic nodes, then one could choose between the two analyses on the basis of the Subjacency Condition. Subjacency would block application of *wh* Movement from the lower $\bar{\text{S}}$ on (63), but not (64).

In short, it is not clear that the grammar of NE has a phrase structure rule NP→$\bar{\text{S}}$. The current theory will allow it and it would be descriptively sufficient; but it seems not to be necessary. However, this indeterminacy could be resolved on diachronic grounds, if it could be shown that changes which occurred simultaneously were the surface consequences of the introduction of this phrase structure rule. The fact that clauses can occur after some prepositions, in surface subject position, as the 'logical subject' of a passive verb, (60a), in pseudo-cleft constructions, etc., is not sufficient to require a phrase structure rule

(63)   (64)

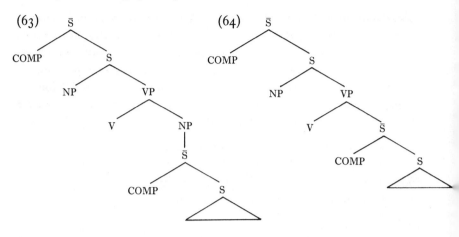

NP → S̄. However, if these possibilities developed simultaneously, one is faced with the choice of claiming that the simultaneity was fortuitous or that these various changes are the surface manifestations of a single change in the abstract grammar, presumably a new rule NP → S̄. It is important to recognize the proper status of such a diachronic argument, that the grammar of NE is known to contain this phrase structure rule as a result of certain changes taking place in, say, the sixteenth century. Clearly one cannot ascribe some kind of 'racial memory' to modern native speakers. The hypothetical simultaneity of these changes (remember that we have not yet discussed any facts concerning the actual changes) argues for the introduction of the phrase structure rule and this argument is directed to the *theory* of grammar. The force of the argument is this: if we look only at the relevant synchronic data and the current version of the theory of grammar, the correct description is not fully determined; there may or may not be a rule NP → S̄. The simultaneity of certain diachronic changes, however, requires reference to such a rule. Therefore the current version of the theory of grammar is too loose and must be restricted in such a way that the NP → S̄ solution must be chosen and the rival analyses are unavailable to the language learner. Conversely, if the relevant innovations (assuming them to be innovations) did not take place simultaneously, one could construct a somewhat weaker argument against the existence in NE of NP → S̄. If the rule was introduced into the grammar, one would expect to see the relevant surface manifestations appearing together; non-simultaneity would suggest that no such abstract change took place. Such is the logic of the matter.

Apart from the emergence of subject sentential complements, the facts themselves are difficult to determine. First, truly sentential structures (i.e. not including gerunds and OE–ME infinitives) have never occurred freely after prepositions in English. This may be a function of what have been treated as selectional restrictions, but there has been a modest decline in the ability of clauses to occur under a preposition (cf. the list of ME prepositional uses in §4.2). In any case, no significant changes took place as subject sentential complements emerged. Secondly, I do not have good data on the relevant interaction of sentential complements with passive, cleft and pseudo-cleft constructions. That is, I cannot make clear claims about the emergence of sentences such as (65).

(65)   a. he was shocked that she had rented a house
        b. it was that she had rented a house that shocked him
        c. what shocked him was that she had rented a house

To argue for the introduction of NP $\rightarrow \bar{S}$, one would want to show that (65a–c) and clauses governed by prepositions developed at the same time as sentential subjects, i.e. in ENE. To argue against the rule, one might show that these developments did not occur simultaneously. There the matter must rest, pending more adequate data.

4.4 Serial verbs in Kwa

4.4.1 Lest the reader should imagine that categorial re-analyses take place only in English around the fifteenth and sixteenth centuries (it is, after all, a common view that Elizabethan syntax was 'lawless and confused'; cf. Salmon 1965), we turn now to 'serial verbs'. This construction type occurs in many languages, particularly in Africa, and consists characteristically of verb phrases standing side-by-side with the same subject, in the same tense, aspect and mood, agreeing in positive/negative polarity and with no intervening conjunction. The meaning of the serial construction is often not transparently the sum of its parts, as may be seen in these Akan examples drawn from Schachter (1974). Givón (1975b: p66ff) cites a large range of semantic relations.[1]

---

[1] Givón cites serial verbs conveying what might be viewed as various kinds of case-relations: instrumental, benefactive, comitative, etc. Lord (1973) illustrates the difference in semantic transparency between a conjunctive and serial construction in Ewe:
    a. é nò tsì 'he drank water'
    b. é kú 'he died'
    c. é nò tsī éyē wò kú 'he drank water and died'
    d. é nò tsī ku
       he-drank-water-died
       'he drowned'

(66)   a. Kofi gyee Amma dii   c. Kofi yɛɛ adwuma maa Amma
          Kofi-received-Amma-ate   Kofi-did-work-gave-Amma
          'Kofi believed Amma'   'Kofi worked for Amma'
       b. Kofi ware sen Amma
          Kofi-is tall-surpasses-Amma
          'Kofi is taller than Amma'

Africanists have been engaged recently in a lively dispute over these
constructions (for example Ansre 1966, Awobuluyi 1973, Bamgboṣe
1973, Givón 1975b, Hyman 1975, Lord 1973, 1976, Schachter 1974,
Stahlke 1970, Williams 1971). The major issues have been whether
serial verbs are verbs or prepositions and, if verbs, whether they are to
be generated in a subordinate or coordinate clause structure. Most
of the analyses in the literature appeal to deletion-under-identity,
something not permitted in the restrictive theory outlined in §1.4.
I shall assume the correctness of Schachter's (1974) analysis of Akan,
including a phrase structure rule S → NP Aux VP*, where VP*
allows an unlimited number of VPs.[1] Thus (66b) has an initial structure
along the lines of (67).

(67)

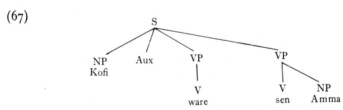

The correct cluster of properties follows from such an analysis: there
can only be one subject NP (68), tense and aspect must be identical
(69a) (compare the non-serial (69b) which has an intervening conjunction), and there is no conjunction or complementizer. Also if all

---

[1] I have modified Schachter's analysis slightly. He postulates a rule S → NP   Aux
VP VP*, and interprets VP* to mean 'zero or more occurrences of VP'. Schachter
assumes that a restrictive theory which does not permit deletion-under-identity
precludes a derivation of serial constructions from reduced clauses. However, this is
false and he fails to consider deriving (66c) from a structure such as (i), where PRO
is a phonologically null element subject to semantic interpretation at surface structure,
where it must be marked as anaphoric to some other NP.
(i) [Kofi yɛɛ adwuma]ₛ AND [PRO maa Amma]ₛ
Although Schachter does not consider it, this analysis can be shown to be inferior
to that of (67). It is important to recognize that the serial constructions represent a
cluster of properties. Therefore, if (i) were adopted, a rule would be needed to delete
the conjunction and PRO would be interpreted as anaphoric to *Kofi* only if the verb
of the second S had the same tense, aspect and mood as the first V. As far as I can
tell, this represents an unwarranted complication of the grammar. Further complications would be needed for sequences of three or more Ss.

serial verbs were derived from reduced clauses, it would be difficult to provide a source for (70); under the proposal adopted here, 'idiomatic' serials like *gye di* (66a) (what Awobuluyi (1967) calls 'splitting verbs') would have a single, discontinuous lexical entry, such as (71) (Schachter 1974: p263; see Jackendoff 1975 for this view of the lexicon and some discussion of discontinuous entries).

(68) *Kofi yɛɛ adwuma Kwaku maa Amma
 Kofi-did-work-Kwaku-gave-Amma

(69) a. *mekɔɔe maba
 I + went – I + have + come
 b. mekɔɔe na maba
 I + went – and – I + have + come
 'I went and I have come back'

(70) Kofi gye di sɛ Amma bɛba
 Kofi-receive-eat-that-Amma-will + come
 'Kofi believes that Amma will come'

(71) gye . . . di [+ V . . . V]
 [+ NP$_x$ Aux __ NP$_y$ __]
 [+ NP$_x$ Aux __ __ S$_y$]
 BELIEVE (x, y)
 Related to *gye* 'receive', *di* 'eat' by morphological
 redundancy rule *i*

Clearly there is much more to be said about the proper analysis of serial verbs, and it may be the case that so-called serial verbs in Yoruba have different properties and require a different analysis from serial verbs in Akan. For details of this analysis the reader is referred to Schachter and to the ensuing debate with Stahlke (pp271–82).

Schachter's analysis of Akan serials, derived from (67), seems to be the best available, constitutes a clear case and provides a suitable reference point to discuss historical changes involving these verbs. As observed on p214n, the support derived from the discussion of deletion-under-identity is misplaced because Schachter did not consider the possibility of deriving serial verbs from a coordinate structure with empty nodes. Strong arguments can be constructed against such an analysis, but they are irrelevant to the aims of this section. Here I am concerned with the categorial status of serial verbs, and they would still be analysed as members of the category verb, regardless of whether they were derived by a reduction of co-ordinate or subordinate clauses. On the other hand, Schachter's analysis appears stronger if one assumes the grammatical theory adopted in this book. The stipulation that there is a component of interpretive rules which derives a logical form from the surface structure, permits a solution to the problem raised at the end of the paper and to some of Stahlke's objections. Schachter's essential claim is that while serial verbs express a large range of semantic relations, their syntax is uniform; the semantic variation cannot be properly adduced to motivate different syntactic structures. In particular there is no need to assign different syntactic structures to what others have distinguished as co-ordinate vs. sub-ordinate serial constructions. For example, the ambiguity of (72) can be captured in much the same way as *persuade* and *promise* are distinguished by Jackendoff (1972) in terms of control properties and lexical semantic features.

(72)   Amma frɛɛ Kofi baae
       Amma-called-Kofi-came
       'Amma called Kofi and came in' OR 'Amma called Kofi to come in'

(73)   a. Ann persuaded Fred to leave
       b. Ann promised Fred to leave

4.4.2   Great caution is required in discussing supposed historical changes when one lacks good historical records of earlier stages of the languages under discussion. Nonetheless, some conclusions can be drawn about the nature of changes affecting serial verbs in the Kwa group. It can be established that categorial changes took place, although the question of the directionality of those changes must be left open.

Consider first some data discussed by Hyman (1971). Igbo, another Kwa language closely related to Akan and Nupe, and the Fe'fe' dialect of Bambileke, a Bantu language, do not have 'serial verbs' but 'consecutive' constructions (74).[1]

----

[1] Givón (1975b) offers the following genetic classification, based roughly on Greenberg (1963):

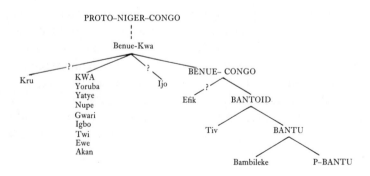

(74) a. ó wèrè ìtè byá (Igbo)
     he took pot &come
   b. à kà láh càk nsà⁀ (Feʼ feʼ)
     he PAST take pot &come
     'he brought the pot'

Consecutive constructions usually involve two or more events occurring one after the other and a 'consecutive verb' is any in such a sequence other than the first; in Feʼ feʼ all consecutive verbs have a consecutive marker, a N-prefix, presumably a reduced form of *ni* 'and then'. Hyman shows that consecutive constructions occur in semantic contexts where other languages such as Nupe and Akan have serials.

(75) Instrumentals
   a. ū lá èbī bā nākà̀ (Nupe)
     he take knife cut meat
   b. ó wèrè m̀mà bèé ánù (Igbo)   'he cut the meat
     he took knife &cut meat   with a knife'
   c. à kà láh pìɛ ncwēe mbáa (Feʼ feʼ)
     he PAST take knife &cut meat

(76) Directionals
   a. ū bīcī lō dzūkó (Nupe)
     he run go market
   b. ó gbàrà ọ́sọ́ gáa áhyà (Igbo)   'he ran to the
     he ran &go market   market'
   c. à kà khúɪa ndūa ngέn ntēe (Feʼ feʼ)
     he PAST run &go market

(77) Comparatives
   a. ū bīcī gã̄ mǐʼ(Nupe)
     he run surpass me
   b. ó gbàra ọ́sọ́ kárịa m̀mú (Igbo)   'he ran faster
     he ran &surpass me   than me'
   c. à kà khúɪa ndūa nšúɪa ā (Feʼ feʼ)
     he PAST run &surpass me

Also the same cluster of syntactic properties arises: there can be indefinitely many consecutive verbs (78), and tense and aspect may not be freely chosen. In Igbo and Feʼ feʼ consecutive verbs are not fully marked for tense, unlike Akan where identical tense markers occur on all serial verbs in a given sequence. However, both Igbo and Feʼ feʼ require identical aspect markers on all verbs; thus if this first verb is in the progressive, all others must have the progressive *ma* marker (< conjunctive + *ba* 'to be') in Fe' fe' and *na* in Igbo (in both languages the marker is optional after the verb 'to take', *làh* in Fe' fe' and *íwè* in Igbo).

(78) à ká sá', njīin ā, nsī sīɛ, nzā wúzā, ndóo sīɛ, nšúᵂa (Fe' fe')
     he PAST come, &see me, &sit down, &eat food, &stand up, &leave
     'he came, saw me, sat down, ate food, stood up and left'

(79) a. ắ múᵘ njóo nšî, mā nzēn (Fe' fe'), he PRES sing song &be dance
       *ắ múᵘ njóo nšî nzēn

      b. ọ́ na éwè m̄mà ná ébè ánụ (Igbo), he BE taking knife &be cutting meat
       *ọ́ na éwè m̄mà ébè ánụ

Also consecutive verbs must have identical subjects and there can be no regular conjunction or complementizer intervening.[1] Consecutive verbs in Igbo and Fe' fe' differ from serial verbs in Akan and Nupe in that the meaning of the sequences is *always* transparently the sum of

---

[1] Here I consider only what are generally referred to in the literature as 'consecutives', as in (i). Hyman deals also with another construction, which he calls 'subjunctive consecutivization' (ii). This construction, however, has quite different properties: it does not have the characteristic N- prefix, a connective *á* (which Hyman calls a subjunctive and imperative marker) may optionally intervene between the two verbs, and the subjects need not be co-referential (in which case the connective *á* is obligatory). I leave the correct analysis of these types as an open and for our purposes irrelevant question.

    (i) à   ká   sá',   nzā   wúzā
        he PAST come &eat food
        'he came and ate'

    (ii) à   ká   sá',   (á)   zā   wúzā
        he PAST come (so that) eat food
        'he came to eat'

    (iii) à   ká   sá',   á   ò ʒū wúzā
        he PAST come so that you eat food
        'he came in order for you to eat'

Hyman's analysis is complicated unnecessarily in two other ways. First, he considers that *láh* in (iv) should be treated as a preposition, partly because of the para-phrases with *mà* 'with' (v) and partly because, 'since it is hardly conceivable how one might physically "take" intelligence, examples such as [(iv)] seem to suggest that *làh* is not being used in its lexical sense'.

    (iv) à   ká   láh   žínù   mfá'
        he PAST take intelligence &work
        'he worked intelligently'.

    (v) à   ká   fá'   mà   žínù
        he PAST work with intelligence
        'he worked with intelligence'

the parts and therefore they never need to be analysed as discontinuous lexical items as in (71). It is important to note that this is a *cluster* of properties; if, for example, the subjects are not co-referential, then there will also be no N-marker.

Hyman assumes a (synchronic) clause-reduction analysis, whereby (78), for example, is derived from an underlying sequence of six co-ordinate clauses by various kinds of deletion-under-identity. Such a solution will not be available under the theory of §1.4, and the fact that there can only be one tense marker, one subject NP and no connectives in any one sequence, suggests an analysis along the lines of Schachter's treatment of serial verbs in Akan. However, the distribution of the conjunctive marker would require a phrase structure rule like (80).

(80) S → NP Aux VP (conj + VP*)

This will ensure that all verbs except the first get the appropriate marker, that there can only be one subject NP, one tense marker, one aspect marker and no connectives. Two alternative formulations might come to mind. The first would postulate the Akan phrase structure rules and introduce the conjunctive marker by transformation. Such a solution is unavailable under the theory adopted here for various reasons. First, the insertion transformation could not be structure-

---

If *làh* is treated as a verb, it is quite regular and occurs in consecutive form as *náh* (vi). The fact that there are paraphrases with *mà* and Hyman finds it difficult to assign a natural metaphorical reading to *làh* in (iv), does not give grounds in the theory adopted here to treat *làh* as anything other than a verb.

(vi) à   kà   núaa   càk,   náh   nsa'
     he   PAST   make   pot   &take   &come
     'he made a pot and brought it'

Secondly, Hyman regards *kwèe(nsì)* 'to join' and *tā'sī* 'to embrace' as auxiliary verbs.

(vii) a. pō   kà   kwée(nsí)   mfá'
         they PAST   join   &work
         'they worked together'
      b. à   kà   thí   píɛ,   nkwée(nsí)   náh   nzā   wúzā
         he   PAST   forge   knife   &join   &take   &eat   food
         'he forged a knife and ate food with them'

(viii) pō   kà   tá'sí   mfá'
       they PAST   embrace   &work
       'they worked together'

He gives no reason for treating these verbs as a separate category, although he seems to have an unspecified semantic criterion in mind. Curiously he notes that 'almost all of the auxiliary markers are clearly verbs in the language. And these auxiliary verbs all take consecutivized main verbs, as seen in [(viia)] and [(viii)]'. If these elements are analysed as verbs, their distribution and form are quite regular.

preserving or local, yet it applies in embedded Ss, which is ruled out by Emonds' principle of structure-preservation. Secondly, if VP is a cyclic node, as it would probably be, this putative transformation would violate the cyclic principle (e.g. Chomsky 1965: p146), which prevents the insertion of morphological material into a configuration dominated by a cyclic node once the cycle of transformational rules has already completed its application on this configuration. Thirdly, the rule would violate the principle specifically of the lexicalist hypothesis, whereby transformations cannot insert lexical material or perform derivational morphology. The second alternative might postulate an additional VP node by a phrase structure rule such as (81).

(81)   S → NP Aux VP
       VP → VP (conj + VP*)

I know of no justification for this additional node; for example, in a structure like (78) I know of no rule which would treat all material to the right of *kà* as a constituent. Suppose that some such rule were discovered; for it to have any relevance to our discussion here, one would need to show that there was no analogous rule operating in Akan, such that a similar, additional VP node would be motivated for the serial constructions. To recapitulate, I know of no evidence for the extra VP node and no way in which serial and consecutive constructions differ which would motivate an extra VP node for, say, serializing languages but not for consecutives.

What emerges from this is that the serial constructions of Akan are very similar to the consecutives of Igbo and Fe' fe'. Since the three languages are genetically closely related, all being of the Kwa sub-group, this is presumably not accidental. Hyman asserts, without argument (and is echoed by Schachter), that the consecutive constructions are the ancestors of the serials: 'In fact there seems to be a natural order of historical evolution from consecutivization to serialization' (1971: p41). I know no evidence to support this. There are three possibilities: either Akan or Igbo and Fe' fe' or some third analysis represents the proto-language. Under any of these three alternatives there has been a change in the phrase structure rules of the Benue–Kwa languages. We shall return to this in a moment, but first we shall consider some other Kwa languages.

4.4.3   There is good reason why Africanists have been in dispute about serial verbs. Akan represents a clear case, but the cognates of the Akan verbs in other Kwa languages are more equivocal in their category status. This is nicely illustrated in the debate between Bamgboṣe (1973) and Awobuluyi (1973). Bamboṣe distinguished two kinds of serial construction: a linking type, which he derived by reduction from underlying clauses, and a modifying type, where the verb does not show the full range of verbal properties and no clause reduction is involved. Awobuluyi analyses most of Bamgboṣe's 'modifying verbs' as regular verbs, adverbs, or prepositions. Throughout the Kwa languages there are many cases of homophony, both inter- and intra-lingual, between verbs and prepositions of the same semantic class. For example, consider the Twi locative verb *wɔ* 'be at' (82). *wɔ* also occurs in the frame [NP VP__ NP]$_s$, as in (83).

(82)   ɔ wɔ mamfẽ,
       he be-at Mamfe
       'he is at Mamfe'

(83)   a. me hũũ no wɔ mamfẽ
          I saw him be-at Mamfe
          'I saw him at Mamfe'

       b. ɔ yɛ adwuma wɔ ɔdan mu
          he do work be-at house inside
          'he is working in the house'

Lord (1973) notes that Twi verbs occurring in this frame are usually conjugated for tense and aspect, and take pronominal and negative prefixes. Thus *wɔ* does not have normal verbal properties; Christaller (1875: p76) noted that *wɔ* and a few other such words with cognate verbs 'have so far stripped off their verbal character and have become mere particles, as they do not assume any prefixes, not even the pro-nominal prefix *me*, nor the negative prefix, except when they are used, not as prepositional auxiliary verbs or particles, but as principal verbs'. Lord notes similar homophonies in Ewe and Gã. Ansre (1966), discussing Ewe, sets up a new category and calls elements like *wɔ* in (83) 'verbids', although 'verbids' seem to have the properties of prepositions. Wester-man (1930: p129) says that 'many verbs when they stand next to others play the part of English prepositions, adverbs, or conjunctions. Now many of these verbs, in playing the part of prepositions, etc., begin to lose their verbal characteristics in that they are no longer conjugated: they thus begin to become form words.' Hence there is evidence that (83a) should be analysed as (84).

(84)

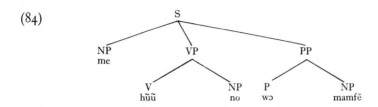

Lord also shows that Yoruba *ní* and Igbo *ná* are clear cases of locative prepositions, cognate with a main verb. The Yoruba verb *ní* is often glossed as 'have, possess' (85).

(85) ó ní ōwó,   he have money,   'he has money'

Igbo has a locative verb *nò*, a verb *ŋwè* 'possess' and an incompletive aspect marker *ná*, as in (86), all presumably cognate with the locative preposition *ná*.[1] *ná* cannot occur as a main verb.

(86) ɔ́ nà èrí ńri ná àyụ̀ ḿmànyá
       he INC eat food, INC drink wine
       'he is eating and drinking wine'

   Lord shows that similar cognate relationships hold between comitative verbs and prepositions. Yoruba *kpèlú* will serve as an illustration, occurring as a verb in (87) and in a serial-like construction in (88). A prepositional analysis must be available for (88) because *kpèlú* + NP in such a context can be fronted in an interrogative (89), as is typical for PPs and impossible for VPs.

(87) fɛ́mī'kpèlú àwō̃ ōlẹ
       Femi SHT be-one-of PL thief
       'Femi is one of the thieves'
(88) ó gé ɛ̄rã̄ kpèlú èsɔ̀
       he cut meat with care
       'he cut the meat with care'
(89) sẹ́ kpèlú ɔ̀wɔ̀ nī wō̃ kí ī
       Q with respect that they greet him
       'was it with respect that they greeted him?'

The conjunction *àtī* 'and' conjoins NPs, PPs but not VPs, and it links *kpèlú* + NP phrases (90).

---

[1] Incompletive or durative markers are often cognate with locatives. Compare ME *he went a-hunting*, where *a* < *on*. Also many languages treat possessives and locatives in parallel fashion (see Lyons 1967 for discussion).

(90) àá   kí ī kpèlú ɔ̀wɔ̀ àtī kpèlú ìrèlè
we + FUT greet him with respect and with humility
'we shall greet him with respect and with humility'

Like most prepositions *kpèlú* can occur without a dependent NP, i.e. adverbially (91), and even reduplicated (92) as a sentence connective.

(91) fémí nī ōrúkɔ̄ mī̃ kpèlú
Femi FOCUS name my also
'Femi is my name too'

(92) kpèlúkpèlú n̄ kò féé lɔ̄
also I NEG wish go
'Also, I did not want to go'

Ewe *kplé* occurs only as a preposition 'with', having no verbal homophone, but a cognate *kpé* 'to meet' (cf. Gã *kpè* 'meet', Fon *kple* 'assemble', Yoruba *kpé* 'assemble', Igbo *kpā* 'collect').

Noting such facts, Lord claims that there was a diachronic development of verb > preposition > adverb, although she offers no historical evidence to support such a claim (cf. Pike 1967 for an identical claim and, again, no historical evidence). In a more recent paper (Lord 1976), she claims that other Kwa serial verbs developed into complementizers. Again she shows interesting cognate relationships in the present-day languages, but offers no evidence to support the alleged direction of the change. She summarizes her case by listing the correspondences of (93), comparing serial verbs with complementizers. A historical relationship between the two classes seems entirely plausible.

(93)

Language		'Say'	Complementizer
Ewe		bé	bé
Yoruba		(kpé)	kpé
		wí	wíkpé
Gã		kèé	ákè
Igbo		ká	ká
		sɨ́	
Asante	⎫	se	sê
Akwapim	⎬ Akan	ka	se
Fante	⎭	ka	dɛ́ɛ̀
Idoma		kà	kà

What emerges from this discussion is that it is likely that category changes have taken place and probably are still in progress involving what have been called serial verbs in the various Kwa languages. Assuming, for example, that the Ewe preposition *kplé* 'with' is cognate with the Yoruba verb *kpèlú*, then three possibilities arise: that the proto-form was a preposition or a verb or something else.[1] Under any of these views, a category change has taken place. Without historical records of earlier stages one cannot specify the direction of the change. It is possible, as assumed by Hyman, Lord, Pike, Schachter and most other writers, that there once were coordinate clauses; restrictions developed, giving rise to a serial analysis as in (67);[2] a category change took place and some serial verbs became prepositions or complementizers; perhaps Lord is right in saying that comitative prepositions preceded instrumentals; finally some of these prepositions became adverbs. However, this sequence is pure speculation.[3] Instead of this development of major to minor category, a reverse process might have taken place. After all, historical records show that the Romance languages underwent two kinds of changes, moving at one stage from 'synthetic' to 'analytic' morphology, and at another stage in the reverse

[1] The fourth possibility, that there was no change, is eliminated by the genetic relationship between the languages. It is possible that the parent language had both a verb *kpèlú* and a homophonous preposition, but normal practice seeks to reconstruct a single source.

[2] Hyman asserts that there was originally a causal relationship between any two verbs in a consecutive construction. In that case, a complication developed in that a wider range of semantic relations became possible, so that in the modern language there are occasional examples of consecutive verbs with no causal relation. Also the verb *bā* 'to be' can occur as a consecutive (*mā* in (i)), but does not have consecutive semantics and cannot be glossed 'and then'.

(i) à   kà   sá'   mā   nzā   wúzā
    he PAST come &be &eat   food

[3] Writers claiming that the direction of change was verb-to-preposition (e.g. Givón, Lord), often adduce as support the assertion that this development took place in Chinese, as shown by Li & Thompson (1974). Conversely, Li & Thompson support their analysis of Chinese with the observation that Lord has shown a parallel historical development in Kwa. However, despite the availability of historical material, Li & Thompson's argument is of the same status as that of Givón, Hyman and Lord, and is based on notions of possible and natural changes. They claim that what were verbs in archaic Chinese are prepositions in modern Mandarin. Grammarians dispute the categorial status of these morphemes in the modern language and have coined the term 'co-verb' to indicate their special status. Unfortunately Li & Thompson offer no syntactic analysis for these elements in archaic Chinese, being content to cite etymological dictionaries which label them as verbs. They offer two arguments: that in the modern language some co-verbs occur with a verbal *-zhe* suffix and that there are homophonous verbs for many co-verbs. As with Kwa, this kind of data does not choose between a verb-to-preposition analysis and preposition-to-verb. Furthermore the arguments that the co-verbs are actually prepositions in the modern language are not compelling. They point to 'the fact that co-verbs have prepositional meanings,' without any independent account of the notion 'prepositional semantics'. Stressing that their claims hold only for surface structure, they also show that co-verbs do not have the same semantic range as serial verbs and offer this as evidence that they are not verbs. Their conclusion may be correct, but it owes nothing to their arguments.

direction. Thus the synthetic Latin future tense *amabo* became the analytic Spanish *amare he*, which in turn became re-synthesized as *amare*. It might be maintained that this dilemma can be resolved by our knowledge of language typologies, but this would be rash for reasons discussed in §3.2 and §7.2. It suffices for our present purposes to show that there were categorial changes of some kind and that they can be viewed as consequences of the Transparency Principle.

Assuming the serial analysis of (67), the categorial changes can be viewed as 'abductive' (Andersen 1973, etc; §3.2). This is illustrated neatly by sentences discussed by Schachter, who considers that serial verbs have developed into auxiliaries and prepositions.

(94) a. Kofi akɔpase
Kofi has + gone + walk
'Kofi has gone for a walk'
b. Kofi nyɛ adwuma wɔ hɔ
Kofi not + does work at there
'Kofi doesn't work there'

kɔ in *akɔpase* is cognate with the verb 'to go', but here occurs as an auxiliary. 'If *kɔ* were a verb, then *kɔ* and *pase* would be members of a serial construction, in which case the perfective prefix *a-* would have to be repeated before *pase*.' In (94b) *wɔ* must be a preposition, although cognate with the verb 'to be (located)'. Here it cannot be construed as a serial verb because it does not agree in positive–negative polarity with the preceding verb. Compare the true serial (95), where each verb is marked as negative (by a homorganic nasal prefix).

(95) a. Kofi nyɛ adwuma mma Amma
Kofi not + does work not + give Amma
'Kofi doesn't work for Amma'
b. onipa no ntumi mba
person the is-not-capable not-come
'the person cannot come'

Therefore, we may compare these structures with the equivalent serializations.

(96) a.

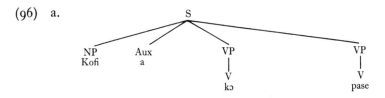

b.

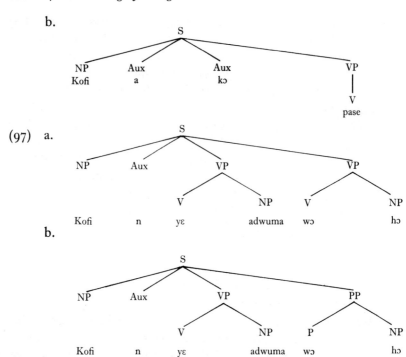

(97) a.

b.

Again, it is no part of our task to make claims about the direction of the change, whether a > b or b > a. Under either interpretation it is an abductive change, a change only in structure. Re-analysis of a serial verb as a complementizer or vice versa is similarly abductive, as can be seen from this Ewe example from Lord (1976).

(98) a.

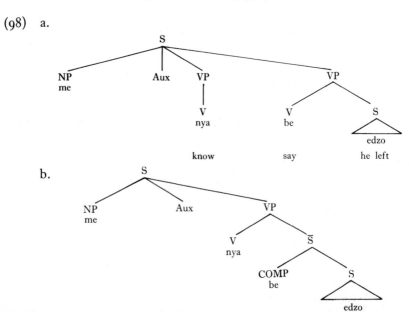

b.

In the absence of historical records, it is impossible to make specific claims about the operation of the Transparency Principle. It is clear that some languages have undergone the change and that others are transitional. In the latter languages the words under discussion have some of the properties of verbs and some of the minor categories; hence the disputes amongst Africanists about the correct categorial analysis. From the comparative data, one may assume that, say, *wɔ* in (97) was originally a verb or preposition which developed exceptional properties; the exceptionality was later eradicated by a category re-analysis. This is now a familiar type of development and presumably was a consequence of the Transparency Principle.

However, this leaves many unanswered questions, particularly why and how the exceptionality developed in the first place. In the absence of records one could postulate many possible scenarios. Givón (1975b) believes that the development is from major to minor category and claims that the fact that serial verbs arise and develop subsequently into prepositions is a function of a SOV-to-SVO word order change and an assumed need for case-markings, based on a reconstructed SOV syntax in Proto-Niger-Congo. This is quite a plausible account but he gives scant consideration to the possibility of a preposition-to-verb change (as in English *to up the ante*); he offers two weak arguments against it (p96): (a) 'when a verb loses much of its semantic contents and becomes a case marker, in due time it also loses much of its phonological material, becomes a bound affix and eventually gets completely eroded into zero. It is thus unlikely that a more crucial portion of the information contents of the utterance (i.e., the semantic contents of a verb) will be entrusted to such a morpheme'. (b) 'Further, while the process of change through depletion is a *predictable* change in language, its opposite (enrichment or addition) is not.' The force of these statements is not clear, nor how one can predict 'change through depletion', and the reader is given no hint. In my view, this kind of claim illustrates the futility of diachronic syntax in the absence of historical records. Givón's arguments for a prior SOV order consist of demonstrations of SOV syntax in the present-day languages, which are said to be predominantly SVO. Irrespective of the validity of the SOV and SVO typologies, no consideration is given to questions of historical priority, specifically to the question of whether the SOV characteristics are relics, as assumed by Givón, or innovations. It is difficult to see how such questions can be approached without historical data. It is sometimes said that we can be guided by supposed 'universals of change', whereby certain kinds of changes are natural and others impossible. However this is specious for two reasons: (a) universals of change can be based only on cases where there are sufficient records to postulate a grammar of an early stage of a language, and this is possible for only a tiny percentage of the world's languages. 'Universals' based on changes in some Indo-European and Semitic languages, Chinese, Tamil, and a few others, should be treated with great caution; (b) even within these language groups, actual changes seem to involve an extremely wide range of formal characteristics and it is by no means clear that there are any limitations, other than those imposed by the theory of grammar (see §3.2 for further discussion). Claims about the development of Proto-Niger-Congo to the present-day attested Kwa languages must remain purely speculative, and therefore I leave open the question of the direction of the changes relating (96a) and (96b), etc. Given the transitional languages where the category status of the words under discussion is unclear, it seems plausible to suggest that the change progressed along the lines of the English modals (chapter 2): exceptional behaviour arose and led to a categorial re-analysis. The direction of re-analysis and the precise point at which the Transparency Principle took effect and forced the re-analysis must remain a mystery, unless crucial historical records become available. If such evidence were available and substantiated the serial verb-to-minor category analysis, light might be shed on the diachronic processes hypothesized by Indo-European philologists, which permitted case and tense desinences to be interpreted as reduced forms of full lexical items.

5 Changes in the lexicon

In this chapter we continue to explore the consequences of the Transparency Principle. We shall look at three changes affecting the lexicon: the demise of the English impersonal verbs, the development of passive constructions, and changes in the Greek verb system. These changes affect the lexicon in different ways and two of them will be shown to follow from the Transparency Principle.

5.1 Impersonal verbs in Middle English[1]

In OE and ME there was a large class of verbs which could occur without surface subjects in the normal position. Following van der Gaaf's compendious 1904 study, we shall call these verbs 'impersonals', glossing over the distinction between 'true impersonals' (weather verbs) and 'quasi-impersonals' (*it seems that Fred left*). These impersonal verbs could be used without an overt surface subject in the normal position (*rains*; *seems that Fred left*). Again, I gloss over the distinction of whether there is truly no surface subject (*rains*) or no subject in the normal position (*seems that Fred left*) and shall refer to both types as subject-less impersonals. These verbs often occurred with an objective NP in the dative or accusative case. We shall pay particular attention here to subject-less impersonals which became personal in later English: *hine hungreð > he hungers, me thynketh I heare > I think that I hear, hine longade > he longed*.

Van der Gaaf claims that *hine hungreð* constructions became obsolete by the end of the fifteenth century. However, he cites examples from Gavin Douglas in the sixteenth; and Visser (1963–73: §43) notes many examples from the works of St Thomas More (written c.1520–34). Therefore it is more accurate to date the final obsolescence from the mid-sixteenth century. The constructions became obsolete in three

[1] Much of this material appeared in slightly different form as part of Lightfoot (1977b).

ways: (a) several of the verbs disappeared from the language during the ME period, (b) many impersonals developed a dummy *it* subject (cf. p178n), and, most interestingly, (c) the pre-verbal NP became re-analysed as a subject, taking on nominative form. The loss of these subject-less impersonals followed two changes which occurred during the ME period: the rigidification of SVO order and the loss of nominal and many verbal inflections. The demise of the subject-less impersonals can be seen as a consequence of these two earlier changes, if we assume the Transparency Principle. (1) illustrates the construction under discussion. These are all subject-less impersonals accompanied by an objective pronoun, which usually occurred pre-verbally.

(1) behofian: us behoueth furst to passe. 1485 Caxton, Chas. Gt 103

chance: at last him chaunst to meete upon the way A faithlesse Sarazin. 1590 Spenser, FQ I ii 12

deynen: ne here to dwell ... deynes me na langer. 1400–50 Alexander 830

greven: thame grevit till heir his name. 1375 Barbour, Bruce xv 541

lacken: though me lacke to purchase Her worthy thank. 1390 Gower, CA (Morley) 446

lician: mee likes ... go see the hoped heaven. 1557 Tottel's Misc. (Arber) 124

lystan: whanne þei shulden slepe, þanne hem lust to wake. c.1450 The Chastising of God's Children (ed. Bazire/Colledge 1957) cx 6

motan: vs muste make lies, for that is nede, Oure-selue to saue. c.1440 York Myst. (Manly, Spec. 1) play xxxviii (The Carpenteres) 321

neden: then needeth us no wepen us for to save. c.1386 Chaucer, ABC 118

scamian: to asken help thee shameth in thyn herte. c.1386 Chaucer, Man of Law's Tale, Prol. 3

semen: so yvel hewed was hir colour Hir semed to haue lyved in langour. c.1400 Rom. R. 214

In OE there were over forty verbs which behaved in this way. Visser (1963–73: §34) notes that many of these verbs fell into disuse before or during the ME period: *(a)grisan, (a)þreotan, belimpan, calan, forscamian, gebyrian, gedafenian, (ge)hreowsian, (ge)limpan, gelustfullian, (ge)mætan, geneah, genyhtsumian, gerisan, (ge)sælan, (ge)spowan, (ge)-swefnian, (ge)tweogan, (ge)tweonian, (ge)weorðan, (ge)yfelian, grullen, mislimpan, (mis)spowan, mistiden, (of)carmian, ofhreowan, ofþyncan, onhagian, sweorcan, þurfan, wlatian.* However some new verbs entered the class in early ME; Visser lists *him irks, him drempte, him nedeth, him repenteth, me reccheth, me seemeth, me wondreth, us mervailleth, me availeth, him booteth, him chaunced, him deynede, him fell, him happened, me lacketh, us moste,* etc. Van der Gaaf (1904: pp12–25) discussed twelve of these ME additions in detail and noted that 'a few verbs already in use in OE underwent a more or less radical change of signifi-cation, and adopted the A construction [accusative or dative + V]: others were formed from existing stems; others, again, were borrowed from Old French and a few from Old Norse' (p12), and in some cases the borrowing transferred a French or Norse personal verb into the impersonal frame *(deynen, repenten, remembren).* This indicates that despite the loss of many of the relevant verbs, the construction was still productive in ME.

In this section most of our attention will be devoted to change (c) above, the re-analysis of some of the impersonals as personal con-structions. Jespersen (MEG III 11.2₁) illustrates the history of the impersonal-to-personal change as in (2).

(2) a. þam cynge licodon peran
     b. the king liceden peares
     c. the king liked pears
     d. he liked pears

In (2a) *peran* is unambiguously the subject and the verb is therefore in the plural. In (2b) the dative marker has disappeared from the first NP, but the verb retains its plural ending. The levelling of nominal inflections gave rise to an identity of form for subject and object NPs, so that after the levelling of the third person singular and plural endings (2c) could be analysed syntactically in two ways: as an SVO structure or as OVS. Thus the loss of inflections on nouns and verbs made (2c) structurally ambiguous and, therefore, permitted a re-analysis. If one assumes the Transparency Principle, the establishment of SVO as the canonical (i.e. initial phrase marker) word order then forced the re-analysis. If a language learner was confronted with the sentence *the king liked the pears*, there would be a tendency to analyse it as SVO; this would conform to the canonical patterns of the language, or to put it in terms of transformational generative grammar, would involve the simplest transformational derivation. More examples of such ambiguous structures are contained in (3).[1]

(3)   a. then Achilles . . . chaunced to sle Philles. c.1400 Destr. Troy 7701
   b. an hound is wo þat ony man goth besyden him in þe-waye. c.1440 Jacob's Well (EETS) LXXXVI 33
   c. who-so list hem for to rede. c.1386 Chaucer, CT B.3509
   d. thenne the kyng dremed a merueillous dreme. 1470–85 Malory p65
   e. God list to shewe his wonderful maracle. c.1386 Chaucer, CT B.447

This syntactic re-analysis (an 'abductive change' in the sense of Andersen 1969, 1972, 1973) took place despite morphological and semantic factors which might have prevented it, by giving the language learner sufficient evidence that this was not SVO but an OVS structure. The morphological restraints lie in parallel constructions with pronouns. Pronouns have distinguished nominative and objective cases throughout their history and one might think that *him liked the pears* was unambiguously OVS, by virtue of the form of the pronoun, and that the existence of this pattern would provide evidence for the possibility of analysing (2c) as OVS in analogous fashion. This did not happen. Such was the force of the Transparency Principle, to require a canonical SVO analysis and the simplest transformational derivation, that even *him liked the pears* was analysed as SVO despite the form of the pronoun. I offer three pieces of evidence for this claim, showing that pre-verbal pronouns in the objective case behaved as subjects.[2]

   (a) Visser (1963–73: §38) notes many instances of pre-verbal objective pronouns triggering verb agreement. If the verb was impersonal, one

---

[1] I beg the question of why OVS constructions survived with these verbs two hundred years after the establishment of underlying SVO order. For some speculation on this, see Noriko McCawley (1976). I also do not address the question of why the impersonal verbs became personal rather than developing a dummy *it* subject (cf. German *es hungert mich*), which would involve a transparent derivation and satisfy the SVO requirement. In general, while there were three ways used to eliminate the subject-less impersonals, I can give no account of why certain verbs were lost, others personalized and others developed a dummy *it* subject. I argued in §3.2 that to demand such predictions from a theory of change is impossibly ambitious.

[2] Butler (1975), taking over claims by Jespersen and Visser, also argues that these objective pronouns were treated as subjects, but he offers no explanation.

would expect third person singular endings; if it was a verb such as *lician* above, normally it would agree in number and person with *pears*. Therefore the revealing examples will be an impersonal verb with a first or second person object pronoun or a verb such as *lician* where the two NPs are of different number or person (4).

(4) a. me think we shal be strong enough. 1534 More, Works (1557)
     b. me-seem my head doth swim. 1571 Damon & Pithias 79

In these examples the verb is agreeing in person and number with the pronoun *me*, despite the fact that it is in the objective case; this indicates that the pronoun is nonetheless analysed as a subject regardless of the clear morphological evidence to the contrary.[1]

  (b) Visser (§31) notes a further construction, illustrated in (5). These seem to be clear cases of impersonals, since the verb is third person singular while there are two NPs in the objective case, neither of which is third person.

(5) a. for certes, lord, so wel us liketh yow. 1386 Chaucer, CT E. 106
     b. sei me loueli lemman, how likes þe me nowþe? c.1350 Will. of
        Palerne 1740

Butler (1975) observes that impersonals could normally enter into one of four types: (i) they may take no complement, *hine hungreð* 'he is hungry'; (ii) they may take a 'causative object', usually in the genitive or with a preposition, *þeah þæt fole þyrste þære lare* 'although that people thirsted for learning', Aelfred, Cura Pastoralis ii 30; *menn scamað for misdædan* 'men are ashamed because of misdeeds', Wulfstan, Homilies lxiv 16; (iii) they may take a *that* clause, or (iv) an infinitival complement. Thus there is no clear way to analyse (5) (but see below). It is most plausible, particularly in the light of (4),

---

[1] One should point out, with Butler, that zero and -*e* also serve as subjunctive endings, so the verb might be a third person singular subjunctive, therefore not agreeing with the pre-verbal NP. However, subjunctives in main clauses are restricted to wishes, commands and the apodoses of counterfactual conditions. The examples cited do not fall into any of these classes.

One should also observe that in some cases forms like (4) exist alongside personal uses of the same verb, so *think* occurred personally and impersonally. The impersonal, OVS forms are not simply eliminated; they survive through ME and cause confusion, so that speakers treat them as SVO in *some* but not all respects. Thus *think* in (4a) is clearly not the personal verb, but the impersonal verb being treated as SVO in terms of number agreement (but not case marking). So with the properties discussed in (b) and (c).

to claim that *us* and *þe* are to be construed as subjects, despite their objective form and the third person ending on the verb. Interestingly, in many instances editors have emended texts to make one of these objectives into nominative form (see Jespersen MEG VII 6.6$_4$). There are many examples which *could* be analysed in the same way, such as (6), but sentences like those in (5) provide the crucial evidence, where one of the objective NPs *must* be interpreted as a subject (i.e. by the time that subject NPs become obligatory). Alternatively, one might assign an initial structure [ ]$_{NP}$ *liketh* [us]$_{NP}$ [yow]$_{NP}$, with a rule preposing *us* after Verb Agreement and Case Assignment. When SVO became the canonical surface word order, such an analysis would be impossible, and sentences such as (5a) would cease to occur – a correct prediction.

(6) þa gelustfullode ðam cyninge heora clæne lif 'their clean life pleased the king'

Jespersen (MEG VII 6.6$_4$) notes similar examples where 'sometimes an expression with the oblique form is followed by a connexion of words that is strictly appropriate only after a nominative' (7).

(7) a. Ase oft ase ich am ischriuen, euer me þuncheð me unschriuen. c.1225 Ancr. R. 332
     b. swetest him þuncheð ham 'they [the nuns] appear to him [God] most lovely' c.1225 Ancr. R. 196

(c) Visser (§38) records cases where an impersonal construction is conjoined with a personal, which seems to indicate that the two types were felt to be parallel (8).

(8) a. but moche now me merueilith, and well may I in sothe. c.1405 Mum and Soþsegger (EETS) ii 1
     b. me is as wo Fer him as ever I was for any man. c.1385 Chaucer, Legend of Good Women 1985

Crucial evidence that such conjoined sentences were regarded as parallel can be found in similar sentences involving null anaphoric functions, or what some linguists might regard as deletion-under-identity (9).

(9) a. þat þou be chaste . . . never — irk to do his wille. c.1340 Rolle of Hampole, The Commandem (Allen) lxxix 219
     b. Arthur loked on the swerd, and — lyked it passynge wel. 1470–85 Malory p74

  c. us sholde neither lakken gold ne gere, But — ben honoured
     whil we dwelten there. c.1374 Chaucer, Troil. IV 1523

  d. us thoughte it was noght worth to make it wys, And — granted
     him withouten moore avys. c.1386 Chaucer, CT A.785

  e. hym happened to be hurte with any arow and — was bown to
     dye. c.1450 Alphab. Tales lvii 19

  f. the kynge (dative) lyked and — loued this lady wel. 1470–85
     Malory p35

In conjoined structures a PRO element may be interpreted as anaphoric to a full NP only if it has the same grammatical function as
the 'trigger'. Hence a PRO subject cannot be interpreted as anaphoric
to an object (10a), even if it is preposed and occurring in the objective
case (10b).

(10) a. *they fired Fred and — is teaching astrology

      b. *$\begin{Bmatrix} \text{Fred} \\ \text{him} \end{Bmatrix}$ they fired and — is teaching astrology

This restriction on the interpretability of abstract elements holds in
ME, as well as NE, but the sentences of (9) are of exactly this form.
We may therefore either say that (9) are exceptions to this restriction,
or take (9) as further evidence that the pre-verbal NP is analysed as a
subject, despite the objective case marking. Notice that (9a)–(9b) show
a subject anaphoric to a putative PRO object, and (9c)–(9f) a putative
object anaphoric to a PRO subject. These sentences provide strong
evidence that the PRO NP of the impersonal verbs in (9a)–(9b) and
the pre-verbal objective pronouns in (9c)–(9f) were analysed as subjects,
yielding parallel conjoined structures and thus permitting the anaphoric
reading.

  So we have three pieces of evidence that the pre-verbal pronouns
with the impersonal verbs were analysed as subjects despite being
morphologically marked as objects.[1] We can see that not only could
(2c) be analysed as SVO, but the pressure for this analysis was strong

---

[1] Butler (1975) discusses this data in the context of proposals by Keenan (1974) who
argues that, while subject NPs in various languages show various characteristics
(they occur clause-initially, trigger verbal agreement, are dominated directly by S,
express agency, etc.), no single property or set of properties is sufficient to define a
subject of a sentence on any universal basis. Rather, 'the subject of a sentence will be
that NP which possesses a solid preponderance of the subject properties relative
to the other NPs in the sentence'. Thus in ME nominative case and triggering verb
agreement are not necessary conditions for subject-hood.

enough to require even *him liked the pears* to be analysed in the same way, despite morphological evidence for an OVS analysis. This pressure stems from the Transparency Principle after the rigidification of SVO order and the loss of inflections, which would have disambiguated (2c).

Not only did the pressure from the Transparency Principle for a standard SVO analysis overcome the countervailing morphological evidence, but also it succeeded against semantic odds, and entailed two semantic changes. As noted earlier, there must be constraints on change from one generation to another, such that communication between successive generations is still possible. This constraint would be challenged by an abductive re-analysis of the type we have discussed. (2b) seems to require an OVS analysis, while (2c) could be analysed as SVO, as we have shown, and the SVO analysis was eventually successful. However this syntactic re-analysis would have the effect of radically changing the meaning. The sentence *the king likes the queen*, originally an OVS structure, means something quite different when analysed as SVO: under the OVS analysis the king senses pleasure and the queen is responsible, but the reverse holds under the SVO analysis. How then was communication possible as the change was in progress across society? The answer is that the meaning of *like* changed from 'to give a pleasurable impression' to 'to receive a pleasurable impression'. Hence *the king likes the queen* with an OVS analysis and *like* meaning 'to give pleasure' would be cognitively synonymous with the same sentence analysed as SVO and the verb interpreted to mean 'to receive pleasure'. Of course, this indeterminacy would arise only in sentences where both NPs were capable of both giving and receiving pleasure. (2c), for example, given the ambiguity of *like*, would be interpreted on the 'receive' reading when analysed as SVO. Jespersen (MEG III 11.2) notes many such verbs which underwent a parallel shift in meaning: *ail, repent, dream, become* (= 'suit'), *matter, belong*, etc. Thus Chaucer's *it reweth me* becomes later English *I rue my ill-fortune*; *but will it not one day in heaven repent you?* becomes *will you not repent...?* This shifting begins at the same time as the syntactic re-analysis; Chaucer, for example, used *rue* in both the 'give' (above) and 'receive' sense, *thou shalt not rewe*, CT A. 3530. The shifting may take place in either direction, so *like* shifted from 'give' to 'receive', while *ail* shifted in the reverse direction: *what does she ayle?* Shakespeare, All's Well II iv 7; *whenever he ails anything*, Southey I 95 > *what ails thee now*,

Scott, OM p170; and, as with *like*, both senses existed side by side for a long period. Thus we may view the shift in meaning of these verbs as a consequence of the syntactic re-analysis; the need to perform such a semantic shift did not thwart the syntactic re-analysis, even when added to the morphological forces outlined above.[1]

In fact, it is arguable that the semantic forces militating against this re-analysis were even stronger, since there was a subtle change in meaning even beyond the semantic shift of *like*, etc. It is usually assumed that [*the king*]$_{\mathrm{NP}}$ [*liked the play*]$_{\mathrm{VP}}$ is not synonymous with *the play pleased the king*, and therefore not with the earlier [*the king liked*]$_{\mathrm{VP}}$ [*the play*]$_{\mathrm{NP}}$, even when one notes the two senses of *like*. This difference may be described by a rule of Subject–Predicate Interpretation, which assigns certain properties to a subject. Presumably semantic changes of this subtlety do not break down communication.

Consider now the transformational derivation of the sentences we have discussed. For the earlier stage, when English was underlyingly SOV, we may postulate (11) as the relevant initial phrase markers (see §4.3 for arguments for generating logical sentential subjects in the rightmost position of the VP). In (11b) a rule of NP Postposing would move *pears* to the right.

(11) a.   b.

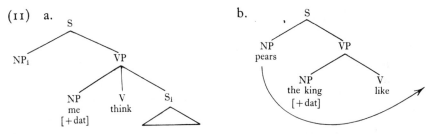

We may posit (12) as the corresponding initial phrase markers for the intermediate stage, after English had adopted underlying SVO order but before the re-analysis and semantic shift had taken place.

---

[1] Notice that if we view the semantic shift as a device to maintain the possibility of successful communication after the syntactic re-analysis, then in Andersen's framework this would be dealt with as an 'adaptive rule'. This raises the question of the formal properties of adaptive rules. If there are no formal constraints on possible adaptive rules, then presumably there are no limits on the way in which two 'adjacent' grammars may differ in their internal structure, except those limits imposed by the general theory of grammar. This seems to be correct, and the theory of change will not be a function of limitations on possible internal differences between adjacent grammars. I argued this in §3.2.

(12)   a.

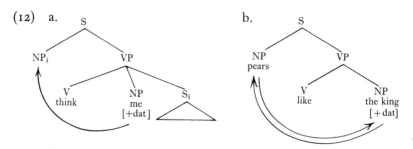

b.

In order to generate the sentences *me thynketh I heare* and *the king liceden peares*, a rule would be needed to move *me* and *the king* into pre-verbal position, as indicated above. One can see that the derivation of *the king liceden peares* from an underlying sequence *peares liceden the king* (12b) would be opaque to the language learner, and difficult to figure out. However, the derivation may have been possible; such a preposing rule was available at this time. (In fact, there may be a problem, insofar as there is no empty NP position for the first movement; this might suffice to disbar permutational processes under the usual requirements for structure-preservation.) We shall call the rule NP Preposing and assume a structural description of (13), where lower case indicates an empty node. We shall return to this rule in some detail in §6.1.

(13)   NP Preposing
       np   X   NP   ⇒ 3   2   t

   Our attention has concentrated on one aspect of the demise of the impersonal verbs, and in terms of the form of the grammar this change affected lexical entries. For example, after the change *think* came to be sub-categorized to occur in the frame NP __ S, where NP could not be empty, and thus initial structures like (12) were no longer possible (in fact, there is a complicating factor with this specific example in that OE had two verbs, the personal *þencan* 'think' and the impersonal *þyncan* 'seem', so this change might be construed as a loss of the impersonal form rather than as a re-analysis; this possibility does not arise with the other examples in (1)). *Like*, on the other hand, underwent no sub-categorization change, since it has always occurred in a NP__ NP slot; in this case the semantic specification changed from 'give pleasure to' to 'receive pleasure from'. Notice that on the assumption that the grammar continued to include rules of NP Preposing and NP Postposing, [NP$_j$ like NP$_i$] could be derived from [NP$_i$ like NP$_j$], as in (12b) (ignoring the problem noted parenthetically above). However, *the king likes the queen* is not ambiguous. This can be accounted for in at least two ways: (a) saying that the syntactic derivation might apply but that semantic interpretation applies only at surface structure and at this point, regardless of the derivational history, the meaning is assigned, specifying that the king receives pleasure from the queen; (b) interpreting the Transparency Principle to be not only a condition on the form of available grammars, but also on the functioning of the rules. In this case, although the grammar has the means to derive $[NP_j$ like $NP_i]$ from $[NP_i$ like $NP_j]$, such a derivation must be debarred on the principle that structures must be analysed in the most transparent fashion. Such an interpretation raises many problems and may be too strong a restriction.

This syntactic change seems not to have been caused by earlier semantic or phonetic changes. It was a consequence of the rigidification of SVO order. The Transparency Principle requires structures to be analysable in the most transparent fashion and the principle apparently exerted sufficient force to bring about the re-analysis despite morphological and semantic restraints, and so it entailed morphological and semantic changes. This re-analysis has been described as a purely formal change affecting the lexical sub-component and I have assumed an autonomous syntax. The change, however, was provoked by a 'functional' factor, the Transparency Principle. The Transparency Principle is a constraint on grammars, which one can see at work in diachronic change, eliminating abstractness and complications on syntactic rules entailed by changes elsewhere in the grammar. The Transparency Principle, then, is a metagrammatical principle restricting the possible syntactic components, as noted earlier, and is entirely consistent with the autonomy thesis.[1]

5.2 Passive constructions

In this section attention will be focussed on the development of so-called passive constructions. As a prelude to the major part of the discussion, I shall first examine the development of the passive in some early Indo-European texts, showing this to be a consequence of the

[1] Harris (1976) argued that the development of subject clitic pronouns in French, usually analysed as a consequence of an earlier phonological change, is in fact motivated by the 'desire' to generalize the canonical word order patterns. I believe that this is a very similar change to the one described here and should be viewed as a change in the syntactic component, provoked by the Transparency Principle.

Transparency Principle. Then I shall turn to passives in the history of English and illustrate a change whereby a lexical rule becomes non-lexical; this will shed some light on the development of the passive in Greek, Latin and Sanskrit.

5.2.1   Most reconstructions of PIE contain a set of verbal desinences called medio-passives, but no endings specifically for the passive voice. Humbert (1945: p100) expresses the standard view: 'le *passif* ne s'est que lentement constitué aux dépens du moyen, auquel il a emprunté la plupart de ses formes'. It will be argued here that the loss of the middle voice as a productive category and the establishment of the passive in Greek follows from the Transparency Principle. The basic observations hold also of Sanskrit and Latin and a similar (but not identical) analysis may be appropriate for analogous developments in these languages.

The medio-passive inflectional category was used to express middle or passive 'meaning'.[1] The middle voice was essentially active and often transitive, but it carried a reflexive notion in that the action of the VP was deemed to be somehow in the interest of the subject of the clause. Thus the active of (14a) contrasts with the middle in (14b) in that in (14b) the action is interpreted to be in the interest of the soldier. Such a distinction is often obscure and difficult to express in an English gloss, but sometimes the middle voice can be translated with a reflexive, as in (14c).

(14)   a. ho stratiótēs loúei tòn híppon 'the soldier washes the horse'
   b. ho stratiótēs loúetai tòn híppon 'the soldier washes the horse (for his own interest)'
   c. ho stratiótēs loúetai 'the soldier washes himself'

---

[1] It is sometimes asserted that these forms expressed only middle meaning in the proto-language and the ability to convey also passive force was an innovation. Lehmann (1974) and Parker (1976) take such a stance, but offer no justification. If this were correct, it would be difficult to imagine an explanation for why and how passive force should be introduced for middle endings in a large number of languages. This seems to be a minority view, which I shall ignore. Chantraine (1953: p179) expresses the usual opinion: 'il semble que, dès l'indoeuropéen, les formes moyennes pouvaient comporter le sens passif [footnote omitted], comme l'indiquent l'indo-arien, l'italique, le celtique, le hittite, le tocharien'. Gothic could be added. This view is shared by Gonda (1951: pp7, 101). A weaker position is that the *fundamental* contrast is active vs. middle, not active vs. passive. Such opinions (e.g. Chantraine 1953: p171; Wackernagel 1926: pp122f) are usually based on the greater frequency of middles in the early texts; Humbert (1945: p107) observes that *Iliad* I has 230 middles and 24 passives, although there are indeterminate cases which urge scepticism about such counts (see (15) below).

Panini called the middle *ātmane padam* 'the expression for oneself', as opposed to the active, which was *parasmai padam* 'the expression for another'. Humbert (1945: p104) comments that

la nuance subjective peut être plus subtile. Pourquoi Agamemnon, quand il propose de mettre à flot une embarcation pour apporter à Chrysès une réparation, dit-il: *nêa mélainan erússomen* [my transliteration – DWL], tandis que, lorsqu'il propose de profiter de la nuit pour mettre toute la flotte en position de départ, il emploie le *moyen: épeita dé ken erusaímetha nêas hapásas?* Logiquement, l'embarcation destinée à Chrysès et la flotte entière font également partie des navires dont il dispose: mais c'est une embarcation *quelconque* qu'il enverra dans le premier cas, tandis que, dans le second, il s'inquiète *personellement* de ses forces navales.

The effect of middle forms is not always so subtle: *nómous títhēmi* (active) 'I impose laws' differs from *nómous títhemai* (middle) 'I set up laws' in that in the active voice the law-giver is somehow external to the governed community. A similar distinction holds between *eirénēn poiô* 'I impose peace' and *eirénēn poioûmai* 'I make peace'. Attaching middle endings to an active (transitive) root would often yield an intransitive, as in (14c), in many cases corresponding to a French or German reflexive: *klínesthai* 's'appuyer sur', *orégesthai* 'se tendre vers', *phéresthai* 'se diriger vers', *loúesthai* 'se laver'. Also there are many roots which are causative in the active and intransitive (often inchoative) in the middle: *hístēmi* 'set': *hístamai* 'stand'; *óllumi* 'kill': *óllumai* 'die'; *peíthō* 'persuade': *peíthomai* 'obey'; *paúō* 'stop': *paúomai* 'desist'. This active: middle semantic contrast, such as it is, was retained for longer in Greek than in Sanskrit and is totally absent in Latin.

These middle or medio-passive forms were also used to express passive 'meaning'. i.e. where the surface subject is understood as bearing the same thematic function as the object of the corresponding active form. This is usually the function labelled 'Theme' by Jackendoff (1972), 'Patient' by Traugott (1972a) and 'Objective' by Fillmore (1968). While in the classical language it can often be said that a form such as *loúetai* is 'ambiguous' between a middle or passive reading, in earlier Greek there is sometimes indeterminacy rather than ambiguity; the verb is intransitive, and it makes little semantic difference whether it is read as passive or middle. Here the distinction between passive and middle has not yet emerged and it is best to speak simply of a medio-passive category.[1]

[1] Similar Sanskrit examples are cited by Gonda (1951: p74), e.g. *avaśiṣyate*, which may be glossed as 'he remains' or 'is left', *dhriyate* 'he is steadfast' or 'maintains

(15) a. Diòs d'eteleíeto boulḗ 'the will of Zeus was accomplished/
accomplished itself'. Iliad I 5
   b. tò d'ephélketo meílinon égkhos 'the ashen spear dragged along
after him/was dragged along'. Iliad XIII 597
   c. ōpheleoménōi pròs autoû 'benefiting from him/being bene-
fitted by'. Herodotus II 68
   d. blábetai dé te goúnat'iónti 'his knees fail/are weakened as he
goes'. Iliad XIX 166

Furthermore a clear, semantic opposition between active and passive
was not established in the earliest times. Homer (Iliad II 374) could
write *khersìn huph' hēmetérēisin haloûsá te perthoménē te* '[the city,]
by our hands captive and wasted', where the role of the formally active
haloûsa is quite parallel to that of the passive *perthoménē*. Thus in early
Greek the thematic function of a NP is often unclear, as with the will
of Zeus in (15a), which may be an Agent or a Theme. However there are
many examples in the earliest texts where the middle forms are carrying
clearly passive force. Note, for example, the formulaic opposition
ollúntōn te kaì olluménōn 'those killing and those being killed'. The
non-middle, i.e. passive, reading is required if the sentence contains an
agent other than the subject; this would be marked most commonly
by *hupó* + the genitive or dative case:[1] *hōs d'hupò laílapi pâsa kelainḕ*
bébrithe khthṓn 'as the whole black earth is oppressed by/beneath a
storm' (Iliad XVI 384). In such a context the subject could not be
interpreted agentively. Lyons (1968: p375) observes that 'the "middle"
voice can "merge" with the passive under the "non-agentive" interpretation of the subject; and this seems to have been the point du départ
for the subsequent development of passive constructions in the Indo-
European languages'. Chantraine (1953: p179) describes the similar
semantics of middle and passive as 'le passif exprime que le sujet
subit l'action. Le moyen assume un rapport particulier avec le sujet . . .'
Similarly Kuryłowicz (1964: p74) notes that 'the fundamental fact is

himself', cf. Vendryes (1921: p122), Wackernagel (1926: pp90ff). Forms such as
mriyate 'dies' or 'is killed' are sometimes cited in this connection. However, this is
to be misled by the glosses. While *mriyate* is medio-passive in form, it is also a
fourth class verb which has the *-ya-* infix. Friedrich (1960: p62) cites similar examples
from Hittite where active form may assume medio-passive force, e.g. *kitta* is glossed
as 'er liegt' or 'er wird gelegt'.

[1] There are other possibilities and agents may be expressed with the genitive, *hupó*+
genitive, *hupó*+ dative, or just the dative: *hormḗtheìs theoû*, Odyssey VIII 499;
hup'androphónoio Lukoúrgou theinómenai bouplêgi, Iliad VI 134–5; *hupò Patróklōi . . .*
kteinómenos, Iliad XVI 490–1; *Akhilḗï damastheís*, Iliad XXII 55.

that the middle use is not to be distinguished from the passive use in *bipartite* constructions', i.e. when there is no agent expressed or assumed.

Summarizing, *loúetai* might mean either 'washes (for himself)' or 'is washed', and likewise Sanskrit *bharisyate* 'he will carry (for himself)' or 'he will be carried'. In the course of the history of Greek, these forms gradually ceased to carry middle force and became associated uniquely with the passive voice. For the future tenses new passive forms were developed. Thus the present tense passive form *blép-etai* is a reflex of the PIE medio-passive and in classical times had middle or passive force, but the aorist tense *ebléphthēn* is assumed to represent an innovation and to convey only passive 'meaning'. We shall show that this standard view represents a gross oversimplification, but it is true of Greek and other related languages (Sanskrit, Latin, etc.) that the passive voice desinences developed largely from the proto medio-passive inflections.

Even if there was a clear opposition between active and middle in the parent language, this distinction was obscured even in the earliest Greek texts. There are many apparent synonyms where one verb is inflected with active endings, the other with middle, such as *háptomai* and *thiggánō* 'I touch'. For several verbs Homer uses active and middle forms in what seems to be free variation, so we find *akoúō* alongside *akoúomai*, *lámpō* and *lámpomai*, *horô* and *horômai*, *spérkhō* and *spérkhomai*, etc. He uses the root *tek-* 'to give birth' 71 times in the active and 21 times in the middle and in one instance uses both forms side by side with no meaning difference.

(16)   óphra ídēi hoîos Zēnòs gónos enthád'hikánō, hòs prôton Mínoa *téke* Krétēi epíouron: Mínōs d'aû *téketh*'huiòn amúmona Deukalíōna.
'so that you might know as what kind of son of Zeus I have come here, [Zeus] first begat Minos, warden of Crete; and Minos begat a son, noble Deucalion'. Iliad XIII 449

phêmi has a third singular aorist *éphē* (active) or *pháto* (middle) and a participle *phámenos* (middle, 12 occurrences) or *phás* (active, 3 occurrences). Sometimes the choice between active and middle forms might be influenced by metrical considerations; Chantraine (1953: p174) notes a preference for middle participles and observes that these forms fit nicely into dactylic patterns: *sperkhómenos*, *agapazómenos*, etc. Also many verbs occur only in the middle ('media tantum') and show no alternations: *keîmai, hépomai, phébomai, ákhnumai, odúromai, hédomai, ákhthomai, boúlomai, médomai, eúkhomai,* and many others. Furthermore, later, in the classical language, one finds verbs which carry active endings for their present tense and middle for the future (Smyth (1920: §806) lists 74): *akoúō:akoúsomai.* Therefore, on these grounds alone it may be assumed that even in Homer the formal distinction of active and middle desinences was by no means semantically transparent.

Further complication arises when one looks at those forms which are supposed to be distinctively passive, namely the *-thē-* forms for the future and aorist. First, it is worth noting that these characteristically passive forms, both Greek innovations, were introduced at different times: the *-thē-* aorists occur in Homer, but the *-thē-* futures do not occur until after Hesiod (Palmer 1962: p124; Humbert 1945: p108). Although Homeric Greek had a formal distinction between what are called middle and passive aorists, the formal distinction was semantically opaque. One finds middle aorists in a passive function, although they are all examples of the older type of aorist: *eblémēn, ektámēn* and *eskhómēn;* for example, *prìn blêsthai Menélaon* (Iliad IV 115), *apéktato pistòs hetaîros* (Iliad XV 437), *pân d'eksēránthē pedíon, skhéto d'aglaòn húdōr* (Iliad XXI 345). Palmer (1962) observes that 'it is noteworthy that no middle of an *s*-aorist [i.e. the later form] is used in a passive function, which suggests that the above usages are fossilized survivals'. This persists into later Greek and *eskhómēn* (middle) is far more common as a passive 'I was possessed' than the formal passive *eskhéthēn* (as in, say, Euripides, Hippolytus 27); Herodotus IV 84 uses *elipómēn* with the force of a passive: *autoû elíponto.* Conversely, aorists in *-thē-* were not used solely as passives. Palmer (1962: p123) notes that in Homer 'about a quarter of the *-thē-* aorists are purely passive', and Smyth (1920: §802) that originally neither *-ēn* nor *-thēn* was passive in meaning. In fact during the history of Greek many middle aorists were supplanted by *-thē-* forms. *dúnamai* has two aorists, *edunéthēn* and *edunésthēn.* The middle forms *dieleksámēn* and *apekrinámēn* are replaced by *dielékhthēn* and *apekríthēn.* Palmer (1962) notes that 'we find a gradual expansion of the passive type at the expense of the middle. Thus we find not only *ēidésthēn,* the Attic aorist of *aidéomai,* but also *ēide(s)sámēn,* while for *hédomai, éramai, ágamai* Homer has only *hēsámēn, ērassámēn, ēgassámēn* as against Attic *hésthēn, ērásthēn, ēgásthēn.*' Throughout Greek many verbs use the future middle forms as passive, Smyth (1920: §808–9) lists 36 examples and a further 21 with two forms (e.g. *ágō:áksomai, akhthḗsomai*), both of which are used with passive force. Nonetheless there was an increasing tendency to associate the -*thē*- forms with passive meaning, as indicated by a textual emendation by Aristophanes (Clouds 1357); alluding to fragment 13 of Simonides, *epéksath'ho Kriòs ouk aeikéōs*, he substituted *epékhthē* for *epéksato*.

Summarizing, the inherited system involved a formal distinction of active vs. medio-passive endings. However, in the earliest Greek texts this formal distinction was semantically opaque. Gradually the medio-passive forms came to be associated uniquely with passive 'meaning' and new, distinctively non-middle forms were introduced for the future and aorist passives. This change can be illuminated and explained partially by the Transparency Principle.

The grammar of earliest Greek involved opacity of a kind that was eliminated by the subsequent demise of the middle voice and the tendency of the old medio-passive desinences to denote only passive relations. This opacity can be shown in two quite different ways. Consider Parker's (1976) observation that the ancient languages under-going this change all had underlying OV order and, like most SOV languages, did not require an overt subject morpheme since the verbal inflections were rich enough to indicate the person and number of the subject.[1] Therefore, since some nominal forms have identical endings for the nominative and accusative cases, certain sentences were liable to an ambiguous analysis. Parker cites the Sanskrit *amṛtaṃ cakre* which might be construed with *cakre* as a third person middle and *amṛtam* as an object, glossed as 'he made the immortality potion', or with *amṛtam* as the subject of the passive voice *cakre*, glossed 'the immortality potion was made'. An analogous sentence from Greek, liable to the same double analysis, would be *tò ástu amúnetai* 'he defends the city' or 'the city is defended'. In fact, sometimes there was the possibility of a triple analysis if the NP could be construed as the subject

---

[1] While Parker's observation is correct, his analysis is deficient. He claims that 'passive meaning' represents an innovation, and that medially inflected verbs acquire passive meaning as a historical change. However, his explanation crucially assumes that passive *structures* (his figure 2) are already independently motivated before the development of passive meaning, which is what he wants to explain. The only evidence offered for this is the citation of some sentences from Modern English. There is a gap in the logic here. Also his 'explanation' is predicated on the assumption that abductive changes involving new constituent analyses may not entail changes of meaning. This assumption is falsified by the changes involving English impersonal verbs. In §5.1 we demonstrated that structural changes involved simultaneous changes in the meaning of *like*, etc.

of a middle verb: *tò ástu amúnetai* 'the city defends (itself)', or 'he defends the city', or 'the city is defended'.

(17)   a.   b.   c.

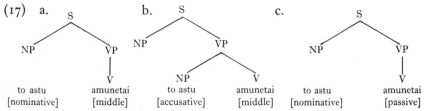

to astu	amunetai	to astu	amunetai	to astu	amunetai
[nominative]	[middle]	[accusative]	[middle]	[nominative]	[passive]

In this case one finds opacity in the sense of what Anttila (1972) calls 'surface ambiguity'. The loss of the middle interpretation for *amúnetai* eliminates the opacity in that *tò ástu amúnetai* would then be analysable only as in (17c). Given certain plausible assumptions, it can be shown that this opacity in the grammar of early Greek arose as a result of earlier changes. If this is correct, the loss of the middle voice may be viewed as a therapeutic response to this newly developed opacity, and thus as a consequence of the Transparency Principle. We shall consider two assumptions about changes taking place between PIE and early Greek, which entailed the opacity which in turn provoked the subsequent loss of the middle voice.

It must be borne in mind that once one ventures back before early Greek, one enters the speculative realm of prehistory. Therefore, the assumptions we are about to entertain cannot be firmly substantiated. However, consider first the hypothesis that PIE had an underlying word order of SVO and that there was a change in the base order before the earliest texts of Greek, which point to a base-generated SOV. For evidence in favour of such a position see Friedrich (1976), Miller (1975), Vennemann (1974). Assuming an underlying SVO order (and no optional transformation permuting verb and object), *tò ástu amúnetai* would be liable only to two possible analyses, namely (17a) and (17c). Only after the change to an underlying SOV order would the possibility arise of the three analyses of (17). Thus if it is correct to assume a SVO-to-SOV base change, it can be seen that such a change would have the effect of increasing opacity and structural ambiguity in the derivations with which we are here concerned; it might be argued that such a development brought the opacity to an intolerable level. In any case, this opacity was eliminated by the loss of the middle voice: after the eventual loss of the middle, *tò ástu amúnetai* could be analysed only as in (17c). In fact there were two stages to the loss of the middle voice: first the middle inflections ceased to be semantically distinct from the active, and eventually the endings themselves were lost, except where they carried passive sense. The first stage was almost complete by the classical period (fifth century BC) and by this time there were very few verbs which could occur with both active and middle inflections and carry the earlier semantic distinctions. *loúō* and *amúnō* are two of the few examples.[1] At this point the active vs. middle inflectional distinction is unpredictable and redundant. A verb would be entered in the lexicon with a specification of its inflectional class (active or middle) and of whether it is transitive or intransitive. There-fore, any medially inflected verb will be liable to an analysis such as (17a) or (17b), according to whether it is transitive or not, but not to both. This reduces the opacity to the level which obtained before the pre-Greek SVO-to-SOV base change.[2] After the loss of the middle as a morphological class, the second stage, the opacity was eliminated altogether and (17c) became the only possible analysis for *tò ástu amúnetai*.

The second relevant set of changes between PIE and earliest Greek created opacity of a different kind. We shall begin our account of this with the observation that in Homer there are very few 'full' passives, i.e. instances of a verb with (medio-)passive morphology and an agent expressed by a preposition or case-marking (usually *hupó* + genitive). *hupó* + genitive occurs quite frequently indicating an agent,[3] but the overwhelming majority of such instances are with intransitive verbs as in (18), which do not show medio-passive morphology.

(18)　a. en koníēisi pésoien hup'andrási dusmenéessin 'in the dust they may fall at the hands of ill-disposed men'. Iliad VI 453

　　　b. épaskhon hup'Árēos palamáōn '(which) they endured at the hands of Ares'. Iliad III 128

　　　c. huph'Héktoros androphónoio thnḗiskontes 'dying before man-slaying Hector'. Iliad I 242

---

[1] Similar developments took place in Sanskrit, of which Speyer (1886: p238) notes that 'instances of medial meaning conveyed by medial forms seem to be found especially in the older texts'. After this time some verbs were lexically marked to take middle endings, but this had no semantic significance. The Latin deponents reflect a similar stage of development. Verbs such as *sequor* 'follow', *reminiscor* 'remember', which have only medio-passive endings, do not fall into any recog-nizable semantic class.

[2] This is a crude and much oversimplified way of quantifying opacity.

[3] *Hupó* also conveys other senses, notably the locative 'under', and sometimes it is not clear whether a given *hupó* phrase is to be interpreted locatively or agentively.

    d. hupò rhipês ... ekserípēi drûs 'an oak is uprooted by a
stroke [of Zeus]'. Iliad XIV 414

This indicates that in Homeric Greek agentive phrases are not to be derived
by a postposing rule. If the overwhelming majority of verbs occurring
with the agentive marker were intransitive, then for these verbs at least
there would be no other underlying position in which the surface subject
could be generated; that is, the NP serving as surface subject must also
serve as the initial, i.e. deep structure, subject. Therefore agentives could
not be generated as initial subjects and must be base-generated in a PP
or with an oblique case. Since agentive phrases must be base-generated
in place in most of the contexts in which they occur, it is difficult to
imagine what would lead an analyst to postulate a movement rule for
those contexts which are analogous to the late Greek passive constructions. It would seem most economical to exploit fully the possibility of
base-generated agentives, and hence not to invoke an unnecessary movement rule. I shall assume that this is correct for Homeric Greek.

    Consider now whether there was in Homeric Greek a rule of NP
*Pre*posing. Some verb roots could occur transitively or intransitively,
as in (19), and this syntactic alternation sometimes correlated with
differences in the gradation of the root vowel.

(19)   a. [Zeùs] kaì álkimon ándra phobeî 'he puts even the brave man
       to flight'. Iliad XVI 689
    b. hoi d'ephébonto katà mégaron 'they fled through the hall'.
       Odyssey XXII 299

Chantraine (1953: p171) notes that 'l'emploi absolu de certaines
verbes generalement transitifs est notable: [Iliad XI 722] *potamòs
Minuëïos eis hála bállōn . . .*'. *éhkō*, used absolutely, occurs passim,
hízō 'sit' (e.g. Iliad XX 15), *dinéō* 'turn' (e.g. Iliad XVIII 494) *phúō*
'sprout' (e.g. Iliad VI 149), etc. It is for these verbs that a movement
analysis might be justified. Thus (19a) might be derived from a structure
such as (20a) and (19b) from (20b).

(20) a.   b.

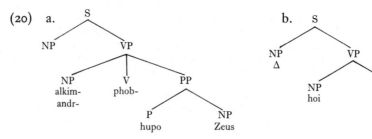

This is a possible description of these verbs. I shall postpone the question of whether a transformational movement analysis is preferable to a lexical rule relating Δ *frightened Agamemnon* to *Agamemnon became frightened*, returning to this question in detail later in the section. Let us assume such a movement analysis as a framework for discussing the facts. If the object NP, or the Theme (Jackendoff 1972), moves into subject position there will be the appropriate root vowel quality. Therefore, the basic observation captured by the NP Preposing rule is that for certain verbs the thematic function associated with the object NP of a transitive verb can also occur as the subject NP of the corresponding intransitive. Under the usual assumptions about the proto-language, this relationship correlated with variations in the quality of the root vowel of the verb; ablaut alternations distinguished transitive causatives (19a) from intransitive inchoatives (19b). To put it differently, in the inherited system the application of NP Preposing was consistently marked by ablaut variations. It is normally assumed that the PIE causatives had -*o*- vocalism in the root vowel. Kuryłowicz (1956: p87; 1964: p86–8) lists pairs such as Greek *phébomai* 'fear': *phobéō* 'frighten', *seúō*:*so(u)óō*, 'hasten', *phérō*:*phoréō* 'carry', *trémō*: *troméō* 'shake', *trépō*:*tropéō* 'turn', Slavic *ležati* 'lie':*ložiti* 'lay', *sěditi* 'sit':*saditi* 'set', Latin *memini* 'remember':*moneo* 'warn', Gothic *sit(j)an*:*satjan*, etc. The Greek alternations occur frequently in Homer, but are not productive after that time.

Between PIE and early Greek the inherited correlation between ablaut variations and NP Preposing was opacified in two ways. First, the ablaut system became defunct as a productive morphological process. This may have resulted partly from earlier phonological changes such as the loss of the laryngeals, the digamma and intervocalic -*s*-, which obscured the morphological relations.[1] As a result of these phonological changes the inherited -*mi* verb system became more complex morphologically and was gradually eliminated in favour of the -*o* system. Second, NP Preposing applied with some verbs with middle inflections. In other words, NPs could occur as the surface subject of a medially inflected verb in the same thematic function as would hold of the direct object of the corresponding active verb. Consider *hélko: hélkei tò égkhos* 'he drags along the spear' vs. *tò égkhos hélketai* 'the spear is

---

[1] The laryngeals and intervocalic -*s*- had already been lost, but the digamma is still extant in Homer. Palmer (1962: p101) reports that 'it has been calculated that against 3354 places where the influence of the digamma is metrically evident, there are 617 places where it is neglected'.

dragged along'. One often finds active causatives corresponding to middle intransitives, such as *phobéō*:*phébomai* above, and such relations obtain from the earliest texts. In many instances the active, two-place form is an innovation based on the older intransitive middle: *agállomai* 'boast' is older than *agállō* 'praise', *théromai* 'become warm' antedates *thérō* 'warm', *maínomai* 'rage' precedes *maínō* 'infatuate'. Similarly the Latin intransitive *conflictari* is older than the active and transitive *conflictare* 'to shatter', which occurs first in Pliny and Tacitus; *plector* 'suffer pain' is older than *plecto* 'punish' (for further examples see Delbrück: 1893–1900: vol. IV pp427ff; Wackernagel 1926: pp129f). However, not all middle verbs involved NP Preposing; in *ho stratiốtēs loúetai*, for example, the subject has the thematic function of Agent, whereas the object of the active *loúei* will always be Theme, indicating that *ho stratiốtēs* has not undergone NP Preposing over *loúetai*. Therefore the grammar of early Greek has been opacified by these changes: there is no longer a clear morphological marker correlating with application of NP Preposing. Application of the rule correlates sometimes with -*e*- vocalism in inchoative:causative pairs, and sometimes with middle desinences; but many verbs with middle forms or roots with -*e*- vocalism have not undergone NP Preposing.

The subsequent changes in Greek eliminated this opacity. The ablaut system was lost as a productive morphological process, so that pairs such as *phobéō*:*phébomai* were eventually eliminated, and the middle voice was lost and supplanted by the passive.[1] By the 'passive' we mean a construction where the underlying object occurs as a surface

---

[1] If the ablaut system was quite productive in the parent language as a marker of NP Preposing, then it might be the case that NP Preposing changed from being a transformational rule and became lexical. Further evidence along these lines may be constructed on the basis of the development of the verbal adjective in -*teos*, expressing necessity. When used with a personal subject, this has passive force: *potamós tis hēmîn esti diabatéos* 'a river must be crossed by us' Xenophon A. II iv 6. Smyth (1920: §2151) notes that such forms are permitted 'only when the verb from which it is derived takes the accusative'. Such restrictions are typical of the 'local' nature of lexical rules, as discussed below. Normal passives and the corresponding active (impersonal) verbal adjective occur with objects in any case: *tôn boskēmátōn epimelē-téon* 'it is necessary to take care of flocks' Xenophon M. II i 28. The personal verbal adjective is a post-Homeric development and the first attestation is *phateîon* in Hesiod Theo 310. We shall discuss such a lexical vs. transformational distinction at length in §§5.2.2–3 and provide evidence for a converse change in English, whereby a lexical rule develops a transformational counterpart. However, there is not enough relevant data available for this early stage of Greek to make the investigation of such a question productive. The next two sections will illustrate the range of data which is necessary in order to make such a claim for English.

subject and the verb carries medio-passive inflections (supplemented by distinctively passive endings for the future and aorist tenses). As a result of these changes, application of NP Preposing was again correlated with a morphological indicator, viz. the passive inflections. Therefore it can be said that throughout the history of Greek, 'NP Preposing' in structures like (20) correlated with a special, morphological marking on the verb: first signalled by the ablaut system, later by the adoption of medio-passive endings on transitive verbs. We have noted above that the middle voice began to decline from early times and the middle endings ceased to convey middle semantics in productive fashion. It seems that as this decline began, they acquired a new function, that of distinctively marking passives, i.e. verbs whose underlying objects occurred as surface subjects, or, put differently, verbs which had undergone NP Preposing.

What has been put forward here does not purport to be a full explanation for the loss of the middle voice in Greek.[1] It is important to recognize that the 'explanation' is after-the-fact. However, it has been shown that opacity introduced as a result of putative changes taking place between PIE and early Greek was eliminated by the subsequent loss of the middle voice. Therefore the loss of the middle could follow from the Transparency Principle if this principle were formulated in such a way as to characterize as intolerable the opacity resulting from the changes in pre-Greek. Clearly this would be a desirable formulation, providing a partial account of the loss of the middle. However, much more is needed before one has a proper formulation of the opacity involved. For example, it will be necessary to resolve the question posed earlier concerning the choice between a transformational rule of NP Preposing and a lexical redundancy rule. Furthermore, attention

---

[1] An alternative explanation for the development of passives has been offered by Lehmann (1974). Like Parker, Lehmann assumes that passive meaning was not present in PIE and that 'the passive as a separate category developed . . . primarily from the middle' (p184); his account runs into the difficulties observed on p240 n. Lehmann (p129) associates the development of passives with an OV-to-VO word order change, neglecting the fact that Sanskrit (and its daughters Hindi, Bengali, etc.) developed passives without ever adopting an underlying or predominant VO order. Parker points to two further problems in Lehmann's claims that middles used reflexively assumed passive force because reflexives and passives are scarcely distinguishable semantically (p129) (cf. English *John shot himself* vs. *John was shot*, which are surely quite distinct), and that the passive arose as a separate category as a result of the inclusion of instrumental and agentive expressions with medially inflected verbs (p183), when in fact the earliest occurrences of passives were overwhelmingly agentless, as noted above.

must be paid to certain aspectual distinctions and it is possible that we do not have sufficient data available. For example, one might claim that the middle voice was normally stative and for that reason could not readily co-occur with agents. Such issues can be clarified by considering some developments involving passive constructions in English, where we have sufficient data to make some interesting claims about the nature of the changes.

5.2.2 We shall now take a brief theoretical interlude, develop a perspective and then return to the history of passive constructions. In chapter 1 it was asserted that syntactic change could be studied most profitably within the context of a restrictive theory of grammar. Our work has been conducted within the framework of the EST. This theory permits at least four classes of rules which are relevant to the present domain of inquiry: phrase structure rules, transformations, lexical redundancy rules and rules of semantic interpretation. The form and function of each rule class must be constrained, unless this abundance of rule classes is to turn into a true embarras de richesses, to the point that the theory permits an excessive range of grammars. We shall consider here the distinction between transformations and lexical redundancy rules. The discussion will draw on Wasow (1977), who showed that criteria for distinguishing these rule classes lead to surprising and correct predictions.

Wasow proposed five distinguishing criteria: 1. (root and local) transformations can change structure, unlike lexical redundancy rules, which cannot. 2. Transformations do not change node labels, whereas lexical redundancy rules may relate items of different grammatical categories. 3. Transformations are 'non-local' in that they map entire phrase markers into other phrase markers and are blind to grammatical relations, whereas lexical rules are 'local' in the sense that they may refer only to those elements which condition a word's initial structure environment. For example, if the lexical rule applies to a verb, it may refer only to those NPs which bear a grammatical relation to the verb in question. 4. Transformations may have as their input the output of an earlier transformation, while lexical rules apply before any transformations and cannot be fed in this way. 5. Transformations are more productive than lexical rules and have few or no genuine exceptions; in a given structural configuration, a lexical rule may apply only if certain lexical items are present.

Armed with these criteria, Wasow examined two proposals for dealing with causative:inchoative relations, as discussed in §5.2.1. Fiengo (1974) proposed that such relationships should be captured by a transformational rule of NP Preposing which moves an object into an empty subject NP, as illustrated in (21).[1] Jackendoff (1975: p659) proposed that the relationship be handled by a lexical redundancy rule (22), which expresses the fact that the subject of the intransitive form corresponds to, i.e. has the same selectional restrictions, thematic function, etc. as, the object of the transitive form.

(21)   np melted the ice $\Rightarrow$ the ice melted

(22) $\begin{bmatrix} +V \\ +[NP_1 \underline{\quad}] \\ NP_1 W \end{bmatrix} \leftrightarrow \begin{bmatrix} +V \\ +[NP_2 \underline{\quad} NP_1] \\ NP_2 \text{ CAUSE } (NP_1, W) \end{bmatrix}$

Wasow noted that both analyses can be formulated within the EST and that they express the same facts. He then demonstrated elegantly that adopting criteria 1–5 offers a principled means of choosing between these analyses and therefore reduces the class of available grammars.

The first two criteria are irrelevant to this choice since NP Preposing neither changes or produces structure nor alters node labels. Wasow's demonstration turns crucially on the third criterion: if the causative rule is lexical, then it should relate only underlying direct objects to subjects. Critical evidence concerns sentences such as (23), where under the transformational analysis (23b) would be derived from an underlying (23c).

(23)   a. the champion showed John's inexperience
       b. John's inexperience showed
       c. np showed John's inexperience

The transformational analysis would incorrectly permit a parallel derivation of (24a) from (24b), where *John's inexperience* is in post-verbal position although it is not the direct object. If, however, the rule is lexical, it will not operate on (24b) because *John's inexperience* bears no grammatical relation to the verb *show* and therefore 'Criterion 3 would prevent the subject of the intransitive form from being related to the complement subject of the transitive form.'

[1] It is important to recognize that NP Preposing is a rule of great generality, involved in the derivation of several construction types. Therefore it is not appropriate to compare its role in the derivation of inchoatives with another device (22), set up exclusively to relate inchoative and causatives, without also considering its other functions in the grammar as a whole. We return to NP Preposing in §6.1.

(24) a. *John's inexperience showed to be a major shortcoming
      b. np showed John's inexperience to be a major shortcoming
      c. the champion showed John's inexperience to be a major
          shortcoming

Secondly, Wasow considers examples like (25), where the transformational analysis would derive (25b) from an underlying (25d).

(25) a. they dropped the rope 100 feet
      b. the rope dropped 100 feet
      c. they dropped John the rope
      d. np dropped the rope 100 feet

Unfortunately, (26a) could be derived in parallel fashion from (26b).

Although [(26a)] is a grammatical sentence of English, it is doubtful whether anyone would want to derive it from [(26b)], since *John* in [(26a)] is the agent, not the goal of *drop*. Assuming that any analysis of causatives must capture the correspondence between the intransitive subject and the transitive object, the derivation of [(26a)] from [(26b)] must be excluded, for no such correspondence holds. A lexical causative rule conforming to criterion 3 would, of course, exclude such a derivation of [(26a)], since *John* is the indirect object, not the direct object, in examples like [(25c)]. (Wasow 1977: p332)

(26) a. John dropped the rope
      b. np dropped John the rope

Furthermore, on the assumption that (25c) is transformationally derived by Dative Movement, then the fourth criterion will prevent a lexical rule from relating (26a) to (26b), since it prescribes that lexical rules cannot be fed by transformations.[1] If there is no rule of Dative Movement, as suggested below, (25c) would be eliminated by the requirement that causative forms involve direct, not indirect objects. Finally, the causative:inchoative relationship shows great lexical irregularity and therefore a lexical analysis would be supported by the fifth criterion. Wasow illustrates the idiosyncrasy as follows.

(27) a. John $\begin{Bmatrix} \text{dropped} \\ \text{lowered} \end{Bmatrix}$ the rope

---

[1] Similarly, one might assume that there is an intermediate structure *np expected John [t to win]*$_S$, where *John* has been extracted from the lower S by a transformation of Raising. In that case, no lexical rule could relate such a structure to a passive *John was expected t to win*, because criterion 4 prescribes that no lexical rule may be fed by a transformation. However, the arguments for such a rule are faulty, as shown by Bresnan (1976b) and Lightfoot (1976a).

b. the rope $\begin{Bmatrix} \text{dropped} \\ \text{*lowered} \end{Bmatrix}$

(28) a. John $\begin{Bmatrix} \text{shattered} \\ \text{demolished} \end{Bmatrix}$ the light bulb

b. the light bulb $\begin{Bmatrix} \text{shattered} \\ \text{*demolished} \end{Bmatrix}$

(29) a. John $\begin{Bmatrix} \text{darkened} \\ \text{tinted} \end{Bmatrix}$ his hair

b. his hair $\begin{Bmatrix} \text{darkened} \\ \text{*tinted} \end{Bmatrix}$

(30) a. we $\begin{Bmatrix} \text{moved} \\ \text{transported} \end{Bmatrix}$ the boxes

b. the boxes $\begin{Bmatrix} \text{moved} \\ \text{*transported} \end{Bmatrix}$

In this way Wasow showed that criteria 1–5 for distinguishing lexical from transformational rules uniformly favour a lexical treatment of causatives.

Later in the paper Wasow turns to passive constructions and argues that the grammar of Modern English has two rules dealing with passives, one lexical and one transformational. He shows first that some passive participles are adjectives while others are verbs. Arguments that passive participles may be adjectives are based on statements such as (31).

(31) i. some occur in prenominal adjective position (*the broken jar*)

ii. some occur as complements to verbs like *act, become, look, sound* (*he seemed annoyed at us*)

iii. some occur with an *un-* prefix which is not tolerated by the corresponding active verb (*her whereabouts are unknown*: *they unknow her whereabouts*)

iv. some may co-occur with *very* which is an intensifier applicable to adjectives (i.e. those whose semantics permit such quantification) and not with verbs: *very red*: **he very reddened*

On the other hand, there are equally good reasons for believing that some passive participles are not adjectives. Wasow constructs arguments based on (32) and (33).

(32) the judgments of a. (where *(...) indicates ungrammatical if the parenthesized material is not present) follow from b. only if there is a transformational derivation.

    a. the church was given *($5); $5 was given (to the church)

    b. someone gave the church *($5); someone gave $5 (to the church)

(33) passive participles may be followed by predicative expressions which may not follow adjectives (*John is considered a fool*: **John is obvious a fool*)

On this basis Wasow postulates two rules relating actives and corresponding passives. According to criteria 1–5 only a lexical rule can relate adjectival passives to actives because, for example, transformations are not permitted to change grammatical categories. On the other hand, only a transformational rule may operate on non-adjectival passives and on examples like (34) where the derived subject bears no grammatical relation to the passive verb (see criterion 3).

(34)   a. a monster is believed to live in Loch Ness

     b. there is believed to be a monster in Loch Ness

Therefore criteria 1–5 force Wasow to postulate two rules relating actives and passives.

    Such a treatment makes various predictions about the clustering of properties: (a) 'passives whose derived subjects are not their underlying direct objects should be unable to exhibit adjectival behaviour', (b) 'criterion 4 predicts that there may be cases in which a transformation feeds the Passive transformation, but that no transformation may feed the lexical passive rule', (c) 'lexical but not transformational passives may undergo lexical rules (e.g. category-changing rules)', (d) 'criterion 5 suggests that lexical passives may exhibit idiosyncrasies not found in transformational passives'.

    The major part of Wasow's paper demonstrates that these predictions are borne out with striking consistency. To illustrate (a) briefly, if the derived subject of a passive verb was the underlying subject of the immediately lower verb (e.g. *John was believed to be popular*), the phrase must be the result of the transformational passive, not the lexical rule. Therefore, the passive phrase will not show adjectival properties. This is borne out in that it cannot occur prenominally (35) or as the complement to verbs like *act* or *seem* (36), cannot occur as an *un*-passive (37) and cannot occur with a degree modifier without *much* (38).

(35)   a. *the thought to be a genius scientist . . .

     b. *the found to be not guilty driver . . .

36) a. there $\begin{Bmatrix} \text{is} \\ \text{*seems} \end{Bmatrix}$ believed to be corruption in high places

b. Mary $\begin{Bmatrix} \text{is} \\ \text{*appears} \end{Bmatrix}$ thought to be a genius

c. John $\begin{Bmatrix} \text{is} \\ \text{*sounds} \end{Bmatrix}$ considered to be a scoundrel

d. Nixon $\begin{Bmatrix} \text{was} \\ \text{*acted} \end{Bmatrix}$ found to be not guilty

(37) a. John is unknown
b. John is known to be a communist
c. *John is unknown to be a communist

(38) a. we were very *(much) expected to be model citizens
b. the war was very *(much) believed to be wrong

To illustrate prediction (d), it can be noted that lexical passives are more exceptional in that, unlike their non-lexical analogues (39), they may require adverbial modifiers (40) and use unpredictable prepositions to mark the NP corresponding to the subject of the corresponding active (*annoyed at, bored with, contained in, elated at, frightened at, horrified at, interested in, known to, overjoyed at, pissed off at, relieved at, surprised at, tired of, upset with*).

(39) a. an example was constructed by the teacher
b. these specimens were found by students
c. two errors were noticed by every reviewer
d. this book was read by the entire class
e. the chicken was killed by the butcher

(40) a. a ?? (carefully) constructed example illustrated the point
b. these specimens look *(recently) found
c. two *(widely) noticed errors have been corrected
d. this *(rarely) read book is a gem
e. the chicken smells *(freshly) killed

Wasow's analysis predicts that (lexical) passives with prepositions other than *by* will not occur in environments requiring a transformational derivation (41).

(41) a. John is known $\begin{Bmatrix} \text{to} \\ \text{by} \end{Bmatrix}$ everyone

b. John is known to be a CIA agent

c. John is known $\begin{Bmatrix} ??\text{to} \\ \text{by} \end{Bmatrix}$ everyone to be a CIA agent

This description claims that *Fred was infuriated* has two surface structure analyses, whereby *infuriated* is either an adjective (lexical passive) or a verb (transformational passive). This sentence is also ambiguous and may refer to a state or an event. Wasow suggests that the adjectival analysis tends to be associated with the stative reading.

In this way a rich set of implicational statements emerges. The clustering of properties is not something which has to be learned and analysed on a one-by-one basis, but rather it follows naturally within the framework of a theory distinguishing lexical and transformational rules in a principled way. In a conceptually restricted theory, allowing only one class of rules, the clustering of properties would presumably have to be stipulated explicitly.

5.2.3   If Wasow's analysis is correct, then one wants to know why the grammar of English should contain two rules with such a degree of overlapping in function. Some history may help come to grips with this question. I shall assume that Wasow's analysis is fundamentally correct, although revisions will be proposed, and I shall argue that the transformational passive is an innovation and was not present in the grammars of earlier English; the earlier grammars contained only the lexical version of passives. My discussion will draw heavily on Visser's lengthy analysis of passive constructions throughout English, and my argument will be based on the simultaneity of various changes.

On the assumptions developed in §5.2.2, the following sentences may be used as the bases for arguments that there must be a non-lexical passive rule in NE. (Such sentences were the basis for the original arguments for a passive transformation in Chomsky 1955, where it was noted that selectional restrictions give only a very weak argument.)

(42)   a. John was given a book
       b. John was expected to win
       c. advantage has been taken of John
       d. John was helped
       e. John was considered a fool
       f. John was arrested at 3pm by the police

On the assumption that the lexical passive relates the direct object of an active construction to the surface subject of a passive, the subjects of (42) will not be related by such a rule to the object of an active. In (42a) *John* is an underlying indirect object and, before being passivizable, i.e. relatable to a subject of *be given*, must be moved first into post-verbal position; *someone gave John a book*.[1] Such a sentence, or intermediate structure, cannot be related to (42a) by a lexical rule because such rules cannot be fed by transformations. On the other hand, a transformational rule will make the necessary relationship, since transformational rules are blind to grammatical (and thematic) relations and any sequence np V NP will meet the requirements of the rule, regardless of the origin or function of the NP. Similarly with (42b), a transformational rule will be able to move *John* into subject position of *be expected* because it is in the post-verbal slot and therefore meets the structural description of such a rule; the fact that it is not a direct object is irrelevant to a transformational rule. However no lexical rule could relate *John* in *I expect John to win* to the subject of *be expected* in (42b), simply because *John* bears no grammatical or thematic relation to *expect*. In (42c) Wasow assumes that *advantage* bears no relation to *take*, and in (42d) *John* can be related only to an underlying indirect object since *help* does not tolerate a direct object; such a relationship cannot be effected by the lexical passive rule, which operates only on direct objects. (42e) can be derived only by application of a transformational rule because in general adjectives cannot be followed directly by a NP and therefore the base rules should not generate a structure *John was* $[considered]_{Adj}$ $[a fool]_{NP}$; the lexical passive operates only on adjectival participles. Finally, on the assumption that adjectival (and lexical) passives are stative, non-statives such as (42f) must be derived differently, such as by application of a transformation. We shall argue later that some of these assumptions are incorrect, and some revisions will be made.

(i) *Indirect passives.* We examine now the history of these and some other constructions, turning first to examples like (42a), where the subject of the passive is related to an indirect object of an active verb

---

[1] This analysis is not necessarily correct. Alternatively *someone gave John a book* may be base-generated and related to *someone gave a book to John* by a lexical rule. I shall not choose between these alternatives here, but the fact that the putative transformation of Dative Movement is of such limited productivity and the occurrence of sentences like *the book was given him* suggest that a lexical analysis may be appropriate. If a lexical analysis is adopted, (42a) will not undergo the lexical rule if the definition of 'direct object', which is crucial to the formulation of the rule, does not include a post-verbal NP which is lexically relatable to an indirect object. Such a definition would correspond to the views of the traditional grammars.

taking both a direct and indirect object. The history of such constructions is well documented. First, let us note that the corresponding passive on the direct object, *a book was given to John*, was common from the earliest times: *Herodian ... þatt fra Filippe ræfedd ... wass ... & gifenn till Herode*, c.1200 Orm. 19,827. One also finds *he had a book given (to) him*: *Bot of Oðer wommen tua [he] Had four suns geten him*, 14c. Cursor M. 3900. However, the 'indirect passive' (Visser's term for a passive whose subject corresponds to the indirect object of an active verb) is a more recent construction. Jespersen (MEG III 15.2) says that this construction is extremely rare before the NE period. This view is echoed by many writers and is consonant with the claim that the transformational passive represents a fairly recent innovation in the grammar of English. In fact Jespersen's statement needs amplification and is disputed by Visser. Early English *ic gēaf him an boc* 'I gave him a book' had an impersonal as in (43).

(43)   a.   him was given a book
        b.   the king was given a book

Visser (1963–73: §1966) notes that in (43a) 'the passive sentence opens with the indirect object, clearly recognizable as such because of its form (a dative). In type [(43b)] it is in the zero case, yet was, in the beginning, still apprehended as the indirect object'. This can be demonstrated when the two NPs are of different number and the verb is in a tense which distinguishes third person singular and plural; in that event the form of the verb indicates which NP is viewed as subject: *the king were given books*. Visser (§1967) claims that 'the origin of [the indirect passive] may be seen as a consequence of the very frequent use – in late Old English and subsequently – of nouns without any outward sign of their indirect object character at the head of the sentence, i.e. in the place proper to the subject', as in (43b). In this view, which is described in detail by Jespersen (MEG IV 15.2), the development is analogous to that of *me thinks > I think*, discussed in §5.1. However, even with the proviso that sentence-initial NPs were often indirect objects, there are a few clear examples from late ME of NPs which are the subject of a passive verb and correspond to an underlying indirect object.[1]

---

[1] These examples are not without difficulty. Jespersen (MEG III 15.3) found (44a) 'rather doubtful'. He expected *have* rather than *am* and speculated that *one* should be read as an adjective modifying *I*, rather than as a direct object. If this is correct,

(44) a. all my shepe ar gone, I am not left one. c.1460 Towneley
Pl. ci 24

b. he was gyvyn the gre be my lorde kynge Arthure. c.1470
Malory, Works (ed. Vinaver) p699

c. if Sir Thomas thynk that he shuld be alowyd mor, he shall be.
1422–1509 Paston Letters (Gairdner) vol. 1 p252

d. I was offered iiij marcs to lese my tytle in the said tythes.
c.1479 Stonor Letters (Camden) no. 245 p83

Visser provides a long list of examples, but on inspection almost all
involve a sentential object and therefore are not instances of indirect
passives (45); these are parallel to NE *John was persuaded to leave*, where
John originates in immediately post-verbal position, is contained within
the same VP as *persuade* and therefore may fairly be construed as a
direct object.

(45) a. And afterward this knyght was bode appere. c.1386 Chaucer,
CT C.1030

b. ytte am I graunted . . . to justifie & juge all þe Iewes. c.1430
York Plays CCLXXI 23

c. he was comaunded for to sey. c.1450 Generides (EETS) 439

Therefore, it seems to be the case that towards the end of the fifteenth
century there are just a few examples of the type *he was given a book*,
where the subject must be construed as corresponding to an underlying
indirect object. Some of these examples involve textual difficulties
(see p260n), and it is remarkable that many of the attestations are
drawn from the Paston Letters. The following verbs occur in an indirect
passive construction before 1500: *allow*(1422), *learn*(= 'teach') (1422),
offer(1422), *proffer*(1422), *teach*(1434), *pay*(1440), *bring*(1450), *yield*

I could be a direct object of *leave* and the example could be handled by the lexical
rule.

In (44b) Caxton's edition reads *him* for *he* and treats the expression as an impersonal passive. Such impersonal passives have been subjected to much editorial
activity and they have often been emended to personal constructions, as was also
the fate of many impersonal verbs of the type discussed in §5.1. This may be another
such example. It is surprising that impersonals should have occasioned such editorial
disapproval. Clear cases of impersonals were common in OE: *eft ðurh ðone witgan
wæs gecid hierdum* (dative) 'after by that wise man there was a rebuking to the
shepherds'. Parallel constructions occur in Modern German: *dir sei dafür herzlich
gedankt* 'to you may there be hearty thanks for it'.

Jespersen (MEG) observed that almost all the early examples with *give* involve
phrases like *I am given to understand*. Here *I* is a direct object and there is no alter-
nating *someone gives to me to understand*, where *me* appears as an indirect object.

(1449), *leave*(1460), *grant*(1460), *give*(1470), *ask*(1490).[1] However, in the sixteenth century the indirect passive begins to occur frequently, and some additional verbs start to tolerate the construction; *say, threaten, adjudge, foretell* and *show.* The construction seems to be well entrenched at this point and steadily extends its domain over subsequent history. In the seventeenth century the construction occurs for the first time with *allow, demand, advance, licence, enjoin, appoint*; in the eighteenth century with *interdict, serve, order, make (amends), lead (a dance), lend*; in the nineteenth with *bid, pardon, secure, owe, allowance, cause, prescribe, deal, leave, assign, play (a trick), allot*; in the twentieth with *accord, advise, assure, award, charge, deny, do, feed, find, fulfil, get, guarantee, grudge, hand, hit, issue, keep, recommend, send, set, stand, strike, take, tip, vote, wish, write.* These lists include some verbs which no longer tolerate indirect passives in NE, but they are nonetheless included here in order to illustrate the extent to which the construction was productive.

Some caution is in order because there is considerable dialectal and stylistic variation. For example, the sentences of (46) are used by established authors of this century, but not all speakers would assent to their grammaticality.

(46) a. she would have been ordered air and sunlight and activity. G. K. Chesterton
      b. she was not grudged that humble place. Compton Mackenzie
      c. he had been stood a drink. G. Warwick Deeping
      d. I was recommended another doctor. W. S. Allen
      e. the purchaser is guaranteed better terms. The Times 1954
      f. I must be forgiven these memories of the past. Graham Greene

Jespersen (MEG III p309) claimed that 'it would probably be difficult to find examples like these: he was *written* a letter, *sent* a note, *telegraphed* the number, or she was *got* a glass of wine or *done* any injustice', although most speakers would now accept all (with the substitution of *radioed* for *telegraphed*). Many grammarians, particularly authors of school grammars, have condemned the construction. Sweet (1900: vol. II p118) says 'we still hesitate over and try to evade such passive constructions as *she was given a watch* . . . because we still feel that

---

[1] Again, for the reasons given above, it is necessary to abstract away from the longer lists provided by Visser. Nonetheless it is instructive to compare these dates with the earliest examples of indirect passives cited by Jespersen (MEG) *offer* (1593), *teach* (1731), *pay* (1713), *give* (1600).

she . . . [is] in the dative, not the accusative relation'. Compare Onions (1904: p41), and Stokoe (1937: p78), who comments that 'it is strictly speaking wrong to make the Indirect Object of the Active idiom the Subject in the Passive idiom'. Grammarians before Sweet usually do not even mention the indirect passive. Kirschner (1957) provides an extensive list of verbs occurring in the indirect passive and calls several of them Americanisms: *accredit, adjudge, administer, appoint, apportion, assure, attribute, bequeath, cable, concede, envy, furnish, land, loan, mail, phone, provide, restore, sell, stand, supply, tender, vote, wire, wish, write.* Some of these occur in Visser's lists, under British authors as early as Shakespeare and Goldsmith. Other grammarians claim that nowadays the indirect passive is the preferred form. Allen (1947: p276) says 'when the verb in the active voice takes two objects, it is more usual in English to make the personal object the subject of the passive voice'. Strang (1970: p151) comments that the development of the indirect passive 'is one aspect of a yet wider tendency, namely to prefer human, especially first person subjects where possible'. Quirk et al. (1972: p346) echo this and claim that the indirect passive is more common than the direct form with verbs taking two objects. Given the attitude of earlier grammarians, one might infer that the lists of permitted indirect passives might err on the side of conservatism; literary texts may have avoided a usage which occurred more freely in popular usage.

However, while there is much dialectal and stylistic variation, from the data presented it is clear that the indirect passive represents an innovative construction; it was not present in ME and began to occur from the late fifteenth century onwards. This is consistent with the claim that the transformational passive was introduced to the grammar of English in the early modern period and that ME had only the lexical passive rule.

The historical facts tally with such a theoretical claim on the assumption that the lexical passive rule relates the direct object of an active verb to the subject of a corresponding passive, where 'direct object' is taken to mean one of two things: either a NP in immediate post-verbal position in the initial phrase marker (if *I gave John the book* is derived by a transformation of Dative Movement) or a post-verbal NP which cannot be lexically related to an indirect object (if *I gave John the book* is base-generated and related by a lexical rule to *I gave a book to John*). So the definition of 'direct object' depends on whether they can be transformationally derived. Given the definition of lexical rules adopted here, there is probably no transformational rule of Dative Movement in the grammar of NE; if there is such a rule, it has many lexical exceptions, as has often been noted, and involves lots of meaning differences. Notice that both definitions include under the rubric of direct object those base-generated post-verbal NPs which appear in the dative case in earlier English. Therefore, the italicized NPs in (47) will count as direct objects, despite the dative case forms, and will be relatable to the subject of a passive as in (48).[1] In these examples no other NP counts as a direct object regardless of whether it is an accusative (f. *þis*), genitive (d. *synna*), dative (e. *heafde*); therefore no other NP can be related to a passive subject. Interestingly there is an alternative impersonal passive for (47 a, b, c), where the direct object is 'retained' in the dative case and there is no subject NP (49) (for examples see above (43); Visser 1963–73: §1959, 1964, 1965; Jespersen MEG III 15.2 for examples).

(47)   a. mon *him* ofteah þara claþa 'someone took-away from-him his clothes'
       b. mon strake *him* (*hine*) off his leg
       c. they banished *him* the realm
       d. mon geclænsaþ *hine* eallra synna 'someone cleanses him of all his sins'
       e. mon *hine* heafde becearf 'someone cut him his head = beheaded him'
       f. Silvestere lærde *hine* þis 'S. taught him this'

(48)   a. he was oftogen þara claþa
       b. he was stricken off his leg
       c. he was banished the realm
       d. he wyrþ eallra synna geclænsod
       e. he wæs heafde becorfen
       f. he wæs læred þis fram Silvestre

(49)   a. him wæs oftogen þara claþa
       b. him was stricken off his leg
       c. him was banished the realm
       d. me was toold

Visser (§1980) lists verbs which he calls 'the antonyms of *give*, such as *ætbreoðan, bidælan, forbeodan, ofteon, forniman, beniman, deprive, excuse, save, spare, defend, bereave, deny, reave, rob, spoil, prohibit,* etc.', and notes that they allow personal passives from early times, unlike

[1] See Jespersen (MEG) for many more examples.

give. This follows from the definitions of direct object given above. Passives like (50) corresponded to the actives of (51) and there are no (contemporary) alternatives such as (52). Therefore the passive subject corresponds to the direct object of a corresponding active, as defined and therefore the relationship can be effected by a lexical rule.

(50) a. why should than our ley men be forboden the gospel? 1533 More, Works (1557) F14
  b. is wretchedness depriv'd that benefit? 1605 Shakespeare, Lear iv vi 61
  c. Death shall be deceiv'd his glut. 1667 Milton, PL 10, 989
  d. Mrs Privett was spared the washing-up. 1959 Norman Collins, Bond Street Story

(51) a. they forbade our laymen the gospel
  b. they deprived him (of) that benefit
  c. they deceived Death (of) his glut
  d. they spared Mrs Privett the washing-up

(52) a. *they forbade the gospel to our laymen
  b. *they deprived that benefit to them
  c. *they deceived the glut to Death
  d. *they spared the washing-up to Mrs Privett

(ii) *Non-local passives.* Constructions such as (42b) *John was expected to win* cannot be related to an active form by a lexical rule because *John*, the subject of the passive verb, bears no grammatical or thematic relation to it. Therefore, if OE and ME had only a lexical and not a transformational passive, such sentences should not occur in these periods. This is predicated on the assumption that the alternative initial phrase marker is of the form: *np expected [John to win]*$_S$. On the other hand one would expect to find sentences like *John was persuaded to win*, relatable to *someone persuaded John [PRO to win]*$_S$, where *John* is the direct object of *persuade* and therefore in a position to be related by a lexical rule to the subject of a passive *persuade*.[1]

The historical facts are unclear. The handbooks usually fail to distinguish the two types. Visser, for example, under the heading of the type *his Majesty was thought to be out of danger, he was seldom seen to smile* (1963–73: §2137), claims that 'the number of [such passives] in Old, Middle and Modern English is immense', but immediately

---

[1] For discussion of this difference in the strict subcategorization of NE *persuade* and *expect*, see Chomsky (1965). There are various reasons to make such a distinction; see p267n.

adds 'in almost all cases the subject of the passive represents the *direct* object [Visser's emphasis] in the active parallel'. Indeed, almost all of his subjoined examples seem to be of this type (53); he also conflates sentences with a *that* complementizer like (54), where the passive subject clearly corresponds to a direct object of the related active.

(53) a. you were not bid to speak. 1603 Shakespeare, Measure v i 77
      b. so longe he wooed the matter that Coueyes owne capitaynes were inveagled to betraie theire lorde. 1571 Campion, History of Ireland (ed. Vossen) p82 35
(54) a. the beggar was comanded . . . That he ferst chese. c.1390 Gower, CAV 2414
      b. ich was preid and e-charged . . . þat y schuld preche to ʒe. c.1389–1400 Three ME Sermons (ed. Grisdale) p79 937

For OE, Callaway (1913: p59) notes that the uninflected infinitive occurs only with the passive of *aliefan* 'allow', *(ge)fremman* 'make', *(ge)seon* 'see', and *hatan* 'command', and that the inflected infinitive occurs only with the passive of *deman* 'condemn', *forbeodan* 'forbid', and *(ge)myngian* 'remind'.

(55) ða wæs heo gesegen mid . . . beorhtnesse leohtes scinan 'she was seen to shine . . . ' Bede cclvi 6

Of these verbs only the subject of passive *(ge)seon* could be construed as corresponding to something other than a direct object. Similarly Jespersen (MEG v 19.3) discusses *expect*-types like *he is seen to nod, he was believed to have a bedroom at the back* alongside *persuade*-types *they were permitted to land, a Christian is commanded to be just in all his dealings.*

Despite the confusion of the handbooks, we may conclude that passives of *persuade*-type verbs occur frequently at all stages of English. Similarly active verbs with infinitival complements are very common and Visser (§2079, 2081) provides copious examples of active verbs of mental perception and saying in OE and ME. However, passive instances of these verbs with infinitival complements are extremely rare. By Callaway's account, in OE only 'see' can be passive, and Visser and Jespersen's lengthy lists include very few ME examples of the relevant type. The passive 'see' may be by analogy with Latin *videor*, which is passive in form but often glossed as 'seem'. The occurrence in ME of these few examples is troublesome for the notion that there was no transformational passive at this time, on the assumption that the relevant verbs were two-place predicates, as they are in NE. (Anthony Warner informs me that such passives are well-attested in the Wycliffe Bible.) However, there is evidence that some verbs which are two-place predicates in NE, could be treated as three-place in ME. The OE custom of using a *that*-clause after a passive verb (Visser §2137) survived into ME and ENE, so that one finds sentences of the form of (56). In addition it is common to find forms like (57), perhaps under the influence of Greek.

(56)   John was expected that he would win
(57)   you know the lilies of the field how they neither toil nor spin

Expect and *know* must be treated as two-place predicates in NE, but such examples show that they could occur as three-place predicates in ME. Given such a possibility one is free to claim that (rare?) passives like *John was expected to win* are related by lexical rule to *np expected John that he would win*, which is an independently required structure on the evidence of (56) and (57).[1]

   (iii) *Complex verbs*. The usual definitions of 'direct object' are thrown into disarray by so-called idiomatic expressions such as *find fault with John*. Traditional grammarians equivocate over whether *fault* is the direct object of *find* or *John* the direct object of the complex verb *find fault with*. Generative grammars often analyse these as $[[find]_V [fault]_{NP} [with]_P]_V [John]_{NP}]_{VP}$ (e.g. Bresnan 1972: p147). Wasow claims that *John* is a direct object of the complex verb and can therefore be related to a subject of a passive *be found fault with*. His discussion implies, although does not state explicitly, that *fault* is not a direct object of *find* and therefore cannot be related lexically to a subject of *be found with John* in *fault was found with John*; such a relationship can be effected only by a transformational rule. His evidence lies in

---

[1] I cannot go further with this claim because of lack of crucial data. Three reasons for assigning NE *persuade* and *expect* different structures are (a) that *expect* but not *persuade* is 'voice transparent', (b) that NP+ infinitive following *expect* behaves as a constituent, but not when following *persuade*, and (c) one finds *persuade NP that S* and *expect that S*, but not *expect NP that S*. For ME, I assume but cannot establish that (i) is not semantically equivalent to (ii), if indeed (ii) was a possible structure. I do not know whether (iii) was possible; compare NE (iv).
   (i) John was expected that he would examine Bill
   (ii) Bill was expected that John would examine him
   (iii) I expected John with all confidence that he would win
   (iv) I persuaded John with good arguments to visit his mother

the contrast between (58) and (59), which suggests that *taken advantage of* can occur as an adjective, while *taken of John* cannot.

(58)   a.   *advantage sounds easily taken of John
       b.   *an example seemed (unfairly) made of John
(59)   a.   John sounds easily taken advantage of
       b.   John seemed unfairly made an example of

This evidence is not very persuasive. Notice first that deleting the adverbs renders (59a) of doubtful grammaticality and (59b) positively ungrammatical. Visser (§1986) lists 119 examples of such complex verbs but almost none can occur in the passive after verbs like *seem, sound,* which are lexically sub-categorized for a following adjectival phrase. For example, Visser cites passives of *dance attendance on, find fault with, fall in love with, lay eyes on, make fun of, set fire to, pay attention to,* etc., but these cannot occur in the relevant construction.

(60)   a.   *Martha seems danced attendance on
       b.   *Martha seems found fault with
       c.   *Martha seems fallen in love with
       d.   *Martha seems laid eyes on
       e.   *Martha seems made fun of
       f.   *the house seems set fire to
       g.   *Martha seems paid attention to

Of the 119, only those in (61) are permitted after *seem,* etc., in my speech, although none of them is much better than marginal.

(61)   a.   ?Martha seems got rid of
       b.   the problem seems lost sight of
       c.   Martha seems made a fool of
       d.   the proposal seems made nonsense of
       e.   this seems taken heed of
       f.   this seems taken note of

Furthermore the remaining properties of adjectival passives lend no support to the invocation of a lexical rule. Neither passive of these idioms tolerates the *un*-passive (62); this follows from the fact that the internal verbs do not permit the prefix (*unmade, *untaken, *unfound, *unlaid,* etc.) and therefore neither supports nor imperils the lexical analysis. Degree adverbs seem impossible in either their adjectival or verbal form (63), and neither form of the passive occurs prenominally (64).[1]

(62)   a. *advantage was untaken of the offer

       b. *the offer was untaken advantage of

(63)   a. *advantage was very (much) taken of us

       b. *fault was very (much) found with the idea

(64)   a. *the taken advantage of offer was refused

       b. *taken of the offer advantage was disappointing

Therefore, for these idioms there is no evidence that either form of the passive should be subsumed under a lexical rule; in fact, (62)–(64) provide evidence to the contrary. Perusal of Visser's list indicates that almost all examples permit a passive like (65a), whereas the (65b) type is more spasmodic and is often possible only when the direct object is preceded by words like *any, no, little, hardly any,* etc., or if the verb is negated.

(65)   a. John was found fault with

       b. fault was found with John

If exceptional behaviour is characteristic of lexical and not transformational rules, this might indicate the reverse of Wasow's claim: that (65a) should be transformationally derived, while a lexical rule should relate (65b) to its corresponding active. However, it is always hard to distinguish what is truly exceptional behaviour from what merely appears to be exceptional to one mechanism in the grammar but in fact follows from other factors.[2]

Correct historical consequences follow from the claim that (65a) and (65b) are both derived by a passive transformation and that neither *fault* nor *John* are direct objects (and therefore cannot be related by a lexical rule to a passive subject), and that there was no passive transformation before the modern period. Both forms of the passive are extremely rare almost to the point of non-existence in OE and ME, but begin to occur with great frequency in the sixteenth century. Jespersen (MEG III 15.7) says that he has found only two examples

---

[1] The latter property is not crucial since in general only 'simple' adjectivals can occur pre-nominally: *the obvious plan* vs. **the obvious to her plan*.

[2] For example, the following passives are not possible: **shame was cried over his folly,* **attendance was danced on Mary, *the better was got of Fritz*. The impossibility of such passives may be a function of *be cried over NP, be danced on NP, be got of NP* being impossible predicates, and therefore may follow from an independent characterization of a 'possible predicate'.

before the eighteenth century. In fact, rare examples can be found from as early as the fourteenth century (66) and Visser cites many instances from the sixteenth century.

(66)   a. noght is mad of Crists word. 14c. Cursor M. 23,860
       b. rule vs by rightwisnes . . . , at no fawte with vs founden be.
           c.1400 Destr. Troy 4850
       c. þei fauȝte I-fere, al-be no mencioun Be made þer-of. c.1420
           Lydgate, Troy IV 4263

Given the transformational analysis adopted here, the absence of such passives in OE and ME lends support to the claim that the passive transformation was introduced only in the sixteenth century.

(iv) *Benefactives.* Wasow claimed that *help* and *thank* (one could add *obey*) sub-categorized only an indirect object, and therefore *John was helped* was derived transformationally and could not be related lexically to a corresponding active. From this it followed that *helped* could only be a verbal form and not adjectival, and therefore that it could not occur prenominally, as a complement to a verb like *seem*, with an *un-* prefix, or with an adjectival degree modifier.

(67)   a. *a (recently) helped person is often good-humoured
       b. *John seems helped by many people
       c. *John was unhelped
       d. John was very *(much) helped by her suggestions

Visser (1963-73: §1933) notes that 'Old English sentences containing a verb + an indirect object . . . kept in their *beon* + past participle transforms the indirect object unaltered, i.e. in the dative': *ðæm mæg beon . . . geholpen* 'they may be helped', Aelfred, Cura Pastoralis xxviii 5. However, most verbs taking a dative also permitted an accusative object with no change of meaning, and therefore one finds personal passives *he wæs geborgen* alongside *him wæs geborgen*. As noted with parallel pairs involving impersonal verbs (§5.1), this is an area of grammar which has led to much editorial activity and many textual emendations. For instance, G. P. Krapp's edition of the Junius MS has **swa hie gecyðde wæron* 'so they were shown', Daniel 431, and then the author notes (p227) 'Schmidt reconstruct[s] to read *swa him gecyðed wæs*'. Therefore these constructions provide no evidence one way or the other on the question of whether there was a lexical and/or transformational passive. If the verbs are free to occur with a direct (accusative) object, then a personal subject of a passive can be related lexically to the object NP. However, *he was helped, thanked, obeyed* also occur in ME, as one would expect if the lexical rule operated on direct objects, where 'direct object' is defined independently of case forms and refers to an immediately post-verbal NP dominated by VP (see above). We are therefore left with the curious situation that *he was helped* was lexically related to *np helped him* in ME, and, if Wasow is right, transformationally related in NE. This might be explainable, but it is a more serious problem that *helped, thanked, obeyed* show only one adjectival property in ME. That is, sentences of the form of (67) would also, as far as I know, be ungrammatical in ME, with the exception of (67c); the OED cites *unhelped, unthanked* and *unobeyed*. Furthermore, OE *he wæs geholpen* seems to have had only a non-stative interpretation, as in NE. Therefore, *helped* shows no distinctively adjectival characteristics apart from the ability to occur with *un-* and one is left with no explanation for why it occurs as a passive participle from such an early date, when only adjectival, lexical passives were available. These passives occur from the thirteenth century.

(68) a. thanked hie be. c.1200 Vices and Virtues xcvii 5
      b. he shal ben holpen wel i-nouh to lede a shrewede lijf. c.1330 Why Werre (in Wright, Political Songs of England) p204
      c. he shall be holpen. c.1386 Chaucer, Legend of Good Women 1984

Since lexical passives are characteristically exceptional, one is free to claim that these are adjectival passives, but that they are exceptional in not occurring prenominally, as a complement to verbs like *seem*, with an adjectival degree modifier, and with stative force. But this runs the risk of reducing the enterprise to taxonomy and unfalsifiability.

(v) *Predicatives.* Predicative expressions such as *he was ordained deacon, considered a traitor* have occurred frequently from the earliest times (69).

(69) a. Ic Theodor ... wæs ... sended biscop Contwara burge cirican. Aelfred, Bede (Miller) cclxxvi 15
      b. þe king was hoten aþelwold. c.1300 Havelok 108
      c. Charles þe eldere ... was icrowned imperour of pope John c.1387 Trevisa, tr. Higden vi 365

Wasow argues that such constructions must be transformationally derived. If this is correct one would expect them not to occur in ME, before the introduction of the passive transformation, which, we argue, took place around the fifteenth to sixteenth centuries. A major reason for deriving such passives transformationally is that adjectives in general cannot occur in the frame [NP be __ NP], and lexical passives involve only adjectival participles. However, it may be necessary to permit deverbative adjectives to occur in such a context or in a frame [NP be __ P NP] (cf. (70)), where the preposition may be deleted optionally.

(70)   a.   there weren they dubbed to knyhtes echone. c.1410 Lovelich, Merlin (ed. Kock) 25,772
       b.   she shall be condemned for a heretic. 1681 Dryden, Spanish Friar (Mermaid) 1 ii
       c.   we are held as outlaws. 1611 Shakespeare, Cymb. IV ii 67

Wasow's evidence for treating such forms non-adjectivally is not very strong. They do not appear prenominally for independent reasons, namely that no adjective + complement occurs prenominally, as noted earlier. Complements to verbs like *seem, sound, act* are liable to well-known trans-Atlantic dialect differences. *He seems a hero, he sounds a musician* are generally supposed to be acceptable to British speakers and not so to Americans; the OED cites many examples from 1225 onwards. Correspondingly British speakers usually accept sentences like (71), where a past participle is followed by a predicative NP and occurs as a complement to *seem*, etc., in an adjectival environment (although I am not sure how freely they occur or whether they should be treated as some kind of analogical formation, more or less like *John is speakable to*, etc., which one sometimes hears).

(71)   a.   Edward already acts ordained (as) a deacon
       b.   John seems considered (as) a fool
       c.   John sounds elected (as) President

Such examples are no worse without the *as*, as Wasow's analysis would predict since [be __ NP] is supposed not to be an adjectival environment, unlike [be __ P NP]. These forms cannot occur with an *un-* prefix, but this is not a good diagnostic for adjective-hood; many participles can occur prenominally and as a complement to *seem*, but not with an *un-* prefix.

(72)   a.   the murdered President
       b.   John acts murdered in the next scene

> c. *John was unmurdered

(73)   a. the uprooted plant
>   b. the plant looks uprooted
>   c. *the plant was unuprooted

Also these forms cannot occur with the adjectival or verbal degree modifier.

(74)   a. *Edward was very (much) ordained deacon
>   b. *John is very (much) considered a genius
>   c. *the child was very (much) named Harry

Hence there seems to be no good reason not to treat these forms as adjectival. The fact that they may be interpreted statively as in (75) argues for the possibility of such an adjectival analysis.

(75)   a. the villain is called Ratman
>   b. John is considered a genius

This analysis must be preferred to Wasow's because it introduces less exceptionality to the grammar and because what exceptionality there is is in 'the right place'. The exceptionality lies in the fact that the relevant verbs cannot occur with an *un-* prefix and they tolerate no degree adverb. Such exceptionality is not surprising for lexical redundancy rules. Wasow's analysis involves exceptions insofar as the verbal participles can occur in an adjectival environment as a complement to verbs like *seem*, take no degree adverb, but are liable to a stative interpretation. This constitutes more exceptions, and transformational rules are characteristically supposed to be unexceptional. If such an adjectival analysis is adopted we may say that deverbative adjectives (unlike non-deverbatives) may occur in the frame [NP be __ P NP] and deverbatives allow an optional deletion of the preposition, as in (71).

Whatever the mechanism, there is good evidence for treating participles in constructions like (42e) as adjectives and therefore as relatable to a corresponding active by the lexical rule. In that case, one is not surprised to find that such constructions occurred in ME, before the introduction of the transformational passive.

(vi) *Stative-dynamic readings.* The ambiguity of many passive phrases between a stative and dynamic reading is well-known. *The food was eaten* may mean that at a certain moment somebody ate the food or that the food had already been eaten. Wasow seeks to associate the stative reading with the adjectival analysis and the dynamic reading with the transformational derivation, although it is by no means clear that such a correlation can be successfully effected.

One finds dynamic (76) and stative (77) passives from the earliest times.

(76) heo þa geascade, þæt þære arwyrðan abbudissan lichoma wæs in cirican broht & geseted 'then she found out that the body of the abbess was brought to the church and buried there'. Aelfred, Bede (Miller) cclxxxviii 30

(77) seo Asia on ælca healfe heo is befangen 'Asia is surrounded on both sides'. Aelfred, Orosius xii 12

However, Visser (1963–73: §1909) gives the usual view that

originally the statal pattern was the normal one, for the simple reason that in Primitive Germanic *wesan/beon* . . . was a notional verb with the sense 'to exist', 'to be (t)here' while the past participle functioned as a predicative adjunct with adjectival import . . . This replacement of the static connotation by the dynamic connotation . . . was naturally a very slow process and not complete until after a period of vacillation and wavering, which may have begun in Old English.

In short, dynamic passives of the form *be* + past participle are very rare in OE and not common in ME. This is consistent with the *tendency* of the dynamic reading to be associated with the transformational passive, and with my historical claim that the transformational passive was introduced only in the early modern period.

The development of this stative vs. dynamic ambiguity has never been adequately explained, as often noted. It is clearly related to the demise of *weorþan* + past participle, which was unambiguously dynamic, presumably as a result of the meaning of *weorþan* 'become'. The availability of *weorþan* alongside *wesan* and *beon* originally kept dynamic and stative passives distinct. The distinction was eliminated even before the loss of *weorþan*, as is illustrated by two, almost adjacent entries in the Parker Chronicle, where there seems to be no semantic distinction: *her Oswine kyning w@s ofslægen*, anno 651 and *her Onna cyning weard ofslægen*, anno 654. Traugott (1972a: p83) notes that Aelfric uses only *wes-* and *beo-* + past participle in his Grammar, but uses *weorþ-* in his Lives and Homilies very frequently; she speculates that there was a stylistic distinction whereby *weorþan* was less formal. As the *wearþ* vs. *wæs* semantic distinction was lost, so new markers were introduced.[1]

---

[1] Traugott (1972a: p83) claims that in OE stativity was marked by adjectival endings. She cites (i) and (ii).

(i) on þære ilcan tide wurdon twegen æþelingas *afliemde* (adjective) of Sciþþian

For example, Visser (§§1875–81) demonstrates in detail how forms like *the house was* (*a*, *an*, *at*, or *in*) *building* came to take on (dynamic) passive force, as in (78).

(78) a. great preparations *are making* to send forces to Guernsey. 1601–1704 Hatton Correspondence (ed. Thompson) vol. vi p174

    b. no marvel, If I found check in our great work within, When such affairs as these *were managing*. 1610 Jonson, Alchemist iv iii 66

    c. their very names *were blotting out*. 1890 Dickens, Tale of Two Cities ii p73

    d. the horses *are harnessing*. C. Bronte, Jane Eyre p323

Visser shows that a passive interpretation is certainly permissible by the time of ME and slowly becomes more common in the period 1500–1800 (the prepositional form dropped out in the sixteenth century), even though it is condemned as 'a vitious expression' in Johnson's Dictionary (1755). The construction is unambiguously non-stative throughout its history. It was still frequently attested in the nineteenth century,[1] but quickly begins to decline as a further innovation develops, *is being* + past participle, which dates from the second half of the eighteenth century and was in its turn roundly condemned by grammarians until the end of the nineteenth century (for citations see Visser: §2158, Jespersen MEG iii 13.7). Another method of disambiguation arises from the development of *get* forms, which denotes the dynamic

'at that same time were two princes put-to-flight from Scythia'. Aelfred, Orosius xliv 24

    (ii) hu II æþelingas wurdon *afliemed* (no inflection) of Sciþþium 'how two princes were put-to-flight from Scythia' Aelfred, Orosius i 25

She assumes that *afliemed* is a verbal (participle) form. However, it is by no means clear even that there is a stative vs. dynamic distinction in (i) and (ii), or that it could be generalized. The notion is difficult to test because, as noted by Traugott, the adjectival forms were not manifested in the nominative masculine singular, and nominative and accusative neuter singular; therefore many examples are ambiguous: *an æþeling wurde afliemed of Scyþþian* 'one prince was put to flight from Scythia'. Since case markings were dysfunctional at this time, one would want to see further arguments for the claim that *afliemde* in (i) is an adjective, as distinct from *afliemed* in (ii).

1 The construction survives to the present day in isolated expressions like $5 *is wanting, owing, missing*; these exist alongside the so-called passivals, *the clothes are drying, the glass shattered*, which are not restricted to progressive aspect. When this construction was productive it was usually ambiguous between an active and passive reading, which was perhaps a reason for its demise: *she was shooting*.

reading and is equivalent to the older *weorþan: the book got written*.
Strang (1970: pp150–1) notes that the periphrastic expressions developing from the sixteenth century serve to disambiguate passive phrases:
the modern *is taken, is being taken, has been taken* and *gets taken* distinguish shades of meaning which could all be expressed by *is taken* in
the sixteenth century. Despite the availability of these various expressions, *the food was eaten* is still ambiguous and it seems that the language
has, in a sense, never fully recovered from the loss of the *wearþ* vs.
wæs distinction.

(vii) *Agent phrases*. Given our distinguishing criteria for lexical and
transformational rules and the diachronic claim that English originally
had merely a lexical passive, developing a transformational passive only
in ENE, one is not surprised to find that agents could be marked in a
variety of ways in ME and that the *by*-phrase became standard later.
Until the sixteenth century the agent could be marked by the dative
case (OE only), or the prepositions *among, at, between, betwixt, by, for,
from, mid, of, on* (OE), *through, to, with*. For any given example it is
sometimes not clear whether one is dealing with an 'instrumental'
NP or one which would serve as a subject in the corresponding active,
but evidently there was a far greater variety of expressions before ENE.
(79) provides some clear examples; Visser (§§1988–2000) offers lengthy
lists.

(79)   a. Sur, I wulde be shreven at you & at no noder. c.1450. Alphab.
          Tales xlix 16
       b. thanne seide Artheur . . . that for him discouered scholde hit
          neuere be, Ne non thyng to hire he wolde diserye. c.1410.
          Lovelich, Merlin (ed. Kock) 12,383
       c. I . . . am defoyled with falsehed and treson thorow sir Bors
          and sir Ector. c.1470 Malory, Works (ed. Vinaver) p528

This variety was eliminated and after the sixteenth century *by* is the
standard form, although, predictably, one still finds other prepositions
being used with lexical passives like *John was interested in Beethoven,
known to Wagner, and surprised at Mahler.*

(viii) *Prepositional passives*. A further argument for our proposition
can be constructed on diachronic changes involving constructions where
the passive subject corresponds to an immediately post-verbal PP.

(80)   a. the bed was slept in
       b. the book was alluded to

c. the strategy was decided on
d. the plan was talked about
e. the meal was paid for
f. the target was shot at
g. the player was hooted at

In NE such passives occur quite freely and, in general, the verb forms do not show adjectival properties, which suggests a transformational analysis. By and large, these forms do not occur prenominally (81), as a complement to verbs like *seem* (82) (although here there seems to be dialectal variation and my judgments are often hazy), with *un-* prefixes (83), or with *very* (84). Furthermore, they usually carry a dynamic reading and the agent phrase is consistently marked with *by*.

(81) a. *the slept in bed
      b. *the alluded to book
      c. *the decided on strategy
      d. *the talked about plan
(82) a. the bed looks slept in
      b. *the book sounds alluded to
      c. ?the strategy seems decided on
      d. *the plan seems talked about
(83) a. *the bed was unslept in
      b. *the book was unalluded to
      c. *the strategy was undecided on
      d. *the plan was untalked about
(84) a. the bed was very *(much) slept in
      b. the book was very *(much) alluded to
      c. the strategy was very *(much) decided on
      d. the plan was very *(much) talked about

The evidence of (81)–(84) indicates that prepositional passives should be transformationally derived. There are, however, isolated instances of prepositional passives in certain adjectival environments (85) and (82 a, c). These examples do not show the full range of adjectival properties. Thus while *lived in* can occur after *looks* in (85a), it cannot occur prenominally or modified by *very*. One solution is to list such phrases as exceptional adjectives, occurring in certain of the usual environments but not in others. After all, all other major categories have lexical items with prepositional adjuncts (e.g. verb-particle constructions, nouns like *drop-out*, *lean-to* and prepositions like *out of*), so it seems natural to posit adjectives with such adjuncts.

(85) a. this house looks lived in
      b. your scheme was unheard of
      c. ?*Aspects* is the most referred to book

The history of prepositional passives lends support to this analysis and to the claim that the transformational passive was introduced in the fifteenth to sixteenth centuries. The handbooks say that there are no instances before 1300, although Visser (§1950) has found two examples. Van der Gaaf (1930: p19) found eleven examples from the fourteenth century; Visser adds a few more.[1] The construction begins to spread rapidly in the fifteenth and sixteenth centuries and Visser (§§1952–3) cites 68 new forms from the fifteenth century, and 124 from the sixteenth. For example, *be agreed on, be aimed at, be asked for* occur for the first time in the sixteenth century. Visser comments that at this point 'it was well on its way to become one of the commonest usages in the language. It appears to have been a special favourite in familiar letters and other texts written in a colloquial style.' The construction has continued to be more widely attested and to occur with ever more numerous combinations of verbs and prepositions. Even today there are many combinations which cannot occur in a passive construction (86), but this is often due to other factors.[2] See, for example, the discussion of the ambiguous *John decided on the boat* in Chomsky (1965: p142).

(86) a. *he was suggested to that he leave
      b. *the tree was painted under
      c. *Nixon was written a book about

[1] This construction must be distinguished from the frequent OE examples where a preposition preceded the verb and (at least in print) is separate from it: *ðy læs hie weorðen up ahæfene*, Aelfred, Cura Pastoralis cxcvii 3. I take these to be particle-verb constructions. One should also mention the construction with *withal* (*they were fought withal*), where the corresponding active always has *with* (*people fought with them*).

[2] For example, (86a) might be ruled out by something like Kuno's (1973) 'clause non-final incomplete constituent' constraint, if such a theory could be substantiated. This precludes fragments of constituents (such as stranded prepositions) anywhere other than in clause-final position. (86c) would be ruled out by a revised version of the A-over-A constraint in Chomsky (1977) or by most standard formulations of passive. There are of course other possibilities, but those cited have some independent motivation. Sentences like (86c) could not arise in OE and ME if there was no transformational passive, therefore such principles would not be needed for these constructions.

Our argument that the transformational passive was introduced in the fifteenth to sixteenth centuries has consisted in a demonstration, firstly, that before that time all the occurring passive forms had the properties and distribution of adjectives and were properly relatable to a corresponding active by a lexical rule, and, secondly, that the non-adjectival passives were introduced simultaneously during the period 1450–1550. There is a major fallacy in the argument as presented so far, which is that we have defined the properties of a lexical rule partly in terms of the distribution of NE adjectives. We then proceeded to see if these properties, so defined, held of ME passives. It is important to see that this is a fallacious mode of argumentation unless it is also demonstrated that ME adjectives have the same relevant distribution as their NE counterparts (recall the history of English quantifiers §4.1). Put differently, one needs to show that the ME passives had the relevant properties of ME, not NE adjectives. Such a case can be made, but some observations are necessary. ME adjectives and passive forms could occur prenominally, after verbs such as *seem, sound, look,* and with an *un-* prefix. In fact, in the sixteenth century, even non-passive past participles could occur prenominally, as in *sour turned wine* (1548), *new comen up matter* (1562), *a gone man* (1598). Both adjectives and passive forms also occurred postnominally (87) and even in comparative and superlative form (88), rendering the parallelism more extensive.

(87) a. kyng crouned. c.1400 Mandeville XII 23
      b. by the fruyte of the tre forbeden. c.1410 Nich. Love, Mirrour Lyf Jesu Chr. (ed. Powell) 33
(88) a. the hop bushe is called . . . of ye Barbarus writers humulus, of the later learneder writer Iupulus. 1562 Turner, Herbal vol. II p43
      b. the damnedest body. 1603 Shakespeare, Measure III i 96
      c. the weather-beatenest Cosmographicall Starre-catcher of em all. 1607. Dekker, A knight's conjuring, done in earnest ii D I D

However, in one respect the parallelism is more restricted: ME past participles could not occur with the adjectival intensifier *very*. Visser (§1127) cites only three examples from before the eighteenth century, but it becomes common from then on. The expression was denounced by many grammarians and labelled an Americanism in 1873 by Fitzedward Hall (*Modern English* p54). Visser (§§1127–69) offers documentation of further parallelisms between ME participles and ME adjectives, such as the ability to occur as a noun, with a -*lice* suffix, and adverbially with -*ly*. Consequently it can be seen that ME passives had the relevant properties not only of NE but also ME adjectives, and therefore that the fallacy does not arise.

The argument developed here, like those of earlier sections, has made crucial use of the simultaneity of the changes discussed. It is claimed, for example, that the innovations all follow from the intro-duction of a transformational passive, a special case of the more general rule of NP Preposing (§6.1). The simultaneity of the changes, all first occurring between 1450 and 1550, may be fortuitous or may indicate that they are the various surface manifestations of a single change in the abstract grammar. We have shown here that current versions of the EST make descriptions available whereby the changes may be related and their simultaneity be explained. This could not have been done in earlier versions of generative grammar where lexical and transformational rules were not distinguished, and therefore is to the credit specifically of the EST.[1] There are, of course, many aspects of the history of English passives which have not been touched on here. In particular, we have looked only at examples of *be* + past participle where the subject corresponds to, i.e. could occur as, a post-verbal NP if the verb were active. We have not looked at the OE inflected passive (which sur-vives into ME with *hatan* 'be called') or at similar constructions which lack the past participle form and are analogous to some examples of the Greek middle; *the house is to let, John is easy to see, $5 is wanting*. None-theless some light has been shed on the development of passives and we have accounted for the simultaneity of the changes taking place between 1450 and 1550 by making use of the distinction between lexical and transformational rules within the context of the EST. Of course, we have not explained why a transformational passive rule should be introduced at this time, in addition to the already existing lexical rule.

5.2.4 §5.2.1 and §5.2.3 are complementary in that they discuss the origin and development of the 'passive voice' in Greek and some

---

[1] However, one thing which does not follow from the EST is the apparent gradual spread of some of the constructions discussed. For example, it was noted that 68 new forms of the prepositional passive occur in the fifteenth century, a further 124 in the sixteenth, more in the seventeenth, and so on. Lest this be adduced as support for some principle of lexical diffusion, one should calculate the chances of all the presently possible combinations being attested in the fifteenth century, given the limited corpus of available texts. This apparent gradualness is probably an artifact of the restrictions on our data.

aspects of the spread of the corresponding English construction.
We have shown first that the development of the Greek 'passive voice',
i.e. the association of inherited medio-passive desinences with application of NP Preposing, was a function of the Transparency Principle.
That is, given certain earlier changes, we can explain the development
of the passive in terms of a limitation on possible grammars. Secondly,
a set of simultaneous changes in the distribution of passive expressions
in English has been accounted for in terms of some formal machinery
within the EST. In this case, claims have been made about the proper
formulation of the changes but not about *why* the changes took place.
For various reasons we are not in a position to explain the English
change or to account for the extending domain of the Greek passives.
In some areas a full account is precluded by a lack of data. For example,
often it is difficult or impossible to determine the aspect of a sentence,
but it is clear that aspectual distinctions have played an important role
in the development of passives. We have seen something of the role
of aspect in the English developments, but there is reason to believe
also that aspect was equally influential in Greek. Kuryłowicz (1964:
pp56ff) argues that the IE perfect and medio-passive endings had a
common origin. A special relationship between perfect and passive is a
recurring feature which shows up, for example, in the Romance
languages after the replacement of Latin *laudatur* by *laudatus est*,
the source of the Romance present passives, which then overlapped
formally with the perfect active and passive. This in turn relates to the
habeo vs. *esse* perfects (French *avoir* vs. *être*). Similar developments
took place in Germanic and in Modern Greek, where the aorist passive
has taken on formal characteristics of the Classical perfect: *krúbō*
has an aorist passive *krúphtēke*, where the -*ēk*- morpheme was once
characteristic of the perfect tense. Wackernagel (1926: p168) thought
that there was a semantic association between the perfect and medio-
passive present, a notion which was developed by Chantraine (1927:
pp26ff). Before them, Dionysios Thrax (*Ars Grammatica*) cited perfects
and medio-passives side by side, *pépēka, diéphthora, epoiēsámēn,
egrapsámēn*, as examples of the middle voice. It is certainly the case,
as noted by Smyth (1920: §1735), Chantraine (1953: p182) and others,
that in Homer there are far more perfect middles used with passive
force than any other middle tenses. The nature of this perfect:medio-
passive relationship is unclear and it remains a mystery that these two
categories should be formally related repeatedly but not continuously

through the history of the IE languages. Another curious correlation is that of passives and causatives. Whitney (1885: pxxxiv) noted parallelisms between the passive and the increasing frequency of causatives in Sanskrit texts, which suggest that passives somehow arise from the existence of causatives. Chantraine (1953: p179) claims that 'un point important est la coexistence d'un actif causatif avec un moyen intransitif', citing pairs such as *hístēmi*:*hístamai* 'stand'. The status of such relationships is beyond my present understanding.

5.3   The Greek moods

So far we have seen two kinds of change involving the lexicon: a change in the strict sub-categorization frame of a class of (once impersonal) verbs together with a predictable reversal of meaning for some of these verbs, and the introduction of a transformational rule in a sense parallel to an already existing lexical rule. We turn now to another type of lexical change, which I suspect is fairly common. This concerns a morphological category which is lost and is replaced some time later by a new inflectional system which, as far as one can tell, serves exactly the same function within the grammar as the former system. Such changes are difficult to explain.

We shall consider the example of the Greek mood system, particularly the subjunctive. I shall first list the major uses of the subjunctive in Classical Greek, give a brief characterization of the mood, which accounts for its use in these environments, and then turn to Modern Greek.

5.3.1   By the subjunctive mood we refer to a formal category, a distinctive set of verbal desinences. The Classical Greek subjunctive was marked by one of the intrinsically long vowels, *ē* or *ō*. When used in a main clause the subjunctive commonly indicated a voluntative expression which may take on imperative force, (89), or a 'deliberative question', sometimes called a 'question of appeal' (90).

(89)   a.   hoi árkhontes apokteínōsi tòn Sōkrátē 'let the commissioners put Socrates to death'
       b.   mē toûto poiête 'do not do this'
(90)   tí poiômen 'what are we to do?'

The subjunctive introduced by the double negative *ou mḗ* denoted what is often described as a tentative assertion, being a somewhat watered down version of *ou* and the future indicative, according to most accounts. When introduced by mè̄ ou the subjunctive denoted an emphatic prohibition, a stronger version of mḗ and the subjunctive, the usual form of a negative command. In each of these two cases the future indicative could also be used instead of the subjunctive with no apparent change in meaning.

In dependent clause types one finds a great variety of mood uses. (a) The subjunctive may be used in complement constructions to certain higher verbs, notably to those which belong to the meaning class of desire, fear, prevention and precaution.

(91) a. phobeîtai mè̄ ouk *eisélthēi* 'he is afraid that he will not come in'
      b. eulabeîtai hópōs mè̄ toûto *poiêî* 'he takes care that he won't do this'
      c. légei hópōs mè̄ *eisélthēi* 'he says that he will not come in'

(b) The subjunctive is used in a purpose clause introduced by the conjunctions *hína, hōs* or *hópōs*. The indicative is used only if the purpose is 'unreal'.

(92) a. epēlthe hína tòn Sōkrátē *ídēi* 'he came in order to see Socrates'
      b. áksion ên ákousai, hína *ḗkousas* (indicative) autôn dialego-ménōn 'it would have been worthwhile listening, in order that you might have heard them discussing'

(c) In conditional sentences the subjunctive mood is used in the protasis of an open condition referring to the future; for present and past reference, the indicative is used. In a counterfactual conditional one finds the indicative and the verb in the apodosis is accompanied by a modal particle *án*.

(93) a. eàn *epélthēi* (subjunctive), ópsetai tòn Sōkrátē 'if he comes, he will see Socrates'
      b. ei *epê̂lthen* (indicative), eîden tòn Sōkrátē 'if he came, he saw Socrates'
      c. ei epê̂lthen (indicative), eîden àn tòn Sōkrátē 'if he had come, he would have seen Socrates'

(d) The subjunctive with the particle *án* is used in relative, temporal and conditional clauses of indefinite or prospective reference.

(94) a. hòs àn *epélthēi* dialégetai tôi Sōkrátei 'whoever comes talks with Socrates'
      b. hótan *epélthēi* dialégetai tôi Sōkrátei 'whenever he comes, he talks with Socrates'

c. eàn *epélthēi* dialégetai tôi Sōkrátei 'if (ever) he comes, he talks with Socrates'

d. meneî héōs àn *éksēi* dialégesthai 'he will stay until it is possible to talk'

Furthermore, in all the cases discussed the optative is normally used instead of the subjunctive if the higher verb is in a past tense. In case (d) *án* is never used with the optative.

The subjunctive is clearly some kind of future tense. Its main clause uses are all future-referring and it occurs as a complement-type only to future-referring verbs. Verbs of desire, prevention and precaution are all inherently future-directed, but verbs of fear are not. It is only when verbs of fear refer to the future that they take a subjunctive complement-type; when referring to the present or past they take an indicative (95).

(95)   phoboûmai mḕ toûto ékouse (indicative) 'I am afraid that he heard it'

Purpose clauses are intrinsically future-directed and the subjunctive is used in other adverbial clauses only when they refer to the future or are indefinite. It is also worth noting that in several contexts the subjunctive and the future indicative are interchangeable, and in the pre-Classical language one finds subjunctives being used equivalently to a future indicative in main clauses. In saying that the subjunctive was a form of the future tense, I agree with Goodwin (1889) and Hahn (1953).[1] However, while I have viewed futurity as a necessary component of the semantics of subjunctives, Hahn regarded it also as sufficient and repeatedly asserted that subjunctives were 'futures and nothing else'. On the use of the subjunctive to express indefiniteness in adverbial and relative clauses, she said (1953: p9):

---

[1] Many linguists have sought either the basic or the original meaning of the Greek moods. Delbrück's seminal 1871 study characterized the subjunctive Grundbegriff as voluntative and the optative as the mood of wish, although by the time that he wrote his *Vergleichende Syntax der indogermanischen Sprachen* some twenty-five years later, he distinguished a volitive and prospective subjunctive, which he did not relate, and optatives of wish, prescription and potentiality, of which the latter two were derived from the first. Humbert comes to the same conclusion as Delbrück, arguing that basically and originally the subjunctive was the mood of the will and the optative the one of wish. However, Gonda (1956) contended that the optative is the mood of 'contingency' and the subjunctive the mood of 'visualization', and that the moods had no temporal significance. For more on these analyses and their deficiencies, see Lightfoot (1975b: pp14ff).

it is very easy to associate the general condition with the future condition ...
[The indefinite use] can be accounted for, it seems to me, precisely on the
assumption that these subjunctives were originally futures, and in no other
way whatever. The point is that what is always true is true of both present
and future, and, since the future represents a period of far greater extent
than the present, it is natural enough to select a tense describing it for a
habitual or repeated action belonging to the present-future sphere.

It is indeed the case that in many languages futures and indefinites can be expressed by identical verbal categories. Nonetheless
the Greek subjunctive and future indicative were not always interchangeable.

I have argued (Lightfoot 1975b) that the subjunctive occurred as a
future tense where there was no existential presupposition; where there
was such a presupposition, the future indicative was used. When making
a statement 'it will snow tomorrow' one makes an assumption about
reality, whereas there is no such assumption in a voluntative expression
(89) or a deliberative question (90). In a construction like (91b), 'he
takes care that he won't do this', the speaker may or may not assume
that in fact 'he won't do this'. This analysis claims that if such an
existential presupposition is made, the future indicative will be used;
otherwise, the subjunctive. In a sentence such as (92a) no assumption
is made about whether or not he in fact saw Socrates, unlike (92b)
where the 'unreal purpose' indicates that there is an existential presupposition, namely a negative one, that you did not hear them discussing; therefore the subjunctive cannot be used here. Reason clauses,
introduced by *because*, Greek *dióti*, etc., necessarily involve an existential
presupposition (see Lightfoot 1975b: ch.4), and therefore when referring to the future will have the future indicative and not the
subjunctive. In future conditionals like (93a) the speaker is non-
committal as to whether or not the protasis is existential. As an
alternative to (93a) one could have a parallel sentence where the verb
of the protasis is future indicative instead of subjunctive. The grammars say of such sentences that they are 'more vivid' or involve
a proposition of great certainty; under this analysis the speaker or
writer would be viewed as supposing that in fact he will come. If the
protasis is assumed to be *counter*factual, again an existential presupposition is involved and the subjunctive could not be used: *if he were
to be champion, he would be rich* (assumption: he will not be champion). It seems then, that the subjunctive mood in Classical Greek

can be characterized as a future tense used where there is no existential presupposition.[1]

Something should be said about the optative, which is closely related to the subjunctive. Grammars often assert that the optative is a 'weaker form' or a 'less vivid' version of the subjunctive. In the dependent uses of the subjunctive listed above, it may usually be replaced by the optative if the main verb is in a past tense, as already noted. In addition, the optative is used in a future conditional of 'remote possibility', i.e. where it is assumed that the protasis will not be fulfilled. It is also used in a reason clause when the reason is 'unreal', when the author or speaker of the sentence does not presuppose the reason to be true.

(96)   eisễlthon eis tàs Athếnas dióti boúlointo (optative) tỗi Sōkrátei dialégesthai 'they came to Athens on the grounds that they wanted to talk with Socrates'

The optative may also be used in indirect discourse dependent on a main verb in the past tense. Here it is an alternative to the indicative and the alternation appears to entail no difference in meaning.

(97)   eîpen hóti hoi árkhontes $\begin{Bmatrix} apékteinan \text{ (indicative)} \\ apokteínaien \text{ (optative)} \end{Bmatrix}$ tòn Sōkrátē 'he said that the commissioners had put Socrates to death'

In main clauses the optative characteristically denotes a wish (98), and in conditional clauses if the verbs of the protasis and apodosis are in the optative, the conditional is future-referring and viewed as only a remote possibility (99).

(98)   *apokteínoien* tòn Sōkrátē 'if only they would kill Socrates'
(99)   ei *epélthoi, ídoi* àn tòn Sōkrátē 'if he were to come (unlikely), he would see Socrates'

---

[1] For details of this analysis see Lightfoot (1972, 1975b: ch.4). There it is demonstrated that certain syntactic environments require an existential presupposition (complements to factive verbs like *know*, *regret* and *because* clauses) and some preclude such a presupposition (open conditionals and indefinite subordinate clauses), while many environments are neutral in this regard and may or may not involve this kind of commitment. It follows from the analysis that a future indicative will occur in a construction requiring such a presupposition, the subjunctive where it is precluded, and either a subjunctive or future indicative in neutral environments. In these earlier works the description was couched in terms of 'abstract verbs', a device which I now believe to play no role in a properly formulated grammar (see p287n).

It seems appropriate to view the optative as a syntactically conditioned variant of the subjunctive, replacing it when dominated by a past tense verb. This accounts for most of the subordinate uses. It is notable that in many languages wishes and remote conditionals are expressed with past tense forms: *if I was/became President, si j'étais président.* French uses a future stem with past tense endings for remote conditionals: *s'il était président, il serait content.* Without understanding the basis for this, it seems plausible to suggest that although there is no dominating verb in these constructions the optative may nonetheless be viewed pre-theoretically, in some loose way, as a past tense variant of the subjunctive.[1] The use of the optative in indirect discourse and to denote an 'unreal reason', above, are beyond the scope of this analysis.

Classical Greek, then, had two future tenses which were distinguished by the presence or absence of an existential presupposition. The future indicative was used where the event was assumed to be virtually certain; the subjunctive was used elsewhere. Such a distinction is by no means necessary. English, for example, has various forms which may refer to the future but their distribution seems to be unrelated to the existential presupposition which plays the distinguishing role in Classical Greek.

(100)   a. John $\begin{Bmatrix} may \\ will \\ must \end{Bmatrix}$ *arrive* tomorrow

        b. John *arrives* tomorrow

        c. John wants *to arrive* tomorrow

        d. John intends *arriving* tomorrow

        e. John *is arriving* tomorrow

---

[1] In Lightfoot (1972, 1975b) it was shown that the relevant data followed if one assumed higher 'abstract verbs' with certain properties. It later turned out that the abstract verbs postulated involved a large degree of idiosyncratic behaviour and therefore served only as taxonomic devices rather than as methods for capturing generalizations; the putative generalizations were not very extensive. This view was anticipated in some objections to abstract verbs cited in the earlier works. Here I assume that subjunctives will be generated freely in the syntax and will be interpreted by semantic rules as indicating future time and absence of an existential presupposition. If a subjunctive is so interpreted in an environment which requires an existential, there will be incompatibility in the semantic interpretation and the derivation will be characterized as ill-formed. The precise formulation of these rules would represent a considerable undertaking and is irrelevant to the limited aims of this section.

5.3.2   In the subsequent development of Greek, the optative, in this analysis a syntactically conditioned variant of the subjunctive, was lost quite early. Even by the time of the New Testament the distribution of the optative had been greatly eroded. Blass & Debrunner (1954: §§384–6) report that wishes may still be expressed with the optative, although there is 'a strong tendency to use the imperative instead of the optative'. The potential optative, accompanied by the particle *án* in a main clause, has disappeared from the vernacular and is replaced by a variety of constructions: future indicative, deliberative subjunctive, etc. The optative of indirect discourse is almost non-existent; it never occurs in relatives or purpose clauses, and only once in a temporal clause. The indefinite optative in subordinate clauses has been supplanted by *án* with the imperfect or aorist indicative.

The Classical subjunctive was also lost as a separate morphological category. The steps by which this took place are not known, but the loss was presumably a result of certain phonological changes. Compare the present tense indicative with the subjunctive (101) and the future indicative with the aorist subjunctive (102).[1]

(101)   a. present indicative

active	middle
gráph-ō	gráph-omai
gráph-eis	gráph-ei
gráph-ei	gráph-etai
gráph-omen	graph-ómetha
gráph-ete	gráph-esthe
gráph-ousi	gráph-ontai

    b. present subjunctive

active	middle
gráph-ō	gráph-ōmai
gráph-ēis	gráph-ēi
gráph-ēi	gráph-ētai
gráph-ōmen	graph-ómetha

---

[1] Blass & Debrunner (1954: §363) note that the conflation was underway by New Testament Greek and that the aorist subjunctive and future indicative were interchangeable, so that *eípō soi* (aorist subjunctive) may be equivalent to *erô soi* (future indicative) 'I shall tell you'. They point to several such cases from the Alexandrian version of the Old Testament: *aposteílō se . . . kaì eksákseis*, Ex. iii 10, where a subjunctive is conjoined with a future indicative and both have future time reference. They analyse this as a consequence of the phonetic levelling of *-sei* with *-sēi*, *-seis* with *-sēis*, and *-somen* with *-sōmen*.

gráph-ēte   gráph-ēsthe
gráph-ōsi   gráph-ōntai

(102)   a.   future indicative

active	middle
gráps-ō	gráps-omai
gráps-eis	gráps-ei
gráps-ei	gráps-etai
gráps-omen	graps-ómetha
gráps-ete	gráps-esthe
gráps-ousi	gráps-ontai

       b.   aorist subjunctive

active	middle
gráps-ō	gráps-ōmai
gráps-ēis	gráps-ēi
gráps-ēi	*gráps-ētai*
gráps-ōmen	gráps-ōmetha
gráps-ēte	*gráps-ēsthe*
gráps-ōsi	gráps-ōntai

The relevant phonological changes are those which collapsed the distinction between short and long *o*, both being pronounced as [o] and reduced *ei*, *ē* and *ēi* to a high front vowel [i] (the *i* of the 'long diphthongs' (*ēi*, etc.) ceased to be pronounced in the second century BC (cf. Allen 1974: p83), and for this reason came to be written 'subscript', i.e. ῃ, etc., in Byzantine times). After such changes the present and aorist subjunctive were distinct from the present and future indicative respectively only in the italicized forms. These changes were under way by the Christian era; Dionysios Thrax in the second century BC testifies that iotas of the long diphthongs were not pronounced, and Allen observes that confusion between *ē* and *i* in Attic inscriptions begins around 150 AD.

However, despite the loss of the morphological category, Modern Greek has preserved the Classical distinction between two kinds of future tense, and has continued to express with one set of desinences the non-existential future and subordinate sentences of indefinite reference. The Modern Greek verb system is quite different from its Classical antecedent. Each verb has two stems, an indicative and what some grammarians call an 'indefinite', which is essentially an aspectual distinction between continuous and punctual respectively.

The so-called indefinite is the morphological descendent of the Classical future tense indicative/aorist subjunctive. These indicative forms may be prefaced with *thá* and serve as a future tense, or they may be prefaced with *ná* and serve as a 'subjunctive'.[1]

The *ná* construction, the so-called subjunctive, occurs in a restricted range of roles, which are almost identical to the distribution of the Classical subjunctive.

(i) Thumb (1912: pp126f) characterizes the main clause uses of the Modern Greek subjunctives as deliberative, voluntative, optative and imperative (103). The Classical double negative constructions cease to occur, although a tentative assertion may be expressed with *ísōs* or *tákhatis* + subjunctive (104); compare the Classical *ou mḗ* + subjunctive.

(103)   a. tí nà soû'pô; 'what am I to say to you?'
        b. ho nómos ná'nai prôtos hodēgós 'let the law be your first guide'
        c. (eíthe) nà zésēi khília khrónia 'may he live a thousand years'
        d. nà pápsēis sto eksês 'stop from now on'

(104)   ísōs nà tò broûme 'perhaps we may find it'

(ii) In complement clauses the *ná* forms occur under the same class of verbs which in Classical Greek permitted a subjunctive complement type: desire, fear, prevention and precaution (105).

---

[1] I take 'subjunctive' to be co-extensive with the *ná* forms, but some grammars distinguish special subjunctive endings even for Modern Greek. For example, Thumb (1912: §213) cites the indicative as *dénō, déneis, dénei, dénome* (or *dénoume*), *dénete, dénoun(e)*, and the subjunctive as *na + dénō, dénēis, dénēi, dénōme* (or *dénoume*), *dénete, dénoun(e)*. However, given the phonetic equivalence in Greek of long and short *o*, and of *ei* and *ēi*, this is a purely orthographic distinction. The same holds of the indefinite subjunctive, whose endings are phonetically identical to the indefinite indicative (present tense). Despite citing these paradigms, Thumb notes that 'as far as terminations are concerned the Subjunctive is perfectly identical with the Indicative' (§179), that 'the subjunctive [desinence] is, of course, the rule with *ná*' (§268) and can occur only with a particle *ná*, *thá*, or *ás* (§179). To distinguish classes of endings in this fashion is to perpetuate a Classical distinction long after it has ceased to have any phonological basis. This illustrates the conservativeness of Thumb's orthography, noted above. In general it may be noted that the language described by Thumb, from whom my examples are drawn, though 'demotic' in character, sometimes tends to be archaistic as well as dialectal; and the former factor is reflected in his spellings, which are often at variance with general modern practice. In view of the many irregularities in current spelling, arising principally from mergers in the vowel system, a phonemic transcription gives a truer representation of the modern forms: but the 'historical' spellings used by Thumb have a certain value in the diachronic context, provided that the above-mentioned mergers are borne in mind; and I have therefore simply transliterated Thumb's spellings into roman (including, for example, in addition to the vowel distinctions, the superfluous 'breathing' *h*, the representation of *β* as *b* rather than *v*, and of εv as *eu* rather than *ev*).

(105) a. thélō nà grápsō 'I want to write'
       b. phoboûmai nà mḕ érthēi 'I am afraid that he will come'
       c. m'empódises na gráphō 'you prevented me from writing'
       d. prósekse (nà) mḕn péseis 'take care not to fall'

However, the Modern Greek verb has no infinitive form and some of the functions of the Classical infinitive have been assumed by the new *ná* forms. With many verbs the Classical infinitive and subjunctive were apparently interchangeable as complement types, but some verbs permitted only an infinitival complement. Where such verbs now allow a *ná* complement, this represents 'an extension of *ná* compared to the Classical subjunctive. In addition to the above uses, *ná* occurs as a complement to verbs of saying (but only when conveying a demand or wish; therefore this is consistent with the analysis of the Classical subjunctive given above), perception and causation (106). It also occurs as a subject to verbs like *gínetai* 'it happens', *prépei* 'it is proper, necessary', and can occur as a nominalization when preceded by the definite article (107).

(106) a. toû eîpan nà pēgaínēi stò spíti tou 'they said to him to go home'
       b. kaneìs dèn toùs eîden potè nà kánoun tò stauró 'nobody ever saw them making the cross'
       c. thà kámete tòn kósmon nà sâs pistépsēi 'you will make the world believe you'

(107) a. prépei nà douleúēis 'you must work'
       b. tò nà agapaîs eînai prâgma phusikó 'to love is a natural thing'

(iii) As for other subordinate clauses, the *ná* form may occur in relative clauses, just as the Classical subjunctive could, and express prospective sense (108). The relative marker may sometimes be omitted (108c).

(108) a. ánthrōpoi poû nà prosékhōntai 'men who are to be watched'
       b. glôssa poû nà moiáksēi me tḕn arkhaía 'a language to resemble the ancient'
       c. êrthen hē óra nà pethánēi 'the hour came to die'

(iv) In adverbial clauses the *ná* form is used in prospective temporal and conditional clauses, as was the Classical subjunctive (109). *Ná* is optional in these expressions, just as in the Classical language one found the subjunctive, future indicative or, with certain conjunctions, the infinitive. With conditional clauses it is worth noting that the *ná* form occurs only in the protasis, and cannot be used in a counterfactual condition (109e), again reflecting the usage of the Classical subjunctive.

(109) a. pheúga, prì nà soû súroun thúmiató 'flee before they scatter incense on you'
       b. dèn tòn áphēse, protoû nà tēs horkistêi 'she did not let him go before he swore to her'
       c. hôste nà bgêi stēn pórta tēs, ebgêken hē psukhê tēs 'before she came to the door, her soul departed'
       d. nà tón idêis, thà tón lupēthêis 'if you see him, you will pity him'
       e. àn tò êkseura, dè thà rōtoûsa 'if I had known, I should not have asked'

Purpose clauses may be expressed with the *ná* forms, sometimes preceded by an 'intensifying' *giá* (110).

(110) a. êrta nà ksegoreutô 'I came to confess'
       b. mè ponērià peripátei (già) nà mè sè noiôsoun 'go with care so that they will not notice you'

(v) The *ná* forms also occur in indefinite relative, temporal and conditional clauses, again reinforcing the analogy with the Classical subjunctive.

(111) a. hópoios kaì nà éblepe tò Sōkrátē, étan eutukhisménos 'whoever saw Socrates was happy'
       b. hópote kaì nà éblepe tò Sōkrátē, étan eutukhisménos 'whenever he saw Socrates, he was happy'
       c. nà phérēi neró, tèn emalónene 'if (ever) she fetched water, he would scold her'

(vi) There is a further use of *ná* which is worth noting. It occurs in consecutive clauses 'if the consequence is only imaginary or expected' (Thumb 1912: §279): *kaì tóso prâgma eînai poû nà 'pêis* 'it is an important enough matter for you to speak about it'; *thà phōnákso dunatá, poû hólos ho kósmos nà m'akoúsēi* 'I shall speak loud enough for all the world to hear me'.

It seems accurate to say that the Modern Greek subjunctive, the *ná* form, mirrors fairly precisely the usage of the Classical subjunctive, and in particular, the opposition between the *ná* and *thá* forms has the same basis as that between the Classical subjunctive and future indicative, being based on the presence or absence of an existential presupposition. Since the Classical and Modern subjunctives are not etymologically related and since this distinction between two ways of referring to the future is by no means a necessary one, it is interesting to speculate on why Greek, having lost its early subjunctive category as a result of phonological changes, developed a new morphological class with almost exactly the same distribution and semantic interpretation as the old subjunctive. It is usually assumed (e.g. by Meillet 1937, Gonda 1956, etc.) that the Classical Greek subjunctive was conservative and reflected the PIE usage. The subjunctive in Latin, for example, had quite a different usage, indicating (if the usual assumption is correct) that the distribution of the PIE subjunctive was changed out of all recognition. If Latin could tolerate such a change, why did Greek, when it lost its subjunctive, replace what was lost with a new formal category having the same distribution and interpretation? That question must be left in abeyance because we have little information on the intermediate stages between New Testament and Modern Greek (the New Testament usage was almost identical to the Classical), and therefore cannot draw reliable conclusions about what else was going on in the grammar at the time that the replacement took place, or indeed how the replacement took place. We are in no position to point to the causes of the introduction of the new category, for example, to ask whether the new *ná* forms were a response to some derivational opacity which had arisen in the grammar of Greek as a result of earlier changes. Although we have discussed this change in pre-theoretic fashion and have made no claims about the grammar of Greek and the formal representation of the changes, there is nonetheless an instructive conclusion to be drawn.

It is sometimes claimed that phonological changes can 'cause' syntactic changes. For example, many grammarians view the phonological changes affecting final unstressed syllables in OE (fixing of stress on the initial syllable in Proto-Germanic, reduction of final unstressed vowels to schwa and, eventually, loss of final schwa) as causing the demise of the case system, which in turn had many further ramifications and, in the opinion of some, entailed the word order shift of SOV to SVO, which then entailed a shifting of V-Aux to Aux-V, etc. An alternative view, to which we shall return in §7.2, holds that phonological changes cannot produce such far-reaching effects in this manner, and that the OE case system was already dysfunctional before the phonological changes took effect.

The Greek developments discussed here support the latter view. General phonological changes eliminated a distinct verbal category, but a new category was introduced with the same distribution and interpretation. Therefore, the destructive phonological changes did not affect the internal structure of the syntax and semantics except to entail the development of a new set of exponents for a future tense not subject to an existential presupposition. In a sense, with the introduction of the *ná* forms, the relevant effects of the phonological changes collapsing [o] and [ō], [ē], [ēi] and [ei], i.e. the loss of the subjunctive category as a distinct set of desinences, were nullified as far as the syntactic and semantic components were concerned. Presumably a similar response was available in principle to the grammar of OE: as the phonological changes wreaked their syntactic havoc, so the grammar could have developed a new set of case markers making the essential distinctions and being immune to the effects of the phonological changes. Something like this seems to be what happened in Greek.[1]

Therefore, in discussing the causes of syntactic change, one has to ask whether the grammar which would result from the application of the changes was so 'marked' or so low rated (by the evaluation metric) as to be an impossible grammar of a natural language. The resulting grammar might violate various necessary properties, such as the Transparency Principle. If this is the case, further therapeutic changes will be needed. There are various possibilities and it might be argued that the development of SVO word order was a therapeutic response to some damage done by the loss of the OE case endings, where 'damage' is interpreted to refer to a new grammar which would, without some further therapeutic change, violate some defining property of a possible grammar of natural language. One such option, illustrated here, is to reinstate the relevant syntactic category with a new set of exponents. This illustrates that it is not enough to point to some levelling phonological changes as an explanation for the loss of some syntactic category; syntactic systems can survive such erosion by introducing new forms which undo the destructive effects of the changes.

---

[1] After the discussion of the English quantifiers in §4.1, one should be cautious about claiming categorial identity on the basis of identical distribution in different historical stages of the language. However, in this example, we are clearly dealing with verbal categories in both Classical and Modern Greek and therefore can legitimately speak of replacement of one set of markers by a new set while the category designation, 'subjunctive', remains constant.

6 On cyclic transformations

Most of the early work on diachronic syntax in a generative perspective concentrated on changes in the transformational sub-component, and this work presupposed a theory of grammar which permitted a wide range of transformations in any one particular grammar. The essentially taxonomic character of this approach has already been discussed in chapter 1. In contrast, current work in EST has proposed severe limitations on the form and function of transformational rules, and Chomsky (1977) has hypothesized that two rules, NP Preposing and *wh* Movement, constitute 'the core of English syntax'. These rules play a role in the derivation of many different construction types and subsume what have been regarded as several diverse transformations. This reflects an abstract view of grammar of a very specific nature. If the theory of grammar permits English to have only two cyclic transformations, each with a very simple and general formulation, the possibilities for diachronic change in this sub-component will be limited and therefore the burden of work for diachronic studies will be shifted from the earlier emphasis. In this chapter we shall examine first NP Preposing and then some changes in the structure of the complementizer position, which affect application of *wh* Movement, and which in turn have implications for many different construction-types. The specific formal properties of this kind of abstract grammar are the subject-matter of this chapter.

6.1 NP Preposing

6.1.1 NP Preposing has been the subject of much recent discussion (Chomsky 1973, 1975: ch. 3, 1976, 1977; Fiengo 1974, etc.). For the purposes of initial discussion I shall postulate the structural description of (1), considering revisions later.[1] This structural description is very

---

[1] I assume that 'end variables' are available by convention and do not need to be stipulated in the structural description of individual rules. I also assume that cyclic rules are not annotated as optional or obligatory; what have been viewed as obligatory transformations are rules whose failure to apply yields an uninterpretable surface structure. See Fiengo (1974) for discussion.

general but I assume conditions on the application of transformational rules (of the general type outlined in Chomsky 1973, etc.), a set of interpretation rules and the so-called 'trace theory of movement rules', which will avoid misgeneration. But the conditions for operation are not at issue here. The rule simply moves a NP to the left and it is structure-preserving, shifting the NP to a position where it could have been generated directly by the phrase structure rules (the lower case indicates an empty NP position). In early discussion of NP Preposing, the rule was assumed to play a role in the derivation of passive sentences and nominalizations (2), 'middle' and what Sweet (1900) calls 'passival' constructions (3), subject-to-subject raising (4), and in '*tough* Movement' sentences (5).

(1)   NP Preposing
      np   X   NP $\Rightarrow$ 3   2   t
(2)   a. Rome was destroyed t
      b. Rome's destruction t
(3)   ice melts t, the book sells t well
(4)   John seems [t to be happy]
(5)   John is easy [to please t]

   NP Preposing plays a role in the derivation of several sentence-types. If we distinguish Harrisian from Chomskyan transformations, NP Preposing would be a rule only under a Chomskyan definition. Speaking loosely and somewhat inaccurately, Harrisian transformations map sentences into other sentences, while Chomskyan transformations map abstract structures into other abstract structures.[1] Hence most Harrisian transformations may be associated with a 'construction-type' in the traditional sense. There is a passive construction and a passive transformation, a pseudo-cleft construction and a pseudo-cleft transformation, a *wh*-question construction and a *wh*-question formation rule. Dougherty (1975) has argued that this is also true of most transformational grammars allegedly written in a Chomskyan framework, but that is because generative transformationalists have carried over the practice of taxonomic transformationalists, the arguments of *Syntactic structures* notwithstanding. NP Preposing is a very different rule, and compatible only with a generative transformational theory. Dougherty argued that within a generative transformational framework it makes no sense to ask of a certain transformation whether or not it

---

[1] For discussion see Chomsky (1968: p54 n10).

is a meaning-changing rule, whereas it does make sense to pose such a question within a taxonomic transformational system.[1] NP Preposing clearly is compatible with a syntax which operates independently of considerations of meaning and use, and since it plays a role in the generation of many different constructions, one may assume that it is not uniquely associated with a particular semantic property. In (2)–(5) the thematic functions of the moved NPs are quite different; in fact the only common property is that the NP ends up in subject position, but this is irrelevant to the semantics because, assuming there to be a rule which assigns certain semantic properties to a subject NP, subject NPs will be defined at surface structure quite independently of NP Preposing. After all, most surface subjects do not arise as a result of NP Preposing. Furthermore, NP Presposing may move a NP but not render it a surface subject, e.g. (6), (7) and the first application in the derivation of (8).

(6) who do you want t to be arrested t
(7) there was a student arrested t
(8) John seems t to have been arrested t

Assuming that NP Preposing is not uniquely associated with some semantic property, the rule will be incompatible with the strongest versions of semantically based grammars, such as one which, claiming that there is no distinction between syntax and semantics, asserts that there can be no purely syntactic rule which does not also play a determined role in the semantics of a given sentence. It is not incompatible, of course, with a weaker version which asserts that one may distinguish syntactic and semantic rules and even syntactic rules with semantic conditions, but that the various classes of rules may be intermingled and have no independence of domain or manner of application. Arguments for the reality of such a NP Preposing rule will constitute an argument against the strongest theses concerning the alleged inseparability of syntax and semantics, such as Montague Grammar and most versions of Generative Semantics as outlined by Lakoff (1971).

Before discussing this rule from a diachronic point of view, I shall

---

[1] 'Chomsky's transformations relate an abstract object with a surface structure sentence. The underlying structure is not a 'paraphrase' of the surface structure in any definable sense. The question in Chomsky's system, as he formulates the problem, is: "What aspects of the syntactic structure correlate with what aspects of the semantic interpretation?"' (Dougherty 1975: p142).

dispute two claims made for it in the earlier literature, namely that it plays a role in the derivation of middle and passival constructions like (3) and *tough* Movement sentences like (5). Fiengo (1974) argued that under the trace theory of movement rules the sentences of (3) should have a (simplified) initial phrase marker as in (9).

(9)   a.   b.

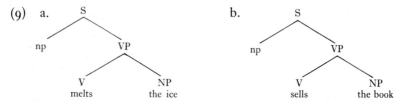

If the subject NPs are lexically filled in the initial phrase marker, a causative and agentive reading will be derived from (9a) and (9b) respectively: *Fred melts the ice, Fred sells the book*. In §5.2 we developed a principled distinction between lexical and transformational rules and, following Wasow, argued that, given the criteria postulated, the relationship between causatives and inchoatives should be captured lexically and not by a transformational rule.[1] Secondly, so-called *tough* Movement sentences like (5) have been analysed in various ways. Some linguists have argued for a deletion rule (Lasnik & Fiengo 1974, Lightfoot 1974a), others for a movement rule designed just for these constructions (Postal & Ross 1971), but Chomsky (1973) argued that the relevant structures should be derived by application of the general rule of NP Preposing. Many people pointed out severe problems with Chomsky's analysis and more recently he has proposed that they should be derived by application of *wh* Movement (Chomsky 1977).[2]

---

[1] Sweet (1900) labels sentences like *the book sells well, the door doesn't lock*, 'passivals'. Visser (1963–73: §1914) characterizes these as present-day English expressions, but they certainly were very productive in ENE and Shakespeare used the construction with many verbs which will not tolerate it today: *one of our French wither'd peares, it lookes ill, it eates drily*, All's Well I i 176; *thy glasse will shew thee how thy beauties wear*, Sonnets lxxvii 1 (see Jespersen (MEG III 16.8) for a long list of such constructions).

The causative/de-causative relationship (*Fred melts the ice/the ice melts*) also enjoyed its most productive period in the sixteenth century. Caxton uses as causatives *cease* (*I ceased him* = 'I caused him to cease'), *learn, possess* (= 'put in possession'), *succumb* (= 'subject'), *sit* (= 'set'), *tarry* (= 'delay'), etc. Similarly Shakespeare uses many verbs as causatives where this is no longer possible: *decrease, fall, fear, fly, increase, issue, perish, remember, sup*, etc. In earlier English, of course, the causative/de-causative relation had been indicated by ablaut, which survives in pairs such as *fell : fall, set : sit*.

[2] The history of constructions like (5) is difficult to determine. Jespersen (MEG III 11.6₁) cites several examples from Chaucer, but there seem to be few cases prior

Therefore, assuming firstly a lexical treatment of de-causatives (or 'middles') and passivals, and secondly Chomsky's *wh* Movement analysis of (5), NP Preposing is not as general as the earliest literature indicated and, in the grammar of NE, it is crucially involved only in the derivation of passives and subject-to-subject raising.[1]

6.1.2 If one assumes that the grammar of NE contains a rule of NP Preposing, one may ask how that rule was introduced historically. There seems to be no motivation for the rule in the grammars of the earliest stages, as we shall see below, so it must have been introduced at some point. The rule could have been introduced in a number of ways: it might have suddenly sprung fully armed from the head of Zeus; it might have developed first as a restricted transformation, gradually extending its range of application in some principled way; perhaps it developed as a non-structure-preserving rule applying only in root Ss and then was assimilated into the grammar, gradually acquiring the more restrictive properties of a standard transformational rule. No doubt there are further possibilities. The second scenario would represent a curious development from the point of view of the theory presupposed here, which claims that transformational rules must be few in number and maximally simple and general in form, being subject to severe constraints on their function. In fact, it seems that the first and simplest case holds, that the rule was introduced to the grammar of some stage of English in more or less its present form. Hence the argument for the correctness of NP Preposing is this: saying that there is such a rule and that the rule was introduced at some point yields an explanation for a set of diverse changes occurring simultaneously in the history of English. At this stage of English the grammar changed

to that. Also it becomes increasingly difficult to distinguish clear cases of what used to be regarded as a deletion process (*he was too fat to have on the team*) from cases where movement must be involved. In ME and ENE it was at least as common to find the verb of the embedded clause in the passive voice: *Suche thynges as shal be profytable to be knowne*, More, Works U33; *things were hard to be distinguished*, Stevenson M33. Chomsky (1973: p265) discusses an unconvincing way of blocking such derivations. But these constructions would involve subject-to-subject raising rather than *tough* Movement, if we were to distinguish two such rules.

[1] NP Preposing *might* be involved also in the derivations of (i) and (ii), if the rules of Extraposition and Genitive Movement are re-analysed as leftward movement rules; see below, §6.1.3. However, this is not a crucial involvement: it may be unnecessary to invoke any movement analysis for 'extraposition' relations and (ii) may be derived by a minor movement rule.

   (i) *that John left* is obvious t
   (ii) a *picture* of John's t

to yield a new output; positing the introduction of (1) gives an account of the simultaneity of the changes in the output. That is, the properties related by NP Preposing also cluster together in their diachronic development.

Subject-to-subject raising constructions like (4) have been discussed recently by Kageyama (1975). Kageyama distinguished two putative rules: Subject Raising into Object Position and Raising to Subject Position (RS). He claimed that RS did not exist in OE, but was established in late ME. Traugott (1972a: p102) took a similar view, pointing out that in OE 'unquestionable instances of subject-raising with verbs like *þync-* 'seem' are hard to find. Their rarity appears to be more than chance textual skewing as translators clearly had difficulty with finding the correct OE form to correspond with Latin subject-raised structures.' Sentences such as *ne geþyncð þe swelc gewin noht lustbære* 'not seems to-you such a battle not agreeable', Orosius xciv 30, could be treated as involving subject-raising or as having a subject complement. However, as Traugott indicates, the number agreement in parallel structures like *þonne þuhte* (singular) *eow þas tida* (plural) *beteran* 'then seemed to-you those times better', Orosius cxx 10, requires a subject complement analysis. Traugott later asserts (p152) that subject-raising was a late ME development. Likewise Jespersen (MEG III 11) claimed that constructions such as *John happened to come, John chanced to come, John was certain to come* all arise for the first time in late ME. *He is sure to come* did occur from earlier times but under the meaning that 'he was sure that he would come', cf. *he was eager to please*, where a deletion analysis would be appropriate but not a preposing rule. Jespersen distinguished two lines of development for 'RS verbs': verbs such as *happen, seem, chance* were impersonal verbs taking a dative object, as discussed above, unlike *sure, certain, unlikely*, where there was never a dative 'experiencer'. Therefore it may be the case that the subject-raising constructions with *sure*, etc., developed under the influence of types like *John happened to leave*. The development of *John happened to leave* was part of the demise of the impersonal verbs already discussed. Notice that if *John happened to leave* results from the application of NP Preposing, *John* must be moved not from the dative position but from the subject of the lower clause. Crucial evidence exists in sentences where the dative and embedded subject are not co-referential (10). Here the dative cannot be preposed: **he happened that his life was ended.*

(10) a. þa gelamp *him* þæt his lif wearð geendod 'then happened him that his life was ended'. OE Blick. Hom. x

b. *me* þyncheð þæt me fæder nis no whit felle 'it seems to me that my father is not...', c. 1205 Layamon, Brut 3290

c. it chaunced *him* that as he passed through Oxfoorde, the scholars picked a quarrell unto his servauntes. 1568 Grafton: OED

Passive constructions were discussed in detail in §5.2, where it was argued that a transformational derivation represented an innovation in late ME–ENE. Until then the grammar contained only a lexical rule to relate actives and passives, and NP Preposing played no role in this construction. Furthermore, at the earliest stages of English, when the base order was SOV, a movement analysis would not be possible for quite general reasons. Keenan (1975) claimed that it is a universal principle that the passive transformation in an OV language is not a movement rule. From a different point of view, it seems to be a plausible constraint on transformational rules that no rule can be formulated such that it will only change structure without re-ordering elements (Chomsky 1973, Lightfoot 1976a); this eliminates the possibility of a rule changing (11) into (12). This constraint is implicit in work as early as Chomsky (1965), which restricted transformations to operations of deletion, permutation, substitution and addition. Even such a loose definition of transformations would not permit a rule to be formulated which would map (11) into (12), where (a) is the structure for passives and (b) for subject-to-subject raising.[1]

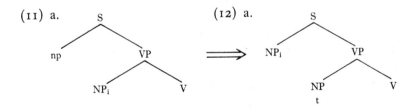

(11) a. / (12) a.

---

[1] This may be a 'generous' interpretation. It assumes (a) that transformations refer only to linear analyses and not to higher structure, (b) that a transformation can perform only one of the four operations listed, particularly that no transformation can simultaneously substitute and delete, and (c) that 'permutation' means re-ordering of two non-null elements. I am not sure that it is fair to attribute these three conditions to the '*Aspects* theory'.

(11) b.   (12) b.

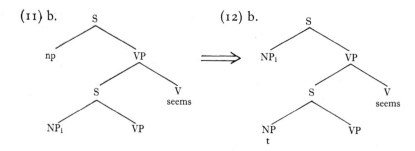

Therefore NP Preposing could be involved in the derivation of passive sentences only after the SOV-to-SVO base change. Canale (1978) dates this change in the late twelfth century. From this point onwards, passive sentences *could* be generated via transformations. Strong evidence for the availability of a movement analysis in NE has been presented in §5.2; there is no such corresponding evidence for early ME. We concluded that a movement analysis became necessary only in late ME.

Consistent with this are passive nominalizations such as *Rome's destruction*, which would require a movement analysis and could not be treated lexically. At all stages of English the 'object' of NPs has been generated postnominally, i.e. *the destruction of Rome*, even in the SOV period. However, one finds these nouns being preposed only from late ME. The earliest case I know of is *he [deofol] tihte þæra Iudeiscra manna heortan to Cristes slege* 'to the slaying of Christ', Aelfric i 26. But they start to occur readily only in Chaucer, and Shakespeare uses them very productively, including with many nouns which no longer tolerate preposing in NE. Jespersen (MEG v 7.5₄) cites several examples: *I burn with thy desire* = 'desire for thee', 1 Hen. VI i ii 108; *least I be suspected of your carriage from the court* = 'of carrying you from the court' Cymb. IV iv 190; *In my despite* = 'despite me' Titus i i 361; *thou didst denie the golds receit*, Err. II ii 17; *a great man's memory may outliue his life half a year*, Hamlet III ii 140. Meanwhile subject NPs had occurred in prenominal possessive form from earliest records, *the Goth's destruction of Rome*.

Consider now the impersonal verbs which were re-analysed as personals. In §5.1 we argued that for the earliest stage, when English had an underlying SOV order, the relevant initial phrase markers were as in (13). In (13b) a rule of NP Postposing would move *pears* to the right.

(13) a.

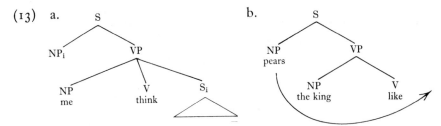

The corresponding initial phrase markers for the later stage, after English had adopted underlying SVO order but before the re-analysis and semantic shift had taken place, were as in (14).

(14) a.

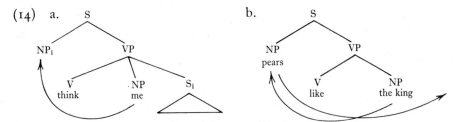

In order to generate *me thynketh I heare* and *the king liceden peares*, a rule would be needed to move *me* and *the king* into pre-verbal position, as indicated. The necessary rule would be NP Preposing, as formulated in (1), subject to all the usual conditions, Specified Subject, Subjacency, etc. – a matter to which we shall return. NP Preposing was not involved with these verbs until after the SOV-to-SVO base change had taken effect. At this stage NP Preposing served to move *me* in structures like (14a) and *the king* in (14b). After the re-analysis of these verbs, whereby they became 'personal' (being derived from structures like (15)), NP Preposing was no longer involved. Hence NP Preposing applied in these constructions only during the ME period.[1]

---

[1] Assuming the criteria developed in §5.2 for distinguishing lexical from transformational rules, this operation on impersonal verbs could be effected by either a lexical rule or a structure-preserving transformation. There is no change of category involved, which would require a lexical analysis, nor does the rule operate on NPs bearing no grammatical or thematic relation to the intervening verb, which would require a transformational derivation. In such a case the current theory is loose enough to permit either alternative, which points to what is perhaps an undesirable indeterminacy. Here I invoke the NP Preposing transformation because of the simultaneity of the innovations with those affecting passives and subject-to-subject raising. If there were no simultaneity, I should be free to claim that the relevant impersonal constructions were related by a lexical rule. Therefore, the impersonal data is consistent with the claim that NP Preposing was introduced in ME, rather than constituting strong support for it.

(15)   a.   b.

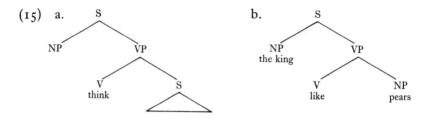

In this section I have indicated that the NE properties related by the rule of NP Preposing (passives and subject-to-subject raising) behave alike from the point of view of historical change, in that they enter the language simultaneously. Furthermore, in its earliest days the rule was of more general application and played a role in the derivation of the impersonals *me thynketh I heare*, etc. Add to this the two phenomena handled by the rule of Intraposition, motivated in §4.3 for the derivation of sentences like *to leave would be a nuisance* and split constructions like *the king's son of England*; it seems reasonable to treat this rule as a special case of NP Preposing, reformulated to move Ss as well as NPs, and one would then have an account for why these two kinds of patterns were introduced at about the same time as the products of NP Preposing discussed here. The rough simultaneity of all these innovations, involving five different construction-types, constitutes support for a grammar relating the cluster of properties handled by NP Preposing (although it must be said that the relevant dates are not as spectacularly uniform as with the English modals, discussed in chapter 2). NP Preposing is the best suggestion I know for relating these phenomena and this rule is compatible with an autonomous syntax as prescribed by the EST, but not with the strongest versions of semantically based grammars.[1] If these arguments are correct, they also militate against one particular version of the EST, which turns out to be too restrictive. To this we now proceed.

6.1.3   Following Emonds (1976) we may distinguish three classes of transformations: root, structure-preserving and local. If we assume the trace theory of movement rules and the correctness of Chomsky's (1977) proposal that NP Preposing and *wh* Movement constitute the core of English syntax, the possibility arises of eliminating the class

---

[1] Notice that no explanation has been provided for why NP Preposing developed. In particular, it has not been shown that it was a function of the Transparency Principle. In a sense the rule is foreshadowed by the already existing lexical rule relating passive and active forms, but it is not clear how that helps in the quest for an explanation.

of structure-preserving transformations. This in itself would be a desirable move and would reduce the class of available grammars.

The trace theory of movement rules introduced a minor notational change that an element, when moved, leaves behind a trace, t, as illustrated in (1). Then there is a surface structure condition requiring all cases of bound anaphora, of which traces are one instance, to be preceded and commanded by an appropriate antecedent.

Such an interpretive principle is needed independently for the distribution of reciprocals, reflexives and expressions such as *his way* in (16c); this will serve to distinguish between (16) and (17)–(18). In (17) the bound expression is not preceded or commanded by any NP, and in (18) not by an appropriate NP.

(16) a. the men voted for each other
      b. the men washed themselves
      c. the man lost his way
(17) a. *each other voted for the men
      b. *themselves washed the men
      c. *he lost the man's way
(18) a. *the woman voted for each other
      b. *the woman washed themselves
      c. *the woman lost his way

In general, traces should have the distribution of bound anaphoric expressions. For some early discussion of trace theory and its motivation, see Chomsky (1975: ch.3).

One consequence of trace theory is the recent proposal that what were formerly viewed as many different transformations are in fact instantiations of either NP Preposing or *wh* Movement. It seems fair to infer from the discussion that these are the only leftward movement rules, i.e. of the cyclic, structure-preserving class. It is also the case that cyclic rightward movement rules are uncommon in the linguistic literature and with proper analysis it may turn out that the few extant examples may be unwarranted.[1] There is a good deal of evidence for

---

[1] There are other rightward movement rules referred to in the literature, such as Heavy NP Shift (Ross 1967, Postal 1974, etc.), Right Node Raising (Postal 1974, etc.). These 'rules' remain unformulated and it is by no means clear that they are well-motivated transformations; if they are, they have unusual properties which would require a general loosening of the restrictions on a possible rule of grammar. It is worth noting that there are no 'unbounded' rightward movement rules in English (Ross 1967). More plausible cases of rightward movement are Extraposition

this position. For example, the four most commonly discussed right-ward movement rules can be eliminated. *There* Insertion and Extraposition each leave a designated morpheme in the position from which the NP is moved (19); this has been viewed by some linguists as a process whereby a trace is 'spelled out' as *there* or *it*. These two transformations effect a relationship between two positions, each of which is clearly marked in surface structure. Presumably these rules can be reformulated as interpretive processes associating the two positions.

(19)   a. there is a bicycle standing by the wall
       b. it seems that Fred left

Several people have argued convincingly for base-generating the agent phrases of passive constructions to the right of the verb or nominalization, thereby dispensing with the right movement rule (Bresnan 1972, Freidin 1975, Hornstein 1977a). Similarly Dresher & Hornstein (1979) have given several good reasons to re-formulate Siegel's (1974) Genitive Movement rule. Siegel proposed a rule moving *John's* to the right and relating the structures of (20); Dresher & Hornstein (1979) motivate a leftward movement rule, illustrated by (21), and demonstrate the superiority of this analysis.[1]

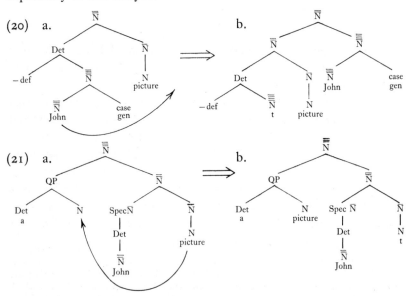

of PP and Extraposition of S within NP (*a review was published of Bill's book*; *the only novel by Tolstoy that I like*), but there are difficulties even with these 'rules'.

[1] Such a leftward movement analysis was considered by Stockwell, Schachter & Partee (1973) and rejected by them. Their reasons for rejecting it evaporate under the enriched surface structures permitted by the trace theory of movement rules.

Therefore, there is some evidence to suggest that rightward movement rules may be dispensable. If NP Preposing and *wh* Movement can be eliminated, there will be no cyclic movement rules in the grammar of English and we may hypothesize that the theory of grammar may be restricted in such a way as to preclude structure-preserving movement rules in principle (compare the discussion of base-generating *wh* elements in the last section of Chomsky 1973; likewise the end of Chomsky 1976).

So can these rules be dispensed with without adding corresponding complexity elsewhere in the grammar? Notice that they each leave a full NP preceding and commanding its trace. If there is no further movement, the trace will be properly bound in surface structure; if there is further movement, the original trace will be properly bound in surface structure by the trace left by the subsequent movement. Therefore it seems reasonable to hypothesize that 'traces' may be generated randomly, i.e. that they may occur under any N generated by the phrase structure rules, but that in surface structure they must be properly bound, i.e. be preceded and commanded by a NP. This will distinguish the ill-formed (22a) from (22b). In (23) the trace is preceded and commanded by *John* but the association of *t* and *John* cannot be effected by the Bound Anaphora Interpretation rule because it is blocked by the Specified Subject Constraint (23a) and the Propositional Island Constraint (23b). Thus in most cases this hypothesis has the same consequences as the movement analyses.

(22) a. t likes chemistry
     b. John seems t to be popular

(23) a. John wanted [Mary to see t]
     b. John believed [that t left]

One virtue of this hypothesis is that it is no longer necessary to distinguish the abstract, phonologically null elements *t* and *PRO*.[1]

---

[1] This represents a very considerable virtue. Some studies within the framework of the trace theory of movement rules have postulated a proliferating inventory of different phonologically null elements (notably Fiengo 1974). Whatever the merits of the theory, those various 'sounds of silence' are troublesome, particularly when one bears in mind that most proponents of the EST would argue against the abstract grammars postulated in the late 1960s by the 'generative semanticists', on the grounds that they involved a very loose theory of transformations and therefore imposed a heavy burden on the language learner. If the EST is not to run the risk of imposing an equally heavy burden, the inventory of abstract elements must be reduced or the abstract elements must be shown to have manifestly different properties. Collapsing *t* and *PRO* is a step in the right direction. For discussion see Chomsky (1977), Lightfoot (1977a).

Rather, a single element will be generated randomly and will be subject to the condition that it be interpretable at surface structure, i.e. that it be preceded and commanded by some NP. So far, then, dispensing with NP Preposing and *wh* Movement does not seem to be an implausible move.

However, the Subjacency Condition appears to present an obstacle for this hypothesis. Subjacency, preventing rules from affecting two elements separated by more than one cyclic node, was formulated to apply only to extraction rules and therefore would apply to NP Preposing and *wh* Movement and not to the interpretive rule associating abstract elements with fully specified NPs. The structures of (24) and (25) have been taken to indicate that the interpretive rules associating reflexives and reciprocals with lexical NPs, and specifying disjoint reference, are not subject to Subjacency and can operate on elements separated by more than one cyclic node.

(24) a. John wants [PRO to try [PRO to begin [PRO to wash himself]]]
      b. the men want [PRO to try [PRO to begin [PRO to wash each other]]]
      c. *I want [PRO to try [PRO to begin [PRO to wash me]]]
(25) a. John told [stories about [pictures of himself]]
      b. the men told [stories about [pictures of each other]]
      c. *I told [stories about [pictures of me]]

Chomsky (1973: p247) formulated Subjacency as (26), stipulating that it 'applies only to extraction rules, that is, to rules that move some item from the position Y to the superior position X'.

(26) No rule can involve X, Y, X superior to Y, if Y is not subjacent to X

If Subjacency applies to NP Preposing and *wh* Movement but not to the interpretive rule associating abstract elements with specified NPs, the two hypotheses under consideration will have different empirical consequences. For example, if there is a rule of *wh* Movement, it will be blocked by Subjacency from yielding a structure like (27), moving *wh* across two intervening cyclic nodes. But if 'traces' are generated randomly, an interpretive rule will not be blocked from associating *t* with *who* and the structure will incorrectly be characterized as well-formed.

(27) who did John tell [stories about [pictures of *t*]]

However, this problem turns out to be specious. NP Preposing never interacts crucially with Subjacency, and incorrect derivations can always be ruled out without appeal to this condition. This can be shown in two ways. Firstly, consider the structural description of (1). This was the earliest formulation of NP Preposing, when it was viewed as being sufficiently general to subsume '*tough* Movement' sentences. Under that view an NP could move over *be easy for Fred PRO to please*, etc., and the rule was formulated with an intervening variable. However, if these sentences no longer involve application of NP Preposing, the rule can be formulated without a variable, as in (28). In passive constructions a verb or nominal may intervene with the further possibility of only a preposition (29c); in subject-to-subject raising cases there can be at most a verb and a preposition phrase (29d).

(28) $\text{np} \begin{Bmatrix} N \\ V \end{Bmatrix} (\begin{Bmatrix} P \\ PP \end{Bmatrix}) \text{ NP} \Rightarrow 4 \quad 2 \quad 3 \quad t$

(29) a. the city *was destroyed* t
      b. the city's *destruction* t
      c. the bed *was slept in* t
      d. John *seems to Linda* t to be incompetent

If (28) is the correct formulation and there is no intervening variable the rule will never apply over more than one cyclic node, and this will follow from its structural description.

Second, even if we retain the more general structural description of (1), incorrect derivations can be eliminated without appeal to Subjacency. Normally *John was expected to appear to win* would be derived from an initial (30a) by two successive applications of NP Preposing, yielding (30b). If *John* were to move directly to the highest np (31a) (violating Subjacency), the derivation would be blocked by Emonds' theory of empty nodes, which requires them to be filled at some point in the derivation. If the lower NP were lexically specified (31b), the movement would be blocked by the Specified Subject Constraint. If the lower NP were an abstract element, the movement would be permitted if the PRO were controlled by *John* (31c), but it would be blocked by the usual version of the Specified Subject Constraint if the PRO were controlled by some other NP (31d). The movements illustrated in (32) would be blocked by the A-over-A condition.

(30)   a. np was expected [np to appear [John to win]]
     b. John was expected [t to appear [t to win]]

(31)   a. John was expected [np to appear [t to win]]
     b. np was expected [Bill to appear [John to win]]
     c. John was expected [PRO to appear [t to win]]
     d. np was persuaded Bill [PRO to appear [John to win]]

(32)   a. *John seems PRO to read [stories about t]$_{NP}$
     b. *John was read [stories about t]$_{NP}$

If Subjacency generally affects cyclic NP extraction rules but NP Preposing only vacuously, then under the assumptions of this section there is only one further rule which will be subject to the constraint, namely the generalized *wh* Movement. In this event there is no reason to formulate a general condition, since it applies only to one rule. Therefore if the two rules were eliminated and *wh* elements and traces were generated randomly, i.e. under any N or COMP, one could impose a constraint on the interpretability of elements in COMP, which would have the same effect as the former Subjacency and COMP-to-COMP conditions. (33) will suffice to distinguish the structures of (34) and (35).

(33)   an element in COMP must be associated with an abstract element either in its own cyclic domain or in the next lowest COMP (where 'its own cyclic domain' means in the same $\bar{S}$ and separated from $\bar{S}$ by no more than one intervening NP node)

(34)   a. [who]$_{COMP}$ [did you meet t]$_S$
     b. [who]$_{COMP}$ [did you see [pictures of t]$_{NP}$]$_S$
     c. *[who]$_{COMP}$ [did you hear [stories about [pictures of t]$_{NP}$]$_{NP}$]$_S$

(35)   a. [who]$_{COMP}$ did you believe [[t]$_{COMP}$ Mary saw t]$_{\bar{S}}$
     b. *[t]$_{COMP}$ did you believe [[who]$_{COMP}$ Mary saw t]$_{\bar{S}}$
     c. *[t]$_{COMP}$ did you believe [[t]$_{COMP}$ Mary saw t]$_{\bar{S}}$
     d. *[who]$_{COMP}$ did you believe [[ ]$_{COMP}$ Mary saw t]$_{\bar{S}}$

(34) illustrates the force of 'in its own cyclic domain'. In (35a) *who* is associated with the *t* in the next lowest COMP, which is in turn associated with the *t* in its own cyclic domain. In (35b) the *t* in the higher COMP cannot be associated with an abstract element in its own cyclic domain or in the next lowest COMP, because there is none available; if there were (35c), the highest *t* would not be 'interpretable' because there is no fully specified NP preceding and commanding it. In (35d) there is no abstract element with which *who* may be associated, i.e. in its cyclic domain or in the lower COMP. Therefore, (35b, c, d) are ill-formed surface structures.

Under Emonds' hypothesis, that the output of a structure-preserving transformation should be generable by the independently motivated phrase structure rules, the question clearly arises of whether such transformations are dispensable if their outputs can be base-generated. Several linguists have speculated along these lines (e.g. Brame 1976; Bresnan 1978; Chomsky 1973: §17; 1976; Freidin 1975), but it appeared to be necessary to retain transformations for a variety of reasons. However, under the trace theory of movement rules, it seems plausible to eliminate this class of rules, exploiting the enriched notion of surface structures and the possibility of permitting semantic interpretation rules to have access only to surface structure syntactic analyses. Notice a matter of logic: it is not necessary to argue for the superiority of a grammar including (33) over one with NP Preposing, *wh* Movement, and the COMP-to-COMP and Subjacency conditions. Notational equivalence will suffice for us to prefer the former grammar, because it permits a more restrictive *theory* of grammar, namely one which makes structure-preserving transformations unavailable. If it should turn out that new interpretive principles are needed, then the issue would probably be purely notational; as far as I can see, such principles are not needed.

In outlining this possibility many assumptions have been made, some of which are controversial. It is therefore not possible to claim with conviction that the elimination of structure-preserving transformations can be successfully effected. In §5.2 we argued for a principled distinction between lexical and structure-preserving transformational rules and showed that making such a distinction yielded correct predictions about English and an insightful account of some historical changes. It is not clear whether the right predictions will continue to be made if the cyclic movement rules are eliminated and viewed as instantiations of the interpretive rule dealing with bound anaphoric expressions. For example, while transformations cannot relate different categories it is not obvious that a similar constraint will hold of interpretive rules. If it does not hold, the question arises of whether the correct consequences follow from a lexical passive rule and, instead of NP Preposing, a general interpretive rule relating *John* and *t* in a surface structure like *John was arrested t*. We shall leave this as an open question.

While the elimination of a class of transformations is an attractive prospect from many points of view, on the evidence of §6.1.2 a theory precluding structure-preserving transformations such as NP Preposing may be too restrictive. We have shown that one can account for the simultaneity of various late ME changes by saying that they are the consequences of the introduction of a new transformation, NP Preposing. If such transformations are precluded in principle, it is difficult to see how to account for the nature of the diachronic data. It is not possible to claim that a new interpretive rule was introduced since the rule associating a bound anaphoric expression with a full NP higher and to the left is much more general and deals with more cases than those handled by NP Preposing. Nor can one claim that the structural description of the interpretive rule was extended to deal with configurations of a full NP preceding and commanding a trace, since one must assume that the rule already capable of treating instances where the higher NP happened to be a *wh* word. Certainly one finds examples of *wh* words preceding and commanding the position in which they must be understood, and in no other relation to that position. Therefore, it is difficult to see how an appropriate Bound Anaphora Interpretation rule could be formulated for the earlier stage of the language; it would associate bound anaphoric expressions with NPs higher and to the left, but one particular bound anaphoric expression, namely *t*, could be associated only with one particular kind of NP, a *wh* element.

So far we have assumed that if there are two grammars of a certain stage of a language, we shall prefer the one which permits an account of the simultaneity of some changes leading to or following from that stage (allowing one to specify a single change in the abstract grammar, the consequences of which are the surface changes which occurred simultaneously). This assumption has been the basis for a series of arguments about the form of particular grammars and about restrictions imposed by a general theory of grammar. At some points we have adduced support for restrictions imposed by current versions of the EST; at other points we have argued for further restrictions, imposing a requirement that derivations must be subject to a Transparency Principle, which entails that the transformational sub-component may effect only fairly minimal changes on a given phrase marker. On the same assumptions, we now have an argument *against* a further restriction on available grammars. A theory of grammar precluding structure-preserving transformations, although plausible from certain points of view, turns out to be too restrictive and does not permit the formulation of a grammar of ME which allows an account of the simultaneity of the changes discussed in §6.1.2.

The fact that the simultaneity of the changes discussed can be captured by specifying the introduction of a NP Preposing transformation turns out to be an interesting claim with relation to theories of grammar. Such a diachronic claim is compatible with current conceptions of the EST, but not with several other modern theories of grammar. In particular, it is incompatible with a Harrisian conception of transformational grammar, with most versions of semantically based grammars and with a more restrictive version of the EST, which debars structure-preserving transformations. Under the assumptions developed in this book, proponents of such theories will have to seek an alternative account of the simultaneity of the late ME changes.

6.2 wh Movement

6.2.1 In this section we shall examine some changes affecting the distribution of the complementizer *that*, particularly in interrogative and relative constructions involving a *wh* word.[1] The changes in surface patterns may be described in various ways; we shall argue that the correct description is in terms of changes in the possible (surface) constituent membership of a node COMP. The argument will appeal to the simultaneity of relevant surface changes and to restrictions on possible grammars imposed by current versions of the EST. The discussion will illustrate the consequences of studying diachronic syntax in the context of a restrictive theory of grammar, as opposed to the earlier tendency to describe surface changes exclusively as the consequence of changes in the formulation of transformational rules, where transformational rules could have many different formal properties.

Before discussing the proper description of changes occurring in ME, I shall demonstrate briefly that in a relative clause (36a), *that* is a complementizer, just as it is in an object complement like (36b), and then I shall proceed to outline a treatment of complementizers and *wh* constructions.

(36) a. the runner that Percy trained came first
      b. Achilles said that Briseis was best

---

[1] This section owes much to initial work by Lydia White (1976). There are many aspects of complementizers and of relative and interrogative clauses which are not discussed here. I am interested mostly in the interaction between these areas of grammar and I hope that what is omitted does not have crucial consequences for the analyses outlined. No doubt some of the analysis should be modified in the light of Chomsky & Lasnik (1977), which I received after this section was completed. I have not yet worked out the full implications of their analysis and confine myself to a few parenthetical comments.

Traditional grammarians often took ME *that* as a reflex of the OE demonstrative pronoun *þæt* and treated it as a relative pronoun, being an alternative to *who, which* (Curme 1931, Einenkel 1916, Lohmann 1880, Mossé 1945, Onions 1904). Jespersen (MEG III 165–7), Klima (1964a), Bresnan (1972) and others have viewed *that* in (36a) as a marker of subordination, a 'complementizer'. The latter view, which I take to be correct, asserts that a *that* introducing a relative clause has the properties and distribution of a clause marker and not of a pronoun. The following six reasons support this position.

(i) Unlike *wh* words, *that* cannot occur as the object of a preposition when introducing a relative clause (37); in general NPs may occur freely after prepositions.

(37) a. the track on which he ran had six lanes
      b. the track which he ran on had six lanes
      c. *the track on that he ran had six lanes
      d. the track that he ran on had six lanes

(ii) Geoghegan (1975), citing an unpublished paper by Downing, points to dialects which distinguish (38) from the ungrammatical (39). On the assumption that *which* is base-generated only within a NP, there is no possible source for (39), since there is no available empty NP node from which the clause-initial *which* could have been moved; hence the ungrammaticality.[1] There is no such problem with the sentences of (38), for which an initial phrase marker can be provided by appeal to independently needed phrase structure rules. Here the anaphoric NP of the relative clause is neither preposed by *wh* Movement nor deleted under identity and hence is phonologically realized as a pronoun; such derivations appear to be acceptable in certain dialects.

---

[1] If, as suggested in the last section, there are no cyclic movement rules and *wh* Movement proves to be a fiction, a distinction between (38) and (39) still emerges. Under this view, the *wh* element would be base-generated in COMP and all other NP slots may also be filled. However, such a structure would be uninterpretable because, as discussed in §6.1 and below, the relative clause semantic interpretation rule requires a head noun followed by a *wh* link and then an 'open sentence', containing a NP 'gap', i.e. a trace t. On the other hand, in (38) there is in surface structure no *wh* element to be so associated with a trace. In most dialects the interpretive rules apply at shallow structure, i.e. before the *wh* word is optionally deleted, and therefore there is a *wh* word to be interpreted; the dialect discussed by Downing might be described as permitting interpretation at *surface* structure, after *wh* Deletion.

(38) a. that's the problem *that* I asked you to find out from Fred
about it
   b. I got some seeds *that* I didn't know how tall they grew
(39) a. *that's the problem *which* I asked you to find out from Fred
about it
   b. *I got some seeds *which* I didn't know how tall they grew

(iii) *That* cannot occur in a 'headless' relative, unlike *wh* words
(40). If the *wh* words are NPs and *that* is not, one can distinguish a
rule (44b) which deletes only *wh* elements where they are preceded by
a NP. Notice that *wh* Deletion, as formulated, will not apply in a headless relative, because the *wh* word would then be preceded by PRO,
an abstract element which, like all such abstract elements, is 'invisible'
to syntactic rules on the assumptions of §1.4. (Chomsky & Lasnik
(1977) present a simpler analysis: any element in COMP may be
deleted freely, with the principle of recoverability blocking deletion of
anything with semantic content. Thus deletion may occur in relative
clauses, but not in direct or indirect questions or in appositive relatives,
where a raising analysis (or equivalent) is not possible. This suffices to
rule out (40c), etc.)

(40) a. you'll get what you want
   b. you'll get who you want
   c. *you'll get that you want

(iv) In general relative pronouns can occur as indefinites with an
-ever suffix, *whoever, whatever, whichever*, but **thatever* is not found.
(v) The clear case of the complementizer *that* (36b) and the *that*
introducing relative clauses can be phonologically reduced to [ðət] or
[t], unlike the demonstrative *that* and the pronouns *which, who* and
what, which cannot be so reduced. Compare (41) and (42), where
reduction can occur on both instances of *that* in (41), but on neither
what nor the demonstrative *that* in (42). Bresnan (1971) has argued
that only 'syntactic dependents' undergo reduction of this type;
clitics, prepositions and complementizers could be defined as 'dependents', but not nouns or adjectives.

(41) I know *that* you ran the way *that* we planned
(42) *that* track isn't *what* it's cracked up to be

(vi) If the relative *that* were a form of the demonstrative, one would expect it to be inflected at least for number and to appear as *those* when the relativized NP was plural.[1]

Assuming, then, that *that* in (36a) is a complementizer and noting the arguments of Bresnan (1970) to the effect that a COMP node must occur in initial phrase markers for the purpose of strict sub-categorization and cannot be introduced by transformational rule (as proposed by Rosenbaum 1967, Lakoff 1968 and others), we shall adopt the phrase structure rules of (43), the cyclic transformations of (44) and a spelling or 'house-keeping' rule (45).

(43)   a. $\overline{S} \rightarrow$ COMP   S

b. COMP $\rightarrow (\left\{\begin{matrix} PP \\ NP \\ AdjP \\ Conj \end{matrix}\right\}) \pm$ WH

(44)   a. *wh* Movement
          [   ]$_{COMP}$ X   wh $\Rightarrow$ 3   2   t
       b. *wh* Deletion
          [NP   wh   X]$_{NP} \Rightarrow$ 1 $\varnothing$ 3

(45)   [   ]$_{COMP} \rightarrow$ *that*

Note that COMP is obligatory in any $\overline{S}$ and in the initial phrase marker may contain a conjunction like *if*, *when*, etc., or an empty NP, PP or AdjP; therefore *wh* Movement is a structure-preserving transformation, moving a *wh* phrase into the COMP position under an empty NP or PP. The fact that *wh* Movement is cyclic and subject to the Subjacency Condition entails that a sentence like *who do you think Kirsten said*

---

[1] Note also that *that* introduces only restrictive relatives, not appositives. While restrictive relatives are clearly subordinate clauses, appositives have some characteristics of coordinate structures, which may be related to the non-occurrence of the 'subordinator' *that* (but see the parenthetical comment on p315). This is not to suggest that appositive relatives be derived from coordinate structures in the initial phrase marker, as suggested by Ross (1967) and others. The rule moving such a coordinate S under a NP would violate all known constraints on movement rules, such as the Specified Subject and Subjacency Conditions and Ross' Complex NP and Coordinate Structure Constraints, as suggested by sentences (i) and (ii).
   (i) Linda believes [the claim [that Susan, who is tall, is a pigmy]]$_{NP}$
   (ii) Linda plays chess and Susan, who is tall, badminton
Geoghegan (1975) offers a fallacious argument for the view that *that* in (36a) is not a pronoun, based on the fact that it cannot be inflected, but she fails to note that *which* and, in most dialects, *who* are also uninflected, although she treats them as pronouns. An argument might be constructed on the basis of the inability of *that* to tolerate a genitive marker, although *which* shares this inability.

Heidi saw? would be derived by successive applications of the rule, as indicated in (46).

(46)  [[who]$_{COMP}$do you think [[t]$_{COMP}$Kirsten said [[t]$_{COMP}$[Heidi saw t]$_s$]$_{\bar{s}}$]$_s$]$_{\bar{s}}$]

There are many reasons to adopt such a successive cyclic analysis. For example, impermissible derivations like (47) will be blocked by Subjacency since the offending movement would cross two intervening cyclic nodes, as indicated, and NPs do not allow a COMP in initial position which would otherwise act as an escape hatch, like the middle COMP in (46). Therefore, it is not necessary to appeal to an otherwise unnecessary island contraint such as Ross' Complex NP Constraint. For discussion and further arguments see Chomsky (1977) and Lightfoot (1977a).[1]

(47) a. [who]$_{COMP}$do you believe [the claim [[that]$_{COMP}$Heidi saw t]$_{\bar{s}}$]$_{NP}$

   b. [who]$_{COMP}$did you hear [the story about [a picture of t]$_{NP}$]$_{NP}$

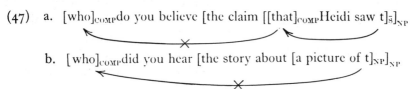

The successive cyclic nature of *wh* Movement is an essential ingredient of Chomsky's (1977) proposal, briefly outlined in §1.4, to treat what have hitherto been viewed as many separate transformations as special cases of *wh* Movement and to subsume Ross' Complex NP, Co-ordinate Structure and *wh* Island Constraints under the already needed Subjacency and Specified Subject Conditions.

[1] I leave open the question of whether (45) is truly a transformational rule or a 'housekeeping' rule, as claimed by Chomsky (1973 n53). The matter is discussed speculatively below. In (45) I omit various conditions imposed by Chomsky (1973) on his analogous rule (199.d); these restrictions seem to be unnecessary. If *that* is inserted into a COMP which is specified as + WH, an uninterpretable structure will result if we assume the interpretive rule for interrogatives outlined in chapter 1; therefore it is redundant to specify in (45) that COMP must be − WH. If a *wh* element moves through a COMP, as in (48), leaving a trace, the structural description for (45) will still be met if, following the proposals of §1.4, traces are 'invisible' to syntactic rules.

   I assume that semantic interpretation takes place at shallow structure, before the application of rules like *wh* Deletion. In which case, one may pose the question of whether such rules, applying between shallow and surface structure, fall into the same formal class as other transformations. Chomsky & Lasnik (1977) define a level of 'surface structure' which is the input to semantic interpretation rules and precedes all deletion rules; this is a novel definition of surface structure but corresponds to the view adopted here, where our 'shallow structure' is equivalent to Chomsky & Lasnik's 'surface structure'.

In the analysis of (43)–(45) I assume that $+$WH (essentially the 'Q' of Baker 1970) underlies direct and indirect questions, whereas $-$WH underlies relatives and ordinary complement clauses. These features will permit the strict sub categorization necessitated by the observations of Bresnan (1970) and they will play an important role in the semantic interpretation of relative clauses, embedded questions and statements. Furthermore, if a lexical NP is inserted into COMP by the base rules, it will be uninterpretable since it will bear no thematic relation to any verb in the structure (unless associated with a base-generated t, under the assumption that there are no movement rules; perhaps an additional statement would be needed to eliminate this possibility); thematic relations are assigned in terms of the position of a NP in the initial phrase marker (recoverable at surface structure under the trace theory of movement rules). Furthermore, Chomsky (1977) points out that 'the rule of interpretation for relatives requires that the relative be taken as an open sentence satisfied by the entity referred to by the NP in which it appears'. Therefore, if all the NP positions in a relative structure are filled by lexical material, there will be no open sentence and the interpretation rule will be unsatisfied. The relative interpretive rule will require also that in shallow structure (crucially before *wh* Deletion) COMP is occupied by a *wh* element, constituting a link between the head NP and the position in the embedded clause, now marked by t, where it must be understood; the corresponding interpretive rule in the grammar of ME will not require such a link since at that stage acceptable relatives could apparently be derived by on-site deletion-under-identity of the lower NP, as we shall see. If a $-$WH COMP is not filled by a *wh*-phrase or a conjunction, it may optionally be realized as *that*, inserted by rule (45) (otherwise null or *for*). Recall from §4.2 that *for* in *it would bother her for me to see you* or *this is the person for you to see* is base-generated under the preposition slot in COMP. We may assume further that *whether* derives from *wh* Movement on *wh + either*, and (with Bresnan 1972) that headless relatives like *he got what he wanted* derive from full relatives with non-lexical heads: *he got [PRO [he wanted wh]$_S$]$_{NP}$.*[1]

For illustration I now provide two sample derivations.

---

[1] The correct analysis of 'headless' relatives may be as given on p315, but there are reasons to postulate a raising rule. Under this view the head NP would be moved first into COMP and then raised to the empty position. This raising rule would spell out any *wh* word marked [$-$animate] as *what*; this would account for the use of *what* only in headless relatives and the absence there of *which*.

(48) a. to whom did you say (that) Kirsten gave it?

   b. [[to whom]$_{PP}$]$_{COMP}$did you say [[[[t]$_{PP}$]$_{COMP}$Kirsten gave it t]$_{\bar{s}}$

                                                                        $-$WH

(49) a. I saw the woman (that) you met

   b. I saw [the woman[[[who]$_{NP}$]$_{COMP}$you met t]$_{\bar{s}}$]$_{NP}$

                                        $-$WH

     $\emptyset$

In (48) *wh* Movement preposes the PP *to whom* successively to the
highest COMP. The COMPs contain a PP and the movements are
structure-preserving. If the COMPs had contained NPs, only *who did
you say (that) Kirsten gave it to?* could be derived, where only the NP
is moved; if both COMPs contained neither NP nor PP, no movement
would be possible, yielding the 'echo question' *you said that Kirsten
gave it to whom?*; if the lower COMP contained a NP and the higher
COMP a PP or zero, one would derive [PP]$_{COMP}$ *you said* [*who*]$_{-WH}$
Kirsten gave it to t, which is ill-formed in that the empty PP has not
been filled at any point in the derivation and a *wh* element is left at
surface structure in a COMP marked $-$WH; if the highest COMP
contains NP and the lower is null, again no movement is possible,
since *who* cannot move directly to the highest COMP without violating
the Specified Subject Condition. Given the structure of (48b) and two
successive applications of *wh* Movement, the lower COMP may be
spelled out as *that*, since it contains no lexical material and abstract
elements are invisible to syntactic rules. In (49b) *wh* Movement applies
in structure-preserving fashion, yielding *the woman whom you met*.
This may be followed by *wh* Deletion, which in turn may be followed
by the rule inserting *that* since there would be no lexical material in
COMP after application of *wh* Deletion. If *wh* Deletion did not apply,
that could not be inserted since COMP would contain lexical material
(in addition to the feature $-$WH) and the structural description of (45)
would not be met. Notice that the structural description of *wh* Deletion
(44b) ensures that it applies only to structures underlying relative
clauses. For further details of this analysis, including some motivation
and justification, see Chomsky (1973).[1]

[1] I have modified Chomsky's treatment in various ways. For example, I do not
postulate his 'Surface Exclusion Filter' (1973: (203)) nor his first condition on the
rule of *that* Insertion (199.d). These ensure the presence of some relative marker
when the subject of the embedded clause has been relativized. However, this is
not needed in the grammar if one assumes that Bever & Langendoen's perception
strategy, sketched below, plays some filtering role. Chomsky (1977), observing the

6.2.2   One consequence of the above analysis is that in any given clause *for, that* and *wh* elements are mutually exclusive in the COMP position. This was not always so and we turn now to relevant data from earlier stages of English. We shall deal first with ME, because that will help to elucidate the OE data, and we examine regular complement clauses, relatives, embedded questions and adverbial clauses.

In ME, ordinary complement clauses could be introduced by *that.* As in OE and NE, *that* was optional in most contexts.

(50)   a. hure goostely fadur . . . seid þat she must foryeve þe pore woman. ME Sermons
   b. and she desyreth of hym that he schuld shewe you the endentures mad betwen the knyght . . . and hym. Paston Letters

Relative clauses could be introduced by an optional *that,* which was indeclinable and, as in OE and NE, could not be preceded by a preposition. It occurred in all other contexts, whether the head noun was animate or inanimate, or whether the clause was restrictive or non-restrictive (51). Relatives were also introduced by *which, whose* and *whom* (52), although this represented a ME innovation.[1] *Which* first occurred as a relative in the twelfth century, becoming entrenched in the fourteenth, and was followed soon by *whose* and *whom.* Traugott (1972a) and Geoghegan (1975) note that *which* was used at first almost exclusively with prepositions, so the new relative words served only for oblique cases; *who* did not occur as a relative until ENE, as we shall see below.[2]

occurrence of *which that,* etc., in ME says that 'there are a number of apparently, rather idiosyncratic rules that determine the phonetic realization of the items in COMP. A formulation given in Chomsky (1973) can be considerably improved and extended, but I will not go into the matter here.' The improved and extended version appears in Chomsky & Lasnik (1977), who distinguish cases like Bever & Langendoen's *the horse raced past the barn fell* from *John is here is surprising,* where the former is really grammatical and will be understood with prompting or in an appropriate context; the latter is ungrammatical and is so characterized by a filter (linked to a perceptual strategy). If one allows perceptual strategies to play a filtering role, as suggested in §1.5, it is not clear that one needs the distinction drawn by Chomsky & Lasnik.

[1] The *wh* pronouns could be omitted under certain conditions, as could *that.* Thus elliptical or 'asyndetic' relatives developed for the first time. The conditions for permissible asyndetic relatives were subject to historical change, as noted below. Lohmann (1880) and Flebbe (1878) are good sources of data on this, and Lohmann argues that the changing conditions for ellipses are related to the OV-to-VO word order change.

[2] *Wh* relatives first arose in the twelfth century and Hewett (1904) reports that in Wyclif's Bible of 1384 the overwhelming majority of relative clauses were introduced by *that*: 801 examples (76%), compared to 171 instances of *which* (16%), the remaining 8% being made up of *who* and *whose.* However, Tyndale's Bible of 1526 had 562 cases of *which* (50%) and 503 occurrences of *that* (44%).

(51) a. besechyng her *that* is the cause of this translation. 1485 Caxton
    b. demest þou nat ... þat al þing þat profiteþ is good. c.1386
       Chaucer, Boethius
(52) a. that is my nece and called is Crysede, *Which* som men wolden
       don oppressioun. c.1386 Chaucer, Troil. II 1418
    b. and now thou woldest falsely been about To love my lady,
       whom I love and serve. c.1386 Chaucer, Knight's Tale 1142

Two properties of ME relatives which distinguish them from NE
are (a) the possibility of *that* immediately following *wh* relative words,
not only the newly introduced pronouns *which, whose* and *whom* but
also after the older *while* and *when* (53), and (b) the fact that *who* did
not exist as a relative pronoun until the sixteenth century, after the use
of *that* with *wh* words had begun to decline. Klima (1964a: p271) notes
that it is a well-known fact about ME syntax that 'during the period
of Chaucer, nominative *who* ... does not occur as a relative pronoun
introducing *attributive* relative clauses [i.e. relatives with lexical heads]
and thus it follows, as is in fact the case, that *who that* does not occur
in that function'. Keyser (1975: p10) cites several authorities for such
a view. There are rare instances of *who that* in late ME, but *who* is
always indefinite, equivalent to *whoever* and occurring in a headless
relative (54).[1] Originally *which* served for inanimate and animate
nouns, and became restricted to inanimates only in the seventeenth
century.

(53) a. thy zodiak of thin Astralabie is shapen as a compas *wich* þat
       contenith a large brede. c.1386 Chaucer, Astrolabie
    b. only the sight of hire *whom that* I serve ... wolde han suffised
       right ynough for me. c.1386 Chaucer, Knight's Tale 1231

[1] Rydén (1966) catalogues the first occurrences of *who* as an anaphoric relative. However, Meier (1967) examines closely what grammarians have called the earliest
examples of the relative *who* and argues that those cited by Jespersen, Curme,
Mustanoja, Winkler and the OED are all either pseudo-relatives to an indefinite
men or generic indefinites equivalent to *whoever*. He dates the first occurrences
from the sixteenth century and points to the works of Roger Ascham: the 119
pages of the *Toxophilus* in 1545 had no instances of a relative *who*, while *The Schole-
master* (c.1565, 126 pp) had 54 examples. *Who* ousted *which* completely by 1700 with
personal antecedents.
   There were other forms of relatives, such as *the which* (N) (i), which has excited
much comment from grammarians, and *that* or even *which* followed by a pronoun (ii).
    (i) there are other Troyans that thou dreams't not of, the whiche for sport sake
       are content to do the profession some grace. Shakespeare, Henry IV
    (ii) as a good friend of mine has frequent made remark to me, which her name ...
       is Harris. Dickens, Martin Chuzzlewit

    c. syk lay the gode man, *whos that* the place is. c.1386 Chaucer,
       Sumnour's Tale 1768

    d. in the mene *while þat* I stille recorded þise þinges wiþ my
       self ... I saw ... a woman of ful gret reuerance. c.1386
       Chaucer, Boethius

(54)   for we all see that it is Goddes wille that he shalle be our
       kynge, and *who that* holdeth agaynst it we wille slee hym.
       1470–85 Malory, Tale of King Arthur

ME embedded questions also occur with the *wh* element alone or
followed by *that* (55). *Who* is found in these constructions, although it
did not occur in ME relative clauses.

(55) a. men shal wel knowe *who that* I am. 1485 Caxton, R67
    b. ne kepe I nat to seye *who* wrastleth best naken, with oille
       anoynt, ne *who that* baar hym best in no disjoynt. c.1386
       Chaucer, Knight's Tale 2960
    c. ye desire to knowe *whedyr that* I shulde abide here stille or
       nowe. 1422–1509 Paston Letters (Gairdner) II 254

That also occurred optionally in various adverbial clauses, following
the usual clause marker (56)–(58). For further examples see Klima
(1964a: pp267ff) and Geoghegan (1975: pp48ff).

(56) a. *whan that* Aprille with his shoures soote ... c.1386 Chaucer,
       CT A. Prol. 1
    b. to-morwe, *whan* ye riden by the weye ... c.1386 Chaucer,
       CT A. Prol. 780

(57) a. for *gif that* shrewdness maketh wretches ... c.1386 Chaucer,
       Boethius
    b. and shame it is, *if* a prest take keep, a shiten shepherde and a
       clene sheep. c.1386 Chaucer, CT A. Prol. 504

(58) a. *whil* I have tyme and space, *er that* I further in this tale pace.
       c.1386 Chaucer, CT A. Prol. 36
    b. yet wolde he have a ferthyng *er* he wente. c.1386 Chaucer,
       CT A. Prol. 255

It is clear that the analysis adopted for NE in §6.2.1 will not suffice
for ME, because ME *that*, subordinating conjunctions and *wh* elements
are not mutually exclusive in COMP.

    Continuing to catalogue facts without analysis, we turn now to OE.
In OE, complement clauses were marked with *þæt*, *þe*, both or zero

(59). This is analogous to the parallel constructions in ME and NE. þe and þæt appear to be usually interchangeable in all constructions, although þæt gradually supplants þe in the course of OE and þe was very rare as an introducer of ordinary complement clauses like (59).

(59) a. hio gelyf'ð to hire bearnon þæt hi willon lyhton for hyre saulle 'she trusts to her children that they will free them for her soul's sake'. Anglo-Saxon Wills

   b. wen ic talige, gif þæt gegangeð, þæt þe gar nymeth, hild heoru-grimme Hreþles eaferan . . . þæt þe Sae-Geatas selran nebban to geceasenne 'I count it probable that if it should happen that the spear, grim battle, should sweep away the son of Hrethel, the Sea-Geats will not be seeking for a better man'. Beowulf 1845

   c. swa ic wat he minne hige cuðe 'so I know (that) he could perceive my intention'

OE had no specifically relative pronoun (Curme (1911) argued that also proto-Germanic had no relative pronoun) and clauses were introduced most commonly by the indeclinable þe (60a), or by an inflected form of the demonstrative pronoun *se*, where the case is determined by its function in the relative clause (60b), or by a combination of the two (60c). In most cases there is a gap in the relative clause, where the head NP must be understood (sometimes a pronoun occurs in the 'gap' position). The latter type was rare in early OE but came to be increasingly common. Indefinite relatives could be formed in one of these three ways or with the *wh* interrogative pronoun (more accurately 'hw-' at this time), which was the only permissible context for a *wh* word in OE relatives (61). Klima (1964a: p256), citing Jespersen (MEG III), notes that in OE the only relative clauses occurring at all freely with no relative marker are where the missing constituent is the subject (62), a point to which we shall return.

(60) a. þonne ealra oþra kyninga þe in middangearde æfre wæron . . . 'then all the other kings who were ever on earth . . . '. Letter of Alexander the Great[1]

---

[1] The 'gap' in such forms may reflect a genitive or dative ((i)–(iii)).

   (i) under þæm twæm consulum þe oðer wæs haten Favius 'under the two consuls of whom the second was called Favius'

   (ii) of ðæm mere ðe Truso standeþ in stade 'from the sea on whose shores T. stands'

b. ða com of ðæm wætre an nædre, *seo* wæs ungemetlice micel
'then came out of the water an adder who was immense'.
Aelfred, Orosius[1]

c. hwæt se ðonne unryhtlice talað, *se þe* talað ðæt he sie unscyldig
'he argues, therefore, wrongly, who argues that he is innocent'.
Gregory's Pastoral Care

(61) swa *hwa* swa þe genyt þusend staþe, ga mid him oðre twa þusend
'whoever compels you to go one mile, go with him two miles'.

(62) tha gelamp hit . . . þæt se eorl Waleram . . . ferde fram his an
castel Belmunt het, to his an other castel Watteuile 'then it
happened that Earl W. went from his one castle, which was
called B., to his other castle W.'. Peterborough Chronicle anno
1124

Embedded questions had a *wh* word, unaccompanied by the complementizers *þe* or *þæt*.

(63) hi nysten *hwæþer* he . . . þat þing worhte 'they did not know
whether he did that thing'. Guthlac

Adverbial clauses could have the complementizer (64), although it
could also be omitted (64a). Sometimes the complementizer consisted
of a preposition + demonstrative pronoun + *þe*, as in (65).

(64) a. ic an þæt lond at Lauenham mine dohter childe *gif þæt*
God wille þæt heo ani haueð and *gif* heonon ne habbe gange it
into stoke 'I grant that land at Lavenham to my daughter's
child, if (that) God wills that she have any and if she has none
let it go to stoke'. Anglo-Saxon Wills

(iii) mon sceolde ælcne mon hatan be þam deore *þe* he gelicost wære 'one should
call each man by the animal to which he is most similar'
This would seem to be an opaque structure and was certainly rare and destined
to die out completely. The opacity was often reduced by retaining a pronoun in
the gap. This was done most often when the gap represented an oblique case, again
illustrating that these were the most difficult to process. Mossé (1945) cites (iv).
(iv) nis nu cwicra nan *þe* ic *him* modsefan minne durre sweotule asecgan 'there is
no living soul that I can express my feelings to him'
þe could never be immediately preceded by a preposition, as noted by Bøgholm
(1939) and others. The preposition could be stranded, as in (v).
(v) on þæm æhtum *þe* heora speda *on* beoth 'in those possessions that their
wealth lies in'

[1] I follow most traditional grammarians in classifying sentences of this type as involving a relative clause. Some evidence against an alternative that such clauses with
a demonstrative pronoun might perhaps be analysed as paratactic is that they usually
had OV word order, which was characteristic of subordinate clauses.

b. and ic an þæt Aethelfled bruke þe lond þer *wile þe* hire lef beth 'and I grant that A. use the land there while (that) it is agreeable to her'. Anglo-Saxon Wills

c. *þeah þe* he his magum nære arfæst æt ecga gelacum 'though he were not kind to his kinsman in the play of edges [= battle]'. Beowulf

d. hit biþ eac geornlic, þæt mon hearlice gnide þone hnescestan mealmstan, *æfter þæm þæt* he þence þone soelestan hwetstan on to geræcceanne 'it will also be desirable that one grind the softest sandstone, if he thinks to achieve the best whetstone'. Aelfred, Orosius

(65) þa sceap him fylgeath *fortham þe* hig cnawath his stefn 'the sheep follow him because they know his voice'. John x 4 (Gospels in West Saxon, MS Corpus Christi College, Cambridge)

As with the ME data, it is clear that the analysis adopted for NE complementizers will not be correct for OE, where *þe* and *þæt* are mutually exclusive neither with clause introducers for adverbial clauses nor with some relative forms. However, there are differences between OE and ME, as in the fact that in OE *wh* forms may not be followed by *þæt*, and the 'interrogative' forms *hwæt, hwylc, hwa* and the oblique *hwone* and *hwam*, antecedents of NE *what, which, who*, do not occur as relatives.

To summarize, throughout the period discussed complement clauses could occur with a *that* (or *þe*) complementizer, and adverbial clauses had an optional *that* (or *þe*) after the introducing conjunction. In OE, relative clauses could be introduced by the complementizer *þe* or *þæt*, by a demonstrative pronoun or by a demonstrative followed by *þe*. OE embedded questions had *wh* forms, which were never accompanied by a complementizer. ME had relatives introduced by the complementizer *þæt*, by *wh* forms (except *who*, which did not occur freely) and by *wh* forms accompanied by *þæt*. ME embedded interrogatives had *wh* forms with an optional *þæt*. Finally in ENE relatives were introduced by either the complementizer or a relative pronoun but not both, and interrogatives never had the complementizer.

Proceeding now to some analysis, note that at all stages the clause introducers *þe* and *þæt* could not be inflected, be preceded immediately by a preposition[1] or occur with an indefinite suffix such as OE, ME

---

[1] That is to say the complementizer *that* cannot be preceded by a preposition internal to the relative clause (i). This is to be distinguished from examples like (ii), pointed

swa or NE -*ever*. Klima (1964a: p275) points out that until Elizabethan times and Defoe (from whom Jespersen (MEG v 393, 398) cites examples) 'the conjunctive element *that* was also employed optionally in the place of a subordinate conjunction that would otherwise be duplicated in conjoined clauses' (66). Therefore, the conclusion that *that* in (36a) is a complementizer and not a pronoun seems to carry over for its OE and ME antecedents.

(66) a. but for the rym ys lyght and lewed, yit make hyt sumwhat agreable, *though* some vers faile in a sillable and *that* I do no diligence to shewe craft. c.1386 Chaucer, HF III 1096

   b. men sholde him brennen in a fyr so reed *if* he were founde or *that* men myghte hym spye. c.1386 Chaucer, Second Nun's Tale 314

   c. but *now* I am returned, and *that* warre-thoughts haue left their places vacant, in their rooms come thronging soft and delicate desires. Shakespeare, Much Ado I i 311

   d. *when* in your motion you are hot and dry – as make your bouts more violent to that end – and *that* he calls for drink, I'll have prepared him a chalice for the nonce. Shakespeare, Hamlet IV vii 157

The facts to be accounted for are that while the NE COMP may contain no more than one lexical phrase, either the complementizer *that* or a subordinating conjunction or a *wh* phrase or *for* or zero, the OE and ME COMPs contained up to two lexical positions. From the earliest times, COMP could consist of a subordinating conjunction and *þe* or *þæt* (*if þæt*, etc.). In the course of OE *se þe* relatives developed. In the thirteenth century the further possibility arose of a preposition + *that*, where the preposition governed the whole clause and could not be construed as governing *that* interpreted as a relative pronoun. Jespersen (MEG III p27) points out that *ere that* replaces OE *ær þæm þe*, where *þæm* is the dative of the demonstrative and *þe* the usual

out by Mustanoja (1960), where *that* is a NP equivalent to *that which*, *which* having been deleted in a context which would be impossible in NE. It should also be distinguished from cases such as (iii), where the preposition governs the whole clause, as was permitted quite freely in ME.

   (i) *the man *to that* she gave it was tall

   (ii) for thou shalt trumpe alle the contrayre of *that* they han done wel or fayre. Chaucer, HF 1630

   (iii) his horses are bred better, for *besides that* they are faire with their feeding, they are taught their mannage. Shakespeare, As You Like It I i 12 complementizer. He notes that *off that, forr thatt, thurrh thatt, fra thatt*, etc. are found in the Ormulum (c.1200), and *after that, before that, but that, by that, er that, for that, save that, sith that, til that* in Chaucer. In the fourteenth and fifteenth centuries *wh* relatives developed and there arose the further possibility of *that* following a *wh* relative and interrogative pronoun. This was very popular in the fifteenth century but proved short-lived and died out rather suddenly. In the sixteenth century the innovations of the last two hundred years were lost and the only 'double-barrelled' possibilities were a subordinating conjunction or some prepositions + *that*.

I propose that the grammar of ME had precisely the same phrase structure rules as those specified in (43) for NE, the same rule of *wh* Movement (44a), but no rule of *wh* Deletion. The 'spelling' rule for inserting *that* was as in (67), whereby *þæt* may be inserted in COMP regardless of what is already there. This permits the surface patterns of (68). Compare the NE rule (45), which inserts *that* only if COMP is already empty.

(67) $\emptyset \rightarrow þæt/[\text{X} \underline{\quad}]_{\text{COMP}}$

(68) a. I said [[(that)]$_{\text{COMP}}$ he had come]$_{\bar{\text{S}}}$
    b. I would have waited [[if (that)]$_{\text{COMP}}$ he had come]$_{\bar{\text{S}}}$
    c. I asked [[who (that)]$_{\text{COMP}}$ was there]$_{\bar{\text{S}}}$
    d. the man [[who (that)]$_{\text{COMP}}$ I saw]$_{\bar{\text{S}}}$ was tall
    e. the man [[(that)]$_{\text{COMP}}$ I saw]$_{\bar{\text{S}}}$ was tall
    f. the man came [[after]$_{\text{P}}$ [[(that)]$_{\text{COMP}}$ Fred left]$_{\bar{\text{S}}}$]$_{\text{PP}}$

There are four comments to be made about this analysis.

(i) It will be noted in (68f) that prepositions governing a full clause are not construed as part of COMP; I assume a phrase structure rule for ME:

$\text{PP} \rightarrow \text{P} \begin{Bmatrix} \text{NP} \\ \bar{\text{S}} \end{Bmatrix}$. Prepositions could govern clauses with complementizers from the thirteenth to sixteenth centuries (following Emonds (1972), I take gerunds to be NPs). For NE I assume a rule $\text{PP} \rightarrow \text{P} \begin{Bmatrix} \text{NP} \\ \text{S} \end{Bmatrix}$, whereby a preposition may govern a clause without a complementizer. This accounts for the absence of complementizers (**before that John came, Mary left*) and the inability of *wh* elements to escape from such clauses (**who did you go before Mary saw t*).[1] We shall return to this analysis below.

---

[1] I take *if, when, although, because*, as clear cases of conjunctions, and *before, since, except, for* as clear cases of prepositions. Only the latter are free to occur with either a clause or a NP ((i)–(ii)).

(ii) An alternative formulation might base-generate *that* as the rightmost constituent of COMP and postulate an optional rule of *that* Deletion. I see little to choose between such an alternative and the analysis adopted here. (Recently Chomsky & Lasnik (1977) have argued for a rule deleting elements in COMP freely, except where blocked by the principle of recoverability; this may be better than either of these alternatives.) The two proposals may be notationally equivalent, but one may be preferred on general theoretical grounds. For example, the rules of *that* Insertion and *that* Deletion will each be subject to various idiosyncratic restrictions: *that* is obligatory in subject complements (**John left is obvious*) and after verbs like *quip, complain* (**Fred quipped John left*). These restrictions may fall out on general, perhaps perceptual grounds, and therefore not be stated as specifications on the rule of, say, *that* Insertion. However, supposing that the rules must be specified in this way and be made subject to 'lexical governance', it might be the case that 'house-keeping rules' but not transformational rules can be so restricted and that house-keeping rules can only insert and not delete material of this type. In this hypothetical situation one would have a reason to prefer the insertion house-keeping rule. Given some well-articulated notions of simplicity, one might argue for the insertion rule by claiming that base-generating *that* and then deleting it was less economical, in some defined sense of 'economical'. However, this is purely speculative and I have no good reason to prefer one of these analyses over the other. An insertion rule is well-motivated for the grammars of OE and NE and I adopt a similar rule for ME only to facilitate exposition.

(iii) In not postulating a rule of *wh* Deletion (44b) for ME, I follow

(i) her desire for gin (to be available) disturbed Fred
(ii) Susan left before the meeting (began)

However, there is disagreement amongst linguists in this area and there are several unclear cases. Emonds (1976), for example, treats all these elements as prepositions. On the other hand Bresnan (1972) treats *than* and *as* in comparative clauses as complementizers; but White (1976) points to sentences like *nothing could be more absurd than that a prince should marry*, which under Bresnan's analysis would presumably contain two elements in COMP, which is otherwise impossible. Bresnan might assign a structure [[*that a prince should marry*]$_\bar{S}$]$_{NP}$; a similar analysis might be adopted for phrases like *the question of* [[*whether they went*]$_\bar{S}$]$_{NP}$. I discussed the plausibility of a rule NP → $\bar{S}$ in §4.3. For reasons not to treat *than* and *as* as complementizers, see Chomsky & Lasnik (1977: app. 1). Both analyses correctly predict that *wh* elements cannot be extracted without violating the Specified Subject Condition because there is no escape-hatch available, either because COMP is filled by *because, since*, etc., or because (under my analysis) NE prepositions can govern only S, where no COMP is available. However, this is an area of grammar which has not been subjected to much careful discussion, and it is best not to be dogmatic.

Grimshaw (1975a) in supposing that ME relatives are derived either by application of *wh* Movement or by on-site deletion of a co-referential NP. One might describe the facts in terms of an obligatory 'pied-piping' convention in Chaucerian English. The relevant sentences are those of (69) and (70).

(69) a. this bok of which (that) I make mencioun
      b. this bok that I make mencioun of
(70) a. *this bok which (that) I make mencioun of
      b. *this bok of that I make mencioun

If relative clauses always involved *wh* Movement with subsequent deletion of the *wh* word or *that*, both of the deletion rules would be applicable to (69) after *wh* Movement has applied. This would permit the ungrammatical sentences of (70). Grimshaw argues that pied-piping is obligatory in ME and that sentences like (69b) involve not *wh* Movement but deletion-under-identity of *the book*. If pied-piping is obligatory and *wh* elements cannot be deleted, the sentences of (70) will not be generated. Similar facts hold of interrogatives: *about what did you speak?* but **what did you speak about?*[1]

(iv) As noted above, in earlier English the relative pronoun and *that* could each be omitted if the missing NP was the subject of the clause. This was rare in OE, but quite frequent from the thirteenth century. Bever & Langendoen (1972) point to a further condition, that

---

[1] This analysis is not uncontroversial. Firstly as a matter of data, there are a few isolated cases of stranded prepositions, usually *in* occurring in the form *inne*, and some examples with two occurrences of the preposition: *til that knyght of which I speke of thus*. Also, in discussing the types *a daughter in whom I delite* and *a daughter whom I delite in* Visser (1963–73: §411) notes contra Grimshaw that 'when the relative pronoun is *whom* or *(the) which* the preposition is placed either before the pronoun or at the end of the clause. Both types are represented in English from the beginning of the Middle English period on.' Secondly, consider NE sentences like (i), where *he* cannot be interpreted as anaphoric to *the man*. Such sentences have been explained in two ways, neither of which would be available under Grimshaw's deletion analysis: Postal (1971) postulated a *wh* Constraint, which stipulates that *wh* elements cannot move over 'coreferential' elements and therefore predicts that the *wh* word co-referential with *the man* is not co-referential with any intervening element and therefore that *he* cannot refer to *the man*. Wasow (1972) accounts for the same facts by treating a trace *t* left by a movement rule as a name; therefore *he* cannot refer to *t* in (i) or to *Bill* in (ii) because it precedes and commands the name. Both analyses depend crucially on a movement analysis. If such sentences occur in ME with the same interpretations, it is not clear how they could be handled by Grimshaw's analysis.
  (i) the man that he said Susan saw t
  (ii) he said Susan saw Bill

the antecedent should be a NP following the main verb. Therefore in ME (71) would be well-formed, unlike (72).

(71)   a. Harry ate the baklava ___ was disintegrating
       b. Harry is a man ___ likes baklava

(72)   *the girl ___ ate the baklava become fat

Our analysis of ME relatives will generate (72). However, Bever & Langendoen (1972) show that the unacceptability of (72) at any stage of English is due to other factors. They argue that a perceptual strategy interprets a NP-V sequence (where V is a finite verb) as the beginning of a clause. 'Thus, if the first verb introduced a relative clause there had to be some marker present in surface structure.' Chomsky & Lasnik (1977) formulate this as a surface filter: $*[NP \text{ tense } VP]_{NP}$.[1] There is much more to be said about such elliptical or 'asyndetic' relatives and the historical changes in the conditions for permissible omission of the relative markers. Lohmann's (1880) careful study of this associates the changing conditions with the OV-to-VO word order change, and Flebbe (1878) has some interesting comparative data noting that almost all the Germanic languages have at some stage permitted such ellipses under various conditions, while today only Danish, Swedish and English do so. Eighteenth-century grammarians engaged in lively debates about the conditions for deletion of relative markers in 'correct' usage. However this intriguing area of grammar seems not to be directly relevant to the problem in hand and I omit further discussion.

Turning now to the grammar of OE, I propose the phrase structure rule of (73) and an insertion rule (74).

$$(73) \quad COMP \rightarrow (\left\{\begin{matrix} PP \\ NP \\ Conj. \end{matrix}\right\}) \pm WH$$

$$(74) \quad \varnothing \rightarrow \left\{\begin{matrix} þe \\ þæt \end{matrix}\right\} / [(Conj)\_\_\_]_{COMP}$$

---

[1] Bever & Langendoen's account makes crucial reference to the changing role of inflections as marking the function of NPs like *baklava* in (71); the restriction (surface filter) developed as nominal inflections were lost. They note a few counterexamples to the claim that it has never been possible to have a V-initial relative clause modifying a subject NP. Sentences like (ii) are probably quite common in casual speech. Chomsky & Lasnik (1977) note sentences like (iii), frequent in dialects of Black English.

    (i) those men[___ blush not in actions blacker than the night] will shun no course ... Shakespeare, Pericles

    (ii) anybody [___ knows Harry]'d say the same

    (iii) the man [(who) saw Bill] he a fool

In (73) NP and PP provide a position for the demonstrative pronoun in sentences like (60b), where I assume that a fronting rule applies (arguably a special case of *wh* Movement. See Traugott (1972a: p104) for the possibility of *se* relatives headed by a PP; likewise indirect questions could be headed by a PP). (60a) is to be derived by a rule of deletion-under-identity, as with analogous ME sentences. These rules will permit surface structures of the form of (75).

(75) a. she said [[(that)]$_{COMP}$ he left]$_{\bar{S}}$
      b. he came [[if (that)]$_{COMP}$ it rained]$_{\bar{S}}$
      c. the man [[to-him]$_{COMP}$ she gave the book]$_{\bar{S}}$ was tall
      d. he [[that]$_{COMP}$ did it]$_{\bar{S}}$ will succeed

(75d) is analogous to sentences like (60c) with *se þe*, where *se* is construed as a member of the higher clause. Here *that* must be inserted, but there is no need for an annotation to the rule (74), since the obligatoriness of *that* or *þe* follows from Bever & Langendoen's perceptual strategy briefly outlined above. I assume that in OE prepositions could be followed by NPs but not by Ss, accounting for the absence (until the thirteenth century) of forms like (68f) *after (that) Fred left*. I assume that *wh* Movement existed in the grammar of OE in the same form as obtains in NE (44a). In OE *hw-* forms have only an interrogative interpretation and can surface only in a +WH COMP (and are not followed by *þe* or *þæt*); therefore if they were base-generated in a relative clause structure and then fronted by *wh* (or *hw*) Movement, into a −WH COMP, they would not be interpretable. The consequence of this is that *hw-* relatives would be characterized as uninterpretable, therefore ill-formed. Finally, although under current theories there was some indeterminacy in ME, for OE a *that* Insertion rule is to be preferred to base-generating *þe* and *þæt* in COMP and postulating a deletion rule. Such a deletion rule would be much more complex than our insertion rule (74), since it would have to specify that deletion was obligatory after a NP or PP in COMP and optional elsewhere. This system correctly characterizes that, like ME and unlike NE, OE permitted double-barrelled COMPs, but consisting only of a conjunction and *þe* or *þæt*.

The analyses adopted here are summarized in table 1. The division into OE, ME, ENE and NE is only an approximation. For example, the phrase structure rule permitting PPs to dominate $\bar{S}$s was introduced in the thirteenth century and was lost in the late sixteenth or early

TABLE I

	OE	ME	ENE	NE
Phrase structure	$\bar{S} \to$ COMP S			
	COMP $\to \left(\left\{\begin{array}{l}\text{PP} \\ \text{NP} \\ \text{Conj}\end{array}\right\}\right)$ ±WH	COMP $\to \left(\left\{\begin{array}{l}\text{PP} \\ \text{NP} \\ \text{AdjP} \\ \text{Conj}\end{array}\right\}\right)$ ±WH		
	PP $\to$ P NP	PP $\to$ P $\left\{\begin{array}{l}\text{NP} \\ \bar{\text{S}}\end{array}\right\}$	PP $\to$ P $\left\{\begin{array}{l}\text{NP} \\ \text{S}\end{array}\right\}$	
Transformations	*wh* Movement			
	[ ]$_{\text{COMP}}$ X wh $\Rightarrow$ 1 2 t			
	deletion-under-identity		*wh* Deletion	
	[$_{\text{NP}}$ [X NP Y]$_{\bar{\text{S}}}$]$_{\text{NP}} \Rightarrow$ 1 2 $\emptyset$ 4		[$_{\text{NP}}$ wh X]$_{\text{NP}} \Rightarrow$ 1 $\emptyset$ 3	
	pronoun fronting			
	[ ]$_{\text{COMP}}$ X se $\Rightarrow$ 1 2 t			
Housekeeping	$\emptyset \to \left\{\begin{array}{l}\textit{þe} \\ \textit{þæt}\end{array}\right\}$ /[(Conj) ___]$_{\text{COMP}}$	$\emptyset \to \textit{þæt}$ /[X ___]$_{\text{COMP}}$	$\emptyset \to \textit{that}$ /[(Conj) ___]$_{\text{COMP}}$	$\emptyset \to \textit{that}$ /[___]$_{\text{COMP}}$

seventeenth century and therefore its life-span coincides only roughly with the usual definitions of ME (1150–1500). I have distinguished *that* Insertion rules for ENE and NE, but the date for the re-formulation of the rule is not clear and may not coincide with the end of ENE (1700). *That* continued to occur freely after conjunctions in the seventeenth century; some instances are found in the eighteenth century (76) and a few survive into modern times (77).

(76) a. he could not do that by any means, *for that* it would put the whole island into confusion. Defoe, Robinson Crusoe
     b. he had heard a medical gentleman . . . say *how that* snuff-taking was bad for the eyes. Dickens, Nicholas Nickleby

(77) now (that) spring is here . . .

The life-span of the *þæt* Insertion rule cited as ME coincides quite accurately with the ME period. *Wh* relatives are found from early ME and *þæt* may follow them from their first occurrence; the last examples of *which that*, etc., are from the very end of the ME period.

6.2.3 It follows from these analyses that COMP could contain two items until the end of the early modern period, although there was some variation in what the first of those items could be: only a conjunction or demonstrative pronoun in OE, conjunction or *wh* word in ME, and a conjunction in ENE. Given this account of the changes (alternatives will be considered in §6.2.4), we can see that some of the changes may be ascribed to analogical levelling of surface structure patterns and to the effects of the Transparency Principle; a partial causal chain may be set up without undue speculation. Consider first the changes taking place within OE: the *se þe* form of the relative occurs only in late OE (a fact not codified in table 1), supplanting the form with the demonstrative alone. Towards the latter part of the OE period the demonstrative pronouns (a) underwent the loss of inflections which affected the language generally as the case system was lost (see chapter 7), and (b) suffered analogical levelling in that the sibilant forms *se* and *seo* (nominative singular masculine and feminine) assumed fricatives like the rest of the paradigm, becoming *þe, þeo* by analogy to *þæt*, etc. At the time of this levelling *þe* was increasingly common as a marker of subordination, perhaps as a consequence of the fact that as SVO order began to develop in subordinate clauses, main and subordinate clauses were no longer distinguished by word order (formerly VO in main clauses and OV in subordinate). As a result of the levelling, the new nominative singular of the demonstrative, which at the same time was being extended to serve a new function as a definite article, was homophonous with the complementizer *þe*. In many relatives it would now be unclear whether the *þe* was a nominative demonstrative, an article or a complementizer, which would often yield parsing difficulties and lack of transparency. Perhaps as a consequence of this, the demonstrative ceased to occur at the head of a relative clause and the rule of Pronoun Fronting was lost (this 'rule' may be a special case of more general word order permutation or 'scrambling' rules). With the loss of this form, relatives would be introduced only by the *þe* complementizer. Clauses of this type, however, were ambiguous or difficult to analyse when the deleted NP was in the genitive or dative (78). Such sentences are rare and the difficulty was often avoided by failing to delete the lower NP, which occurred in pronominal form (79) (see p323n).

(78)   . . . for mine soule & for mine louerde *þat ic under begeat* . . .and for alle þe mannes soule *þe ic forþingiae* 'for my soul and for that of my lord that I acquired [land] under and for the souls of all men that I intercede for'. Anglo-Saxon Wills

(79)   eaðig bið se wer, þe his tohopa bið to Drihtne 'blessed be the man, that his hope is in the Lord'

This 'explanation' is, of course, after-the-fact, but sentences like (78) are exceedingly rare, where anaphoric pronouns occur they are usually in an oblique case as in (79), and as Pronoun Fronting was lost, so a new form of relative with *se þe* developed, which suggests that there may have been such a functional 'gap' in the system and that relatives introduced only by a complementizer were in a sense insufficient.

Perhaps as a partial consequence of the instability of the demonstrative pronouns at this time, new relative forms developed exploiting the *wh* pronouns which had hitherto been used only as interrogatives and indefinite (headless) relatives. *Which* occurred from early ME, followed soon by the oblique forms *whose* and *whom*, but *who* developed only in the sixteenth century. The *wh* forms first occurred where the co-referential noun was in an oblique case or was the object of a preposition. The lateness of *who* is consistent with the after-the-fact explanation above, because its environment (i.e. a subject NP) was the least ambiguous; that is, a relative clause introduced by *that* and with a deleted subject NP would present none of the parsing difficulties outlined above and would permit a less opaque analysis. Perhaps it was introduced, albeit so late, as a result of analogical levelling: of the interrogative pronoun paradigm, this had been the only form not to occur as a relative. With the new *wh* relatives in ME *that* was retained, so the innovative *which that* surface patterns were similar to the former *se þe*.

As the *wh* relatives developed, two further changes took place, both presumably by analogical extension: the *that* complementizer began to appear after interrogative pronouns in embedded questions and after prepositions governing a full clause. At this stage *þæt* was apparently viewed as a marker of subordination, in a sense replacing the VO $\sim$ OV word order alternation which had formerly distinguished main and subordinate clauses. *þæt* had become more common in this role since it could now be used in the most common relative clause structures and a relative marker (either a *wh* word or *þæt*) was now necessary in new contexts. Here I refer to sentences like (71), *Harry ate the baklava___was disintegrating*, where, following the analysis of Bever & Langendoen (1972), after the loss of inflections marking *the baklava* as the object of *ate*, a relative clause marker became necessary, given the general perceptual tendency to interpret a NP-V sequence as subject-verb. With these developments, it seems not implausible to attribute the rise of P-*þæt*-S and interrogative-*þæt*-S structures as due to analogical extension of *þæt*, which came to be viewed as a general marker of subordination. I see no way in which these two developments follow in any stricter sense from earlier changes.[1] Indeed, formerly prepositions had never governed finite, complementizer-initial clauses in any form, nor can they in the grammar of NE.

As pointed out by Jespersen, *þæt* often seems to be redundant in the new, ME system. Double-barrelled COMPs in relative clauses were a temporary phenomenon (as were prepositions governing finite clauses): *se þe* occurred freely only in late OE and *which that* forms were obsolete by ENE. Geoghegan (1975: p57) is tempted to explain this in functional terms:

[1] Imputing changes to analogy in such a way constitutes a psychological claim, although no 'psychological evidence' has been offered and it is hard to know what would constitute valid evidence of this type. The evidence is purely linguistic and lies in the simultaneity of changes which, although not the reflex of a single formal change in the grammar, can be viewed as related in terms of surface structure patterns.

only when there was danger of a loss of information, or when unfamiliarity with new forms could cause ambiguity, were such 'redundant' patterns widespread. The same reasoning can be used to explain the [temporary] patterns [of complementizers followed by anaphoric pronouns, as in p323n]. It appears that once the speakers of Middle English had become accustomed to the use of *wh* words . . . *that* was no longer needed to signal the subordinate status of the relative clause.

There is much speculation underlying this view, but there is also some substance to it, as we have indicated, insofar as certain aspects of the changes can plausibly be viewed as functions of the Transparency Principle. It may even be correct that the 'redundant' *that* was a crutch which served to help speakers of a language undergoing a set of major transitions involving word order changes, loss of inflections and much more. However, if this view is correct, one is left with the puzzling fact that conjunctions like *after, before, if* and *while* were the most retentive of *that* and occurred with it freely in the seventeenth century and even into modern times, although these conjunctions were manifestly introducers of subordinate clauses.[1]

6.2.4 The reader will have observed in table 1 that the ME changes are instantiated in the grammar as three distinct differences from the grammar of OE: a new phrase structure rule for PP, a new *þæt* Insertion rule and the loss of Pronoun Fronting. These are simultaneous changes, whose net effect is that *þæt* can occur after any element in COMP and after a preposition governing the whole clause. At the end of §6.2.3 the new phrase structure rule for PPs and the fact that interrogative pronouns could be followed by *that* were interpreted as analogical extensions, dependent on the new *which that* relatives. Elsewhere in this book I have argued that the simultaneity of a set of surface changes may argue for the uniqueness of the change in the abstract grammar,

---

[1] The historical claims in this sub-section have no bearing on the proposals of Chomsky (1977) to extend the domain of *wh* Movement and to subsume under it various 'rules' involved in the derivation of topicalized sentences, clefts, comparatives and infinitival constructions. Only in relatives and interrogatives does the *wh* element surface; in the other sentence-types *wh* is usually deleted obligatorily. I assume that this holds also of earlier stages of English, although there is not much relevant data available. Given the nature of the surviving texts there are few examples of topicalized sentences and even clefts and comparatives, which are characteristic of less formal styles of language. Since *wh* is moved into COMP, there will be no subordinating conjunction which would otherwise occupy the slot to be filled by the moved *wh*; and since it is deleted obligatorily, there will be no possibility of *which that* structures at surface. Therefore double-barrelled COMPs will not arise in such constructions and no predictions are made.

and I have argued for particular forms and theories of grammar on the basis of whether they allow a unique formulation of the simultaneous surface changes. That is not to say, of course, that all simultaneous surface changes *must* be instantiations of a single change in the formal grammar; rather that, ceteris paribus, one will prefer a grammar relating a family of changes. Here the various surface changes follow from two or maybe three changes in the formal grammar.[1] I know of no proposal that there is a single abstract change which would relate the various changes in permitted surface patterns, although, given the recent proposals of Chomsky & Lasnik (1977), it might be possible to formulate this as a single change in the surface filter for COMP; I have not yet worked out the details. There are alternative accounts, to which we now turn, but both must be rejected. I shall comment only on selected aspects of these alternatives, with a view to making a general point at the end.

Geoghegan (1975 p58f) postulates rules of *that* Insertion and *that* Deletion for all stages of English. 'The presence of [*that* Insertion] in the derivation of relative clauses is necessary if *that* is indeed a signal of subordination, because such a word could not be present in deep structure.' No reason is given and one is left to wonder what definition of deep structure precludes *that* being base-generated. She assumes that *that* must be present as a 'trigger' for a rule producing OV order in subordinate clauses. She thus tacitly presupposes a theory of transformations which allows rules to be formulated so that they apply only to subordinate clauses, in a sense a reversal of Emonds' root/non-root distinctions and in any case an idiosyncratic theory which requires some articulation. 'Even in those Old English subordinate clauses in which *þe* or *þæt* did not appear overtly, it must have

---

[1] There is no reason to require a one-to-one relationship between a change in surface patterns and a change in a formal grammar. As noted in chapter 3, a 'single' surface change may be a reflex of a grammar which has undergone several formal changes, all interrelated to some degree, and conversely many apparently diverse surface changes may be a consequence of the addition, loss or re-formulation of a single rule. Also the re-analysis of the English modals involved changes in phrase structure and some transformational rules, and new lexical entries; but under the analysis adopted in §2.2 a unity is discernible and there is a direct causal relation such that the transformational re-formulations follow from and are necessitated by the categorial re-analysis.

If OE Pronoun Fronting is a special case of *wh* Movement, there would be only two changes in the grammar. Under this view relative clauses would look very similar throughout the history of English, falling into two classes: (a) clauses with OE *þe* (ME *þat*) and deletion of the relativized NP or a retained personal pronoun, (b) clauses with OE *se* (ME *wh*) involving a movement and (typically) pied-piping of a preposition.

been present at some point in the derivation [in order to trigger the appropriate word order] . . . *þe* could then be optionally deleted.' Pullum (1976) has referred to the postulation of such analyses as the Duke of York Gambit; the Duke of York, it will be recalled, marched his men to the top of the hill and marched them down again, doing nothing on the way. Pullum argues that such analyses should be invoked only under severely restricted conditions. Geoghegan adopts a similar analysis for NE, inserting *that* by transformation after subordinating conjunctions like *after*, *if* and *before*, and later deleting it even though *that* can *never* appear in such a position in surface structure; such an analysis is akin to rules of absolute neutralization in phonology and involves a form of abstractness which is, by common consent, to be avoided (see, for example, Kiparsky 1968b). It is difficult to know what could persuade a language learner to postulate such an abstract derivation. Therefore, Geoghegan's conclusion that 'most differences between Old and New English relative clauses consequently appear to be only superficial . . . the transformations necessary to derive relative clauses have not changed',[1] is a function of her working methods and certain unstated and unmotivated assumptions about the form of possible grammars. This analysis illustrates a rather extreme case of a common tendency amongst contemporary linguists to postulate 'transformations' arbitrarily with no theory or even explicit account of what transformational rules can and cannot do. It is typical of such analyses to invoke rules with a wide range of formal properties.

Keyser (1975) examined this area of grammar from a diachronic point of view, and claimed that sequences like *which that*

are impossible if *wh*-fronting is (universally) a structure-preserving rule. This follows, of course, since the only way that *that* can appear in a surface string is if the *wh*-word has not been fronted to replace it. If it has been fronted, then the *wh*-word must occupy the COMP position . . . and *that* is prevented from being spelled out. It is therefore counter-evidence to the structure-preserving hypothesis that we find in Middle English [such sequences].

---

[1] Klima (1964a) also claims that the changes between late ME and NE were essentially superficial and involved only the valences of transformational rules. *That* is assumed to be base-generated such that it could follow relative and embedded interrogative pronouns and be deleted optionally in ME and obligatorily in NE. 'The change in the valence of the rule progressed gradually from item to item or class of items to class of items' (p282). Nonetheless, Klima claims that eventually there was a restructuring whereby later generations 'finally failed to abstract a rule comparable to the rule of Late Middle English for the reduction to *that* of repeated conjunctions (an instance of spontaneous change)' (p284).

Keyser goes on to speculate that under this analysis the diachronic change was one whereby *wh* Movement (his '*wh*-fronting') 'was not a structure-preserving rule in Middle English but came to be one in early Modern English'. Such a change would represent, as Keyser notes, a considerable weakening of the theory of grammar. Current versions of the EST incorporating Emonds' structure-preserving principle would predict that no grammar of natural language will have a transformational rule which is neither root nor structure-preserving nor local. *Wh* Movement in ME is clearly neither root nor local; if it is also neither structure-preserving, it can exist only at the cost of weakening the theory of grammar to permit a fourth class of trans-formational rule, an undesirable move. Fortunately there is no reason to adopt such a formulation or to abandon structure-preservation. Keyser's claims are predicated on various assumptions: that *wh* Move-ment is a rule of ME grammar, with the same formulation and mode of operation as in NE; that it is neither root nor local in ME; if it is also not structure-preserving, its existence will serve to disconfirm the universality of Emonds' characterizations of possible transformational rules. However, there is a further assumption: that the structure of COMP in ME is as in NE. This assumption is not discussed, although it is central to Keyser's argument. If the ME COMP can be a two-place structure, dominating a NP or PP node and a slot for *that*, then *wh* Movement will be structure-preserving, as in NE. Such a view is advocated by Klima (1964a), Geoghegan (1975) and White (1976), and is even adopted by Keyser later in his paper when he outlines an alternative hypothesis. Furthermore, the analysis adopted here, whereby *that* may be transformationally inserted into COMP, permits *wh* Movement to be characterized as structure-preserving. *That* Insertion is not structure-preserving but nor is it a movement rule (the structure-preserving principle applies only to movement transformations, not to deletion rules, etc.), and it may not even be a transformation if one may properly distinguish a class of 'housekeeping' rules.

Keyser, having allegedly refuted the structure-preserving principle, proceeds to outline an alternative account of the changes. There are problems with this account,[1] but even if it were equivalent to the

---

[1] White (1976) points out that Keyser's 'maximally simple' rules of *that* Deletion and Relative Pronoun Deletion will permit the generation of NE sentences like (i)–(iii). (i) can be eliminated by Bever & Langendoen's (1972) perceptual strategy, but (ii)–(iii) cannot. These facts all follow from the Surface Exclusion Filter of Chomsky (1973: (203)) and the version in Chomsky & Lasnik (1977), which subsumes

account given here, the latter would be preferred because it is couched within a more restrictive theory of grammar, i.e. one incorporating Emonds' classification of possible rules. To put it differently, if there are two analyses of a given range of data, both of which make only correct predictions and involve a similar degree of complexity, one will prefer the analysis which presupposes the more restrictive theory of possible grammars. This failure to distinguish a theory of grammar from a virtuous particular grammar is revealed by the questions posed by Keyser.

Keyser postulates a (fragment of a) grammar of ME and asks 'how can we account for this change from Stage 1 to the subsequent early Modern English stage in which *who* as a nominative relative appears and in which relative pronoun + *that* does not?' He concludes that an output condition was added to the grammar specifying that 'no clause may contain a *wh*-word directly followed by the subordinate markers *that* or *for* as clause-mates'. In the light of this he asks whether it is possible 'to characterize the class of possible modifications that a grammar can undergo so that one can predict whether a given modification will be expressible as a rule rather than an output condition and vice versa'. Clearly the underlying assumption is that there should be a formal device to express whatever changes take place between two stages of a language, that these formal devices will have specified properties and that a theory of change may be able to predict what kind of formal devices will be introduced for a given set of modifications. This is far too strong a goal for a theory of change, for the reasons given in chapter 3, but, more seriously, it confuses synchrony with diachrony. Keyser argues that the grammar of eighteenth-century English is the grammar of ME with the addition of an output constraint that 'no clause may contain anything followed by *that*'; this permits the desired formal characterization of various changes. The confusion of synchrony and diachrony is revealed in a telling comment that such a grammar of eighteenth-century English 'is obviously not a stable stage of linguistic development' (p14), because a child exposed to the output of such a grammar would have no reason to postulate an underlying *that* in

the Bever & Langendoen cases, where the perceptual strategy 'links' to a grammatical filter, accounting for the ungrammaticalness (as opposed to difficulty in processing; cf. p319n).
  (i) *the man [__ is bald] is tall
  (ii) *Harry is a man [__ likes baklava]
  (iii) *Harry ate the baklava [__ was disintegrating]

contexts where it could never surface; therefore, as Keyser noted, a re-structuring was inevitable. Since this is so, the only reason to postulate such an intermediate stage with the output condition lies in the assumptions made about the form of possible grammatical innovations, as is indicated by the fact that Keyser is obliged to postulate a later re-analysis in any case. Thus diachronic considerations determine the form of the intermediate grammar, whereas it is axiomatic that a synchronic grammar must be established only on the basis of a theory of grammar and the primary data available to a language learner, where primary data do not include information about earlier stages of the language. Recalling the re-analysis discussed in chapter 2 involving English modals, one assumes that on the basis of these assumptions Keyser would be obliged to postulate prior to the re-analysis an intermediate stage, whereby a single formal device was added to the earlier grammar, which would produce the required changes in output. One can only speculate on what such a formal device would look like. This fallacious confusion of synchrony and diachrony stems from a failure to distinguish the role of a theory of grammar from particular grammars. This should be contrasted with an argument·form used at several points in this book: there may be two or more possible descriptions of a certain stage of a language, one of which is consistent with a theory of grammar incorporating some restrictive principle (here, usually the Transparency Principle), such that the restrictive principle may explain the need for a re-analysis leading to the language for which we have two or more descriptions. The restrictive principle derives support from its ability to permit an explanation of why the re-analysis should have taken place in the way that it did. Thus in the case of the English modals we compared two descriptions of NE, one involving a new category modal, the other a set of features. Only under the former description was it possible to specify how the new grammar was more highly valued than its predecessor; that specification appealed to a notion of transparency, restricting possible derivations. It was thereby shown that a theory incorporating a Transparency Principle was able to do something beyond the range of the theory within which the feature-based description was couched, thereby deriving support.

These two alternative accounts by Geoghegan and Keyser have been discussed in order to illustrate some fallacies involved in studying diachronic syntax without reference to a restrictive theory of grammar. The first alternative presupposed such a loose theory that transformations could be postulated in seemingly arbitrary fashion, while the second assumed a restrictive theory and sought to refute it by appeal to some fallacious notions about the appropriate goals for a theory of change, whereby it was assumed that corresponding to a set of changes there should always be a single formal operation affecting the earlier grammar, such as the addition or loss of a transformation or output constraint.

7   *The causes of re-analysis*

> We must concede that the universe we see is a ceaseless creation,
> evolution and destruction of forms and that the purpose of science
> is to foresee that change of form, and if possible, explain it. (René
> Thom, *Stabilité structurelle et morphogenèse* ch. 1A)

In §3.2, in discussing a theory of syntactic change, I have claimed
there are no formally definable limits to the ways in which two consecutive grammars of a given language may differ, beyond those limits
imposed by a theory of grammar. Therefore there are no grounds to
expect a theory of change to delimit the notion of a possible syntactic
change on formal grounds. This, of course, is not to claim that any
grammar may change into any other possible grammar (as defined by
the theory of grammar) over the period of two generations; we claim
only that such lower limits to possible changes are not *formally* prescribed. It is now time to return to this issue.

7.1   Role of surface structure and analogies

7.1.1   Throughout this book we have concentrated our attention on
radical re-analyses, manifested by a set of simultaneous but superficially unrelated changes in admissible surface structures. This is
illustrated nicely by the modals story of §2.2, which consisted of a
re-analysis following on five isolated changes occurring at different
times and affecting different parts of the grammar. The description of
isolated piecemeal changes, such as the development of non-past
interpretations for syntactically past tense forms, the failure of the *to*
infinitive form to spread to the 'complements' of modals, etc., will
have few consequences for the evaluation of grammars. Such changes
can be given a viable account in grammars of many different forms,
and therefore they do not serve as a basis for choosing between grammars. However, families of simultaneous changes provide crucial tests

and in many cases only a very restricted class of grammars can show a relation for any given set of simultaneous changes. So it is by and large only radical re-analyses relating such simultaneous changes, which have interesting implications for conclusions about the correct form of grammars. Hamp (1974) makes the same point: 'most instances of really interesting linguistic change involve multiple changes of various sorts'. In the last three chapters we have illustrated a significant range of re-analyses with quite different formal properties: the introduction of a new category such as Quantifier (§4.1) or Modal (§2.2), the metamorphosis of verb features, [±tense], [±past], to an initial structure constituent (§2.3), changes in phrase structure rules by re-arrangement of already existing categories (§4.3), various kinds of re-formulations of transformations (§2.2, §6.2), introduction of new transformations (§6.1, §5.2), re-ordering and loss of rules (§1.3), changes in strict sub-categorization (§5.1), in lexical redundancy rules (§4.4) and in morphological realization in the example of the Greek moods (§5.3), etc. Several other changes have been mentioned along the way, if not argued for, and furthermore one finds combinations of these changes (see especially chapter 2). The variety of these re-analyses gives substance to the claim in §3.2 that there are no formal limits to possible changes, or that, if there are, they must be very loose, and permissive enough to allow at least the changes noted here.

So far the discussion has been couched mainly in terms of the ways in which the grammars of consecutive generations may differ from each other, and I have proposed one causal principle of change: the Transparency Principle. This is a requirement of the theory of grammar that derivations may be only of a limited degree of complexity. Historical evidence has been adduced for this principle along the lines that if one assumes such a principle one can explain why various re-analyses took place in the history of English and other languages, e.g. the introduction of new categories Modal and Quantifier (with the attendant transformational re-formulations), the new sub-categorization requirements for the ME impersonal verbs (§5.1), introduction of the 'passive' in the early IE languages (§5.2), and the developments of the verbal character of English infinitival complements (§4.2). I shall make no attempt to formalize the Transparency Principle or to give a precise account of the permitted degree of derivational opacity. At this stage I do not have enough evidence to make an exact proposal: although several re-analyses have been examined here, one needs to look at many more – and, of course, re-analyses of this type are not easy to find and must be argued for and justified. Therefore, while precision in this respect is now premature, a reasonable goal for work in diachronic syntax is a characterization of tolerable opacity. In fact, an exact quantification may not be possible, but this does not gainsay the value of the goal. The Transparency Principle will stand as an inductive generalization (see p123) and argument must necessarily be after-the-fact, at least in the historical domain; one argues that the fact that a re-analysis took place at a certain point t in the history of language L suggests that the Transparency Principle, a defining principle of available grammatical analyses, characterizes as unacceptable the degree of derivational opacity which would obtain in some part of the grammar of L, if the grammar at $t-1$ were to develop, say, a further exception feature. Thus in fifteenth-century English, derivations involving 'pre-modal' verbs were opaque to some specifiable extent. At about this time a further change was taking place whereby the *to* infinitives were becoming general in the complements to all verbs other than the pre-modals. If another exception feature were developed, the opacity would be correspondingly increased. This change coincided with a radical re-analysis, manifested by the cluster of seven changes in the early sixteenth century. Thus one may explain the fact that the re-analysis took place at this point by defining the Transparency Principle in such a way that it will permit the opacity in the derivations of the fifteenth century but not in those of the old derivations augmented by one further exception feature dealing with the form of infinitival complements. Given the assumptions about a theory of syntactic change developed in §3.2 (19), such a definition will predict the need for some kind of re-analysis as the *to* infinitive is generalized to the complements of non-pre-modal verbs. An argument of this form provides some insight to the form of the Transparency Principle. Exact predictions will be derivable only when one provides an exact characterization of the tolerance level for opacity and complexity. The principle can be given an exact content only in the light of several such arguments. Its effects will be manifested not only in predictions about the point at which historical re-analyses will occur but also in the range of permitted grammars. It could be refuted by demonstrating that the grammar of language L' does not accord with it; such a refutation will be exactly as convincing as the (fragment of) grammar presented. In helping to delimit the class of available grammars, the Transparency Principle will also make predictions about the nature of the acquisition process, about language pathology and about all other factual domains to which a theory of grammar is responsive. The nature of those predictions will depend on the interpretive mechanisms provided for each of those domains.[1] Under this view, if a theory of grammar is seen in the context of a theory of markedness and incorporates a Transparency Principle and other restrictions on the set of possible grammars (such as Emonds' structure-preservation proposal, the autonomy hypothesis, the Specified Subject condition, etc.), then such a theory is a causal factor for and *provokes* certain kinds of historical re-analyses.

It is perhaps worthwhile distinguishing this notion of transparency from the sense in which Langacker (1977) uses the term. Langacker's 'transparency' is a principle 'that the ideal or optimal linguistic code, other things being equal, will be one in which every surface unit (typically a morpheme) will have associated with it a clear, salient, and reasonably consistent meaning or function, and every semantic element in a sentence will be associated with a distinct and recognizable surface form'. So languages tend towards a one-to-one correspondence between units of form and meaning. This is manifested by the loss of 'morphemes with no obvious meaning or syntactic function', by the loss of allomorphic variation, and by 'the tendency for different kinds of boundaries to occur in the same position in a string' (thus morpheme boundaries occur at syllable boundaries and not in the middle of a syllable, etc.). Of course, a one-to-one correspondence is never achieved, allegedly because of the competing forces of 'signal simplicity' and 'code simplicity'. Signal simplicity 'favours fewer and shorter units of expression', and code simplicity 'pertains to the number of different fixed expressions, patterns, and locutions that a speaker must master, remember and manipulate in language use. The impracticality of having a separate lexical item for every conceivable object, event or situation a speaker is likely to encounter is of course a truism' (p114). Thus Langacker must invoke a balance between these three 'forces', and this is a consequence of defining transparency in terms of *semantic* recoverability, as opposed to the recoverability of abstract, initial *syntactic* structures.

---

[1] In §3.2 we set up the basis of a theory of syntactic change, incorporating a statement that less highly valued grammars are liable to re-analysis. 'Less highly valued' will be specified by the theory of grammar and this is an interpretive statement deriving predictions about historical change from grammatical theory. Similar interpretive statements will be needed as components of theories of acquisition, pathology, etc., in order to derive predictions in those domains from a definition of possible grammars. This elementary point is often overlooked in discussions of predictions allegedly following from grammars in some more direct sense, i.e. without an intervening interpretive statement.

7.1.2   In this book I have argued for a theory of grammar within the broad framework of the Extended Standard Theory. A crucial element is the 'shallowness' of the derivations and the claim that the functional load bearable by the transformational component is severely limited. In §6.1 I even suggested the possibility of eliminating cyclic movement rules, enriching the theory of grammar to proscribe such 'rules' and to make them unavailable for a grammar of a natural language. This becomes possible if one adopts the trace theory of movement rules and a richer conception of surface structure, which may contain phonologically null elements. In this approach the level of surface structure plays a much more important role in the functioning of a grammar than it did under earlier conceptions of transformational generative theory. For example, it is arguable that surface structures are the sole input to the rules of semantic interpretation and that many generalizations can be stated at this level via surface filters or output constraints and even lexical sub-categorization requirements.[1] One would still distinguish initial from surface structures, positing transformations to mediate between them, if there were syntactic generalizations to be captured in that fashion. That is to say, the claim that semantic rules operate only on surface structures does not entail the elimination of transformations as conceived throughout this book; such an entailment would hold only under the somewhat extravagant and certainly non-standard assumption that transformations serve solely to characterize paraphrase relations and that there is a one-to-one correspondence between initial structures and semantic interpretations. For a demonstration that much, perhaps all, semantic interpretation can be determined from the 'enriched' surface structures (i.e. surface structures containing abstract, phonologically null elements) and without reference to initial or intermediate structures, and for an illustration of the role of surface filters, see Chomsky (1977), Chomsky & Lasnik (1977), and Lightfoot (1977a).

The enhanced role of surface structures and the restrictions on the derivational processes have important consequences for the approach to historical change and open up another angle on the huge question of the causes of change. It was noted in §3.3 that analogy plays an extensive role in syntactic change and this has been illustrated at several points: the changes involving the distribution of *wh* elements and complementizers were analysed in terms of analogical extensions (§6.2), and

---

[1] Compare earlier formulations where it was assumed that the input to the semantic rules was initial structures (Katz & Postal 1964), or initial, end-of-cycle and surface structures (Jackendoff 1972).

the sub-categorization change of impersonal verbs to personal (*hine hungreth* > *he hungers*) was viewed as generalizing the newly canonical SVO word order (§5.1). The latter change was described in terms of the Transparency Principle; the earlier word order change, whereby the phrase structure rules generated SVO structures instead of SOV, entailed intolerable opacity in the derivation of certain sentence-types with impersonal verbs, such that the Transparency Principle required the elimination of this opacity. However, this principle of grammar is inextricably intertwined with what others have called analogical extension. The principle imposes an upper limit to irregularity and complexity in derivations and has the effect of entailing historical changes which render the derivations more regular and easier to figure out. This sometimes takes the form of extending already existing patterns, as with the ME impersonal verbs and the *wh* elements co-occurring with complementizers. Of course, this is not an inevitable response to intolerable opacity; the re-analysis introducing a new category of Modal did not extend already existing patterns. Nonetheless it is a frequent response and would include what Kiparsky (1974) calls 'imperfect learning',[1] what Parker (1976) calls 'Mis-assignment of Constituent Structure' (see §5.2), and what Andersen calls 'abductive innovation'.

In a series of papers, Andersen (1969, 1972, 1973, 1974) has distinguished various types of historical change. In Andersen (1974) he provides this table.

(1)   1 Adaptive Innovations
      A   1 Accommodative Innovations
          2 Remedial Innovations
      B Contact
   2 Evolutive Innovations
      A Deductive Innovations
      B Abductive Innovations

Adaptive innovations essentially change the relationship between a given grammar and some other aspect of the communicative system. For example, a new word such as 'laser' or 'quark' might be introduced to label a newly current concept. Another innovation might consist

---

[1] Kiparsky's account of 'imperfect learning' is similar in many respects to Andersen's view of abductive innovation; after all, the underlying idea is a traditional one. Thus imperfect learning is said to take place where the later generation hypothesizes a different grammar from that of the parent generation and where the languages generated are slightly different. Compare p148.

of a rule permitting some sentence which would not otherwise be characterized as well-formed by the speaker's grammar; such rules might be invoked when a speaker confronts a new dialect. Evolutive innovations, on the other hand, are to be accounted for entirely by relations within the speakers' grammars. If one takes the three propositions of a syllogism 'all men are mortal' (the LAW), 'Socrates is a man' (the CASE), and 'Socrates is mortal' (the RESULT), one may distinguish three modes of inference: induction, deduction, and what Charles Sanders Peirce called abduction. Induction proceeds from observed cases and results to establish a law, deduction derives a result from a law and a case, but under abduction (often conflated with induction) one takes an observed result, applies a law and infers a case. Thus noting that Socrates is mortal (i.e. dead), one may invoke the general law that all men are mortal and abduce that Socrates was a man. Andersen (1973) notes that this is a fallible means of reasoning, because one may match the observed result with the wrong law and thereby draw a false conclusion; but Peirce gave it a prominent place in theories of scientific method because of the three modes of inference it alone can generate new ideas and explanations. Andersen points out that abductive reasoning plays an important role in language acquisition, although his discussion is inadequate by virtue of omitting to point out that Peirce's theory of abduction crucially involved a limitation on available hypotheses, i.e. a restrictive theory of grammar, in this case (cf. Chomsky (1968: ch.3) for some discussion):

a learner observes the verbal activity of his elders, construes it as a 'result' – as the output of a grammar – and guesses at what that grammar might be ... [He has a] set of 'laws', which he shares with all members of his species, viz. the properties of his constitution that completely determine the nature of linguistic structure, and hence the relation between a grammar and its output [i.e. a theory of grammar] ...

As he builds up his grammar, in his attempt to explain the utterances he has observed, the learner constantly tests its validity by use of both induction and deduction. He checks new utterances produced by his models against the relevant parts of his grammar, to see whether these new data ('results') can be reconciled with the linguistic structure he has formulated [the posited 'case'] in conformity with the 'laws' of language; this is induction. If they cannot, there can be only one reason: his grammar is inadequate. He will then be prompted to make new abductions to make the grammar conform to the observed facts ... he also speaks, testing his grammar by using it to produce utterances in conformity with the laws of language.

This is deduction, the process by which an abductive inference is evaluated on the basis of the consequences it entails. If his analysis is deficient, the learner's utterances may cause misunderstandings or elicit corrections, which may prompt him to revise his analysis. (Andersen 1973: pp776–7)

By an abductive process a language learner hypothesizes a grammar on the basis of the language of his models and of what he knows would count as a possible grammar. 'If a learner defines any of the structural relations that hold among the elements of his grammar differently from his models, he may be said to have made an *abductive innovation*' (Andersen 1974). Abductive innovations are thus changes in the grammar, therefore covert and only indirectly observable through the consequences entailed. These consequences are the overt changes and are 'deductive innovations'. As an example, Andersen gives the early ME collective singular *cheris*, which could also be analysed as a plural *cheri-s*; this would be an abductive change (the kind of thing which others call 'mis-analysis' or 'misassignment of constituent structure'). The deductive (overt) consequences would be that a new form *cheri* replaces the singular occurrences of *cheris* and the former collective *cheris* comes to occur as the subject of only plural verbs.[1] Andersen stresses that these innovations arise in the course of language acquisition and that 'from the point of view of language acquisition, innovating and non-innovating abductions are equally interesting and equally important objects of study'. Andersen (1974) offers a typology of abductive innovations.

There may also be abductive innovations with no immediate observable consequences. In Lightfoot (1974a) I argued that grammars contain indeterminacy in the sense that a given sentence may have more than one syntactic derivation, even though it is not semantically ambiguous. It was assumed that *John is eager to please* and *John is easy to please* are derived differently, the first involving a deletion rule operating on an initial structure [*John is eager* [*John to please*]], the second being derived by a movement rule from an initial [*np is easy* [Δ *to please John*]]. Then it was shown that certain sentences of the same surface form *John is Adj to V* could and should permit both derivations, although they were not semantically ambiguous. That is, for some sentences there is no unique analysis and they may be derived

---

[1] Such examples can be multiplied with ease. The re-analysis of the collective *pease* as a new singular form *pea+* a plural marker, or of earlier *a napron* as NE *an apron* are along the same lines. Such re-segmentation is an extremely common form of change.

in two or more ways. In some cases the two (or more) analyses may be *required* because each of them in isolation is inadequate to account for the full range of facts. For example, in §4.2 I claimed that sentences of the form *Jude wrote a book for you to sell* may be derived from an initial [*Jude wrote a book for you* [*PRO to sell the book*] or [*Jude wrote a book* [*for you to sell the book*]], where *you* may be construed as a subject of the lower clause or a benefactive to the higher verb. Also, in §5.2 I discussed examples like *they took advantage of Jude*, where *advantage* may be construed as the direct object of the verb *take*, or *Jude* as that of the complex verb *take advantage of*; compare the two passives *advantage was taken of Jude* and *Jude was taken advantage of*. If the initial structure contains [[*take*]$_V$ [*advantage*] $_{NP}$[*of*]$_P$]$_V$ [*Jude*]$_{NP}$ then the indeterminacy lies not in the availability of more than one structure (cf. *Jude wrote a book for you to sell*), but in whether a rule calling for a V-NP sequence is interpreted as applying on the larger or smaller V in this configuration. As a third example, Hankamer (1977) has pointed to a double analysis of reduced *wh* questions. Citing work by Robin Bechofer, he claimed that reduced questions like (2) may be derived via a rule of Sluicing (Ross 1969b) or a rule of Stripping (Hankamer 1971).

(2) I just hired somebody to walk my dog. Oh yeah? Who?

The two analyses have precisely the same consequences in most examples, but there are cases which can be dealt with only by a Sluicing analysis and others which require appeal to Stripping. Thus a reduced question with a stranded preposition betrays application of *wh* Movement and then Sluicing (3), since Sluicing may apply only after *wh* Movement. However, there are other reduced *wh* questions (4) wherein the survivor of the reduction is something which cannot be fronted by *wh* Movement, and therefore cannot be a survivor of Sluicing but can be derived by Stripping.

(3) Slinky Sue just walked in. Oh yeah? Who with?
(4) Dick has a picture of [inaudible] on his desk. A picture of who?

The availability of this kind of indeterminacy or multiple analysis permits abductive innovations.

As a fourth example, recall our discussion of the ME impersonal verbs in §5.1. In the earliest stage sentences like (5a) were to be analysed as OVS and could be glossed as 'pears pleased the king'. In NE (5c) is equally unambiguous in having a SVO analysis, but there was a stage where (5b) was structurally ambiguous and could be treated as OVS with *like* meaning 'to cause pleasure for' or as SVO with *like* meaning 'to derive pleasure from'.

(5) a. þam cynge licodon peran
     b. the king liked pears
     c. he liked pears

Although (5b) could be construed as OVS or SVO, similar sentences might be unambiguous. Examples would be instances where a (case-marked) pronoun was involved (6) or the number of the verb gave away which NP was the subject (7).

(6) a. him liked pears (OVS)
     b. he liked pears (SVO)
(7) a. the king like pears (OVS)
     b. the king likes pears (SVO)

Sentences like those of (6) and (7) occur during the period in which (5b) was structurally ambiguous, and therefore illustrate how abductive innovations take place. At the earliest stage only an OVS analysis was possible for (5a) and sentences like (6a) and (7a) were attested while (6b) and (7b) were not. Then, with the loss of nominal inflections and the collapsing of several verbal forms, 'parallel' sentences like (5b) could be analysed as OVS or SVO – indicating again that grammars permit indeterminacy of analysis. The dual analysis is required by the fact that all the sentences of (6) and (7) occur at this time. The Transparency Principle required that the SVO analysis prevail, for the reasons given in §5.1. Put differently, speakers at the earliest stage abduced only an OVS analysis for (5a); speakers of the next stage abduced either OVS or SVO (as indicated by the occurrence of the novel (6b) and (7b)); and eventually speakers of NE abduced only SVO, as shown by the demise of (6a) and (7a) and the fact that *like* now means only 'to derive pleasure from'. The intermediate stage can be depicted as permitting two analyses A^1 and A^2, which cover an intersecting domain of facts, as in (8).

(8)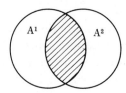

If A^1 is the analysis surviving from earlier times and A^2 is the innovation, then the sequence of historical observables will be that there will first arise some new sentence-types, those of (6b) and (7b) in this example, represented by the unshaded area of A^2. Then the sentence-types covered by the unshaded area of A^1, (6a) and (7a) here, were lost. In this way A^2 replaces A^1 by an abductive innovation, with the deductive consequence of (6b) and (7b) being introduced, (6a) and (7a) becoming obsolete, and *like* undergoing a semantic shift. The fact that A^2 supplanted A^1 is predicted and explained by the Transparency Principle. This particular example can be viewed as an analogical extension, whereby the newly canonical SVO patterns are generalized to what were once impersonal verbs; the new base order is extended by the elimination of the outstandingly complex derivations which would be required in order to continue to generate the old OVS patterns from an underlying SVO structure. Thus we have described the nature of the change (new sub-categorization requirements), the reasons for it (the SOV-to-SVO base change interacting with the Transparency Principle) and the manner in which it took place (an abductive innovation). The net result was a simpler grammar and a more pervasive SVO order in surface structures. Since the theory of grammar, under this view, requires derivations and therefore surface structures to be open to a transparent analysis, surface structures and their analysis clearly play a crucial role in syntactic change and in a description of the causes of change.

This kind of change, whereby a new construction is viewed as a re-analysis of another surface structure pattern, appears often in the traditional literature. For example, Paul (1880: p295) and Wackernagel (1926: pp263f) discuss the Latin accusative and infinitive in these terms, Woodcock (1958: p10, 196–7) the Latin complementizer *quod* from an earlier relative internal accusative,[1] Wackernagel (1926: p265) the Gothic dative and infinitive with *warþ*, and Curme (1931: p191) the English *for ... to* complement construction (see §4.2). Jamison (1976) and Naro (1976) offer more recent accounts of similar phenomena. Naro distinguishes this kind of change from the grammar comparison approach of the generativists, but the distinction is more apparent than real.

Naro examines the *se*-impersonal (9) and *se*-passive constructions

---

[1] Sentences like (i) show the neuter relative pronoun *quod* as an internal accusative, but *quod* came to be perceived as an ordinary complementizer, as indicated by the development of sentences like (ii), where it cannot be treated as an internal accusative.
  (i) miratur (id) quod gaudeo 'he is amazed at that rejoicing which I rejoice'
  (ii) miratur quod caec us sum 'he is amazed that I am blind'

(10) in modern Portuguese. (9) and (10) differ in that (9) occurs only in the third person singular and there is no agreement with the underlying object *estas casas*; the underlying object remains in post-verbal position in unmarked order and there is never any agent phrase in surface structure. In the *se*-passive, however, the verb agrees with the underlying object, and earlier stages allowed agents, although the modern language does not.

(9)   vende-se estas casas 'they are selling these houses'
(10)   vendem-se estas casas 'they are selling these houses'

Naro argues against treating (9) as a variant of (10) without appropriate verb concord (the view of many traditional grammarians), and postulates a lexical item *se*, which can be generated in any NP position in initial structure. *Se* has the feature specification of (11), where [+clitic] and [+nominative] guarantee that, in surface structure, it occurs only as a superficial subject and is cliticized. As justification for [+clitic], Naro points to certain dialects which do not permit this use of *se* with an accusative clitic, whereas it is allowed with non-clitic accusatives or non-accusative clitics. This treatment correctly allows the use of the *se*-impersonal with the *se*-passive (12), derived from an initial (13).

$$(11) \quad \begin{bmatrix} -\text{definite} \\ +\text{human} \\ +\text{3rd person} \\ +\text{group interpretation} \\ +\text{clitic} \\ +\text{nominative} \end{bmatrix}$$

(12)   é-se tentado pelo diablo 'people are tempted by the devil'
(13)   [o diablo]$_{NP}$ [[tenta]$_V$ [se]$_{NP}$ [por np]$_{PP}$]$_{VP}$

The *se*-passive, however, is given quite a different treatment. Naro postulates rules of Agent Postposing, NP Preposing, Object PRO-Fronting and Reflexive.[1]

(14)   Agent Postposing
$$NP_1 \quad Aux \quad V \quad NP_2 \quad P \quad np \Rightarrow t \quad 2 \quad 3 \quad 4 \quad 5 \quad 1$$
(15)   NP Preposing
$$np \quad Aux \quad V \quad NP_2 \quad X \Rightarrow 4 \quad \begin{bmatrix} 2 \\ +\text{pass} \end{bmatrix} \quad 3 \quad t \quad 5$$

---

[1] I reformulate Naro's rules slightly, making them consistent with the form of rules in this book but without making substantive changes. So I incorporate traces in the structural changes and a cliticization in (16).

(16) Object PRO-Fronting
     np Aux V NP X $\Rightarrow$ 4 2 [3, 4] t 5
          [+3rd]   [+pro]

These rules will apply to an initial (17). Agent Postposing will yield (18), which meets the structural description for either NP Preposing, yielding the *ser*-passive (19), or Object PRO-Fronting, which gives (20), which in turn meets the structural description for Reflexive, which produces the *se*-passive (21).

(17) [os examinadores]$_{\text{NP}}$ Past examinar [Dom Nuno]$_{\text{NP}}$ [por np]$_{\text{PP}}$

(18) t Past examinar [Dom Nuno]$_{\text{NP}}$ [por os examinadores]$_{\text{PP}}$

(19) [Dom Nuno]$_{\text{NP}}$ $\begin{bmatrix} \text{Past} \\ +\text{pass} \end{bmatrix}$ examinar t [por os examinadores]$_{\text{PP}}$

(20) [Dom Nuno]$_{\text{NP}}$ $\begin{bmatrix} \text{Past} \\ +\text{pass} \end{bmatrix} \begin{bmatrix} \text{examinar,} & \begin{matrix} \text{Dom} & \text{Nuno} \\ +\text{pro} \end{matrix} \end{bmatrix}$ t [por os examinadores]$_{\text{PP}}$

(21) [Dom Nuno]$_{\text{NP}}$ $\begin{bmatrix} \text{Past} \\ +\text{pass} \end{bmatrix}$ [examinar, se] t [por os examinadores]$_{\text{PP}}$

The surface structures (19) and (21) are realized respectively as *Dom Nuno foi examinado pelos examinadores* and *Dom Nuno examinou-se pelos examinadores* 'Dom Nuno was examined by the examiners'. Naro claims that Object PRO-Fronting is involved in the derivation of Left Dislocation sentences (22), where the pronoun copy is not subsequently reflexivized, because Reflexive is triggered only by a subject NP (cf. (21)).

(22) Sebastiana, eu beijei-a 'Sebastiana, I kissed her'

Naro notes that such a derivation 'synchronically relates [the *se*-passive's] restriction to the third person to a similar restriction of Left Dislocation . . . , as it also synchronically relates the morphological shape of the passivizing particle *se* to the reflexive *se*', and he concludes that 'the impersonal, whatever its diachronic origins, cannot be, in any sense, a synchronic variant of the passive'.

Considering the history of these constructions, Naro argues that the *se*-passive construction was of older provenience but that the *se*-impersonal first appeared in the sixteenth century. The innovation was in a sense foreshadowed: it was of almost the same superficial form as the *se*-passives of a verb-complement construction, and the 'impersonal' semantics of the new form are similar to those of the agent-less passive. Although the resulting surface pattern is similar to the *se*-passive, the two constructions, as indicated above, are viewed as not being transformationally related. Naro proceeds:

> I conclude that the new *se*-impersonal construction can have no connection with a process of Agentization, even if the agent phrase is thought of as deleted. Since it also has no connection with a process of Object Fronting, we reach the important conclusion that THE NEW CONSTRUCTION HAS NO FORMAL CONNECTION WHATEVER WITH EITHER OF THE TRANSFORMATIONS THAT WERE CRITICALLY INVOLVED IN THE DERIVATION OF ITS DIACHRONIC ANCESTOR, the *se*-passive. (p801)

He also notes that in the analyses adopted there is no special relation between the initial, underlying structures of the *se*-passive and the *se*-impersonal, and therefore no formal connection between the underlying forms of the new and old constructions. He then concludes:

> In short, considerations of derivation appear to be incapable of explaining the genesis of the *se*-impersonal.
>
> To understand the appearance of the *se*-impersonal, we must apparently turn away from the strictly formal deep-grammatical structure and transformational mechanisms of the preceding period, and look instead to the surface structure. In other words, rather than looking for structurally determined causes within the grammatical system itself, we must concentrate on the surface form of this system's output. (p802)

Certain surface structure properties of the early classical *se*-passive served as the basis for the development of the *se*-impersonal:

(23) a. the agent phrase was optional
      b. under some circumstances, surface subjects (not only subjects of *se*-passives) could follow their verb
      c. under other circumstances, *se* usually preceded its verb

Therefore, a *se*-passive, which had the *typical* surface form NP_2 V-*se por* NP_1, could surface as *se* V NP_2. Thus, given the unmarked nature of active sentences, it would be natural for a language learner, confronted with a pattern *se* V NP, to analyse it as an active and to treat *se* as a subject (unless, of course, an agent phrase was present, which would preclude an active construal). This would be the simplest hypothesis: it extends the domain of active patterns and involves a minimally complex derivation, which is far simpler than the alternative (24). If the surface form were construed as a *se*-passive, then, given Naro's analysis, it would have to be derived from an initial (24a) by successive applications of Agent Postposing, Agent Deletion, Object PRO-Fronting, Reflexive, Subject Postposing, *se* Preposing. Naro tells us nothing of the form of the last two re-ordering rules, but it is clear that the derivation is enormously complex.

(24)

					Agent Postposing
a.	NP_1 Aux V NP_2 por np				$\Rightarrow$
					Agent Deletion
b.	t Aux V NP_2 por NP_1				$\Rightarrow$
					Object PRO-Fronting
c.	t Aux V NP_2				$\Rightarrow$
					Reflexive
d.	NP_2 Aux [V NP_2] t				$\Rightarrow$
	pro				Subject Postposing
e.	NP_2 Aux V se t				$\Rightarrow$
					se Preposing
f.	t Aux V-se NP_2				$\Rightarrow$
g.	se Aux V NP_2				

Interpreting *se* V NP as an active would involve no movement rules. The language learner would still have to deal with the cliticized character of *se* and its occasionally exceptional surface position, but, as Naro notes, these positional properties would already be familiar from other *se*-constructions. Therefore, we have a situation very much like that of the ME impersonal verbs. A string *se* V NP would be analysed under the earlier grammar as an object-verb-subject structure (where *se* is a derived passivizing particle), and as SVO under the subsequent grammar. The latter analysis is far simpler and (24) is a particularly clear case of the kind of derivation which would be disallowed by the Transparency Principle. Again as with the ME impersonal verbs, there were differences between the two constructions: differences in the unmarked word order of the two types, differences in the verb agreement patterns in that a plural deep object would require a plural verb in the passive form but not in the impersonal, and perhaps some subtle differences in semantics. However, just as the objective form of the initial pronoun in ME *me thinks that I hear* was not enough to prevent it from being parsed as a subject (§5.1), so these differences were sufficiently subtle to be overridden and lost, as the re-analysis or abductive innovation became entrenched.

This re-analysis is remarkably similar in form and motivation to that involving the ME impersonals, and Naro views the change, quite properly, as an analogical extension or regularization in surface structure terms, observing also that 'formal grammatical rules and derivations . . . need not be related in any way to those of the earlier stage', as I argued in §3.2. However, he also asserts that in general syntactic change is 'critically dependent on the surface properties of language and essentially independent of grammatical derivations', and refers to 'the explanatory power of surface factors in syntactic change' as having been 'demonstrated . . . to be superior to that of underlying structures and grammatical derivations'. However, this has not been shown. While it is correct that grammars are constructed afresh by each successive generation and that the grammars of successive generations may have quite extensive, perhaps unlimited, formal differences (within the bounds of the theory of grammar and conforming to the requirement that mutual comprehensibility be preserved), and while it is also true that the development of the *se*-impersonal constitutes an extension of already existing surface patterns, this question must be posed: why did the change take place? Part of the answer must surely be that the re-analysis provided a way to eliminate the extraordinarily complex derivation of (24) (I have throughout assumed the correctness of Naro's analysis). So the Transparency Principle provides part of the explanation insofar as it requires some therapy to be performed to eliminate (24); the principle says nothing about what form the therapy must take.[1] This is where the role of surface structure assumes importance, because in many instances the therapy takes the form of extending some already occurring surface pattern, i.e. such that the relevant forms can be construed as being base-generated without the mediation of several movement rules. The Portuguese *se*-impersonals exemplify this tendency, as do the ME impersonals, etc. Thus, in asserting (correctly) the importance of surface analogies, one should not deny

---

[1] Naro does not indicate how the derivation of (24) came to develop historically, whether it was a consequence of an earlier change in the grammar. Compare the opacity of the ME impersonals, which developed as a consequence of the earlier SOV-to-SVO base word order change.

any role to abstract derivations.[1] The seeds for this re-analysis lay in the complexity of certain derivations, and that complexity is an essential ingredient of any explanation of why the re-analysis took place. There are other changes, e.g. that of the English modals, where the re-analysis is entailed by the Transparency Principle, but where the therapy did not extend already existing patterns and where surface analogies play no detectable role. Therefore one must recognize two ingredients to a proper statement of the causes of syntactic change: the theory of grammar, incorporating the Transparency Principle and interacting with perceptual strategies, will specify low-valued grammars which are liable to undergo a re-analysis which will effect the necessary therapy; in undertaking a particular re-analysis, speakers often generalize already existing surface patterns, perhaps by some kind of (pre-theoretical) analogical process. Again, the causes, mechanisms and effects of a given change must always be carefully distinguished.

The role of analogy in accounts of historical change has given rise to much confusion. The term itself is used in quite different senses. For example, under one traditional use a speaker can be said to produce new sentences *by analogy* with forms already in his inventory. So Bloomfield (1933: p275):

A grammatical pattern (sentence-type, construction, or substitution) is often called an *analogy*. A regular analogy permits a speaker to utter speech-forms which he has not heard; we say that he utters them *on the analogy* of similar forms which he has heard.

Such a notion has been criticized as being essentially taxonomic (notably by Chomsky (1959)). As a theory of language acquisition it predicts the possibility of errors (i.e. deviations from adult forms) which are not attested and, conversely, many of the errors which are made cannot be explained in terms of analogy. Many of these errors can be explained in terms of a theory of grammar allowing abstract levels of representation, whereas analogical theories usually invoke processes of generaliz-

---

[1] In support of his claim, Naro cites Klima's (1964b) account of case-marking, where case comes to depend on *surface* structure position. The grammatical derivations shed no light on the nature of the change because the rules themselves do not change; in some instances they become deprived of input (and therefore become less general), sometimes get more input (and become more general), and sometimes there is no effect on their generality. It is not clear how this constitutes support for Naro's general claim, unless he were to maintain that a reverse change is impossible, whereby case-marking, formerly dependent on surface position, comes to depend on initial structure position of the NP or on thematic functions. I know of no reason to proscribe such a change and Naro offers none.

ation defined on parallel *surface* structures, without access to more abstract representations. So most current work on language acquisition is based on the development of a formal, abstract grammar rather than on analogical processes. But one can view this sense of analogy as not so much refuted as being saved from vacuity by the development and refinement of an explicit and generative theory of a native speaker's linguistic abilities (Vincent 1974). So Chomsky (1959: p56):

> It is easy to show that the new events that we accept and understand as sentences are not related to those with which we are familiar by any simple notion of formal (or semantic or statistical) similarity or identity of grammatical frame. Talk of generalization in this case is entirely pointless and empty. It appears that we recognize a new item as a sentence not because it matches some familiar item in some simple way, but because it is generated by the grammar that each individual has somehow and in some form internalized. And we understand a new sentence, in part, because we are somehow capable of determining the process by which this sentence is derived in the grammar.

A second traditional sense of the term covers what some neogrammarians called 'false analogy', sporadic irregularities of historical change, distinct from regular sound laws. This subsumes re-analyses and the product of abductive innovations. This second use of 'analogy' has also received extensive criticism from some generative historians, who reject all notions associated with analogy. In a much-quoted passage, King (1969: p235) asserts that 'the latter categories, in particular analogy, thereby tend to become terminological receptacles devoid of explanatory power – catchalls for irregularities in the operation of "regular sound laws"'. Such criticisms of analogy, although often overstated as we shall see, stem from the tendency of many historical linguists to invoke analogical processes without suitable restrictions which would distinguish absurd proportions. It is no explanation to say simply that some morpheme has been analogically extended from one class of forms to another, unless it is shown (a) why this morpheme is generalized at the expense of another item which must have had a similar function (e.g. the replacement of *kine* by *cows*), and (b) why, where there are more than two formal classes comprising the grammatical category involved, the morpheme is extended only to one class and not to the others (e.g. in noun declensions, the isolated extension of, say, the Latin *o*-stem genitive singular marker -*i* to the fifth declension, replacing *dies* by *diei*, but not to the third declension, nor extending any other *c*-stem form). Without such restrictions, analogical 'explanations' are arbitrary.[1] Not only is proportional analogy too strong in the above sense, in that it just requires *some* relation between the terms on a proportion and therefore allows non-occurring examples, but Kiparsky (1974) argues that it is also too weak insofar as there are genuine analogical changes where there exist no proportional schemata. He cites the novel 'double' plurals *mices, feets, mens,* 'which are common in American dialects as well as in child language'.

These criticisms boil down to the claim that analogy is too general a notion and cannot be used as the basis for a predictive theory. The appropriate response to this is not to reject the notion out of hand, but to follow Kuryłowicz (1945–9) and Mańczak (1958) and seek to constrain its application. It is probably the case that the notion can never be predictive in the strongest sense. Kuryłowicz (1945–9: p174) uses a now famous image:

Il en est comme de l'eau de pluie qui doit prendre un chemin prévu (gouttières, égouts, conduits) *une fois qu'il pleut.* Mais la pluie n'est pas une nécessité. De même les actions prévues de l''analogie' ne sont pas des nécessités. Etant obligée à compter avec ces deux facteurs différents la linguistique ne peut jamais prévoir les changements à venir.

Defining the gutters along which the rain-water, when it comes, must flow, i.e. constraining the application of analogical processes, is not a trivial task, and the substantive proposals of Kuryłowicz and Mańczak have received critical discussion and a good deal of elaboration. Anttila (1977: pp47ff) shows that there are almost as many proposals for classifying analogical changes as there are linguists who have written on the topic. Work of this type sheds light on the nature of historical changes and on the definitions of possible grammars. However, when one bears in mind the abductive nature of the language learner's grammar construction, the fact that grammars are not passed on with slight modifications from one generation to the next but are constructed anew by each individual child, it is probably a mistake to seek to formalize all aspects of analogical change and certainly fallacious to

---

[1] Kiparsky (1974) shows that the usual view of analogy is loose enough to be invoked to justify changes such as the development of a new form **heye* on the basis of a proportion *ear:hear = eye:x*, or **Mary, who John knows Bill and* on the basis of *John knows Mary:Mary, who John knows = John knows Bill and Mary:x.* However, such changes have not occurred and could not, where, in the second example, a principle of grammar would be contravened (Ross' Co-ordinate Structure Constraint).

represent analogical processes directly in the grammar, following the practice of some generativists.

King (1969), developing proposals of Kiparsky (1965), has sought to re-define analogy as grammar simplification and to eliminate any independent category of analogical change. Levelling was to be regarded as a result of a tendency to formal simplicity of the rule system. Koefoed (1974) has pointed out that generativists constantly modify their notational system so that what is felt to be simple can also be expressed in a simple way. This is based on an assumption that linguistic simplicity is a function of a notational convention and a simplicity metric. For example, Bach (1968) proposes a 'neighbourhood convention' which makes it notationally simpler to write a rule working in two directions than a rule working in just one direction, thus expressing an intuition that the former is more general, and therefore simpler. As evidence, he argues that historical change often takes the form of rule generalization and then points to a change in Old High German whereby a unidirectional assimilation rule becomes bidirectional. So the occurrence of a unidirectional-to-bidirectional change is offered as evidence for the intuition that bidirectional rules are more general. However, Koefoed stresses that if one admits that there are historical changes which optimalize a grammar in one respect but make it less simple, less highly valued, in other respects, as I have argued here at several points, one must abandon efforts to construct a single formalism expressing all kinds of simplicity or give up the hypothesis that diachronic changes necessarily 'simplify'. 'Having observed that the development of languages is determined by a number of conflicting factors, we must consciously choose which of these factors is to be expressed by the formalism. The other factors must stay outside the formalism' (Koefoed 1974: p280) and be stated as extra-formal, or 'functional' principles.

After the somewhat extravagant claims of the 1960s, emphasizing the role in diachrony of the notational conventions of a grammar, more recent work on generative approaches to historical change has sought to develop such extra-formal principles. For example, Bever & Langendoen (1972) invoke a tension between grammatical simplicity and perceptual ease, where the former determines the ease of acquisition and the latter determines the ease of performance. The notational conventions reflect grammatical simplicity and the ease of acquisition, while the characterization of perceptual ease is treated as an extra-formal matter and is not captured by the formal grammar.

As another illustration, Koefoed points to conflict between notions of 'phonetic simplicity' and 'simplicity of the abstract system'. Although they complicate the system, some examples of rule addition can be shown to entail a phonetic simplification. Therefore phonetic simplification has been treated as another extra-formal grammatical principle, along with perceptual ease; these factors are not reflected in the formal notation and are not a function of the formal evaluation measure.

Similarly Kiparsky has more recently posited extra-formal conditions to account for various 'analogical' regularities: constraints on phonotactics, distinctness conditions requiring semantically relevant information to be retained in surface structure, and levelling conditions minimizing allomorphy in paradigms. He claims (1972: p195) that 'all these conditions are functional. Syntagmatic, phonotactic conditions can be related to the requirements of speech production. Retention of functional information in surface structure would appear to be motivated by the requirements of speech perception, and elimination of allomorphy in paradigms by language acquisition.' The validity of such distinctions is not clear to me, nor that of Koefoed's notion of the 'learnability of the abstract system', determined independently of the extra-formal conditions. The learnability of a grammar presumably cannot be determined just from its form, but depends on the relationship between the formal derivations and the surface forms, and on the properties of the Language Acquisition Device or the limits to what counts as a possible grammar. There are also problems involving the proper trading relation between these various notions. For example, Koefoed (1974: p284) sets up an alternative hypothesis to that of Kiparsky and proceeds to show that there is very little to choose between them:

Paradigm regularity is not an independent factor that conflicts with simplicity of the rule system; rather, both are aspects of one notion 'learnability of the abstract system'. So, if we want the notational conventions and evaluation criterion to specify this one notion, paradigm regularity must be translatable into formal simplicity. To the extent that the current notational conventions do not allow for the translation of paradigm regularity into formal simplicity these conventions must be revised.

The early rejection of analogy and the insistence on naive notions of linguistic simplicity stem from a confusion between so-called mechanisms of change, their cause and their effect. There may be various kinds of formal relations between consecutive grammars; I have asserted that there are no formally definable historical constraints, while others have permitted an extremely wide range including rule addition and loss, rule simplification and complication, with re-ordering and re-analysis of the underlying forms which constitute the input to the rules. The simple characterization of the nature of a given change as, say, rule addition, does not *explain* it. This should be self-evident, but Weinreich, Labov & Herzog (1968: p144) found it necessary to comment:

> There was a time when sound changes were being reclassified under the headings of '*additions . . . deletion . . . substitution . . . transposition of phonemes*'. We presume that a repetition of this simplistic exercise in relation to *rules* . . . is not to be taken as the chief contribution of generative theory to historical linguistics. . . . it is far more important to see whether it offers any new perspectives in the *explanation* of changes.

Unfortunately, many generativists have equated explanation with a classification of the possible differences between grammars of successive generations. They have followed the lead of Bloomfield (1933: p385) who asserted that 'the causes of sound change are unknown' and disavowed much interest in the problem of causation.

> There is no more reason for language to change than there is . . . for jackets to have three buttons one year and two the next. (Postal 1968: p283)

> Explanation of the cause of language change is far beyond the reach of any theory ever advanced. (Harris 1969: p550)

> Many linguists, probably an easy majority, have long since given up enquiring into the why of phonological change. (King 1969: p189)

Rule re-ordering may be a correct description of some change but it offers nothing in the way of explanation and says nothing of the cause of the change. As Anttila (1974: p74) puts it, 'it should have been another truism that the loss of a rule cannot be the cause of the change'. Similarly Miller (1973: p686): 'to regard simplification (cf. Kiparsky 1968: §8) as a form of restriction is to confuse the change with the motivation for it'. But there were other cautionary statements: Bever & Langendoen (1972), for example, noted that 'our formal outline of the historical developments is less satisfactory as the basis for an explanation of what has happened. Indeed, there is no general sense in which the changes we outline demonstrate any overall tendency for grammars to evolve in a particular *formal* way [my emphasis – DWL]'. In short, many generative treatments of historical change have shown scant regard for the causes of change or confused the explanation of a change with its mere characterization. Therefore it is little wonder that analogy, which is essentially a causal notion, was given such short shrift. King (1969) provided the clearest illustration of this and marked a turning point. Most of the reviews of the book defended analogy against King's attempt to exorcize it (Bhat 1970, Campbell 1971, Jasanoff 1971, Robinson & van Coetsem 1973), and since that time there has been a growing interest in the matter and an increased effort to constrain the application of analogical processes to prevent their overuse and misuse; this is illustrated by the papers from the First International Conference on Historical Linguistics (Anderson & Jones 1974), notably those by Anttila, Andersen, Campbell, Jeffers, Kiparsky, Koefoed and Vincent.

However, along with the revived interest in, and elaboration of, analogy as an explanatory principle of historical change, one particular orientation deserves some cautionary comment: the claim that analogical processes should be represented directly in the grammar. Hankamer (1972), in a widely cited paper following up a suggestion of Chomsky (1970), argues that analogical rules exist 'and that they must be given the status of grammatical rules'. The evidence is based on certain Turkish time adverbials which have the structure of relative clauses to a head noun such as *zaman*. He refers to constructions like (25) as temporal relatives ('T-Rel') and they have the same structure as an ordinary relative clause (26). The embedded subject is in the genitive case and the verb appears as a participle, marked with a possessive suffix and agreeing in person and number with the subject.

(25) Hasan-ın   gel- diğ- i   zaman
      Hasan [gen]   come [part] [poss]   time
      'when Hasan comes'
(26) Hasan-ın   oku- duğ- u   kitap
      Hasan [gen]   read [part] [poss]   book
      'the book Hasan read'

Sometimes the genitive suffix on the embedded subject may be omitted. Hankamer discusses the contexts in which the genitive does not occur and concludes that 'the T-Rels without genitive ... have a semantic function which may be characterized as "inceptive", or rather that they occur in the context of a main clause which is semantically "inceptive"'.

He then compares another adverbial, formed by adding the suffix -INCE to the uninflected stem of the verb (27).

(27)   Hasan Istanbula gel-ince 'upon Hasan's coming to Istanbul'

He notes that this adverbial 'has a semantic function that can be characterized as "inceptive"; it can occur in conjunction with main clauses of exactly the types that require Genless T-Rels'. Claiming that such a coincidence of distribution 'can hardly be an accident' and would normally be accounted for by positing 'a rule deriving one form from the other',[1] he proceeds to reject for different reasons the analyses of (a) taking the -INCE adverbial as basic and the genitive-less T-Rel as derived from it, and (b) taking genitive-less T-Rels as basic and -INCE adverbials as transformationally derived. The motivation for these analyses is predicated on the assumption that 'not to transformationally relate Genless T-Rels to -INCE adverbials is to claim that their identical distributions are an accident'. Hankamer then captures the generalization by brute force: -INCE adverbials are to be base-generated and T-Rels are derived by the usual rule of Relative Clause Formation. Then the absence of the genitive suffix in certain T-Rels is dealt with by the 'analogical rule' or 'transderivational constraint' of (28).

(28)   The Fake Suffix Rule
        when a T-Rel occurs in an environment which, in another derivation, allows an -INCE adverbial, the sequence − DIK +POSS   NP is reanalysed by analogy to the Suffixed Adverbial as an opaque suffix

'The effect of this rule is that subsequent syntactic transformations treat these T-Rels not as having the structure of Relative Clauses, but rather as if they were Suffixed Adverbials. In particular, the rule which

---

[1] This is a nice illustration of the point made in §6.1, that some generative grammarians have perpetuated a non-generative, Harrisian view of transformations.
   Hankamer (1972: p117) falsely claims that this problem from Turkish 'is exactly that faced by Chomsky' when he invoked analogical rules in Chomsky (1970). Chomsky identified two construction-types: derived nominals (*John's criticism of the book*) and gerundive nominals (*John's criticizing the book*). He then found that some people accepted phrases like *John's criticism of the book before he read it*, which had some of the properties of derived nominals and some of gerundives. He claimed that these were of doubtful grammaticality, and invoked 'analogical' rules to account for them. That is quite different from setting up a rule in order to state explicitly a generalization which the analyst feels to exist. It is also worth noting that Chomsky cited independent evidence for the analogical nature of these sentences: *his criticism of the book before he read it appears on p15*, etc.

inserts the genitive suffix on the subject of a nominalized sentence will not be able to apply'.

The weakening of the theory of grammar to permit such analogical or transderivational rules in the grammars of natural languages vastly extends the expressive power of grammars. One of the problems with the very concept of analogy, as indicated earlier, is its looseness in allowing absurd proportions which never occur (see p361n). Those problems will carry over to any attempt to introduce analogical rules into formal grammars. Once one admits a rule like (28) one admits also the possibility of an immense number of similar rules whereby structures, whether initial, intermediate or surface structures, may be 're-analysed' with reference to any other structure – unless, of course, analogical processes are to be constrained in some way. Hankamer offers no suggestions along these lines and the history of the attempt to constrain the application of analogy in historical linguistics scarcely provides grounds for optimism. Therefore, the introduction of rules like (28) is a priori most undesirable and should be invoked only in the face of compelling evidence. Fortunately, within the framework of the EST, there is an alternative account of the facts as described, which Hankamer did not consider: to allow -INCE adverbials and T-Rels to be generated independently, as proposed, but to invoke an interpretation rule operating on surface structures (like all interpretation rules). Genitive markers will be generated optionally on the subject of nominalizations, including on those in -INCE adverbials. Where the genitive marker does not occur in surface structure, the semantic rule assigns an INCEPTIVE interpretation. If the semantic marker INCEPTIVE occurs with a main verb which, by virtue of its meaning, cannot be inceptive (29), or fails to occur under a verb which cannot be non-inceptive (30), or with the essentially inceptive suffix -INCE (31), a semantic anomaly will result (the kind of thing which Jackendoff 1972 refers to as an 'inconsistency') and the derivation will be marked as ill-formed. A similar inconsistency arises from the occurrence of the inceptive -INCE under a non-inceptive main verb (32).

(29) $\begin{Bmatrix} \text{Hasanın} \\ \text{*Hasan} \end{Bmatrix}$ geldiği zaman, yağmur vardı 'when Hasan came, there was rain'

(30) $\begin{Bmatrix} \text{Hasan} \\ \text{*Hasanın} \end{Bmatrix}$ gediği zaman, şarap içmeğe başlıyacağız 'when Hasan comes, we'll start to drink wine'

(31) $\begin{Bmatrix} \text{Hasan} \\ \text{*Hasanın} \end{Bmatrix}$ gelince, çay içtik 'when Hasan came, we drank tea'

(32)   *Hasan gelince, çay içiyorduk 'when Hasan came, we were drinking tea'

Hankamer refers to three other putative examples of analogical rules, sometimes referred to as 'Let's Pretend' rules. The first concerns complex NPs which do not form islands. Ross' Complex NP Constraint (or Chomsky's Subjacency Condition) should block the extraction in (33a), just as it does in (33b). Hankamer invokes a generalization that 'the ones which do not form islands have paraphrases in which there is a simple verb with a sentential complement' (34).

(33)   a. who is it that Jack has [plans to seduce t]?
        b. *who is it that Jack was discussing [plans to seduce t]?
(34)   who is it that Jack plans to seduce t?

He suggests that 'the non-island-forming behaviour of the constructions in [(33a)] can be accounted for by a "Let's Pretend" rule that allows the sequence V NP, when followed by a sentential complement, to pretend to be a simple verb just in case there is a derivation in which a simple verb occurs with a sentential complement, and which is a paraphrase of the affected sentence'. It is difficult to evaluate this proposal since no analysis is presented. Notice that the re-analysis 'rule' makes reference to paraphrase and is therefore presumably 'global' in that it has access not only to the tree to be changed by application of the rule but also to the output of the semantic interpretation rules operating on (33a) and (34); such globality represents a further vast and undesirable extension of the class of available grammars. Similarly, while *have plans* may be analysed as a simple verb for the purposes of certain movement rules, it must be treated as a V-NP sequence for other rules such as Affix Hopping (or 'Verb Agreement') and Topicalization.[1] But what is missing from Hankamer's brief discussion is an argument that not only *can* (33a) be accounted for by such a rule, but also that it *must* be. Without such an argument or a consideration of alternative analyses, one can scarcely be expected to accept the vast extension of the expressive power of grammars entailed by this proposal.

---

[1] There would be an embarrassing problem for this account if it were shown that there was no such rule as Topicalization, but that topicalized sentences were derived by application of *wh* Movement (see §1.4). In that case, *wh* Movement would sometimes treat *have plans* as indissoluble (**what does John have t to seduce Mary?*), and sometimes as a V-NP sequence: *plans, John has t to seduce Mary (but not ideas)*, which would be derived by moving *wh* from the position marked by *t*, with subsequent *wh* Deletion.

The other two examples of 'Let's Pretend' rules are attributed to Perlmutter and concern Quantifier Floating in French and Clitic Climbing in Spanish. French quantifiers may float down into infinitival clauses allegedly only where there exists a paraphrase with a finite clause, and conversely Spanish clitics may climb to a higher clause from an infinitival complement *unless* there exists a paraphrase with a finite clause. Again discussion is brief, no analysis is offered and no alternative considered (cf. Kayne 1975, Lightfoot 1977a, Quicoli 1976).

Clements (1975) follows the lead of Hankamer (1972) and argues for an analogical rule of Tree Grafting in Ewe. He considers Affix Verb Phrases (AVPs), 'auxiliary' VPs which are morphologically marked for aspect, and claims that while they undergo certain transformational and morphological rules which apply also to NPs, they do not have the distribution of NPs in initial structures. He summarizes his observations in the table (35).

(35)

With respect to	AVPs behave like	
	VPs	NPs
grammatical relations	yes	no
distributional relations	yes	no
selectional restrictions	yes	no
transformational relations	no(?)	yes

After considering various alternatives, he proposes a rule of Tree Grafting in order to capture the noun-like properties of AVPs. AVPs are base-generated as VPs, accounting for their VP-like behaviour with respect to deep structure properties like grammatical and distributional relations and selectional restrictions, and they are subsequently re-analysed as NPs by a rule of Tree Grafting which converts a substructure like (36) to one like (37) by adding nodes to base-generated structures; it does not delete or change node labels.

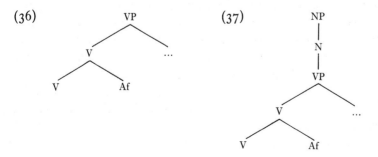

(36)   (37)

Although Clements professes a debt to Hankamer, this is a very different kind of proposal. While a theory permitting grafting rules does extend the expressive power of grammars beyond what would obtain under a theory not permitting such rules, it is not a vast extension. If grafting rules are constrained to operate only on major categories, to apply before all other transformational rules, to add nodes (not deleting or changing nodes) and to add only one node, then the proposal represents only a modest extension to the class of available grammars. Compare this to the vast extensions entailed by Hankamer's proposal for transderivational rules. Furthermore, Clements' Tree Grafting shares certain characteristics with the analyses adopted here in §2.1 and §4.2, whereby *have–be* Raising can move an element from a VP into Aux before application of any transformations and *for*-Phrase Formation can move a subject NP into an empty prepositional phrase. Each of these proposals was designed to capture the mixed character of *has* in (38a) and *John* in (38b), where *has* has some of the properties of an auxiliary and some of a verb and *John* behaves in some ways like a subject of *to win* and in some ways like a PP.

(38)   a.   Mary has won
        b.   it would be surprising for John to win

Clements says that the effect of Tree Grafting is to generalize to AVPs the range of grammatical processes which apply to NPs and that therefore the rule exemplifies analogical extension (not analogical levelling). In that sense the rule can be said to be 'analogical'. However, this is a very loose sense of the term which reduces it almost to uselessness, because in this sense any rule which feeds, i.e. creates environments for, another rule will be called analogical, and that will include most if not all of the cyclic transformations. Such rules might be viewed as part of a *historical* analogical process, but that is quite a different matter. That is, the introduction of such a grafting rule might be one step in a gradual category change, whereby certain morphologically defined elements were once dominated by category X, then by X with a transformationally grafted Y node, and then just by category Y. Thus category Y is analogically extended to dominate new elements and a grammar with a rule grafting Y over X is one intermediate stage in that change. Thus in Ewe it is in principle possible that AVPs once had no nominal properties and later on will have no VP properties and will occur only in initial structure NP contexts.

In the light of our earlier discussion of the indeterminacy of grammars, notice that the facts of Ewe as described by Clements cannot be treated as the reflexes of two co-existent systems. AVPs do not have all the properties of VPs and all the properties of NPs; only in that event could one invoke co-existent systems and indeterminate descriptions. However, an alternative account is not considered by Clements. Following the proposals of Chomsky (1970), one might argue that categories are shorthand labels for feature complexes and that AVPs and NPs share one or more distinctive features. Thus AVPs and NPs would constitute distinct feature complexes in initial structures and any rule affecting both AVPs and NPs would make reference only to the category features distinguishing these two classes from all others. Developing a set of category features for a language is not a trivial task (witness the work on English along these lines by Jackendoff (1977)) and depends on patternings across the grammar. Only when category features have been developed can this alternative account be evaluated, but Clements' data strongly suggest that AVPs and NPs would share some distinctive feature(s).

Whatever the status of this alternative account, there is a clear distinction to be drawn between Hankamer's truly analogical proposal and Clements' Tree Grafting rule, which is analogical only in a very loose sense. Transderivational constraints such as Hankamer's, which make reference to 'parallel' structures in a manner similar to analogical proportions of a traditional kind, entail an immense increase to the expressive power of grammars and therefore represent an undesirable move; they also turn out to be unmotivated, as we have shown. Therefore, while admitting analogy as an explanatory principle for historical change, one does not need to incorporate analogical processes into formal (synchronic) grammars.

Analogy is a principle governing the construction of grammars, influencing the form of grammars, but in no sense directly represented in those grammars. That is, a late ME child, confronted with a pattern *the king likes the queen* (analysed in his parent's grammar as OVS), may choose to analyse it as SVO in accordance with the newly canonical SVO word order elsewhere in his grammar. This may fairly be said to be an analogical re-analysis; but the analogical process, which one might characterize proportionally as *John hit Mary*:SVO = *the king likes the queen*:xVx, is not represented in the grammar of the parent or that of the child. This becomes clear when one thinks of grammar construction or language learning as an abductive process. The parent's grammar analyses *the king likes the queen* as OVS, while the child's grammar treats it as SVO. This has consequences in other areas of the grammar, such as a change in the meaning of *like*, etc. In asking why this historical change has taken place, one may offer two causal factors: first, the Transparency Principle, defined in terms of abstract derivational processes, shows why some re-analysis was necessary since it characterizes the preceding grammar as very low-rated in certain areas (as a result of an earlier SOV-to-SVO word order change); second, the particular re-analysis adopted (which consisted formally of a change in the strict sub-categorization requirements of *thinks* and a semantic reversal of some verbs such as *like*) followed analogical lines in that it extended surface SVO patterns and eliminated the marked OVS patterns. Notice that the *form* of the grammar was not simplified but merely changed, with one sub-categorization frame being substituted for another. What was simplified was the *functioning* of the grammar, so that certain sentences, like *the king likes the queen*, came to have a simpler, more transparent and more accessible transformational derivation. Many syntactic re-analyses are of an analogical nature in that they eliminate derivational opacity by re-construing the sentence involved as derived more transparently by an already existing rule (but not all re-analyses are of this type; compare the English modals discussed in §2.2, where analogy played no role). This does not entail representing analogical processes in the grammar (cf. Hankamer) or building some kind of analogical principle into the theory of grammar. The theory of grammar as proposed here will characterize low-valued grammars, and the theory of change, as developed in §3.2, states that low-valued grammars (including those which violate the Transparency Principle) are liable to historical re-analysis. One could argue for building an analogical principle into the theory of grammar only if one could predict (a) when a change will follow analogical lines (ME impersonals) and when it will not (ENE modals) and (b) what form the analogical proportion will take. That is, why was the *king likes the queen* (OVS) analogized to *John hit Mary* (SVO) and not vice versa, or to *him likes the queen* (i.e. by reconstituting some kind of case-marking), or to some other pattern? Only when these questions are answered will analogy be strong enough to predict the nature of historical re-analyses and to earn itself a place in the pantheon of principles defining possible grammars. This does not seem to be a likely outcome. The major discussions of analogical principles in Havers (1931), Kuryłowicz (1945–9), Mańczak (1958) or, more recently, Esper (1973) and Anttila (1977) do not suggest the prospect of a theory of analogy which is strongly predictive. When one bears in mind the abductive nature of language learning, there is no reason to expect such a theory to be forthcoming, i.e. incorporating principles predicting the form of a re-analysis.

Analogy is not represented directly in grammars nor is it in any way a defining property of the theory of grammar. However, once one distinguishes the causes of a historical re-analysis from its effects and from its formal characterization, then many syntactic re-analyses can be viewed by an analyst as representing analogical extensions of existing surface patterns. That is quite different from claiming that analogy represents a principle of grammar or even a statement in a theory of change. The fact that many re-analyses can be interpreted as analogical extensions does not make analogy a principle of change or anything more than a pre-theoretical concept. On the other hand, the fact that the *form* of re-analyses cannot be predicted beyond imposing very general bounds on possible surface structure extensions, does not belittle the role of analogy in governing language acquisition and therefore historical change. The sub-categorization change involving ME *think*, etc., is illuminated by the Transparency Principle and the observation that the effect of the change was to extend SVO surface patterns. The fact that the former is a defining principle of formal grammars does not make it any more or less illuminative of the change than the fact that SVO patterns come to have a more extensive domain. The usefulness of analogical notions for illuminating syntactic re-analyses in this way will be increased by a theory of grammar such as the one adopted here, which attributes an enhanced functional role to surface structures, compared to earlier versions of generative grammar. Surface analogies clearly play an important role in syntactic re-analyses. If one permits 'enriched' surface structures such that they may contain abstract elements and thereby provide the sole input to semantic rules of interpretation and allow the statement of various generalizations at the level of surface structure via output constraints or the filtering effect of the interpretive rules (see §1.4), then the functional load of surface structures is correspondingly increased. This in turn increases the availability of surface analogies and therefore increases the usefulness of 'analogy' in illuminating re-analyses which have taken place, provoked by the Transparency Principle or other statements of the theory of grammar.

7.2   Independent causation

7.2.1   Caution is in order in discussing the causes of historical change. In the course of this book I have imputed various re-analyses to certain principles of grammar, but there are other causal factors. Two languages of common ancestry will often undergo many parallel changes, but they also characteristically undergo many individual changes. Similarly if two languages show a similar property or construction-type, one language may modify it in some way while the other preserves it unchanged. Therefore, not all changes are predetermined or follow in some necessary way from grammatical principles; if it were otherwise, genetically related languages would be uniform and differences could not develop in the course of time. So causation must be a complex matter and it is an error to look for a single factor as the motivating element for historical change in general. Various things may facilitate or provoke changes and thus be said to be causal factors of some given change, including extraneous factors like language contact and expressivity (to which I shall return below). The fact that the change does not occur whenever the causal factor x is present or, conversely, that the change may occur even when the causal factor x is not present does not indicate that x is not a causal factor. Langacker (1977) observes that 'different factors may trigger the same type of change, and that several different factors may converge in instigating and determining the direction of a given change'. There are various kinds of factors, grammatical, psychological (i.e. analogical), social, etc., and while two or more may coincide to favour some change, they may also conflict and neutralize each other. Discussion of the causes of change often revolves around notions of 'simplicity' or a principle of 'economy of effort'. Langacker and others have sought to refine 'simplicity', breaking it down and claiming that languages tend towards ideals such as 'signal simplicity' (similar to 'economy of effort', and explaining phonological assimilations, simplification of consonant clusters, reduction and elimination of unstressed vowels, etc.), 'perceptual optimality' (conflicting with signal simplicity and requiring adequate distinctions for units of expression), 'constructional simplicity' (elimination of high degrees of markedness), 'transparency' (whereby languages are 'optimal along this parameter to the extent that they show a one-to-one correspondence between units of expression and units of form'), 'code simplicity' (keeping to a manageable level 'the number of different fixed expressions, patterns and locutions that a speaker must master, remember and manipulate in language use'). Such a proliferating inventory of conflicting tendencies provides ready explanations for almost any change, but also runs the risk of rendering the theory of change vacuous and unfalsifiable. If one sets up conflicting principles, one is methodologically bound to provide further principles predicting when a given principle will take precedence over a competitor and vice versa. Work of this type usually stops short of specifying any such precedence relations.

I have taken a somewhat different approach, distinguishing carefully a theory of change from a restrictive theory of grammar. A theory of grammar imposes limits on the kind of system a language learner may postulate in hypothesizing a grammar of his native language. Abductive reasoning plays a critical role in the child's grammar construction and the child is often led to hypothesize a grammar quite different from that of his models; he is led to do this by the theory of grammar with which he is endowed, i.e. by the limits to the kind of system he may set up. Earlier generations may introduce changes in their grammars and thus in their outputs, producing a more highly marked system, one which is in certain respects close to the limits imposed by the theory of grammar. For example, perhaps the effect of the earlier changes has been to lead to transformational derivations of such a degree of complexity as to approach the limits laid down by the Transparency Principle. In such a situation a child is tempted to entertain or 'abduce' a novel and simpler analysis which produces the same or almost the same output as the analysis or 'grammar' of his models. Thus language acquisition is seen as a major locus of historical innovation and that innovation is provoked by the restrictive theory of grammar. This has now been illustrated many times. It has been assumed throughout that radical re-analyses of the internal form of the abstract grammar, abductive innovations, take place only when necessary. More accurately, since grammars may be indeterminate in certain areas (see §7.1), abductive innovations involving (minor) changes in the output of the grammar take place only where necessary (e.g. the re-analyses involving the English modals, impersonal verbs, quantifiers, etc.). Re-analyses do not take place in arbitrary fashion. This is in part a function of the fact that while re-analyses may involve radical and far-reaching changes in the grammar, there can only be minor changes in the output. This in turn is a consequence of the constraint on changes (imposed by the theory of change; see §3.2), that mutual comprehensibility must be preserved between generations. Whether or not two systems are mutually comprehensible is at present and perhaps in principle not formalizable. However, the fact that mutual comprehensibility represents an intuitive and non-formal concept does not render it useless. It serves to impose a highly restrictive limit on the class of possible changes. For example, presumably no grammar with a base-generated SOV word order could undergo a re-analysis of its phrase structure rules to generate initial SVO structures, unless it already had transformational rules changing the basic SOV order to SVO in certain contexts. It follows from this that such word order changes must 'leak' through the grammar and cannot take place without warning. This restriction follows on the assumption that such a far-reaching kind of unannounced change would entail mutually incomprehensible systems. Not all changes, of course, must leak through the grammar. If one assumes that a system with uniform adjective-noun order is not mutually comprehensible with one generating a uniform noun-adjective order, it follows that if one order is to take over from the other in the course of time, this change will be effected gradually in the sense that the innovative order will occur first in restricted contexts, slowly extending its range. However, if a system treating *the king likes the queen* as OVS is mutually comprehensible with one construing it as SVO (under the conditions indicated in §5.1, e.g. that *like* undergoes a shift in meaning), there would be no need for a replacement of one analysis by the other to be gradual; the replacement would be free to occur across-the-board, cataclysmically, since it does not endanger communicability.

This opens up the general question of the gradualness of change, a matter which has caused some confusion in the literature but nonetheless something on which it is de rigueur that every book on historical linguistics must deliver an opinion. Chung (1976) claims that 'the standard generative view of syntactic change [sic] is that it is not gradual but discrete', noting in an Orwellian turn that 'this view is so widely held that it is hard to find explicit mention of it in the literature'. The notion of a 'standard generative view of syntactic change' is a puzzling one when so little work has been done in the area. She refutes this 'standard view' by asserting that 'syntactic change must be actualized gradually', specifically that 'syntactic change is actualized for sentences that undergo superficial rules before it is actualized for sentences that undergo major cyclic rules' (p439). Chung's claim overlaps to a large extent with the claim made in §3.2, that a theory of grammar incorporating some version of Emonds' structure-preserving hypothesis predicts that many changes will enter the language as root transformations, i.e. non-structure-preserving, and only later percolate through the grammar to affect the base rules. If Emonds is correct in claiming that only one root transformation may apply in any root S, it follows that the innovative root transformation will not apply where another (older) root transformation (i.e. non-superficial or 'major cyclic' rule) applies (Chung's category of major cyclic rules seems to overlap largely with Emonds' root transformations). So this kind of gradualness, far from being inconsistent with generative grammar, actually follows from it in direct fashion. However, if one views grammar change as embedded in the acquisitional process and proceeding by abductive innovations on the part of language learners as they hypothesize and construct their grammars, the question of the gradualness of change loses much of its interest. Language learners are free to construct grammars which differ in formally unlimited ways from those of their models; in this sense they may make discrete innovations. This is possible because, while learners are limited to minor changes in outputs by the condition of mutual comprehensibility with their models, small differences in output can correspond to large differences in the abstract grammar and vice versa (see Hale (1974) for discussion with relation to Maori, and Fasold (1976) for a similar claim that substantial changes in rules may lead to only slightly different surface forms). Therefore the nature of the acquisitional process dictates that a learner's output will differ only in minor and often piecemeal ways from that of his models, but his grammar may differ radically.

To return to the main line of argument, radical re-analyses can be viewed as caused by an interaction of (a) the limits on the hypotheses of the language learner, imposed by the theory of grammar, and (b) earlier changes such that resulting grammars have become marked in some area. As the degree of markedness approaches an unacceptable level (as defined by a precise account of the Transparency Principle), so a re-analysis is required. Degrees of markedness are defined by the theory of grammar, including the specification of what constitutes unacceptable markedness. In this sense, the theory of grammar predicts and may be said to play a causal role in historical re-analyses. The requirement of mutual comprehensibility between the system constructed by the language learner and that of his models restricts the availability of re-analysed grammars and limits re-analyses to where they are necessitated by the theory of grammar; thus language learners do not re-analyse arbitrarily.

Two vital ingredients to this approach to the causes of syntactic change are: first a clear distinction between a theory of grammar and a theory of change, where the theory of grammar defines degrees of markedness, including impossibly marked grammars, and the theory of change states that highly marked grammars are liable to re-analysis; and second the assumption that markedness is defined and eliminated in local fashion. As discussed in §3.1, I follow Paul (1880) in assuming that grammars are re-analysed in such a way as to solve essentially local problems; the fact that the re-analysis adopted may lead to markedness, derivational complexity, etc., in other areas of the grammar often does not inhibit the change. In §3.2 I expressed this as a claim that grammars practise therapy rather than prophylaxis. This local character of syntactic change plays an important role in causation in that it permits one change to lead to another. A re-analysis may affect certain constructions and eliminate certain kinds of markedness. However, language learners do not re-design their entire grammar or practise sufficient prudence to check all the implications of a given change for all other areas of the grammar. Consequently a re-analysis eliminating markedness in one area of the grammar may entail increased markedness in another area. This means that changes may often take place in implicational sequences. We have seen several examples of this in earlier chapters.

The re-analysis of the ME impersonal verbs was treated as a consequence of the earlier SOV-to-SVO base word order change, interacting with the Transparency Principle. The introduction of a basic SVO word order no doubt took place in response to some structural 'need' and eliminated markedness which had developed in some areas of the grammar (see below), but it was shown in §5.1 that it entailed a more complex derivation for sentences like *the king likes the queen.* These sentences were subsequently re-analysed in such a way that the complex derivations were eliminated. Therefore, this re-analysis may be viewed as being caused by an interaction of the theory of grammar, specifically the Transparency Principle, and the earlier SOV-to-SVO base change. Thus, by virtue of the Transparency Principle, there is an implicational relationship between these two re-analyses.

The most complex implicational chain discussed here is that involving the English modals. In that example, there were five early changes affecting different parts of the grammar. Whatever the reasons for these changes, the net result in one area of the grammar was that the verbs *may, must, can,* etc., became highly exceptional. The Transparency Principle required some kind of re-analysis and a new modal category was introduced. The introduction of this category was therefore caused by the interaction of the five earlier changes and the Transparency Principle, and eliminated the offending opacity. Notice that this is a weak sense of 'cause': the Transparency Principle proscribes intolerable opacity, but does not specify how it should be eliminated. Therefore, *some* re-analysis was called for, but the form of the re-analysis is not predetermined, nor does it follow from any principle of grammar known to me. However, the introduction of the new category, while eliminating markedness in certain areas, entailed some immediate problems elsewhere. Specifically, if the rules of Negative Placement and Subject-Verb Inversion were to be retained in their old form, new sentence-types would be produced: **John can play not the blues, *play John can the blues?* If *can* is no longer a V, these sentences would be generated by a grammar which continued to require that the negative marker be placed after the first V or that the first V be moved in front of the subject NP; in each instance the first V would be *play* after the re-analysis of *can* as a modal (see §7.3 below). This did not happen, presumably because these innovations would be sufficiently drastic to endanger mutual comprehensibility across generations. Instead, the two transformations were re-formulated to make reference to Aux rather than V; this preserved the old surface forms *John cannot play the blues* and *can John play the blues?* Therefore, this re-formulation of Negative Placement and Subject-Verb Inversion may be said to be caused by an interaction of the introduction of the new category and the requirement that mutual communicability be preserved across generations. Finally, the re-categorization of *can, will, must* as modals seems to have entailed the introduction of new verbal periphrastic elements, *be able to, be going to, have to,* although I cannot suggest any sensible reason for this entailment.

In this way one may find implicational chains of syntactic (and other) changes. Given the local character of re-analysis, one change may lead to another by entailing or helping to entail (along with other changes) intolerable markedness in some other area of the grammar. Therefore, the more restrictive one's theory of grammar, the more implications will follow from a given change. That is, if one postulates very tight limits to permitted derivational opacity, a re-analysis in one area is more likely to cause intolerable markedness elsewhere and therefore to contribute to further changes in the grammar. Given that the orientation of work on the EST since the late 1960s has been to impose the most restrictive possible constraints on the form and functioning of rules of grammars, this work will make predictions about implicational sequences of changes. The extent to which these restrictions are borne out will constitute further evidence for or against the theory. So if one treats conditions on rules within the logic of markedness, as discussed in §1.5, the theory of grammar will specify what 'deviations' constitute an intolerably marked grammar. So the Specified Subject and Subjacency Conditions, for instance, contribute to a specification of more or less marked rules and derivational processes; $\overline{X}$ conventions similarly distinguish natural from unnatural sets of phrase structure rules. Where these proposals are clear enough, they can be tested and refined against historical re-analyses, particularly the implicational relationships holding amongst them. As argued earlier, historical re-analyses constitute a rich and hitherto untapped area for testing and refining theories of grammar, given proper distinctions between theories of change and grammar. Testing grammars in this way is a complicated matter in that grammars must be posited for at least two stages of a language and discussion of the correct grammar must necessarily be somewhat abstract and theory-bound, even where there is an abundance of data. Re-analyses are not primary, observed data, but require argument and justification. To the extent that theories of grammar make successful predictions about diachronic change, so they will derive further plausibility and shed light on our understanding of the nature of change. Using a version of the EST, I have described several re-analyses and some implicational sequences where one change entails another by virtue of some principle of grammar. Principles of grammar therefore play a causal role in provoking certain historical changes. In this sense, a given grammar can be said to be a product of its history. It has the form it does partly as a result of earlier changes, entailing further changes because of the local character of re-analyses and the limits imposed on the kinds of grammars that a language learner may hypothesize.

7.2.2 However, even though the theory of grammar may interact with earlier innovations to cause further re-analyses, this is not a sufficient account of the causes of change. One is still left to wonder why grammars never reach a state of equilibrium or indeed what set off such implicational sequences in the first place. Here one must turn to extra-grammatical causes of change; this is what Andersen calls 'adaptive innovation', which is motivated by the communicative system and is to be distinguished from 'evolutive innovation', motivated by linguistic structure (see §7.1.1). It may be difficult to decide whether an individual historical change is an evolutive or adaptive change, whether it is motivated by the theory of grammar or by extra-grammatical factors, but that does not gainsay the validity of the distinction, which is essential. In the realm of syntax one may appeal to at least three kinds of extra-grammatical causes of change: foreign influence, expressivity and 'after-thought'.[1]

Foreign influence has played a prominent role in many accounts of syntactic change. If a change affects a construction in some language such that it becomes more like a parallel construction in another language, that change might be attributed to and explained by the influence of the second language. This mode of explanation is invoked frequently by Lockwood (1968, 1969), and Fehling (1976) pleads for scholars to make greater use of borrowing as an explanation for parallels across languages. Lockwood considers the Proto-Germanic periphrastic verbs as an imitation of Romance developments, and the reduction of the PIE tense system due to Finno-Ugric influence. Fehling claims that the Greek and Latin accusative + infinitive construction cannot be inherited and represents a borrowing of Latin from Greek. He points to similarities between Semitic (Hebrew) and Western European languages, claiming that the European forms are syntactic calques from Hebrew: the use of *to* as an infinitival and dative marker, the existence of a definite article and two genders, masculine and feminine, the use of *one* as an indefinite article and *man* as indefinite subject. Traugott (1972a) suggests the influence of French and Scandinavian upon the disappearance of grammatical gender in English. Weber (1971) points to the role of Latin in the development of Relative-Noun structures in Germanic. Hyman (1975) attributes some word order

---

[1] I regard perceptual factors as intra-grammatical or at least as causes of change which are internal to the 'system' (see §4.3 for the way in which perceptual factors may influence changes).

changes in African languages to borrowing. Similarly, Lakoff (1968), relying heavily on Brénous' (1895) study of hellenisms in Latin, attributes many changes taking place between Latin and Spanish to the influence of Greek. She noted the close contact between Latin and Greek in imperial times, the tendency of wealthy Romans to employ Greek tutors for their children, etc. She then invoked bilingualism as the explanation for Spanish innovations whereby the new construction was similar in some respect to a Greek expression. This explanation was invoked without any attempt to determine how the new con- struction was first introduced – for example whether it was used by writers particularly susceptible to Greek influence (for a more careful account, compare Coleman (1975)). More recently, Hamp (1975) has claimed that the changes discussed by Bever & Langendoen (1972), concerning the English relative pronoun, might be explained not by general perceptual mechanisms but by borrowing from Welsh. Bever & Langendoen (see §6.2) had shown that important changes had affected the distribution of relative markers between 1400 and 1550, that the relative marker came to be often an invariant form in surface structure (*that, who*), and that it came to be deletable prevailingly in object position as opposed to the earlier deletion of subject relatives. Hamp shows that the new surface structures paralleled closely the comparable Welsh forms. The net effect of various processes in medi- eval Welsh was that a segmental trace of a relative marker *a* occurred only in affirmative clauses and as subject or object, and in these *a* was deleted in rapid speech, leaving only the lenition of the following initial as the overt mark. Lenition was a regular mark of an *object* NP in main clauses, whereas subject lenition occurred only in restricted circumstances and 'falls off in frequency to a vanishing point in Modern Welsh. Thus lenition comes to be a strong mark of object syntax . . . in non-subject syntax the absence of an overt segment for *Rel* was normal. Hence to a bilingual speaker in Britain the suppression of an overt *Rel* segment had a strong linkage with non-subject syntax' (Hamp 1975: p300). Only a minority of English speakers were competent in Welsh, and to explain the English relative pronoun changes as a borrowing of the Welsh patterns would require a demonstration that the innovating forms were first used by bilingual speakers, for the most part in Wales or in the border counties, only later spreading more generally. Hamp offers no such demonstration.

So, while foreign influence has often been invoked as an explanation for syntactic changes (see Weinreich (1953) and Kurath (1972) for comprehensive accounts of alleged borrowings, usually affecting the lexicon, morphology and phonology), it is not enough to show simply that parallel forms exist in two languages whose speakers are in close cultural contact. However, to assert that many of the explanations in the literature are specious as they stand is not to deny that there are genuine cases of borrowing. Nadkarni (1975) offers a persuasive example by showing that a dialect of Konkani, an IE language, has two relative clause constructions, an inherited IE type and another borrowed from Kannada, a Dravidian language. He shows that the borrowed form is supplanting the inherited one and that this change is taking place through bilingual speakers. For four hundred years the speakers of the Saraswat Brahmin dialect of Konkani have been fluently bilingual in Kannada, which has been the language of early schooling, business and administration; the language has been learned early in childhood, almost simultaneously with the mother tongue. In clausal relatives, the usual IE pattern has a relative pronoun and this occurs in all dialects of Konkani and in the other neighbouring IE languages, Hindi, Gujarati and Marathi. However, the Kannada pattern has an interrogative pronoun, which is ungrammatical in all the neighbouring IE languages, except Saraswat Brahmin Konkani. Furthermore, in Kannada $\bar{o}$ is attached to the verb of the relative clause and also occurs as a marker of yes–no questions. Similarly this particular dialect of Konkani attaches a *-ki* suffix to a verb in a relative clause, which otherwise marks yes–no questions; this is the only IE dialect to do this, so it is presumably not an inherited property. Furthermore, relative clauses may usually be extraposed, separated from the head noun (cf. *the man came in who I met yesterday*), in IE languages, but not in Dravidian; Saraswat Brahmin Konkani extraposes the IE-type relative, but not the Dravidian type. Nadkarni argues that the Dravidian type (introduced by an interrogative pronoun, including a yes–no interrogative marker on the verb, and not extraposable) is supplanting the IE type of relative. Most conspicuously, the oblique case forms of the relative pronoun have been lost and so, wherever the relativized NP is in the accusative/dative, genitive, locative, the Dravidian form must be used, i.e. with the interrogative pronoun, which has a full complement of case forms. Nadkarni also claims convincingly that this change cannot plausibly be viewed as structurally induced, as filling some need or structural gap, nor as introducing a new construction with some special stylistic value. He finds no evidence for pidginization or creolization processes. Furthermore, bilingualism is unidirectional and Kannada speakers hardly ever learn Konkani; if they did learn Konkani, they would be regarded as responsible for the Dravidianization on the ground that their Konkani would have had a Kannada substratum. Also code-switching is unavailable as an explanation since the Saraswat Brahmins rarely begin in Konkani and switch to Kannada in mid-sentence, or vice versa. This suggests strongly that borrowing is the only available explanation for the change in the relative clause forms.[1] In the light of Nadkarni's careful analysis, one may conclude that while borrowing is often invoked gratuitously in the literature, there are nonetheless examples of syntactic changes where language contact and borrowing seem to be the best available explanation.

A second kind of extra-grammatical cause of syntactic change is what one might term 'expressivity'. This would include the introduction of novel forms for stylistic effect, such as the 'topicalized' sentences which are common in certain English dialects, where a NP occurs in a marked position and with heavy stress: *Mingus, she heard, but not Miles.* Similarly,. 'dislocation' sentences would fall under the same rubric: *Mingus, I heard him* and *he played cool, Miles.* These forms are still regarded as novel in English and as having a distinct stylistic force; they are common in Yorkshire dialects and with British football commentators. However, such forms characteristically become bleached and lose their novelty value as they become commonly used. This can be illustrated with the parallel dislocation sentences in French: *Pierre, je le connais* and *je le connais, Pierre* were originally stylistically marked alternants of *je connais Pierre* but now they have lost much of their special force and have become relatively unmarked construction-types, to the point that in simple, affirmative main clauses they are the norm and the former unmarked type, *je connais Pierre*, is vanishingly rare. This process is familiar from lexical change, where, to the constant dismay of the purists, adjectives are regularly 'devalued' by a kind of linguistic inflation: 'excellent' comes to mean merely 'good', 'enormous' to mean 'big', and 'fantastic', 'fabulous', etc., lose their original force. As this happens so new superlatives must be invented to describe the end-point on some scale: hence the popular 'ginormous', 'fanta-

---

[1] Nadkarni goes on to hypothesize the conditions necessary for borrowing to induce a successful syntactic change: extensive bilingualism, where the whole community speaks the second language and uses it actively for a wide range of purposes, and the absence of standardizing influences such as a strong literary tradition.

bulous', etc. Similarly metaphors lose their value and become standardized through frequent use, requiring a constant effort on the part of speakers to find new forms with the old surprise value. So in syntax new constructions are introduced, which by their unusual shape have a novelty value and are used for stylistic effect. The special stylistic effect slowly becomes bleached out and the constructions lose their marked force, become incorporated into the normal grammatical processes and thereby require speakers to draw on their creative powers once more to find another new pattern to carry the desired stylistic effect. So sentences such as *Mingus, she heard* seem to be fairly recent innovations and have a special topicalization effect in most dialects;[1] in other dialects, notably those of North Americans with a Yiddish background, the construction has already become bleached of its special effect, like the dislocation sentences of French. This is an important kind of historical change in syntax which has been given very little attention in the literature, perhaps as a consequence of the lack of a real analogue in phonological change.

One further kind of extra-grammatical cause of syntactic change, which could perhaps be subsumed as a special case of 'expressivity', is what Hyman (1975) has called 'after-thought'. This is alleged to play a role in the development of SOV word order to SVO. In addition to the usual SOV patterns one would get after-thought expressions SOVO: *Mingus the ice-cream liked . . . and the rum baba.* Thus in a OV language, after-thoughts permit certain surface occurrences of VO. If in an underlyingly OV language there are rules which allow many surface occurrences of VO forms, the language runs the risk of being re-analysed as underlyingly VO, as we shall discuss in the next section. Therefore, insofar as the after-thought phenomenon is a psychological motivation for VO sequences, it contributes to the opacity of the underlying OV order and therefore may be said to play a causal role in the development of a new VO order, albeit perhaps a minor role.

7.2.3 So far we have identified two classes of explanations for syntactic change: grammatical and extra-grammatical. In the literature one finds also what appears to be a third class: independent diachronic principles. Some writers argue explicitly for such principles, while

---

[1] Again, one must beware of ex tacito arguments. With highly marked constructions it is particularly dangerous to assume that their absence from the surviving texts indicates that they were ungrammatical.

others couch in those terms claims which should prove to be a function of grammatical principles. For example, it is often said that if an OV language changes to become VO, there will also be a re-ordering of V-Aux to Aux-V. This is couched as a principle of change. However, such a diachronic implicational universal would be a result of a theory of grammar which allowed phrase structure rules to generate an underlying Aux-V-O or O-V-Aux, but not O-Aux-V. We shall return to this matter below, but first we shall examine some explicit claims for independent diachronic principles of change. These claims are reminiscent of the notion of 'diachronic process' criticized in §3.2 and often appeal to concepts of 'drift' and typologically 'consistent' languages.

The concept of linguistic 'drift' is due to Sapir (1921: ch.7) who used the term in describing the replacement of *whom* by *who*.

The drift of a language is constituted by the unconscious selection on the part of its speakers of those individual variations that are cumulative in some special direction. This direction may be inferred, in the main, from the past history of the language . . . the changes of the next few centuries are in a sense prefigured in certain obscure tendencies of the present (p166)

the particular drifts involved in the use of *whom* are of interest to us not for their own sake but as symptoms of larger tendencies at work in the language. At least three drifts of major importance are discernible. (p174)

Sapir lists the levelling of the subject–object distinction, the tendency to fixed word order and the development of the invariable word. In positing a 'canalizing' of such 'forces', he poses the question: 'are we not imputing to this history a certain mystical quality?' He does not provide a clear answer to this question nor define these drifts, showing how they relate to the synchronic rules of a language, or to universal considerations, or to diachronic 'processes'. Certainly some of the recent work which has taken up this idea, has treated it in mystical fashion.

Robin Lakoff (1972) examined changes in various IE languages which yield a more analytic surface syntax, and sought to combine Sapir's three drifts into one.

This phenomenon . . . cannot be described by talking about individual changes in transformational rules, in the phrase structure component, in the lexicon, or indeed, in any part of the grammar. Rather, it must be described as a metacondition on the way the grammar of a language as a whole will change . . . 'If there is a choice between a rule and a lexical item to produce a surface structure containing independent segments, as opposed to one containing morphologically bound forms, pick the former'. Speaking metaphorically, it instructs the language to segmentalize where possible . . . (p178)

It is not at all clear where this metacondition exists: neither as part of a grammar nor as a universal condition on the form of grammars. It is not clear how a constraint on change within one language family, a constraint that is not absolute but which is nevertheless influential, is to be thought of. But there is no other way to think of these things: either there is such a metacondition, whatever it is, or all the Indo-European languages have been subject to an overwhelming series of coincidences. (p192)

An only slightly less mystical approach to 'drifts' is one based on Greenberg's word order typologies; this has achieved a certain popularity in recent years. Greenberg (1966), developing ideas of Jakobson (particularly those of Jakobson 1958), postulated a set of implicational universals and quasi-universals based on 'predominant' surface word order patterns. His universals 16 and 17 illustrate the general form.

Universal 16. In languages with dominant order VSO, an inflected auxiliary always precedes the main verb. In languages with dominant order SOV, an inflected auxiliary always follows the main verb.

Universal 17. With overwhelmingly more than chance frequency, languages with dominant order VSO have the adjective after the noun.

On the basis of such implications, there emerged a notion of a 'typologically consistent' language. Thus a 'consistent' SOV language would have post-positions, the orders V-Aux, Adj-N, Genitive-N, Determiner-N, Indirect Object-Direct Object, and it will tend to be heavily inflected. A 'consistent' SVO language would have prepositions and the reverse orders, namely Aux-V, N-Adj, N-Genitive, N-Determiner, Direct Object-Indirect Object, and it will tend not to be heavily inflected.[1] Therefore, if a consistent SOV language were to develop into a consistent SVO type, it would undergo a large number of harmonic changes. Since some of the universals are quasi-universals, e.g. Universal 17 above, it is possible to define hierarchies: if a language acquires property p, it will tend later to acquire property q. The absolute universals, e.g. Universal 16 above, may define simultaneous changes: if a language acquires property p, it simultaneously acquires property q,

[1] This particular formulation is based on Vennemann (1972) who asserts that 'in a syntactically consistent language all grammatically functional word order relation-

since languages with *p* but without *q* do not and presumably cannot exist. Such implicational hierarchies are familiar from the work of 'analogists' like Kuryłowicz, Mańczak and others; Greenberg (1969) examines the hierarchical fashion in which some marked categories of Slavic nominal declensions lost their inflectional signs. Such an approach gives rise also to the notion of a typologically inconsistent language, which has some of the properties of say, a SOV language, and some of a SVO and therefore can be said to be 'in transition' from one type to the other.

This idea underlies much recent work (e.g. many of the papers in Li 1975b, 1976, 1977) and is exemplified by Li (1975a). Li discusses locative phrases, manner-adverbial complements and co-verbs in Modern Mandarin. For example, some morphemes, called 'co-verbs' by Chinese grammarians, have some of the properties of verbs and some of prepositions. These items were all clear cases of verbs in Archaic Chinese and have been developing into prepositions. However, the rate of the change differs from one item to the next: some have lost all their verbal properties, others retain their full verbal status in certain contexts and others are somewhere in between.

Thus the disparate behaviour of a co-verb with respect to these verb features merely represents the different extent to which vestigial properties of verbs are retained by present-day co-verbs. It reflects the different rate of change

ships can be predicted from the relative order of V and O, as in (1)' [footnote omitted].

(1) $\{A, B\}$ $\begin{cases} [A, B] \text{ in OV languages} \\ [B, A] \text{ in VO languages} \end{cases}$ for the following A and B:

		A	B
I	a	object	verb
	b	adverbial	verb
	c	main verb	auxiliary
	d	main verb	modal
	e	main verb	intensional verb
II	a	adjective	noun
	b	relative clause	noun
	c	number marker	noun
	d	genitive	noun
	e	numeral	noun
	f	determiner	noun
III	a	adjective stem	comparison marker
	b	standard	comparative adjective
	c	adverbial	adjective
IV	a	noun phrase	relation marker (adposition, i.e. postposition or preposition)
V	a	indirect object	direct object
	b	temporal adverbial	directional adverbial

of different lexical items in a historical process ... the explanation of such synchronic disparity requires an understanding of diachronic processes. (Li 1975a: p884)

Li's general claim is that various synchronic 'irregularities' of this type are to be 'explained' by the diachronic shift from SVO to SOV typology. This shift 'has been in effect for more than a millennium, and is still an ongoing process'. In considering whether the language will achieve all the characteristics of an SOV typology, he notes that

a diachronic process may continue in a specific direction, but it may also halt and be overtaken by another diachronic process. However, the shift in word order has already carried Mandarin a considerable distance toward the OV typology; and it appears reasonable to assume that the process still has considerable momentum. (p885)

Koch (1974) took a similar approach to parallel changes in several IE languages, arguing that they can be viewed as the symptoms of a more general SOV-to-SVO typological change. The explanation for why English levelled most of its inflections and developed a fixed word order and greater use of 'function words' (prepositions, auxiliaries) was not to be found within the history of English. The traditional explanation for these changes appeals to the erosive effect of phonological change: the fixing of a heavy stress accent on the initial syllable in Proto-Germanic is alleged to have led to a loss of distinctions in final syllables, and hence to the demise of the case system, which in turn entailed a therapeutic fixing of word order and development of function words. This view is held by older writers and is put forward in the most recent work (Kellner 1892: p17; Wyld 1927: p19; Pyles 1964: p152; Vennemann 1975), and was hinted at by Sapir (1921: p175). Following up the work of Strang (1970) and others, Koch discredited this view by showing that OE was structurally much more similar to NE than is usually assumed: despite the availability of case forms and verbal markers, the inflectional system was already dysfunctional, function words were common and word order was the prime signal of grammatical relations (Strang (1970) and Gardner (1971) have satisfactorily refuted the view of, for example, Fries who thought that 'the order of ... words ... has no bearing whatever upon the grammatical relationships involved ... word-order is non-distinctive and connotative' (Fries 1940: p1)). As opposed to the traditional view, Koch argued that 'it is the rising predominance of SVO order in OE that makes the breakdown of the inflectional system possible'; this was based on the assumption, derived from Greenberg's work, that SVO languages characteristically do not have rich (post-positional) inflectional systems. Koch views the Germanic, Romance and Slavic languages, Albanian, Greek and Lithuanian as evolving gradually from SOV to typologically consistent SVO languages. They are evolving at different rates, but they are all on the same slope, steadily acquiring more and more properties which are characteristic of the SVO type. She argues, for example, that Proto-Germanic was in transition from SOV to SVO and that its daughter languages have steadily acquired more SVO properties (although German has also introduced some 'archaic', i.e. SOV features; 'the history of German is bizarre' and it has compounded the structural ambivalence of Proto-Germanic). Noting parallel and more rapid developments in the history of Romance, she claims that the explanation of these changes must be sought in the structure of PIE. At that stage something (unspecified) must have triggered off the SOV-to-SVO change and ever since the daughter languages have relentlessly been doing what was in some sense forced upon them by the parent and gradually perfecting a harmonic SVO typology.

The parallelism of these changes in Germanic, Romance, Lithuanian, etc., is indeed interesting and demands explanation, particularly when compared to converse developments in Mandarin Chinese. However, there are many problems with an explanation in terms of a typological drift. To start with, if the seeds of these changes were sown in PIE, then alongside the parallelisms noted one must also consider divergent developments in other daughter languages: most of the IE daughters preserved predominantly OV order for a long time, and Hindi still does, while Old Irish became VSO. Therefore, there was nothing inevitable about the SOV-to-SVO change in the IE languages in general. Also languages for which we have historical evidence that they have undergone a complete typological shift are vanishingly few and those which have come close to a complete shift, such as Latin-French, have taken several millennia to adopt all the new properties. This has led some workers (e.g. Givón 1971, 1975b) to posit the notion of 'lag', whereby some of the properties of the new typology may not develop until long after some others. For example, typological innovations are said characteristically to affect VP before NPs, so that a language developing a SVO typology will acquire V-O and Aux-V order before it acquires N-Det, N-Gen and N-Adj. Such lags may extend over thousands of years (see the quotation from Li (1975a) above); indeed, French has still not developed N-Det order and shows no sign of doing so, despite being a consistent SVO language in most other respects. Therefore, given the diverse developments in the IE daughter languages and the concept of 'lag', it is certainly oversimplified to posit a simple syntactic drag-chain being set off in the parent language and being relentlessly followed through by the daughters, as suggested by Koch. It is also fallacious to view this kind of drift teleologically (Anttila 1977) or to equate it with grammatical 'conspiracies' or 'targets' (Miller 1973). Since typologically mixed languages exist and are stable over long periods of time, there is no reason to equate typological consistency or purity with phonotactic (surface) constraints such that languages are directed somehow to change towards a pure type, just as phonological rules may 'conspire' to achieve a certain kind of output (e.g. three rules in a grammar all having the effect of eliminating certain kinds of consonant clusters). Therefore, positing a typological shift does not constitute an explanation for the various changes. Languages are learned and grammars constructed by the individuals of each generation. They do not have racial memories such that they know in some sense that their language has gradually been developing from, say, an SOV and towards a SVO type, and that it must continue along that path. After all, if there were a prescribed hierarchy of changes to be performed, how could a child, confronted with a language exactly half-way along this hierarchy, know whether the language was changing from type x to type y, or vice versa? Therefore, when one bears in mind the abductive nature of the acquisitional process, the concept of an independent diachronic universal (i.e. unrelated to the theory of grammar) becomes most implausible. As is always the case, whether the individual changes are part of a more general drift, their causes must be sought either in the grammar which gave rise to them or in extra-grammatical phenomena such as foreign influence, stylistic expressivity, etc.

Each individual change may be due to a variety of factors. That is, while a given change may be entailed by the Transparency Principle, the opacity eliminated by the change may itself be a consequence of various factors, including some earlier changes. Therefore, one should return to the perspective of earlier writers and seek to identify different things which may share responsibility for a given change, despite the impatience shown for this kind of approach by recent proponents of typological drift. Sapir, while acknowledging that the loss of the *who–whom* distinction is part of the general drift towards invariable words and the elimination of the case system, nonetheless isolates four reasons for this particular change: first *whom* was felt not to belong to the set of personal pronouns, which have distinct subject–object forms, but to the set of interrogative and relative pronouns, which show no such distinction; second, the emphatic nature of interrogative pronouns and adverbs militates in favour of their invariableness; third, an objective form rarely occurs in sentence-initial position (*him I saw*); and fourth, [hu:m] is alleged to be phonetically clumsy before the alveolar stops of *do* and *did*. Sapir observes that the value of each factor is variable, depending on the individual and the locution, and that the linguist can never be certain that he has isolated all the determinants of any drift. Similarly Jespersen (MEG III 11.2) gives three reasons for the development of impersonal to personal verbs, discussed in §5.1: the greater interest taken in persons than in things, the formal identity of nominative and oblique cases of nouns, and the impossibility of distinguishing the cases in certain constructions. In §5.1 we gave quite a different account of the latter change, but here I am less interested in the validity of Sapir's or Jespersen's explanations than in the form that they felt an explanation should take; it was not enough to say that the change was part of a general drift towards the loss of the case system, greater analyticity and the rise of the invariable word. While that may indeed have turned out to be the consequence, it had to be explained how that came about. It could not be assumed that the individual changes were in any way goal-oriented, and the general drift was not offered as an explanation for its constituent parts. If different changes affecting different areas of grammar at different times and for different reasons all chanced to contribute to the language's greater analyticity (while of course, other changes did not), so be it; there is no reason to assume that the various changes should be formally related simply because of the overall effect.

Similarly, in looking for the causes of the rise of SVO order in OE, Strang properly looks for several contributing forces, since in general changes cannot be imputed to a single factor. She attributes the change partly to 'factors we may regard as accidental and evolutionary: that is to say, a pattern may come to predominate through a series of co-incidences' and partly to the breakdown of subject–object morphology

(Strang 1970: p312). This is the kind of explanation which would be consistent with the view of syntactic change developed here. In a language undergoing a change from SOV to SVO order, I would expect to find a steadily increasing number of SVO sentences. These would arise in various ways, perhaps by a rule postposing direct objects for the purposes of topicalization or some other such expressive function, since I assume that one of the ways for a speaker to achieve greater expressivity is to adopt a novel or unusual form of construction. SOV languages characteristically have sentential objects in the rightmost positions, probably for the reasons given by Kuno (1974) and discussed in §4.3; if they occurred between the subject and the verb, there would be a risk of multiple centre-embedding and juxtaposition of conjunctions, which seem to cause perceptual problems. This is corroborated by Aitchison (in press) who shows that Homeric and Classical Greek infinitive complements usually followed the main verb, although OV patterns were usual for simple object NPs. Aitchison argues that Greek changed to VO order by virtue of 'a rightwards operations conspiracy which ... snowballed and destroyed the OV [order]'. First infinitival complements occurred in rightmost position and likewise relative clauses in constructions like (39). Such relatives may be moved rightwards by a (probably stylistic) rule analogous to what some linguists call Heavy NP Shift (e.g. Ross 1967, Postal 1974).

(39)   [epithései]$_V$ [phármakh', [há ken paúseisi melaináōn odunáōn]$_{\bar{S}}$]$_{NP}$
       'he will lay on drugs which are to soothe the dark pain'

One also finds postposing of 'reduced relatives' with participles (40) and appositional NPs (41).

(40)   potì dè skêptron bále gaíēi khruseíois hēloisi peparménon
       to a sceptre-he threw-ground-with golden-nails-pierced
       'he threw to the ground the sceptre, studded with golden nails'
(41)   hoì dè Mukḗnas eîkhon, eüktímenon ptolíethron
       who Mycenae held, well-founded citadel.
       'who lived in the sturdy citadel of Mycenae'

Aitchison argues that these patterns permitted an increasing tendency for Heavy NP Shift and 'after-thought' constructions. This was reinforced by gapping and conjunction reduction rules which led to more VO patterns. 'Object Deletion' was a rightward process, and one finds OV + V patterns, but never V + OV.[1] 'Verb deletion', also being generally a rightward process, yielded OV + O patterns, and we find another example of a surface VO form (42).

(42) hoí th'Huríēn enémonto kaì Aulída petréessan
      who Hyria inhabited and Aulis rocky
      'who inhabited Hyria and rocky Aulis'

Thus in Greek for various reasons one has a gradual snowballing of rightwards operations and there arise several examples of VO forms. If VO forms proliferate sufficiently, the language may be re-analysed as underlyingly VO and undergo a change in the phrase structure rules, as in fact eventually happened with Greek.

Stockwell (1977), following McKnight (1928), develops a similar account of the word order change in English. McKnight had attributed the rise of post-verbal complementation in large measure to after-thought: 'To the apparently finished sentence are added a number of explanatory details, afterthoughts; or some element, by reason of close connection with the following clause, may be put after the verb. To motives like these the analytic order probably owes its origin' (1928: p217). Stockwell is less concerned with such psychological motivation, but notes that 'there are a number of structural motivations within the syntax of OE that considerably strengthen the tendency to exbraci-ate', where 'exbraciation' is the rightward movement eliminating nominal and adverbial elements within the brace [v . . . V]. Stockwell proceeds to identify various processes which gave rise to surface sequences SV(O), so that eventually a language learner had sufficient basis to abduce a generalization that 'sentences end with complements, not with verbs'.

If Kuno's (1974) perceptual account is correct, all SOV languages will have the seeds in them for a change to underlying SVO order. This is because they will typically show surface SVO order when the object is sentential, as noted above. If the language develops further 'leaks', as in the case of Greek, such that SVO surface patterns pro-liferate, a base re-analysis becomes possible and eventually necessary by virtue of the Transparency Principle. Given sufficient rightwards derivational operations, there will come a point where derivations can

[1] I retain the familiar term Object *Deletion*, although the EST precludes old-style deletion-under-identity rules. I assume that the phrase structure rules would generate empty categories which could later be interpreted as anaphoric to corres-ponding, lexical categories under appropriate conditions (see §1.4).

be simplified by positing an underlying SVO order. Thus the increasing number of rightwards operations would yield ever greater derivational opacity, which eventually could be reduced by a Thomian catastrophe, a base re-analysis. If the rightwards operations are movement rules and serve a stylistic or expressive function, they will typically not be structure-preserving and will affect main clauses first. And if they are stylistic rules, they will often be subject to various 'pragmatic' conditions. As an indication that a base change has taken place, one would look for a variety of simultaneous changes, most notably a significant increase in the occurrence of the innovating order in non-root, subordinate clauses. See Canale (1978) for an argument that English underwent a base re-analysis in the twelfth century whereby SVO became the base-generated word order. We have seen in earlier chapters that this base change was a causal factor in provoking several further changes in the history of English.

Seen in this light, it is not surprising that IE languages should undergo some parallel changes. If most of the early IE languages were underlyingly SOV, they also allowed some surface SVO forms, as one way of solving some perceptual difficulties (Kuno 1974). Rightward movement rules also provided a means for topicalization and for serializing complex structures in such a way as to avoid 'heavy' elements in the middle of a sentence and thereby entailing more processing difficulties. There was nothing necessary about the development of these rightward derivational processes, but they are not surprising. Given enough surface VO forms, the Transparency Principle would necessitate a re-analysis of the phrase structure rules, as indicated. This re-analysis in turn would entail derivational opacity elsewhere in the grammar, thereby contributing to further changes. The form of these subsequent changes could vary, but they would have to (a) eliminate the offending derivational opacity and (b) maintain comprehensibility between generations; they would therefore be constrained significantly. If one views change in this way, one is not surprised at parallel changes affecting several IE languages independently but one is not obliged to appeal for an explanation to racial memories or mystical metaconditions on linguistic families or goal-oriented clusters of changes. Instead change can be viewed as a function of chance and necessity: it can be viewed as a matter of chance (or at least as due to extra-grammatical factors) that a language should introduce a rightward topicalization rule or resolve one kind of opacity by one re-analysis rather than another; it is a matter of necessity that the grammar should not allow excessive opacity, that surface strings should be processable with minimal perceptual difficulty, and that generations should maintain mutual comprehensibility. The three latter factors respectively force re-analyses at certain points, encourage certain kinds of rules and restrict the possibilities for change in any given grammar. Obviously a restrictive theory of grammar plays a crucial role in prescribing such necessities of change, as through the Transparency Principle. Under a suitably restrictive theory of grammar there will be limited syntactic drag-chains; again, the history of the English modals provides an illustration. The requirement of mutual comprehensibility, a function of the theory of change (§3.2), restricts the class of possible re-analyses. In this way, following Kuryłowicz's analogy, gutters are prescribed for historical changes and the partial similarity of developments in French, English, Greek and Lithuanian is explained. Again, a clear distinction between the roles of a theory of grammar and a theory of change has been crucial. It is the neglect of such a distinction and the failure to work with a sufficiently restrictive theory of grammar which has led others to appeal to mystical conditions, teleological accounts, racial memories and other such 'explanatory' principles.

While the role of drag-chains or implicational sequences of syntactic changes has often been overstated, they do exist and they are of enormous importance for a theory of grammar. That is, there are sets of roughly analogous changes which cluster together in independent languages; many of these clusters cannot be explained by current theories of grammar. Unfortunately the careful work reported in Greenberg (1966) has spawned a mass of loosely argued material purporting to present typological data and implicational hierarchies of changes which demand explanation. In particular, the notion of a typologically consistent language has been made so demanding that very few, if any, languages fulfil all the requirements. Consequently the empirical interest of the concept diminishes. For example, a consistent SVO language is said to have Noun-Adjective order, but the basis for this claim is quite unclear, since there are languages which are typologically consistent in their VP properties (e.g. have Verb-Object, Auxiliary-Verb, Direct Object-Indirect Object orders) but may or may not have the consistent NP properties for a SVO typology. Hamp (1974) expresses the doubts of many linguists when he denies that there is any relation between NP order and that of the major elements of a sentence, although this too may be an excessively strong position.

This kind of work, exemplified by Li's various anthologies (1975b, 1976, 1977), typically conducts its analyses in an informal and inexplicit fashion. Watkins (1976), in a passage cited in part in §3.3, contrasts 'the practical analytic approach of current generative syntax – at best, fine-grained, but more often hair-splitting – with the gross generalizations, the crude Cyclopean techniques of "typological" syntax' and points to the dangers of elevating

some of Greenberg's extremely interesting quasi-universals to the dubious status of an intellectual straitjacket, into which the facts of various Indo-European languages must be fitted, willy-nilly, rightly or wrongly . . .

Where the facts of a given language are clearly inconsistent with one or another ideal type, Lehmann [and many others, e.g. Koch (1974), Li (1975a) above] assumes that the language is 'in transition'; and upon this a superficial 'explanatory' teleological theory of syntactic change is built – as though all living languages were not by definition in transition from one stage to another stage. Nor does the theory in any way 'explain' why some languages undergo these apparently radical changes in syntactic type over a thousand years, while others (like Turkic or Japanese) apparently do not.

So this kind of typological classification often becomes a substitute for analysis and explanation, conducted in terms of 'predominant' word order. Once the claims are translated to the realm of grammar, detailed analysis becomes essential. McCawley (1970) thinks that English is underlyingly VSO, Ross (1970) that it is SOV, and I regard it as SVO in initial structure. Whatever the merits of these three claims, the question of the correct underlying structure for English is not a trivial one to be determined simply by observation. Presumably the same holds for other languages. Gross generalizations about predominant surface word order gloss over crucial problems. For example, throughout the history of English items like *all, many, every* have occurred in the same positions with respect to the noun they modify, but they have nonetheless undergone an important categorial change (see §4.1). Similarly, *may, must, might*, etc., have characteristically preceded the verb they modify since ME and have undergone no positional change in terms of their relations with major constituents, but in §2.2 we showed that there were other changes affecting the relationship of these elements to the rest of the grammar. These changes were provoked by earlier changes and in turn themselves provoked others. All of these developments have played an important role in the history of English and have contributed to Sapir's drift towards greater analyticity.

However, the changes are revealed by the formulation of (partial) grammars; they would not reveal themselves to workers basing their typologies on 'predominant' surface word order patterns and failing to write explicit grammars for the various stages. Therefore, one cannot explain *why* changes in basic word order take place, if one cannot first give an account of *how* the changes came about, specifying the intermediate grammars. Under the typological approach, some of the most fundamental questions are still quite open even for the most extensively studied languages, like English, German and French. For example, if a language changes from one typology to another, say SOV to SVO, it will acquire many different properties and it is often assumed that there is a predetermined order in which these properties are acquired: so Auxiliary-Verb order will be acquired before Noun-Genitive, which in turn will precede Noun-Adjective. However, if the claims are to be made about the underlying order of elements in the initial structure of a generative grammar, the order of these changes is often difficult to establish. Canale (1976) has tried to establish the order of some base changes for English but they are often difficult to pin-point and, again, a lot of fine-grained analysis is needed. Until this is done for a wide range of languages, there are no grounds to suppose that there is a universally determined hierarchy of changes, a prescribed slope which all languages must slide down at varying rates.

Indeed it would be most surprising if it turned out to be possible to define a directionality to historical change in terms of gross surface properties, independently of grammars, and for changes taking place over a long period of time, perhaps millennia. Even if an order is established for, say, English, German and French, caution is needed before making claims of universality. It should always be borne in mind that to describe the progress of a typological shift, one needs historical records for a long time-span. Such records are unavailable for all but a tiny minority of the world's languages, and in §3.3 we showed fundamental problems for any attempt to reconstruct a hypothetical proto-syntax, which prevent one from treating reconstructed 'changes' on a par with changes where the earlier stage is documented – despite the fact that much of the typological approach is based on such reconstructions. Also the typological shifts which are attested are of different types, some SOV to SVO (Latin to French), some vice versa (Chinese, if Li and Thompson are correct) and some in other directions (Celtic, developing a VSO type). Given that these attested histories reflect such a tiny fraction of the total number, one can never be sure that the generalizations based on them are in fact principled and not coincidental.

For example, it is often said that when a language shifts from a SOV to a SVO type, pronominal objects will be slower to adopt the new order than full, lexical NPs and that nominal morphology will also be slow to change and will often reflect the sentential syntax of earlier stages (Givón 1971, Miller 1975, etc.). In support of the first proposition, authors point to French, which retains SOV order where the object is pronominal, although it has SVO order elsewhere (43) (again, abstracting away from other possible surface orders).

(43)   a. je l'aime 'I like him'
       b. j'aime le garçon au nez long 'I like the boy with the long nose'

English nominal compounds are adduced as support for the second proposition, since OV patterns still occur, reflecting the earlier sentential word order: *wind-break, log-roller, traffic-jam, evil-doer*. As noted in §3.3, such propositions often constitute the basis for work reconstructing proto-grammars. These particular claims, although commonly invoked, do not hold even of the attested changes. First, Modern Greek also has SOV order with pronominal objects and SVO with lexical NPs (44), although the clitics are not conservative and do not reflect their earlier order; pronominal clitics in pre-verbal position developed only after SVO order was well-established.

(44)   a.   o kinigòs skótose tòn líko 'the hunter killed the wolf'
       b.   o kinigòs tòn skótose 'the hunter killed it'

Second, while English does have nominal compounds of an OV pattern, there is no reason to assume that this is a relic of an older sentential order which will eventually be replaced by VO forms once the SVO typology is perfected and permeates the grammar fully. Nominals introduced in the Elizabethan period were of a VO pattern, i.e. the innovating type (*pickpocket, turnkey*, etc.; see §3.3), but then the language reverted to OV forms. Whatever the reasons for that reversion, it cannot be said to be a result of the earlier sentential OV word order when an intermediate stage had used VO types productively.

Even if it were the case that one could identify certain constructions as more conservative, more resistant to impending typological change, one could never be sure that this was not just an accident of, say, English and French, and that if historical records of another SVO language happened to be discovered they would not show that it progressed from SOV to SVO harmonics by quite a different route. The extreme paucity of our records means that to claim universality for a hierarchy shared by *all* the attested histories would be as naive as seeking to determine all the legitimate moves of chess from one four-move game. Mere statistics cannot tell one whether such generalizations, even if they hold perfectly where we have relevant data, are coincidental or principled. In reading much of the recent literature on syntactic change (e.g. Li 1975b, 1977, Steever, Walker & Mufwene 1976), one might gain the impression that there is a large body of diachronic universals which must be explained by a theory of grammar and a theory of change. In fact, much of this body of 'data' melts away when one examines the slender basis for the claims that 'typological changes' characteristically affect domain *x* before domain *y*. There is no reason to suppose that in this respect the changes affecting Romance, Germanic, Slavic, Greek, Chinese, and the few other languages with a long documented history, represent the total range of possibilities. One should therefore be cautiously sceptical about attempts to develop theories of grammar and change on the basis of such 'generalizations'. It is unlikely that much understanding will be gained about the causes of change without finer-grained analyses than those which typify the 'typological approach'.

In a powerful critique, Hawkins (1976) has identified further problems with the 'typological approach' and the diachronic theory based on it. He first identifies considerable confusion, stemming from the failure to distinguish unilateral and bilateral implications. The thirty-nine implicational universals of Greenberg (1966) were formulated unilaterally and have been interpreted as such by Canale (1976) and others who have constructed implicational hierarchies. Hawkins claims that many of these should be treated as bilateral implications, even with respect to Greenberg's own data base. This entails quite different predictions. If $P \rightarrow Q$ is a unilateral implication, there will be three possible languages: those having P&Q, $-P\&-Q$, and $-P\&Q$. Whereas the bilateral implication $P \leftrightarrow Q$ permits only two languages, those with P&Q or $-P\&-Q$. This in turn entails quite different predictions about the hierarchies of diachronic changes, if one translates Greenberg's implications into diachronic statements along the lines of Canale (1976). So only if verb-auxiliary > object-verb is a unilateral implication does the possibility arise of a language with object-verb order and auxiliary-verb; this possibility is excluded if the implication is bilateral. In a diachronic change from SOV typology to SVO, one would expect an intermediate stage of object-verb and auxiliary-verb order only if the implication is regarded as unilateral. So Hawkins claims that there is widespread confusion in the literature, with important empirical consequences for language typology. He identifies three further shortcomings in this kind of work: first, the correlations across syntactic domains are not very good and the order of, say, verb and object seems to bear no relation to the order of noun and adjective; second, some language-types have no exemplifications; and third, no distinction is drawn between language-types which have very many exponents and those which have a mere handful. Further-more, as theories of diachronic change these typologies are internally inconsistent if one assumes unilateral implications, as most of the literature does. These theories are what Hawkins calls 'trigger-chain' theories: some property changes and sets off a chain reaction which is defined by Greenberg-type implications. The trigger may be gram-matical, pragmatic or perceptual.[1] So consider an implication $P \to Q$ and a language $-P\&-Q$. If the language acquires property Q first, it will become $-P\&Q$, which is quite consistent with the universal implication and there would be no reason (i.e. following from this implication) for the language to proceed to acquire property P. On the other hand, if property P is acquired first, the chain will be set off, but there will be an intermediate stage $P\&-Q$, which violates the universal on which the chain is allegedly based. Therefore, the trigger, property P, could not be acquired in the first place. Hence such theories

---

[1] Vennemann offers a grammatical trigger: phonological changes reduce morpho-logical distinctions and the order shifts from SOV to SVO to prevent widespread ambiguity whereby NP NP V might be interpreted as SOV or OSV. Given the change in verb position, implicational universals suffice to explain the subsequent order changes. Similarly Li & Thompson (1974) attributed a word order change in Mandarin Chinese to the collapsing of complex sentences into simple ones through the development of co-verbs. Hyman's after-thought is an example of a pragmatic trigger, provoking various elements to occur post-verbally by analogy to the after-thought constructions and thereby getting the chain started. Antinucci, Duranti & Gebart (1976) provide a perceptual trigger: contra Vennemann and others, they claim that in a SOV language the first relation to change is that of a noun and its relative clause. The prenominal relatives of SOV languages are alleged to pose perceptual problems and therefore shift to postnominal position and this triggers off a chain reaction.

must, and usually do, allow for a violation of 'universal' implications in order to get the chain started. Hawkins goes on to show that, not surprisingly, trigger-chain theories as proposed make empirically false predictions about the hierarchy of changes in a general typological shift.

However, there are many implicational universals which are not just statistical tendencies about predominant surface patterns, but are exceptionless and can be interpreted as claims holding of some level of representation in a formal grammar. Where the implications are bilateral, they make predictions about the clustering of diachronic changes. Such implications shed light on the correct theory of grammar. In several sections we have stressed the importance of simultaneous but apparently unrelated changes in surface patterns, and we have used the simultaneity of changes to argue for one formulation of the change over another. Thus we have assumed throughout that simultaneous changes should be related where possible, shown to be the various surface realizations of a single change in the abstract grammar. One would take a similar tack with implicational universals and assume that they should fall out from an appropriate theory of grammar. One can seek explanations for implicational universals in one of two ways: either to show that the implication follows from some general perceptual strategy (see §4.3) or to show that it falls out on formal grounds. For example, suppose that a typologist reported that languages had underlying sequences of either Auxiliary-Verb and Verb-Object or Verb-Auxiliary and Object-Verb, but never either Verb-Auxiliary and Verb-Object or Auxiliary-Verb and Object-Verb. Suppose also that he reported that if a grammar with underlying Verb-Object order changed to one with Object-Verb, it also simultaneously changed Auxiliary-Verb to Verb-Auxiliary, and vice versa; and also that whenever an underlying Object-Verb changed to Verb-Object, Verb-Auxiliary changed also to Auxiliary-Verb. These are the kinds of implications which should fall out from a theory of grammar, and these facts suggest that the correct theory should allow phrase structure rules generating Auxiliary-Verb and Verb-Object, or Verb-Auxiliary and Object-Verb, but no other combination. That in turn suggests an appropriate form for $\overline{X}$ conventions. $\overline{X}$ conventions have two interesting consequences for diachronic syntacticians: they provide a restrictive theory of a possible phrase structure rule, thus constraining possible innovations, and they yield a descriptive mechanism for cross-category generalizations. If under the $\overline{X}$ convention a language has [Spec $\overline{X}$] preceding $\overline{X}$, where X may be N, V, Adj, etc., then (assuming Aux, Det and Degree Adverbs to be 'specifiers' of major categories) it will follow that one will find in that language Aux-V order, Det-N and Degree Adv-Adj. Given conventions of this type, one would not expect to find a language with Aux-V order and N-Det. Diachronically one would expect that if a language changes from V-Aux to Aux-V order, then it will also change from N-Det to Det-N (this prediction is borne out in Germanic). One would not expect a cross-category rule to be introduced which affected different bar levels, e.g. $\overline{\overline{P}}$, $\overline{\overline{N}}$, $\overline{V}$ and Adj. There is much more that could be said about this, but some of the data accumulated by typologists provide tests for a theory of syntactic change incorporating $\overline{X}$ conventions. To the extent that $\overline{X}$ conventions are successful, they account for certain (bilateral) implicational universals, and thus certain clusters of simultaneous changes.

Of course, there are many implicational universals and thus simultaneous changes which cannot be accounted for by current theories of grammar. They demand explanation and constitute challenges for existing theories. While much work remains to be done, it is nonetheless true that as theories are refined and made more restrictive they will make more predictions about the clustering of properties since they will permit a narrower range of available grammars.

Consider a striking example from the recent paper by Chomsky & Lasnik (1977). Under their theory an apparently mysterious correlation follows automatically, that a surface filter (45) proposed in Perlmutter (1971) should hold only for languages lacking a rule of subject-pronoun deletion.

(45) any sentence other than an imperative in which there is a S that does not contain a subject in surface structure is ungrammatical

Assuming the trace theory of movement rules, they formulate the filter as (46), where [$_{NP}$e] is an empty NP, which may be regarded here as a trace left by a movement rule.

(46) *[that [$_{NP}$e]], except in the context: [$_{NP}$ NP – – . . .]

Perlmutter points out that (45) is not universal: Spanish allows (47), but French does not allow (48).

(47) quién creiste que vio a Juan
(48) *qui crois-tu que a vu Jean
In Spanish, but not in French or English, a subject can be deleted (49)

(49)   a.   creo que partió
       b.   je crois qu'il est parti (*crois qu'est parti)
       c.   I think that he left (*think that left)

Chomsky & Lasnik maintain (46) as a universal filter and explain the fact that it is not manifested in languages with a rule of subject-pronoun deletion. The 'surface structure' of (47), prior to deletion, is (47'), just as the surface structure of (49a) is (49a'). (Surface structure is defined here in novel fashion as a level obtaining before the application of deletion rules; see p317n).

(47')   quién tú creiste que [$_{NP}$e] vio a Juan
(49a')   yo creo que él partió

The optional subject deletion rule converts (49a') to (49a) and (47') to (47). By virtue of the deletion, neither (47) nor (49) violates the filter and each is a well-formed sentence. 'In general, if the language permits subject deletion it will delete "empty" subjects of the form [$_{NP}$ e], thus voiding the filter' (p453). French and English have no such deletion rule and therefore no means of avoiding the effects of the filter.[1] The discussion presupposes that deletion rules apply before the filters.

It is reasonable to expect that as the theory of grammar becomes increasingly restrictive as a result of future research, so in narrowing the class of available grammars it will account for more implicational universals and thus clusters of simultaneous changes. It would follow from Chomsky & Lasnik's analysis that if Spanish lost its subject deletion rule one would expect sentences like (47) to become obsolete at the same time. Thus existing implicational statements which can hold of grammars, such as that of Perlmutter (1971), demand explanation; likewise clusters of simultaneous changes. Increasingly restrictive theories of grammar provide some of the desired accounts, as we have just seen. Again we note that work on syntactic change and implicational universals proceeds hand-in-hand with work on restrictive theories of grammar. The two areas of study are inextricably intertwined – or, rather, they should be. I hope that this book has shown

---

[1] Notice that if a language has a subject deletion rule, it must be free to apply to *all* NPs blindly. The proposal does not involve extending the rule so that it applies not only to [yo]$_{NP}$ but also to [e]$_{NP}$. If transformations are by definition blind to the lexical content of categories, they could no more distinguish between [yo]$_{NP}$ and [e]$_{NP}$ than between [el gaucho]$_{NP}$ and [el hermano]$_{NP}$. In fact, in the same paper Chomsky & Lasnik suggest that lexical items are inserted only in surface structures, i.e. after the application of the syntactic transformations (but before semantic interpretation).

how data from diachronic change can shed light on the correct restrictive principles imposed by a theory of grammar, and how the theory of grammar, properly conceived, can explain radical historical re-analyses.

7.3 Conclusion

I have drawn distinctions between a theory of grammar and a theory of change, between changes necessitated by various principles of grammar or perceptual strategies and those provoked by extra-grammatical factors. I have claimed that there are no formal constraints on possible re-analyses beyond the constraints imposed by a theory of grammar. In denying any teleological directionality to change and urging caution in dealing with so-called diachronic universals, I have viewed change as a function of chance and necessity, in much the same way that Monod (1970) views genetic transmission. I can illustrate this by returning for the last time to our paradigm case, the history of the English modals. Recall that there were five early changes, affecting different aspects of the grammar at different times, and making the pre-modals exceptional verbs with the special properties of (50).

(50) i inability to occur with direct objects
   ii inflectional idiosyncrasies
   iii unique form of the infinitive
   iv a past tense without the usual time reference
   v special rule feature for epistemic pre-modals

This was followed by a re-analysis best described as the introduction of a new Modal category, a reformulation of two transformations and the appearance of new lexical items *have to*, *be able to* and *be going to*.

Fragment of OE grammar	Fragment of ENE grammar
S → NP VP	S → NP AUX VP
VP → V (NP)	AUX → T (Modal)
NP → $\begin{Bmatrix} N \\ S \end{Bmatrix}$	VP → (*have-en*) (*be-ing*) V (NP)
Negative Placement	NP → $\begin{Bmatrix} N \\ S \end{Bmatrix}$
NP V X ⇒ NP V neg X	Negative Placement
Subject-Verb Inversion	NP AUX X ⇒ NP AUX neg X
NP V X ⇒ V NP X	Subject-Aux Inversion
	NP AUX X ⇒ AUX NP X

The five early changes leading to the properties of (50) were a function of chance as far as our analysis was concerned. It may turn out that there is a principled reason for why the non-pre-modal preterite-present verbs were lost from the language or transferred to other inflectional classes. That is, it might be shown that this change was a function of some earlier changes and some principle of grammar. Similarly it might be shown that there was good reason for the pre-modals to develop new meanings for their past tense forms which had nothing to do with past time reference, or for *shall, may* and *can* to cease to occur with direct objects. However, I cannot provide reasons for these changes and must regard them provisionally as a function of chance, caused by extra-grammatical factors of some kind (cf. Sapir 1921: ch.7 n9), who speaks of 'relatively random' phenomena in the same sense). The net result of these changes was a situation where the categorial membership of *must, may, will*, etc., was opaque and the degree of opacity approached the limits prescribed by the theory of grammar. Therefore, a therapeutic re-analysis was required – as a matter of necessity, imposed by the theory of grammar. This re-analysis could be of any form, but it must (a) eliminate the intolerable opacity and (b) lead to a grammar permitting mutual comprehensibility with the earlier generation. The first requirement follows from the theory of grammar, the second from the theory of change (§3.2). And, of course, the resulting grammar must conform to the general limits imposed by the theory of grammar. Within these restrictions any solution could be adopted. It was a matter of chance that the solution actually adopted involved a new category; other possibilities could be imagined such as regularizing the form of the pre-modals such that they developed a third person singular -*s* ending and a *to* form for the infinitive, permitting them to look more like regular verbs. With the introduction of a category Modal (and Auxiliary), further changes were required – as a matter of necessity, imposed this time by the theory of change. If there were no further changes, the existing rules of Negative Placement and Subject-Verb Inversion would yield quite different surface patterns, of a kind to strain communicability across generations to breaking-point. A string such as (51) would not meet the old structural descriptions of the two rules and therefore could not occur in negative or interrogative contexts.

(51)   NP   Aux   V

If the intervening Aux were somehow ignored, the existing rules would place the negative after the first verb and invert the first verb, giving new surface forms like (52) and either (53a) or (53b), where the older generation yielded (52′) and (53′).

(52)   John can go not
(53)   a. can go John?
        b. go John can?
(52′)   John cannot go
(53′)   can John go?

Therefore some re-formulation was necessitated by the theory of change in order to prevent a breakdown of communication. Again, the re-formulation must conform to the theory of grammar and yield surface results similar to those produced by the earlier grammar. There were no further constraints, in particular no constraints imposing additional formal limits on the change. It was a matter of chance that the actual solution was as indicated in the fragment of ENE grammar above; again, other possibilities could be imagined.

This illustrates how chance and necessity interact to determine the form of a historical change. Although there are no formal constraints on possible changes, as argued in §3.2, nonetheless radical re-analyses following from the theory of grammar must meet strict conditions: they must lead to a grammar fulfilling the restrictive requirements imposed by the theory of grammar; they must be suitably therapeutic, e.g. eliminate intolerable opacity; they must yield a surface output fairly close to that of the earlier grammars. For any given re-analysis, these requirements impose narrow restrictions on the available options. Therefore, even when one concedes that there are no general formal limits on possible changes of the type sought by Kiparsky, Langacker and most other generativists, it is nonetheless not the case that a grammar can be changed into *any* other grammar by each successive generation. Thus the possibilities for re-analysis are severely limited, but they are not limited formally except as dictated by the theory of grammar. Although there is an element of chance in re-analyses like that involving the English modals, the grammar's room for manoeuvre is limited. This becomes clear when one thinks of the task of each generation of language learners, who must hypothesize or 'abduce' a grammar permitting communication with their models and must do so within the limits which grammars must meet.

Chance also plays a role in changes caused by extra-grammatical factors such as borrowing, or desire for expressivity. Although various conditions must be met in order for borrowing to take place (as indicated in §7.2.2), it was at least in part a matter of chance that the Saraswat Brahmins borrowed Kannada relative clause patterns into Konkani. Similarly, it is in part a matter of chance that some underlying SOV languages topicalize an object NP by moving it to the end of the sentence, thereby yielding a surface SVO form and perhaps contributing to a general snowballing tendency for surface SVO patterns, which may eventually lead to a re-analysis of the phrase structure rules to give SVO order in initial structures; there are, after all, other ways of mark-ing topicalized NPs. However, this element of chance has important consequences for the way one studies diachronic change: it restricts the possibilities for reconstruction of proto-grammars (§3.3), prevents a theory of change from ever being strongly predictive and suggests the impossibility of positing syntactic drag-chains extending over millennia. I have argued that syntactic drag-chains are more limited in scope than is sometimes assumed, and that for re-analyses required by the theory of grammar there is usually a number of possibilities, each with different consequences for other areas of grammar. Likewise there are many possibilities for changes entailed by extra-grammatical factors, again each with different consequences. Therefore, long-term drag-chains are not of much interest and characteristically demand the positing of racial memories or notions of teleological directionality.

Testable predictions about future changes must be treated sceptically, given the extensive role of chance. The best one can do is to predict where a re-analysis will be required by the theory of grammar and to specify the available options for the form that that re-analysis might take. Which option will turn out to be adopted must in many instances remain a matter of chance. However, this view of change has two merits: it contributes to our understanding of the internal history of a given language by explaining (and often discovering) the simultaneity of superficially unrelated changes; it introduces a new mode of argumen-tation for choosing between competing theories and synchronic descrip-tions and therefore contributes to our understanding of the correct theory of grammar. This is based on the deriving of predictions from restrictive theories of grammar about the point at which re-analyses will occur and about the remedial effects which must be achieved.

Bibliography (and index of references)

Abbott, E. A. (1870) *A Shakespearian grammar*. Reprinted 1966. New York: Dover. *pp*175, 183

Aitchison, J. (in press) 'The order of word order change'. *Transactions of the Philological Society*. *pp*393–4

Akmajian, A. (1977) 'The complement structure of perception verbs in an autonomous syntax framework'. In Culicover, Wasow & Akmajian (1977). *p*210

Allen, C. (1975) 'Old English modals'. In Grimshaw (1975b). *pp*99, 106

Allen, W. Sidney (1953) 'Relationship in comparative linguistics'. *Transactions of the Philological Society* 52–108. *p*156

(1974) *Vox Graeca*. 2nd edn. Cambridge: Cambridge University Press. *p*289

Allen, W. Stannard (1947) *Living English structure*. London: Longman. *p*262, 263

Andersen, H. (1969) 'A study in diachronic morphophonemics: the Ukrainian prefixes'. *Language* 45.3, 553–74. *pp*232, 237, 348

(1972) 'Diphthongization'. *Language* 48.1, 11–50. *pp*232, 348

(1973) 'Abductive and deductive change'. *Language* 49.4, 765–93. *pp*148, 151, 225, 232, 348–50, 381

(1974) 'Toward a typology of change: bifurcating changes and binary relations'. In Anderson & Jones (1974). *pp*149, 348, 350, 365

Anderson, J. M. & C. Jones, eds. (1974) *Historical linguistics*. Proceedings of the First International Conference on Historical Linguistics. Amsterdam: North Holland. *pp*vii, 365

Ansre, G. (1966). 'The verbid – a caveat to 'serial verbs''. *Journal of West African Languages* 3.1, 29–32. *pp*214, 221

Antinucci, F., A. Duranti & L. Gebart (1976) 'Relative clause structure, relative clause perception, and the change from SOV to SVO'. Mimeo. Istituto di Psicologia, Rome. *p*401

Anttila, R. (1972) *An introduction to historical and comparative linguistics*. New York: Macmillan. *pp*136, 154, 156, 159, 161–4

(1974) 'Formalization as degeneration in historical linguistics'. In Anderson & Jones (1974). *pp*364–5

(1975) 'Was there a generative historical linguistics?'. In K.-H. Dahlstedt, ed. *The Nordic languages and modern linguistics.* Proceedings of the Second International Conference of Nordic and General Linguistics, University of Umeå, June 1973. Stockholm: Almqvist & Wiksell International. *pp*47, 129

(1977) *Analogy.* The Hague: Mouton. *pp*361, 373, 391

Aronoff, M. (1976) *Word formation in generative grammar. Linguistic Inquiry* monographs no. 1. Cambridge, Mass.: MIT Press. *pp*21, 54

Awobuluyi, O. (1967) 'Studies in the syntax of the standard Yoruba verb'. Unpublished PhD dissertation. Columbia University. *p*215

(1973) 'The modifying serial construction: a critique'. *Studies in African Languages* 4.1, 87–111. *pp*214, 221

Bach, E. (1968) 'Two proposals concerning the simplicity metric in phonology', *Glossa* 2, 128–49. *p*362

Baker, C. L. (1970) 'Notes on the description of English questions: the role of an abstract question morpheme'. *Foundations of Language* 6.2, 197–219. *p*318

Bally, C. (1926) *Le langage et la vie.* Paris: Payot. *p*124

Bamgboṣe, A. (1973) 'The modifying serial construction: a reply'. *Studies in African Linguistics* 4.2, 207–17. *pp*214, 221

Bever, T. G. (1970) 'The cognitive basis for linguistic structure'. In J. R. Hayes, ed. *Cognition and language learning.* New York: Wiley. *p*174

& D. T. Langendoen (1972) 'The interaction of speech perception and grammatical structure in the evolution of language'. In Stockwell & Macauley (1972). *pp*41, 46, 319–20, 329–31, 335, 339–40, 362, 364–5, 382

Bhat, D. N. S. (1970) Review of King (1969). *Indian Linguistics* 31, 49–57. *p*365

Blass, F. & A. Debrunner (1954) *Grammatik des neutestamentlichen Griechisch.* Göttingen: Vandenhoeck & Ruprecht. *p*288

Bloomfield, L. (1926) 'A set of postulates for a science of language'. *Language* 2, 153–64. *p*74

(1933) *Language.* New York: Holt, Rinehart & Winston. *pp*359, 364

(1960) 'The linguistic aspects of science'. *International Encyclopedia of Unified Science* 1.4. Chicago: University of Chicago Press. *p*74

Bøgholm, N. (1939) *English speech from a historical point of view.* Copenhagen: Nyt Nordisk Forlag. *p*324

Botha, R P. (1970) *The methodological status of grammatical argumentation.* The Hague: Mouton. *p*75

(1971) *Methodological aspects of transformational generative phonology.* The Hague: Mouton. *p*75

(1973) *The justification of linguistic hypotheses: a study of non-demonstrative inference in transformational grammar.* The Hague: Mouton. *pp*19, 75

Brame, M. (1976) *Conjectures and refutations in syntax and semantics.* New York: American Elsevier. *p*311

Brénous, J. (1895) *Etude sur les hellénismes dans la syntaxe latine.* Paris. 1965 edn. Rome: 'L'Erma' di Bretschneider. *p*382

Bresnan, J. W. (1970) 'On complementizers: toward a syntactic theory of complement types'. *Foundations of Language* 6.3, 297–321. *pp*316, 318

(1971) 'Contraction and the transformational cycle in English'. Mimeo. *p*315

(1972) 'Theory of complementation in English syntax'. Unpublished PhD dissertation. MIT, Cambridge, Mass. *pp*195, 198, 267, 306, 314, 328

(1976a) 'On the form and functioning of transformations'. *Linguistic Inquiry* 7.1, 3–40. *p*62

(1976b) 'Non-arguments for Raising'. *Linguistic Inquiry* 7.3, 485–501. *p*254

(1978) 'A realistic transformational grammar'. In M. Halle, J. W. Bresnan & G. Miller, eds. *Linguistic theory and psychological reality.* Cambridge, Mass.: MIT Press. *p*311

Bright's Anglo-Saxon Reader (1935) Revised and enlarged by J. R. Hulbert. New York: Holt, Rinehart & Winston. *p*172

Brugmann, K. (1886–95) *Grundriss der vergleichenden Grammatik der indogermanischen Sprachen.* Strassburg: Trübner. *pp*8–9

Butler, M. C. (1975) 'Middle English impersonal constructions and the notion of 'subject of a sentence''. Mimeo. *pp*232–3, 235

Callaway, M. (1913) *The infinitive in Anglo-Saxon.* Washington, D.C.: Carnegie Institution. *pp*186, 266

Campbell, A. (1959) *Old English Grammar.* London: Oxford University Press. *p*172

Campbell, L. (1971) Review of King (1969). *Language* 47.1, 191–209. *p*365

Canale, M. (1976) 'Implicational hierarchies of word order relationships'. In Christie (1976). *pp*98, 107, 398, 400–1

(1978) 'Word order change in OE: base re-analysis in generative grammar'. Unpublished PhD dissertation. McGill University, Montreal. *pp*302, 395

Carden, G. (1976) *English quantifiers: logical structure and linguistic variation.* Taishukan Studies in Modern Linguistics. Tokyo. *pp*1–2, 4, 181

Carlson. A. (1976) 'A diachronic treatment of English quantifiers'. Unpublished MA thesis. McGill University, Montreal. *pp*168–86

Chantraine, P. (1927) *Histoire du parfait grec.* Paris: Champion. *p*281

(1953) *Grammaire homérique.* Paris: Klincksieck. *pp*240, 242–3, 248, 281–2

Chomsky, N. (1955) *Logical structure of linguistic theory.* New York: Plenum [:975]. *pp*11, 15, 20, 43, 46, 83, 258

(1957) *Syntactic structures.* The Hague: Mouton. *pp*11, 43–4, 83, 116

(1959) Review of B. F. Skinner *Verbal behaviour. Language* 35.1, 26–58. *pp*359–60

(1961) 'On the notion 'rule of grammar''. In *Proceedings of the Twelfth Symposium in Applied Mathematics,* vol. 12, *The American Mathematical Society,* Providence, RI, 6–24. *p*145

(1962) 'Current issues in linguistic theory'. In *Proceedings of the IXth International Congress of Linguists*. The Hague: Mouton. *p*62

(1965) *Aspects of the theory of syntax*. Cambridge, Mass.: MIT Press. *pp*20, 40, 54, 220, 265, 278, 301

(1968) *Language and Mind*. New York: Harcourt, Brace & World. *pp*296, 349

(1970) 'Remarks on nominalization'. In R. A. Jacobs & P. S. Rosenbaum, eds. *Readings in English transformational grammar*. Waltham: Ginn & Co. *pp*51, 55, 168, 185, 365–6, 371

(1972a) 'Some empirical issues in the theory of transformational grammar'. In *Studies in semantics in generative grammar*. The Hague: Mouton. *p*55

(1972b) 'Deep structure, surface structure and semantic interpretation'. In *Studies in semantics in generative grammar*. The Hague: Mouton. *pp*86, 88

(1973) 'Conditions on transformations'. In S. Anderson & P. Kiparsky, eds. *A festschrift for Morris Halle*. New York: Holt, Rinehart & Winston. *pp*70, 84, 196, 295–6, 298–9, 301, 307–8, 311, 317, 319–20, 339, 368

(1975) *Reflections on language*. New York: Pantheon. *pp*21, 49, 59, 75, 295, 305

(1976) 'Conditions on rules of grammar'. *Linguistic Analysis* 2, 303–51. *pp*21, 48, 174, 295, 307

(1977) 'On *wh* Movement'. In Culicover, Wasow & Akmajian (1977). *pp*20–1, 57–8, 62, 65, 68, 71, 73–4, 174, 278, 295, 298–9, 304–5, 307, 317–20, 336, 347

Chomsky, N. & M. Halle (1968) *The sound pattern of English*. New York: Harper & Row. *pp*3, 49, 77

Chomsky, N. & H. Lasnik (1977) 'Filters and control'. *Linguistic Inquiry* 8.3, 425–504. *pp*313, 315, 317, 320, 328, 330, 337, 339, 347, 403–4

Christaller, J. B. (1875) *A grammar of the Asante and Fante language, called Tshi*. Reprinted 1964. London: Gregg Press. *p*221

Christie, W., ed. (1976) *Current progress in historical linguistics*. Amsterdam: North Holland. *p*vii

Chung, S. (1976) 'Case marking and grammatical relations in Polynesian'. Unpublished PhD dissertation. Harvard University, Cambridge, Mass. *pp*128, 376–7

Clements, G. N. (1975) 'Analogical re-analysis in syntax: the case of Ewe tree-grafting'. *Linguistic Inquiry* 6.1, 3–52. *pp*369–71

Coleman, R. (1975) 'Greek influence on Latin syntax'. *Transactions of the Philological Society* 101–56. *p*382

Collinge, N. (1960) 'Some reflections on comparative historical syntax'. *Archivum Linguisticum* 12, 79–101. *p*156

Corum, C. (1975) 'A pragmatic analysis of parenthetic conjuncts'. In *Papers from the 11th Regional Meeting of the Chicago Linguistic Society*. Chicago: Chicago Linguistic Society. *pp*43, 73

Culicover, P., T. Wasow & A. Akmajian, eds. (1977) *Formal syntax.* New York: Academic Press.

Curme, G. O. (1911) 'Is the Gothic Bible Gothic?' *Journal of English and Germanic Phonology* 10, 335–54. *p*323

(1931) *Syntax.* Boston: D. C. Heath. *pp*314, 321, 323, 353

Delbrück, B. (1871) *Der Gebrauch des Konjunktivs und Optativs im Sanskrit und Griechischen* (= *Syntaktische Forschungen* vol. i). Halle: Waisenhaus. *p*284

(1893–1900) *Vergleichende Syntax der Indogermanischen Sprachen* (= *Grundriss der vergleichenden Grammatik Indogermanischen Sprachen* vols. iii–v). Strassburg: Trübner. *pp*8, 9, 250

de Rijk, R. (1972) 'Relative clauses in Basque: a guided tour'. In *The Chicago which hunt.* Chicago: Chicago Linguistic Society. *p*126

Dillard, L. (1972) *Black English: its history and usage in the United States.* New York: Vintage Press. *p*126

Dobzhansky, T. (1970) *Genetics of the evolutionary process.* New York: Columbia University Press. *p*68

Dougherty, R. (1974) 'The syntax and semantics of *each other* constructions'. *Foundations of Language* 12, 1–47. *p*182

(1975) 'Harris and Chomsky at the syntax-semantics boundary'. In Hockney et al. eds. *Contemporary research in philosophical logic and linguistic semantics.* Dordrecht: Reidel. *pp*47, 58, 296–7

Dresher, E. (1978) Review of Lass & Anderson (1975). *Language* 54.2, 432–446. *p*77

Dresher, E. & N. Hornstein (1979) 'Trace theory and NP movement rules'. *Linguistic Inquiry* 10.1. *p*306

Dressler, W. (1969) 'Eine textsyntaktische Regel der indogermanischen Wortstellung'. *Zeitschrift für vergleichende Sprachforschung* 83, 1–25. *p*158

(1971) 'Über die Rekonstruktion der indogermanischen Syntax'. *Zeitschrift für vergleichende Sprachforschung* 85, 5–22. *p*156

Einenkel, E. (1916) *Geschichte der englischen Sprache* vol. ii. Strassburg: Trübner. *p*314

Ellegård, A. (1953) *The auxiliary 'do': the establishment and regulation of its use in English.* Stockholm: Almqvist & Wiksell. *pp*117–18

Emonds, J. (1972) 'A reformulation of certain syntactic transformations'. In S. Peters, ed. *Goals of linguistic theory.* Englewood Cliffs, NJ: Prentice-Hall. *pp*190–1, 193, 202–4, 210–11, 327

(1976) *A transformational approach to English syntax: root, structure-preserving and local transformations.* New York: Academic Press. *pp*21, 57, 126–8, 130, 158, 197–8, 202, 220, 304, 311, 328, 337, 339, 377

Erben, J. (1969) '*Tun*, als Hilfsverb im heutigen Deutsch'. In U. Engel, P. Grebe & H. Rupp, eds. *Festschrift für Hugo Moser.* Düsseldorf: Pödagogischer Verlag Schwann. *p*117

Esper, E. A. (1973) *Analogy and association in linguistics and psychology.* Athens: University of Georgia Press. *p*373

Faraci, R. A. (1974) 'Aspects of the grammar of infinitives and *for*-phrases'. Unpublished PhD dissertation. MIT, Cambridge, Mass. *p*198

Fasold, R. W. (1976) 'One hundred years from syntax to phonology'. In Steever, Walker & Mufwene (1976). *pp*147, 377

Fehling, D. (1976) 'Remarks on the role of the syntactical calque in standard languages and the similarity between Classical Greek and Latin syntax'. *Folia Linguistica* 9, 73–84. *p*381

Fiengo, R. W. (1974) 'Semantic conditions on surface structures'. Unpublished PhD dissertation. MIT, Cambridge, Mass. *pp*253, 295, 298, 307

Fiengo, R. W. & H. Lasnik (1973) 'The logical structure of reciprocal sentences'. *Foundations of Language* 9, 447–68. *p*182

Fillmore, C. J. (1968) 'The case for case'. In E. Bach & R. Harms, eds. *Universals in linguistic theory.* New York: Holt, Rinehart & Winston. *p*241

Fischer, P. (1924) 'Zur stellung des Verbs im Griechischen'. *Glotta* 13, 1–11; 189–205. *p*162

Flebbe, Dr (1878) 'Der elliptische Relativsatz im Englischen'. *Archiv für das Studium der neueren Sprachen und Litteraturen* 60, 85–101. *pp*320, 330

Fodor, J. (1970) 'Three reasons for not deriving *kill* from *cause to die*'. *Linguistic Inquiry* 1.4, 429–38. *p*55

Freidin, R. (1975) 'The analysis of passives'. *Language* 51.2, 384–405. *pp*306, 311

Friedrich, J. (1960) *Hethitisches Elementarbuch* vol. I. Heidelberg: Winter. *p*242

Friedrich, P. (1975) *Proto-Indo-European syntax. Journal of Indo-European Studies* monograph no. 1. Hattiesburg, Miss. *pp*vii, 155–7, 162, 246

  (1976) 'The devil's case: PIE as SVO'. In A. Juilland, ed. *Linguistic studies presented to Joseph Greenberg.* Saratoga, Calif.: Anma Libri. *p*246

Fries, C. C. (1940) 'On the development of the structural use of word-order in Modern English'. *Language* 16, 199–208. *p*389

Gardner, F. (1971) *The analysis of syntactical patterns of Old English.* The Hague: Mouton. *p*389

Geoghegan, S. G. (1975) 'Relative clauses in Old, Middle and New English'. *Ohio State University Working Papers in Linguistics* 18, 30–71. *pp*314, 316, 320, 322, 335, 337–9, 341

Givón, T. (1971) 'Historical syntax and synchronic morphology: an archaeologist's field trip'. In *Papers from the 7th Regional Meeting of the Chicago Linguistic Society.* Chicago: Chicago Linguistic Society. *pp*8, 160, 390, 399

  (1975a) 'Toward a discourse definition of syntax'. Mimeo. *p*216

  (1975b) 'Serial verbs and syntactic change: Niger-Congo', in Li (1975b). *pp*199, 213–14, 216–17, 224, 227, 390

(1976) 'Topic, pronoun and grammatical agreement', in Li (1976). *pp*126, 128, 144

Gonda, J. (1951) *Remarks on the Sanskrit passive.* Leiden: Brill. *pp*240–1

(1956) *The character of the Indo-European moods.* Wiesbaden: Harrassowitz. *pp*284, 293

Goodwin, W. W. (1889) *Syntax of the moods and tenses of the Greek verb.* London: Macmillan. *p*284

Green, G. M. (1976) 'Main clause phenomena in subordinate clauses'. *Language* 52.2, 382–97. *p*127

Greenberg, J. H. (1963) *The languages of Africa. IJAL*, vol. II, 29.1; publication no. 25. *p*216

(1966) 'Some universals of grammar with particular reference to the order of meaningful elements'. In J. H. Greenberg, ed. *Universals of language.* Cambridge, Mass.: MIT Press. *pp*vii, 10, 12, 42, 53, 91, 156–7, 199, 205, 387–8, 390, 396–402

(1969) 'Some methods of dynamic comparison in linguistics'. In J. Puhvel, ed. *Substance and structure of language.* Berkeley, Los Angeles: University of California Press. *p*388

Grimshaw, J. (1975a) 'Evidence for relativization by deletion in Chaucerian Middle English'. In Grimshaw (1975b). *p*329

ed. (1975b) *Papers in the history and structure of English.* Amherst: University of Massachusetts, Department of Linguistics.

Hahn, E. A. (1953) *Subjunctive and optative: their origin as futures.* New York: American Philological Association. *pp*284–5

Haiman, J. (1974) *Targets and syntactic change.* The Hague: Mouton. *pp*131–2, 142

Hale, K. (1974) 'Deep-surface canonical disparities in relation to analysis and change'. In H. M. Hoenigswald & R. Longacre, eds. *Current trends in linguistics* vol. XI. The Hague: Mouton. *pp*148, 377

(1976) 'Linguistic autonomy and the linguistics of Carl F. Voegelin'. Mimeo. *p*68

Halitsky, D. (1975) 'Left-branch Ss and NPs in English: a bar notation analysis'. *Linguistic Analysis* 1.3. *p*21

Hall, R. A. (1950) 'The reconstruction of proto-Romance'. *Language* 26.1, 6–27. *p*163

Halle, M. (1962) 'Phonology in generative grammar'. *Word* 18, 54–72. *pp*24, 150

Hamp, E. (1974) 'The major focus in reconstruction and change'. In Anderson & Jones (1974). *pp*344, 396

(1975) 'On the disappearing English relative particle'. In G. Drachman, ed. *Akten der I. Salzburger Frühlingstagung für linguistik.* Tübingen: Narr. *p*382

Hankamer, J. (1971) 'Constraints on deletion in syntax'. Unpublished PhD dissertation. Yale University, New Haven. *p*351

(1972) 'Analogical rules in syntax'. In *Papers from the 8th Regional Meeting of the Chicago Linguistic Society*. Chicago: Chicago Linguistic Society. *pp*365–9, 371–2

(1977) 'Multiple analyses'. In Li (1977). *p*351

Harris, J. W. (1969) 'Sound change in Spanish and the theory of markedness'. *Language* 45.3, 538–52. *p*364

Harris, M. B. (1976). 'The inter-relationship between phonological and grammatical change'. Mimeo. To appear in *Proceedings of the International Conference on Historical Phonology*, Ustronie, Poland. *p*239

Harris, Z. (1951) *Methods in structural linguistics*. Chicago: University of Chicago Press. *p*52

(1957) 'Cooccurrence and transformation in linguistic structure'. *Language* 33.2, 283–340. *pp*47, 58, 296, 313

(1965) 'Transformational theory'. *Language* 41.2, 363–401. *p*47

Havers, W. (1931) *Handbuch der erklärenden Syntax. Ein Versuch zur Erforschung der Bedingungen und Triebkräfte in Syntax und Stilistik*. Heidelberg: Winter. *p*373

Hawkins, J. A. (1976) 'Word order change in relation to the logical status of linguistiç universals'. Mimeo. *pp*400–2

Hermann, E. (1931) *Lautgesetz und Analogie*. Abhandlungen der Gesellschaft der Wissenschaften zu Göttingen, Phil.-Hist. Klasse, Neue Folge 23, 3. Berlin: Weidmannsche Buchhandlung. *p*124

Heusler, A. (1964) *Altisländisches Elementarbuch*. Heidelberg: Winter. *p*25

Hewett, W. T. (1904) 'The historical use of the relative pronouns in English literature'. *Proceedings of the American Philosophical Society* 43, 278–89. *p*320

Higgins, F. R. (1974) 'On J. Emonds' analysis of Extraposition'. In J. Kimball, ed. *Syntax and semantics* vol. II, 149–196. New York: Seminar Press. *p*202

Hirt, H. (1921) *Indogermanische Grammatik*. Heidelberg: Winter. *p*9

Hoenigswald, H. M. (1960) *Language change and linguistic reconstruction*. Chicago: University of Chicago Press. *pp*143, 149, 156

(1966) 'Are there universals of linguistic change?' In J. H. Greenberg, ed. *Universals of language*. Cambridge, Mass.: MIT Press. *p*13

Holton, G. (1973) *Thematic origins of scientific thought*. Cambridge, Mass.: Harvard University Press. *p*75

Hooper, J. & S. Thompson (1973) 'On the applicability of root transformations'. *Linguistic Inquiry* 4.4, 465–97. *p*127

Hornstein, N. (1977a) 'S and the $\overline{\text{X}}$ convention'. *Linguistic Analysis* 3.2, 137–76. *pp*21, 51, 306

(1977b) 'Towards a theory of tense'. *Linguistic Inquiry* 8.3, 521–57. *p*122

Huddleston, R. (1974) 'Further remarks on the analysis of auxiliaries as main verbs'. *Foundations of Language* 11.2, 215–29. *p*98

Humbert, J. (1945) *Syntaxe grecque*. Paris: Klincksieck. *pp*240–1, 244

Hyman, L. (1971) 'Consecutivization in Fe?fe?'. *Journal of African Languages* 10, 29–43. *pp*216–20, 224

(1975) 'On the change from SOV to SVO: evidence from Niger-Congo'. In Li (1975b). *pp*214, 381–2, 385

Itkonen, E. (1974) *Linguistics and metascience.* Studia Philosophica Turkuensia, Fasc. II. Turku: Kokemäki. *p*75

Jackendoff, R. S. (1972) *Semantic interpretation in generative grammar.* Cambridge, Mass.: MIT Press. *pp*59, 84, 92–6, 182, 216, 241, 249, 347

(1975) 'Morphological and semantic regularities in the lexicon'. *Language* 51.3, 639–71. *pp*21, 54, 215, 253

(1977) $\overline{X}$ *syntax: a study of phrase structure. Linguistic Inquiry* monograph no. 2. Cambridge, Mass.: MIT Press. *pp*51, 371

Jacobs, R. A. (1975) *Syntactic change: a Cupan (Uto-Aztecan) case-study.* University of California Publications in Linguistics. Berkeley and Los Angeles: University of California Press. *pp*vii, 155, 166

Jakobson, R. (1929) 'Remarques sur l'évolution phonologique du russe comparée à celle des autres langues slaves'. *Travaux du Cercle de Prague* 2. Reprinted in R. Jakobson, *Selected writings* vol. I. The Hague: Mouton, 1962. *pp*7, 143

(1931) 'Prinzipien der historischen Phonologie'. *Travaux du Cercle de Prague* 4. Revised version, 'Principes de phonologie historique', in R. Jakobson, *Selected writings* vol. I. The Hague: Mouton, 1962. *pp*143, 149

(1958) 'Typological studies and their contribution to historical comparative linguistics'. *Proceedings of the VIIIth International Congress of Linguists,* Oslo. Reprinted in R. Jakobson, *Selected writings* vol. I. The Hague: Mouton, 1962. *p*387

Jamison, S. (1976) 'Functional ambiguity and syntactic change: the Sanskrit accusative'. In Steever, Walker & Mufwene (1976). *p*353

Jankowsky, K. (1972) *The neogrammarians.* The Hague: Mouton. *p*8

Jasanoff, J. (1971) Review of King (1969). *Romance Philology* 25, 74–85. *p*365

Jeffers, R. (1976a) 'Syntactic change and syntactic reconstruction'. In Christie (1976). *pp*155–7, 163–6

(1976b) Review of Lehmann (1974). *Language* 52.4, 982–88. *p*158

(1976c) 'Typological shift and change in complex sentence structure'. In Steever, Walker & Mufwene (1976). *p*161

Jenkins, L. (1972) 'Modality in English syntax'. Unpublished PhD dissertation. MIT, Cambridge, Mass. *p*131

(1977) 'Movement transformations as interpretive rules in the Extended Standard Theory'. In C. Rohrer & N. Ruwet, eds. *Proceedings of the Colloque Franco-Allemand.* Tübingen: Max Niemeyer Verlag. *p*71

Jespersen, O. (1922) *Language: its nature, development and origin.* London: Allen & Unwin, *p*8

(1941) *Efficiency in linguistic change*. Copenhagen: Munksgaard. *p*124

(1909–49) *A modern English grammar on historical principles*, vols. I–VII. London: Allen & Unwin. *pp*47, 111–12, 171, 175, 178–9, 190, 231–2, 234, 236, 260–2, 264, 266, 269–70, 275, 298–300, 302, 314, 321, 323, 326–7, 335, 392

Kageyama, T. (1975) 'Relational grammar and the history of Subject Raising'. *Glossa* 9.2, 165–81. *p*300

Katz, J. J. & P. M. Postal (1964) *An integrated theory of linguistic descriptions*. Cambridge, Mass.: MIT Press. *p*347

Kaye, J. (1973) 'Opacity and recoverability in phonology'. *Canadian Journal of Linguistics* 19.2, 134–49. *p*144

(1975) 'A functional explanation for rule ordering in phonology'. *Papers from the parasession on functionalism*. Chicago: Chicago Linguistic Society. *p*136

Kayne, R. (1975) *French syntax: the transformational cycle*. Cambridge, Mass.: MIT Press. *p*369

Keenan, E. (1974) 'The Functional Principle: generalizing the notion "subject of"'. In *Papers from the 10th Regional Meeting of the Chicago Linguistic Society*. Chicago: Chicago Linguistic Society. *p*235

(1975) 'Some universals of Passive in relational grammar'. In *Papers from the 11th Regional Meeting of the Chicago Linguistic Society*. Chicago: Chicago Linguistic Society. *p*301

Kellner, L. (1892) *Historical outlines of English syntax*. London: Macmillan. *pp*108, 170, 175–6, 178, 389

Kenyon, J. S. (1909) *The syntax of the infinitive in Chaucer*. London: Chaucer Society, 2nd Series XLIV. *p*186

Keyser, S. J. (1975) 'A partial history of the relative clause in English'. In Grimshaw (1975b). *pp*321, 338–42

Kim, W. G. (1976) 'The theory of anaphora in Korean syntax'. Unpublished PhD dissertation. MIT, Cambridge, Mass. *p*67

King, R. D. (1969) *Historical linguistics and generative grammar*. Englewood Cliffs, N.J.: Prentice-Hall. *pp*6, 11, 156, 159, 164, 360, 362, 364–5

Kiparsky, P. (1965) 'Phonological change'. Unpublished PhD dissertation, MIT, Cambridge, Mass. *p*362

(1968a) 'Linguistic universals and linguistic change'. In E. Bach & R. Harms, eds. *Universals in linguistic theory*. New York: Holt, Rinehart & Winston. *pp*13, 17, 143, 147, 364, 407

(1968b) 'How abstract is phonology?' Indiana University Linguistics Club. *pp*13, 338

(1968c) 'Tense and mood in Indo-European syntax'. *Foundations of Language* 4.1, 30–57. *pp*25–7, 142

(1971) 'Historical linguistics'. In W. Dingwall, ed. *A survey of linguistic science*. College Park, Maryland: Linguistics Program, University of Maryland. *pp*136, 144

(1972) 'Explanation in phonology'. In S. Peters, ed. *Goals of linguistic theory*. Englewood Cliffs, NJ: Prentice-Hall. *p*363

(1974) 'Remarks on analogical change'. In Anderson & Jones (1974). *pp*144, 154, 348, 361, 365

Kiparsky, P. & C. Kiparsky (1970) 'Fact'. In M. Bierwich & K.-H. Heidolph, eds. *Progress in linguistics*. The Hague: Mouton. *p*197

Kirschner, G. (1957) 'Recent American influence on standard English: the syntactical sphere'. *Zeitschrift für Anglistik und Amerikanistik* 5, 29–42. *p*263

Kispert, R. J. (1971) *Old English: an introduction*. New York: Holt, Rinehart & Winston. *pp*170, 173

Klima, E. (1964a) 'Studies in diachronic transformational syntax'. Unpublished PhD dissertation. Harvard University. *pp*15, 22–4, 40, 142, 198, 314, 321–3, 326, 338–9

(1964b) 'Relatedness between grammatical systems'. *Language* 40.1, 1–20. *pp*22–4, 34–5, 359

Koch, M. (1974) 'A demystification of syntactic drift'. *Montreal Working Papers in Linguistics* 3. *pp*389–91, 397

Koefoed, G. (1974) 'On formal and functional explanation: some notes on Kiparsky's 'Explanation in phonology''. In Anderson & Jones (1974). *pp*362–3, 365

Koster, J. (1976) 'Remarks on *wh* Movement and the Locality Principle'. Mimeo, University of Amsterdam. *p*67

Koyré, A. (1957) *From the closed world to the infinite universe*. Baltimore: Johns Hopkins Press. *p*18

Kuhn, T. (1962) *The structure of scientific revolutions*. Chicago: Chicago University Press. *p*45

Kuno, S. (1972) 'Natural explanations for some syntactic universals'. NSF Report no. 28. Cambridge, Mass.: Harvard Computation Laboratory. *p*95

(1973) 'Constraints on internal clauses and sentential subjects'. *Linguistic Inquiry* 4.3, 363–85. *p*278

(1974) 'The position of relative clauses and conjunctions'. *Linguistic Inquiry* 5.1, 117–36. *pp*144–7, 209, 393–5

Kurath, H. (1972) *Studies in area linguistics*. Bloomington: Indiana University Press. *p*383

Kuryłowicz, J. (1945–9) 'La nature des procès dits 'analogiques''. *Acta Linguistica* 5, 15–37. *pp*361, 373, 396

(1956) *L'apophonie en indo-européen*. Warsaw: Polska Akademia Nauk. *p*249

(1964) *The inflectional categories of Indo-European*. Heidelberg: Winter. *pp*242–3, 249, 281

Lakatos, I. (1970) 'Falsification and the methodology of scientific research programmes'. In Lakatos & Musgrave (1970). *pp*74–6, 125, 135, 140

Lakatos, I. & A. Musgrave, eds. (1970) *Criticism and the growth of knowledge.* Cambridge: Cambridge University Press. *p*45

Lakoff, G. (1970a) *Irregularity in syntax.* New York: Holt, Rinehart & Winston. *p*55

(1970b) 'Global rules'. *Language* 46.3, 627–39. *p*56

(1970c) 'Repartee, or a reply to 'Negation, Conjunction, and Quantifiers''. *Foundations of Language* 6.3, 389–422. *p*181

(1971) 'On generative semantics', in L. Jakobovits & D. Steinberg, eds. *Semantics.* Cambridge: Cambridge University Press. *p*297

Lakoff, R. T. (1968) *Abstract syntax and Latin complementation.* Cambridge, Mass.: MIT Press. *pp*15, 36–41, 100, 113, 202, 316, 382

(1972) 'Another look at drift'. In Stockwell & Macauley (1972). *pp*386–7

Lane, G. (1949) 'On the present state of Indo-European linguistics'. *Language* 25, 333–42. *p*8, 22

Langacker, R. (1977) 'Syntactic re-analysis', in Li (1977). *pp*124, 149, 346, 374–5, 407

Lasnik, H. (1976) 'Remarks on coreference'. *Linguistic Analysis* 2.1, 1–22. *p*61

Lasnik, H. & R. W. Fiengo (1974) 'Complement object deletion'. *Linguistic Inquiry* 5.4, 535–72. *p*298

Lass, R. (1976) *English phonology and phonological theory.* Cambridge: Cambridge University Press. *p*75

Lass, R. & J. M. Anderson (1975) *Old English phonology.* Cambridge: Cambridge University Press. *pp*77–8

Lehmann, W. P. (1973) 'A structural principle of language and its implications'. *Language* 49.1, 47–66. *p*53

(1974) *Proto-Indo-European syntax.* Austin: University of Texas Press. *pp*vii, 155–8, 165, 240, 251, 397

Li, C. (1975a) 'Synchrony vs. diachrony in language stucture'. *Language* 51.4, 873–86. *pp*8, 388–9, 391, 397

ed. (1975b) *Word order and word order change.* Austin: University of Texas Press. *pp*155, 388, 397, 400

ed. (1976) *Subject and topic.* New York: Academic Press. *pp*388, 397

ed. (1977) *Mechahisms of syntactic change.* Austin: University of Texas Press. *pp*vii, 154–5, 166, 388, 397, 400

Li, C. & S. Thompson (1974) 'Historical change of word order: a case-study in Chinese and its implications'. In Anderson & Jones (1974). *pp*199, 224, 401

(1975) 'The semantic function of word order: a case-study in Mandarin'. In Li (1975b). *p*398

Lightfoot, D. W. (1972) 'Abstract verbs and the development of the Greek mood system'. In *Proceedings of the XIth International Congress of Linguists*, Bologna, 914–22. *pp*286–7

(1974a) 'Indeterminacy in syntax'. *Canadian Journal of Linguistics* 19.2, 150–66. *pp*17, 298, 350–1

(1974b) 'The diachronic analysis of English modals'. In Anderson & Jones (1974). *p*x

(1975a) 'Diachronic syntax: extraposition and deep structure re-analysis'. In E. Kaisse & J. Hankamer, eds. *Proceedings of the 5th meeting of the North-eastern Linguistic Society*. Cambridge, Mass.: Harvard Linguistics Department; and in *Folia Linguistica* 9. *p*x

(1975b) *Natural logic and the Greek moods*. The Hague: Mouton. *pp*284–7

(1976a) 'The theoretical implications of Subject Raising'. *Foundations of Language* 14.2, 257–86. *pp*3, 254, 301

(1976b) 'The base component as a locus of syntactic change'. In Christie (1976). *p*186

(1976c) Review of R. Kempson, *Presupposition and the delimitation of semantics* and D. Wilson, *Non-truth-conditional semantics*. *Journal of Linguistics* 12.2, 324–34. *p*17

(1977a) 'On traces and conditions on rules', in Culicover, Wasow & Akmajian (1977). *pp*65, 197, 307, 317, 347, 369

(1977b) 'Syntactic change and the autonomy thesis'. *Journal of Linguistics* 13.2. *p*229

Lockwood, W. B. (1968) *Historical German syntax*. London: Oxford University Press. *p*381

(1969) *Indo-European philology, historical and comparative*. London: Hutchinson. *p*381

Lohmann, O. (1880) 'Über die Auslassung des englischen Relativpronomens'. *Anglia* 3, 115–50. *pp*314, 320, 330

Lord, C. (1973) 'Serial verbs in transition'. *Studies in African Linguistics* 4.3, 269–96. *pp*213–14, 221–4

(1976) 'Evidence for syntactic re-analysis: from verb to complementizer in Kwa'. In Steever, Walker & Mufwene (1976). *pp*, 214, 223–4, 226

Lyons, J. (1967) 'A note on possessive existential and locative sentences'. *Foundations of Language* 3, 390–96, *p*222

(1968) *Introduction to theoretical linguistics*. Cambridge: Cambridge University Press. *p*242

McCawley, J. D. (1970) 'English as a VSO language'. *Language* 46.2, 286–99. *p*367

(1975) 'The category status of English modals'. *Foundations of Language* 12.4, 597–601. *pp*98, 115

McCawley, N. (1976) 'From OE/ME 'impersonals' to 'personal' constructions: what is a 'subject-less' S?' In Steever, Walker & Mufwene (1976). *p*232

McKnight, G. H. (1928) *The evolution of the English language: from Chaucer to the twentieth century*. Reprinted 1968. New York: Dover. *p*394

Makkai, A. & V. Makkai (1976) 'The nature of linguistic change and modern linguistic theories'. In Christie (1976). *p*4

Mańczak, W. (1958) 'Tendances générales des changements analogiques'. *Lingua* 7, 298–325; 387–420. *pp*361, 373

Meier, H. H. (1967) 'The lag of relative *who* in the nominative'. *Neuphilologus* 51, 277–88. *p*321

Meillet, A. (1937) *Introduction à l'étude des langues indo-européennes*. Paris: Hachette. *pp*156, 165–6, 293

Miller, D. G. (1973) 'On the motivation of phonological change'. In B. Kachru, ed. *Issues in linguistics: papers in honor of Henry and Renée Kahane*. Urbana: University of Illinois. *pp*364, 391

(1975) 'Indo-European: VSO, SOV, SVO or all three?'. *Lingua* 37, 31–52. *pp*156, 246, 399

Monod, J. (1970) *Le hasard et la necessité: essai sur le philosophie naturelle de la biologie moderne*. Paris: Editions du Seuil. *pp*viii, 405

Morin, Y.-C. & M. St Amour (1977) 'Description historique des constructions infinitives de français'. *Montreal Working Papers in Linguistics* 9. *p*3

Mossé, F. (1945) *Manuel de l'anglais du moyen âge: des origines au XIVe siècle*, vols. I–II. Paris: Aubier. *pp*175, 178, 314, 324

Mustanoja, T. (1958) *The English syntactical type 'one the best man' and its occurrence in other Germanic languages*. Helsinki: Mémoires de la Société Neophilologique de Helsinki, vol. xx. *pp*170, 176–7

(1960) *A Middle English syntax*. Helsinki: Mémoires de la Société Neophilologique de Helsinki. *pp*175, 194, 200, 321, 326

Nadkarni, M. V. (1975) Bilingualism and syntactic change in Konkani'. *Language* 51.3, 672–83. *pp*383–4

Naro, A. (1976) 'The genesis of the reflexive impersonal in Portuguese'. *Language* 52.4, 779–810. *pp*6, 353–9

Newmeyer, F. (1975) *English aspectual verbs*. The Hague: Mouton. *p*98

Nichols, P. (1976) 'The *for* complementizer'. Mimeo. UCLA. *p*195

Onions, C. T. (1904) *An advanced English syntax*. New York: Macmillan [= 1971 *Modern English syntax*. London: Routledge, Keegan & Paul]. *pp*263, 314

Palacas, A. L. (1971) 'The higher predicate status of modals and implications for the lexicon'. *Glossa* 5.1, 31–46. *p*98

Palmer, F. R. (1965) *A linguistic study of the English verb*. London: Longman. *p*118

Palmer, L. R. (1954) *The Latin language*. London: Faber & Faber. *p*30

(1962) 'The language of Homer'. In A. J. B. Wace and F. H. Stubbings, eds. *A companion of Homer*. London: Macmillan. *pp*244, 249

Parker, F. (1976) 'Language change and the passive voice'. *Language* 52.2, 449–60. *pp*151, 240, 245–6, 251, 348

Paul, H. (1880) *Prinzipien der Sprachgeschichte*. Halle: Max Niemeyer. *pp*8, 9, 124, 353, 378

Peirce, C. S. (1966) *The collected papers of C. S. Peirce*, ed. C. Hartshorne, P. Weiss & A. Burks. Cambridge, Mass.: Harvard University Press. *pp*74, 349

Perlmutter, D. (1971) *Deep and surface structure constraints in syntax*. New York: Holt, Rinehart & Winston. *pp*403-4

Peters, S. & R. W. Ritchie (1973) 'On the generative power of transformational grammars'. *Information Sciences* 6, 49-83. *pp*viii, 13, 20

Pike, K. (1967) 'Grammar as wave'. Georgetown Monograph Series no. 20, 1-14. *pp*223-4

Pope, M. (1934) *From Latin to modern French*. Manchester: Manchester University Press. *p*161

Popper, K. (1959) *The logic of scientific discovery*. London: Hutchinson. *pp*17, 74-6, 123, 125, 140

(1963) *Conjectures and refutations*. London: Routledge & Kegan Paul. *pp*45, 74-6

(1973) *Objective knowledge*. Oxford: Clarendon Press. *pp*74-6

Posner, R. (1974) 'Ordering of historical phonological rules in Romance'. *Transactions of the Philological Society* 98-127. *p*136

Postal, P. M. (1968) *Aspects of phonological theory*. New York: Harper & Row. *pp*10, 77, 364

(1971) *Cross-over phenomena*. New York: Holt, Rinehart & Winston. *p*329

(1974) *On Raising*. Cambridge, Mass.: MIT Press. *pp*3, 202, 305, 393

Postal, P. M. & J. R. Ross (1971) '¡Tough Movement si, tough Deletion no!' *Linguistic Inquiry* 2.4, 544-6. *p*298

Poutsma, H. (1914) *A grammar of late modern English*. Groningen: Noordhoff. *p*47

(1923) *The infinitive, the gerund and the participles of the English verb*. Groningen: Noordhoff. *p*186

Pullum, G. K. (1975) 'A golden treasury of counterexamples to the Specified Subject Constraint'. Indiana University Linguistics Club. *p*73

(1976) 'The Duke of York gambit'. *Journal of Linguistics* 12.1, 83-102. *p*338

Pullum, G. K. & D. Wilson (1977) 'Autonomous syntax and the analysis of auxiliaries'. *Language* 53.4. *pp*115, 130

Pyles, T. (1964) *The origins and development of the English language*. New York: Harcourt, Brace & Jovanovich. *p*389

Quicoli, C. (1976) 'Conditions on Quantifier Movement in French'. *Linguistic Inquiry* 7.4, 583-607. *p*369

Quirk, R. & C. L. Wrenn (1955) *An Old English grammar*. London: Methuen. *pp*170, 172-3

Quirk, R., S. Greenbaum, G. Leech & J. Svartvik (1972) *A grammar of contemporary English*. London: Longman. *p*263

Radford, A. (1976) 'On the non-transformational nature of syntax: synchronic and diachronic evidence from Romance causatives'. In M. B. Harris, ed.

Romance syntax: synchronic and diachronic perspectives. Manchester: University of Salford. *pp*2–4

Reichenbach, H. (1947) *Elements of symbolic logic.* New York: Macmillan. *p*122

Reiner, E. (1968) *La place de l'adjectif épithète en français.* Vienna: Wilhelm Braumüller, Universitäts-Verlagsbuchhandlung Gmbh. *p*206

Ries, J. (1894) *Was ist Syntax?* Prague: Taussig & Taussig. *p*8

Robinson, O. W. & F. van Coetsem (1973) Review of King (1969). *Lingua* 31, 331–69. *p*365

Rosenbaum, P. S. (1967) *The grammar of English predicate complement constructions.* Cambridge, Mass.: MIT Press. *pp*210, 316

Ross, J. R. (1967) 'Constraints on variables in syntax'. Unpublished PhD dissertation. MIT, Cambridge, Mass. *pp*62, 68, 130, 200, 211, 305, 316–17, 361, 368, 393

(1969a) 'Auxiliaries as main verbs'. In W. Todd, ed. *Studies in philosophical linguistics*, Series 1. Evanston: Great Expectations. *pp*81–92, 95, 98, 113, 115, 125, 133–4

(1969b) 'Guess who?' *Papers from the 5th Regional Meeting of the Chicago Linguistic Society.* Chicago: Chicago Linguistic Society. *p*351

(1970) 'Gapping and the order of constituents'. In M. Bierwisch & K.-H. Heidolph, eds. *Progress in linguistics.* The Hague: Mouton. *p*397

Rydén, M. (1966) *Relative constructions in early sixteenth century English.* Stockholm: Almqvist & Wiksell. *p*321

Salmon, V. (1965) 'Sentence structures in colloquial Shakesperian English'. *Transactions of the Philological Society* 105–40. *pp*5, 213

Samuels, M. L. (1965) 'The role of functional selection in the history of English'. *Transactions of the Philological Society* 15–40. *p*124

Sapir, E. (1921) *Language.* New York: Harcourt. *pp*42, 124, 386, 389, 392, 406

Saussure, F. de (1916) *Cours de linguistique générale.* Paris: Payot. *p*124

Schachter, P. (1974) 'A non-transformational account of serial verbs'. *Studies in African Linguistics*, suppl. 5, 253–71. *pp*213–26

Siegel, D. (1974) 'Topics in English morphology'. Unpublished PhD dissertation. MIT, Cambridge, Mass. *p*306

Sievers, E. (1903) *An Old English grammar*, trans. ed. A. S. Cook. Boston: Ginn. *pp*169–70, 172

Smith, C. (1964) 'Determiners and relative clauses in a generative grammar of English'. *Language* 40.1, 37–52. *p*200

Smyth, H. (1920) *Greek grammar.* Cambridge, Mass.: Harvard. *pp*132, 244, 250, 281

Speyer, J. S. (1886) *Sanskrit syntax.* Reprint 1968. Kyoto: Rinsen-Shoten Bookstore. *p*247

Stahlke, H. (1970) 'Serial verbs'. *Studies in African Linguistics* 1.1, 60–99. *pp*214–16

Steele, S. (1977) 'Clisis and diachrony'. In Li (1977). *p*152

Steever, S., C. Walker & S. Mufwene, eds. (1976) *Diachronic syntax*. Chicago: Chicago Linguistic Society. *pp*vii, 400

Stockwell, R. P. (1976) Reply to Lightfoot (1976b). In Christie (1976). *pp*100, 153, 196

(1977) 'Motivations for exbraciation in Old English'. In Li (1977). *p*394

Stockwell, R. P. & R. Macauley (1972) *Linguistic change and generative theory*. Bloomington: Indiana University Press.

Stockwell, R. P., P. Schachter & B. H. Partee (1973) *The major syntactic structures of English*. New York: Holt, Rinehart & Winston. *pp*199–200, 306

Stokoe, H. R. (1937) *The understanding of syntax*. London: Heinemann. *p*263

Strang, B. M. H. (1970) *A history of English*. London: Methuen. *pp*113, 177–9, 263, 276, 389, 392–3

Strattmann, F. H. (1891) *A Middle-English dictionary*. Oxford: Clarendon Press. *pp*102, 183

Sweet, H. (1900) *A new English grammar: logical and historical*. Oxford: Clarendon Press. *pp*296, 298

Szemerényi, O. (1972) 'A new leaf of the Gothic Bible'. *Language* 48.1, 1–10. *p*6

Tatlock, J. S. P. (1927) *A concordance to the complete works of G. Chaucer and to the Romaunt of the Rose*. Washington: Carnegie Institution. *pp*206–7

Teeter, K. (1974) 'Some Algic etymologies'. *International Journal of American Linguistics* 40.3, 197–201. *p*126

Thom, R. (1972) *Stabilité structurelle et morphogenèse*. New York: Benjamin. *pp*ix, 78, 124, 343, 395

(1973) 'Sur la typologie des langues naturelles: essai d'interpretation psycholinguistique'. In M. Gros, M. Halle & M.-P. Schützenberger, eds. *The formal analysis of natural languages*. The Hague: Mouton. *p*78

Thomason, S. G. (1976) 'What else happens to opaque rules?' *Language* 52.2, 370–81. *p*136

Thorne, J. P. (n.d.) 'The grammar of jealousy: a note on the character of Leontes'. *p*6

Thumb, A. (1912) *Handbook of the Modern Greek vernacular*. Edinburgh: Clark. *pp*290, 292

Traugott, E. [Closs] (1965) 'Diachronic syntax and generative grammar'. *Language* 41.2, 402–15. *pp*15, 24, 28–35, 41, 152, 202

(1969) 'Toward a grammar of syntactic change'. *Lingua* 23, 1–27. *pp*8, 28–35

(1972a) *The history of English syntax*. New York: Holt, Rinehart & Winston. *pp*99, 241, 274–5, 300, 320, 331, 381

(1972b) 'On the notion 'restructuring' in historical syntax'. In *Proceedings of the XIth International Conference of Linguists*, Bologna; and in *Stanford Occasional Papers in Linguistics* no. 2. *p*100 van der Gaaf, W. (1904) *The transition from the impersonal to the personal construction in Middle English.* Heidelberg: Winter. *pp*229–31

(1930) 'The passive of a verb accompanied by a preposition'. *English Studies* 12, 1–24. *p*278

Vendryes, J. (1902) 'Réflexions sur les lois phonétiques'. In *Mélanges linguistiques offerts à Antoine Meillet.* Paris: Klincksieck. *p*7

(1921) *Le langage.* Paris: Renaissance du livre. *p*242

Vennemann, T. (1972) 'Analogy in generative grammar: the origin of word order'. In *Proceedings of the XIth International Congress of Linguists,* Bologna. *pp*387–8

(1974) 'Topics, subjects and word order: from SXV to SVX via TVX'. In Anderson & Jones (1974). *pp*53, 246

(1975) 'An explanation of drift'. In Li (1975b). *pp*389, 401

Vincent, N. (1974) 'Analogy re-considered'. In Anderson & Jones (1974). *pp*360, 365

Visser, F. Th. (1963–73) *An historical syntax of the English language* vols. I–IIIb. Leiden: Brill. *pp*vii, 99, 102, 105, 109–10, 112, 175, 190–4, 200, 229–34, 258, 260, 262–70, 274–6, 278–9, 298, 329

Wackernagel, J. (1926) *Vorlesungen über Syntax.* Basel: Birkhaüser. *pp*9, 240, 242, 250, 281, 353

Wagner, K. H. (1969). *Generative grammatical studies in the Old English language.* Heidelberg: Julius Groog Verlag. *p*99

Wang, W. (1965) 'Two aspect markers in Mandarin'. *Language* 41, 457–70. *p*24

Warburton, I. & N. S. Prabhu (1975) 'Diachronic processes and synchronic grammars'. *Glossa* 9.2, 202–17. *p*8

Washabaugh, W. (1975) 'On the development of complementizers in creolization'. *Stanford Working Papers on Language Universals* 17, 109–40. *p*195

Wasow, T. (1972) 'Anaphoric relations in English'. Unpublished PhD dissertation. MIT, Cambridge, Mass. *pp*70, 329

(1975) 'Anaphoric pronouns and bound variables'. *Language* 51.2, 368–83. *p*61

(1977) 'Transformations and the lexicon'. In Culicover, Wasow & Akmajian (1977). *pp*252–80

Watkins, C. (1963) 'Syntax of the Old Irish verb'. *Celtica* 6, 1–49. *pp*156, 159

(1964) 'Preliminaries to the reconstruction of IE sentence structure'. In *Proceedings of the IXth International Congress of Linguists,* Cambridge, Mass. *pp*156, 163

(1976) 'Toward Proto-Indo-European syntax: problems and pseudo-problems'. In Steever, Walker & Mufwene (1976). *pp*156, 158, 162, 397

Weber, H. (1971) *Das erweiterte Adjectiv- und Partizipialattribut im Deutschen.* Munich: Hüber Verlag. *p*381

Weinreich, U. (1953) *Languages in contact: findings and problems*. New York: Publications of the Linguistic Circle of New York. *p*383

Weinreich, U., W. Labov & M. Herzog (1968) 'Empirical foundations for a theory of language change'. In W. P. Lehmann & Y. Malkiel, eds. *Directions for historical linguistics*. Austin: University of Texas Press. *p*364

Westermann, D. (1930) *A study of the Ewe language*. London: Oxford University Press. *p*221

White, L. (1976) 'Changes in the structure of COMP'. *Montreal Working Papers in Linguistics* 7. *pp*313, 328, 339

Whitney, W. D. (1885) 'Numerical results from indexes of Sanskrit tense and conjugation stems'. *Journal of American Oriental Society* 13, xxxii. *p*282

(1892) 'On Delbrück's Vedic syntax' (Review of B. Delbrück, *Altindische Syntax*). *American Journal of Philology* 13, 271–306. *p*8

(1896) *A Sanskrit grammar*. Boston: Ginn.

Williams, W. (1971) 'Serial verb constructions in Krio'. *Studies in African Linguistics*, Supplement no. 2. *p*214

Woodcock, E. C. (1958) *A new Latin syntax*. Cambridge, Mass.: Harvard University Press. *p*353

Wydler, K. (1956) *Zur Stellung des attributiven Adjectivs vom Latein bis Zum Neufranzösischen*. Doctoral thesis. Zürich: Romanica Helvetica, 53. *p*206

Wyld, H. C. (1927) *A short history of English*. London: Murray. *p*389

Yngve, V. (1960) 'A model and a hypothesis for language structure'. *Proceedings of the American Philosophical Society* 104, 444–66. *p*145

Citation index

Aelfred, 31, 170, 201, 233, 270, 271, 274, 275, 278, 300, 324, 325
Aelfric, 99, 104, 106, 107, 172, 183, 274, 302
Alexander, Alliterative Romance of, 201, 230
Alphabet of Tales, 235, 276
Ancren Riwle, 200, 201, 234
Anglo-Saxon Wills, 323, 324, 325, 334
Aristophanes, 245
Arthur, 105
Ascham, Roger, 180, 231
Aurelio and Isabell, 110

Barbour, John, 230
Bede, 98, 99, 266
Beowulf, 119, 172, 323, 325
Blickling Homilies, 172, 178, 301
Booke of Hawkyng, 173
Bronte, Charlotte, 275
Butler, Charles, 118

Campion, Edmund, 266
Caxton, William, 230, 261, 298, 321, 322
Chanson de Roland, 206
Chapman, George, 173
Chastysing of goddes chyldren, 230
Chaucer, Geoffrey, 33, 99, 104, 176, 177, 200, 205, 207, 208, 230, 232, 233, 234, 235, 236, 261, 271, 298, 302, 321, 322, 326, 327
Chesterton, Gilbert K., 262
Chronicon Vilod., 174
Cloud of Unknowing, 105
Collins, Norman, 265
Cooper, Thomas, 110, 180
Cranmer, Thomas, 110
Cursor Mundi, 173, 176, 201, 260, 270
Cynewulf, 172

Damon and Pithias, 233
Deeping, Warwick, 262
Defoe, Daniel, 333

Dekker, Thomas, 279
Demosthenes, 25
Destruction of Troy, 232, 270
Dickens, Charles, 275, 321, 333
Digby Mysteries, 102
Dionysios Thrax, 281, 289
Douglas, Gavin, 184, 229
Dreambook, 201
Dryden, John, 272

Euripides, 244

Fenton, Geoffrey, 112
Fielding, Henry, 118
Fortescue, Thomas, 174

Genesis (Caedmon), 169, 172
Generides, 261
Gospels in W. Saxon, 172, 173, 325
Gower, John, 230, 266
Grafton, Richard, 301
Greene, Graham, 262
Gregory, 324
Grenewey, Richard, 180
Guthlac, 324

Hakewill, William, 184
Hatton Correspondence, 275
Havelok the Dane, 99, 201, 271
Henry the Minstrel, 101
Herodotus, 242, 244
Hesiod, 244, 250
Hexameron of St Basil, 201
Hoccleve, Thomas, 101
Holland, Philemon, 174
Hooker, Richard, 112
Hurd, Bp Richard, 104

Iliad (Homer), 162, 240, 241, 242, 243, 244, 247, 248, 393
Interlinear Rule of St Benet, 200

Jacob's Well, 232

Jamieson, John, 102
Johnson, Samuel, 275
Jonson, Ben, 275

King Alexander, 323
Kingsley, Charles, 101
Krapp, G. P., 270

Lambeth Homilies, 176, 184
Lawman, 170, 176
Layamon, 174, 183, 301
Le Livre de Melibée et Prudence, 208
Linacre, 110
Lindisfarne Gospels, 200
Love, Nicholas, 279
Lovelace, Richard, 101
Lovelich, Henry, 272, 276
Lydegate, John, 174, 184, 270
Lyly, John, 180

Mackenzie, Compton, 262
Malory, Sir Thomas, 232, 234, 235, 261,
    276, 322
Mandeville, Bernard, 279
Mannyng, Robert, 173, 178
Maugham, Somerset, 184
Mencius, 121
ME Sermons, 320
Milton, John, 265
Miracle Plays, 173
Monk of Evesham, 112
More, Sir Thomas, 110, 118, 119, 229,
    233, 265, 299
Mum and Sopsegger, 234

Nashe, Thomas, 205
Norton, Thomas, 174

Odyssey (Homer), 242, 248
OE Chronicles, 169, 172, 201, 204
OE Miscellany, 183
Ormulum, 176, 260, 327

Panini, 241
Parker Chronicle, 274
Parsons, B., 180
Partenay, The Romance of, 118
Paston Letters, 205, 261, 320, 322
Pecock, Reginald, 174
Peterborough Chronicle, 184, 324
Philips, Ambrose, 101
Piers Plowman, 176
Pliny, 250
Pottenham, 173

Ramsey, Allan, 103
Riddles (Grein), 173
R. Glouc., 173
Robinson, Francis K., 103
Rolle of Hampole, Richard, 234
Romaunt of the Rose, 230
Rushworth Gospels, 99
Rutherford, Samuel, 103

Saxon Leechdoms, 169, 170
Scott, Sir Walter, 103, 105, 237
Secreta Secretorum, 200
Shakespeare, William, 108, 175, 180, 183,
    184, 205, 236, 263, 265, 266, 272,
    279, 298, 302, 321, 326
Simonides, 245
Sir Ferumbras, 178
Sir Tristrem, 102
Smollett, Tobias, 105
Southey, Robert, 236
Speculum Guy, 200
Spenser, Edmund, 175, 180, 230
Stapleton, Thomas, 201
State Papers of Henry VIII, 184
Stevenson, 299
Stonor Letters and Papers, 261
Swift, Jonathan, 31, 184
Synge, 118

Tacitus, 250
Tale of MacDatho's Pig, 25
Tennyson, Alfred Lord, 102
Three ME Sermons, 266
Thucydides, 25
Tottel's Miscellany, 230
Townley Mysteries, 108, 261
Trevisa, John de, 112–13, 271
Turner, William, 279
Tyndale, William, 183

Vanbrugh, Sir John, 105
Vices and Virtues, 176, 271

Webbe, Bp George, 180
William of Palerne, The Romance of, 233
Wodehouse, P. G., 5
Wright, Thomas, 271
Wulfstan, 201, 233
Wycherley, William, 105
Wyclif, John, 173, 183, 267, 320

Xenophon, 25, 250

York Plays, 230, 261